International Student Edition

BUSINESS ACCOUNTING 2

Seventh Edition

Frank Wood BSc (Econ), FCA
and
Alan Sangster BA, MSc, CA, Cert TESOL

D1301060

PITMAN
PUBLISHING

London · Hong Kong · Johannesburg · Melbourne · Singapore · Washington DC

PITMAN PUBLISHING
128 Long Acre, London WC2E 9AN
A Division of Pearson Professional Limited

Seventh edition published in Great Britain 1996

© Frank Wood 1967
© Longman Group UK Limited 1973, 1979, 1989, 1993
© Pearson Professional Limited 1996

British Library Cataloguing in Publication Data
A CIP catalogue record for this book is available on request from the British Library.

ISBN 0–273–61983–7

10 9 8 7 6 5 4 3 2

Typeset by Land & Unwin (Data Sciences) Limited, Bugbrooke
Printed and bound in Singapore

The Publishers' policy is to use paper manufactured from sustainable forests.

Contents

Full contents

Preface to the seventh edition

This is the second volume of the textbook. It completes the coverage of the financial accounting part of quite a few examinations in accounting. As examination syllabuses are constantly being revised, it would not make sense to be too specific as to which chapters would be needed by students taking each of the various examinations.

The examining bodies whose students will find the book of most value include:

The various Institutes of Chartered Accountants
Association of Chartered Certified Accountants
Chartered Institute of Management Accountants
Institute of Chartered Secretaries and Administrators
Association of Accounting Technicians
London Chamber of Commerce and Industry
Royal Society of Arts Examinations Board

This volume examines all the current accounting standards (both *Statements of Standard Accounting Practice* – SSAPs – and *Financial Reporting Standards* – FRSs) in as much detail as is needed by most students at this level. However, where they represent a complete examination paper, some students will need a much more detailed knowledge of them than a textbook of this kind can provide. In this case, students would be well advised to refer to a specialist textbook on the topic, or to the standards themselves.

We would like to thank all those who suggested changes, many of which have been incorporated within this edition. In particular, we are indebted to Michael Siaw Jun Choi for providing us with a great deal of useful information.

We wish to acknowledge the permission to use past examination papers granted by the Institute of Chartered Accountants in England and Wales, the Chartered Association of Certified Accountants, the Chartered Institute of Management Accountants, the Association of Accounting Technicians, the Institute of Chartered Secretaries and Administrators, the University of London, the Associated Examining Board, the Joint Matriculation Board and the Welsh Joint Education Committee.

As in previous editions, all answers to questions are the product of our own work and have not been supplied by any of the examining bodies. To this end, we would like to thank Christina Mulligan for her efforts in ensuring the accuracy of the answers provided.

Frank Wood and Alan Sangster

Also available free to lecturers who adopt **Business Accounting:**

Teacher's Manual (0 273 62305 2) A time-saving Teacher's Manual, including fully displayed answers to all questions with the suffix 'A' in the texts, is available free of charge to lecturers who recommend *Business Accounting* Volumes 1 or 2 on their courses.

OHP Masters (0 273 62544 6) Paper masters for OHPs of relevant diagrams in the text are also available if lecturers adopt the text.

EQL Multiple Choice Question software *Volume 1* (0 273 62546 2)

EQL Multiple Choice Question software *Volume 2* (0 273 62547 0)

Other books in the Frank Wood series:

Business Accounting Multiple Choice Question Book (0 273 62545 4)

Business Accounting *Volume 1* (0 273 61980 2)

Business Accounting: Irish Edition (0 273 60499 6)

Business Accounting: Irish Edition, Multiple Choice Question Book (0 273 60832 0)

Frank Wood's Business Accounting NVQ Level 2 Accounting *Student's Workbook* (0 273 60188 1)

Frank Wood's Business Accounting NVQ Level 3 Accounting *Student's Workbook* (0 273 60446 5)

Frank Wood's Book-Keeping and Accounts (0 273 03770 6)

Part 1

SPECIAL ACCOUNTS

Introduction

This part is concerned with five items that are treated in a similar way, irrespective of the form of business involved, along with a chapter that rounds off the material covered in *Business Accounting 1* on partnership accounts.

1

Joint venture accounts

Objectives

After you have studied this chapter, you should:

● *understand what is meant by the term 'joint venture'*

● *know how to make the entries in the accounts for a joint venture*

1.1 Nature of joint ventures

Sometimes a particular business venture can best be done by two or more firms joining together to do it instead of doing it separately. The joining together is for that one venture only, it is not joining together to make a continuing business.

Such projects are known as **joint ventures**. For instance, a merchant might provide the capital, the transport to the markets and the selling skills. The farmer grows the produce. The profits or losses are then shared between them in agreed ratios. It is like a partnership, but only for this one transaction. There may be several joint ventures between the same firms, but each one is a separate venture. The agreements for each venture may be different from each other.

1.2 Accounting for large joint ventures

For large-scale joint ventures, a separate bank account and separate set of books are kept. In such cases the calculation of profit is not difficult. It is similar to preparing a set of final accounts in an ordinary firm.

1.3 Accounting for smaller joint ventures

No separate set of books or separate bank accounts are kept for smaller joint ventures. Each party will record in his own books only those transactions with which he has been concerned. Exhibit 1.1 gives an example of such a joint venture.

Exhibit 1.1

White of London and Green of Glasgow enter into a joint venture. White is to supply the goods and pay some of the expenses. Green is to sell the goods and receive the cash, and pay the remainder of the expenses. Profits are to be shared equally.

Details of the transactions are as follows:

		£
White supplied the goods costing		1,800
White paid wages		200
White paid for storage expenses		160
Green paid transport expenses120		
Green paid selling expenses		320
Green received cash from sales of all the goods		3,200

Stage 1

White and Green will each have entered up his part of the transactions. White will have opened an account named 'Joint Venture with Green'. Similarly, Green will have opened a 'Joint Venture with White' account. The double entry to these joint venture accounts will be:

In White's books:

Payments by White:	Debit joint venture with Green
	Credit cash book
Good supplied:	Debit joint venture with Green
	Credit purchases

In Green's books:

Payments by Green:	Debit joint venture with White
	Credit cash book
Cash received by Green:	Debit cash book
	Credit joint venture with White

At this point the joint venture accounts in each of their books will appear as follows:

White's books (in London)

Joint Venture with Green

	£		
Purchases	1,800		
Cash: wages	200		
Cash: storage expenses	160		

Green's books (in Glasgow)

Joint Venture with White

	£		£
Cash: transport expenses	120	Cash: sales	3,200
Cash: selling expenses	320		

Stage 2

At this stage, White and Green know only the details in their own set of books. They do not yet know what the details are in the other person's books.

This means that they cannot yet calculate profits, or find out how much cash has to be paid or received to close the venture. To do this they must each send a copy of their joint venture accounts to the other person.

Each person will then draw up a memorandum joint venture account, to include all the details from each joint venture account. This is now shown:

White and Green
Memorandum Joint Venture Account

	£	£		£
Purchases		1,800	Sales	3,200
Wages		200		
Storage expenses		160		
Transport expenses		120		
Selling expenses		320		
Net profit:				
White (one-half)	300			
Green (one half)	300	600		
		3,200		3,200

The memorandum joint venture account is not a double entry account. It is drawn up only (a) to find out the shares of net profit or loss, and (b) to help calculate the amounts payable and receivable to close the venture.

Stage 3

The net profit shares for White and Green need to be brought into their books. This is as follows:

White's books
Debit share of profit to joint venture with Green's account
Credit White's profit and loss account

Green's books
Debit share of profit to joint venture with White's account
Credit Green's profit and loss account

After these entries the joint venture accounts are balanced down. These will show:

(a) If the balance carried down is a credit balance, the person has received more from the joint venture than he should keep. He will then have to pay that amount to the other person to close the venture.
(b) If the balance carried down is a debit balance, the person has received less from the joint venture than he should get. He will then need to receive cash from the other person to close the venture.

The joint venture accounts now completed can be shown.

White's books (in London)

Joint Venture with Green

	£		£
Purchases	1,800	Balance c/d	2,460
Cash: wages	200		
Cash: storage expenses	160		
Share of profit transferred			
to profit and loss account	300		
	2,460		2,460
Balance b/d	2,460	Cash in settlement from Green	2,460

Green's books (in Glasgow)

Joint Venture with White

	£		£
Cash: transport expenses	120	Cash: sales	3,200
Cash: selling expenses	320		
Share of profit transferred			
to profit and loss account	300		
Balance c/d	2,460		
	3,200		3,200
Cash in settlement to White	2,460	Balance b/d	2,460

New terms

Joint ventures (p.3): Business agreements under which two businesses join together for a set of activities and agree to share the profits.

Main points to remember

1 When two or more businesses join together for a particular business venture, and do not form a permanent business entity, they have entered into a joint venture.

2 Larger joint ventures operate a separate bank account and books dedicated to the project.

3 The participants in smaller joint ventures rely on their own bank accounts and books to run and record their part of the project, using a *memorandum joint venture account* to pass the details of their part of the project to the other participant(s).

Review questions

Note: Questions with the letter A shown after the question number do NOT have answers shown at the back of the book. Answers to the others are shown on page 582 onwards.

1.1 Ollier and Avon enter a joint venture, to share profits or losses equally, resulting from dealings in second-hand cars. Both parties take an active part in the business, each recording his own transactions. They have no joint banking account or separate set of books.

19X3
Jan   1   Ollier buys three cars for £900.
 „   31   Ollier pays for repairs and respraying of vehicles £60.
Mar   1   Avon pays garage rental £20 and advertising expenses £10.
Apr 12   Avon pays for licence and insurance renewal of vehicles, £36.
Aug 10   Avon buys a vehicle in excellent condition for £100.
 „   31   Ollier sells the four vehicles, to various clients, the sales being completed on this date, totalling £1,600.

Show the relevant accounts in the books of both partners.

1.2A Mr Carter entered into a joint venture with Mr Thomas for the purchase and sale of bicycles. They agreed that profits and losses should be shared equally.

The following transactions took place:

(*a*) Mr Carter purchased bicycles for £88,900 and paid carriage £273.
(*b*) Mr Thomas purchased bicycles for £7,560 and paid carriage £51.
(*c*) Mr Thomas paid to Mr Carter £40,000.
(*d*) Mr Carter sold bicycles for £73,400 and sent a cheque for £30,000 to Mr Thomas.
(*e*) Mr Thomas sold for £10,230 all the bicycles he had purchased.
(*f*) The unsold bicycles in the possession of Mr Carter were taken over by him at a valuation of £26,000.
(*g*) The amount due from one venturer to the other was paid and the joint venture was dissolved.

You are required to prepare:
(*i*) a statement to show the net profit or loss of the joint venture, and
(*ii*) the accounts for the joint venture in the books of Mr Carter and Mr Thomas.

1.3 Plant, Hoe & Reap entered into a joint venture for dealing in carrots. The transactions connected with this venture were:

19X1
Jan   8   Plant rented land cost £156.
 ,,   10   Hoe supplied seeds cost £48.
 ,,   17   Plant employed labour for planting £105.
 ,,   19   Hoe charged motor expenses £17.
 ,,   30   Plant employed labour for fertilising £36.
Feb 28   Plant paid the following expenses: Sundries £10, Labour £18, Fertiliser £29.
Mar 17   Reap employed labour for lifting carrots £73.
 ,,   30   Sale expenses London paid by Reap £39.
 ,,   31   Reap received cash from sale proceeds gross £987.

You are required to show the joint venture accounts in the books of Plant, Hoe & Reap. Also show in full the method of arriving at the profit on the venture which is to be apportioned: Plant seven-twelfths; Hoe three-twelfths; Reap two-twelfths.

Any outstanding balances between the parties are settled by cheque on 30 April.

1.4A Wild, Wood and Bine enter into a joint venture for dealing in antique brass figures. The following transactions took place:

19X4
Mar   1   Wild rented a shop, paying 3 months' rent £150.
 ,,   2   Wood bought a motor van for £2,700.
 ,,   4   Wood bought antiques for £650.
 ,,   15   Bine received cash from sale proceeds of antiques £3,790.
 ,,   28   Wild bought antiques for £1,200.
Apr 11   Motor van broke down. Bine agreed to use his own van for the job, until cessation of the joint venture, at an agreed charge of £400.
 ,,   13   Motor van bought on Mar 2 was sold for £2,100. Proceeds were kept by Wild.
 ,,   15   Sales of antiques, cash being kept by Wood £780.
 ,,   18   Lighting bills paid for shop by Bine £120.
 ,,   30   Bine bought antiques for £440.
May   4   General expenses of shop paid for £800, Bine and Wild paying half each.
 ,,   19   Antiques sold by Bine £990, proceeds being kept by him.
 ,,   31   Joint venture ended. The antiques still in stock were taken over at an agreed valuation of £2,100 by Wood.

You are required to show the joint venture accounts in the books of each of the three parties. Show in full the workings needed to arrive at the profit on the venture. The profit or loss was to be split: Wood one-half; Wild one-third; Bine one-sixth. Any outstanding balances between the parties were settled on 31 May 19X4.

2
Bills of exchange

Objectives

After you have studied this chapter, you should:

● *understand what is meant by the term 'bill of exchange',
  how they are used, and by whom*

● *know how to make the entries in the accounts for a bill
  of exchange*

2.1 Nature of bills of exchange

When goods are supplied to someone on credit, or services performed for him, then that person becomes a **debtor**. The creditor firm would normally wait for payment by the debtor. Until payment is made the money owing is of no use to the creditor firm as it is not being used in any way. This can be remedied by **factoring** the debtors, which involves passing the debts over to a finance firm. They will pay an agreed amount for the legal rights to the debts.

Another possibility is that of obtaining a bank overdraft, with the debtors accepted as part of the security on which the overdraft has been granted.

Yet another way that can give the creditor effective use of the money owing to him is for him to draw a **bill of exchange** on the debtor. This means that a document is drawn up requiring the debtor to pay the amount owing to the creditor, or to anyone nominated by him at any time, on or by a particular date. He sends this document to the debtor who, if he agrees to it, is said to 'accept' it by writing on the document that he will comply with it and appends his signature. The debtor then returns the bill of exchange to the creditor. This document is then legal proof of the debt. The debtor is not then able to contest the validity of the debt except for any irregularity in the bill of exchange itself.

2.2 How bills of exchange are used

The creditor can now act in one of three ways:

1 He can negotiate the bill to another person in payment of a debt. That person may also renegotiate it to someone else. The person who possesses the bill at maturity, i.e. the date for payment of the bill, will present it to the debtor for payment.

2 He may 'discount' it with a bank. 'Discount' here means that the bank will take the bill of exchange and treat it in the same manner as money deposited in the bank account. The bank will then hold the bill until maturity when it will present it to the debtor for payment. The bank will make a charge to the creditor for this service, known as a **discounting charge**.

3   The third way open to the creditor is for him to hold the bill until maturity when he will present it to the debtor for payment. In this case, apart from having a document which is legal proof of the debt and could therefore save legal costs if a dispute arose, no benefit has been gained from having a bill of exchange. However, action **1** or **2** could have been taken if the need had arisen.

2.3 The parties to a bill of exchange

The creditor who draws up the bill of exchange is known as the **drawer**. The debtor on whom it is drawn is the **drawee**, when accepted he becomes the **acceptor**, while the person to whom the bill is to be paid is the **payee**. In fact, it may be recognised that a cheque is a special type of bill of exchange where the drawee is always a bank and, in addition, is payable on demand. This chapter, however, refers to bills of exchange other than cheques.

To the person who is to receive the money on maturity of the bill of exchange the document is known as a **bill receivable**, while to the person who is to pay the sum due on maturity it is known as a **bill payable**.

2.4 Dishonoured bills

When the debtor fails to make payment on maturity the bill is said to be dishonoured. If the holder is someone other than the drawer then he will have recourse against the person who has negotiated the bill to him, that person will then have recourse against the one who negotiated it to him, and so on until final recourse is had against the drawer of the bill for the amount of money due on the bill. The drawer's right of action is then against the acceptor.

On dishonour, a bill is often **noted**. This means that the bill is handed to a lawyer acting in his capacity as a notary public, who then re-presents the bill to the acceptor. The notary public then records the reasons for it not being discharged. The notary public's fee is known as a **noting charge**. With a foreign bill, in addition to the bill being noted, it is necessary to **protest** the bill in order to preserve the holder's rights against the drawer and previous endorsers. **Protest** is the term which covers the legal formalities needed.

The action to be taken by the drawer depends entirely upon circumstances. Often the lack of funds on the acceptor's part is purely temporary. In this case the drawer will negotiate with the acceptor and agree to draw another bill, or substitute several bills of smaller amounts with different maturity dates, for the amount owing, frequently with an addition for interest to compensate for the extended period of credit. Negotiation is the keynote; it must not be thought that acceptors are always sued when they fail to make payment. They are customers, and where future dealings with them are expected to be profitable harsh measures are certainly to be avoided. Legal action should be the last action to be considered. Any interest charged to the acceptor would be debited to his account and credited to an Interest Receivable Account.

2.5 Discounting charges and noting charges

From the acceptor's point of view the discounting of a bill is a matter wholly for the drawer or holder to decide. He, the acceptor, has been allowed a term of credit and will pay the agreed price on the maturity of the bill. Therefore the discounting charge is not one that he should suffer; this should be borne wholly by the person discounting the bill.

On the other hand, the noting charge has been brought about by the acceptor's default. It is equitable that his account should be charged with the amount of the expense of **noting** and **protesting**.

2.6 Retired bills

Instead of waiting until maturity, bills may be retired, i.e. not allowed to run until maturity. They may be paid off before maturity, in which case a rebate is often allowed because the full term of credit has not been taken; or else renewed by fresh bills being drawn and the old ones cancelled. The new bills often include interest because the term of credit has been extended.

2.7 Examples of bookkeeping entries

Exhibit 2.1

1 Drawer's Books

Goods had been sold by D Jarvis to J Burgon on 1 January 19X6 for £400. A bill of exchange is drawn by Jarvis and accepted by Burgon on 1 January 19X6, the date of maturity being 31 March 19X6. The following accounts show the entries necessary:

(a) If the bill is held by the drawer until maturity when the drawee makes payment.

J Burgon

19X6		£	19X6		£
Jan 1	Sales	400	Jan 1	Bill receivable	400

Bills Receivable

19X6		£	19X6		£
Jan 1	J Burgon	400	Mar 31	Bank	400

Bank

19X6		£		
Mar 31	Bills receivable	400		

(b) Where the bill is negotiated to another party by the drawer, in this case to IDT Ltd on 3 January 19X6.

J Burgon

19X6		£	19X6		£
Jan 1	Sales	400	Jan 1	Bill receivable	400

Bills Receivable

19X6		£	19X6		£
Jan 1	J Burgon	400	Jan 3	IDT Ltd	400

(c) If the bill is discounted with the bank, in this case on 2 January 19X6, the discounting charges being £6.

J Burgon

19X6		£	19X6		£
Jan	1 Sales	400	Jan	1 Bill receivable	400

Bills Receivable

19X6		£	19X6		£
Jan	1 J Burgon	400	Jan 2 Bank		400

Bank

19X6		£	19X6		£
Jan	2 Bills receivable	400	Jan	2 Discounting charges	6

Discounting Charges

19X6		£	
Jan	2 Bank	6	

2 Acceptor's Books

The instances (a), (b) and (c) in the drawer's books will result in similar entries in the acceptor's books. From the acceptor's point of view two things have happened, first the acceptance of the bill, and second its discharge by payment. The fact that (a), (b) and (c) would result in different payees is irrelevant so far as the acceptor is concerned.

D Jarvis

19X6		£	19X6		£
Jan	1 Bills payable	400	Jan	1 Purchases	400

Bills Payable

19X6		£	19X6		£
Mar 31 Bank		400	Jan	1 D Jarvis	400

Bank

			19X6		£
			Mar 31 Bill payable		400

2.8 Dishonoured bills and accounting entries

These can be illustrated by reference to Exhibit 2.2.

Exhibit 2.2

On 1 April 19X7 A Grant sells goods for £600 to K Lee, a bill with a maturity date of 30 June 19X7 being drawn by Grant and accepted by Lee on 2 April 19X7. On 30 June

19X7 the bill is presented to Lee, but he fails to pay it and it is therefore dishonoured. The bill is noted, the cost of £2 being paid by Grant on 7 July 19X7.

The entries needed will depend on whether or not the bill had been discounted by Grant.

1 Drawer's Books

Where the bill had not been discounted or renegotiated:

K Lee

19X7		£	19X7		£
Apr	1 Sales	600	Apr	2 Bills receivable	600
Jun	30 Bill receivable – dishonoured	600			
Jul	7 Bank: Noting charge (a)	2			

Bills Receivable

19X7		£	19X7		£
Apr 2 K Lee		600	Jun 30 K Lee – bill dishonoured		600

Bank

			19X7		£
			Jul	7 Noting charges – K Lee (a)	2

Note:
(a) As the noting charges are directly incurred as the result of Lee's default, then Lee must suffer the cost by his account being debited with that amount.

Where the bill has been discounted with a bank:

The entries can now be seen as they would have appeared if the bill had been discounted on 5 April 19X7, discounting charges being £9.

K Lee

19X7		£	19X7		£
Apr	1 Sales	600	Apr	2 Bill receivable	600
Jun	30 Bank – bill dishonoured (c)	600			
Jul	7 Bank: Noting charge	2			

Bills Receivable

19X7		£	19X7		£
Apr	2 K Lee	600	Apr	5 Bank	600

Bank

19X7		£	19X7		£
Apr	5 Bills receivable	600	Apr	5 Discounting charges (b)	9
			Jun	30 K Lee – bill dishonoured (c)	600
			Jul	7 Noting charges – K Lee	2

Discounting Charges

19X7		£	
Apr 5 Bank (*b*)		9	

Notes:

(*b*) The discounting charges are wholly an expense of A Grant. They are therefore charged to an expense account. Contrast this with the treatment of the noting charges.

(*c*) On maturity the bank will present the bill to Lee. On its dishonour the bank will hand the bill back to Grant, and will cancel out the original amount shown as being deposited in the bank account. This amount is then charged to Lee's personal account to show that he is still in debt.

2 Acceptor's Books

The entries in the acceptor's books will not be affected by whether or not the drawer has discounted the bill.

A Grant

19X7		£	19X7		£
Apr 1 Bill payable		600	Apr 1 Purchases		600
			Jun 30 Bill payable – dishonoured		600
			Jul 7 Noting charge (*d*)		2

Bills Payable

19X7	£	19X7	£
Jun 30 A Grant – bill dishonoured	600	Apr 1 A Grant	600

Noting Charges

19X7		£	
Jul 7 A Grant (*d*)		2	

Note:

(*d*) The noting charges will have to be reimbursed to A Grant. To show this fact A Grant's account is credited while the Noting Charges Account is debited to record the expense.

2.9 Bills receivable as contingent liabilities

The fact that bills had been discounted, but had not reached maturity by the balance sheet date, could give an entirely false impression of the financial position of the business unless a note to this effect is made on the balance sheet. That such a note is necessary can be illustrated by reference to the following balance sheets.

Balance Sheet as at 31 December 19X7

	£	(a) £	£	(b) £
Fixed assets		3,500		3,500
Current assets:				
Stock	1,000		1,000	
Debtors	1,200		1,200	
Bills receivable	1,800		–	
Bank	500		2,300	
	4,500		4,500	
Less Current liabilities	3,000		3,000	
Working capital		1,500		1,500
		5,000		5,000
		£		£
Financed by:				
Capital		5,000		5,000

Balance sheet (a) shows the position if £1,800 of bills receivable were still in hand. Balance sheet (b) shows the position if the bills had been discounted, ignoring discounting charges. To an outsider, balance sheet (b) seems to show a much stronger liquid position with £2,300 in the bank. However, should the bills be dishonoured on maturity the bank balance would slump to £500. The appearance of balance sheet (b) is therefore deceptive unless a note is added, e.g. 'Note: There is a contingent liability of £1,800 on bills discounted at the balance sheet date.' This note enables the outsider to view the bank balance in its proper perspective of depending on the non-dishonour of the bills discounted.

New terms

Bill of exchange (p. 9): A document drawn up by the drawer which requires his debtor, the drawee, to accept the bill, agreeing to pay a specified sum to the person called the payee on the due date specified.

Acceptor (p. 10): The drawee, when he accepts the bill, becomes the acceptor, thereby accepting liability to pay the debt.

Dishonoured bill (p. 10): Where the acceptor fails to pay his debt on the due date.

Contingent liability (p. 15): Until the acceptor pays his debt owing on the bill, the drawer will have a liability for the contingency that the bill will be dishonoured.

Main points to remember

1 Bills of exchange enable businesses to obtain money owing to them in advance of the date when the debtor is expected to clear his debt.

2 They are also a form of evidence should the amount due be disputed later.

3 Bills of exchange are not a guarantee that a debt will be honoured.

Review questions

2.1   N Gudgeon sells goods to two companies on July 1 19X7.

To R Johnson Ltd	£2,460
To B Scarlet & Co Ltd.	£1,500

He draws bills of exchange on each of them and they are both accepted.

He discounts both of the bills with the bank on July 4 19X7, and suffers discounting charges of £80 on Johnson's bill and £65 on Scarlet's bill. On September 1 19X7 the bills mature and Johnson Ltd meets its liability. Scarlet's bill is dishonoured and is duly noted on September 4, the noting charge being £6.

Show the above in the necessary accounts:

(*a*) In the books of Gudgeon.
(*b*) In the books of Scarlet Ltd and of Johnson Ltd.

2.2A   P Cummings buys goods from T Victor Ltd on January 21 19X7 for £2,900 and from C Bellamy & Co for £4,160. Bills are drawn on him and he accepts them.

T Victor Ltd discount their bill with their bank on January 29, the discounting charge being £110.

C Bellamy & Co simply keep their bill waiting for maturity.

On maturity of the bills on April 21 19X7, Cummings duly meets (pays) Bellamy's bill. He is unable to pay Victor's bill and it is accordingly dishonoured. Victor duly has it noted on April 28 19X7, the noting charge being £10.

Show the entries necessary in:

(*a*) The books of P Cummings.
(*b*) The books of T Victor Ltd.
(*c*) The books of C Bellamy & Co.

2.3   KC owed TM £960. KC accepted a bill of exchange at three months' date for this amount. TM discounted it for £948.

Before the due date of the bill TM was informed that KC was unable to meet the bill and was offering a composition of 37.5 per cent of each £ to his creditors. This offer was accepted and cash equivalent to the composition was received.

Show the ledger entries to record the above in TM's ledger.

2.4   Draw up a sales ledger control account for the month of August 19X6 from the following:

19X6			£
Aug	1	Balances (Dr)	12,370
		Balances (Cr)	105
		Totals for the month:	
		Sales journal	16,904
		Returns inwards journal	407
		Cheques received from customers	15,970
		Bills receivable accepted	1,230
		Cash received from customers	306
		Bad debts written off	129
		Cash discounts allowed	604
		Bill receivable dishonoured	177
Aug	31	Balances (Cr)	88
		Balances (Dr)	?

Note: This question is being asked because it contains entries for bills of exchange.

2.5 A purchases ledger control account should be drawn up for February 19X7 from the following:

19X7			£
Feb	1	Balances (Dr)	33
		Balances (Cr)	8,570
		Totals for month:	
		Purchases journal	11,375
		Returns outwards journal	568
		Bills payable accepted by us	1,860
		Cheques paid to suppliers	9,464
		Cash paid to suppliers	177
		We were unable to meet a bill payable on maturity and it was therefore dishonoured	800
		We agreed to suffer noting charge on dishonoured bill	20
Feb	28	Balances (Dr)	47
		Balances (Cr)	?

Note: This question is being asked because it contains entries for bills of exchange.

2.6A Indicate by journal entries how the following would appear in the ledger accounts of (*a*) Noone, (*b*) Iddon.

19X8
Jan 1 Iddon sells goods £420 to Noone, and Noone sends to Iddon a three months' acceptance for this amount.

„ 1 Iddon discounts the acceptance with the Slough Discount Co. Ltd, receiving its cheque for £412.

Feb 29 One-third of Noone's stock, valued at £3,600, is destroyed by fire. Noone claims on the underwriters at Lloyds with whom he is insured.

Apr 1 The underwriters admit the claim for £3,000 only as the total stock was only insured for £9,000.

„ 4 In view of Noone's difficulties Iddon meets the acceptance due today by giving his cheque for £420 to the Slough Discount Co. Ltd; he draws on Noone a further bill for one month for £430 (to include £10 interest) which Noone accepts.

„ 9 Noone receives cheque from the underwriters in settlement of the admitted claim.

May 7 Noone's bank honours the acceptance presented by Iddon as due today.

2.7A Enter the following in the appropriate ledger accounts of R Smith:

19X0
Jan 5 R Smith sold goods to P Thomas, £320, and Thomas accepted Smith's bill for three months for this amount.

„ 6 R Smith discounted Thomas's bill at the London Discount Co. for £304, and pays this amount into his account at the bank.

Apr 8 The London Discount Co. notified Smith that Thomas's bill had been dishonoured. Smith at once sent a cheque to the London Discount Co. for the full amount of the bill plus £3 charges.

„ 14 Smith agreed that Thomas's bankers should accept a further bill for one month for the total amount owing plus £10 interest, and received the new acceptance.

May 18 Smith's bank informed him the new bill had been paid.

2.8A On 1 June 19X2, X purchased goods from Y for £860 and sold goods to Z for £570. On the same date, X drew a bill (No. 1) at three months on Z for £400 and Z accepted it. On 12 June 19X2, Z drew a bill (No. 2) at three months on Q for £150 which Q accepted. On 14 June, Z endorsed bill No. 2 over to X and, on 16 June, X endorsed this bill over to Y.

On 20 June, X accepted a bill (No. 3) at three months for £720 drawn by Y in full settlement of his account, including interest. On 23 June, Y discounted bill No. 3 at his bank.

On 17 September, Y informed X that Q's acceptance had been dishonoured and X sent a cheque for £150 to Y. The other bills were paid on the due dates.

On 20 September, X received a cheque from Z for half the amount due from him.

Show the entries to record these transactions in the ledger and cash book of X.

2.9A Balances and transactions affecting a company's control accounts for the months of May 19X2 are listed below:

	£	
Balances at 1 May 19X2:		
Sales ledger	9,123	(debit)
	211	(credit)
Purchase ledger	4,490	(credit)
	88	(debit)
Transactions during May 19X2:		
Purchases on credit	18,135	
Allowances from suppliers	629	
Receipts from customers by cheque	27,370	
Sales on credit	36,755	
Discounts received	1,105	
Payments to creditors by cheque	15,413	
Contra settlements	3,046	
Allowances to customers	1,720	
Bills of exchange receivable	6,506	
Customers' cheques dishonoured	489	
Cash receipts from credit customers	4,201	
Refunds to customers for overpayment of accounts	53	
Discounts allowed	732	
Balances at 31 May 19X2:		
Sales ledger	136	(credit)
Purchases ledger	67	(debit)

Required:

(a) Explain the purposes for which control accounts are prepared.

(b) Post the sales ledger and purchases ledger control accounts for the month of May 19X2 and derive the respective debit and credit closing balances on 31 May 19X2.

(Association of Certified Accountants)

3

Consignment accounts

Objectives

After you have studied this chapter, you should:

- *understand what is meant by the term 'consignment account', how such accounts are used, and by whom*

- *know how to record the entries for consignment accounts*

3.1 Nature of a consignment

When a trader sells goods directly to customers, whether they are in his home country or overseas, these are ordinary sales. However, a trader may send goods to an agent to sell them for him. These goods are said to be sent on **consignment**. The main features are:

(a) The trader sends the goods to the agent. The goods do not belong to the agent; his job is to sell them for the trader. The goods are owned by the trader until they are sold. The trader sending the goods is called the **consignor**. The agent is called the **consignee**.

(b) The agent will store the goods until they are sold by him. He will have to pay some expenses, but these will later be refunded by the trader.

(c) The agent will receive a commission from the trader for his work.

(d) The agent will collect the money from the customers to whom he sells the goods. He will pay this over to the trader after deducting his expenses and commission. The statement from the agent to the trader showing this is known as the *account sales*.

Consignment accounts are to be found mainly in overseas trade.

3.2 Consignor's (the trader's) records

For each consignment to an agent a separate consignment account is opened. Think of it as a trading and profit and loss account for each consignment. The purpose is to calculate the net profit or loss on each consignment.

Goods consigned and expenses paid by the consignor

Double entry needed:

Goods consigned (a)   Debit consignment account
                               Credit goods sent on consignment account

Expenses paid (b)   Debit consignment account
                               Credit cash book

Expenses of the agent (consignee) and sales receipts

When the sales have been completed the consignee will send an account sales to the consignor. This will show:

		£	£
Sales			xxx
Less	Expenses	xxx	
	Commission	xxx	xxx
Balance now paid			xxx

The consignor enters these details in his books. The double entry needed is:

Sales (*c*):	Debit consignee's account
	Credit consignment account
Expenses of consignee (*d*):	Debit consignment account
	Credit consignee's account
Commission of consignee (*e*):	Debit consignment account
	Credit consignee's account
Cash received from consignee (*f*):	Debit cash
	Credit consignee's account

Against each type of entry needed, (*a*) to (*f*) are shown. These will be used in Exhibit 3.1.

Exhibit 3.1

Wills of London, whose financial year ends on 31 December, consigned goods to Adams, his agent in Canada. All transactions were started and completed in 19X5.

(*a*) January 16: Wills consigned goods costing £500 to Adams.
(*b*) February 28: Wills paid carriage to Canada, £50.

Adams, the consignee, sends an account sales on 31 July when all the goods have been sold. It shows:

(*c*) Sales amounted to £750.
(*d*) Adams' expenses were: Import duty, £25.
　　　　　　　　　　　　　　 Distribution expenses, £30.
(*e*) Commission had been agreed at 6 per cent of sales. This amounted to £45.
(*f*) Adams paid balance owing, £650.

Wills' books:

Consignment to Adams, Ottawa, Canada

19X5		£	19X5		£
Jan 16	Goods sent on consignment (*a*)	500	Jul 31 Sales (*c*)		750
Feb 28	Bank: carriage (*b*)	50			
Jul 31	Adams: Import duty (*d*)	25			
	Distribution (*d*)	30			
„ 31	Adams: Commission (*e*)	45			
„ 31	Profit on consignment (transferred to profit and loss account)	100			
		750			750

Goods sent on Consignment

		19X5		£
		Jan 16	Consignment to Adams (*a*)	500

Cash Book

19X5		£	19X5		£
Jul 31	Adams (consignee) (*f*)	650	Feb 28	Consignment to Adams: Carriage (*b*)	50

Adams (Consignee)

19X5		£	19X5		£
Jul 31	Consignment: Sales (*c*)	750	Jul 31	Consignment:	
			„ 31	Import duty (*d*)	25
			„ 31	Distribution (*d*)	30
			„ 31	Commission (*e*)	45
			„ 31	Bank (*f*)	650
		750			750

You can see that the main features are:

(*a*) The consignment account is a trading and profit and loss account for one consignment.

(*b*) The consignee's (Adams) personal account is used to show double entry for items concerning him. All of these details have been shown on the account sales he sent after selling the goods.

3.3 Consignee's (the agent's) records

The only items needed in the consignee's records will be found from the account sales he sent to the consignor after the goods have been sold.

He does not enter, in his double entry, the goods received on consignment. They never belong to him. His job is to sell the goods. Of course he will keep a note of the goods, but not in his double entry account records.

The double entry needed is:

Cash from sales of consignment (*c*):	Debit cash book Credit consignor's account
Payment of consignment expenses (*d*):	Debit consignor's account Credit cash book
Commission earned (*e*):	Debit consignor's account Credit profit and loss account
Cash to settle balance shown on account sales (*f*):	Debit consignor's account Credit cash book

Exhibit 3.2

Taking the details shown in Exhibit 3.1 the account sales sent by Adams (consignee) to Wills (consignor) would appear as follows:

Account Sales (converted into £ sterling)		
		Adams, Ottawa, Canada. 31 July 19X5
To Wills London.		
		£
Sale of goods received on consignment (c)		750
Less Charges:	£	
Import duty (d)	25	
Distribution costs (d)	30	
Commission (e)	45	100
Bank draft enclosed (f)		650

The double entry accounts in the books of the consignee (Adams) follow:

Wills (Consignor)

19X5	£	19X5	£
Jul 31 Bank:		Jul 31 Bank: Sales (c)	750
Import duty (d)	25		
Distribution (d)	30		
„ 31 Commission transferred to profit and loss (e)	45		
„ 31 Bank (f)	650		
	750		750

Cash Book

19X5	£	19X5	£
Jul 31 Wills: Sales (c)	750	Jul 31 Wills: Import duty (d)	25
		„ 31 Wills: Distribution (d)	30
		„ 31 Wills: To settle account (f)	650

Profit and Loss Account (Adams)

		£
	Commission on consignment from Wills (e)	45

You will see that the account of Wills in Adams' books in Exhibit 3.2 contains exactly the same details as that of Adams in Wills' books in Exhibit 3.1. Obviously the debits and credits are on opposite sides in the two sets of accounts.

3.4 Bad debts and consignments

Normally, when an agent sells the goods of the consignor he will collect the sale money from the customer. If the customer does not pay his account, the money in respect of this does not have to be paid by the agent to the consignor.

To make certain he does not have such bad debts, the consignor may pay an extra commission to the agent. When this happens the money for the debt will have to be paid by the agent even though he has not collected it. This extra commission is called **del credere commission.**

3.5 Consignor's accounting period and incomplete consignments

In this chapter we have looked at consignments which were all sold by the agent before the financial year end of the consignor. For instance, if a consignor's account year ends annually on 31 December, all goods consigned in 19X4 will have been sold by 31 December 19X4.

Sometimes this will not be true. We could have sent goods to the agent in September 19X4, and the final sales may be in March 19X5. When the consignor prepares his final accounts up to 31 December 19X4, there will be an incomplete consignment at the date of the balance sheet.

3.6 Accounting for incomplete consignments

The main difference between a completed consignment at the balance sheet date and an uncompleted one is that the unsold stock has to be valued and carried down to the following period. This stock will appear in the balance sheet of the consignor as a current asset. Such a case is shown in Exhibit 3.3.

Exhibit 3.3

(a) Farr of Chester consigns 10 cases of goods costing £200 per case to Moore in Nairobi on 1 July 19X4.

(b) Farr pays £250 for carriage and insurance for the whole consignment on 1 July 19X4.

Farr receives an interim account sales with a bank draft from Moore on 28 December 19X4. It shows (converted into £ sterling):

(c) Moore has sold 8 cases of goods for £400 each = £3,200.

(d) Moore has paid a total of £150 for landing charges and import duties on receipt of the whole consignment.

(e) Moore has paid selling costs, in respect of the 8 cases sold, of £160.

(f) Moore has deducted his commission of 10 per cent in respect of the 8 cases sold = 10% × £3,200 = £320.

(g) Moore encloses bank draft of £2,570. This is made up of (c) £3,200 − (d) £150 − (e) £160 − (f) £320 = £2,570.

Farr now wishes to balance off his consignment account at his financial year end, 31 December 19X4, and to transfer the profit to date to his profit and loss account.

The consignment account will appear as follows:

Farr's books:

Consignment to Moore

19X4		£	19X4		£
Jul 1	Goods on consignment (a)	2,000	Dec 28	Moore: Sale of part consignment (c)	3,200
„ 1	Bank: Carriage and insurance (b)	250	„ 31	Value of unsold stock (h) c/d	480
Dec 28	Moore: Landing charges and import duties (d)	150			
	Selling costs (e)	160			
	Commission (f)	320			
„ 31	Profit on consignment to profit and loss	800			
		3,680			3,680
19X5					
Jan 1	Value of unsold stock (h) b/d	480			

Note:	(h)	Value of unsold stock at 31 December 19X4:		£	£
		Goods: 2 cases × £200 each			400
		Add Proportion of expenses belonging to 2 unsold cases out of 10 received			
		(b) Carriage 2/10 × £250		50	
		(d) Landing charges and duties 2/10 × £150		30	80
					480

There is no proportion of (e) selling costs £160 or (f) commission £320 added to the valuation of the 2 unsold cases. This is because both of these expenses were only for the sale of the 8 cases, and nothing to do with the 2 unsold cases.

The profit and loss account for Farr for the year ended 31 December 19X4 will include the consignment profit of £800. The balance sheet as at 31 December 19X4 will include the consignment stock of £480 as a current asset.

The consignee's account, Moore's, can be shown in Farr's books as:

Moore

19X4		£	19X4		£
Dec 28	Consignment: Sales (c)	3,200	Dec 28	Consignment expenses:	
				Landing charges etc. (d)	150
				Selling costs (e)	160
				Commission (f)	320
				Bank (g)	2,570
		3,200			3,200

3.7 Final completion of consignment

When the remainder of the consignment is sold, the consignment account can be closed. This will be done by transferring the final portion of profit or loss to the consignor's profit and loss account. The details will be found in the final account sales which the consignee will have sent to the consignor.

Taking the completion of the consignment in Exhibit 3.3 as an example, the following details were obtained from the final account sales dated 31 March 19X5.

(*i*)   The final 2 cases of goods were sold for £380 each = £760.
(*j*)   Selling costs for these 2 cases were £70.
(*k*)   Commission deducted at 10 per cent = 10% × £760 = £76.
(*l*)   Bank draft sent for £614. Made up of (*i*) £760 − (*j*) £70 − (*k*) £76 = £614.

The consignment account can now be shown.

Farr's books:

Consignment to Moore

19X5		£	19X5		£
Jan 1	Value of unsold stock (*h*) b/d	480	Mar 31	Moore: Sale of remainder (*i*)	760
Mar 31	Moore:				
	Selling costs (*j*)	70			
	Commission (*k*)	76			
„ 31	Profit to profit and loss	134			
		760			760

New terms

Consignment (p. 19): Selling goods through an agent.

Consignor (p. 19): The person sending goods on consignment.

Consignee (p. 19): The person receiving the goods on consignment.

Del credere commission (p. 23): Extra commission payable to an agent who will promise to pay for any bad debts.

Main points to remember

1   Goods sent to an agent on consignment continue to belong to the consignor until they are sold.

2   The consignee, or agent, sells the goods and collects the money due from customers.

3   The money collected is passed to the consignor after deduction of expenses and commission.

Review questions

3.1   On 8 February 19X5 PJ, a London trader, consigned 120 cases of goods to MB, an agent in New Zealand.

The cost of the goods was £25 a case. PJ paid carriage to the port £147 and insurance £93.

On 31 March 19X5 PJ received an *account sales* from MB, showing that 100 cases had been sold for £3,500 and MB had paid freight, at the rate of £2 a case, and port charges amounting to £186. MB was entitled to a commission of 5 per cent on sales. A *sight draft* for the net amount due was enclosed with the *account sales*.

You are required to show the accounts for the above transactions in the ledger of PJ and to show the transfer to profit and loss account at 31 March 19X5.

(Institute of Chartered Secretaries and Administrators)

3.2A   (*a*) Explain the differences between a consignment and a sale.
  (*b*) 100 cases of goods costing £3,500 were sent on consignment by X Limited to Y Limited on 1 February 19X7. At the same time, X Limited paid delivery expenses of £100 and insurance of £20. On 1 March 19X7 an interim account sales was received from Y Limited showing that 80 cases had been sold for £63 each and that storage charges of £180 and selling expenses of £100 had been deducted from the account. After also deducting the commission on sales which was agreed at 5 per cent of the gross sales, Y Limited settled the balance due to X Limited for goods sold by a bank draft.

Required:
(*i*)   Prepare the interim account sales, and
(*ii*) the consignment account in the books of X Limited.

3.3   On 15 November 19X5, Hughes consigned 300 cases of wooden items to Galvez of Madrid. On 31 December 19X5, Galvez forwarded an account sales, with a draft for the balance, showing the following transactions:

1   250 cases sold at £20 each and 50 at £18 each.
2   Port and duty charges £720.
3   Storage and carriage charges £410.
4   Commission on sales 5% + 1% del credere.

Required:
(*a*) Prepare the account sales, and
(*b*) Show the consignment inward account in the books of Galvez. Ignore interest.

3.4   Stone consigned goods to Rock on 1 January 19X6, their value being £12,000, and it was agreed that Rock should receive a commission of 5 per cent on gross sales. Expenses incurred by Stone for freight and insurance amount to £720. Stone's financial year ended on 31 March 19X6, and an account sales made up to that date was received from Rock. This showed that 70 per cent of the goods had been sold for £10,600 but that up to 31 March 19X6, only £8,600 had been received by Rock in respect of these sales. Expenses in connection with the goods consigned were shown as being £350, and it was also shown that £245 had been incurred in connection with the goods sold. With the account sales, Rock sent a sight draft for the balance shown to be due, and Stone incurred bank charges of £12 on 10 April 19X6, in cashing same.

Stone received a further account sales from Rock made up to 30 June 19X6, and this showed that the remainder of the goods had been sold for £4,800 and that £200 had been incurred by way of selling expenses. It also showed that all cash due had been received with the exception of a debt for £120 which had proved to be bad. A sight draft for the balance due was sent with the account sales and the bank charged Stone £9 on 1 July 19X6, for cashing same. You are required to write up the necessary accounts in Stone's books to record these transactions.

(Institute of Chartered Accountants)

3.5A   Fleet is a London merchant. During the financial year to 31 March 19X8, he sent a consignment of goods to Sing, his agent in Bali. The details of the transaction were as follows:

(*a*) On 1 April 19X7, 1,000 boxes were sent to Sing. These boxes had originally cost Fleet £20 each.

(b) Fleet's carriage, freight and insurance costs of the consignment paid on 30 April 19X7 amounted to £2,000.

(c) During the voyage to Bali, ten boxes were lost. On 30 September 19X7, Fleet received a cheque for £220 as compensation from his insurance company for the loss of the boxes.

(d) On 1 March 19X8, Fleet received £20,000 from Sing.

(e) Both Fleet and Sing's accounting year end is 31 March.

(f) On 15 April 19X8, Fleet received the following interim account sales from Sing:

Interim Account Sales

The Water Front
Gama
Bali

31 March 19X8
Consignment of goods sold on behalf of Fleet, London: 950 boxes of merchandise.

	£	£	£
Sales:			
950 boxes at £30 each			28,500
Charges:			
Distribution expenses (at £2 per box)		1,900	
Landing charges and import duty (at £1 per box)		990	
Commission (5% × £28,500)		1,425	4,315
			24,185
Less amount previously sent			20,000
Net proceeds per draft enclosed			£4,185

31 March 19X8
Sing (signed)
Bali

Required:
Prepare the following ledger accounts for the year to 31 March 19X8:

(a) in Fleet's books of account:
    (i) goods sent on consignment account;
    (ii) consignment to Sing's account;
    (iii) Sing (consignee) account;

    and

(b) in Sing's books of account:
    (i) Fleet (London) account;
    (ii) commission account.

(*Association of Accounting Technicians*)

4

Branch accounts

Objectives

After you have studied this chapter, you should:

- *know two methods of recording the entries relating to branch accounts*
- *be aware of the issues relating to foreign branch accounts*

4.1 Accounting records and branches

When we look at accounting records to show transactions at the branches of an organisation, we have a choice of two main methods. These are:

(*a*) the head office keeps all the accounting records, or
(*b*) each branch has its own full accounting system.

It is easier to understand branch accounts if these two main methods are dealt with separately.

4.2 If the head office maintains all the accounts

The accounts are used for three main purposes:

(*a*) to record transactions showing changes in assets, liabilities and capital;
(*b*) to ascertain the profitability of each branch;
(*c*) in addition, if possible, to check whether anyone at the branches is stealing goods or cash.

This third purpose is very important for firms that have many branches. The people who manage or work in these branches are receiving and paying out large sums of money. In addition they may be handling large amounts of stocks of goods.

The branch or branches may be a considerable distance away from the head office. This may mean that the manager, or any of his staff, may think that they can steal things without being caught.

4.3 Methods for checking stock and cash

If a firm with only a few branches sells only very expensive cars, it would be easy to check on purchases and sales of the cars. The number of cars sold would not be very great. Checking that cars or money have not been stolen would be easy. However, a firm such as a store with branches selling many thousands of cheap items could not be checked so easily. To keep a check on each carton of salt or bag of flour sold would be almost impossible. Even if it could be done, such checking would cost too much.

The accounting answer to this problem is to record all transactions at the branch in terms of selling prices. Then for each accounting period, it should be possible to check whether the closing stock is as it should be.

For a small branch, for example, you may be given the following figures:

	£
Stock on hand at 1 January – at selling price	500
January – Goods sent to the branch by the head office – at selling price	4,000
January – Sales by the branch – obviously at selling price	3,800

The calculation of the closing stock becomes:

	£
Opening Stock 1 January (selling price)	500
Add Goods sent to the branch (selling price)	4,000
Goods which the branch had available for sale (selling price)	4,500
Less Goods sold (selling price)	3,800
Closing stock at 31 January should therefore be (selling price)	700

4.4 Allowances for deficiencies

In every business there will be:

(a) Wastage of goods for some reason. Goods may be damaged or broken, or they may be kept too long or somehow waste away.
(b) Stealing by customers, especially in the retail business.
(c) Thefts by employees.

No one can be certain how much stock is wasted or stolen during a period. Only experience will enable a firm to make a good estimate of these losses.

4.5 The double column system

At regular intervals, obviously at least once a year but usually more frequently, the head office may draft a trading and profit and loss account for each branch. The trading account can be shown with two columns, one in which goods sent to the branch or in stock are shown at cost price, i.e. the normal basis for any business. This column is therefore part of a normal trading account for the branch. The other column will show all trading account items at selling price. This column allows deficiencies in trading to be compared with the normal deficiency allowed for wastages, etc. It is not a part of the double entry recording; it is a memorandum column for control purposes only.

Exhibit 4.1

This is drafted from the following details for a firm which sells goods at a uniform mark-up of 33⅓ per cent on cost price:

	£
Stock 1 Jan 19X8 (at cost)	1,200
Goods sent to the branch during the year (at cost)	6,000
Sales (selling price)	7,428
Stock 31 Dec 19X8 (at cost)	1,500
Expenses	1,000

Allowances for wastage, etc., one per cent of sales.

<table>
<tr><td colspan="9" align="center">Branch Trading and Profit and Loss Account for the year ended
31.12.19X8</td></tr>
<tr><td></td><td colspan="2" align="center">At
selling
price</td><td></td><td></td><td colspan="2" align="center">At
selling
price</td></tr>
<tr><td></td><td>£</td><td>£</td><td></td><td></td><td>£</td><td>£</td></tr>
<tr><td>Stock 1 Jan 19X8</td><td>1,600</td><td>1,200</td><td>Sales</td><td></td><td>7,428</td><td>7,428</td></tr>
<tr><td>Goods from head office</td><td>8,000</td><td>6,000</td><td>Deficiency (difference)</td><td></td><td>172</td><td></td></tr>
<tr><td></td><td>9,600</td><td>7,200</td><td></td><td></td><td></td><td></td></tr>
<tr><td>Less Stock 31 Dec 19X8</td><td>2,000</td><td>1,500</td><td></td><td></td><td></td><td></td></tr>
<tr><td></td><td>7,600</td><td>5,700</td><td></td><td></td><td></td><td></td></tr>
<tr><td>Gross profit c/d</td><td></td><td>1,728</td><td></td><td></td><td></td><td></td></tr>
<tr><td></td><td>7,600</td><td>7,428</td><td></td><td></td><td>7,600</td><td>7,428</td></tr>
<tr><td>Expenses</td><td></td><td>1,000</td><td>Gross profit b/d</td><td></td><td></td><td>1,728</td></tr>
<tr><td>Net profit</td><td></td><td>728</td><td></td><td></td><td></td><td></td></tr>
<tr><td></td><td></td><td>1,728</td><td></td><td></td><td></td><td>1,728</td></tr>
</table>

As the actual deficiency of £172 exceeds the amount expected, i.e. one per cent of £7,428 = £74, an investigation will be made.

This method is suitable where all the sales are for cash, there being no sales on credit.

4.6 The stock and debtors system

Further adjustments are needed when there are credit sales as well as cash sales. There are two ways of making the entries. These are:

(a) using memoranda columns only to keep a check on stock, in a similar way to that shown in 4.5;
(b) building the control of stock fully into the double entry system. This is often called an integrated system.

We can now examine both of these methods.

Using the following basic data, Exhibit 4.2 shows the records when the memoranda method is used, while Exhibit 4.3 shows the records when the integrated method is in use.

Data: A branch sells all its goods at a uniform mark-up of fifty per cent on cost price. Credit customers are to pay their accounts directly to the head office.

		£
First day of the period:		
Stock (at cost)	(A)	2,000
Debtors	(B)	400
During the period:		
Goods sent to the branch (at cost)	(C)	7,000
Sales – Cash	(D)	6,000
Sales – Credit	(E)	4,800
Cash remitted by debtors to head office	(F)	4,500
At the close of the last day of the period:		
Stock (at cost)	(G)	1,800
Debtors	(H)	700

The letters A to H beside the figures have been inserted to identify the entries in Exhibit 4.3. The entries for each of the above items will have the relevant letter shown beside it.

Memoranda columns method

Exhibit 4.2

Branch Stock

	Selling price memo. only			*Selling price memo. only*	
	£	£		£	£
Stock b/fwd	3,000	2,000	Sales: Cash	6,000	6,000
Goods sent	10,500	7,000	Credit	4,800	4,800
Gross profit to			Stock c/d	2,700	1,800
profit and loss		3,600			
	13,500	12,600		13,500	12,600
Stock b/d	2,700	1,800			

Branch Debtors

	£		£
Balances b/f	400	Cash	4,500
Branch stock	4,800	Balance c/d	700
	5,200		5,200
Balance b/d	700		

Goods Sent to Branches

	£		£
Transfer to head office trading account	7,000	Branch stock	7,000

Cash Book

	£	
Branch stock – cash sales	6,000	
Branch debtors	4,500	

The branch stock account is thus in effect a trading account, and is identical to the type used in the double column system. In addition, however, a branch debtors account is in use.

The balance of the goods sent to the branches account is shown as being transferred to the head office trading account. This figure is deducted from the purchases in the head office trading account, so that goods bought for the branch can be disregarded when the gross profit earned by the head office is calculated.

The integrated system

The integrated system introduces the idea that the gross profit earned by a firm can be calculated by reference to profit margins only. A simple example illustrates this point. Assume that a self-employed travelling salesman sells all his goods at cost price plus 25 per cent for profit. At the start of a week he has £4 stock at cost, he buys goods costing £40, he sells goods for £45 (selling price) and he has goods left in stock at the end of the week which had cost him £8. A normal trading account based on this data is shown below.

Trading Account for the week ended...

	£		£
Opening stock	4	Sales	45
Add Purchases	40		
	44		
Less Closing stock	8		
Cost of goods sold	36		
Gross profit	9		
	45		45

This could, however, also be shown as:

	£
Profit made when opening stock is sold	1
Profit made when purchases are sold	10
Profit made when all goods are sold	11
But he still has left unsold goods (cost £8) on which the profit still has to be realised	2
Therefore profit realised	9

This could be expressed in account form as:

Salesman's Adjustment Account

	£		£
Gross profit	9	Unrealised profit b/f	1
Unrealised profit c/d	2	Goods bought	10
	11		11

The integrated system uses an adjustment account which is needed because goods sent to the branch are shown at cost price in a 'goods sent to branches account'. In the branch stock account these goods are shown at selling price. Obviously if one entry is made at cost price and the other at selling price, the accounts would not balance. To correct this, an extra account called a branch adjustment account is opened. The entries in this account are in respect of the profit content only of goods.

The branch stock account acts as a check upon stock deficiencies. The branch adjustment account shows the amount of gross profit earned during the period.

Exhibit 4.3 shows the accounts needed for the integrated system from the same information on pages 30–31 used to complete Exhibit 4.2. In this example a stock deficiency does not exist. The letters A to H in Exhibit 4.3 conform to the letters A to H shown against the information on page 31.

Exhibit 4.3

Branch Stock (Selling Price)

		£			£
Balance b/f	(A)	3,000	Sales: Cash	(D)	6,000
Goods sent to branch	(C)	10,500	Credit	(E)	4,800
			Balance c/d	(G)	2,700
		13,500			13,500
Balance b/d	(G)	2,700			

Branch Debtors (Selling Price)

		£			£
Balances b/f	(B)	400	Cash	(F)	4,500
Branch stock	(E)	4,800	Balances c/d	(H)	700
		5,200			5,200
Balances b/d	(H)	700			

Goods Sent to Branches (Cost Price)

	£			£
Transfer to head office trading account	7,000	Branch stock	(C)	7,000

Branch Adjustment (Profit Content)

		£			£
Gross profit to profit and loss		3,600	Unrealised profit b/f	(A)	1,000
Unrealised profit c/d	(G)	900	Branch stock – goods sent	(C)	3,500
		4,500			4,500
			Unrealised profit b/d	(G)	900

The opening and closing stocks are shown in the branch stock account at selling price. However, the balance sheet should show the stock at cost price. The previous balance sheet should therefore have shown stock at cost £2,000. This is achieved by having a compensating £1,000 credit balance brought forward in the branch adjustment account so that the debit balance of £3,000 in the branch stock account, when it comes to being shown in the balance sheet, has the £1,000 credit balance deducted to show a net figure of £2,000. Similarly, at the close of the period the balance sheet will show stock at £1,800 (branch stock debit balance £2,700 *less* branch adjustment credit balance £900).

4.7 The stock and debtors integrated system – further considerations

Returns

Goods may be returned:

(*a*) from the branch stock to the head office;
(*b*) from the branch debtors to the branch stock;
(*c*) from the branch debtors to the head office.

Exhibit 4.4

To examine the entries needed, suppose a firm sells goods at cost plus 25 per cent profit, and according to the categories stated the following goods were returned, all prices shown being selling prices: (*a*) £45, (*b*) £75, (*c*) £15. The entries needed are:

Branch Stock (Selling Price)

		£				£
Returns from debtors	(*b*)	75	Returns to head office	(*a*)		45

Branch Adjustment (Profit Loading)

		£
Returns from branch	(*a*)	9
Returns from debtors	(*c*)	3

Goods Sent to Branches (Cost Price)

		£
Returns from branch	(*a*)	36
Returns from debtors	(*c*)	12

Branch Debtors (Selling Price)

				£
	Returns to branch	(*b*)		75
	Returns to head office	(*c*)		15

Entries (*b*) both being in accounts shown at selling price were two in number, i.e. £75 Dr and £75 Cr; entries (*a*) and (*c*) each needed entries in three accounts, (*a*) being £45 Cr and £9 Dr and £36 Dr, (*c*) being £15 Cr and £12 Dr and £3 Dr.

4.8 If each branch maintains full accounting records

This method is rarely used in firms with many branches. It is more common in a firm with just one or two or a few branches, and is particularly relevant if a branch is large enough to warrant employing a separate accounting staff.

A branch cannot operate on its own without resources, and it is the firm that provides these in the first instance. The firm will want to know how much money it has invested in each branch, and from this arises the concept of branch and head office current accounts. The relationship between the branch and the head office is seen as that of a debtor/creditor. The current account shows the branch as a debtor in the head office records, while the head office is shown as a creditor in the branch records.

The current accounts are used for transactions concerned with supplying resources to the branch or in taking back resources. For such transactions full double entry records are needed both in the branch records and in the head office records, i.e. each item will be recorded twice in each set of records. Some transactions will, however, concern the branch only, and these will merely need two entries in the branch records and none in the head office records. Exhibit 4.5 shows several transactions and the records needed.

Exhibit 4.5

A firm with its head office in London opened a branch in Manchester. The following transactions took place in the first month:

(A) Opened a bank account at Manchester by transferring £1,000 from the London bank account.

(B) Bought premises in Manchester, paying by cheque drawn on the London bank account, £5,000.

(C) Manchester bought a motor van, paying by cheque £600 from its own bank account.

(D) Manchester bought fixtures on credit from A B Equipment Ltd, £900.

(E) London supplied a machine valued at £250 from its own machinery.

(F) Manchester bought goods from suppliers, paying by cheque on its own account, £270.

(G) Manchester's cash sales banked immediately in its own bank account, £3,000.

(H) Goods invoiced at cost to Manchester during the month by London (no cash or cheques being paid specifically for these goods by Manchester), £2,800.

(I) A cheque is paid to London by Manchester as general return of funds, £1,800.

(J) Goods returned to London by Manchester – at cost price, £100.

The exact dates have been deliberately omitted. It will be seen later that complications arise because of differences in the timing of transactions. Each transaction has been identified by a capital letter. The relevant letter will be shown against each entry in the accounts.

Head Office Records (in London)

Manchester Branch Current Account

		£			£
Bank	(A)	1,000	Bank	(I)	1,800
Bank – premises	(B)	5,000	Returns from Branch	(J)	100
Machinery	(E)	250			
Goods sent to Branch	(H)	2,800			

Bank

		£			£
Manchester Branch	(I)	1,800	Manchester Branch	(A)	1,000
			Manchester premises	(B)	5,000

Machinery

					£
			Manchester Branch	(E)	250

Goods sent to Branch

		£			£
Returns from Branch	(J)	100	Manchester Branch	(H)	2,800

Branch Records (in Manchester)

Head Office Current Account

		£			£
Bank	(I)	1,800	Bank	(A)	1,000
Returns	(J)	100	Premises	(B)	5,000
			Machinery	(E)	250
			Goods from Head Office	(H)	2,800

Bank

		£			£
Head Office	(A)	1,000	Motor van	(C)	600
Cash sales	(G)	3,000	Purchases	(F)	270
			Head Office	(I)	1,800

Premises

		£	
Head Office	(B)	5,000	

Motor Van

		£	
Bank	(C)	600	

Fixtures

		£	
A B Equipment Ltd	(D)	900	

A B Equipment Ltd

				£
	Fixtures	(D)		900

Machinery

		£	
Head Office	(E)	250	

Purchases

		£	
Bank	(F)	270	

Sales

			£
	Bank	(G)	3,000

Goods from Head Office

		£			£
Head Office	(H)	2,800	Head Office – returns	(J)	100

It can be seen that items C, D, F and G are entered only in the Manchester records. This is because these items are purely internal transactions and are not concerned with resources flowing between London and Manchester.

4.9 Profit or loss and current accounts

The profit earned by the branch (or loss incurred by it) does not belong to the branch. It belongs to the firm and must therefore be shown as such. The head office represents the central authority of the firm and profit of the branch should be credited to the Head Office Current Account, any loss being debited.

The branch will therefore draw up its own trading and profit and loss account. After agreement with the head office the net profit will then be transferred to the credit of the Head Office Current Account. The head office in its own records will then debit the Branch Current Account and credit its own profit and loss account. Taking the net profit earned in Exhibit 4.5 as £700, the two sets of books would appear thus:

Head Office Records (in London)

London Profit and Loss Account

		£
	Net profit earned by the Manchester Branch	700

Manchester Branch Current Account

	£		£
Bank	1,000	Bank	1,800
Bank: premises	5,000	Returns from Branch	100
Machinery	250		
Goods sent to Branch	2,800		
Net profit to main profit and loss account	700	Balance c/d	7,850
	9,750		9,750
Balance b/d	7,850		

Branch Records (in Manchester)

Manchester Profit and Loss Account

	£	
Net profit carried to the Head Office Current Account	700	

Head Office Current Account

	£		£
Returns to Head Office	100	Bank	1,000
Bank	1,800	Premises	5,000
		Machinery	250
		Goods from Head Office	2,800
Balance c/d	7,850	Profit and loss account	700
	9,750		9,750
		Balance b/d	7,850

4.10 The combined balance sheet

After the trading and profit and loss accounts have been drawn up a balance sheet is required for the whole firm. The branch will send its trial balance to the head office which will add the assets in its own trial balance to those in the branch trial balance to give the total for each type of asset to be shown in the balance sheet, and a similar procedure will be carried out for the liabilities.

In the trial balances the Head Office Current Account will be a debit balance while the Branch Current Account will be a credit balance, e.g. the two figures of £7,850 in the London and Manchester books. These therefore cancel out and are not shown in the combined balance sheet. This is in order, as the two balances do not in fact represent assets or liabilities, but are merely a measure of the resources at the branch.

4.11 Items in transit

It was stated earlier that the timing of transactions raised complications. Obviously a cheque sent by a Manchester branch one day would probably arrive in London the next day, while goods sent from London to Manchester, or returned from Manchester to London, could well take longer than that. Both the head office and the branch will have entered the transactions at the dates of remittance or receipt, and as the remittance from one place will occur on one day and the receipt occur at the other place on another day, then where items are in transit at the end of a financial period each set of records will not contain identical figures. This will mean that the balances on the current accounts will not be equal to one another.

It is, however, necessary to have identical amounts of balances on the current accounts so that they will cancel out when the combined balance sheet is prepared. As the two sets of records contain some figures which are different from each other they must somehow be reconciled so that the balances carried down are the same. Which set of figures are to be altered? The answer is one of expediency. It would be normal to find the most experienced accountants at the Head Office, and therefore the amendments should all be made in the Head Office books instead of leaving it to junior accountants at the branches who would be more likely to make mistakes. Also if there are several branches the problems of communicating specific instructions to several accountants some distance away make it easier for all amendments to be made at the Head Office.

Exhibit 4.6 is for a second month of the business shown in Exhibit 4.5. However, whereas there were no items in transit at the end of the first month, this does not hold true at the conclusion of the second month.

Exhibit 4.6

Head Office records (showing current accounts only)	£
Goods sent to Branch	3,700
Cheques received from Branch	2,950
Returns received from Branch	440

Branch records	
Goods received from Head Office	3,500
Cheques sent to Head Office	3,030
Returns sent to Head Office	500

It may be assumed that the net profit as shown by the profit and loss account of the branch is £800.

Branch Records (in Manchester)

Head Office Current Account

	£		£
Bank	3,030	Balance b/fwd	7,850
Returns to Head Office	500	Goods from Head Office	3,500
Balance c/d	8,620	Net profit	800
	12,150		12,150
		Balance b/d	8,620

Head Office Records (in London)

Manchester Branch Current Account

		£			£
Balance b/fwd		7,850	Bank	(B)	2,950
Goods sent to Branch	(A)	3,700	Returns received	(C)	440
Net profit		800			

At this point the following items are observed to be in transit at the end of the period (these should be confirmed to ensure that they are not merely errors in accounting records):

1 Goods sent to the branch amounting to £200 (£3,700 – £3,500).
2 Cheques sent by the branch amounting to £80 (£3,030 – £2,950).
3 Returns from the branch amounting to £60 (£500 – £440).

(**A**) needs amending to £3,500. This is done by crediting the account with £200.
(**B**) needs amending to £3,030. This is done by crediting the account with £80.
(**C**) needs amending to £500. This is done by crediting the account with £60.

As these are items in transit they need to be taken to the period in which they arrive, i.e. the next month. This is effected by carrying them down as balances into the next period. The branch current account will now be completed.

It may appear at first sight to be rather strange that all the items in transit are shown as debit balances. However, it must be appreciated that goods (including returns) and money in transit are assets of the firm at the end of a financial period. That they are in transit is merely stipulating that the assets are neither at the head office nor at the branch but are somewhere else. Assets are always shown as debit balances and there is no reason why it should be different just because they have not reached their destination on a certain date.

Manchester Branch Current Account

	£		£
Balance b/fwd	7,850	Bank	2,950
Goods sent to branch	3,700	Returns received	440
Net profit	800	Goods in transit c/d	200
		Cheques in transit c/d	80
		Returns in transit c/d	60
		Balance c/d	8,620
	12,350		12,350
Balance b/d	8,620		
Goods in transit b/d	200		
Cheques in transit b/d	80		
Returns in transit b/d	60		

All of these four balances are shown in the trial balance. When the combined balance sheet is being prepared the balance of the two current accounts, i.e. in this case £8,620, will cancel out as it is a debit balance in one trial balance and a credit balance in the other. The goods in transit £200 and the returns in transit £60, both being goods, are added to the stock in the balance sheet. This is because stock is made up of the following items:

At the end of the second month:

	£
Stock at London	
Add Stock at Manchester	
Add Stocks in transit (£200 + £60)	260
Total stock	

Similarly, the balance for cheques or remittances in transit is added to the bank balances at London and Manchester:

	£
Bank balance at London	
Add Bank balance in Manchester	
Add Remittances in transit	80

This is rather like a man who has £14 in one pocket and £3 in another. He takes a £5 note from the pocket containing the larger amount and is transferring it to his other pocket when someone asks him to stay perfectly still and calculate the total cash in his possession. He therefore has:

	£
Pocket 1	9
Pocket 2	3
Cash in transit	5
	17

4.12 Items in transit and the balance sheet

Using the figures already given in Exhibit 4.6 but adding some further information, trial balances for London Head Office and the Manchester Branch are now shown in Exhibit 4.7 after the profit and loss accounts have been drawn up for the second month.

Exhibit 4.7

	Trial Balances as at 29 February 19X8			
	London Head Office		*Manchester Branch*	
	Dr	*Cr*	*Dr*	*Cr*
	£	£	£	£
Premises	10,000		5,000	
Machinery	2,000		400	
Fixtures	3,100		1,400	
Motor vans	1,500		900	
Closing stock	3,800		700	
Debtors	1,100		800	
Bank	12,200		600	
Head Office Current Account				8,620
Branch Current Account	8,620			
Goods in transit	200			
Cheques in transit	80			
Returns in transit	60			
Creditors		1,300		1,180
Capital account as at 1 Jan 19X8		37,860		
Net profit for the two months (Branch £1,500 + Head Office £2,000)		3,500		
	42,660	42,660	9,800	9,800

The combined balance sheet can now be drawn up.

Balance Sheet as at 29 February 19X8

	£	£
Fixed assets		
Premises		15,000
Machinery		2,400
Fixtures		4,500
Motor vans		2,400
		24,300
Current assets		
Stocks	4,760	
Debtors	1,900	
Bank	12,880	
	19,540	
Less Current liabilities		
Creditors	2,480	
Working capital		17,060
		41,360

Capital

		£		£
Balance at 1 January 19X8				37,860
Add Net profit:				
London				2,000
Manchester				1,500
				41,360

Notes:

		£			£
Stocks:	London	3,800	Bank:	London	12,200
	Manchester	700		Manchester	600
	In transit		In transit		80
	(£200 + £60)	260			
		4,760			12,880

4.13 Foreign branch accounts

The treatment of the accounts of foreign branches is subject to only one exception from that of branches in your own country. This is concerned with the fact that when the trial balance is drawn up by the branch then this will be stated in a foreign currency. To amalgamate these figures with your own country's figures will mean that the foreign branch figures will have to be translated into your currency.

There are rules for general guidance as to how this can be done. SSAP 20: *Foreign currency translation* gives rules for organisations to follow. These are the ones which will be shown. (Before you read further you should check whether or not this topic is part of your examination requirements.)

The amount of a particular currency which one can obtain for another currency is known as the exchange rate. Taking an imaginary country with a currency called *chips*, there might be a general agreement that the exchange rate should stay about 5 chips to equal £1. At certain times the exchange rate will exactly equal that figure, but due to all sorts of economic reasons it may well be 5.02 chips to £1 on one day and 4.97 chips to £1 several days later. In addition, some years ago there may have been an act of devaluation by one of the countries involved; the exchange rate could well have then been 3 chips to £1. To understand more about exchange rates and devaluation the reader of this book would be well advised to consult a relevant economics textbook.

It is clear, however, that all items in the trial balance should not be converted to your currency on the basis of the exchange rate ruling at the date of the trial balance. The rules in SSAP 20 have been devised in an attempt to bring about conversion into your currency so as not to distort reported trading results.

4.14 Conversion rules per SSAP 20

1 (a) Fixed assets at the exchange rate ruling when the assets were bought. This method is known as the **temporal method**. If fixed assets have been bought on different dates, then different rates will have to be used for each separate purchase.
   (b) Depreciation on the fixed assets at the same rate as the fixed assets concerned.
2 Current assets and current liabilities – at the rate ruling at the date of the trial balance. This is known as the **closing method**.
3 Opening stock in the trading account – at the rate ruling at the previous balance sheet date.

4   Goods sent by the head office to the branch, or returns from the branch – at the actual figures shown in the Goods Sent to Branches Account in the head office books.
5   Trading and profit and loss account items, other than depreciation, opening and closing stocks, or goods sent to or returned by the branch – at the average rate for the period covered by the accounts.
6   The Head Office Current Account – at the same figures as shown in the Branch Current Account in the Head Office books.

4.15 Conversion of trial balance figures

When the conversion of the figures into your currency is completed, the totals of the debit and credit sides of your currency trial balance will not normally be equal to one another. This is due to different exchange rates being taken for conversion purposes. A balancing figure will therefore be needed to bring about the equality of the totals. For this purpose a **difference on exchange account** will be opened and a debit entry made therein if the lesser total is on the debit side of the trial balance. When the head office redrafts the profit and loss account any debit balance on the difference on exchange account should be transferred to it as an expense. A credit balance on the difference on exchange account should be transferred to the credit of the profit and loss account as a gain.

In consolidated accounts, special rules are applied for foreign exchange conversion.

Exhibit 4.8

An example of the conversion of a trial balance into UK currency is now shown. The branch is in Flavia, and the unit of currency is the Flavian dollar. The exchange rates needed are:

(a)   On 1 January 19X3, 10 dollars = £1
(b)   On 1 January 19X5, 11 dollars = £1
(c)   On 1 January 19X8, 17 dollars = £1
(d)   On 31 December 19X8, 15 dollars = £1
(e)   If no further information were given the average rate for 19X8 would have to be taken as (c) + (d) ÷ 2, i.e. 16 dollars = £1. This is not an advisable procedure in practice; the fact that the average has been calculated from only two readings could mean that the average calculated might be far different from a more accurate one calculated from a larger number of readings.

Trial Balance as on 31 December 19X8

	Dr (dol)	Cr (dol)	Exchange rates	Dr £	Cr £
Fixed assets:					
Bought 1 Jan 19X3	10,000		10=£1	1,000	
Bought 1 Jan 19X5	8,800		11=£1	800	
Stock 1 Jan 19X8	6,800		17=£1	400	
Expense accounts	8,000		16=£1	500	
Sales		32,000	16=£1		2,000
Goods from Head Office	21,900		£ per account in Head Office books	1,490	
Head Office current account		43,000	£ per account in Head Office books		3,380

Debtors	9,000		15=£1	600	
Creditors		4,500	15=£1		300
Bank	15,000		15=£1	1,000	
	79,500	79,500		5,790	5,680
Difference on exchange account					110
				5,790	5,790

The stock at 31 December 19X8 is 12,000 dollars. When the trading account is drawn up this will be converted at 15 dollars = £1, i.e. £800.

Main points to remember

1 There are two main methods used to record transactions of the branches of an organisation:
   (a) all accounting records are kept by the head office.
   (b) each branch has its own full accounting system.

2 Foreign branch figures need to be translated using the principles set down in SSAP 20: *Foreign currency translation.*

Review questions

4.1 Octopus Ltd, whose head office is at Cardiff, operates a branch at Swansea. All goods are purchased by head office and invoiced to and sold by the branch at cost plus 33⅓ per cent.

Other than a sales ledger kept at Swansea, all transactions are recorded in the books at Cardiff.

The following particulars are given of the transactions at the branch during the year ended 28 February 19X7.

	£
Stock on hand, 1 March 19X6, at invoice price	4,400
Debtors on 1 March 19X6	3,946
Stock on hand, 28 February 19X7, at invoice price	3,948
Goods sent from Cardiff during the year at invoice price	24,800
Credit sales	21,000
Cash sales	2,400
Returns to head office at invoice price	1,000
Invoice value of goods stolen	600
Bad debts written off	148
Cash from debtors	22,400
Normal loss at invoice price due to wastage	100
Cash discount allowed to debtors	428

You are required to write up the branch stock account and branch total debtors account for the year ended 28 February 19X7, as they would appear in the head office books.

(*Institute of Chartered Accountants*)

4.2 A Co. Ltd has a branch in Everton at which a full set of books are kept. At the end of the year the following is a summary of the transactions between the branch and the head office as recorded in the latter's books:

	£
Balance due from branch 1 January	20,160
Cash received from branch	30,000
Goods supplied to branch	23,160
Goods returned by branch	400
Expenses paid on behalf of branch	6,000

At 30 June the branch profit and loss account showed a net profit of £3,500.

(*a*) Show the above items as they would appear in the ledger of the head office.
(*b*) How can any resulting balance from these figures be proved, and what does it indicate?

4.3 RST Limited is a family-controlled company which operates a chain of retail outlets specialising in motor spares and accessories.

Branch stocks are purchased by a centralised purchasing function in order to obtain the best terms from suppliers.

A 10 per cent handling charge is applied by head office to the cost of the purchases, and branches are expected to add 25 per cent to the resulting figure to arrive at normal selling prices, although branch managers are authorised to reduce normal prices in special situations. The effect of such reductions must be notified to head office.

On 1 April 19X6, a new branch was established at Derham. The following details have been recorded for the year ended 31 March 19X7:

	£
Purchase cost to head office of stock transferred to Derham	82,400
Derham branch sales: cash	89,940
credit	1,870
Stocks transferred from Derham to other branches, at normal selling prices	3,300
Authorised reductions from normal selling prices during the year	2,250

All records in respect of branch activities are maintained at head office, and the branch profit margin is dealt with through a branch stock adjustment account.

Required:
(*a*) Prepare:
  (*i*) the branch stock account (maintained at branch selling prices);
  (*ii*) the branch stock adjustment account.
  The *book stock* should be taken for this part of the question.
(*b*) List four of the possible reasons for the stock difference revealed when a physical stocktaking at the Derham branch on 31 March 19X7 showed stock valued at selling prices amounting to £14,850.
(*c*) State which of the following is the figure to be included in RST Limited's balance sheet at 31 March 19X7, for Derham branch stock:
  (*i*) £11,138
  (*ii*) £11,880
  (*iii*) £10,800
  (*iv*) None of these.

Justify your choice with appropriate calculations.

(*Chartered Institute of Management Accountants*)

4.4A Paper Products has a head office in London and a branch in Bristol. The following information has been extracted from the head office books of account as at 31 March 19X6:

Information relating to the branch

Balances	Opening £000		Closing £000
Branch bank account (positive balance)	3		12
Branch debtors	66		81
Branch stock (at transfer price)	75		90
Transactions during the year		£000	
Bad debts written off		15	
Branch general expenses			
(paid from bank branch account)		42	
Cash received from credit customers and banked		390	
Cash sales banked		120	
Cash transferred from branch to head office bank account		459	
Credit sales		437	
Discounts allowed to credit customers		9	
Goods returned by credit customers		8	
Goods returned from branch			
(at transfer price from head office)			30
Goods sent to branch			
(at transfer price from head office)			600

Information relating to head office

Balances	Opening £000		Closing £000
Stock	180		220
Transactions during the year		£000	
Bad debts written off		24	
Cash sales		1,500	
Credit sales		2,000	
Discounts allowed to credit customers		29	
General expenses		410	
Goods returned by credit customers		40	
Purchases		2,780	

Additional information:

1 Most of the accounting records relating to the branch are kept by the head office in its own books of account.
2 All purchases are made by the head office, and goods are invoiced to the branch at selling price, that is, at cost price plus 50 per cent.

Required

(a) Write up the following ledger accounts for the year to 31 March 19X6, being careful to bring down any balances as at that date:
   (i) branch stock account;
   (ii) goods sent to branch account;
   (iii) branch stock adjustment account;
   (iv) branch debtors account; and
   (v) branch bank account.
(b) Compile Paper Products' trading, and profit and loss account for the year to 31 March 19X6.
(c) Examine briefly the merits and demerits of Paper Products' method of branch bookkeeping including comments on the significance of the 'balancing figure' in the branch stock account.

(Association of Accounting Technicians)

4.5 Packer and Stringer were in partnership as retail traders sharing profits and losses: Packer three-quarters, Stringer one-quarter. The partners were credited annually with interest at the rate of 6 per cent per annum on their fixed capitals; no interest was charged on their drawings.

Stringer was responsible for the buying department of the business. Packer managed the head office and Paper was employed as the branch manager. Packer and Paper were each entitled to a commission of 10 per cent of the net profits (after charging such commission) of the shop managed by him.

All goods were purchased by head office and goods sent to the branch were invoiced at cost.

The following was the trial balance as on 31 December 19X4.

| | Head Office Books | | Branch Books | |
	Dr	Cr	Dr	Cr
	£	£	£	£
Drawings accounts and fixed capital accounts:				
Packer	2,500	14,000		
Stringer	1,200	4,000		
Furniture and fittings, at cost	1,500		1,100	
Furniture and fittings, provision for depreciation as at 31 December 19X3		500		350
Stock on 31 December 19X3	13,000		4,400	
Purchases	37,000			
Goods sent to branches		18,000	17,200	
Sales		39,000		26,000
Provision for doubtful debts		600		200
Branch and head office current accounts	6,800			3,600
Salaries and wages	4,500		3,200	
Paper, on account of commission			240	
Carriage and travelling expenses	2,200		960	
Administrative expenses	2,400			
Trade and general expenses	3,200		1,800	
Sundry debtors	7,000		3,000	
Sundry creditors		5,800		400
Bank balances	600			1,350
	81,900	81,900	31,900	31,900

You are given the following additional information:
(a) Stocks on 31 December 19X4, amounted to: head office £14,440, branch £6,570.
(b) Administrative expenses are to be apportioned between head office and the branch in proportion to sales.
(c) Depreciation is to be provided on furniture and fittings at 10 per cent of cost.
(d) The provision for doubtful debts is to be increased by £50 in respect of head office debtors and decreased by £20 in the case of those of the branch.
(e) On 31 December 19X4 cash amounting to £2,400, in transit from the branch to head office, has been recorded in the branch books but not in those of head office; and on that date goods invoiced at £800, in transit from head office to the branch, had been recorded in the head office books but not in the branch books.

Any adjustments necessary are to be made in the head office books.

You are required to:

(a) prepare trading and profit and loss accounts and the appropriation account for the year ended 31 December 19X4, showing the net profit of the head office and branch respectively;

(b) prepare the balance sheet as on that date; and

(c) show the closing entries in the branch current accounts giving the make-up of the closing balance.

Income tax is to be ignored.

(*Institute of Chartered Accountants*)

4.6A L R, a trader, commenced business on 1 January 19X9, with a head office and one branch.

All goods were purchased by the head office and goods sent to the branch were invoiced at a fixed selling price of 25 per cent above cost. All sales, both by the head office and the branch, were made at the fixed selling price.

The following trial balance was extracted from the books at the head office at 31 December 19X9.

Trial Balance

	£	£
Capital		52,000
Drawings	1,740	
Purchases	123,380	
Sales		83,550
Goods sent to branch (at selling price)		56,250
Branch current account	24,550	
Fixed assets	33,000	
Debtors and creditors	7,980	11,060
General expenses	8,470	
Balance at bank	3,740	
	202,860	202,860

No entries had been made in the head office books for cash in transit from the branch to head office at 31 December 19X9, £1,000.

When the balances shown below were extracted from the branch books at 31 December 19X9, no entries had been made in the books of the branch for goods in transit on that date from head office to branch, £920 (selling price).

In addition to the balances which can be deduced from the information given above, the following balances appeared in the branch books on 31 December 19X9.

	£
Fixed assets	6,000
General expenses	6,070
Debtors	7,040
Creditors (excluding head office)	1,630
Sales	51,700
Balance at bank	1,520

When stock was taken on 31 December 19X9, it was found that there was no shortage at the head office, but at the branch there were shortages amounting to £300, at selling price.

You are required to prepare trading and profit and loss accounts (*a*) for head office and (*b*) for the branch, as they would have appeared if goods sent to the branch had been invoiced at cost, and a balance sheet of the whole business as on 31 December 19X9.

Head office and branch stocks are to be valued at cost.

Ignore depreciation of fixed assets.

(*Institute of Chartered Secretaries and Administrators*)

4.7   Nion is a retail stock outlet operating from a head office in London and a branch in Brighton. The following trial balances have been extracted from the books of account as at 31 October 19X1.

	Head Office Books		Branch Books	
	Dr	Cr	Dr	Cr
	£	£	£	£
Drawings	40,000			
Fixed assets: at cost	350,000		100,000	
accumulated depreciation				
(at 1 November 19X0)		140,000		30,000
Stock (at 1 November 19X0)	8,000		20,000	
Provision for unrealised profit		4,000		
Purchases	914,000			
Goods sent to branch at invoiced value		380,000	375,000	
Sales		850,000		437,000
Provision for doubtful debts		9,000		2,500
Head office/branch current accounts	175,000			120,000
Distribution expenses	80,500		5,000	
Administrative expenses	200,000		16,500	
Trade debtors	60,000		60,000	
Trade creditors		50,000		
Cash and bank balances	15,500		13,000	
Capital		410,000		
	£1,843,000	£1,843,000	£589,500	£589,500

Additional information:

1   All goods are purchased by the head office. Those goods sent to the branch are invoiced at cost plus 25 per cent.

2   Stocks were valued at 31 October 19X1 as being at head office, £12,000; and at the branch, £15,000 at their invoiced price.

3   Depreciation is to be provided for the year on the fixed assets at a rate of 10 per cent on the historic cost.

4   The provision for doubtful debts is to be maintained at a rate of 5 per cent of outstanding trade debtors as at the end of the financial year.

5   As at 31 October 19X1, there was £50,000 cash in transit from the branch to the head office; this cash was received in London on 3 November 19X1. There was also £5,000 of goods in transit at invoice price from the head office to the branch; the branch received these goods on 10 November 19X1.

Required:

Prepare in adjacent columns: (*a*) the head office, and (*b*) the branch trading and profit and loss accounts for the year to 31 October 19X1; and a **combined** balance sheet for Nion as at that date.

Notes:
(*i*) a combined trading and profit and loss account is NOT required; and
(*ii*) separate balance sheets for the head office and the branch are also NOT required.

(*Association of Accounting Technicians*)

4.8A Star Stores has its head office and main store in Crewe, and a branch store in Leek. All goods are purchased by the head office. Goods are invoiced to the branch at cost price plus a profit loading of 20 per cent. The following trial balances have been extracted from the books of account of both the head office and the branch as at 31 December 19X9:

	Head Office		Branch	
	Dr	*Cr*	*Dr*	*Cr*
	£000	£000	£000	£000
Administrative expenses	380		30	
Distribution costs	157		172	
Capital (at 1 January 19X9)		550		
Cash and bank	25		2	
Creditors and accruals		176		20
Current accounts	255			180
Debtors and prepayments	130		76	
Motor vehicles:				
at cost	470		230	
accumulated depreciation at 31 December 19X9		280		120
Plant and equipment:				
at cost	250		80	
accumulated depreciation at 31 December 19X9		120		30
Proprietor's drawings during the year	64			
Provision for unrealised profit on branch stocks				
at 1 January 19X9		5		
Purchases	880			
Sales		1,200		570
Stocks at cost/invoiced amount at 1 January 19X9	80		30	
Transfer of goods to the branch/				
from the head office		360	300	
	£2,691	£2,691	£920	£920

Additional information:
1   The stocks in hand at 31 December 19X9 were estimated to be as follows:

	£000
At head office (at cost)	100
At the branch (at invoiced price)	48

In addition, £60,000 of stocks at invoiced price had been despatched to the branch on 28 December 19X9. These goods had not been received by the branch until 5 January 19X0 and so they had not been included in the branch books of account.
2   On 31 December 19X9, the branch had transferred £15,000 of cash to the head office bank, but this was not received in Crewe until 2 January 19X0.

Required:
(*a*) Prepare in adjacent columns and using the vertical format: (*i*) the head office, and (*ii*) the branch trading and profit and loss accounts for the year to 31 December 19X9 (*note:* a combined profit and loss account is NOT required); and
(*b*) prepare in the vertical format, Star Stores' balance sheet as at 31 December 19X9 (*note:* separate balance sheets for the head office and the branch are NOT required).

(*Association of Accounting Technicians*)

4.9   EG Company Limited, a manufacturing business, exports some of its products through an overseas branch whose currency is 'florins', which carries out the final assembly operations before selling the goods.

The trial balances of the head office and branch at 30 June 19X8 were:

	Head Office £	Head Office £	Branch 'Fl.'	Branch 'Fl.'
Freehold buildings at cost	14,000		63,000	
Debtors/creditors	8,900	9,500	36,000	1,560
Sales		104,000		432,000
Authorised and issued capital		40,000		
Components sent to branch		35,000		
Head office/branch accounts	60,100			504,260
Branch cost of sales			360,000	
Depreciation provision, machinery		1,500		56,700
Head office cost of sales (including goods to branch)	59,000			
Administration costs	15,200		18,000	
Stock at 30 June 19X8	28,900		11,520	
Profit and loss account		2,000		
Machinery at cost	6,000		126,000	
Remittances		28,000	272,000	
Balance at bank	4,600		79,200	
Selling and distribution costs	23,300		28,800	
	220,000	220,000	994,520	994,520

The following adjustments are to be made:

1   The cost of sales figures include a depreciation charge of 10 per cent per annum on cost for machinery.
2   A provision of £300 for unrealised profit in branch stock is to be made.
3   On 26 June 19X8 the branch remitted 16,000 'Fl.'; these were received by the head office on 4 July and realised £1,990.
4   During May a branch customer in error paid the head office for goods supplied. The amount due was 320 'Fl.' which realised £36. It has been correctly dealt with by head office but not yet entered in the branch books.
5   A provision has to be made for a commission of 5 per cent of the net profit of the branch after charging such commission, which is due to the branch manager.

The rates of exchange were:

At 1 July 19X7	10 'Fl.' = £1
At 30 June 19X8	8 'Fl.' = £1
Average for the year	9 'Fl.' = £1
On purchase of buildings and machinery	7 'Fl.' = £1

You are required to prepare, for internal use:
(a)   detailed operating accounts for the year ended 30 June 19X8;
(b)   combined head office and branch balance sheet as at 30 June 19X8;
(c)   the branch account in the head office books, in both sterling and currency, the opening balance on 1 July 19X7 being £25,136 (189,260 'Fl.').
Taxation is to be ignored.

(*Chartered Institute of Management Accountants*)

4.10 OTL Ltd commenced business on 1 January 19X0. The head office is in London and there is a branch in Highland. The currency unit of Highland is the Crown.

The following are the trial balances of the head office and the Highland branch as at 31 December 19X0:

	Head Office		Highland Branch	
	£	£	Crowns	Crowns
Branch account	65,280			
Balances at bank	10,560		66,000	
Creditors		21,120		92,400
Debtors	18,480		158,400	
Fixed assets (purchased 1 January 19X0)	39,600		145,200	
Head office account				316,800
Profit and loss account (net profit for year)		52,800		79,200
Issued share capital		86,400		
Stocks	26,400		118,800	
	160,320	160,320	488,400	488,400

The trial balance of the head office was prepared before any entries had been made in respect of any profits or losses of the branch.

Remittance from head office to branch and from branch to head office were recorded in the books at the actual amounts paid and received.

The rates of exchange were:

On 1 January 19X0	5 crowns = £1
Average rate for year 19X0	4.4 crowns = £1
On 31 December 19X0	4 crowns = £1

Required:
(a) The trial balance of the Highland branch as at 31 December 19X0, in sterling.
(b) The closing entries, as at 31 December 19X0, in the branch account in the books of the head office.
(c) A summary of the balance sheet of OTL Ltd as at 31 December 19X0.
Ignore depreciation of fixed assets.
Ignore taxation.

(*Institute of Chartered Secretaries and Administrators*)

4.11A Home Ltd is incorporated in the UK and rents mobile homes to holidaymakers in this country and in Carea. The company has a head office in London and a branch in Carea where the local currency is 'Mics'. The following balances are extracted from the books of the head office and its 'self-accounting' branch at 31 December 19X4.

	Head Office £	Branch Mics
Debit balances		
Fixed assets at cost	450,000	900,000
Debtors and cash	17,600	36,000
Operating costs	103,700	225,000
Branch current account	42,600	
	613,900	1,161,000

Credit balances		
Share capital	200,000	–
Retained profit, 1 January 19X4	110,800	–
Sales revenue	186,300	480,000
Creditors	9,700	25,000
Head office current account	–	420,000
Accumulated depreciation	107,100	236,000
	613,900	1,161,000

The following information is provided regarding exchange rates, some of which is relevant.

The fixed assets of the branch were acquired when there were 8 Mics to the £. Exchange rates ruling during 19X4 were:

	Mics to the £
1 January	6
Average	5
31 December	4

There are no cash or goods in transit between head office and branch at the year end.

Required:
The final accounts of Home Ltd for 19X4. The accounts should be expressed in £s sterling and, for this purpose, the conversion of Mics should be made in accordance with the temporal method of translation as specified in SSAP 20: *Foreign currency translation*.

(*Institute of Chartered Secretaries and Administrators*)

5

Hire purchase accounts

Objectives

After you have studied this chapter, you should:

● *know what distinguishes 'hire purchase' from outright purchase*

● *know what distinguishes 'hire purchase' from a lease*

● *know how to record the entries relating to hire purchase transactions*

5.1 Nature of hire purchase

Hire purchase is a means of buying assets. Instead of paying at the time of purchase, or shortly afterwards, a hire purchase contract is different. The essential differences are:

(*a*) The asset does not belong to the purchaser when it is received from the supplier. Instead it belongs to the supplier providing the hire purchase.

(*b*) The purchaser will pay for the item by instalments over a period of time. This may be for as long as two or three years, or longer.

(*c*) The hire purchase price will be higher than the price would have been if paid immediately, i.e. the cash price. The extra money paid is for interest.

(*d*) The asset does not legally belong to the purchaser until two things happen:
  (*i*) the final instalment is paid, and
  (*ii*) the purchaser agrees to a legal option to buy the asset.

If the purchaser wants to, he could stop paying the instalments. He would then have to give the asset back to the seller. He would not be able to get a refund of instalments already paid.

If the purchaser is unable to continue paying the instalments, the seller could normally repossess the asset. The seller would keep all the instalments already paid.

5.2 Law of hire purchase

The Hire Purchase Act 1964 governs all hire purchase transactions.

5.3 Interest payable on hire purchase

When each payment is made on a hire purchase contract, it will consist of the following:

(a) part of the instalment will be paying off part of the amount owing for the cash price of the asset;

(b) the other part of the instalment will be for the interest that has accrued for the period of time.

The total payment (a) + (b) made for each instalment may either be of equal amounts or unequal amounts.

Exhibit 5.1 Unequal instalments

(a) A machine is bought from A King at the start of year 1. Cash price is £2,000.

(b) Hire purchase price is £2,300.

(c) Payable in 2 annual instalments at the end of each year. Each instalment to be £1,000 plus interest accrued for that year.

(d) Rate of interest is 10 per cent per annum.

			£
Year 1:	Cash price	(A)	2,000
	Add Interest 10% of (A) £2,000		200
			2,200
	Less Instalment paid		1,200
	Owing at end of year 1	(B)	1,000
Year 2:	*Add* Interest 10% of (B) £1,000		100
			1,100
	Less Instalment paid		1,100
	Owing at end of year 2		– –

Exhibit 5.2 Equal instalments

The facts are the same as in Exhibit 5.1, except that each instalment is £1,152. (Each figure of interest is rounded down to the nearest £.)

			£
Year 1:	Cash price	(A)	2,000
	Add Interest 10% of (A) £2,000		200
			2,200
	Less Instalment paid		1,152
	Owing at end of year 1	(B)	1,048
Year 2:	*Add* Interest 10% of (B) £1,048		104
			1,152
	Less Instalment paid		1,152
	Owing at end of year 2		– –

The interest for year 1 is the same for both equal or unequal instalments, as the whole of the cash price is owed in both cases for a full year.

5.4 Accounting for hire purchase

Accounting treats assets bought on hire purchase as though they belonged immediately to the purchaser.

This is because businesses normally buy assets on hire purchase with the intention of paying all the instalments, so that the asset finally will belong to them. As they mean to keep the asset and legally own it on the final payment, accounting enters it as though legal ownership occurred on purchase.

This is an illustration of the use of the 'substance over form' concept. Legally the firm does not yet own the asset (form), yet for all intents and purposes it does from an economic point of view (substance).

The total purchase price is split into two parts for the accounts:

(a) *cash price*: this is the amount to be debited to the fixed asset account;
(b) *interest*: this is an expense of borrowing money and needs charging to an expense account, i.e. hire purchase interest account.

As interest accrues over time, each period should be charged only with the interest accrued for that period. This is shown in Exhibit 5.3.

Exhibit 5.3

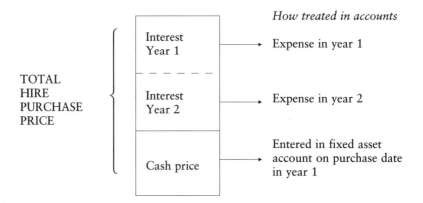

5.5 Illustrations of purchaser's accounts

The double entry needed is:

(A)	Cash price:	Debit fixed asset
		Credit supplier
(B)	Hire purchase interest:	Debit hire purchase interest
	(for each period's interest)	Credit supplier
(C)	Hire purchase instalments:	Debit supplier
		Credit cash book
(D)	Charge interest to profit and loss:	Debit profit and loss
		Credit hire purchase interest

We can now look at the accounts which would have been used to enter the facts as in Exhibit 5.1.

Letters shown against the entries are as shown above.

Machinery

			£		
Year 1					
Jan 1 A King	(A)	2,000			

Hire Purchase Interest

			£				£
Year 1				Year 1			
Dec 31 A King	(B)	200		Dec 31 Profit and loss	(D)	200	
Year 2				Year 2			
Dec 31 A King	(B)	100		Dec 31 Profit and loss	(D)	100	

A King

		£				£
Year 1			Year 1			
Dec 31 Bank	(C)	1,200	Jan 1 Machinery	(A)	2,000	
Dec 31 Balance c/d		1,000	Dec 31 HP interest	(B)	200	
		2,200			2,200	
Year 2			Year 2			
Dec 31 Bank	(C)	1,100	Jan 1 Balance b/d		1,000	
			Dec 31 HP interest	(B)	100	
		1,100			1,100	

Cash Book

					£
		Year 1			
		Dec 31 A King	(C)	1,200	
		Year 2			
		Dec 31 A King	(C)	1,100	

Profit and Loss Account (Extracts)

		£	
Year 1 Hire purchase interest	(D)	200	
Year 2 Hire purchase interest	(D)	100	

5.6 Depreciation and assets bought on hire purchase

Depreciation is based on the cash price. The interest does not enter depreciation calculations.

5.7 Balance sheets and assets bought on hire purchase

In the balance sheet for a sole trader or partnership, fixed assets being bought on hire purchase can be shown as follows:

Fixed assets	£	£
Machinery at cost		20,000
Less Owing on hire purchase	6,000	
„ Depreciation to date	10,000	16,000
		4,000

In Exhibit 5.1 above, if the machinery had been depreciated using the straight line method at 20 per cent, the balance sheet entries would have been:

Balance Sheet (end of year 1)

Fixed assets	£	£
Machinery at cost		2,000
Less Owing on hire purchase (*a*)	1,000	
„ Depreciation to date	400	1,400
		600

Note: (*a*) is balance of A King's account.

Balance Sheet (end of year 2)

Fixed assets	£	£
Machinery at cost	2,000	
Less Depreciation to date	800	1,200

Note: at the end of year 2 there was nothing owing to A King for hire purchase.

However, in company balance sheets this is *not* allowed. A change introduced first by the 1981 Companies Act is that an amount owing on a hire purchase contract cannot now be deducted from the value of the asset in the balance sheet. This still applies with the later Companies Acts.

5.8 A fully worked example

Exhibit 5.4 illustrates hire purchase more fully. It covers three years of hire purchase and shows the balance sheet figures.

Exhibit 5.4

(*a*) A machine is bought by K Thomas for £3,618, hire purchase price, from Suppliers Ltd on 1 January 19X3.
(*b*) It is paid by 3 instalments of £1,206 on 31 December of 19X3, 19X4 and 19X5.
(*c*) The cash price is £3,000.
(*d*) Rate of interest is 10 per cent.

The letters (A) to (F) refer to the description of entries following the account.

Machinery

19X3		£
Jan 1 Suppliers Ltd	(A)	3,000

Suppliers Ltd

19X3			£	19X3				£
Dec 31	Bank	(B)	1,206	Jan 1	Machinery	(A)	3,000
„ 31	Balance c/d	(D)	2,094	Dec 31	HP interest	(C)	300
			3,300					3,300
19X4				19X4				
Dec 31	Bank	(B)	1,206	Jan 1	Balance b/d	(D)	2,094
„ 31	Balance c/d	(D)	1,097	Dec 31	HP interest	(C)	209
			2,303					2,303
19X5				19X5				
Dec 31	Bank	(B)	1,206	Jan 1	Balance b/d	(D)	1,097
				Dec 31	HP interest	(C)	109
			1,206					1,206

Hire Purchase Interest

19X3			£	19X3			£
Dec 31	Suppliers Ltd	(C)	300	Dec 31	Profit and loss	(E)	300
19X4				19X4			
Dec 31	Suppliers Ltd	(C)	209	Dec 31	Profit and loss	(E)	209
19X5				19X5			
Dec 31	Suppliers Ltd	(C)	109	Dec 31	Profit and loss	(E)	109

Provision for Depreciation: Machinery

19X3			£
Dec 31	Profit and loss	(F)	600
19X4			
Dec 31	Profit and loss	(F)	600
19X5			
Dec 31	Profit and loss	(F)	600

Balance Sheets as at 31 December

		£	£	£
19X3	Machinery (at cost)		3,000	
	Less Depreciation	600		
	„ Owing on hire purchase agreement	2,094		
			2,694	306
19X4	Machinery (at cost)		3,000	
	Less Depreciation to date	1,200		
	„ Owing on hire purchase agreement	1,097		
			2,297	703
19X5	Machinery (at cost)		3,000	
	Less Depreciation to date		1,800	1,200

Description of entries:

(A) When the asset is acquired the cash price is debited to the asset account and the credit is in the supplier's account.
(B) The instalments paid are credited to the bank account and debited to the supplier's account.
(C) The interest is credited to the supplier's account for each period as it accrues, and it is debited to the expense account, later to be transferred to the profit and loss account for the period (E).
(D) The balance carried down each year is the amount of the cash price still owing.
(F) Depreciation provisions are calculated on the full cash price, as the depreciation of an asset is in no way affected by whether or not it has been fully paid for.

The balance sheet consists of balance (A), the cash price, *less* balance (F), the amount of the cash price apportioned as depreciation, *less* balance (D), the amount of the cash price still owing at each balance sheet date.

5.9 The seller's books: apportionment of profits

There are many ways of drawing up the final accounts of a business which sells goods on hire purchase. The method used should be the one most suitable for the business.

The total profit for the seller of goods on hire purchase breaks down as follows:

	£
Profit on item sold: Cash price *less* cost	xxx
Profit made because of interest charged	xxx
	xxx

In Exhibit 5.4, Suppliers Ltd sold a machine to K Thomas. Assume that the machine had cost Suppliers Ltd £2,100. The total profit upon the final instalment being paid is:

		£	£
Profit on sale of machine:	Cash price	3,000	
	Cost	2,100	900
Profit earned by charging interest:	19X3	300	
	19X4	209	
	19X5	109	618
Total profit over 3 years			1,518

Apportionment of profit on sale

There are two main methods of dealing with the problem of how to split the £900 profit on sale of the machine:

(a) It is considered profit in the period in which it was first sold to the purchaser. In this case the £900 would all be shown as profit for 19X3.
(b) The profit is divided among the three years.

The ratio is calculated as follows:

$$\frac{\text{Cash received in period}}{\text{Total cash to be received}} \times \text{Profit}$$

In this case the profits will be shown as:

19X3 $\dfrac{£1,206}{£1,206 \times 3} \times £900 = \frac{1}{3} \times £900 = £300$

19X4 $\dfrac{£1,206}{£1,206 \times 3} \times £900 = \frac{1}{3} \times £900 = £300$

19X5 $\dfrac{£1,206}{£1,206 \times 3} \times £900 = \frac{1}{3} \times £900 = £300$

Total profit on sale for three years   £900

This case shows equal profits because equal instalments were paid each year. Unequal payments would result in unequal profits.

Apportionment of interest to profit and loss account

The interest accrued for each period should be taken into profit calculations. As the amount owed reduces, so does the interest:

	£
Year 19X3	300
Year 19X4	209
Year 19X5	109
Total interest for the three years	618

5.10 The seller's books: accounts needed

We can now look at Exhibit 5.5 taking the details from Exhibit 5.4 as it would appear in the seller's books. Items (A) to (C) have already been shown in Exhibit 5.4.

Exhibit 5.5

(A) The machine was sold on 1 January 19X3 to K Thomas on hire purchase terms. Cash price was £3,000 plus hire purchase interest.
(B) Hire purchase interest was at a rate of 10 per cent.
(C) There are to be 3 instalments of £1,206 each, receivable on 31 December of 19X3, 19X4 and 19X5. These were paid by K Thomas on the correct dates.
(D) This was the only hire purchase sale during the 3 years.
(E) The profit on the cash price is to be shown as profits for 19X3, the year in which the sale was made.
(F) The cost of the machine to Suppliers Ltd was £2,100.

Hire Purchase Sales

19X3		£	19X3			£
Dec 31	Trading	3,000	Jan 1	K Thomas	(A)	3,000

K Thomas

19X3			£	19X3			£
Jan 1	Sales	(A)	3,000	Dec 31	Bank	(C)	1,206
Dec 31	HP interest	(B)	300	„ 31	Balance c/d		2,094
			3,300				3,300
19X4				19X4			
Jan 1	Balance b/d		2,094	Dec 31	Bank	(C)	1,206
Dec 31	HP interest	(B)	209	„ 31	Balance c/d		1,097
			2,303				2,303
19X5				19X5			
Jan 1	Balance b/d		1,097	Dec 31	Bank	(C)	1,206
Dec 31	HP interest	(B)	109				
			1,206				1,206

Hire Purchase Interest

19X3			£	19X3			£
Dec 31	Trading		300	Dec 31	K Thomas	(B)	300
19X4				19X4			
Dec 31	Trading		209	Dec 31	K Thomas	(B)	209
19X5				19X5			
Dec 31	Trading		109	Dec 31	K Thomas	(B)	109

Cost of Hire Purchase Goods

19X3			£	19X3		£
Jan 1	Bank	(F)	2,100	Dec 31 Trading		2,100

Cash Book

19X3			£	19X3			£
Dec 31	K Thomas	(C)	1,206	Jan 1	Hire purchase goods	(F)	2,100
19X4							
Dec 31	K Thomas	(C)	1,206				
19X5							
Dec 31	K Thomas	(C)	1,206				

Trading Accounts
Year ended 31 December 19X3

	£		£
Cost of goods sold	2,100	Hire purchase sales	3,000
		Hire purchase interest	300

Year ended 31 December 19X4

			£
		Hire purchase interest	209

Year ended 31 December 19X5

	£
Hire purchase interest	109

In Exhibit 5.5 all the profit was taken as being earned in 19X3. If we decided to take the profit as being earned when the instalments are received, then the only account which would be altered would be the trading account. All the other accounts would be exactly the same as in Exhibit 5.5.

The amendments needed are shown as Exhibit 5.6.

Exhibit 5.6

Trading Accounts
Year ended 31 December 19X3

	£		£
Cost of goods sold	2,100	Hire purchase sales	3,000
Hire purchase profit suspense		Hire purchase interest	300
profit not yet earned	600		

Year ended 31 December 19X4

			£
	Hire purchase profit suspense		
	profit for 19X4	(H)	300
	Hire purchase interest		209

Year ended 31 December 19X5

			£
	Hire purchase profit suspense		
	profit for 19X5	(H)	300
	Hire purchase interest		109

Hire Purchase Profit Suspense

19X4			£	19X3			£
Dec 31 Trading	(H)		300	Dec 31 Trading	(G)		600
Dec 31 Balance c/d			300				
			600				600
19X5				19X5			
Dec 31 Trading	(H)		300	Jan 1 Balance b/d			300

The double entry needed was:

(G) In year of sale:	Debit trading account with profits carried to future years
	Credit hire purchase profit suspense
(H) In following years:	Debit hire purchase profit suspense with profits earned in each year
	Credit trading account

The entries for hire purchase interest have not changed.

5.11 Repossessions

When customers stop paying their instalments before they should do, the goods can be taken away from them. This is called **repossession**. The amounts already paid by the customers will be kept by the seller.

The repossessed items should be entered in the books of the seller, as they are now part of his stock, but they will not be valued as new stock. The items must be valued as used goods.

Exhibit 5.7 shows how the accounts must be changed.

(a) On 1 January 19X4 we buy 15 calculators for £300 each.

(b) On 1 January 19X4 we sell 12 of them for a cash price of £480 plus £120 interest to be paid = £600 total.

(c) 24 monthly instalments are to be paid of £25 each = £600.

(d) Because of the difficulties of apportioning interest, each instalment is taken to include £5 interest, i.e. 24 × £5 = £120 interest.

(e) On 1 November 19X4, after 10 instalments have been received, a customer who bought 2 calculators cannot pay any more instalments. Both calculators are returned by him. We do not have to repay the instalments paid by him.

(f) The 2 calculators returned are valued at £140 each. Also in stock on 31 December 19X4 are 3 of the calculators bought on 1 January 19X4 for £300 each and still valued at that.

(g) Profit is to be calculated based on the number of instalments paid.

Exhibit 5.7

Trading Account for the year ended 31 December 19X4

		£			£
Purchases	(*i*)	4,500	Sales at cash price	(*ii*)	4,800
Less Stock	(*v*)	1,180	Hire purchase interest	(*iii*)	600
Cost of goods sold		3,320	Instalments received		
			on repossessions	(*iv*)	500
Provision for unrealised					
profit	(*vi*)	900			
Gross profit	(*vii*)	1,680			
		5,900			5,900

Notes: Calculations are made as follows:

(*i*) 15 × £300 each = £4,500.

(*ii*) 10 were sold (and not returned) at cash price of £480 each.

(*iii*) Interest on 10 sold (and not returned) × £5 × 12 months = £600.

(*iv*) 10 instalments paid (including interest) on 2 calculators = 10 × £25 × 2 = £500.

(*v*) Stock = new items 3 × £300 = £900
repossessed items 2 × £140 = £280
£1,180

(*vi*) Profit per calculator = cash price £480 – cost £300 = £180
To be paid: 12 instalments out of 24 = ½ profit = £90
Number sold and not returned, 10 × £90 = £900

(*vii*) Gross profit can be checked:

Earned to date 10 × £90		=	£900
Interest earned to date £5 × 10 × 12 months		=	£600
Profit on repossessions:			
Instalments received	£500		
Loss of value on repossessions			
Cost 2 × £300	£600		
Value taken back	£280	= £320	£180
			£1,680

5.12 SSAP 21: Accounting for leases and hire purchase contracts

In August 1984 SSAP 21 was issued. The background was stated in the following terms.

Leasing and hire purchase contracts are means by which companies finance the right to use of the purchase of fixed assets. In the UK there is normally no provision in a lease contract for legal title to the leased asset to pass to the lessee during the term of a lease. In contrast, under a hire purchase contract the hirer may acquire legal title by exercising an option to purchase the asset upon fulfilment of certain conditions (normally the payment of an agreed number of instalments).

Lessors fall into three broad categories. They may be companies, including banks and finance houses, which provide finance under lease contracts to enable a single customer to acquire the use of an asset for the greater part of its useful life; they may operate a business which involves the renting out of assets for varying periods of time probably to more than one customer; or they may be manufacturer or dealer lessors who use leasing as a means of marketing their products, which may involve leasing a product to one customer or to several customers. As a lessor and lessee are both parties to the same transaction it is appropriate that the same definitions should be used and the accounting treatment recommended should ideally be complementary. However, this will not mean that the recorded balances in both financial statements will be the same, because the pattern of cash flows and the taxation consequences will be different.

Leases can appropriately be classified into **finance leases** and **operating leases**. The distinction between a finance lease and an operating lease will usually be evident from the substance of the contract between the lessor and the lessee. A finance lease usually involves repayment to a lessor by a lessee of the full cost of the asset together with a return on the finance provided by the lessor. As such, a lease of this type is normally non-cancellable or cancellable only under certain conditions, and the lessee enjoys substantially all the risks and rewards associated with the ownership of an asset, other than the legal title.

An operating lease involves the lessee paying a rental for the hire of an asset for a period of time which is normally substantially less than its useful economic life. The lessor retains the risks and rewards of ownership of an asset in an operating lease and normally assumes responsibility for repairs, maintenance and insurance.

Briefly, this standard requires that a finance lease should be accounted for by the lessee as if it were the purchase of the property rights in an asset with simultaneous recognition of the obligation to make future payments, in the same way that a hire purchase is normally accounted for. Under an operating lease, only the rental will be taken into account by the lessee. The standard recognises that the substance of a transaction rather than its legal form should govern the accounting treatment.

New terms

Hire purchase agreements (p. 54): These are legal agreements by which an organisation can obtain the use of an asset in exchange for payment by instalment.

Finance lease (p. 65): This is an agreement whereby the lessee enjoys substantially all the risks and rewards associated with ownership of an asset other than legal title.

Operating lease (p. 65): This is an agreement whereby the lessor retains the risks and rewards associated with ownership and normally assumes responsibility for repairs, maintenance and insurance.

Main points to remember

1 Hire purchase is a means of buying assets where:
   (a) the asset does not belong to the purchaser until the final instalment is paid *and* the purchaser agrees to a legal option to buy the asset; *but*
   (b) for accounting purposes, the asset is treated immediately as if it belonged to the purchaser.

2 Each payment made on a hire purchase contract is part interest and part payment of the cash price of the asset.

Review questions

5.1 An engineering concern purchased machines on the HP system over a period of three years paying £846 down on 1 January 19X3, and further annual payments of £2,000 due on 31 December 19X3, 19X4 and 19X5.

The cash price of the machine was £6,000, the vendor company charging interest at 8 per cent per annum on outstanding balances.

Show the appropriate ledger accounts in the purchaser's books for the three years and how the items would appear in the balance sheet at 31 December 19X3; depreciation at 10 per cent per annum on the written-down value is to be charged and interest calculated to the nearest £.

5.2A On 1 January 19X3 J Donkins bought a machine (cash price £2,092) from CD & Co. Ltd on the following hire purchase terms. Donkins was to make an immediate payment of £600 and three annual payments of £600 on 31 December in each year. The rate of interest chargeable is 10 per cent per annum.

Donkins depreciates this machinery by 10 per cent on the diminishing balance each year.

(a) Make the entries relating to this machine in Donkins' ledger for the years 19X3, 19X4 and 19X5. (All calculations are to be made to the nearest £.)
(b) Show how the item machinery would appear in the balance sheet as at 31 December 19X3.

5.3 Bulwell Aggregates Ltd wish to expand their transport fleet and have purchased three heavy lorries with a list price of £18,000 each. Robert Bulwell has negotiated hire purchase finance to fund this expansion, and the company has entered into a hire purchase agreement with Granby Garages plc on 1 January 19X1. The agreement states that Bulwell Aggregates will pay a deposit of £9,000 on 1 January 19X1, and two annual instalments of £24,000 on

31 December 19X1, 19X2 and a final instalment of £20,391 on 31 December 19X3.

Interest is to be calculated at 25 per cent on the balance outstanding on 1 January each year and paid on 31 December each year.

The depreciation policy of Bulwell Aggregates Ltd is to write off the vehicles over a four-year period using the straight line method and assuming a scrap value of £1,333 for each vehicle at the end of its useful life.

The cost of the vehicles to Granby Garages is £14,400 each.

Required:
(a) Account for the above transactions in the books of Bulwell Aggregates Ltd, showing the entries in the profit and loss account and balance sheet for the years 19X1, 19X2, 19X3 and 19X4.
(b) Account for the above transactions in the books of Granby Garages plc, showing the entries in the hire purchase trading account for the years 19X1, 19X2, 19X3. This is the only hire purchase transaction undertaken by this company.

Calculations to the nearest £.

(*Association of Accounting Technicians*)

5.4A J York was acquiring two cars under hire purchase agreements, details of which are as follows:

Registration number	JY 1	JY 2
Date of purchase	31 May 19X6	31 October 19X6
Cash price	£18,000	£24,000
Deposit	£3,120	£4,800
Interest (deemed to accrue evenly over the period of the agreement)	£1,920	£2,400

Both agreements provided for payment to be made in 24 monthly instalments commencing on the last day of the month following purchase.

On 1 September 19X7, vehicle JY 1 became a total loss. In full settlement on 20 September 19X7:

(a) an insurance company paid £12,500 under a comprehensive policy; and
(b) the hire purchase company accepted £6,000 for the termination of the agreement.

The firm prepared accounts annually to 31 December and provided depreciation on a straight line basis at a rate of 20 per cent per annum for motor vehicles, apportioned as from the date of purchase and up to the date of disposal.

All instalments were paid on due dates.

The balance on the hire purchase company account in respect of vehicle JY 1 is to be written off.

You are required to record these transactions in the following accounts, carrying down the balances as on 31 December 19X6 and 31 December 19X7:
(a) Motor vehicles;
(b) Depreciation;
(c) Hire purchase company;
(d) Assets disposal.

5.5 On 30 September 19X7, B Wright, who prepares final accounts annually to 30 September, bought a motor lorry on hire purchase from the Vehicles and Finance Co. Ltd. The cash price of the lorry was £3,081. Under the terms of the hire purchase agreement, Wright paid a deposit of £1,000 on 30 September 19X7, and two instalments of £1,199 on 30 September, 19X8 and 19X9. The hire vendor charged interest at 10 per cent per annum on the balance outstanding on 1 October each year. All payments were made on the due dates.

Wright maintained the motor lorry account at cost and accumulated the annual provision for depreciation, at 25 per cent on the diminishing balance method, in a separate account.

You are required to:
(a) prepare the following accounts as they would appear in the ledger of B Wright for the period of the contract:
  (i) Vehicles and Finance Co Ltd;
  (ii) Motor lorry on hire purchase;
  (iii) Provision for depreciation of motor lorry;
  (iv) Hire purchase interest payable;
(b) show how the above matters would appear in the balance sheet of B Wright at 30 September 19X8.

The Vehicles and Finance Co. Ltd prepares final accounts annually to 30 September, on which date it charges B Wright with the interest due.
Make calculations to the nearest £.

5.6 S Craven started business on 1 October 19X5 selling machines of one standard type on hire purchase terms. During the year to 30 September 19X6 he purchased machines at a uniform price of £60 and sold 1,900 machines at a total price under hire purchase agreements of £100 per machine, payable by an initial deposit of £30 and 10 quarterly instalments of £7.
The following trial balance was extracted from Craven's books as at 30 September 19X6.

	£	£
Capital		76,000
Drawings	4,000	
Fixed assets	10,000	
Purchases	120,000	
Cash collected from customers		83,600
Rent, rates and insurance	4,500	
Wages	8,600	
General expenses	10,270	
Balance at bank	10,630	
Sundry trade creditors		8,400
	168,000	168,000

The personal accounts of customers are memorandum records (i.e. they are not part of the double entry system).
Craven prepares his annual accounts on the basis of taking credit for profit (including interest) in proportion to cash collected from customers.
Prepare Craven's hire purchase trading account and a profit and loss account for the year ended 30 September 19X6 and a balance sheet as at that date.
Ignore depreciation of fixed assets.

5.7 RJ commenced business on 1 January 19X8. He sells refrigerators, all of one standard type, on hire purchase terms. The total amount, including interest, payable for each refrigerator, is £300. Customers are required to pay an initial deposit of £60, followed by eight quarterly instalments of £30 each. The cost of each refrigerator to RJ is £200.
The following trial balance was extracted from RJ's books as on 31 December 19X8.

Trial Balance

	£	£
Capital		100,000
Fixed assets	10,000	
Drawings	4,000	
Bank overdraft		19,600
Creditors		16,600
Purchases	180,000	
Cash collected from customers		76,500
Bank interest	400	
Wages and salaries	12,800	
General expenses	5,500	
	£212,700	£212,700

850 machines were sold on hire-purchase terms during 19X8.

The annual accounts are prepared on the basis of taking credit for profit (including interest) in proportion to the cash collected from customers.

You are required to prepare the hire purchase trading account, and the profit and loss account for the year 19X8 and balance sheet as on 31 December 19X8.

Ignore depreciation of fixed assets.

Show your calculations.

(Institute of Chartered Secretaries and Administrators)

5.8A Object Limited is a retail outlet selling word processing equipment both for cash and on hire purchase terms. The following information has been extracted from the books of account as at 31 August 19X6:

	Dr £	Cr £
Authorised, issued and fully paid share capital		
(ordinary shares of £1 each)		75,000
Administration and shop expenses	130,000	
Cash at bank and in hand	6,208	
Cash received from hire purchase customers		315,468
Cash sales		71,000
Depreciation of premises and equipment (at 1 September 19X5)		45,000
Hire purchase debtors (at 1 September 19X5)	2,268	
Premises and equipment at cost	100,000	
Profit and loss account (at 1 September 19X5)		8,000
Provision for unrealised profit (at 1 September 19X5)		1,008
Purchases	342,000	
Stock (at 1 September 19X5)	15,000	
Trade creditors		80,000
	£595,476	£595,476

Additional information:

1 The company's policy is to take credit for gross profit (including interest) for hire purchase sales in proportion to the instalments collected. It does this by raising a provision against the profit included in hire purchase debtors not yet due.

2 The cash selling price is fixed at 50 per cent and the hire purchase selling price at 80 per cent respectively above the cost of goods purchased.

3 The hire purchase contract requires an initial deposit of 20 per cent of the hire purchase selling price, the balance to be paid in four equal instalments at quarterly intervals. The first instalment is due three months after the agreement is signed.

4 Hire purchase sales for the year amounted to £540,000 (including interest).
5 In February 19X6 the company repossessed some goods which had been sold earlier in the year. These goods had been purchased for £3,000, and the unpaid instalments on them amounted to £3,240. They were then taken back into stock at a value of £2,500. Later on in the year they were sold on cash terms for £3,500.
6 Depreciation is charged on premises and equipment at a rate of 15 per cent per annum on cost.

Required:
Prepare Object Limited's trading, and profit and loss account for the year to 31 August 19X6, and a balance sheet as at that date.
   Your workings should be submitted.

(*Association of Accounting Technicians*)

5.9A On 1 January 19X6, F Limited commenced business selling goods on hire purchase. Under the terms of the agreements, an initial deposit of 20 per cent is payable on delivery, followed by four equal quarterly instalments, the first being due three months after the date of sale. During the year sales were made as follows:

	Cost price	HP Sales price
	£	£
10 January	150	225
8 March	350	525
12 May	90	135
6 July	200	300
20 September	70	105
15 October	190	285
21 November	160	240

The goods sold in July were returned in September and eventually sold in November for £187 cash. All other instalments are paid on the due dates.

It may be assumed that:

(a) gross profit and interest are credited to profit and loss account in the proportion that deposits and instalments received bear to hire purchase price, or
(b) the cost is deemed to be paid in full before any credit is taken for gross profit and interest.

You are to prepare for the first year of trading, a hire purchase trading account compiled firstly on assumption (a) and secondly on assumption (b) and give the relevant balance sheet entries under each assumption.
   Workings should be clearly shown.

(*Chartered Institute of Management Accountants*)

5.10A On 1 January 19X7, Carver bought a machine costing £20,000 on hire purchase. He paid a deposit of £6,000 on 1 January 19X7 and he also agreed to pay two annual instalments of £5,828 on 31 December in each year, and a final instalment of £5,831 on 31 December 19X9.
   The implied rate of interest in the agreement was 12 per cent. This rate of interest is to be applied to the amount outstanding in the hire purchase loan account as at the beginning of the year.
   The machine is to be depreciated on a straight line basis over five years on the assumption that the machine will have no residual value at the end of that time.

Required:
(a) Write up the following accounts for each of the three years to 31 December 19X7, 19X8 and 19X9 respectively:
  (i)   machine account;
  (ii) accumulated depreciation on machine account; and
  (iii) hire purchase loan account; and
(b) show the balance sheet extracts for the year as at 31 December 19X7, 19X8 and 19X9 respectively for the following items:
  (i)   machine at cost;
  (ii) accumulated depreciation on the machine;
  (iii) long-term liabilities: obligations under hire purchase contract; and
  (iv) current liabilities: obligations under hire purchase contract.

(*Association of Accounting Technicians*)

5.11 Dundas Limited purchased a machine under a hire purchase agreement on 1 January 19X8. The agreement provided for an immediate payment of £2,000, followed by five equal instalments of £3,056, each instalment to be paid on 30 June and 31 December respectively.

The cash price of the machine was £10,000. Dundas estimated that it would have a useful economic life of five years, and its residual value would then be £1,000.

In apportioning interest to respective accounting periods, the company uses the 'sum of digits' method.

Required:
(a) Write up the following ledger accounts for each of the three years to 31 December 19X8, 19X9 and 19X0 respectively:
  (i)   machine hire purchase loan account; and
  (ii) machine hire purchase interest account; and
(b) show the following balance sheet extracts relating to the machine as at 31 December 19X8, 19X9 and 19X0 respectively:
  (i)   fixed assets: machine at net book value;
  (ii) creditors: amounts payable within one year – obligation under hire purchase contract; and
  (iii) creditors: amounts falling due after more than one year – obligation under hire purchase contract.

(*Association of Accounting Technicians*)

6

Partnership dissolution

Objectives

After you have studied this chapter, you should:

● *know what happens upon dissolution of a partnership*

● *know how to record the entries relating to the dissolution of a partnership*

6.1 Need for dissolution

Reasons for dissolution include the following:

(*a*) The partnership is no longer profitable, and there is no longer any reason to carry on trading.

(*b*) The partners cannot agree between themselves how to operate the partnership. They therefore decide to finish the partnership.

(*c*) Factors such as ill-health or old age may bring about the close of the partnership.

6.2 What happens upon dissolution

Upon **dissolution** the partnership firm stops trading or operating. Then, in accordance with the Partnership Act 1890:

(*a*) the assets are disposed of;

(*b*) the liabilities of the firm are paid to everyone other than partners;

(*c*) the partners are repaid their advances and current balances – advances are the amounts they have put in above and beyond the capital;

(*d*) the partners are paid the final amounts due to them on their capital accounts.

Any profit or loss on dissolution would be shared by all the partners in their profit and loss sharing ratios. Profits would increase capitals repayable to partners. Losses would reduce the capitals repayable.

If a partner's final balance on his capital and current accounts is in deficit, he will have to pay that amount into the partnership bank account.

6.3 Disposal of assets

The assets do not have to be sold to external parties. Quite often one or more existing partners will take assets at values agreed by all the partners. In such a case the partner may not pay in cash for such assets; instead they will be charged to his capital account.

6.4 Accounting for partnership dissolution

The main account around which the dissolution entries are made is known as the realisation account. It is this account in which it is calculated whether the realisation of the assets is at a profit or at a loss.

Exhibit 6.1 shows the simplest of partnership dissolutions. We will then look at a more difficult example in Exhibit 6.2.

Exhibit 6.1

The last balance sheet of A and B, who share profits A two-thirds : B one-third is shown below. On this date they are to dissolve the partnership.

Balance Sheet at 31 December 19X6

	£	£		£
Fixed assets				
Buildings		10,000	Capitals: A	12,000
Motor vehicle		2,000	B	6,000
		12,000		18,000
Current assets			*Current liabilities*	
Stock	3,000		Creditors	2,000
Debtors	4,000			
Bank	1,000	8,000		
		20,000		20,000

The buildings were sold for £10,500 and the stock for £2,600. £3,500 was collected from debtors. The motor vehicle was taken over by A at an agreed value of £1,700, but he did not pay any cash for it. £2,000 was paid to creditors. The costs of the dissolution were paid which were £200.

The accounting entries needed are:

(A) Transfer book values of all assets to the realisation account:
Debit realisation account
Credit asset accounts

(B) Amounts received from disposal of assets:
Debit bank
Credit realisation account

(C) Values of assets taken over by partner without payment:
Debit partner's capital account
Credit realisation account

(D) Creditors paid:
Debit creditors' accounts
Credit bank

(E) Costs of dissolution:
Debit realisation account
Credit bank

(F) Profit or loss on realisation to be shared between partners in profit and loss sharing ratios:
If a profit: Debit realisation account
Credit partners' capital accounts
If a loss: Debit partners' capital accounts
Credit realisation account

(G) Pay to the partners their final balances on their capital accounts:
Debit capital accounts
Credit bank

The entries are now shown. The letters (A) to (G) as above are shown against each entry:

Buildings

		£				£
Balance b/f		10,000	Realisation	(A)		10,000

Motor Vehicle

		£				£
Balance b/f		2,000	Realisation	(A)		2,000

Stock

		£				£
Balance b/f		3,000	Realisation	(A)		3,000

Debtors

		£				£
Balance b/f		4,000	Realisation	(A)		4,000

Realisation

		£					£
Assets to be realised:			Bank: Assets sold				
Buildings	(A)	10,000	Buildings	(B)			10,500
Motor vehicle	(A)	2,000	Stock	(B)			2,600
Stock	(A)	3,000	Debtors	(B)			3,500
Debtors	(A)	4,000	Taken over by partner A:				
Bank:			Motor vehicle	(C)			1,700
Dissolution costs	(E)	200	Loss on realisation		£		
			A 2/3	(F)	600		
			B 1/3	(F)	300		900
		19,200					19,200

Bank

		£				£
Balance b/d		1,000	Creditors	(D)		2,000
Realisation: Assets sold			Realisation: Costs	(E)		200
Buildings	(B)	10,500	Capitals: to clear			
Stock	(B)	2,600	A	(G)		9,700
Debtors	(B)	3,500	B	(G)		5,700
		17,600				17,600

Creditors

		£		£
Bank	(D)	2,000	Balance b/f	2,000

A: Capital

		£		£
Realisation: Motor	(C)	1,700	Balance b/f	12,000
Realisation: Share of loss	(F)	600		
Bank: to close	(G)	9,700		
		12,000		12,000

B: Capital

		£		£
Realisation: Share of loss	(F)	300	Balance b/f	6,000
Bank: to close	(G)	5,700		
		6,000		6,000

The final balances on the partners' capital accounts should always equal the amount in the bank account from which they are to be paid. For instance, in the above exhibit there was £15,400 in the bank from which to pay A £9,700 and B £5,700. If the final bank balance does not pay out the partners' capital accounts exactly, you will have made a mistake somewhere.

6.5 Accounting: a more detailed example

Exhibit 6.1 did not show the more difficult accounting entries. A more difficult example appears in Exhibit 6.2.

The extra information is:

(a) Any provision such as bad debts or depreciation is to be transferred to the credit of the asset account: see entries (A) in Exhibit 6.2.
(b) Discounts on creditors – to balance the creditors' account, transfer the discounts on creditors to the credit of the realisation account: see entries (F) in the exhibit.
(c) Transfer the balances on the partners' current accounts to their capital accounts: see entries (I) of the exhibit.
(d) A partner who owes the firm money because his capital account is in deficit must now pay the money owing: see entries (J) of the exhibit.

Exhibit 6.2

On 31 December 19X8, P, Q and R decided to dissolve their partnership. They had always shared profits in the ratio of P 3 : Q 2 : R 1.

Their goodwill was sold for £3,000, the machinery for £1,800 and the stock for £1,900. There were three motor cars, all taken over by the partners at agreed values, P taking one for £800, Q one for £1,000 and R one for £500. The premises were taken over by R at an agreed value of £5,500. The amounts collected from debtors amounted to

£2,700 after bad debts and discounts had been deducted. The creditors were discharged for £1,600, the difference being due to discounts received. The costs of dissolution amounted to £1,000.

Their last balance sheet is summarised as:

Balance Sheet as at 31 December 19X8

	£	£	£			£	£
Fixed assets				Capital account:	P		6,000
Premises			5,000		Q		5,000
Machinery			3,000		R		3,000
Motor vehicles			2,500				14,000
			10,500				
Current assets				Current accounts:	P	200	
Stock		1,800			Q	100	
Debtors	3,000				R	500	800
Less Provision				*Current liabilities*			
for bad				Creditors			1,700
debts	200	2,800					
Bank		1,400	6,000				
			16,500				16,500

The accounts recording the dissolution are shown below. A description of each entry follows the accounts, the letters (A) to (K) against each entry indicating the relevant descriptions.

Premises

	£			£
Balance b/f	5,000	Realisation	(B)	5,000

Machinery

	£			£
Balance b/f	3,000	Realisation	(B)	3,000

Motor Vehicles

	£			£
Balance b/f	2,500	Realisation	(B)	2,500

Stock

	£			£
Balance b/f	1,800	Realisation	(B)	1,800

Debtors

	£			£
Balance b/f	3,000	Provisions for bad debts	(A)	200
		Realisation	(B)	2,800

Realisation (S)

		£			£
Assets to be realised:			Bank: Assets sold		
Premises	(B)	5,000	Goodwill	(C)	3,000
Machinery	(B)	3,000	Machinery	(C)	1,800
Motor vehicles	(B)	2,500	Stock	(C)	1,900
Stock	(B)	1,800	Debtors	(C)	2,700
Debtors	(B)	2,800	Taken over by partners:		
Bank: Costs	(G)	1,000	P: Motor car	(D)	800
Profit on realisation:	(H)		Q: Motor car	(D)	1,000
		£	R: Motor car	(D)	500
P	600		R: Premises	(D)	5,500
Q	400		Creditors: Discounts	(F)	100
R	200	1,200			
		17,300			17,300

Creditors

		£		£
Bank	(E)	1,600	Balance b/f	1,700
Realisation (Discounts)	(F)	100		
		1,700		1,700

Bank (S)

		£			£
Balance b/f		1,400	Creditors	(E)	1,600
Realisation: Assets sold			Realisation: Costs	(G)	1,000
Goodwill	(C)	3,000	P: Capital	(K)	6,000
Machinery	(C)	1,800	Q: Capital	(K)	4,500
Stock	(C)	1,900			
Debtors	(C)	2,700			
R: Capital	(J)	2,300			
		13,100			13,100

P Capital (S)

		£			£
Realisation: Motor car	(D)	800	Balance b/f		6,000
Bank	(K)	6,000	Current account		
			transferred	(I)	200
			Realisation: Share of		
			profit	(H)	600
		6,800			6,800

Provision for Bad Debts

		£		£
Debtors	(A)	200	Balance b/f	200

P Current Account

		£			£
P: Capital	(I)	200	Balance b/f		200

Q Current Account

		£			£
Q: Capital	(I)	100	Balance b/f		100

Q Capital (S)

		£			£
Realisation: Motor car	(D)	1,000	Balance b/f		5,000
Bank	(K)	4,500	Current account transferred	(I)	100
			Realisation: Share of profit	(H)	400
		5,500			5,500

R Capital (S)

		£			£
Realisation: Motor car	(D)	500	Balance b/f		3,000
Realisation: Premises	(D)	5,500	Current account transferred	(I)	500
			Realisation: Share of profit	(H)	200
			Bank	(J)	2,300
		6,000			6,000

R Current Account

		£			£
R: Capital	(I)	500	Balance b/f		500

Description of transactions:

(A) The provision accounts are transferred to the relevant asset accounts so that the net balance on the asset accounts may be transferred to the realisation account. Debit provision accounts. Credit asset accounts.

(B) The net book values of the assets are transferred to the realisation account. Debit realisation account. Credit asset accounts.

(C) Assets sold. Debit bank account. Credit realisation account.

(D) Assets taken over by partners. Debit partners' capital accounts. Credit realisation account.

(E) Liabilities discharged. Credit bank account. Debit liability accounts.

(F) Discounts on creditors. Debit creditors' account. Credit realisation account.

(G) Costs of dissolution. Credit bank account. Debit realisation account.

(H) Profit or loss split in profit/loss-sharing ratio. Profit – debit realisation account. Credit partners' capital accounts. The opposite if a loss.

(I) Transfer the balances on the partners' current accounts to their capital accounts.

(J) Any partner with a capital account in deficit, i.e. debits exceeding credits, must now pay in the amount needed to cancel his indebtedness to the partnership firm. Debit bank account. Credit capital account.

(K) The credit balances on the partners' capital accounts can now be paid to them. Credit bank account. Debit partners' capital accounts.

The payments made under (K) should complete the payment of all the balances in the partnership books.

6.6 The rule in *Garner* v *Murray* (does not apply in Scotland)

It sometimes happens that a partner's capital account finishes up with a debit balance. Normally the partner will pay in an amount to clear his indebtedness to the firm. However, sometimes he will be unable to pay all, or part, of such a balance. In the case of *Garner* v *Murray* in 1904 (a case in England) the court ruled that, subject to any agreement to the contrary, such a deficiency was to be shared by the other partners *not* in their profit- and loss-sharing ratios but in the ratio of their 'last agreed capitals'. By 'their last agreed capitals' is meant the credit balances on their capital accounts in the normal balance sheet drawn up at the end of their last accounting period.

It must be borne in mind that the balances on their capital accounts after the assets have been realised may be far different from those on the last balance sheet. Where a partnership deed is drawn up it is commonly found that agreement is made to use normal profit-and-loss-sharing ratios instead, thus rendering the *Garner* v *Murray* rule inoperative. The *Garner* v *Murray* rule does not apply to partnerships in Scotland.

Before reading further you should check whether or not this topic is in the requirements for your examinations.

Exhibit 6.3

After completing the realisation of all the assets, in respect of which a loss of £4,200 was incurred, but before making the final payments to the partners, the balance sheet appears:

Balance Sheet

	£	£
Cash at bank		6,400
		6,400
Capitals: R	5,800	
S	1,400	
T	400	
	7,600	
Less Q (debit balance)	1,200	6,400
		6,400

According to the last balance sheet drawn up before the dissolution, the partners' capital account credit balances were: Q £600; R £7,000; S £2,000; T £1,000; while the profits and losses were shared Q 3 : R 2 : S 1 : T 1.

Q is unable to meet any part of his deficiency. Each of the other partners therefore suffer the deficiency as follows:

$$\frac{\text{Own capital per balance sheet before dissolution}}{\text{Total of all solvent partners' capitals per same balance sheet}} \times \text{Deficiency}$$

This can now be calculated.

$$\text{R} \quad \frac{£7,000}{£7,000 + £2,000 + £1,000} \times £1,200 = \quad £840$$

$$S \qquad \frac{£2,000}{£7,000 + £2,000 + £1,000} \times £1,200 = \qquad £240$$

$$T \qquad \frac{£1,000}{£7,000 + £2,000 + £1,000} \times £1,200 = \qquad £120$$

$$\overline{£1,200}$$

When these amounts have been charged to the capital accounts, then the balances remaining on them will equal the amount of the bank balance. Payments may therefore be made to clear their capital accounts.

	Credit balance B/fwd		Share of deficiency now debited		Final credit balances
	£		£		£
R	5,800	–	840	=	4,960
S	1,400	–	240	=	1,160
T	400	–	120	=	280
Equals the bank balance					6,400

6.7 Piecemeal realisation of assets

Frequently the assets may take a long time to realise. The partners will naturally want payments made to them on account as cash is received. They will not want to wait for payments until the dissolution is completed just for the convenience of the accountant. There is, however, a danger that if too much is paid to a partner, and he is unable to repay it, then the person handling the dissolution could be placed in a very awkward position.

To counteract this, the concept of prudence is brought into play. This is done by:

(a) Treating each receipt of sale money as being the final receipt, even though more could be received.

(b) Any loss then calculated so far to be shared between partners in profit-and-loss-sharing ratios.

(c) Should any partner's capital account after each receipt show a debit balance, then he is assumed to be unable to pay in the deficiency. This deficit will be shared (failing any other agreement) between the partners using the *Garner v Murray* rule.

(d) After payments of liabilities and the costs of dissolution the remainder of the cash is then paid to the partners.

(e) In this manner, even if no further money were received, or should a partner become insolvent, the division of the available cash would be strictly in accordance with the legal requirements. Exhibit 6.4 shows such a series of calculations.

Exhibit 6.4

The following is the summarised balance sheet of H, I, J and K as at 31 December 19X5. The partners had shared profits in the ratios H 6:I 4:J 1:K1.

Balance Sheet as at 31 December 19X5

	£
Assets	8,400
	8,400
Capitals:	
H	600
I	3,000
J	2,000
K	1,000
Creditors	1,800
	8,400

On 1 March 19X6 some of the assets were sold for cash £5,000. Out of this the creditors' £1,800 and the cost of dissolution £200 are paid, leaving £3,000 distributable to the partners.

On 1 July 19X6 some more assets are sold for £2,100. As all of the liabilities and the costs of dissolution have already been paid, then the whole of the £2,100 is available for distribution between the partners.

On 1 October 19X6 the final sale of the assets realised £1,200.

First distribution: 1 March 19X6	H		I		J		K	
	£		£		£		£	
Capital balances before dissolution	600		3,000		2,000		1,000	
Loss if no further assets realised: Assets £8,400 – Sales £5,000 = £3,400 + Costs £200 = £3,600 loss								
Loss shared in profit/loss ratios	1,800		1,200		300		300	
	1,200	Dr	1,800	Cr	1,700	Cr	700	Cr
H's deficiency shared in *Garner* v *Murray* ratios		³⁄₆	600	²⁄₆	400	¹⁄₆	200	
Cash paid to partners (£3,000)			1,200		1,300		500	

Second distribution: 1 July 19X6	H		I		J		K	
	£		£		£		£	
Capital balances before dissolution	600		3,000		2,000		1,000	
Loss if no further assets realised – Assets £8,400 – Sales (£5,000 + £2,100) = £1,300 + Costs £200 = £1,500 loss								
Loss shared in profit/loss ratios	750		500		125		125	
	150	Dr	2,500	Cr	1,875	Cr	875	Cr
H's deficiency shared in *Garner* v *Murray* ratios			75		50		25	
			2,425		1,825		850	
Less First distribution already paid			1,200		1,300		500	
Cash now paid to partners (£2,100)			1,225		525		350	

Third and final distribution: 1 October 19X6	H	I	J	K
	£	£	£	£
Capital balances before dissolution	600	3,000	2,000	1,000
Loss finally ascertained: Assets £8,400 – Sales (£5,000 + £2,100 + £1,200) = £100 + Costs £200 = £300 loss				
Loss shared in profit/loss ratios	150	100	25	25
	450 Cr	2,900 Cr	1,975 Cr	975 Cr
(No deficiency now exists on any capital account)				
Less First and second distributions	–	2,425	1,825	850
Cash now paid to partners (£1,200)	450	475	150	125

In any subsequent distribution following that in which all the partners have shared, i.e. no partner could then have had a deficiency left on his capital account, all receipts of cash are divided between the partners in their profit- and loss-sharing ratios. Following the above method would give the same answer for these subsequent distributions but obviously an immediate division in the profit-and-loss-sharing ratios would be quicker. The reader is invited to try it to satisfy him/herself that it would work out at the same answer.

New terms

Dissolution (p. 72): When a partnership firm ceases operations and its assets are disposed of.

The *Garner* v *Murray* rule (p. 79): If one partner is unable to make good a deficit on his capital account, the remaining partners will share the loss in proportion to their last agreed capitals, not in the profit/loss-sharing ratio.

Main points to remember

1 Upon dissolution, a partnership firm stops trading or operating, any profit or loss on dissolution being shared by the partners in their profit-sharing ratio.

2 The *Garner* v *Murray* rule does not apply to partnerships in Scotland.

Review questions

6.1 S, W and M are partners. They share profits and losses in the ratios of ⅖, ⅖ and ⅕ respectively.

For the year ended 31 December 19X6 their capital accounts remained fixed at the following amounts:

	£
S	6,000
W	4,000
M	2,000

They have agreed to give each other 10 per cent interest per annum on their capital accounts.

In addition to the above, partnership salaries of £3,000 for W and £1,000 for M are to be charged.

The net profit of the partnership before taking any of the above into account was £25,200.

You are required to draw up the appropriation account of the partnership for the year ended 31 December 19X6.

6.2A Draw up a profit and loss appropriation account for Winn, Pool and Howe for the year ended 31 December 19X7, and balance sheet extracts at that date, from the following:

(i)   Net profits £30,350.
(ii)   Interest to be charged on capitals: Winn £2,000; Pool £1,500; Howe £900.
(iii) Interest to be charged on drawings: Winn £240; Pool £180; Howe £130.
(iv)   Salaries to be credited: Pool £2,000; Howe £3,500.
(v)   Profits to be shared: Winn 50%; Pool 30%; Howe 20%.
(vi)   Current accounts: Winn £1,860; Pool £946; Howe £717.
(vii) Capital accounts: Winn £40,000; Pool £30,000; Howe £18,000.
(viii) Drawings: Winn £9,200; Pool £7,100; Howe £6,900.

6.3 Moore and Stephens, who share profits and losses equally, decide to dissolve their partnership as at 31 March 19X1. Their balance sheet on that date was as follows:

	£		£
Capital account: Moore	2,000	Buildings	800
Stephens	1,500	Tools and fixtures	850
	3,500	Debtors	2,800
Sundry creditors	2,750	Cash	1,800
	6,250		6,250

The debtors realised £2,700, the buildings £400 and the tools and fixtures £950. The expenses of dissolution were £100 and discounts totalling £200 were received from creditors.

Prepare the accounts necessary to show the results of the realisation and of the disposal of the cash.

6.4   X, Y and Z have been in partnership for several years, sharing profits and losses in the ratio 3:2:1. Their last balance sheet which was prepared on 31 October 19X1 is as follows:

Balance Sheet of X, Y and Z
as at 31 October 19X1

	£			£
Capital X	4,000	*Fixed assets*		
Y	4,000	At cost	20,000	
Z	2,000	*Less* Depreciation	6,000	
	10,000			14,000
		Current assets		
		Stock	5,000	
		Debtors	21,000	
Current liabilities				
Bank	13,000			
Creditors	17,000			26,000
	30,000			
	£40,000			£40,000

Despite making good profits during recent years they had become increasingly dependent on one credit customer, Smithson, and in order to retain his custom they had gradually increased his credit limit until he owed the partnership £18,000. It has now been discovered that Smithson is insolvent and that he is unlikely to repay any of the money owed by him to the partnership. Reluctantly X, Y and Z have agreed to dissolve the partnership on the following terms:
(i)   The stock is to be sold to Nelson Ltd for £4,000.
(ii) The fixed assets will be sold for £8,000 except for certain items with a book value of £5,000 which will be taken over by X at an agreed valuation of £7,000.
(iii) The debtors, except for Smithson, are expected to pay their accounts in full.
(iv) The costs of dissolution will be £800 and discounts received from creditors will be £500.
      Z is unable to meet his liability to the partnership out of his personal funds.

Required:
(a) the realisation account;
(b) the capital accounts to the partners recording the dissolution of the partnership.

(*Associated Examining Board*)

6.5A The following trial balance has been extracted from the books of Gain and Main as at 31 March 19X2; Gain and Main are in partnership sharing profits and losses in the ratio 3 to 2:

	£	£
Capital accounts:		
Gain		10,000
Main		5,000
Cash at bank	1,550	
Creditors		500
Current accounts:		
Gain		1,000
Main	2,000	
Debtors	2,000	
Depreciation: Fixtures and fittings		1,000
Motor vehicles		1,300
Fixtures and fittings	2,000	
Land and buildings	30,000	
Motor vehicles	4,500	
Net profit (for the year to 31 March 19X2)		26,250
Stock, at cost	3,000	
	£45,050	£45,050

In appropriating the net profit for the year, it has been agreed that Main should be entitled to a salary of £9,750. Each partner is also entitled to interest on his opening capital account balance at the rate of 10 per cent per annum.

Gain and Main have decided to convert the parnership into a limited company, Plain Limited, as from 1 April 19X2. The company is to take over all the assets and liabilities of the partnership, except that Gain is to retain for his personal use one of the motor vehicles at an agreed transfer price of £1,000.

The purchase consideration will consist of 40,000 ordinary shares of £1 each in Plain Limited, to be divided between the partners in profit-sharing ratio. Any balance on the partners' current accounts is to be settled in cash.

You are required to:
Prepare the main ledger accounts of the partnership in order to close off the books as at 31 March 19X2.

(*Association of Accounting Technicians*)

6.6A A, B & C are partners sharing profits and losses in the ratio 2:2:1. The balance sheet of the partnership as at 30 September 19X7 was as follows:

	£		£	£
Freehold premises	18,000	Capital accounts		
Equipment and machinery	12,000	A	22,000	
Motor cars	3,000	B	18,000	
Inventory*	11,000	C	10,000	
Debtors	14,000			50,000
Bank	9,000	Loan account – A		7,000
		Creditors		10,000
	£67,000			£67,000

* *Author's note*: Inventory is another word for stock.

The partners agreed to dispose of the business to CNO Limited with effect from 1 October 19X7 under the following conditions and terms:

(*i*) CNO Limited will acquire the goodwill, all fixed assets and the inventory for the purchase consideration of £58,000. This consideration will include a payment of £10,000 in cash and the issue of 12,000 10 per cent preference shares of £1 each at par, and the balance by the issue of £1 ordinary shares at £1.25 per share.

(*ii*) The partnership business will settle amounts owing to creditors.

(*iii*) CNO Limited will collect the debts on behalf of the vendors.

Purchase consideration payments and allotments of shares were made on 1 October 19X7.

The partnership creditors were paid off by 31 October 19X7 after the taking of cash discounts of £190.

CNO Limited collected and paid over all partnership debts by 30 November 19X7 except for bad debts amounting to £800. Discounts allowed to debtors amounted to £400.

Required:

(*a*) Journal entries (including those relating to cash) necessary to close the books of the partnership, and

(*b*) Set out the basis on which the shares in CNO Limited are allotted to partners.
Ignore interest.

(*Institute of Chartered Secretaries and Administrators*)

6.7   Amis, Lodge and Pym were in partnership sharing profits and losses in the ratio 5:3:2. The following trial balance has been extracted from their books of account as at 31 March 19X8:

	£	£
Bank interest received		750
Capital accounts (as at 1 April 19X7):		
Amis		80,000
Lodge		15,000
Pym		5,000
Carriage inwards	4,000	
Carriage outwards	12,000	
Cash at bank	4,900	
Current accounts:		
Amis	1,000	
Lodge	500	
Pym	400	
Discounts allowed	10,000	
Discounts received		4,530
Drawings:		
Amis	25,000	
Lodge	22,000	
Pym	15,000	
Motor vehicles:		
at cost	80,000	
accumulated depreciation (at 1 April 19X7)		20,000
Office expenses	30,400	
Plant and machinery:		
at cost	100,000	
accumulated depreciation (at 1 April 19X7)		36,600
Provision for bad and doubtful debts		
(at 1 April 19X7)		420
Purchases	225,000	
Rent, rates, heat and light	8,800	
Sales		404,500
Stock (at 1 April 19X7)	30,000	
Trade creditors		16,500
Trade debtors	14,300	
	£583,300	£583,300

Additional information:
(a) Stock at 31 March 19X8 was valued at £35,000.
(b) Depreciation on the fixed assets is to be charged as follows:
    Motor vehicles – 25 per cent on the reduced balance.
    Plant and machinery – 20 per cent on the original cost.
    There were no purchases or sales of fixed assets during the year to 31 March 19X8.
(c) The provision for bad and doubtful debts is to be maintained at a level equivalent to 5 per cent of the total trade debtors as at 31 March 19X8.
(d) An office expense of £405 was owing at 31 March 19X8, and some rent amounting to £1,500 had been paid in advance as at that date. These items had not been included in the list of balances shown in the trial balance.
(e) Interest on drawings and on the debit balance on each partner's current account is to be charged as follows:

	£
Amis	1,000
Lodge	900
Pym	720

(f) According to the partnership agreement, Pym is allowed a salary of £13,000 per annum. This amount was owing to Pym for the year to 31 March 19X8, and needs to be accounted for.
(g) The partnership agreement also allows each partner interest on his capital account at a rate of 10 per cent per annum. There were no movements on the respective partners' capital accounts during the year to 31 March 19X8, and the interest had not been credited to them as at that date.

Note: The information given above is sufficient to answer part (a) (i) and (ii) of the question, and notes (h) and (i) below are pertinent to requirements (b) (i), (ii) and (iii) of the question.

(h) On 1 April 19X8, Fowles Limited agreed to purchase the business on the following terms:
   (i)   Amis to purchase one of the partnership's motor vehicles at an agreed value of £5,000, the remaining vehicles being taken over by the company at an agreed value of £30,000;
   (ii) the company agreed to purchase the plant and machinery at a value of £35,000 and the stock at a value of £38,500;
   (iii) the partners to settle the trade creditors: the total amount agreed with the creditors being £16,000;
   (iv) the trade debtors were not to be taken over by the company, the partners receiving cheques on 1 April 19X8 amounting to £12,985 in total from the trade debtors in settlement of the outstanding debts;
   (v)   the partners paid the outstanding office expense on 1 April 19X8, and the landlord returned the rent paid in advance by cheque on the same day;
   (vi) as consideration for the sale of the partnership, the partners were to be paid £63,500 in cash by Fowles Limited, and to receive 75,000 in £1 ordinary shares in the company, the shares to be apportioned equally amongst the partners.
(i) Assume that all the matters relating to the dissolution of the partnership and its sales to the company took place on 1 April 19X8.

Required:
(a) Prepare:
   (i)   Amis', Lodge's and Pym's trading, profit and loss and profit and loss appropriation account for the year to 31 March 19X8;
   (ii) Amis', Lodge's and Pym's current accounts (in columnar format) for the year to 31 March 19X8 (the final balance on each account is to be then transferred to each partner's respective capital account);
   and

(b) Compile the following accounts:
  (i) the partnership realisation account for the period up to and including 1 April 19X8;
  (ii) the partners' bank account for the period up to and including 1 April 19X8; and
  (iii) the partners' capital accounts (in columnar format) for the period up to and including 1 April 19X8.

Note: Detailed workings should be submitted with your answer.

(Association of Accounting Technicians)

6.8A Proudie, Slope and Thorne were in partnership sharing profits and losses in the ratio 3:1:1. The draft balance sheet of the partnership as at 31 May 19X6 is shown below:

	£000 Cost	£000 Depreci- ation	£000 Net book value
Fixed assets			
Land and buildings	200	40	160
Furniture	30	18	12
Motor vehicles	60	40	20
	£290	£98	192
Current assets			
Stocks		23	
Trade debtors	42		
Less Provision for doubtful debts	1		
		41	
Prepayments		2	
Cash		10	
		76	
Less Current liabilities			
Trade creditors	15		
Accruals	3		
		18	
			58
			£250
Financed by:			
Capital accounts			
Proudie		100	
Slope		60	
Thorne		40	
			200
Current accounts			
Proudie		24	
Slope		10	
Thorne		8	
			42
			242
Loan			
Proudie			8
			£250

Additional information:
1 Proudie decided to retire on 31 May 19X6. However, Slope and Thorne agreed to form a new partnership out of the old one, as from 1 June 19X6. They agreed to share profits and losses in the same ratio as in the old partnership.

2 Upon the dissolution of the old partnership, it was agreed that the following adjustments were to be made to the partnership balance sheet as at 31 May 19X6.

(a) Land and buildings were to be revalued at £200,000.

(b) Furniture was to be revalued at £5,000.

(c) Proudie agreed to take over one of the motor vehicles at a value of £4,000, the remaining motor vehicles being revalued at £10,000.

(d) Stocks were to be written down by £5,000.

(e) A bad debt of £2,000 was to be written off, and the provision for doubtful debts was then to be adjusted so that it represented 5 per cent of the then outstanding trade debtors as at 31 May 19X6.

(f) A further accrual of £3,000 for office expenses was to be made.

(g) Professional charges relating to the dissolution were estimated to be £1,000.

3 It has not been the practice of the partners to carry goodwill in the books of the partnership, but on the retirement of a partner it had been agreed that goodwill should be taken into account. Goodwill was to be valued at an amount equal to the average annual profits of the three years expiring on the retirement. For the purpose of including goodwill in the dissolution arrangement when Proudie retired, the net profits for the last three years were as follows:

	£000
Year to 31 May 19X4	130
Year to 31 May 19X5	150
Year to 31 May 19X6	181

The net profit for the year to 31 May 19X6 had been calculated before any of the items listed in 2 above were taken into account. The net profit was only to be adjusted for items listed in 2(d), 2(e) and 2(f) above.

4 Goodwill is not to be carried in the books of the new partnership.

5 It was agreed that Proudie's old loan of £8,000 should be repaid to him on 31 May 19X6, but any further amount owing to him as a result of the dissolution of the partnership should be left as a long-term loan in the books of the new partnership.

6 The partners' current accounts were to be closed and any balances on them as at 31 May 19X6 were to be transferred to their respective capital accounts.

Required:

(a) Prepare the revaluation account as at 31 May 19X6.

(b) Prepare the partners' capital accounts as at the date of dissolution of the partnership, and bring down any balances on them in the books of the new partnership.

(c) Prepare Slope and Thorne's balance sheet as at 1 June 19X6.

(*Association of Accounting Technicians*)

6.9 Lock, Stock and Barrel have been in partnership as builders and contractors for many years. Owing to adverse trading conditions it has been decided to dissolve the partnership. Profits are shared Lock 40 per cent, Stock 30 per cent, Barrel 30 per cent. The partnership deed also provides that in the event of a partner being unable to pay off a debit balance the remaining partners will treat this as a trading loss.

The latest partnership balance sheet was as follows:

	Cost	Depreciation	
Fixed tangible assets	£	£	£
Freehold yard and buildings	20,000	3,000	17,000
Plant and equipment	150,000	82,000	68,000
Motor vehicles	36,000	23,000	13,000
	206,000	108,000	98,000
Current assets			
Stock of land for building		75,000	
Houses in course of construction		115,000	
Stocks of materials		23,000	
Debtors for completed houses		62,000	
		275,000	
Current liabilities			
Trade creditors	77,000		
Deposits and progress payments	82,000		
Bank overdraft	132,500		
		291,500	
Excess of current liabilities over current assets			(16,500)
			81,500
Partners' capital accounts			
Lock		52,000	
Stock		26,000	
Barrel		3,500	
			81,500

During the six months from the date of the latest balance sheet to the date of dissolution the following transactions have taken place:

	£
Purchase of materials	20,250
Materials used for houses in course of construction	35,750
Payments for wages and subcontractors on building sites	78,000
Payments to trade creditors for materials	45,000
Sales of completed houses	280,000
Cash received from customers for houses	225,000
Payments for various general expenses	12,500
Payments for administration salaries	17,250
Cash withdrawn by partners: Lock	6,000
Stock	5,000
Barrel	4,000

All deposits and progress payments have been used for completed transactions.

Depreciation is normally provided each year at £600 on the freehold yard and buildings, at 10 per cent on cost for plant and equipment and 25 per cent on cost for motor vehicles.

The partners decide to dissolve the partnership on 1 February 19X7 and wish to take out the maximum cash possible, as items are sold. At this date there are no houses in course of construction and one-third of the stock of land had been used for building.

It is agreed that Barrel is insolvent and cannot bring any money into the partnership. The partners take over the partnership cars at an agreed figure of £2,000 each. All other vehicles were sold on 28 February 19X7 for £6,200. At the same date stocks of materials were sold for £7,000, and the stock of the land realised £72,500. On 30 April 19X7 the debtors paid in full and all the plant and equipment was sold for £50,000.

The freehold yard and buildings realised £100,000 on 1 June 19X7, on which date all remaining cash was distributed.

There are no costs of realisation or distribution.

Required:

(a) Prepare a partnership profit and loss account for the six months to 1 February 19X7, partners' capital accounts for the same period and a balance sheet at 1 February 19X7.
(b) Show calculations of the amounts distributable to the partners.
(c) Prepare a realisation account and the capital accounts of the partners to the final distribution.

(*Chartered Association of Certified Accountants*)

6.10A Grant and Herd are in partnership sharing profits and losses in the ratio 3 to 2. The following information relates to the year to 31 December 19X0:

	Dr	Cr
	£000	£000
Capital accounts (at 1 January 19X0):		
Grant		300
Herd		100
Cash at bank	5	
Creditors and accruals		25
Debtors and prepayments	18	
Drawings during the year:		
Grant (all at 30 June 19X0)	40	
Herd (all at 31 March 19X0)	40	
Fixed assets: at cost	300	
: accumulated depreciation (at 31 December 19X0)		100
Herd – salary	10	
Net profit (for the year to 31 December 19X0)		60
Stocks at cost (at 31 December 19X0)	90	
Trade creditors		141
Trade debtors	223	
	£726	£726

Additional information:

1 The partnership agreement allows for Herd to be paid a salary of £20,000 per annum, and for interest of 5 per cent per annum to be paid on the partners' capital account balances as at 1 January in each year. Interest at a rate of 10 per cent per annum is charged on the partners' drawings.

2 The partners decide to dissolve the partnership as at 31 December 19X0, and the business was then sold to Valley Limited. The purchase consideration was to be 400,000 £1 ordinary shares in Valley at a premium of 25p per share. The shares were to be issued to the partners on 31 December 19X0, and they were to be shared between them in their profit-sharing ratio.

The sale agreement allowed Grant to take over one of the business cars at an agreed valuation of £10,000. Apart from the car and the cash and bank balances, the company took over all the other partnership assets and liabilities at their book values as at 31 December 19X0.

3 Matters relating to the appropriation of profit for the year to 31 December 19X0 are to be dealt with in the partners' capital accounts, including any arrears of salary owing to Herd.

Required:
(*a*) Write up the following accounts for the year to 31 December 19X0:
  (*i*) the profit and loss appropriation account;
  (*ii*) Grant and Herd's capital accounts; and
  (*iii*) the realisation account.
(*b*) Prepare Valley's balance sheet as at 1 January 19X1 immediately after the acquisition of the partnership and assuming that no further transactions have taken place in the meantime.

(*Association of Accounting Technicians*)

Part 2

COMPANIES

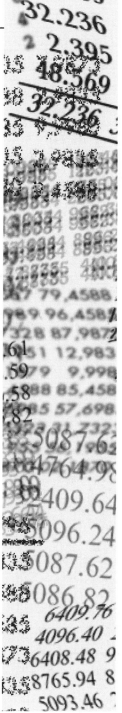

Introduction

This part is concerned with the accounts and financial
statements of limited companies. It considers how
various accounting transactions should be entered in
the books and how the financial statements should be
presented, including the requirements of the
Companies Acts and of accounting standards.

7

Limited companies: general background

Objectives

After you have studied this chapter, you should:

- *be aware of the legal nature of limited companies*
- *be aware of the statutory framework governing limited companies*
- *be aware of some of the major characteristics of limited companies*

7.1 Preliminary study

An introduction was made to the accounts of limited companies in Volume 1. It was intended to show some of the basic outlines of the final accounts of limited companies to those people who would be finishing their studies of accounting with the completion of Volume 1. This volume now carries the study of limited companies accounting to a more advanced stage.

7.2 The Companies Acts

The Acts of Parliament now governing limited companies are the Companies Acts 1985 and 1989. The 1989 Act both adds to and amends the 1985 Act, so that both Acts have to be read together. In this volume we cannot deal with many of the complicated issues arising from the Companies Acts: these are better left until the reader has reached a more advanced stage in his/her studies.

The Companies Acts are the descendants of modern limited liability company legislation which can be traced back to the passing of the Companies Act 1862. This Act was a triumph for the development of the limited liability principle which had been severely restricted since the so-called 'Bubble Act' of 1720, this latter Act being the remedy for a multitude of spectacular frauds perpetrated behind the cloak of limited liability. Not until 1862 was general prejudice overcome, and the way paved for the general use of the limited liability principle which is now commonplace. Company law therefore consists of the Companies Acts 1985 and 1989, together with a considerable body of case law which has been built up over the years. It must be borne in mind that there are still a number of chartered companies in existence which were incorporated by Royal Charter, such as the Hudson's Bay Company, or else which were formed by special Acts of Parliament.

7.3 Changes in company law

Over the last 20 to 30 years the United Kingdom has made many changes in its company law. This has been brought about because of the obligation to observe the company law directives issued by the Council of the European Community. Such changes do not eliminate completely the differences in company law throughout the European Union, but they have considerably reduced such differences and have provided minimum standards to be observed.

The 1985 and 1989 Companies Acts lay down detailed rules of the format of the final accounts of limited companies. These will be considered later.

Banks and insurance companies do not come under the same legislation as that for other companies. A separate part of the 1989 Act deals with banks, whilst insurance companies are the subject of a special directive.

7.4 Other forms of company

The Companies Acts also cover companies with unlimited liability. These are now very rarely met in practice. Also covered are companies limited by guarantee, which may or may not have a share capital, but the Companies Act 1985 forbids the future formation of such companies, if they have a share capital. Both of these types of limited company are relatively unimportant, and therefore any future reference to a 'limited company' or merely a 'company' will be concerned with limited liability companies of the normal type.

7.5 Separate legal entity

The outstanding feature of a **limited company** is that, no matter how many individuals have bought shares in it, it is treated in its dealings with the outside world as if it were a person in its own right: it is said to be a separate 'legal entity'. Just as the law can create this separate legal person, then so also can it eliminate it, but its existence can only be terminated by using the proper legal procedures. Thus the identity of the shareholders in a large concern may be changing daily as shares are bought and sold by different people. On the other hand, a small private company may have the same shareholders from when it is incorporated (the day it legally came into being), until the date when liquidation is completed (the cessation of the company, often known also as 'winding up' or being 'wound up'). A prime example of its identity as a separate legal entity is that it may sue its own shareholders, or in turn be sued by them.

The legal formalities by which the company comes into existence can be gleaned from any textbook on company law. It is not the purpose of this book to discuss company law in any great detail; this is far better left to a later stage of one's studies. As companies must, however, comply with the law, the essential company law concerning accounting matters will be dealt with in this book as far as is necessary.

What is important is that the basic principles connected with company accounts can be seen in operation. In order that the student may not be unduly confused, points which very rarely occur, or on which the legal arguments are extremely involved and may not yet have been finally settled, will be left out completely or merely mentioned in passing. This means that some generalisations will bear closer scrutiny when accounting studies reach a more advanced stage.

7.6 Memorandum and Articles of Association

Each company is governed by two documents, known as the **Memorandum of Association** and the **Articles of Association**, generally referred to as the **memorandum** and the **articles**. The memorandum consists of five clauses for private companies, and six for public companies, which contain the following details:

1 The name of the company.
2 The part of the UK where the registered office will be situated.
3 The objects of the company.
4 A statement (if a limited liability company) that the liability of its members is limited.
5 Details of the share capital which the company is authorised to issue.
6 A public limited company will also have a clause stating that the company is a public limited company.

The memorandum is said to be the document which discloses the conditions which govern the company's relationship with the outside world.

7.7 Limited liability

The principle of limited liability underlying clause 4 has been of the utmost importance in industry and commerce. It is inconceivable that large business units, such as Imperial Chemical Industries Ltd or Great Universal Stores Ltd, could have existed except for a very few instances. The investor in a limited company, who therefore buys shares in it, is a shareholder. The most he can lose is the money he has paid for the shares, or where he has only partly paid for them, then he is also liable for the unpaid part in addition. With public companies, where their shares are dealt in on a Stock Exchange, he can easily sell them whenever he so wishes. The sale of a share in a private company is not so easily effected.

7.8 Classes of shares

The main classes of shares are **ordinary** shares and **preference** shares. Unless clearly stated in the Memorandum or Articles of Association, preference shares are assumed to be of the cumulative variety already described in Volume 1.

There are also a variety of other shares. The rights attaching to these shares are purely dependent on the skill and ingenuity of the draftsman of the Memorandum and Articles of Association. An entirely new type of share may be created provided it does not contravene the law.

The shares which carry the right to the whole of the profits remaining after the preference shares (and any other fixed dividend shares) have been paid a dividend are often known as the equity share capital or as **equities**.

Until 1981 the only type of share which could be bought back from the shareholders by the company itself were redeemable preference shares. This has changed completely, and will be considered in detail in Chapter 9.

7.9 Distributable profits

In Volume 1, Chapter 41, the calculation of dividends from profits available for distribution was described. This means that there should be some way of knowing what **distributable profits** are.

In the Companies Acts there is a definition of **realised profits** and **realised losses**. This definition also applies for the purpose of calculating a company's distributable profits. A company's realised profits and losses are defined as 'those profits and losses which are treated as realised in the accounts, in accordance with principles generally accepted with respect to the determination of realised profits and losses for accounting purposes at the time when those accounts are prepared'. In accounting, the realisation concept recognises profit or loss at the point when a contract is made in the market to buy or sell assets.

7.10 Table A

Besides the Memorandum of Association, every company must also have Articles of Association. Just as the memorandum governs the company's dealings with the outside world, the articles govern the relationships which exist between the members and the company, between one member and the other members, and other necessary regulations. The Companies Act has a model set of articles known as Table A. A company may, if it so wishes, have its articles exactly the same as Table A, commonly known as 'adopting Table A', or else adopt part of it and have some sections altered. The adoption of the major part of Table A is normal for most private companies. In accounting textbooks, unless stated to the contrary, the accounting examples shown are usually on the basis that Table A has been adopted.

Table A lays down regulations concerning the powers of the directors of the company. On the other hand, the company may draft its own regulations for the powers of directors. Any such regulations are of the utmost importance when it is realised that the legal owners of the business, the shareholders, have entrusted the running of the company to the directors. The shareholders' own rights are largely limited to attending Annual General Meetings and having voting rights thereat, although some shares do not carry voting rights. The Companies Acts make the keeping of proper sets of accounting records and the preparation of Final Accounts compulsory for every company. In addition the accounts must be audited, this being quite different from a partnership or a sole trader's business where an audit is not compulsory at all.

Companies having limited liability, whether they are private or public companies, have to send a copy of their Final Accounts, drawn up in a prescribed manner, to the Registrar of Companies. Public companies must submit Accounts within seven months of their financial year end; private companies within ten months of their year end. Chapters 15–17 are concerned with stating the accounting requirements of the Companies Acts.

7.11 Public companies and the Stock Exchange

The shares of most of the public companies are dealt in on one or other of the recognised Stock Exchanges. The shares of private companies cannot be bought and sold on any Stock Exchange, as this would contravene the requirements for the company being recognised as a 'private' company. The sale and purchase of shares on the Stock Exchanges have no effect on the accounting entries made in the company's books. The only entry made in the company's books when a shareholder sells all, or some, of his shares to someone else, is to record the change of identity of the shareholders. The price at which shares were sold on the Stock Exchange does not enter into the company's books. While no accounting entries are necessary, probably apart from a small charge being made to the shareholder to compensate the company for administrative expenses in recording the change of identity caused by the share transfer and the completion of certain legal documents by the company, the price of the shares on the Stock Exchange has repercussions on the financial policy of the company. If some new shares are to be issued, what price they are to be issued at will be largely dependent on the Stock Exchange valuation. If another firm is to be taken over by the company, part of the purchase price being by the means of shares in the company, then the Stock Exchange value will also affect the value placed upon the shares being given. A takeover bid from another firm may well be caused because the Stock Exchange value of the shares has made a takeover seem worthwhile. It must be recognised that the Stock Exchanges are the 'second-hand market' for a company's shares. The company does not actually sell (normally called **issue**) its shares by using the Stock Exchange as a selling place. The company issues new shares directly to the people who make application to it for the shares at the time when the company has shares available for issue. The company does not sell to, or buy from, the Stock Exchanges. This means that the shares of a public company sold and bought on Stock Exchanges are passing from one shareholder to another person who will then become a shareholder. Apart from the effect upon the financial policies of the firm the double entry accounts of the company are not affected.

7.12 Stocks and shares

Later in this book you are shown the procedure whereby the shares of a company may be made into **stock**. Thus 500 ordinary shares of £1 each may be made into £500 stock. The dividends paid on the shares or the stock would be the same, and the voting powers would also be the same. Apart from administrative convenience there is really no difference between shares and stock.

New terms

Limited company (p. 95): A form of organisation established under the Companies Acts as a separate legal entity, and required to comply with the provisions of the Acts. The members of the company, known as shareholders, are only liable to pay the full price of the shares – not for any further amount, i.e. their liability is limited.

Memorandum of Association (p. 97): The document that discloses the conditions governing a company's relationship with the outside world.

Articles of Association (p. 97): The document that arranges the internal relationships, for example, between members of the company, and the duties of directors. The Companies Act gives a model known as Table A.

Main points to remember

1 Limited companies are governed by the Companies Acts.

2 Limited companies are each a separate legal entity.

3   Each company is governed by two documents:
    (a) the Memorandum of Association; and
    (b) the Articles of Association.

4   Investors in limited companies can only lose the amount they paid (plus any amount still unpaid if the shares are only part-paid) when they acquired their investment in the company, i.e. they have 'limited liability'.

8

The issue of shares and debentures

Objectives

After you have studied this chapter, you should:

● *understand the terminology relating to the issue of shares and debentures*

● *be aware of the steps in the process of issuing of shares and debentures*

● *know how to record the accounting entries relating to the issue of shares and debentures*

8.1 The issue of shares

In the case of public companies a new issue of shares can be very costly indeed, and the number of shares issued must be sufficient to make the cost worthwhile. However, for simplicity, so that the principles are not obscured by the difficulties of grappling with large amounts, the numbers of shares shown as issued in the illustrations that follow will be quite small.

Shares can be issued being payable for (*a*) immediately on application, or (*b*) by instalments. The first instances will be of shares being paid for immediately. Issues of shares may take place on the following terms connected with the price of the shares:

(*a*) Shares issued at par. This would mean that a share of £1 nominal value would be issued for £1 each.

(*b*) Shares issued at a premium. In this case a share of £1 nominal value would be issued for more than £1 each, say for £3 each.

(*c*) Until a change made in an earlier Companies Act, dated 1980, shares could have been issued at a discount. This is now expressly forbidden.

8.2 Share premiums and discounts

This will all seem rather strange at first. How can a £1 share, which states that value on the face of it, be issued for £3 each, and who would be foolish enough to buy it? The reasons for this apparently strange state of affairs stem from the Companies Act requirement that the share capital accounts always show shares at their nominal value, irrespective of how much the shares are worth or how much they are issued for. To illustrate this, the progress of two firms can be looked at, firm A and firm B. Both firms started in business on 1 January 19X1 and issued 1,000 ordinary shares each of £4 nominal value at par. Ignoring any issue expenses, the balance sheets on that date would appear:

Firms A Ltd and B Ltd

Balance Sheet as at 1 January 19X1

	£
Bank	4,000
Capital	4,000

Five years later, on 31 December 19X5, the balance sheets show that the companies have fared quite differently. It is to be assumed here, for purposes of illustration, that the balance sheet values and any other interpretation of values happen to be identical.

£4,000 capital is needed by A Ltd, and this is to be met by issuing more ordinary shares. Suppose that another 1,000 ordinary shares of £4 nominal value each are issued at par. Column (*a*) shows the balance sheet before the issue, and column (*b*) shows the balance sheet after the issue has taken place.

A Ltd Balance Sheets (Solution 1) as at 31 December 19X5

	(*a*) £	(*b*) £
Fixed and current assets (other than bank)	9,000	9,000
Bank	1,000	5,000
	10,000	14,000
Financed by:		
Ordinary share capital	4,000	8,000
Profit and loss	6,000	6,000
	10,000	14,000

Now the effect of what has happened can be appreciated. Before the new issue there were 1,000 shares. As there were £10,000 of assets and no liabilities, then each share was worth £10. After the issue there are 2,000 shares and £14,000 of assets, so that now each share is worth £7. This would be extremely disconcerting to the original shareholders who see the value of each of their shares fall immediately by £3.

On the other hand, the new shareholder who has just bought shares for £4 each sees them rise immediately to be worth £7 each. Only in one specific case would this be just, and that is where each original shareholder buys an equivalent number of new shares. Otherwise this obviously cannot be the correct solution. What is required is a price which is equitable as far as the interests of the old shareholders are concerned, and yet will attract sufficient applications to provide the capital required. As in this case the balance sheet value and the real value are the same, the answer is that each old share was worth £10 and therefore each new share should be issued for £10 each. The balance sheets will now appear:

A Ltd Balance Sheets (Solution 2) as at 31 December 19X5

	(a) £	(b) £
Fixed and current assets (other than bank)	9,000	9,000
Bank	1,000	11,000
	10,000	20,000
Financed by:		
Ordinary share capital (at nominal value)	4,000	8,000
Share premium (*see* note below)		6,000
Profit and loss	6,000	6,000
	10,000	20,000

Thus in (*a*) above 1,000 shares own between them £10,000 of assets = £10 each, while in (*b*) 2,000 shares are shown as owning £20,000 of assets = £10 each. Both the old and new shareholders are therefore satisfied with the bargain that has been made.

Note: The **share premium** shown on the capital side of the balance sheet is needed, ignoring for a moment the legal requirements to be complied with in company balance sheets, simply because the balance sheet would not balance without it. If shares are stated at nominal value, but issued at another price, the actual amount received increases the bank balance, but the share capital shown is increased by a different figure. The share premium therefore represents the excess of the cash received over the nominal value of the shares issued.

The other, B Ltd, has not fared so well. It has, in fact, lost money. The accumulated losses are reflected in a debit balance on the profit and loss appropriation account as shown in the following balance sheet at (*c*). It can be seen that there are £3,000 of assets to represent the shareholders' stake in the firm of 1,000 shares, i.e. each share is worth £3 each. If more capital was needed 1,000 more shares could be issued. From the action taken in the previous case it will now be obvious that each new share of £4 nominal value would be issued for its real value of £3 each, were it permitted to do so. The balance sheets would appear:

B Ltd Balance Sheets (correct solution) as at 31 December 19X5

	(c)	(d)
Fixed and current assets (other than bank)	2,000	2,000
Bank	1,000	4,000
Discounts on shares (*see* below)		1,000
Profit and loss – debit balance	1,000	1,000
	4,000	8,000
Ordinary share capital	4,000	8,000

Once again, as the share capital is shown at nominal value, but the shares issued at a different figure, the difference being **discounts on shares** must be shown in order that the balance sheet may balance. It is, of course, not actually an asset, it is merely a balancing figure needed because the entries already made for an increase in the ordinary share capital and the increase in the bank balance have been at different figures. The figure for discounts on shares therefore rectifies the double entry 'error'.

Although shares cannot now be issued at a discount, there will very occasionally still be items in company balance sheets for discounts on shares issued before 1980. Although not listed as an item in the balance sheet formats per the 1985 Companies Act, a separate heading will have to be inserted to accommodate the item.

For the purpose of making the foregoing explanations easier it was assumed that balance sheet values and other values were the same. This is very rarely true for all the assets, and in fact there is more than one other 'value'. A balance sheet is a historical view of the past based on records made according to the firm's interpretation and use of accounting concepts and conventions. When shares are being issued it is not the historical view of the past that is important, but the view of the future. Therefore the actual premiums and discounts on shares being issued is not merely a matter of balance sheet values, but on the issuing company's view of the future and its estimate of how the investing public will react to the price at which the shares are being offered.

It is to be noted that there are no restrictions on issuing shares at par or at a premium.

The actual double entry accounts can now be seen.

8.3 Shares payable in full on application

The issue of shares in illustrations (1), (2) and (3) which follow are based on the balance sheets that have just been considered.

1 Shares issued at par

1,000 ordinary shares with a nominal value of £4 each are to be issued. Applications, together with the necessary money, are received for exactly 1,000 shares. The shares are then allotted to the applicants.

Bank

		£	
Ordinary share applicants	(A)	4,000	

Ordinary Share Applicants

		£			£
Ordinary share capital	(B)	4,000	Bank	(A)	4,000

Ordinary Share Capital

			£
	Ordinary share applicants	(B)	4,000

It may appear that the ordinary share applicants account is unnecessary, and that the only entries needed are a debit in the bank account and a credit in the ordinary share capital account. However, applicants do not always become shareholders; this is shown later. The applicant must make an offer for the shares being issued, accompanied by the necessary money: this is the application. After the applications have been vetted the allotments of shares are made by the company. This represents the acceptance of the offer by the company and it is at this point that the applicant becomes a shareholder. Therefore (A) represents the offer by the applicant, while (B) is the acceptance by the company. No entry must therefore be made in the share capital account until (B) happens, for it is not until that point that the share capital is in fact in existence. The share applicants account is therefore an intermediary account pending allotments being made.

2 Shares issued at a premium

1,000 ordinary shares with a nominal value of £4 each are to be issued for £10 each (*see* A Ltd previously). Thus a premium of £6 per share has been charged. Applications and the money are received for exactly 1,000 shares.

Bank

	£	
Balance b/fwd	1,000	
Ordinary share applicants	10,000	

Ordinary Share Applicants

		£		£
Ordinary share capital	(A)	4,000	Bank	10,000
Share premium	(B)	6,000		
		10,000		10,000

Share Premium

		£
Ordinary share applicants	(B)	6,000

Ordinary Share Capital (A Ltd)

		£
Balance b/fwd		4,000
Ordinary share applicants	(A)	4,000

Note: (A) is shown as £4,000 because the share capital is shown at nominal value and not as total issued value. (B) The £6,000 share premiums must therefore be credited to a share premium account to preserve double entry balancing.

3 Shares issued at a discount (prior to 1980)

1,000 ordinary shares with a nominal value of £4 each are to be issued for £3 each (*see* B Ltd previously). Thus a discount of £1 per share is being allowed. Applications and the money are received for exactly 1,000 shares.

Bank

	£	
Balance b/fwd	1,000	
Ordinary share applicants	3,000	

Ordinary Share Applicants

	£		£
Ordinary share capital	4,000	Bank	3,000
		Discounts on shares	1,000
	4,000		4,000

Ordinary Share Capital

			£
		Balance b/fwd	4,000
		Ordinary share capital	4,000

Discounts on Shares

	£		
Ordinary share applications	1,000		

4 Oversubscription and undersubscription for shares

When a public company invites investors to apply for its shares it is obviously very rare indeed if applications for shares equal exactly the number of shares to be issued. Where more shares are applied for than are available for issue, then the issue is said to be **oversubscribed**. Where fewer shares are applied for than are available for issue, then the issue has been **undersubscribed**.

With a brand-new company a minimum amount is fixed as being necessary to carry on any further with the running of the company. If the applications are less than the minimum stated, then the application monies must be returned to the senders. This does not apply to an established company. If therefore 1,000 shares of £1 each are available for issue, but only 875 shares are applied for, then only 875 will be issued, assuming that this is above the fixed minimum figure. The accounting entries will be in respect of 875 shares, no entries being needed for the 125 shares not applied for, as this part does not represent a transaction.

The opposite of this is where the shares are oversubscribed. In this case some sort of rationing is applied so that the issue is restricted to the shares available for issue. The process of selecting who will get how many shares depends on the policy of the firm. Some firms favour large shareholders because this leads to lower administrative costs. Why the costs will be lower will be obvious if the cost of calling a meeting of two companies each with 20,000 shares is considered. H Ltd has 20 shareholders with an average holding of 1,000 shares each. J Ltd has 1,000 shareholders with an average holding of 20 shares each. They all have to be notified by post and given various documents including a set of the final accounts. The cost of printing and sending these is less for H Ltd with 20 shareholders than for J Ltd with 1,000 shareholders. This is only one example of the costs involved, but it will also apply with equal force to many items connected with the shares. Conversely, the directors may prefer to have more shareholders with smaller holdings, one reason being that it decreases the amount of voting power in any one individual's hands. The actual process of rationing the shares is then a simple matter once a policy has been agreed. It may consist of scaling down applications, of drawing lots or some other chance selection, but it will eventually bring the number of shares to be issued down to the number of shares available. Excess application monies will then be refunded by the company.

An issue of shares where 1,000 ordinary shares of £1 nominal value each are to be issued at par payable in full, but 1,550 shares are applied for, will appear as follows:

Bank

	£		£
Ordinary share applicants	1,550	Ordinary share applicants (refunds)	550

Ordinary Share Applicants

	£		£
Bank	550	Bank	1,550
Ordinary share capital	1,000		
	1,550		1,550

Ordinary Share Capital

			£
		Ordinary share applicants	1,000

8.4 Issue of shares payable by instalments

The shares considered so far have all been issued as paid in full on application. Conversely, many issues are made which require payment by instalments. These are probably more common with public companies than with private companies. It should be noted that a public company is now not allowed to allot a share unless there has been paid on it a sum equal to at least one-quarter of its nominal value plus the whole of any premium.

The various stages, after the initial invitation has been made to the public to buy shares by means of advertisements (if it is a public company), etc., are as follows:

(A) Applications are received together with the application monies.

(B) The applications are vetted and the shares allotted, letters of allotment being sent out.

(C) The excess application monies from wholly unsuccessful applicants, or, where the application monies received exceed both the application and allotment monies required, wholly and partly unsuccessful applicants, are returned to them. Usually, if a person has been partly unsuccessful, his excess application monies are held by the company and will reduce the amount needed to be paid by him on allotment.

(D) Allotment monies are received.

(E) The next instalment, known as the first call, is requested.

(F) The monies are received from the first call.

(G) The next instalment, known as the second call, is requested.

(H) The monies are received from the second call.

This carries on until the full number of calls have been made, although there is not usually a large number of calls to be made in an issue.

The reasons for the payments by instalments become obvious if it is realised that a company will not necessarily require the immediate use of all the money to be raised by the issue. Suppose a new company is to be formed: it is to buy land, erect a factory, equip it with machinery and then go into production. This might take two years altogether. If the total sum needed was £1,000,000, the allocation of this money could be:

Ordinary Share Capital

	£
Cost of land, payable within 1 month	300,000
Cost of buildings, payable in 1 year's time	200,000
Cost of machinery, payable in 18 months' time	200,000
Working capital required in 2 years' time	300,000
	1,000,000

The issue may therefore well be on the following terms:

	Per cent
Application money per share, payable immediately	10
Allotment money per share, payable within 1 month	20
First call, money payable in 12 months' time	20
Second call, money payable in 18 months' time	20
Third call, money payable in 24 months' time	30
	100

The entries made in the share capital account should equal the amount of money requested to that point in time. However, instead of one share applicants account, this is usually split into several accounts to represent the different instalments. For this purpose application and allotment are usually joined together in one account, the application and *allotment account*, as this cuts out the need for transfers where excess *application monies* are held over and set off against allotment monies needed. When allotment is made, and not until then, an entry of £300,000 (10 per cent + 20 per cent) would be made in the share capital account. On the first call an entry of £200,000 would be made in the share capital account, likewise £200,000 on the second call and £300,000 on the third call. The share capital account will therefore contain not the monies received, but the amount of money requested. Exhibit 8.1 now shows an instance of a share issue.

Exhibit 8.1

A company is issuing 1,000 7 per cent preference shares of £1 each, payable 10 per cent on application, 20 per cent on allotment, 40 per cent on the first call and 30 per cent on the second call. Applications are received for 1,550 shares. A refund of the money is made in respect of 50 shares, while for the remaining 1,500 applied for, an allotment is to be made on the basis of 2 shares for every 3 applied for (assume that this will not involve any fractions of shares). The excess application monies are set off against the allotment monies asked for. The remaining requested instalments are all paid in full. The letters by the side of each entry refer to the various stages outlined earlier.

Bank

		£			£
Application and allotment:			Application and		
Application monies	(A)	155	allotment refund	(C)	5
Allotment monies					
(£1,000 × 20% *less* excess					
application monies £50)	(B)	150			
First call	(F)	400			
Second call	(H)	300			

Application and Allotment

		£			£
Bank – refund of			Bank	(A)	155
application monies	(C)	5	Bank	(B)	150
Preference share capital	(B)	300			
		305			305

First Call

		£			£
Preference share capital	(E)	400	Bank	(F)	400

Second Call

		£			£
Preference share capital	(G)	300	Bank	(H)	300

7 per cent Preference Share Capital

	£			£
		Application and allotment	(B)	300
		First call	(E)	400
Balance c/d	1,000	Second call	(G)	300
	1,000			1,000
		Balance b/d		1,000

If more than one type of share is being issued at the same time, e.g. preference shares and ordinary shares, then separate share capital accounts and separate application and allotment accounts and call accounts should be opened.

8.5 Forfeited shares

Sometimes, although it is probably fairly rare in recent times, a shareholder fails to pay the calls requested from him. The Articles of Association of the company will probably provide that the shareholder will have his shares forfeited, provided that certain safeguards for his protection are fully observed. In this case the shares will be cancelled, and the instalments already paid by the shareholder will be lost to him.

After the forfeiture, the company may reissue the shares, unless there is a provision in the Articles of Association to prevent it. There are certain conditions as to the prices at which the shares can be reissued. These are that the amount received on reissue plus the amount received from the original shareholder should at least equal (*a*) the called-up value where the shares are not fully called up, or (*b*) the nominal value where the full amount has been called up. Any premium previously paid is disregarded in determining the minimum reissue price.

Exhibit 8.2

Take the same information as that contained in Exhibit 8.1, but instead of all the calls being paid, Allen, the holder of 100 shares, fails to pay the first and second calls. He had already paid the application and allotment monies on the required dates. The directors conform to the provisions of the Articles of Association and (A) Allen is forced to suffer the forfeiture of his shares. (B) The amount still outstanding from Allen will be written off. (C) The directors then reissue the shares at 75 per cent of nominal value to J Dougan. (D) Dougan pays for the shares.

First Call

	£			£
Preference share capital	400	Bank		360
		Forfeited shares	(B)	40
	400			400

Second Call

		£			£
Preference share capital		300	Bank		270
			Forfeited shares	(B)	30
		300			300

7 per cent Preference Share Capital

		£			£
Forfeited shares	(A)	100	Application and allotment		300
Balance c/d		900	First call		400
			Second call		300
		1,000			1,000
			Balance b/d		900
Balance c/d		1,000	J Dougan	(C)	100
		1,000			1,000
			Balance b/d		1,000

Forfeited Shares

		£			£
First call	(B)	40	Preference share capital	(A)	100
Second call	(B)	30			
Balance c/d		30			
		100			100
J Dougan (*see* following note)		25	Balance c/d		30
Balance c/d		5			
		30			30

Bank

		£			
First call (£900 × 40%)		360			
Second call					
(£900 × 30%)		270			
J Dougan	(D)	75			

J Dougan

		£			£
Preference share capital		100	Bank	(D)	75
			Forfeited shares (discount on		
			reissue) – *see* following note		25
		100			100

Note: The transfer of £25 from the forfeited shares account to J Dougan's account is needed because the reissue was entered in the preference share capital account and Dougan's account at nominal value, i.e. following standard practice of a share capital account being concerned with nominal values, but Dougan was not to pay the full nominal price. Therefore the transfer of £25 is needed to close his account.

The balance of £5 on the forfeited shares account can be seen to be: cash received from original shareholder on application and allotment £30 + from Dougan £75 = £105. This is £5 over the nominal value so that the £5 appears as a credit balance. This is usually stated to be either transferred to a profit on reissue of forfeited shares account, but it really cannot be thought that this is followed in practice for small amounts. More normally it would be transferred to the credit of a share premium account.

8.6 Calls in advance and in arrear and the balance sheet

At the balance sheet date some shareholders will not have paid all the calls made. These are collectively known as **calls in arrear**. On the other hand, some shareholders may have paid amounts in respect of calls not made by the balance sheet date. These are **calls in advance**.

Calls in arrear, i.e. **called-up share capital not paid**, is to be shown in the balance sheet in one of the positions shown in the format per the 1985 Companies Act (*see* Chapter 16). There is no specified place for calls in advance, so this will be inserted in the balance sheet as an extra heading.

8.7 Rights issues

The costs of making a new issue of shares can be quite high. A way to reduce the costs of raising new long-term capital in the form of issuing shares may be by way of a **rights issue**. To do this the company circularises the existing shareholders, and informs them of the new issue to be made and the number of shares which each one of them is entitled to buy of the new issue. In most cases the shareholder is allowed to renounce his rights to the new shares in favour of someone else. The issue is usually pitched at a price which will make the rights capable of being sold, i.e. if the existing shareholder does not want the shares he can renounce them to A who will give him £x for the right to apply for the shares in his place, a right that A could not otherwise obtain. If any shareholder does not either buy the shares or transfer his rights, then the directors will usually have the power to dispose of such shares not taken up by issuing them in some other way.

8.8 Debentures

A **debenture** is a bond, acknowledging a loan to a company, usually under the company's seal, which bears a fixed rate of interest. Unlike shares, which normally depend on profits out of which to appropriate dividends, debenture interest is payable whether profits are made or not.

A debenture may be redeemable, i.e. repayable at or by a specified date. Conversely it may be irredeemable, redemption only taking place when the company is eventually liquidated, or in a case such as when the debenture interest is not paid within a given time limit.

People lending money to companies in the form of debentures will obviously be interested in how safe their investment will be. In the case of some debentures, the debenture holders are given the legal right that on certain happenings they will be able to take control of specific assets, or of the whole of the assets. They can then sell the assets and recoup the amount due under their debentures, or deal with the assets in ways specified in the deed under which the debentures were issued. Such debentures are known as being secured against the assets, the term **mortgage** debenture often being used. Other debentures carry no prior right to control the assets under any circumstances. These are known as **simple** or **naked** debentures.

8.9 The issue of debentures

The entries for the issue of debentures are similar to those for shares. It would, however, certainly not be the normal modern practice to issue debentures at a premium. If the word 'debentures' appears instead of 'share capital', then the entries in the accounts would be identical.

8.10 Shares of no par value

It can be seen that the idea of a fixed par value for a share can be very misleading. For anyone who has not studied accounting, it may well come as a shock to find that a share with a par value of £1 might in fact be issued for £5. If the share is dealt in on the Stock Exchange they might find a £1 share selling at £10 or even £20, or equally well it may sell for only 10p.

Another disadvantage of a par value is that it can give people entirely the wrong impression of the activities of a business. If a par value is kept to, and the dividend based on that, then with a certain degree of inflation the dividend figure can look excessive. Many trade union leaders would howl with disapproval if a dividend of 100 per cent were declared by a company. But is this so excessive? Exhibit 8.3 gives a rather different picture.

Exhibit 8.3

Allen bought a share 40 years ago for £1. At the time he was satisfied with a return of 5 per cent on his money. With a 5 per cent dividend he could buy a certain amount of goods which will be called x. Forty years later to buy that same amount of goods, x, he would need, say, 20 times as much money. Previously £5 would have bought x, now it would take £100. To keep his dividend at the same level of purchasing power he would need a dividend now of 100 per cent, as compared with the 5 per cent he was receiving 40 years ago.

In the United States of America, Canada and Belgium as well as other countries, no par value is attached to shares being issued. A share is issued at whatever price is suitable at the time, and the money received is credited to a share capital account.

New terms

Share premium (pp. 101–3): Where a share is issued at a price above its par, or nominal value, the excess is known as a premium.

Share discount (pp. 101–3): Where a share was issued at a price below its par, or nominal value, the shortfall was known as a discount. However, it is no longer legal under the Companies Acts to issue shares at a discount.

Rights issue (p. 111): An issue of shares to existing shareholders.

Debenture (pp. 111–2): A bond or document acknowledging a loan to a company, normally under the company's seal and carrying a fixed rate of interest.

Shares at no par value (p. 112): Shares which do not have a fixed par, or nominal value.

Main points to remember

1   Shares may be issued either:

(*a*) at par, or nominal value – i.e. a £1 ordinary share would be issued in exchange for payment of £1, or

(*b*) at a premium – i.e. if a £1 ordinary share were issued at a premium of 25p, it would cost the buyer £1.25 (and the 25p would be put into the issuing company's *share premium* account).

2   The accounting entries made on the issue of debentures are identical to the accounting entries made on the issue of shares.

Review questions

8.1   A limited company has a nominal capital of £120,000 divided into 120,000 ordinary shares of £1 each. The whole of the capital was issued at par on the following terms:

	Per share
Payable on application	£0.125
Payable on allotment	£0.25
First call	£0.25
Second call	£0.375

Applications were received for 160,000 shares and it was decided to allot the shares on the basis of three for every four for which applications had been made. The balance of application monies were applied to the allotment, no cash being refunded. The balance of allotment monies were paid by the members.

The calls were made and paid in full by the members, with the exception of a member who failed to pay the first and second calls on the 800 shares allotted to him. A resolution was passed by the directors to forfeit the shares. The forfeited shares were later issued to D Regan at £0.90 each.

Show the ledger accounts recording all the above transactions, and the relevant extracts from a balance sheet after all the transactions had been completed.

8.2   Badger Ltd has an authorised capital of £100,000 divided into 20,000 ordinary shares of £5 each. The whole of the shares were issued at par, payments being made as follows:

	£
Payable on application	0.5
Payable on allotment	1.5
First call	2.0
Second call	1.0

Applications were received for 32,600 shares. It was decided to refund application monies on 2,600 shares and to allot the shares on the basis of two for every three applied for. The excess application monies sent by the successful applicants is not to be refunded but is to be held and so reduce the amount payable on allotment.

The calls were made and paid in full with the exception of one member holding 100 shares who paid neither the first nor the second call and another member who did not pay the second call on 20 shares. After requisite action by the directors the shares were forfeited. They were later reissued to B Mills at a price of £4 per share.

You are to draft the ledger accounts to record the transactions.

8.3 The authorised and issued share capital of Cosy Fires Ltd was £75,000 divided into 75,000 ordinary shares of £1 each, fully paid. On 2 January 19X7, the authorised capital was increased by a further 85,000 ordinary shares of £1 each to £160,000. On the same date 40,000 ordinary shares of £1 each were offered to the public at £1.25 per share payable as to £0.60 on application (including the premium), £0.35 on allotment and £0.30 on 6 April 19X7.

The lists were closed on 10 January 19X7, and by that date applications for 65,000 shares had been received. Applications for 5,000 shares received no allotment and the cash paid in respect of such shares was returned. All shares were then allocated to the remaining applicants pro rata to their original applications, the balance of the monies received on applications being applied to the amounts due on allotment.

The balances due on allotment were received on 31 January 19X7, with the exception of one allottee of 500 shares and these were declared forfeited on 4 April 19X7. These shares were reissued as fully paid on 2 May 19X7, at £1.10 per share. The call due on 6 April 19X7 was duly paid by the other shareholders.

You are required
(a) To record the above-mentioned transactions in the appropriate ledger accounts; and
(b) To show how the balances on such accounts should appear in the company's balance sheet as on 31 May 19X7.

(*Chartered Association of Certified Accountants*)

8.4A During the year to 30 September 19X7, Kammer plc made a new offer of shares. The details of the offer were as follows:

1   100,000 ordinary shares of £1 each were issued payable in instalments as follows:

	Per share £
On application at 1 November 19X6	0.65
On allotment (including the share premium of £0.50 per share) on 1 December 19X6	0.55
On first and final call on 1 June 19X7	0.30
	£1.50

2   Applications for 200,000 shares were received, and it was decided to deal with them as follows:
    (a) to return cheques for 75,000 shares;
    (b) to accept in full applications for 25,000 shares; and
    (c) to allot the remaining shares on the basis of three shares for every four shares applied for.

3   On the first and final call, one applicant who had been allotted 5,000 shares failed to pay the due amount, and his shares were duly declared forfeited. They were then reissued to Amber Ltd on 1 September 19X7 at a price of £0.80 per share fully paid.

Note: Kammer's issued share capital on 1 October 19X6 consisted of 500,000 ordinary shares of £1 each.

Required:
Record the above transactions in the following ledger accounts:

(a) ordinary share capital;
(b) share premium;
(c) application and allotment;
(d) first and final call;
(e) forfeited shares; and
(f) Amber Ltd's account.

(*Association of Accounting Technicians*)

8.5 M Limited has an authorised share capital of £1,500,000 divided into 1,500,000 ordinary shares of £1 each. The issued share capital at 31 March 19X7 was £500,000 which was fully paid, and had been issued at par. On 1 April 19X7, the directors, in accordance with the company's Articles, decided to increase the share capital of the company by offering a further 500,000 ordinary shares of £1 each at a price of £1.60 per share, payable as follows:

On application, including the premium	£0.85 per share
On allotment	£0.25 per share
On first and final call on 3 August 19X7	£0.50 per share

On 13 April 19X7, applications had been received for 750,000 shares and it was decided to allot the shares to applicants for 625,000 shares, on the basis of four shares for every five shares for which applications had been received. The balance of the money received on application was to be applied to the amounts due on allotment. The shares were allotted on 1 May 19X7, the unsuccessful applicants being repaid their cash on this date. The balance of the allotment money was received in full by 15 May 19X7.

With the exception of one member who failed to pay the call on the 5,000 shares allotted to him, the remainder of the call was paid in full within two weeks of the call being made.

The directors resolved to forfeit these shares on 1 September 19X7, after giving the required notice. The forfeited shares were reissued on 30 September 19X7 to another member at £0.90 per share.

You are required to write up the ledger accounts necessary to record these transactions in the books of M Limited.

(*Chartered Institute of Management Accountants*)

8.6A Applications were invited by the directors of Grobigg Ltd for 150,000 of its £1 ordinary shares at £1.15 per share payable as follows:

	Per share
On application on 1 April 19X8	£0.75
On allotment on 30 April 19X8 (including the premium of £0.15 per share)	£0.20
On first and final call on 31 May 19X8	£0.20

Applications were received for 180,000 shares and it was decided to deal with these as follows:

1 To refuse allotment to applicants for 8,000 shares.
2 To give full allotment to applicants for 22,000 shares.
3 To allot the remainder of the available shares pro rata among the other applicants.
4 To utilise the surplus received on applications in part payment of amounts due on allotment.

An applicant, to whom 400 shares had been allotted, failed to pay the amount due on the first and final call and his shares were declared forfeit on 31 July 19X8. These shares were reissued on 3 September 19X8 as fully paid at £0.90 per share.

Show how the transactions would be recorded in the company's books.

(*Chartered Association of Certified Accountants*)

9

Companies purchasing and redeeming their own shares and debentures

Objectives

After you have studied this chapter, you should:

- *understand, in the context of shares and debentures, the difference between the terms 'purchasing' and 'redeeming'*

- *be aware of the alternative ways in which a company may purchase or redeem its own shares and debentures*

- *know the difference between the purchase/redemption opportunities available to private companies, and those available to other companies*

- *know how to record the accounting entries relating to the purchase and the redemption of shares and debentures*

9.1 Purchasing and redeeming own shares

To a student the words 'purchasing' and 'redeeming' may appear to be exactly the same as far as this chapter is concerned. To all intents and purposes it is the same, for it involves an outflow of cash by the company to get back its own shares and then cancel them. However, from a rather more legal and precise point of view, 'redeeming' means the buying back of shares which were originally issued as being 'redeemable' in that the company stated when they were issued that they would be, or could be, redeemed (i.e. bought back by the company). The terms of the 'redemption' (buying back) would be stated at the time when the shares were issued. However, when shares are issued and are not stated to be 'redeemable' then, when they are bought back by the company it is then said to be the 'purchase' of its shares by the company, usually in the open market.

Until 1981 a company in the United Kingdom could not in normal circumstances 'purchase' its own shares. In addition 'redemption' was limited to one type of share, **redeemable preference shares**. This had not been the case in the United States and Europe for many years where companies had, with certain restrictions, been allowed to buy back their own shares. The basic reason why this was not allowed in the UK was the fear that the interests of creditors could be adversely affected if the company used its available cash to buy its own shares, thus leaving less to satisfy the claims of the creditors. The possibilities of abuse with preference shares was considered to be less than with ordinary shares, thus it was possible to have redeemable preference shares.

Now, under the Companies Acts, a company may, if it is authorised to do so by its articles of association:

(*a*) Issue redeemable shares of any class (preference, ordinary, etc). Redeemable shares include those that are to be redeemed on a particular date as well as those that are merely liable to be redeemed at the discretion of the shareholder or of the company. There is an important proviso that a company can only issue redeemable shares if it has in issue shares that are *not* redeemable. Without this restriction a company could issue only redeemable shares, then later redeem all of its shares, and thus finish up without any shareholders.

(*b*) 'Purchase' its own shares (i.e. shares that were not issued as being redeemable shares). Again there is a proviso that the company must, *after* the purchase, have other shares in issue at least some of which are not redeemable. This again is to stop the company redeeming its whole share capital and thus ceasing to have members. The company must have, after the purchase, at least two members.

9.2 Advantages of purchase and redemption of shares

Certainly there are quite a few possible advantages of a company being able to buy back its own shares. These are strongest in the case of private companies. For public companies the main advantage is that those with surplus cash resources could find it useful to be able to return some of this surplus cash back to its shareholders by buying back some of its own shares, rather than have pressure put on them to use such cash in uneconomic ways.

For private companies the main possible advantages would appear to be overcoming snags which occur when a shareholder cannot sell his shares on the 'open market', i.e. a stock exchange. This means that:

(*a*) It will help shareholders who have difficulties in selling their shares to another individual to be able to realise their value when needed, for any reason.

(*b*) People will be more willing to buy shares from private companies. The fear of not being able to dispose of them previously led to finance being relatively difficult for private companies to obtain from people outside the original main proprietors of the company.

(*c*) In many 'family' companies cash is needed to pay for taxes on the death of the shareholder.

(*d*) Shareholders with grievances against the company can be bought out, thus contributing to the more efficient management of the company.

(*e*) Family-owned companies will be helped in their desire to keep control of the company when a family shareholder with a large number of shares dies or retires.

(*f*) Similar to public companies, as described above, the company could return unwanted cash resources back to its shareholders.

(*g*) For both private companies, and for public companies whose shares are not listed on a stock exchange, it may help boost share schemes for employees, as the employees would know that they could fairly easily dispose of the shares instead of being stuck with them.

9.3 Accounting entries

The accounting entries for either 'purchase' or 'redemption' of shares are exactly the same, except that the word 'Redeemable' will appear as the first word in the title of the accounts for shares that are redeemable. The figures to be entered will naturally be affected by the **terms** under which shares are redeemed or purchased, but the actual type of **location** of the debits and credits to be made will be the same.

The reader will more easily understand the rather complicated entries needed if s/he understands the reasoning behind the Companies Acts. The protection of the creditor was uppermost in the minds of Parliament. The general idea is that **capital** should not be returned to the shareholders, except under certain circumstances. If capital is returned to the shareholders, thus reducing the cash and bank balances, then the creditors could lose out badly if there was not then sufficient cash/bank balances to be able to pay their claims. Thus the shareholders, seeing that things were not progressing too well in the company, could get their money out possibly at the expense of the creditors.

There are dividends which can quite legitimately be paid to the shareholders out of distributable profits, but the idea is to stop the shareholders withdrawing their capital. Included under the general heading of 'capital' for this purpose are those particular reserves which cannot be used up for the payment of cash dividends. There are special exceptions to this, namely the reduction of capital by public companies (*see* Chapter 13) and the special powers of a private company to purchase or redeem its own shares out of capital (*see* later in this chapter), but apart from these special cases the company law regulations are intended to ensure that capital figures do not fall when shares are redeemed or purchased. This general purpose is behind the accounting entries which are now to be examined.

9.4 Rules for redemption or purchase

It is important to note that in *all* cases shares can only be redeemed or purchased when they are fully paid.

The safeguards for the protection of 'capital' contained in the Companies Acts may be summarised as follows.

9.5 Nominal value

In respect of the **nominal** value of shares redeemed or purchased, either (*a*) there must be a new issue of shares to provide the funds for redemption or purchase or (*b*) sufficient distributable profits must be available (i.e. a large enough credit balance on the appropriation account) which could be diverted from being used up as dividends to being treated as used up for the purpose of redeeming or purchasing the shares. Therefore, when shares are redeemed or purchased other than out of the proceeds of a new issue, then, and only then, the amount of distributable profits treated as being used up by the nominal value of shares redeemed or purchased is debited to the appropriation account and credited to a **capital redemption reserve**. (Before 1981 this was called a capital redemption reserve fund. The use of the word 'fund' has now been dropped.) Thus the old share capital will equal the total of the new share capital *plus* the capital redemption reserve. The capital redemption reserve is a 'non-distributable' reserve. This means that it cannot be transferred back to the credit of the appropriation account, and so increase the profits available for distribution as cash dividends. The process of diverting profits from being usable for dividends means that the non-payment of the dividends leaves more cash in the firm against which creditors could claim if necessary.

Note: In all the examples which follow, the shares being redeemed/purchased could either be redeemable shares or those not specifically stated to be redeemable. Obviously, in a real company, the titles of the accounts would state which shares were redeemable.

To get the reader used to journal entries, and then seeing the effect on the face of the balance sheet, journal style entries will be shown first, followed by the balances for the balance sheet.

Exhibit 9.1

£2,000 preference shares are redeemed/purchased at par, a new issue of £2,000 ordinary shares at par being made for the purpose.

		Dr £	Cr £
(A1)	Bank	2,000	
(A2)	Ordinary share applicants		2,000
	Cash received from applicants		
(B1)	Ordinary share applicants	2,000	
(B2)	Ordinary share capital		2,000
	Ordinary shares allotted		
(C1)	Preference share capital	2,000	
(C2)	Preference share purchase*		2,000
	Shares to be redeemed/purchased		
(D1)	Preference share purchase*	2,000	
(D2)	Bank		2,000
	Payment made to redeem/purchase shares		

Note: In all the examples which follow, the shares being purchased/redeemed are preference shares. In fact they could be any type of share, ordinary, preference, preferred ordinary, etc. The shares to be redeemed/purchased are transferred to a preference share purchase account. In fact if they were being redeemed it would be a preference share redemption account. It will make it easier to follow if the answers are standardised.

	Balances before £		Effect Dr £		Cr £	Balances after £
Net assets (except bank)	7,500					7,500
Bank	2,500	(A1)	2,000	(D2)	2,000	2,500
	10,000					10,000
Ordinary share capital	5,000			(B2)	2,000	7,000
Ordinary share applicants	–	(B1)	2,000	(A2)	2,000	–
Preference share capital	2,000	(C1)	2,000			–
Preference share purchase	–	(D1)	2,000	(C2)	2,000	–
	7,000*					7,000*
Profit and loss	3,000					3,000
	10,000					10,000

*Notice: total 'capitals' remain the same.

Exhibit 9.2

£2,000 preference shares redeemed/purchased at par, with no new issue of shares to provide funds for the purpose. Therefore an amount equal to the nominal value of the shares redeemed *must* be transferred from the profit and loss appropriation account to the credit of a capital redemption reserve.

		Dr £	Cr £
(A1)	Preference share capital	2,000	
(A2)	Preference share purchase		2,000
	Shares to be redeemed/purchased		
(B1)	Preference share purchase	2,000	
(B2)	Bank		2,000
	Cash paid as purchase/redemption		
(C1)	Profit and loss appropriation	2,000	
(C2)	Capital redemption reserve		2,000
	Transfer per Companies Act 1985, Section 45		

	Balances before		Effect Dr		Effect Cr	Balances after
	£		£		£	£
Net assets (except bank)	7,500					7,500
Bank	2,500			(B2)	2,000	500
	10,000					8,000
Ordinary share capital	5,000					5,000
Preference share capital	2,000	(A1)	2,000			–
Preference share purchase	–	(B1)	2,000	(A2)	2,000	–
Capital redemption reserve	–			(C2)	2,000	2,000
	7,000*					7,000*
Profit and loss	3,000	(C1)	2,000			1,000
	10,000					8,000

*Notice: total 'capitals' (share capital + non-distributable reserves) remain the same at £7,000.

Exhibit 9.3

£2,000 preference shares redeemed/purchased at par, being £1,200 from issue of ordinary shares at par and partly by using appropriation account balance.

		Dr £	Cr £
(A1)	Bank	1,200	
(A2)	Ordinary share applicants		1,200
	Cash received from applicants		
(B1)	Ordinary share applicants	1,200	
(B2)	Ordinary share capital		1,200
	Ordinary shares allotted		
(C1)	Profit and loss appropriation	800	
(C2)	Capital redemption reserve		800
	Part of redemption/purchase not covered by new issue, to comply with Companies Act 1985		
(D1)	Preference share capital	2,000	
(D2)	Preference share purchase		2,000
	Shares being redeemed/purchased		
(E1)	Preference share purchase	2,000	
(E2)	Bank		2,000
	Payment made for redemption/purchase		

	Balances before £		Effect Dr £		Effect Cr £	Balances after £
Net assets (except bank)	7,500					7,500
Bank	2,500	(A1)	1,200	(E2)	2,000	1,700
	10,000					9,200
Ordinary share capital	5,000			(B2)	1,200	6,200
Ordinary share applicants	–	(B1)	1,200	(A2)	1,200	–
Preference share capital	2,000	(D1)	2,000			–
Preference share purchase	–	(E1)	2,000	(D2)	2,000	–
Capital redemption reserve	–			(C2)	800	800
	7,000*					7,000*
Profit and loss	3,000	(C1)	800			2,200
	10,000					9,200

*Notice: total 'capitals' remain the same.

9.6 Premiums

The next requirement under the Companies Acts is that when shares are being redeemed/purchased at a premium, but they were *not* originally issued at a premium, then an amount equal to the premium *must* be transferred from the appropriation account to the credit of the share purchase/redemption account. This again is to divert profits away from being distributable to being part of 'capital'.

Exhibit 9.4

£2,000 preference shares which were originally issued at par are redeemed/purchased at a premium of 20 per cent. There is no new issue of shares for the purpose. In this example the ordinary shares had been originally issued at a premium, thus the reason for the share premium account being in existence. However, it is *not* the ordinary shares which are being redeemed and therefore the share premium *cannot* be used for the premium on redemption/purchase of the preference shares.

		Dr £	Cr £
(A1)	Preference share capital	2,000	
(A2)	Preference share purchase		2,000
	Shares being redeemed/purchased		
(B1)	Profit and loss appropriation	400	
(B2)	Preference share purchase		400
	Premium on purchase/redemption of shares *not* previously issued at premium		
(C1)	Profit and loss appropriation	2,000	
(C2)	Capital redemption reserve		2,000
	Transfer because shares redeemed/purchased out of distributable profits		
(D1)	Preference share purchase	2,400	
(D2)	Bank		2,400
	Payment on purchase/redemption		

	Balances before £		Effect Dr £		Cr £	Balances after £
Net assets (except bank)	7,500					7,500
Bank	2,500			(D2)	2,400	100
	10,000					7,600
Ordinary share capital	4,500					4,500
Preference share capital	2,000	(A1)	2,000			–
Preference share purchase	–	(D1)	2,400	(A2)	2,000	–
				(B2)	400	
Capital redemption reserve	–			(C2)	2,000	2,000
Share premium	500					500
	7,000*					7,000*
		(C1)	2,000			
Profit and loss	3,000	(B1)	400			600
	10,000					7,600

*Notice: total 'capitals' remain the same.

Under the Companies Acts, when shares are being redeemed or purchased at a premium, *and* they were originally issued at a premium, *and* a new issue of shares is being made for the purpose, then the share premium account *can* have an amount calculated as follows transferred to the credit of the share purchase/redemption account. This is shown as (E).

Share Premium Account

				£
	Balance before new issue		(A)	xxx
Add	Premium on new issue		(B)	xxx
	Balance after new issue		(C)	xxx
	Amount that *may* be transferred		(E)	
	is lesser of:			
	Premiums that were received when it first issued the shares now being redeemed/purchased (D)	xxx		
	or			
	Balance after new issue (C) above	xxx		
	Transfer to share purchase/redemption		(E)	xxx
	New balance for balance sheet (could be nil)			xxx

Where the amount being deducted (E) is *less* than the premium paid on the *current* redemption or purchase, then an amount equivalent to the difference must be transferred from the debit of the appropriation account to the credit of the share purchase/redemption account. (An instance of this is shown in Exhibit 9.5.) This again diverts profits away from being distributable.

Exhibit 9.5

£2,000 preference shares originally issued at a premium of 20 per cent now being purchased/redeemed at a premium of 25 per cent. The position can be shown in three different companies if for the purpose of purchase/redemption:

- Company 1 issues 2,400 ordinary £1 shares at par;
- Company 2 issues 2,000 ordinary £1 shares at 20 per cent premium;
- Company 3 issues 1,600 ordinary £1 shares at 50 per cent premium.

Share Premium Account

		Company 1 £	Company 2 £	Company 3 £
Balance before new issue	(A)	150[1]	400	400
Premium on new issue			400	800 (B)
Balance after new issue	(C)	150	800	1,200
Amount transferable to share purchase/ redemption is therefore lower of (C) or original premium on issue (£400)		150[2]	400[2]	400[2]
New balance for balance sheet		–	400	800

Notes:

1   In Company 1 it is assumed that of the original £400 premium the sum of £250 had been used up to issue bonus shares (*see* Chapter 13 later).

2   As these figures are less than the premium of £500 *now* being paid, the differences (Company 1 £350; Companies 2 and 3 £100 each) must be transferred from the debit of the appropriation account to the credit of the preference share/purchase redemption account.

Journal entries:

	Company 1 Dr £	Company 1 Cr £	Company 2 Dr £	Company 2 Cr £	Company 3 Dr £	Company 3 Cr £
(A1) Bank	2,400		2,400		2,400	
(A2) Ordinary share applicants		2,400		2,400		2,400
Cash received from applicants						
(B1) Ordinary share applicants	2,400		2,400		2,400	
(B2) Ordinary share capital		2,400		2,000		1,600
(B3) Share premium		–		400		800
Ordinary shares allotted						
(C1) Preference share capital	2,000		2,000		2,000	
(C2) Preference share purchase		2,000		2,000		2,000
Shares being redeemed/purchased						
(D1) Share premium account	150		400		400	
(D2) Preference share purchase		150		400		400
Amount of share premium account used for redemption/purchase						
(E1) Profit and loss appropriation	350		100		100	
(E2) Preference share purchase		350		100		100
Excess of premium payable over amount of share premium account usable for the purpose						
(F1) Preference share purchase	2,500		2,500		2,500	
(F2) Bank		2,500		2,500		2,500
Amount paid on redemption/purchase						

Exhibit 9.6

The following balance sheets for the three companies of Exhibit 9.5 are given *before* the purchase/redemption. The balance sheets are then shown *after* purchase/redemption.

Balance Sheets (*before* redemption/purchase)

	Company 1 £	Company 2 £	Company 3 £
Net assets (except bank)	7,500	7,500	7,500
Bank	2,500	2,500	2,500
	10,000	10,000	10,000
Ordinary share capital	4,850	4,600	4,600
Preference share capital	2,000	2,000	2,000
Share premium	150	400	400
	7,000	7,000	7,000
Profit and loss account	3,000	3,000	3,000
	10,000	10,000	10,000

Balance Sheets (*after* redemption/purchase)

	Company 1 £	Company 2 £	Company 3 £
Net assets (except bank)	7,500	7,500	7,500
Bank	2,400	2,400	2,400
	9,900	9,900	9,900
Ordinary share capital	7,250	6,600	6,200
Share premium	–	400	800
	7,250	7,000	7,000
Profit and loss account	2,650	2,900	2,900
	9,900	9,900	9,900

9.7 Private companies: redemption or purchase of shares out of capital

The earlier Companies Act of 1981 introduced a *new* power for a *private* company to redeem/purchase its own shares where *either* it has insufficient distributable profits for the purpose *or* it cannot raise the amount required by a new issue. Previously it would have had to apply to the court for **capital reduction** as per Chapter 13. The 1981 legislation made it far easier to achieve the same objectives, both in terms of time and expense. This is carried on in the current Companies Acts.

A book on company law should be read for the detail of the various matters which must be dealt with. A very brief outline may be given as follows:

(*a*) The company must be authorised to do so by its Articles of Association.

(*b*) Directors must certify that, after the **permissible capital payment**, the company will be able to carry on as a going concern during the next twelve months, and be able to pay its debts immediately after the payment and also during the next twelve months.

(*c*) Auditors to make a satisfactory report.

(*d*) Permissible capital payment is the amount by which the price of redemption or purchase exceeds the aggregate of (i) the company's distributable profits and (ii) the proceeds of any new issue. This means that a private company should use its available profits and any share proceeds before making a payment out of capital.

9.8 Permissible capital payments

(*a*) Where the permissible capital payment is *less* than the nominal value of shares redeemed/purchased, the amount of the difference *shall* be transferred to the capital redemption reserve from the appropriation account (or undistributed profits).

(*b*) Where the permissible capital payment is *greater* than the nominal value of shares redeemed/purchased, *any* non-distributable reserves (e.g. share premium account, capital redemption reserve, revaluation reserve, etc.) or fully paid share capital can be reduced by the excess.

This can best be illustrated by taking two companies, R and S, with similar account balances *before* the purchase/redemption, but redeeming on different terms:

Exhibit 9.7

Company R	Before £		Dr £		Cr £	After £
Net assets (except bank)	2,500					2,500
Bank	7,500			(B2)	4,000	3,500
	10,000					6,000
Ordinary shares	1,000					1,000
Preference shares	4,000	(A1)	4,000			–
Non-distributable reserves	2,000					2,000
Capital redemption reserve				(C2)	3,000	3,000
Preference share purchase	–	(B1)	4,000	(A2)	4,000	
	7,000					
Profit and loss	3,000	(C1)	3,000			
	10,000					6,000

Preference shares redeemed at par £4,000. No new issue.

Therefore pay	£4,000
Less Profit and loss account	£3,000
Permissible capital payment	£1,000
Nominal amount shares redeemed/purchased	£4,000
Less Permissible capital payment	£1,000
Deficiency to transfer to capital redemption reserve (C1 and C2)	£3,000

(A1) and (A2) represents transfer of shares redeemed/purchased.
(B1) and (B2) represents payment to shareholders.

Company S	Before £		Dr £		Cr £	After £
Net assets (except bank)	2,500					2,500
Bank	7,500			(D2)	7,200	300
	10,000					2,800
Ordinary share capital	1,000					1,000
Preference shares	4,000	(A1)	4,000			–
{ Non-distributable reserves	2,000	(C1)	200			1,800
{ Capital redemption reserve	–					–
Preference share purchase		(D1)	7,200	(A2)	4,000	
				(B2)	3,000	
				(C2)	200	
	7,000					2,800
Profit and loss	3,000	(B1)	3,000			–
	10,000					2,800

Preference shares redeemed/purchased at premium 80%. No new issue.

Therefore pay	£7,200
Less Profit and loss account	£3,000
Permissible capital payment	£4,200
Permissible capital payment	£4,200
Less Nominal amount redeemed/purchased	£4,000
Excess from *any* of non-distributable reserves (or capital) (C1 and C2)	£200

(A1) and (A2) represents shares redeemed/purchased.
(B1) and (B2) is transfer to redemption/purchase account of part of source of funds.
(D1) and (D2) is payment to shareholders.

9.9 Cancellation of shares purchased/redeemed

All shares purchased/redeemed must be cancelled immediately. They cannot be kept in hand by the company and traded in like any other commodity.

9.10 Redemption of debentures

Unless they are stated to be irredeemable, debentures are redeemed according to the terms of the issue. The necessary funds to finance the redemption may be from:

(*a*) an issue of shares or debentures for the purpose;
(*b*) the liquid resources of the company.

As it resembles the redemption of redeemable preference shares, when the redemption is financed as in (*a*), no transfer of profits from the profit and loss appropriation account to a reserve account is needed. However, when financed as in (*b*) it is good accounting practice, although not legally necessary, to divert profits from being used as dividends by transferring an amount equal to the nominal value redeemed from the debit of the profit and loss appropriation account to the credit of a reserve account.

Redemption may be effected:

1 by annual drawings out of profits;
2 by purchase in the open market when the price is favourable, i.e. less than the price which will have to be paid if the company waited until the last date by which redemption has to be carried out;
3 in a lump sum to be provided by the accumulation of a sinking fund.

These can now be examined in more detail.

Regular annual drawings out of profits

(a) When redeemed at a premium

In this case the source of the bank funds with which the premium is paid should be taken to be (*a*) the share premium account, or if this does not exist, or the premium is in excess of the balance on the account, then any part not covered by a share premium account is deemed to come from (*b*) the profit and loss appropriation account. Exhibit 9.8 shows the effect on a balance sheet where there is no share premium account, while Exhibit 9.9 illustrates the case when a share premium account is in existence.

Exhibit 9.8

Starting with the *before* balance sheet, £400 of the debentures are redeemed at a premium of 20 per cent.

Balance Sheets

	Before	+ or −	After
	£	£	£
Other assets	12,900		12,900
Bank	3,400	− 480 (A)	2,920
	16,300		15,820
Share capital	10,000		10,000
Debenture redemption reserve	−	+ 400 (B)	400
Debentures	2,000	− 400 (A)	1,600
Profit and loss	4,300	− 400 (B)	
		− 80 (A)	3,820
	16,300		15,820

Exhibit 9.9

Starting with the *before* balance sheet, £400 of the debentures are redeemed at a premium of 20 per cent.

Balance Sheets

	Before	+ or −	After
	£	£	£
Other assets	13,500		13,500
Bank	3,400	− 480 (A)	2,920
	16,900		16,420
Share capital	10,000		10,000
Share premium	600	− 80 (A)	520
Debenture redemption reserve	−	+ 400 (B)	400
Debentures	2,000	− 400 (A)	1,600
Profit and loss	4,300	− 400 (B)	3,900
	16,900		16,420

In both Exhibits 9.8 and 9.9 the debenture redemption reserve account is built up each year by the nominal value of the debentures redeemed each year. When the whole issue of debentures has been redeemed, then the balance on the debenture redemption reserve account should be transferred to the credit of a general reserve account. It is, after all, an accumulation of undistributed profits.

(b) Redeemed – originally issued at a discount

The discount originally given was in fact to attract investors to buy the debentures, and is therefore as much a cost of borrowing as is debenture interest. The discount therefore needs to be written off during the life of the debentures. It might be more rational to write it off to the profit and loss account, but in fact accounting custom, as permitted by law, would first of all write it off against any share premium account or, secondly, against the profit and loss appropriation account.

The amounts written-off over the life of the debentures are:

(*a*) equal annual amounts over the life of the debentures; or

(*b*) in proportion to the debenture debt outstanding at the start of each year. Exhibit 9.10 shows such a situation.

Exhibit 9.10

£30,000 debentures are issued at a discount of 5 per cent. They are repayable at par over five years at the rate of £6,000 per annum.

Year	Outstanding at start of each year	Proportion written off		Amount
	£			£
1	30,000	$30/90 \times £1,500$	=	500
2	24,000	$24/90 \times £1,500$	=	400
3	18,000	$18/90 \times £1,500$	=	300
4	12,000	$12/90 \times £1,500$	=	200
5	6,000	$6/90 \times £1,500$	=	100
	90,000			1,500

Redeemed by purchase in the open market

A sum equal to the cash actually paid on redemption should be transferred from the debit of the profit and loss appropriation account to the credit of the debenture redemption reserve account. The sum actually paid will of course have been credited to the cash book and debited to the debentures account.

Any discount (or profit) on purchase will be transferred to a reserve account. Any premium (or loss) on purchase will be deemed to come out of such a reserve account, or if no such account exists or it is insufficient, then it will be deemed to come out of the share premium account. Failing the existence of these accounts any loss must come out of the profit and loss appropriation account. It may seem that purchase would not be opportune if the debentures had to be redeemed at a premium. However, it would still be opportune if the premium paid was not as high as the premium to be paid if the final date for redemption was awaited.

Redemption of debentures by a sinking fund

Where debentures are issued which are redeemable (and most are redeemable) consideration should be given to the availability of cash funds at the time.

This method involves the investment of cash outside the business. The aim is to make a regular investment of money which, together with the accumulated interest or dividends, is sufficient to finance the redemption of the debentures at the requisite time.

Before calculations become too involved a simple proposition can be examined. As each period's interest (or dividend) is received, then that amount is immediately reinvested. Apart from the reinvestment of interest the other money taken for investment is to be an equal amount each period. This being so, if the money is to be invested at 5 per cent per annum, and the debenture is £500 to be redeemed in five years' time, then how much should be taken for investment each year? If £100 were taken each year for five years, then this would amount to more than £500 because of the interest and of the interest on the reinvested interest. Most readers will recognise this as money being invested at compound interest. Therefore something less than £100 per annum is needed. The exact amount can be calculated by the use of the compound interest formula. Chapter 33 illustrates how the amount needed can be calculated. As these calculations are left until later in the book, a summarised set of tables is now shown to help the student at this stage.

Annual sinking fund instalments to provide £1

Years	3%	3½%	4%	4½%	5%
3	0.323530	0.321933	0.320348	0.318773	0.317208
4	0.239028	0.237251	0.235490	0.233744	0.232012
5	0.188354	0.186481	0.184627	0.182792	0.180975
6	0.154597	0.152668	0.150761	0.148878	0.147017
7	0.130506	0.128544	0.126609	0.124701	0.122819
8	0.112456	0.110476	0.108527	0.106609	0.104721
9	0.098433	0.096446	0.094493	0.092574	0.090690
10	0.087230	0.085241	0.083291	0.081378	0.079504

The table gives the amount required to provide £1 at the end of the relevant number of years. To provide £1,000 multiply by 1,000; to provide for £4,986 multiply by 4,986.

9.11 Double entry records for sinking fund

When the annual instalment has been found, the double entry needed each year is:

Annual instalment:
    Dr Profit and loss appropriation
        Cr Debenture redemption reserve
Investment of 1st instalment:
    Dr Debenture sinking fund investment
        Cr Bank
Interest/dividends on sinking fund investment
    Dr Bank
        Cr Debenture redemption reserve
Investment of second and later instalments (these consist of equal annual instalment plus interest/dividend just received)
    Dr Debenture sinking fund investment
        Cr Bank

Exhibit 9.11

Debentures of £10,000 are issued on 1 January 19X1. They are redeemable five years later on 31 December 19X5 on identical terms. The company therefore decides to set aside an equal annual amount, which at an interest rate of 5 per cent will provide £10,000 on 31 December 19X5. According to the table £0.180975 invested annually will provide £1 in five years' time. Therefore £0.180975 × 10,000 will be needed annually = £1,809.75.

Profit and Loss Appropriation for years ended 31 December

(19X1) Debenture redemption reserve 1,809.75	
(19X2) Debenture redemption reserve 1,809.75	
(19X3) Debenture redemption reserve 1,809.75	
(19X4) Debenture redemption reserve 1,809.75	
(19X5) Debenture redemption reserve 1,809.75	

Debenture Redemption Reserve

	£	19X1	£
		Dec 31 Profit and loss	1,809.75
		19X2	
19X2		Dec 31 Bank interest	
Dec 31 Balance c/d	3,709.99	(5% of £1,809.75)	90.49
		Dec 31 Profit and loss	1,809.75
	3,709.99		3,709.99
		19X3	
		Jan 1 Balance b/d	3,709.99
		Dec 31 Bank interest	
19X3		(5% of £3,709.99)	185.49
Dec 31 Balance c/d	5,705.23	Dec 31 Profit and loss	1,809.75
	5,705.23		5,705.23
		19X4	
		Jan 1 Balance b/d	5,705.23
		Dec 31 Bank interest	
19X4		(5% of £5,705.23)	285.26
Dec 31 Balance c/d	7,800.24	Dec 31 Profit and loss	1,809.75
	7,800.24		7,800.24
		19X5	
		Jan 1 Balance b/d	7,800.24
		Dec 31 Bank interest	
19X5		(5% of £7,800.24)	390.01
Dec 31 Debentures now redeemed	10,000.00	Dec 31 Profit and loss	1,809.75
	10,000.00		10,000.00

Debenture Sinking Fund Investment

19X1	£		£
Dec 31 Bank	1,809.75		
19X2			
Dec 31 Bank (*see* note (*a*))	1,900.24		
19X3			
Dec 31 Bank (*see* note (*b*))	1,995.24		
19X4		19X5	
Dec 31 Bank (*see* note (*c*))	2,095.01	Dec 31 Cash: Sale of investment	7,800.24
	7,800.24		7,800.24

Notes:
Cash invested

	(*a*)	(*b*)	(*c*)
	£	£	£
The yearly instalment	1,809.75	1,809.75	1,809.75
Add interest received reinvested immediately	90.49	185.49	285.26
	1,900.24	1,995.24	2,095.01

Bank (extracts)

19X1		£	19X1		£
Jan 1	Debentures (issued)	10,000.00	Dec 31	Debenture sinking fund investment	1,809.75
19X2			19X2		
Dec 31	Debenture redemption reserve (interest on investment)	90.49	Dec 31	Debenture sinking fund investment	1,900.24
19X3			19X3		
Dec 31	Debenture redemption reserve (interest on investment)	185.49	Dec 31	Debenture sinking fund investment	1,995.24
19X4			19X4		
Dec 31	Debenture redemption reserve (interest on investment)	285.26	Dec 31	Debenture sinking fund investment	2,095.01
19X5			19X5		
Dec 31	Debenture redemption reserve (interest on investment)	309.01	Jan 1	Debentures (redemption)	10,000.00

Debentures

19X6		£	19X1		£
Jan 1	Bank (redemption)	10,000.00	Jan 1	Bank	10,000.00

The instalment for 19X5 is not in fact invested, nor is the interest received on 31 December 19X5 reinvested. The money to redeem the debentures is required on 1 January 19X6, and there is not much point (even if it were possible, which would very rarely hold true) in investing money one day only to withdraw it the day afterwards. The amount required is £10,000 and is available from the following sources:

	£
Dec 31 19X5 Sale of investment	7,800.24
„ 31 19X5 Interest received but not reinvested	390.01
„ 31 19X5 The fifth year's instalment not invested	1,809.75
	10,000.00

Sometimes debentures bought in the open market are not cancelled, but are kept 'alive' and are treated as investments of the sinking fund. The annual appropriation of profits is credited to the sinking fund account, while the amount expended on the purchase of the debentures is debited to the sinking fund investment account. Interest on such debentures is debited to the profit and loss account and credited to the sinking fund account, thus the interest, as far as the sinking fund account is concerned, is treated in the same fashion as if it was cash actually received by the firm from an outside investment. The sum expended on investments will then be equal to the annual appropriation + the interest on investments actually received + the interest on debentures kept in hand.

9.12 Convertible loan stock

Particularly in periods of high inflation the attractions to lenders to provide funds at reasonable rates of interest is much reduced as they stand to lose significantly on the real value of the funds lent, since the repayment of the loan is normally fixed at its original cash value. One way of attracting lenders has been to give them the right to convert their loan into shares. The right can usually be exercised once a year over a stated number of years at a given rate of conversion from loan to shares. The value of the conversion right will depend on the performance of the shares in the market. If the shares increase in value significantly, the conversion value will increase and attract the lender to opt into shares. If the shares do badly, the lender can retain the loan stock with its higher levels of security.

The accounting entries are as previously described for the redemption of the loan. The value of the shares issued to meet the redemption will be fixed under the terms of the original agreement by reference to the market prices at specified dates.

New terms

Capital redemption reserve (p. 118): A 'non-distributable' reserve created when shares are redeemed or purchased other than from the proceeds of a fresh issue of shares.

Sinking fund (p. 127): An external fund set up to meet some future liability such as the redemption of debentures. Cash is paid into the fund at regular intervals to accumulate with compound interest to the required future sum.

Main points to remember

1   The accounting entries made on the redemption or purchase by a company of its own shares are the same, except that the word 'redeemable' will appear as the first word in the title of the accounts for shares that are redeemed.

2   In order to protect creditors, companies *must* still have irredeemable shares in issue after undertaking any purchase or redemption of its own shares.

3   A company cannot redeem or purchase its own shares unless they are fully paid.

4   The rules on reserves to use when purchasing or issuing their own shares at a premium are less strict for private companies.

5   Debentures are redeemed according to the terms of their issue.

Review questions

9.1   Exercises (*a*) to (*e*) inclusive are based on the following commencing balance sheet.

RSV Ltd
Balance Sheet

	£
Net assets (except bank)	20,000
Bank	13,000
	33,000
Preference share capital	5,000
Ordinary share capital	15,000
Share premium	2,000
	22,000
Profit and loss	11,000
	33,000

Note also that each of exercises (*a*) to (*e*) are independent of each other. They are not cumulative.

(*a*)   RSV Ltd, per 9.1, redeems £5,000 preference shares at par, a new issue of £5,000 ordinary shares at par being made for the purpose. Show the balance sheet after completion of these transactions. Workings are to be shown as journal entries.

(*b*)   RSV Ltd, per 9.1, redeems £5,000 preference shares at par, with no new issue of shares to provide funds. Show the balance sheet after completing the transaction. Workings: show journal entries.

(*c*)   RSV Ltd, per 9.1, redeems £5,000 preference shares at par. To help finance this an issue of £1,500 ordinary shares at par is effected. Show the balance sheet after these transactions have been completed; also show the necessary journal entries.

(*d*)   RSV Ltd, per 9.1, redeems £5,000 preference shares at a premium of 25 per cent. There is no new issue of shares for the purpose. In this question the share premium account is taken as being from the issue of ordinary shares some years ago. Show the balance sheet after these transactions have been completed, and the supporting journal entries.

(*e*)   RSV Ltd, per 9.1, redeems £5,000 preference shares at a premium of 40 per cent. There is an issue of £7,000 ordinary shares at par for the purpose. The preference shares had originally been issued at a premium of 30 per cent. Show the balance sheet after these transactions have been completed, and also the supporting journal entries.

9.2A   Exercises (*a*) to (*e*) inclusive are based on the same commencing balance sheet, as follows:

BAR Ltd

Balance Sheet

	£
Net assets (except bank)	31,000
Bank	16,000
	47,000
Preference share capital	8,000
Ordinary share capital	20,000
Share premium	4,000
	32,000
Profit and loss	15,000
	47,000

Note also that exercises (*a*) to (*e*) are independent of each other. They are not cumulative.

(*a*) BAR Ltd, per 9.2A, purchases £10,000 of its own ordinary share capital at par. To help finance this £7,000 preference shares are issued at par. Show the necessary journal entries and the balance sheet after the transactions have been completed.

(*b*) BAR Ltd, per 9.2A, purchases £12,000 of its own ordinary shares at a premium of 20 per cent. No new issue of shares is made for the purpose. It is assumed that the share premium account is in respect of the issue of preference shares some years before. Show the balance sheet after the transactions have been completed, and also the supporting journal entries.

(*c*) BAR Ltd, per 9.2A, purchases all the preference share capital at par. These shares were not originally redeemable preference shares. There is no new issue of shares to provide funds. Show the requisite journal entries, and the closing balance sheet when the transaction has been completed.

(*d*) BAR Ltd, per 9.2A, purchases £12,000 of its own ordinary shares at par, a new issue of £12,000 preference shares at par being made for the purpose. Show the journal entries needed and the balance sheet after completing these transactions.

(*e*) BAR Ltd, per 9.2A, purchases £6,000 ordinary shares at a premium of 50 per cent. They had originally been issued at a premium of 20 per cent. There is an issue of £10,000 preference shares at par for the purpose. Show the amended balance sheet, together with the journal entries.

9.3   A company's balance sheet appears as follows:

	£
Net assets (except bank)	12,500
Bank	13,000
	25,500
Preference share capital	5,000
Ordinary share capital	10,000
Non-distributable reserves	6,000
	21,000
Profit and loss	4,500
	25,500

Required:
(a) If £6,000 of the ordinary shares were purchased at par, there being no new issue of shares for the purpose, show the journal entries to record the transactions and the amended balance sheet.
(b) If, instead of (a), £6,000 ordinary shares were purchased at a premium of 100 per cent, there being no new issue of shares for the purpose, show the journal entries to record the transactions and the amended balance sheet.

9.4A Debentures of £30,000 are issued on 1 January 19X3. Redemption is to take place, on equal terms, four years later. The company decides to put aside an equal amount to be invested at 5 per cent which will provide £30,000 on maturity. Tables show that £0.232012 invested annually will produce £1 in four years' time.

You are required to show:
(a) debenture redemption reserve account;
(b) debenture sinking fund investment account;
(c) debentures account;
(d) profit and loss account extracts.

9.5 Some years ago M plc had issued £375,000 of 10 per cent debentures 19X6/19X0 at par. The terms of the issue allow the company the right to repurchase these debentures for cancellation at or below par, with an option to redeem, at a premium of 1 per cent, on 30 September 19X6. To exercise this option the company must give three months' notice which it duly did on 30 June 19X6 indicating its intention to redeem all the debentures outstanding at 30 September 19X6.

M plc had established a sinking fund designed to accumulate the sum of £378,750 by 30 September 19X6 and had appropriated profits annually and invested these, together with the interest from such investments and the profits made on any realisations from time to time. A special No 2 bank account was established specifically to deal with the receipts and payments relating to the debentures and the sinking fund.

By 30 June 19X6 annual contributions amounting to £334,485, together with the interest on the sinking fund investments of £39,480, had all been invested except for £2,475 which remained in the No 2 bank account at that date.

The only investments sold, prior to 30 June 19X6, had cost £144,915 and realised £147,243. This was used to repurchase debentures with a par value of £150,000.

Transactions occurring between 1 July and 30 September 19X6 were:
(i) interest received on the sinking fund investments:

7 July – £1,756
13 September – £1,455

(ii) proceeds from the sale of investments:

2 August – £73,215 (book value was £69,322)
25 September – £160,238 (remaining investments)

(iii) redemption of all the debentures, on 30 September, with the exception of £15,000 held by B Limited. The company had received notice of a garnishee order.*
(iv) M plc deposited with the W Bank plc the sum of £15,150 on 30 September 19X6.

You are to ignore debenture interest and income tax.

You are required, from the information given above, to prepare the ledger accounts (including the No 2 bank account) in the books of M plc for the period 30 June to 30 September 19X6, showing the transfer of the final balances to the appropriate accounts.

Note – Garnishee Order
This order, issued by the court, instructs M plc not to release the money owing to B Limited until directed by the court to do so.

(*Chartered Institute of Management Accountants*)

9.6A The following information relates to White Rabbit Trading plc:

Summarised Balance Sheet as at 31 January 19X7

	£000
Fixed assets	2,400
Investments	120
Net current assets	1,880
	4,400
Financed by:	
Capital and reserves	
Ordinary shares of 50p each fully paid	2,000
Redeemable shares of £1 each (19X7/19X1)	500
Share premium	200
Revaluation surplus	400
Profit and loss account	900
	4,000
Long-term liabilities	
8% debentures (19X7/19X0)	400
	4,400

On 1 February 19X7 the company closed the list of applications for 400,000 ordinary shares at a premium of 50p. The shares were to be paid for as follows: 60p on application, 25p on allotment and 15p on the first and final call, which was to be made on 1 May 19X7. A total of £1,320,000 was received, the shares were allotted and £1,032,000 was returned to unsuccessful applicants. The call money was received by 31 May from all shareholders, with the exception of two shareholders, one of whom had been allotted 500 shares. The other subscriber for 100 shares still owed £25 for allotment in addition to the call money. Eventually both lots of shares were forfeited and reissued to an existing shareholder for a payment of £500 which was duly received.

At a board meeting on 15 February 19X7 the directors decided to make a fresh issue of 500,000 £1 redeemable shares at a premium of 60p, and to redeem all of the existing redeemable shares at a premium of 40p. The shares had originally been issued for £1.20 each. All moneys due on application were duly received by 31 March 19X7, and the redemption took place on 6 April 19X7.

In January 19X5 White Rabbit Trading plc had purchased, for cash, 80,000 25p ordinary shares in March Hares Ltd for £25,000, and this is included in investments on the balance sheet at 31 January 19X7. On 1 April 19X7 the company purchased 400,000 out of a total issue of 500,000 25p ordinary shares in March Hares Ltd, by exchanging 200,000 of its own ordinary shares.

The 8 per cent debentures were redeemed on 15 May 19X7 at a 10 per cent premium, and on the same date £500,000 7 per cent debentures (19X0/19X3) were issued at a discount of 5 per cent.

Required:
Show the full journal entries to record the above events, including cash/bank transactions, in the books of White Rabbit Trading plc.

(Chartered Association of Certified Accountants)

9.7 During the year to 30 September 19X9, Popham plc issued 100,000 £1 ordinary shares. The terms of the offer were as follows:

19X9		£
31 March	on application	0.30 (including the premium)
30 April	on allotment	0.70
30 June	first and final call	0.20

Applications were received for 200,000 shares. The directors decided to allot the shares on the basis of 1 for every 2 shares applied for and apply the excess application money received against the amount due on allotment.

All amounts due on application and allotment were received on the due dates, with the exception of one shareholder who had been allotted 10,000 shares, and who defaulted on the first and final call. These shares were forfeited on 31 July 19X9, and reissued on 31 August 19X9 at a price of £1.10 per share.

Required:
Write up the above details in the books of account of Popham plc using the following ledger accounts:

(*i*)   application and allotment;
(*ii*) first and final call; and
(*iii*) investment – own shares.

(*Association of Accounting Technicians*)

9.8A   Alas plc has an authorised share capital of 150,000 ordinary shares of £10 each. Upon incorporation, 50,000 shares were issued and fully paid. The company has decided to issue another 50,000 shares, the details of which are as follows:

	Per share £
Upon:	
Application	3
Allotment (including a premium of £5)	8
First call	2
Final call	2
	15

Additional information:
1   Applications were received for 85,000 shares out of which 10,000 shares were rejected, the cash being returned immediately to the applicants. The remaining applicants were allotted two shares for every three shares applied for, and the surplus application money was carried forward to the allotment stage.
2   The total amount due on allotment was duly received.
3   All cash due at the first call was received, but the final call resulted in 5,000 shares being forfeited. These shares were subsequently reissued at a price of £13 per share.

Required:
Compile the following ledger accounts:
(*a*) ordinary share capital;
(*b*) ordinary share applications;
(*c*) ordinary share allotment;
(*d*) share premium;
(*e*) ordinary share first call;
(*f*) ordinary share final call;
(*g*) investments – own shares (originally known as the forfeited shares account).

9.9 The following information relates to Grigg plc:

1 On 1 April 19X8 the company had £100,000 10 per cent debentures in issue. The interest on these debentures is paid on 30 September and 31 March.

2 The debenture redemption fund balance (relating to the redemption of these debentures) at 1 April 19X8 was £20,000. This fund is being built up by annual appropriations of £2,000. The annual appropriation (along with any dividends or interest on the investments) is invested on 31 March.

3 Debenture redemption fund investments can be realised at any time in order to purchase debentures in the open market either at or below par value. Such debentures are then cancelled.

4 On 31 December 19X8 £10,000 of investments were sold for £11,400, and the proceeds were used to purchase debentures with a par value of £12,000.

5 Dividends and interest on redemption fund investments during the year to 31 March 19X9 amounted to £1,600.

6 The cost of dealing with the above matters and any taxation effects may be ignored.

Required:
Write up the following ledger accounts for the year to 31 March 19X9:
(*a*) 10 per cent debentures;
(*b*) debenture redemption fund;
(*c*) debenture redemption fund investments;
(*d*) debenture redemption; and
(*e*) debenture interest.

(*Note*: the debenture redemption fund is sometimes known as a **sinking fund**.)

10

Limited companies taking over other businesses

Objectives

After you have studied this chapter, you should:

- know how to record the accounting entries relating to a limited company taking over another business

- be aware of the difference in the accounting treatment of takeovers by limited companies of sole traders, partnerships and limited companies

- be aware of the two methods whereby a limited company may take over another limited company

- know how to deal with pre-incorporation profits and losses

10.1 Introduction

Limited companies will often take over other businesses which are in existence as going concerns. The purchase considerations may either be in cash, by giving the company's shares to the owners, by giving the company's debentures, or by any combination of these three factors.

It must not be thought that because the assets bought are shown in the selling firm's books at one value the purchasing company must record the assets taken over in its own books at the same value. The values shown in the purchasing company's books are those values at which the company is buying the assets, such values being frequently quite different than those shown in the selling firm's books. As an instance of this, the selling firm may have bought premises many years ago for £1,000 but they may now be worth £5,000. The company buying the premises will obviously have to pay £5,000 and it is therefore this value that is recorded in the buying company's books. Alternatively, the value at which it is recorded in the buying company's books may be less than that shown in the selling firm's books. Where the total purchase consideration exceeds the total value of the identifiable assets then such excess is the goodwill, and will need entering in a goodwill account in the purchasing company's books. Should the total purchase consideration be less than the values of the identifiable assets, then the difference would be entered in a capital reserve account.

Before the accounting entries necessary to record the purchase of a going business are looked at, it must be pointed out that such recording of the transactions is the simple end of the whole affair. The negotiations that take place before agreement is reached, and the various strategies undertaken by the various parties, are a study in themselves. The accounting entries are in effect the 'tip of the iceberg', i.e. that part of the whole affair which is seen by the eventual reader of the accounts.

10.2 Taking over a sole trader's business

It is easier to start with the takeover of the simplest sort of business unit, that of a sole trader. Some of the balance sheets shown will be deliberately simplified so that the principles involved are not hidden behind a mass of complicated calculations.

Exhibit 10.1

Earl Ltd is to buy the business of M Kearney. The purchase consideration is to be £6,000 cash, the company placing the following values on the assets taken over – Machinery £3,000, Stock £1,000. The goodwill must therefore be £2,000, because the total price of £6,000 exceeds the values of Machinery £3,000 and Stock £1,000 by the sum of £2,000. The company's balance sheets will be shown before and after the takeover, it being assumed that the transactions are all concluded immediately.

M Kearney

Balance Sheet

	£
Machinery	1,700
Stock	1,300
	3,000
Capital	3,000

Earl Ltd

Balance Sheet(s)

	Before £	+ or – £	After £
Goodwill		+2,000	2,000
Machinery	11,000	+3,000	14,000
Stock	5,000	+1,000	6,000
Bank	9,000	–6,000	3,000
	25,000		25,000
Share capital	20,000		20,000
Profit and loss	5,000		5,000
	25,000		25,000

Exhibit 10.2

Suppose the purchase had been made instead by issuing 7,000 shares of £1 each at par to Kearney. The goodwill would then be £7,000 – assets taken over £4,000 = £3,000. The balance sheets of Earl Ltd would be:

Earl Ltd

Balance Sheets

	Before £	+ or – £	After £
Goodwill		+3,000	3,000
Machinery	11,000	+3,000	14,000
Stock	5,000	+1,000	6,000
Bank	9,000		9,000
	25,000		32,000
Share capital	20,000	+7,000	27,000
Profit and loss	5,000		5,000
	25,000		32,000

Exhibit 10.3

If the purchase had been made by issuing 5,000 shares of £1 each at a premium of 50 per cent, then the total consideration would have been worth £7,500, which, if the assets of £4,000 are deducted, leaves goodwill of £3,500. The balance sheets would then be:

Earl Ltd

Balance Sheet(s)

	Before £	+ or – £	After £
Goodwill		+3,500	3,500
Machinery	11,000	+3,000	14,000
Stocks	5,000	+1,000	6,000
Bank	9,000		9,000
	25,000		32,500
Share capital	20,000	+5,000	25,000
Share premium		+2,500	2,500
Profit and loss	5,000		5,000
	25,000		32,500

Exhibit 10.4

Now if the purchase had been made by the issue of 1,000 shares of £1 each at a premium of 40 per cent, £3,000 worth of 7 per cent debentures at par and £4,000 in cash, then the total purchase consideration would be shares valued at £1,400, debentures valued at £3,000 and cash £4,000, making in all £8,400. The assets are valued at £4,000, the goodwill must be £4,400. The balance sheets would appear:

Earl Ltd

Balance Sheet(s)

	Before £	+ or – £	After £
Goodwill		+4,400	4,400
Machinery	11,000	+3,000	14,000
Stocks	5,000	+1,000	6,000
Bank	9,000	–4,000	5,000
	25,000		29,400
Share capital	20,000	+1,000	21,000
Share premium		+400	400
Profit and loss	5,000		5,000
Debentures		+3,000	3,000
	25,000		29,400

In each of Exhibits 10.1 to 10.4 it has been assumed that all transactions were started and completed within a few moments. The fact is that an intermediary account would be created but then closed almost immediately when the purchase consideration was handed over. Taking Exhibit 10.3 as an example, there will be a credit in the share capital account and in the share premium account, and debits in the goodwill, machinery and stock accounts. Nevertheless, shares cannot be issued to goodwill, machinery or stocks. They have in fact, been issued to M Kearney. This means that there should have been an account for M Kearney, but that the balance on it was cancelled on the passing of the purchase consideration. The actual accounts for Exhibit 10.3 were as follows in the books of Earl Ltd:

Share Premium

		£
	M Kearney	2,500

Share Capital

Balance c/d	25,000	Balance b/fwd	20,000
		M Kearney	5,000
	25,000		25,000
		Balance b/d	25,000

Profit and Loss

		£
	Balance b/fwd	5,000

Goodwill

	£	
M Kearney	3,500	

Machinery

	£		£
Balance b/fwd	11,000		
M Kearney	3,000	Balance c/d	14,000
	14,000		14,000
Balance b/d	14,000		

Stock

	£		£
Balance b/d	5,000		
M Kearney	1,000	Balance c/d	6,000
	6,000		6,000
Balance c/d	6,000		

(In fact, the £1,000 would probably be entered in the purchases account. It does, however, obviously increase the actual amount of stock.)

Bank

	£		
Balance b/fwd	9,000		

M Kearney

	£		£
Consideration passing:		Assets taken over	
Share capital	5,000	Goodwill	3,500
Share premium	2,500	Machinery	3,000
		Stock	1,000
	7,500		7,500

Some accountants would have preferred to use a business purchase account instead of a personal account such as that of M Kearney.

Sometimes the company taking over the business of a sole trader not only pays a certain amount for the assets but also assumes responsibility for paying the creditors in addition. Take the case of a sole trader with assets valued at Premises £5,000 and Stock £4,000. To gain control of these assets the company is to pay the sole trader £11,000 in cash, and in addition the company will pay off creditors £1,000. This means that the goodwill is £3,000, calculated as follows:

		£
Paid by the company to gain control of the sole trader's assets:		
Cash to the sole trader		11,000
Cash to the sole trader's creditors		1,000
		12,000
The company receives assets:	£	
Premises	5,000	
Stock	4,000	
		9,000
Excess paid for goodwill		3,000

10.3 Partnership business taken over by a limited company

The entries are basically the same as for those of taking over a sole trader. The main difference is the distribution of the purchase consideration. In the case of a sole trader s/he gets all of it. In a partnership it has to be divided between the partners.

This means that in a partnership a realisation account will have to be drawn up to calculate the profit or loss on sale of the partnership business. The profit or loss on sale will then be shared between the partners in their profit/loss-sharing ratios.

The double entry needed in the partnership books is:

(A) Transfer assets being disposed of to realisation account:
                Dr Realistion
                    Cr Assets (various)
(B) Enter purchase price:
                Dr Limited company (purchaser)
                    Cr Realisation
(C) If profit on sale:
                Dr Realisation
                    Cr Partners' capitals (profit-sharing ratio)
(D) If loss on sale:
                Dr Partners' capitals (profit-sharing ratio)
                    Cr Realisation
(E) Receipt purchase price:
                Dr Cash
                Dr Shares (if any) in limited company
                Dr Debentures (if any) in limited company
                    Cr Limited company (purchaser)
(F) Final settlement with partners:
                Dr Partners' capital and current accounts
                    Cr Cash
                    Cr Shares (if any) in limited company
                    Cr Debentures (if any) in limited company

Entries for these are illustrated in Exhibit 10.5.

Exhibit 10.5

Kay and Lee were in partnership, sharing profits and losses in the ratio 2:1 respectively. The following was their balance sheet as at 31 December 19X4.

Kay and Lee
Balance Sheet as at 31 December 19X4

Fixed assets:		£
Buildings		30,000
Motor vehicles		15,000
		45,000
Current assets:		
Stock	8,000	
Debtors	6,000	
Bank	1,000	15,000
		60,000
Capitals: Kay	32,000	
Lee	16,000	48,000
Current accounts: Kay	3,000	
Lee	4,000	7,000
Current liabilities:		5,000
Creditors		60,000

On 1 January 19X5 Cayley Ltd was to take over the assets, other than bank. The purchase price is £80,000, payable by £60,000 in £1 shares in Cayley Ltd at par, plus

£20,000 cash. Kay and Lee will pay off their own creditors. Shares are to be divided between the partners in their profit-sharing ratio.

First we will see the closing entries in the accounts of Kay and Lee. The only asset account shown will be that of the bank account. The creditors' accounts are also not shown. The letters in brackets refer to the description of the double entry already given.

Books of Kay and Lee:

Realisation

		£			£
Assets taken over:			Cayley Ltd	(B)	80,000
Buildings	(A)	30,000			
Motor vehicles	(A)	15,000			
Stock	(A)	8,000			
Debtors	(A)	6,000			
Profit on realisation:					
Kay ⅔	(C)	14,000			
Lee ⅓	(C)	7,000 21,000			
		80,000			80,000

Cayley Ltd

		£			£
Realisation: sale price	(B)	80,000	Bank	(E)	20,000
			Shares in Cayley Ltd	(E)	60,000
		80,000			80,000

Shares in Cayley Ltd

		£			£
Cayley Ltd	(E)	60,000	Capitals: Kay	(F)	40,000
			Lee	(F)	20,000
		60,000			60,000

Capitals

		Kay £	Lee £			Kay £	Lee £
Shares in Cayley	(F)	40,000	20,000	Balances b/f		32,000	16,000
Bank	(F)	6,000	3,000	Profit on realisation	(C)	14,000	7,000
		46,000	23,000			46,000	23,000

Current Accounts

		Kay £	Lee £			Kay £	Lee £
Bank	(F)	3,000	4,000	Balances b/f		3,000	4,000

Bank

		£		£
Bank b/f		1,000	Creditors	5,000
Cayley Ltd	(E)	20,000	Capitals: Kay	6,000
			Lee	3,000
			Current accounts: Kay	3,000
			Lee	4,000
		21,000		21,000

Note: It would have been possible to transfer the balances of the current accounts to the capital accounts before settlement.

Assuming that Cayley values the buildings at £41,000 and stock at £7,000 its balance sheet at 1 January 19X5 would appear as (B) under. The items shown under (A) were the balances before the takeover.

Balance Sheet(s)

	(A) *Before* £	+ £	– £	(B) *After* £
Goodwill				11,000
Buildings	50,000	41,000		91,000
Motor vehicles	25,000	15,000		40,000
Stock	28,000	7,000		35,000
Debtors	17,000	6,000		23,000
Bank	30,000		20,000	10,000
	150,000	69,000	20,000	210,000
Share capital (£1 shares)	100,000	60,000		160,000
Profit and loss	40,000			40,000
Creditors	10,000			10,000
	150,000	60,000		210,000

10.4 The takeover of a limited company by another limited company

One company may take over another company by one of two methods:

1 By buying all the assets of the other company, the purchase consideration being by cash, shares or debentures. The selling company may afterwards be wound up: either the liquidators may distribute the purchasing company's shares and debentures between the shareholders of the selling company, or else the shares and debentures of the buying company may be sold and the cash distributed instead.

2 By giving its own shares and debentures in exchange for the shares and debentures of the selling company's share and debenture holders.

Exhibit 10.6 is an illustration of each of these methods.

Exhibit 10.6

The following are the balance sheets of three companies as at the same date.

Balance Sheets

	R Ltd £	S Ltd £	T Ltd £
Buildings	13,000	–	1,000
Machinery	4,000	2,000	1,000
Stock	3,000	1,000	2,000
Debtors	2,000	1,000	3,000
Bank	1,000	2,000	3,000
	23,000	6,000	10,000
Share capital (£1 shares)	18,000	3,000	5,000
Profit and loss	2,000	1,000	4,000
Current liabilities	3,000	2,000	1,000
	23,000	6,000	10,000

R takes over S by exchanging with the shareholders of S two shares in R at a premium of 10 per cent for every share they hold in S.

R takes over T by buying all the assets of T, the purchase consideration being 12,000 £1 shares in R at a premium of 10 per cent, and R will pay off T's creditors. R values T's assets at Buildings £2,000, Machinery £600, Stock £1,400, Debtors £2,500, and the Bank is £3,000, a total of £9,500.

R's deal with the shareholders of S means that R now has complete control of S Ltd, so that S Ltd becomes what is known as a subsidiary undertaking of R Ltd, and will be shown as an investment in R's balance sheet.

On the other hand, the deal with T has resulted in the ownership of the assets resting with R. These must therefore be added to R's assets in its own balance sheet. As R has given 12,000 £1 shares at a premium of 10 per cent plus taking over the responsibility for creditors £1,000, the total purchase consideration for the assets taken over is £12,000 + £1,200 (10 per cent of £12,000) + £1,000 = £14,200. Identifiable assets as already stated are valued at £9,500, therefore the goodwill is £14,200 – £9,500 = £4,700.

The distinction between the acquisition of the two going concerns can be seen to be a rather fine one. With S the shares are taken over, the possession of these in turn giving rise to the ownership of the assets. In the books of R this is regarded as an investment. With T the actual assets and liabilities are taken over so that the assets now directly belong to R. In the books of R this is therefore regarded as the acquisition of additional assets and liabilities and not as an investment (using the meaning of 'investment' which is used in the balance sheets of companies). The balance sheet of R Ltd therefore becomes:

R Ltd

Balance Sheet

	Before £		+ or – £		After £
Goodwill		+(T)	4,700		4,700
Buildings	13,000	+(T)	2,000		15,000
Machinery	4,000	+(T)	600		4,600
Investment in S at cost		+	6,600		6,600
Stock	3,000	+(T)	1,400		4,400
Debtors	2,000	+(T)	2,500		4,500
Bank	1,000	+(T)	3,000		4,000
	23,000				43,800
Share capital	18,000	+(S)	6,000		
		+(T)	12,000	=	36,000
Share premium		+(S)	600		
		+(T)	1,200	=	1,800
Profit and loss	2,000				2,000
Current liabilities	3,000	+(T)	1,000		4,000
	23,000				43,800

No entry is necessary in the books of S Ltd, as it is merely the identity of the shareholders that has changed. This would be duly recorded in the register of members, but this is not really an integral part of the double entry accounting system.

If, however, T Ltd is now liquidated, then a realisation account must be drawn up and the distribution of the shares (or cash if the shares are sold) to the shareholders of T Ltd must be shown. Such accounts would appear as follows:

Books of T Ltd

Realisation

	£		£
Book values of assets disposed of:		R Ltd: Total purchase	
Buildings	1,000	consideration	14,200
Machinery	1,000		
Stock	2,000		
Debtors	3,000		
Bank	3,000		
Profit on realisation transferred			
to sundry shareholders	4,200		
	14,200		14,200

Share Capital

	£		£
Sundry shareholders	5,000	Balance b/fwd	5,000

Profit and Loss

	£		£
Sundry shareholders	4,000	Balance b/fwd	4,000

Creditors

	£		£
R Ltd – taken over	1,000	Balance b/fwd	1,000

R Ltd

	£		£
Realisation:		Creditors	1,000
Total consideration	14,200	Sundry shareholders: 12,000	
		£1 shares received at premium	
		of 10 per cent	13,200
	14,200		14,200

Sundry Shareholders

	£		£
R Ltd: 12,000 £1 shares at premium		Share capital	5,000
of 10 per cent	13,200	Profit and loss	4,000
		Profit on realisation	4,200
	13,200		13,200

It can be seen that the items possessed by the sundry shareholders have been transferred to an account in their name. These are (a) the share capital which obviously belongs to them, (b) the credit balance on the profit and loss account built up by withholding cash dividends from the shareholders, and (c) the profit on realisation which they, as owners of the business, are entitled to take. As there were 5,000 shares in T Ltd, and 12,000 shares have been given by R Ltd, then each holder of 5 shares in T Ltd will now be given 12 shares in R Ltd to complete the liquidation of the company.

10.5 The exchange of debentures

Sometimes the debentures in the company taking over are to be given in exchange for the debentures of the company being taken over. This may be straightforward on the basis of £100 debentures in company A in exchange for £100 debentures in company B. However, the problem often arises where the exchange is in terms of one or both sets of debentures being at a discount or at a premium. The need for such an exchange may be twofold:

(a) To persuade the debenture holders in Company B to give up their debentures some form of inducement may be needed, such as letting them have A's debentures at a discount even though they may well be worth the par value.

(b) There may be a difference in the debenture interest rates. For instance, a person with a £100 7 per cent debenture would not normally gladly part with it in exchange for a £100 6 per cent debenture in another company. The first debenture gives him/her £7 a year interest, the second one only £6 per year. Thus the debenture in the second company may be issued at a discount to redeem the debenture in the first company at a premium. As the amount of interest is only one factor – there are also others such as the certainty of the debenture holder regaining his/her money if the firm had to close down – the precise terms of the exchange cannot be based merely on arithmetical calculations of interest rates, but it is one of the measures taken when negotiating the exchange of debentures.

Exhibit 10.7

1 D Ltd is to give the necessary debentures at a discount of 10 per cent required to redeem £9,000 debentures in J Ltd at a premium of 5 per cent. The problem here is to find exactly what amount of debentures must be given by D Ltd.

Answer:

$$\text{Total nominal value of debentures Ltd to be redeemed (exchanged)} \times \frac{\text{Redeemable value of each £100 debenture of J Ltd}}{\text{Issue value of each £100 debenture of D Ltd}}$$

= Total nominal value of D Ltd to be issued

$$= £9,000 \times \frac{105}{90} = £10,500$$

Thus, to satisfy the agreement, debentures of D Ltd of a total nominal value of £10,500 are issued at a discount of 10 per cent to the debenture holder of J Ltd.

2 H Ltd is to give the necessary debentures at par to redeem £5,000 debentures in M Ltd at a premium of 4 per cent.

$$£5,000 \times \frac{104}{100} = \text{Debentures of £5,200 nominal value are given by H Ltd at par.}$$

10.6 Profit (or loss) prior to incorporation

Quite frequently companies take over businesses from a date which is actually before the company was itself incorporated. It could be that two persons enter into business and start trading with the intention of running the business as a limited company. However, it takes more than a few days to attend to all the necessary formalities before the company can be incorporated. Obviously it depends on the speed with which the formation is pushed through and the solution of any snags which crop up. When the company is in fact incorporated it may enter into a contract whereby it adopts all the transactions retrospectively to the date that the firm (i.e. with two persons it was a partnership) had started trading. This means that the company accepts all the benefits and disadvantages which have flowed from the transactions which have occurred. The example used was that of a brand-new business; it could well have been an old-established business that was taken over from a date previous to incorporation.

Legally a company cannot earn profits before it comes into existence, i.e. is incorporated, and therefore to decide what action will have to be taken, such profits will first of all have to be calculated. Any such profits are of a capital nature and must be transferred to a capital reserve account, normally titled **Pre-Incorporation Profit Account** or **Profit Prior to Incorporation Account**. That this should be so is apparent if it is realised that, though the actual date from which the transactions have been adopted falls before the date of incorporation, the price at which the business is being taken over is influenced by the values of the assets, etc., at the date when the company actually takes over, i.e. the date of incorporation. Suppose that Doolin and Kershaw start a business on 1 January 19X5 with £1,000 capital, and very shortly afterwards Davie and Parker become interested as well, and the four of them start to form a company in which they will all become directors, Davie and Parker to start active work when the company is incorporated. The company is incorporated on 1 May 19X5 and the original owners of the business, Doolin and Kershaw, are to be given shares in the new company to compensate them for handing over the business. If they know, not necessarily with precision, that the original £1,000 assets will have grown to net assets of £6,000, then they most certainly would not part with the business to the company for £1,000. Ignoring goodwill they would want £6,000 of shares. Conversely, if the net assets have shrunk to

£400, would Davie and Parker be happy to see £1,000 of shares handed over? This means that the price at which the business is taken over is dependent on the expected value at the date of the company incorporation, and not on the value at the date on which the company is supposed to take over. Taking the case of the increase in net assets to £6,000 the £5,000 difference is made up of profits. If these profits could be distributed as dividends, then in effect the capital payment of £6,000 in shares is being part used up for dividend purposes. This is in direct contradiction to the normal accounting practice of retaining capital intact (the accountant's meaning of 'capital' and not the meaning given to 'capital' by the economist). The £5,000 profits must therefore be regarded as not being available for dividends. They are thus a capital reserve.

Although the profit cannot be regarded as free for use as dividends, any such loss can be taken to restrict the dividends which could be paid out of the profits made after incorporation. This is the concept of prudence once again coming into play, and if the price paid on takeover was misjudged and a high figure was paid, and it was discovered later that a loss had been made, then the restriction of dividends leads to the capital lost being replaced by assets held back within the firm. Alternatively the amount of the pre-incorporation loss could be charged to a goodwill account, as this is also another way of stating that a higher price has been paid for the assets of the firm than is represented by the value of the tangible assets taken over.

It is possible for the profits up to the date of incorporation to be calculated quite separately from those after incorporation. However, the cost of stocktaking etc. may be felt to be not worth while merely to produce accounts when in fact the accounts could be left until the normal financial year end. This is invariably the case in examination questions. Therefore when the accounts for the full financial year are being made up, they will consist of profits before and after incorporation. The accounts must therefore be split to throw up the two sets of profit (or loss), so that distinction can be made between those profits usable, and those not usable, for dividend purposes. There is no hard-and-fast rule as to how this shall be done. Known facts must prevail, and where an arbitrary apportionment must be made it should meet the test of common sense in the particular case. Exhibit 10.8 shows an attempt to calculate such profits.

Exhibit 10.8

Slack and King, partners in a firm, are to have their business taken over as from 1 January 19X4 by Monk Ltd which is incorporated on 1 April 19X4. It was agreed that all profits made from 1 January 19X4 should belong to the company, and that the vendors be entitled to interest on the purchase price from 1 January to date of payment. The purchase price was paid on 30 April 19X4, including £1,600 interest. A profit and loss account is drawn up for the year ended 31 December 19X4. This is shown as column (X). This is then split into before incorporation, shown as column (Y), and after incorporation as column (Z). The methods used to apportion the particular items are shown after the profit and loss account, the letters (A) to (I) against the items being the references to the notes. These particular methods must definitely not be used in all cases for similar expenses; they are only an indication of different methods of apportionment. The facts and the peculiarities of each firm must be taken into account, and no method should be slavishly followed. Assume for this example that all calendar months are of equal length.

Monk Ltd

Profit and Loss Account for the year ended 31 December 19X4

		(X) Full year		(Y) Pre-incorporation		(Z) After	
		£	£	£	£	£	£
Gross profit	(A)		38,000		8,000		30,000
Less:							
Partnership salaries	(B)	1,000		1,000			
Employees' remuneration	(C)	12,000		3,000		9,000	
General expenses	(C)	800		200		600	
Commission on sales	(D)	1,700		200		1,500	
Distribution expenses	(E)	1,900		400		1,500	
Bad debts	(F)	100		20		80	
Bank overdraft interest	(G)	200				200	
Directors' remuneration	(H)	5,000				5,000	
Directors' expenses	(H)	400				400	
Debenture interest	(H)	500				500	
Depreciation	(C)	1,000		250		750	
Interest paid to vendors	(I)	1,600		1,200		400	
			26,200		6,270		19,930
Net profit			11,800				
Transferred to capital reserves					1,730		
Carried down to the appropriation account							10,070

Notes:

(A) For the three months to 31 March sales amounted to £40,000, and for the remaining nine months they were £150,000. Gross profit is at a uniform rate of 20 per cent of selling price throughout the year. Therefore the gross profit is apportioned (Y) 20 per cent of £40,000 = £8,000, and (Z) 20 per cent of £150,000 = £30,000.

(B) The partnership salaries of the vendors, Slack and King, obviously belong to (Y), because that is the period of the partnership.

(C) These expenses, in this particular case, have accrued evenly throughout the year and are therefore split on the time basis of (Y) three-twelfths, (Z) nine-twelfths.

(D) Commission to the salesmen was paid at the rate of ½ per cent on sales up to 31 March, and 1 per cent thereafter. The commission figure is split:

(Y) ½ per cent of £40,000	=		200
(Z) 1 per cent of £150,000	=		1,500
			1,700

(E) In this particular case (but not always true in every case) the distribution expenses have varied directly with the value of sales. They are therefore split:

$$(Y) \frac{Y \text{ sales}}{\text{Total sales}} \times \text{Expenses} = \frac{40,000}{190,000} \times £1,900 = \frac{4}{19} \times £1,900 = £400$$

$$(Z) \frac{Z \text{ sales}}{\text{Total sales}} \times \text{Expenses} = \frac{150,000}{190,000} \times £1,900 = \frac{15}{19} \times £1,900 = £1,500$$

(F) The bad debts were two in number:
  (*i*) in respect of a sale in January, the debtor dying penniless in March, £20;
  (*ii*) in respect of a sale in June, the debtor being declared bankrupt in December, £80.

(G) The bank account was never overdrawn until June, so that the interest charged must be for period (Z).

(H) Only in companies are such expenses as directors' salaries, directors' expenses and debenture interest to be found. These must naturally be shown in period (Z).

(I) The interest paid to the vendors was due to the fact that the company was receiving all the benefits from 1 January but did not in fact pay any cash for the business until 30 April. This is therefore in effect loan interest which should be spread over the period it was borrowed, i.e. three months to (Y) and 1 month to (Z).

New terms

Pre-incorporation profits or losses (p. 151): Profits or losses which arise immediately before a limited company is legally incorporated. Any such profits will be treated as 'capital profits' not for distribution while, for sake of prudence, any such losses will be set against post-incorporation profits.

Main points to remember

1   The basic accounting entries are the same whether a limited company takes over a sole trader or a partnership.

2   Limited companies may take over other limited companies either:
    (a) by buying all the assets of the other company; or
    (b) by giving its own shares and debentures in exchange for the shares and debentures of the company being taken over.

3   Pre-incorporation profits are not available for distribution.

Review questions

10.1 Checkers Ltd was incorporated on 1 April 19X5 and took over the business of Black and White, partners, as from 1 January 19X5. It was agreed that all profits made from 1 January should belong to the company and that the vendors should be entitled to interest on the purchase price from 1 January to date of payment. The purchase price was paid on 31 May 19X5 including £1,650 interest.

The following is the profit and loss account for the year to 31 December 19X5:

	£		£
Salaries of vendors	1,695	Gross profit	28,000
Wages and general expenses	8,640		
Rent and rates	860		
Distribution expenses	1,680		
Commission on sales	700		
Bad debts	314		
Interest paid to vendors	1,650		
Directors' remuneration	4,000		
Directors' expenses	515		
Depreciation	£		
Motors	1,900		
Machinery	575		
	2,475		
Bank interest	168		
Net profit	5,303		
	28,000		28,000

You are given the following information:

1 Sales amounted to £20,000 for the three months to 31 March 19X5 and £50,000 for the nine months to 31 December 19X5. Gross profit is at a uniform rate of 40 per cent of selling price throughout the year, and commission at a rate of 1 per cent is paid on all sales.
2 Salaries of £1,695 were paid to the vendors for their assistance in running the business up to 31 March 19X5.
3 The bad debts written off are:
   (*a*) a debt of £104 taken over from the vendors;
   (*b*) a debt of £210 in respect of goods sold in August 19X5.
4 On 1 January 19X5 motors were bought for £7,000 and machinery for £5,000. On 1 March 19X5 another motor van was bought for £3,000 and on 1 October 19X5 another machine was added for £3,000. Depreciation has been written off motors at 20 per cent per annum, and machinery 10 per cent per annum.
5 Wages and general expenses and rent and rates accrued at an even rate throughout the year.
6 The bank granted an overdraft in June 19X5.

Assuming all calendar months are of equal length:

(*a*) set out the profit and loss account in columnar form, so as to distinguish between the period prior to the company's incorporation and the period after incorporation;
(*b*) state how you would deal with the profit prior to incorporation;
(*c*) state how you would deal with the results prior to incorporation if they turned out to be a net loss.

10.2 On 31 December 19X6 Breeze Ltd acquired all the assets, except the investments, of Blow Ltd.

The following are the summaries of the profit and loss account of Blow Ltd for the years 19X4, 19X5 and 19X6:

	19X4	19X5	19X6		19X4	19X5	19X6
Motor expenses	1,860	1,980	2,100	Trading profits	22,050	25,780	25,590
Depreciation of plant				Investment income	290	340	480
and machinery	4,000	3,200	2,560	Rents received	940	420	–
Bank overdraft interest	180	590	740	Profit on sale of			
Wrapping expenses	840	960	1,020	property		4,800	
Preliminary expenses							
written off	–	690	–				
Net profit	16,400	23,920	19,650				
	23,280	31,340	26,070		23,280	31,340	26,070

The purchase price is to be the amount on which an estimated maintainable profit would represent a return of 25 per cent per annum.

The maintainable profit is to be taken as the average of the profits of the three years 19X4, 19X5 and 19X6, after making any necessary adjustments.

You are given the following information:
(a) The cost of the plant and machinery was £20,000. It is agreed that depreciation should have been written off at the rate of 12½ per cent per annum using the straight line method.
(b) A form of new plastic wrapping material introduced on to the market means that wrapping expenses will be halved in future.
(c) By a form of long-term rental of motor vehicles, it is estimated that motor expenses will be cut by one-third in future.
(d) Stock treated as valueless at 31 December 19X3 was sold for £1,900 in 19X5.
(e) The working capital of the new company is such that an overdraft is not contemplated.
(f) Management remuneration has been inadequate and will have to be increased by £1,500 a year in future.

You are required to set out your calculation of the purchase price. All workings must be shown. In fact, your managing director, who is not an accountant, should be able to decipher how the price was calculated.

10.3 CJK Ltd was incorporated on 15 December 19X9 with an authorised capital of 200,000 ordinary shares of £0.20 each to acquire as at 31 December 19X9 the business of CK, a sole trader, and RP Ltd, a company.

From the following information you are required to prepare:
(a) the realisation and capital accounts in the books of CK and RP Ltd showing the winding up of these two concerns;
(b) the journal entries to open the books of CJK Ltd, including cash transactions and the raising of finance;
(c) the balance sheet of CJK Ltd after the transactions have been completed.

The balance sheet of CK as at 31 December 19X9 is as follows:

Balance Sheet

	£
Freehold premises	8,000
Plant	4,000
Stock	2,000
Debtors	5,000
Cash	200
	19,200
Capital	16,000
Creditors	3,200
	19,200

The assets (excluding cash) and the liabilities were taken over at the following values: freehold premises £10,000, plant £3,500, stock £2,000, debtors £5,000 less a bad debts provision of £300, goodwill £7,000, creditors £3,200 less a discount provision of £150. The purchase consideration, based on these values, was settled by the issue of shares at par.

The balance sheet of RP Ltd as at 31 December 19X9 is as follows:

Balance Sheet

	£
Freehold premises	4,500
Plant	2,000
Stock	1,600
Debtors	3,400
	11,500
Share capital: 10,000 shares at £0.40 each	4,000
Revenue surplus	2,500
Creditors	1,500
Bank overdraft	3,500
	11,500

The assets and liabilities were taken over at book value with the exception of the freehold premises which were revalued at £5,500. The purchase consideration was a cash payment of £1 and three shares in CJK Ltd at par in exchange for every two shares in RP Ltd.

Additional working capital and the funds required to complete the purchase of RP Ltd were provided by the issue for cash of:

(i)   10,000 shares at a premium of £0.30 per share;
(ii) £8,000 7 per cent debenture stock at 98.

The expenses of incorporating CJK Ltd were paid, amounting to £1,200.

(*Chartered Institute of Management Accountants*)

10.4A The balance sheet of Hubble Ltd as at 31 May 19X0 is shown below.

Hubble Ltd

	£	£
Fixed assets:		
Freehold premises at cost		375,000
Plant and machinery at cost		
Less Depreciation £48,765		101,235
Motor vehicles at cost		
Less Depreciation £1,695		6,775
		483,010
Current assets:		
Stock-in-trade	102,550	
Debtors	96,340	
Cash in hand	105	
		198,995
		682,005
Authorised share capital		
650,000 ordinary shares of £1 each		650,000
Issued share capital:		
400,000 ordinary shares of £1 each fully paid		400,000
Profit and loss account		180,630
		580,630
Current liabilities		
Trade creditors	63,200	
Bank overdraft	38,175	
		101,375
		682,005

Hubble Ltd agreed to purchase at this date the freehold premises, plant and machinery and stock of A Bubble at agreed valuations of £100,000, £10,000 and £55,000, respectively. The purchase price was to be fully settled by the issue to Bubble of 120,000 ordinary shares of £1 each in Hubble Ltd, and a cash payment to Bubble of £25,000. Bubble was to collect his debts and to pay his creditors.

Hubble Ltd sold one of its own premises prior to taking over Bubble for £75,000 (cost £55,000) and revalued the remainder at £400,000 (excluding those acquired from Bubble).

You are required to:
(a) show the journal entries, including cash items, in the books of Hubble Ltd to give effect to the above transactions; and
(b) show the balance sheet of Hubble Ltd after completing them.

(*Chartered Association of Certified Accountants*)

10.5A From the following information you are required to:
(a) prepare a statement apportioning the unappropriated profit between the pre-incorporation and post-incorporation periods, showing the basis of apportionment;
(b) show the share capital and profits on the balance sheet of the company as at 31 March 19X0.

VU Limited was incorporated on 1 July 19X9 with an authorised share capital of 60,000 ordinary shares of £1 each, to take over the business of L and Sons as from 1 April 19X9.

The purchase consideration was agreed at £50,000 for the net tangible assets taken over, plus a further £6,000 for goodwill.

Payment was satisfied by the issue of £30,000 8 per cent debentures and 26,000 ordinary shares both at par, on 1 August 19X9. Interest at 10 per cent per annum on the purchase consideration was paid up to this date.

The company raised a further £20,000 on 1 August 19X9 by the issue of ordinary shares at a premium of £0.25 per share.

The abridged profit and loss account for the year to 31 March 19X0 was as follows:

	£	£
Sales:		
1 April 19X9 to 30 June 19X9	30,000	
1 July 19X9 to 31 March 19Y0	95,000	
		125,000
Cost of sales for the year	80,000	
Depreciation	2,220	
Directors' fees	500	
Administration salaries and expenses	8,840	
Sales commission	4,375	
Goodwill written off	1,000	
Interest on purchase consideration, gross	1,867	
Distribution costs (60 per cent variable)	6,250	
Preliminary expenses written off	1,650	
Debenture interest, gross	1,600	
Proposed dividend on ordinary shares	7,560	
		115,862
Unappropriated profit carried forward		9,138

The company sells one product only, of which the unit selling price has remained constant during the year, but due to improved buying the unit cost of sales was reduced by 10 per cent in the post-incorporation period as compared with the pre-incorporation period.

Taxation is to be ignored.

(*Chartered Institute of Management Accountants*)

10.6A Rowlock Ltd was incorporated on 1 October 19X8 to acquire Rowlock's mail order business, with effect from 1 June 19X8.

The purchase consideration was agreed at £35,000 to be satisfied by the issue on 1 December 19X8 to Rowlock or his nominee of 20,000 ordinary shares of £1 each, fully paid, and £15,000 7 per cent debentures.

The entries relating to the transfer were not made in the books which were carried on without a break until 31 May 19X9.

On 31 May 19X9 the trial balance extracted from the books is:

	£	£
Sales		52,185
Purchases	38,829	
Wrapping	840	
Postage	441	
Warehouse rent and rates	921	
Packing expenses	1,890	
Office expenses	627	
Stock on 31 May 19X8	5,261	
Director's salary	1,000	
Debenture interest (gross)	525	
Fixed assets	25,000	
Current assets (other than stock)	9,745	
Current liabilities		4,162
Formation expenses	218	
Capital account – Wysocka, 31 May 19X8		29,450
Drawings account – Wysocka, 31 May 19X8	500	
	85,797	85,797

You also ascertain the following:
1   Stock on 31 May 19X9 amounted to £4,946.
2   The average monthly sales for June, July and August were one-half of those for the remaining months of the year. The gross profit margin was constant throughout the year.
3   Wrapping, postage and packing expenses varied in direct proportion to sales, whilst office expenses were constant each month.
4   Formation expenses are to be written off.

You are required to prepare the trading and profit and loss account for the year ended 31 May 19X9 apportioned between the periods before and after incorporation, and the balance sheet as at that date.

(*Chartered Institute of Management Accountants*)

11

Taxation in company financial statements

Objectives

After you have studied this chapter, you should:

- know why profit per the profit and loss account is normally different from assessable profit for corporation tax calculations

- know when advanced corporation tax (ACT) is payable

- know how ACT affects the calculation of 'mainstream corporation tax'

- be aware of the rules of ACT set-off

- be aware of what to do with irrecoverable ACT

- be aware of how ACT and tax credits relate to companies and individuals

- be aware of how income tax on interest affects companies and individuals

- understand how the 'imputation system' operates

- understand how and why deferred tax is relevant to capital allowances

11.1 Introduction

This chapter is concerned with the entries made in the financial statements of firms in respect of taxation. It is not concerned with the actual calculation of the taxes. Taxation legislation is now extremely complex and contains many exceptions to the general rules applicable to companies. It is impossible in a book at this level to delve into too many of the complications, and it should therefore be appreciated that, as far as companies are concerned, though the facts in this chapter apply to the great majority of limited companies, there are some other complications in a small minority of cases.

Taxation that affects companies can be split between:

1 Direct taxes, payable to the Inland Revenue, this being the government department responsible for the calculation and collection of the taxes. For a company these taxes

are corporation tax and income tax. SSAP 8 deals with the treatment of taxation in company financial statements, and will be adhered to in this chapter.

2   Value added tax, abbreviated as VAT. This has been dealt with in Volume 1.

11.2 Limited companies: corporation tax and income tax

The tax which limited companies suffer is known as corporation tax. It is legally an appropriation of profits, it is not an expense, and it should therefore be shown in the profit and loss appropriation account. Two law cases, many years ago, did in fact settle any arguments as to whether it was an expense or appropriation, both cases being decided in favour of the view that it was an appropriation of profits.

When a company makes profits, then such profits are assessable to corporation tax. It does not mean that corporation tax is payable on the net profits as shown in the financial statements. What it does mean is that the corporation tax is assessable on the profit calculated after certain adjustments have been made to the net profit shown according to the profit and loss account. These adjustments are not made in the actual financial statements, they are made in calculations performed quite separately from the drafting of financial statements. Suppose that K Ltd has the following profit and loss account:

K Ltd Profit and Loss Account for the year ended 31 March 19X8

	£	£
Gross profit		100,000
Less: General expenses	30,000	
Depreciation of machinery	20,000	
		50,000
Net profit		50,000

The depreciation provision for machinery is the accounting figure used for the financial statements. It is not usually the same figure as that allowed by the Inland Revenue for the depreciation of the machinery. The allowances made for depreciation by the Inland Revenue are known as **capital allowances**. These are calculated by rules which usually vary at one point or another from the methods applied by the company in determining depreciation provisions.

A detailed study of a textbook on taxation would be necessary to see exactly how capital allowances are calculated. In some fairly rare cases, hardly ever found in large or medium-sized concerns but probably more common in very small firms, the capital allowances are calculated and the financial provision for depreciation is taken at the same figure. In the case of K Ltd, assume that the capital allowances amount to £27,000, and that the rate of corporation tax is 40 per cent on assessable profits. The calculation of the corporation tax liability would be:

	£
Net profit per the financial statements	50,000
Add Depreciation provision not allowed as a deduction for corporation tax purposes	20,000
	70,000
Less Capital allowances	27,000
Adjusted profits assessable to corporation tax	43,000

As the corporation tax is assumed to be at the rate of 40 per cent of assessable profits, the corporation tax liability will be £43,000 × 40 per cent = £17,200. Sometimes the adjusted profits are greater than the net profits shown in the financial statements, but may equally well be less. This illustrates the fact that it is relatively rare for the external observer to be able to calculate the corporation tax payable merely by knowing the net profit made by the company. In fact, there are also other items besides depreciation provisions that need adjusting to find the correct assessable profits for corporation tax purposes. All that is needed here is the understanding that profit per the profit and loss account is normally different from assessable profit for corporation tax calculations.

11.3 The rate of corporation tax

The rate of corporation tax is fixed by the Chancellor of the Exchequer in his Budget, presented to Parliament in November of each year. In the Budget, the corporation tax rates are fixed covering the period from 1 April before the budget until 31 March the year following. This rate is to be applied to the assessable profits of companies earned during this period. Thus a rate of 25 per cent announced in November 19X4 covers the assessable profits earned from 1 April 19X4 to 31 March 19X5. A company whose financial year end is not 31 March will, therefore, span two governmental financial years, and will need to apportion its taxable profits across the two periods.

Exhibit 11.1

Company T Ltd: adjusted profits for the year ended 31 December 19X8 = £160,000.

Rates of corporation tax:
For the government financial year ended 31.3.19X8, 45 per cent.
For the government financial year ended 31.3.19X9, 40 per cent.

	£
3 months' profit 1.1.19X8 to 31.3.19X8	
3/12 months × £160,000 = £40,000 × 45 per cent	18,000
9 months' profit 1.4.19X8 to 31.12.19X8	48,000
9/12 months × £160,000 = £120,000 × 40 per cent	66,000

11.4 Corporation tax – when payable

From 1 April 1990, all companies have a payment date of 9 months after the end of each accounting period. For the rest of this chapter, although companies with relatively small profits can pay tax at a lower rate than companies with greater profits, unless mentioned otherwise, for the purposes of illustration, corporation tax will be assumed to be at the rate of 40 per cent.

11.5 Advance corporation tax

Basic features

When a company pays a dividend, a sum equal to a fraction of that figure must be paid to the Inland Revenue by the company as **advance corporation tax**, abbreviated as ACT.

There used to be a formula for the fraction which varied as the basic rate of income tax changed. That formula does not now apply. For all payments of ACT from 6 April 1994, the rate of ACT is 20 per cent. However, the ACT rate applies to the gross figure before

ACT. This means that when calculated with reference to the dividend actually paid it is 20 per cent of the gross dividend paid, i.e. 25 per cent of the net dividend (or, Gross dividend 100% – ACT 20% = Net dividend paid 80% × 25% = ACT 20% + Net dividend paid 80% = Gross dividend 100%).

Therefore the payments due of ACT on the following net dividends actually paid to shareholders would be:

Net dividend paid to shareholders	ACT which will have to be paid to the Inland Revenue
£	£
4,000	1,000
20,000	5,000
300,000	75,000

ACT is, in fact, a prepayment of the main or 'mainstream' corporation tax bill (MCT) of a company. The mainstream corporation tax can only be ascertained after the end of the quarter (or 'return period') in which it occurred. Thus a company that paid a dividend on 20 May 19X4 would be required to pay the ACT 14 days after the end of the quarter ending 30 June 19X4, i.e. on 14 July 19X4.

The four return periods end on 31 March, 30 June, 30 September and 31 December, and there is a fifth at the end of the company's accounting period. ACT payable on dividends paid ('franked payments') during a return period is offset against ACT recoverable on dividends received ('franked investment income') in the same return period.

When a company is due to pay its corporation tax bill, it adjusts the amount it sends to the Inland Revenue by the amount of ACT it has paid or reclaimed during the relevant period.

Exhibit 11.2

Three companies with income chargeable to corporation tax of £100,000 have dividend policies whereby they distribute:

(a) nothing;
(b) 50 per cent of available income;
(c) 100 per cent of available income.

	(a)		(b)		(c)	
	Profits	Tax	Profits	Tax	Profits	Tax
	£	£	£	£	£	£
Taxable	100,000		100,000		100,000	
Corporation tax 40%	40,000	40,000	40,000	40,000	40,000	40,000
	60,000		60,000		60,000	
Dividend – net cash paid to shareholder	Nil		30,000		60,000	
ACT payable on net dividend (25%)		–		7,500		15,000
Mainstream corporation tax (MCT)		40,000		32,500		25,000

Restrictions on set-offs of ACT against mainstream corporation tax

There is a limit to how much ACT can be set off against MCT. The limit is calculated as follows:

	£
Take company's profits assessable to corporation tax, say (a)	£100,000
ACT limit = ACT rate (20%) × (a) = 20% × £100,000 =	£20,000

Any ACT not set off against mainstream corporation tax for the period can be carried back and set off against corporation tax for the past six years. Any excess which then still exists can be carried forward against future corporation tax liabilities without any time limit.

Exhibit 11.3

Given corporation tax at 40 per cent the following would be the MCT for three companies with distributions of A £90,000, B £60,000, and C £30,000:

	Company A		Company B		Company C	
	£	£	£	£	£	£
Taxable profits		100,000		75,000		50,000
Basic corporation tax 40%		40,000		30,000		20,000
Less ACT on distribution:						
Lower of:						
(i) ACT on distributions:						
£90,000 × 25%	22,500					
£60,000 × 25%			15,000			
£30,000 × 25%					7,500	
or (ii) ACT limit of:						
20% × £100,000	20,000					
20% × £75,000			15,000			
20% × £50,000					10,000	
ACT set-off therefore is		20,000		15,000		7,500
Mainstream corporation tax		20,000		15,000		12,500

(a) The ACT on distributions is based on the net dividend paid times the ACT rate on net dividends of 25 per cent.

(b) The ACT limit is based on the taxable profits times the ACT rate (on gross dividends) of 20 per cent.

The unrelieved ACT of £2,500 for Company A is available for relief in another accounting period. Companies B and C received full relief for ACT.

Proposed dividends

(a) The ACT which may be offset against the basic MCT liability **relates to dividends paid (less received) during the accounting period** irrespective of the period for which the dividends are payable.

(b) **ACT is due only when a dividend is paid**, not when it is proposed. It follows that ACT on a dividend proposed at the end of an accounting period will be offset against the basic MCT liability of the next following accounting period (i.e. of the period in which the dividend is paid). Thus ACT on a dividend proposed at the end of a company's accounting period on 31 March 19X4 and paid on 3 June 19X4 will be offset against the basic MCT liability of the accounting period ending 31 March 19X5; it will not be available to offset the MCT on the profits of the accounting period ending 31 March 19X4, even though it arose on dividends paid in respect of that period.

Writing-off irrecoverable ACT

Any irrecoverable ACT (i.e. ACT the recoverability of which is not reasonably certain and foreseeable) should be written-off in the profit and loss account in which the related dividend is shown.

There are two different views on the presentation in the profit and loss account of irrecoverable ACT written-off. One view is that irrecoverable ACT should be treated as part of the tax charge upon the company to be deducted in arriving at profits after tax (known as the net basis); the other is that the irrecoverable ACT, being a cost stemming from the payment of a dividend, should be treated as an appropriation like the dividend itself (known as the nil basis). Of the two methods, the first is supported by SSAP 8 as the appropriate accounting treatment because unrelieved ACT constitutes tax upon the company or group, as opposed to tax on the shareholders, and is not an appropriation of profits. It is appreciated, however, that some readers or analysts of financial statements may wish for their purposes to regard irrecoverable ACT in some other manner. The amount of irrecoverable ACT should therefore be disclosed separately if material.

11.6 Income tax

As already stated, companies do not pay income tax, instead they suffer corporation tax. In the case of a sole trader income tax is not directly connected with the business, as the calculation of it depends on whether the sole trader is married or not, the number of dependants s/he may have and their ages, the amount and type of other income received by him/her, etc. It should therefore be charged to the drawings account.

The income tax charged upon a partnership is also subject to the personal situation of the partners. The actual apportionment of the tax between the partners must be performed by someone who has access to the personal tax computations; it most certainly is not apportioned in the partners' profit-sharing ratios. When the apportionment has been made each partner should have the relevant amount debited to his drawings account. Sole traders and partnerships are not liable to corporation tax.

Income tax does, however, come into the financial statements of limited companies in that the company, when paying charges such as debenture interest or some types of royalty, will deduct income tax from the amount to be paid to the debenture holder or royalty owner. This figure of income tax is then payable by the company to the Inland Revenue. This means simply that the company is acting as a tax collector on behalf of the Inland Revenue.

Suppose, for example, that the company has a thousand different debenture holders. It is far easier for the Inland Revenue if the company pays only the net amount (i.e. the amount of debenture interest less income tax) due to each debenture holder and then pays the income tax deducted, in one figure, to the Inland Revenue. This saves the Inland Revenue having to trace a thousand debenture holders and then collect the money from them. It obviously cuts down on the bad debts that the Inland Revenue might suffer, it makes it more difficult to evade the payment of income tax, plus it makes it cheaper for the Inland Revenue to administer the system. This system is based on the same principles as PAYE on wages or salaries.

For clarity, throughout the rest of this chapter it will be assumed that the basic rate of income tax is 25 per cent. The real rate will obviously differ from time to time. In addition, where an individual has a high or low income he/she will pay rates of income tax which may differ from 25 per cent. However, even though individual debenture holders may have to pay income tax at higher rates, or indeed pay lower rates or no income tax at all, a company will generally deduct income tax at the basic rate.

This means that if a company had 8 per cent debentures amounting to £100,000 then, assuming that the debenture interest was payable in one amount, cheques amounting to a total of £6,000 (8 per cent of £100,000 = £8,000 less 25 per cent income tax, £2,000 = £6,000) will be paid to the debenture holders. A cheque for £2,000 will then be paid to the Inland Revenue by the company. Assume that debenture holder AB is liable on his income to income tax at the rate of 25 per cent, and that he receives interest of £75 net (i.e. £100 gross less income tax £25), on his debenture of £1,250 then he has already suffered his rightful income tax by deduction at the source. He will not get a further bill from the Inland Revenue for £25 tax, he has already suffered the full amount due by him, and the company will have paid the £25 income tax as part of the total income tax cheque of £2,000.

On the other hand, debenture holder CD may not be liable to income tax because his income is low, or he may have a large number of dependants or other such circumstances for which he obtains relief from having to pay any income tax. If he has a debenture of £1,000 he will receive a cheque for interest amounting to £60 (i.e. £80 gross, less income tax £20). As he is not liable to income tax, but as £20 of his money has been included in the total cheque paid by the company to the Inland Revenue of £2,000, then he will be able to claim a refund of £20 from the Inland Revenue. Such a claim is made direct to the Inland Revenue, the company having nothing to do with the refund.

Another debenture holder, EF, is liable to a higher rate of income tax of 40 per cent on his income. If he has a debenture of £25,000, then the company will pay a cheque to him of £1,500 (£2,000 gross less income tax £500). In fact, he is really liable for £800 income tax (£2,000 at 40 per cent) on this income. As £500 income tax has been taken from him and handed over by the company in the total cheque of £2,000 income tax paid to the Inland Revenue, eventually the Inland Revenue will send an extra demand for income tax of £300 to EF (£800 liable less £500 already paid). The company will have nothing to do with this extra demand.

11.7 Income tax on interest

Of course, a company may well have bought debentures or may own royalties, etc., in another company. This may mean that the company not only pays charges, such as debenture interest, but also receives similar items from other companies. The company will receive such items net after income tax has been deducted. When the company both receives and pays such items, it may set off the tax already suffered by it from such interest, etc. received against the tax collected by it from its own charges, and pay the resultant net figure of income tax to the Inland Revenue.

The figures of charges to be shown as being paid or received by the company in the company's own profit and loss account are the gross charges, i.e. the same as they would have been if income tax had never been invented. An exhibit will now be used to illustrate this more clearly.

Exhibit 11.4

RST Ltd has 7 per cent debentures amounting to £10,000 and has bought a £4,000 debenture of 10 per cent in a private company, XYZ Ltd. During the year cheques amounting to £525 (£700 less 25 per cent) have been paid to debenture holders, and a cheque of £300 (£400 less 25 per cent) has been received from XYZ Ltd. Instead of paying over the £175 income tax deducted on payment of debenture interest, RST Ltd waits until the cheque is received from XYZ Ltd and then pays a cheque for £75 (£175 collected by it less £100 already suffered by deduction by XYZ Ltd) to the Inland Revenue in settlement.

Debenture Interest Payable

	£		£
Cash	525	Profit and loss	700
Income tax	175		
	700		700

Debenture Interest Receivable

	£		£
Profit and loss	400	Cash	300
	–	Income tax	100
	400		400

Income Tax

	£		£
Unquoted investment income	100	Debenture interest	175
Cash	75		–
	175		175

It may well have been the case that although the income tax had been deducted at source from both the payment out of the company and the amount received, no cash has been paid specifically to the Inland Revenue by the company by the balance sheet date. This means that the balance of £75 owing to the Inland Revenue will be carried down as a credit balance and will be shown under current liabilities in the balance sheet.

11.8 Corporation tax and the imputation system

When a dividend is paid by a company, this is done without any specific deduction of tax of any kind from the dividend payment. However, the dividend has been paid out of the balance of profits remaining after corporation tax has been charged. In addition, although this has not been deducted specifically from the dividend cheques, a sum equal to 25 per cent of the net dividend has to be paid as advance corporation tax. The final part of what is called the imputation system is that the recipient of the dividend is entitled to a tax credit. The tax credit will equal 25 per cent of the net dividend received (on the assumption of 25 per cent income tax rate).

This works out as follows. An individual, not a company, who has 640 shares of £1 each in a company will receive a dividend cheque of £64 if the company pays a dividend of 10 per cent on its shares. When he declares the income on his tax return he will have to show the figure of the actual income received plus a tax credit equal to 25 per cent of that figure, i.e. in this case £64 + 25 per cent of £64 = £80. Assuming an income tax rate of 25 per cent, he might expect to have to pay £20 income tax on this income of £80, which is £4 greater than the tax credit available to him as a result of the ACT paid by the company who paid him the dividend. However, the rules were changed with affect from 5 April 1993 to restrict the tax liability of individuals on dividends received to 20 per cent of the gross dividend, providing they are not liable to higher rate tax. If they are, the liability is the difference between the higher rate and the tax credit rate. In other words, if the higher rate were 40 per cent, the higher rate tax payer would have to pay 20 per cent of the gross dividend over and above the 20 per cent already deducted as ACT. In this example, that would represent another £16.

On the other hand, if his personal reliefs are such that he would not have to pay any income tax at all, then he will be able to get a refund of the £16 tax credit from the Inland Revenue.

When it comes to companies buying shares in other companies there are a few differences. Some terminology is necessary here. **Franked investment income** consists of the dividend received, plus the tax credit, by a UK resident company from another UK resident company. A **franked payment** is a dividend, plus the relevant advance corporation tax, payable by a UK resident company.

As far as the franked investment income is concerned the double entry is as follows:

Cash received:
    Dr Bank
        Cr Investment income
Tax credit:
    Dr Tax on profit on ordinary activities
        Cr Investment income

This means that if company A received a dividend of £600 from company B there will also be a tax credit of £150 (25 per cent of £600). The financial statements will appear as:

Bank

	£
Investment income	600

Investment Income

	£		£
Profit and loss	750	Bank	600
	–	Tax on profit on ordinary activities	150
	750		750

The profit and loss account will therefore include £750 investment income, while the £150 tax will be included in the total figure of taxation which will include corporation tax.

So far as the calculation of the payment of ACT by company A is concerned, it will be able to deduct the figure of £150 from its next ACT payment. This is for the *calculation part* only, it does not affect the basic double entry.

Although the payments of advance corporation tax are affected as stated, the full payment of corporation tax liability will be affected only as regards the allocation of it between the advance corporation tax part and the mainstream part.

Dividends proposed, and not paid, at the year end are simply shown gross, as are dividends receivable but not yet actually received. No entry is made for tax in these cases.

11.9 Deferred taxation

It was pointed out earlier in the chapter that *profits per the financial statements* and *profits on which tax is payable* are often quite different from each other. The main reasons for this are:

(*a*) The figure of depreciation shown in the profit and loss account may be far different from the Inland Revenue's figure for 'capital allowances', which is *their* way of calculating allowances for depreciation.

(b) Some items of expense charged in the profit and loss account will not be allowed by the Inland Revenue as expenses. Examples are political donations, fines for illegal acts, and expenses of entertaining UK customers.

Timing differences

In the case of capital allowances under (a) above, the amount of 'depreciation' charged for an asset over the years will eventually equal the amount allowed by the Inland Revenue as 'capital allowances'. Where the difference lies is in the periods when these items will be taken into account.

For instance, let us take an asset which will be used for three years and then put out of use. It costs £4,800 and will be sold three years later for £2,025. The depreciation rate is to be 33⅓ per cent straight line. Inland Revenue capital allowances are 25 per cent reducing balance.

Years ended 5 April	19X2	19X3	19X4	Total
	£	£	£	£
Depreciation in accounts	925	925	925	2,775
Capital allowances in tax calculations	1,200	900	675	2,775
Timing differences	+275	−25	−250	nil

Let us suppose that profits for each year, after charging depreciation, amounted to £1,000. A comparison of profits per financial statements and profits for tax purposes becomes as follows:

Years ended 5 April	19X2	19X3	19X4	Total
	£	£	£	£
Profits per accounts after depreciation	1,000	1,000	1,000	3,000
Profits for tax purposes	725	1,025	1,250	3,000
Differences	−275	+25	+250	nil

As you can see, profits have in fact remained the same at £1,000; it is the timing difference of capital allowances which gives different figures for tax purposes. Taking the point of view that profits of £1,000 per year give a more sensible picture than the £725, £1,025 and £1,250 per the Inland Revenue calculations, the company's way of depreciating is probably more suitable than the Inland Revenue's method which does not vary between different companies.

You may well be asking if it matters at all. Analysts and potential investors and shareholders themselves place a great reliance on *earnings per share after tax* (EPS). Suppose that corporation tax was 40 per cent for each of the three years and that there were 10,000 shares. This would give the following figures:

Tax based on 'real profits', i.e. company's calculations:

	19X2	19X3	19X4
	£	£	£
Profits per accounts before taxation	1,000	1,000	1,000
Less Corporation tax (40%)	400	400	400
Profit after tax	600	600	600
Earnings per share ÷ 10,000	6.0p	6.0p	6.0p

Tax based on Inland Revenue calculations:

	19X2 £	19X3 £	19X4 £
Profits per accounts before tax	1,000	1,000	1,000
Less Corporation tax:			
40% × £725	290		
40% × £1,025		410	
40% × £1,250			500
Profits after tax	710	590	500
Earnings per share ÷ 10,000	7.1p	5.9p	5.0p

In truth each of the years has been equally as profitable as any other, as shown by the company's calculation of 6.0p earnings per share each year. On the other hand, if no adjustment is made, the financial statements when based on actual tax paid would show 7.1p, 5.9p and 5.0p. This could confuse shareholders and would-be shareholders.

So as not to distort the picture given by financial statements, the concept of deferred taxation was brought in by accountants. This was given approval in SSAP15: *Accounting for deferred taxation*. The double entry is as follows:

1   In the years when taxation is lower than it would be on comparable accounting profits:

   Dr Profit and loss appropriation account
      Cr Deferred taxation account

with the amount of taxation understated.

2   In the years when taxation is higher than it would be on comparable accounting profits:

   Dr Deferred taxation account
      Cr Profit and loss appropriation account

with the amount of taxation overstated.

We will now look at Exhibit 11.5 to see how the profit and loss appropriation account and deferred taxation account would have been drawn up for the example given above. To make the exhibit follow the wording for published company financial statements, instead of 'Profit per financial statements before taxation' we will call it instead 'Profit on ordinary activities before taxation'.

Exhibit 11.5

Profit and Loss Appropriation Account for the years ended 5 April

	19X2 £	£	19X3 £	£	19X4 £	£
Profit on ordinary activities before taxation		1,000		1,000		1,000
Tax on profit on ordinary activities:						
Corporation tax	290		410		500	
Deferred taxation	110	400	(10)	400	(100)	400
Profit on ordinary activities after taxation		600		600		600

For purposes of shareholders, stock exchange analysts, would-be shareholders, etc. the profit after taxation figures on which earnings per share (EPS) would be calculated is the figure of £600 for each of the three years. The distortion has thus been removed.

Assuming that corporation tax is payable on 1 January following each accounting year end, the accounts for corporation tax and deferred tax would be as follows:

Corporation Tax

	£		£
19X2		**19X2**	
Apr 5 Balance c/d	290	Apr 5 Profit and loss appropriation	290
	290		290
19X3		**19X2**	
Jan 1 Bank	290	Apr 6 Balance b/d	290
		19X3	
Apr 5 Balance c/d	410	Apr 5 Profit and loss appropriation	410
	700		700
19X4		**19X3**	
Jan 1 Bank	410	Apr 6 Balance b/d	410
		19X4	
Apr 5 Balance c/d	500	Apr 5 Profit and loss appropriation	500
	910		910
		19X4	
		Apr 6 Balance b/d	500

Deferred Taxation

	£		£
19X2		**19X2**	
Apr 5 Balance c/d	110	Apr 5 Profit and loss appropriation	110
	110		110
19X3		**19X2**	
Apr 5 Profit and loss appropriation	10	Apr 6 Balance b/d	110
Apr 5 Balance c/d	100		
	110		110
19X4		**19X3**	
Apr 5 Profit and loss appropriation	100	Apr 6 Balance b/d	100
	100		100

The balance sheets would appear:

	19X2 £	19X3 £	19X4 £
Creditors: amounts falling due within one year			
Corporation tax	290	410	500
Provisions for liabilities and charges			
Deferred taxation*	110	100	–

*Any Advance Corporation Tax (ACT) recoverable would be shown as a deduction from this figure.

Permanent differences

Differences in profits for accounts purposes and those for tax purposes because of non-allowable items such as political donations, entertaining expenses etc., are not adjusted for.

A fully worked example

Exhibit 11.6 shows the accounts in which tax will be involved for the first year of a new company, Harlow Ltd. Exhibit 11.7 follows with the second year of that company. This should make your understanding easier – to consider one year alone very often leaves students with many unanswered questions in their minds.

The tax rates used are: corporation tax 35 per cent, income tax 25 per cent.

Exhibit 11.6

Harlow Ltd has just finished its first year of trading on 31 December 19X4. Corporation tax throughout was 35 per cent, the ACT rate was 20 per cent and income tax was 25 per cent. You are given the following information:

(A) Net trading profit for the year was £165,000, before adjustment for debenture interest.
(B) Debenture interest (net) of £12,000 was paid on 31 December 19X4 and (C) the income tax deducted was paid on the same date.
(D) An ordinary interim dividend of 10 per cent on the 210,000 £1 ordinary shares was paid on 1 July 19X4, and (E) the requisite ACT on 1 October 19X4.
(F) A proposed final ordinary dividend of 25 per cent for the year is to be accrued.
(G) Depreciation of £12,000 has been charged before arriving at net trading profit. Capital allowances of £37,000 have been approved by the Inland Revenue. Account for timing differences.
(H) Corporation tax on the first year's trading is expected to be £38,500.

You are required to:
(*a*) show double-entry accounts (other than bank) to record the above;
(*b*) prepare extracts from the profit and loss account and balance sheet.

Exhibit 11.7 will carry on to Harlow Ltd's second year in trading.

Debenture Interest

19X4		£	19X4		£
Dec 31 Bank	(B)	12,000	Dec 31 Profit and loss		16,000
Dec 31 Income tax	(C)	4,000			
		16,000			16,000

Income Tax

19X4		£	19X4		£
Dec 31 Bank	(C)	4,000	Dec 31 Debenture interest	(C)	4,000

Ordinary Dividends

19X4		£	19X4		£
Jul 1	Bank (D)	21,000	Dec 31 Profit and loss		73,500
Dec 31	Accrued c/d	52,500			
		73,500			73,500

Deferred Taxation

19X4	£	19X4		£
Dec 31 Balance c/d	8,750	Dec 31 Profit and loss*	(G)	8,750

*(G) allowed £37,000 but only charged £12,000
= £25,000 × 35% corporation tax deferred = £8,750.

Corporation Tax

19X4	£	19X4		£
Dec 31 Balance c/d	38,500	Dec 31 Profit and loss	(H)	38,500

Advance Corporation Tax

19X4	£	19X4	£
Oct 1 Bank (25% × £21,000) (E)	5,250	Dec 31 Balance c/d	5,250

Profit and Loss Account (extracts) for the year ended 31 December 19X4

		£	£
Net trading profit	(A)		165,000
Less Debenture interest	(B)		16,000
Profit on ordinary activities before taxation			149,000
Corporation tax	(H)	38,500	
Deferred taxation	(G)	8,750	47,250
Profit on ordinary activities after taxation			101,750
Less Dividends on ordinary shares:			
Interim paid 10 per cent	(D)	21,000	
Proposed final dividend 25 per cent		52,500	
			73,500

Balance Sheet (extracts) as at 31 December 19X4

Creditors: amounts falling due within one year	£
Proposed ordinary dividend	52,500
Corporation tax	38,500
Deferred tax (£8,750 − ACT recoverable £5,250)	3,500

Exhibit 11.7

Harlow Ltd, as per Exhibit 11.6, has now finished its second year of trading. From 19X4 there will be four balances (concerned with the exhibit) to be brought forward. These accounts are:

Proposed ordinary dividend	(A)	Cr	£52,500
Corporation tax	(B)	Cr	£38,500
Deferred taxation	(C)	Cr	£8,750
ACT recoverable	(D)	Dr	£5,250

The following information is given to you:

(E) The proposed ordinary dividend £52,500 was paid on 1 March 19X5.

(F) The ACT was paid on 1 June 19X5. Corporation tax remains at 35 per cent, the ACT rate is still 20 per cent and income tax remains at 25 per cent.

(G) Shares had been bought in STU Ltd and franked investment income in the form of a dividend of £1,500 (excluding tax credits) was received on 31 August 19X5.

(H) An interim dividend of 15 per cent on the 210,000 £1 ordinary shares was paid on 1 July 19X5 and (I) the ACT on it paid on 30 September 19X4.

(J) Debentures had been bought in RRR Ltd and interest (net) of £4,500 was received on 30 December 19X5.

(K) Harlow Ltd paid its own debenture interest (net) of £12,000 on 31 December 19X5, and (L) the income tax account (net) was paid on the same date.

(M) The corporation tax due for 19X4 was paid on 30 September 19X5.

(N) A final ordinary dividend for the year of 30 per cent was proposed. This will be paid in March 19X6.

(O) Corporation tax for the year ended 31 December 19X5 is expected to be £41,300.

(P) Depreciation of £28,000 has been charged in the accounts, while capital allowances amounted to £22,000.

(Q) Net trading profit after deducting depreciation but before adjusting for the above was £178,000.

It would have been quite possible to open a tax on profit on ordinary activities account and transfer tax items to there, prior to closing to the profit and loss account. We will now use this method.

Ordinary Dividends

19X5		£	19X5		£
Mar 1	Bank	(E) 52,500	Jan 1	Balance b/f	(A) 52,500
Jul 1	Bank interim	(H) 31,500	Dec 31	Profit and loss	94,500
Dec 31	Accrued c/d	(N) 63,000			
		147,000			147,000

(Franked) Investment Income

19X5		£	19X5		£
Dec 31	Profit and loss	1,875	Aug 31	Bank	(G) 1,500
			Aug 31	Tax on profit on ordinary activities	375
		1,875			1,875

Debenture Interest Payable

19X5		£	19X5		£
Dec 31	Bank	(K) 12,000	Dec 31	Profit and loss	16,000
Dec 31	Income tax	4,000			
		16,000			16,000

Debenture Interest Receivable

19X5			£	19X5			£
Dec 31	Profit and loss		6,000	Dec 30	Bank	(J)	4,500
				Dec 30	Income tax		1,500
			6,000				6,000

Income Tax

19X5			£	19X5			£
Dec 30	Debenture interest receivable		1,500	Dec 31	Debenture interest payable		4,000
Dec 31	Bank	(L)	2,500				
			4,000				4,000

Deferred Taxation

19X5			£	19X5			£
Dec 31	Tax on profit on ordinary activities (6,000 × 35%)	(P)	2,100	Jan 1	Balance b/f	(C)	8,750
Dec 31	Balance c/d		6,650				
			8,750				8,750

Advance Corporation Tax

19X5			£	19X5		£
Jan 1	Balance b/f	(D)	5,250	Sep 30 Corporation tax – set-off*		5,250
Jan 1	Bank 25% × 52,500	(F)	13,125	Dec 31 Balance c/d		20,625
Sep 30	Bank 25% × 31,500 – 1,500 (FII)	(I)	7,500			
			25,875			25,875

*Note: only the ACT paid in 19X4 can be set off against the tax for 19X4.

Corporation Tax

19X5			£	19X5			£
Sep 30	ACT (recovered)		5,250	Jan 1	Balance b/f	(B)	38,500
Sep 30	Bank	(M)	33,250	Dec 31	Tax on profit on ordinary activities	(O)	41,300
Dec 31	Accrued c/d		41,300				
			79,800				79,800

Tax on Profit on Ordinary Activities

19X5			£	19X5			£
Aug 31	Franked investment income		375	Dec 31	Deferred taxation	(P)	2,100
Dec 31	Corporation tax	(O)	41,300	Dec 31	Profit and loss		39,575
			41,675				41,675

Profit and Loss account (extracts) for the year ended 31 December 19X5

		£	£
Net trading profit	(Q)		178,000
Add Debenture interest received		6,000	
Franked investment income		1,875	7,875
			185,875
Less Debenture interest payable			16,000
Profit on ordinary activities before taxation			169,875
Tax on profit on ordinary activities			39,575
Profit on ordinary activities after taxation			130,300
Less Dividends on ordinary shares			
Interim paid 15 per cent		31,500	
Proposed final dividend		63,000	94,500

Balance Sheet (extracts) as at 31 December 19X5

Creditors: amounts falling due within one year	£
Proposed ordinary dividend	63,000
Corporation tax	41,300
Deferred tax (6,650 – ACT recoverable 20,625)	(13,975)

New terms

Corporation tax (p. 162): A form of direct taxation levied on the profits of companies. The rate is determined each year in the Finance Act.

Advance corporation tax (p. 163): A payment in advance of the main corporation tax due which arises when dividends are paid. The rate is the same as the basic income tax.

Imputation system (p. 168): When a dividend is paid a tax credit based on the basic income tax rate is allowed to the recipient. This is the case, even though companies pay corporation tax not income tax.

Deferred taxation (p. 169): Timing differences arise between the accounting treatment of events and their taxation results. Deferred taxation accounting adjusts the differences so that the accounts are not misleading.

Main points to remember

1   Profit per the profit and loss account is normally different from assessable profit for corporation tax calculations.

2   Advanced corporation tax (ACT) is payable 14 days after the end of the 'return period' in which it arose.

3   ACT represents advance payment of taxation and the amount of ACT paid to the Inland Revenue is deducted from the corporation tax due in order to arrive at the amount of 'mainstream corporation tax' due for the period.

4   ACT set-off is restricted to the amount found by multiplying the taxable profits by the ACT rate.

5   Irrecoverable ACT should be written off in the profit and loss account for the period in which the related dividend is shown.

6   Deferred tax eliminates the differences that arise as a result of depreciation being replaced by capital allowances when calculating corporation tax payable.

Review questions

For those taking examinations with little tax content, questions 11.5 and 11.6A will be sufficient for your purposes.

11.1 Long Acre Ltd has just finished its first year of trading to 31 December 19X3. Corporation tax throughout was 35 per cent, the ACT rate was 20 per cent and income tax 25 per cent. You are given the following information:

(i)   Net trading profit, after adjustment for (ii) but before other adjustments, was £220,000.
(ii)   Depreciation of £50,000 was charged in the accounts. Capital allowances amounted to £90,000.
(iii) An interim dividend of 5 per cent on 400,000 £1 ordinary shares was paid on 1 July 19X3.
(iv)   ACT on (iii) was paid on 30 September 19X3.
(v)   Debenture interest of £9,600 (net) was paid on 31 December 19X3.
(vi)   Income tax deducted from debenture interest was paid on 31 January 19X4.
(vii) A final dividend of 7½ per cent was proposed for the year.
(viii) Corporation tax for the year was estimated to be £90,000.

You are required to:
(a)   draw up the double-entry accounts recording the above (except bank);
(b)   show the relevant extracts from the profit and loss account and the balance sheet.

Note that question 11.2A is concerned with the second year of trading for Long Acre Ltd.

11.2A Long Acre Ltd has just finished its second year of trading to 31 December 19X4. Balances per 11.1 need to be brought forward into this question. Tax rates are the same as for 19X3.
   The following information is available:

(i)   The proposed final dividend for 19X3 (see 11.1) was paid on 31 January 19X4.
(ii)   ACT on (i) was paid on 31 March 19X4.
(iii) Shares in Covent Ltd were bought on 1 January 19X4. A dividend of £2,400 (excluding tax credits) was received on 30 September 19X4. This is franked investment income.
(iv)   Debentures in Covent Ltd were bought 1 July 19X4. Debenture interest of £7,200 (net) was paid to us on 31 December 19X4.
(v)   Debenture interest of £9,600 (net) was paid by us on 31 December 19X4.
(vi)   Income tax owing to the Inland Revenue for 19X4 was not paid by us until 19X5. The 19X3 income tax had been paid on 30 January 19X4.
(vii) An interim dividend of 7½ per cent on 400,000 £1 ordinary shares was paid by us on 10 July 19X4.
(viii) ACT on (vii) was paid by us on 10 October 19X4.
(ix)   A final dividend of 17½ per cent was proposed for the year.
(x)   Depreciation of £70,000 was charged in the accounts. Capital allowances amounted to £96,000.
(xi)   Net trading profit (before taking into account (iii), (iv), and (v)) was £360,000.
(xii) The corporation tax due for 19X3 was paid on 1 October 19X4. Corporation tax for the year to 31 December 19X4 is expected to be £95,000.

You are required to:
(a) Draw up the double entry accounts recording the above (except bank).
(b) Show the relevant extracts from the profit and loss account for the year and balance sheet at the year end.

Question 11.3 is a typical professional examination question. It is not easy. Remember to bring forward the balances from the previous year which will often have to be deduced. The letters (A) to (N) against the information will make it easier for you to check your answer against that given at the back of the book.

11.3 Corporation tax for financial years 19X1, 19X2, and 19X3 was 35 per cent, the ACT rate was 20 per cent and income tax for each year was 25 per cent.

(A) Barnet Ltd's draft profit and loss account for the year ended 31 December 19X2 shows net trading profit of £560,000. This figure is before taking into account (B) and (C1) and (C2).
(B) Debenture interest paid on 30 November 19X2 (gross) was £80,000. Ignore accruals.
(C1) Fixed rate interest received is £24,000 net, excluding tax credits. Date received 31 October 19X2. Ignore accruals.
(C2) A dividend of £900 was received from CD Ltd on 1 September. This is franked investment income.
(D) Depreciation, already charged before calculating net trading profit, was £50,000. This compares with £90,000 capital allowances given by the Inland Revenue. There is to be full provision for all timing differences for 19X2.
(E) The income tax bill (net) in respect of (B) and (C1) was paid on 15 December 19X2.
(F) Preference dividend paid on 30 June 19X2 £18,000.
(G) Ordinary interim dividend paid 15 July 19X2 £75,000.
(H) Proposed final ordinary dividend for 19X2 (paid in 19X3) was £120,000.
(I) Proposed final ordinary dividend for 19X1 (paid 31 March 19X2) was £90,000.
(J) There was a credit balance on deferred taxation account on 31 December 19X1 of £67,000.
(K) Mainstream tax for 19X1 had been provided for at £115,000 but was finally agreed at £112,000 (paid on 30 September 19X2).
(L) Corporation tax for 19X2 is estimated to be £154,000.
(M) ACT is paid in each case two months after dividends paid.
(N) ACT paid in 19X1 but which had not been set-off against corporation tax in 19X1 amounted to £49,000.

You are required to enter up the following accounts for the year ended 31 December 19X2 for Barnet Ltd: Deferred tax; Income tax; Interest receivable; Debenture interest; Franked investment income; Advance corporation tax; Corporation tax; Tax on profit on ordinary activities; Preference dividends; Ordinary dividends; Profit and loss account extract. Also Balance sheet extracts as at 31 December 19X2.

11.4A KK Ltd has a trading profit, before dealing with any of the undermentioned items, for the year ended 31 December 19X9 of £200,000. You are to complete the profit and loss and appropriation account for the year.

(a) The standard rate of income tax is taken as being 30 per cent.
(b) KK Ltd has bought £80,000 of 10 per cent debentures in another company. KK Ltd receives its interest, less income tax, for the year on 15 December 19X9.
(c) KK has issued £150,000 of 8 per cent debentures, and pays interest, less income tax for the year on 20 December 19X9.
(d) No cheque has been paid to the Inland Revenue for income tax.
(e) KK Ltd has a liability for corporation tax, based on the year's profits for 19X9, of £97,000.

(*f*) KK Ltd owns 60,000 ordinary shares of £1 each in GHH Ltd, and receives a cheque for the dividend of 20 per cent in November 19X9. GHH Ltd is neither a subsidiary company nor a related company.

(*g*) KK Ltd proposed a dividend of 15 per cent on the 100,000 ordinary shares of £1 each, payable out of the profits for 19X9.

(*h*) Transfer £20,000 to general reserve.

(*i*) Unappropriated profits brought forward from last year amounted to £19,830.

11.5 BG Ltd has a trading profit for the year ended 31 December 19X7, before dealing with the following items, of £50,000. You are to complete the profit and loss account and appropriation account.

(*a*) The standard rate of income tax is taken as being 30 per cent.

(*b*) BG Ltd had £40,000 of 9 per cent debentures. It sent them cheques for debenture interest for the year less income tax, on 31 December 19X7.

(*c*) BG Ltd had bought £10,000 of 11 per cent debentures in another company. It received a year's interest, less income tax, on 30 December 19X7.

(*d*) No cheque has been paid to the Inland Revenue for income tax.

(*e*) BG Ltd had bought 15,000 ordinary shares of £1 each in MM Ltd. MM Ltd paid a dividend to BG Ltd of 20 per cent on 30 November 19X7. MM Ltd is a 'related company'.

(*f*) BG Ltd had a liability for corporation tax, based on profits for 19X7, of £24,000.

(*g*) BG proposed a dividend of 30 per cent on its 70,000 ordinary shares of £1 each, out of the profits for 19X7.

(*h*) Transfer £5,000 to general reserve.

(*i*) Unappropriated profits brought forward from last year amounted to £9,870.

11.6 The following information relates to Kemp plc for the year to 31 March 19X0:

	£m
1 Dividends	
Proposed final ordinary dividend for the year to 31 March 19X9 paid on 31 August 19X9	28
Interim ordinary dividend paid on 31 December 19X9	12
Proposed final ordinary dividend for the year 31 March 19X0 to be paid on 31 July 19X0	36
2 Advance corporation tax	
Credit balance at 1 April 19X9	7
3 Deferred taxation account	
Credit balance at 1 April 19X9	3
During the year to 31 March 19X0 a transfer of £5 million was made from the profit and loss account to the deferred taxation account.	
4 Tax rates	
Corporation tax 35 per cent	
Income tax 25 per cent	
5 Assume that all advance corporation tax is recoverable against corporation tax.	

Required:

Write up the following accounts for the year to 31 March 19X0, being careful to insert the appropriate date for each entry, and to bring down the balances as at 31 March 19X0:

(*i*) ordinary dividends;

(*ii*) advance corporation tax; and

(*iii*) deferred taxation.

(*Association of Accounting Technicians*)

11.7A   The following figures appeared in W Ltd's balance sheet at 31 March 19X2:

Current liability – corporation tax	£600,000
Deferred taxation	£300,000
Less advance corporation tax recoverable	(50,000)
	£250,000

During the year ended 31 March 19X3, W Ltd made a payment of £520,000 to the Collector of Taxes in settlement of the company's mainstream corporation tax for the year ended 31 March 19X2. Dividend payments totalling £60,000 were made during the year ended 31 March 19X2 and a further dividend of £200,000 had been proposed at the year end.

Two dividend payments were made during the year ended 31 March 19X3. A payment of £200,000 was made in respect of the final dividend for the year ended 31 March 19X2. An interim dividend of £40,000 was paid in respect of the year ended 31 March 19X3. These payments were made in May 19X2 and September 19X2 respectively. The directors have provided a final dividend of £240,000 for the year ended 31 March 19X3.

W Ltd received a net dividend of £12,000 from a UK quoted company. This was received in August 19X2.

W Ltd's tax advisers believe that corporation tax of £740,000 will be charged on the company's profits for the year ended 31 March 19X3. This amount is net of the tax relief of £104,000 which should be granted in respect of the extraordinary loss which the company incurred during the year. It has been assumed that corporation tax will be charged at a rate of 35%. The basic rate of income tax was 25%. The ACT rate is 20%.

It has been decided that the provision for deferred tax should be increased by £20,000. No provision is to be made in respect of timing differences of £400,000.

You are required:
(a) to prepare the note which will support the figure for the provision for corporation tax in W Ltd's published profit and loss account the for the year ended 31 March 19X3;
(b) to calculate the liabilities for mainstream corporation tax and advance corporation tax which will appear in W Ltd's published balance sheet at 31 March 19X3;
(c) to prepare the deferred tax note which will support the figure for the liability which will appear in W Ltd's published balance sheet at 31 March 19X3.

(*Chartered Institute of Management Accountants*)

12

Provisions, reserves and liabilities

Objectives

After you have studied this chapter, you should:

● *be aware of the difference between a 'provision' and a 'liability'*

● *be aware of the difference between revenue and capital reserves*

● *know how capital reserves may be used*

● *know what normally comprises distributable profit*

12.1 Provisions

A **provision** is an amount written-off or retained by way of providing for depreciation, renewals or diminution in value of assets, or retained by way of providing for any known liability of which the amount cannot be determined with 'substantial' accuracy. This therefore covers such items as **provisions for depreciation**. A **liability** is an amount owing which can be determined with substantial accuracy.

Sometimes, therefore, the difference between a provision and a liability hinges around what is meant by 'substantial' accuracy. Rent owing at the end of a financial year would normally be known with precision; this would obviously be a liability. Legal charges for a court case which has been heard, but for which the lawyers have not yet submitted their bill, would be a provision. The need for the distinction between liabilities and provisions will not become obvious until Chapter 15, where the requirements of the Companies Acts regarding disclosures in the final accounts are examined.

12.2 Revenue reserves

A **revenue reserve** is where an amount has been voluntarily transferred from the profit and loss appropriation account by debiting it, thus reducing the amount of profits left available for cash dividend purposes, and crediting a named **reserve account.** The reserve may be for some particular purpose, such as a **foreign exchange reserve account** created just in case the firm should ever meet a situation where it would suffer loss because of devaluation of a foreign currency, or it could be a **general reserve account.**

Such transfers are, in fact, an indication to the shareholders that it would be unwise at that particular time to pay out all the available profits as dividends. The resources represented by part of the profits should more wisely and profitably be kept in the firm, at least for the time being. Revenue reserves can be called upon in future years to help swell the profits shown in the profit and loss appropriation account as being available for dividend purposes. This is effected quite simply by debiting the particular reserve account and crediting the profit and loss appropriation account.

12.3 General reserve

A general reserve may be needed because of the effect of inflation. If in the year 19X3 a firm needs a working capital of £4,000, the volume of trade remains the same for the next three years but the price level increases by 25 per cent, then the working capital requirements will now be £5,000. If all the profits are distributed, the firm will still only have £4,000 working capital which cannot possibly finance the same volume of trade as it did in 19X3. Transferring annual amounts of profits to a general reserve instead of paying them out as dividends is one way to help overcome this problem. On the other hand it may just be the convention of conservatism asserting itself, with a philosophy of 'it's better to be safe than sorry', in this case to restrict dividends because the funds they would withdraw from the business may be needed in a moment of crisis. This is sometimes overdone, with the result that the firm has excessive amounts of liquid funds being inefficiently used, whereas if they were paid out to the shareholders, who after all are the owners, then the shareholders could put the funds to better use themselves.

This then leaves the question of the balance on the profit and loss appropriation account if it is a credit balance. Is it a revenue reserve? There is no straightforward answer to this; the fact that it has not been utilised for dividend purposes could mean that it has been deliberately held back and as such could be classified as a revenue reserve. On the other hand, there may be a balance on the account just because it is inconvenient to pay dividends in fractions of percentages.

12.4 Capital reserves

A **capital reserve** is normally quite different from a revenue reserve. It is a reserve which is not available for transfer to the profit and loss appropriation account to swell the profits shown as available for cash dividend purposes. Most capital reserves can never be utilised for cash dividend purposes; notice the use of the word 'cash', as it will be seen later that bonus shares may be issued as a 'non-cash' dividend.

The ways that capital reserves are created must therefore be looked at.

Capital reserves created in accordance with the Companies Acts

The Companies Acts state that the following are capital reserves and can never be utilised for the declaration of dividends payable in cash:

(*a*) capital redemption reserve – *see* Chapter 9;
(*b*) share premium account – *see* Chapter 8;
(*c*) revaluation reserve – where an asset has been revalued then an increase is shown by a debit in the requisite asset account and a credit in the Revaluation Account. The recording of a reduction in value is shown by a credit in the asset account and a debit in the Revaluation Account.

Capital reserves created by case law

Distributable profits per the Companies Acts have been described earlier in this volume. The definition includes the words 'in accordance with principles generally accepted'. As accounting develops and changes there will obviously be changes made in the 'principles generally accepted'.

There are quite a few law cases decided to establish exactly whether an item would be a distributable profit or not and therefore available for cash dividend purposes. This makes the difference as to whether an item should be transferred to a capital reserve account as not being distributable, or else to a revenue reserve account if it is distributable. These cases will have to be studied at the more advanced stages of accounting, and so will not be dealt with here.

12.5 Capital reserves put to use

These can only be used in accordance with the Companies Acts. The following description of the actions which can be taken assumes that in fact the articles of association are the same as Table A for this purpose, and that therefore there are no provisions in the articles to prohibit such actions.

Capital redemption reserve (for creation *see* Chapter 9)

(a) To be applied in paying up unissued shares of the company as fully paid shares. These are commonly called 'bonus shares', and are dealt with in Chapter 13.
(b) Can be reduced only in the manner as to reduction of share capital (*see* Chapter 13).
(c) Can be reduced, in the case of a private company, where the permissible capital payment is greater than the nominal value of shares redeemed/purchased (*see* Chapter 9).

Share premium account (for creation *see* Chapter 8)

(a) The same provision referring to bonus shares as exists with the capital redemption reserve.
(b) Writing off preliminary expenses.
(c) Writing off expenses and commission paid on the issue of shares or debentures.
(d) In writing off discounts on shares or debentures issued (for creation of these accounts, *see* Chapter 8).
(e) Providing any premium payable on redemption or purchases of shares or debentures.

Revaluation reserve

Where the directors are of the opinion that any amount standing to the credit of the revaluation reserve is no longer necessary then the reserve must be reduced accordingly. An instance of this would be where an increase in the value of an asset had been credited to the revaluation account, and there had subsequently been a fall in the value of that asset.

The revaluation reserve may also be reduced where the permissible capital payment exceeds the nominal value of the shares redeemed/purchased.

Profits prior to incorporation (for creation *see* Chapter 10)

These can be used for the issuing of bonus shares, in paying up partly paid shares, or alternatively they may be used to write down goodwill or some such similar fixed asset.

Created by case law

These can be used in the issue of bonus shares or in the paying up of partly paid shares.

12.6 Distributable profit

Distributable profits have already been defined. Accounting Standards will apply unless they come into conflict with the Companies Acts themselves.

Normally the revenue reserves, including any credit balance on the profit and loss account, would equal distributable profit.

Development costs

Under Section 269, any development costs which have been capitalised have to be deducted from distributable profits, *unless* there are special circumstances justifying the capitalisation. Normally this means that SSAP 13 (Research and development) will apply.

Depreciation on revalued assets

There is a conflict here between SSAP 12 (Depreciation) and the Companies Acts. The Companies Acts require depreciation on revalued assets to be based on the revalued amounts. However, the Companies Acts allow the extra depreciation because of the revaluation to be *added back* when calculating distributable profit.

Distributions in kind

Where a company makes a non-cash distribution, for example by giving an investment, and that item (i.e. in this case the investment) has been revalued, it could generally be said that part of the distribution was unrealised profit locked into investment. However, the Companies Acts allow this because the 'unrealised' profit is 'realised' by the distribution (from the company's viewpoint, anyway).

12.7 Distributions and auditors' reports

The Companies Acts prohibit any particular distribution if the auditor's report is qualified, with one exception. That is that if the amount involved is *not* material and the auditor agrees to this fact, then distribution of an item can take place.

If a distribution is unlawfully made, any member knowing it to be so could be made to repay it. If the company could not recover such distributions then legal proceedings could be taken against the directors.

New terms

Provision (p. 182): An amount written-off or retained by way of providing for depreciation, renewals or diminution in value of assets, or retained by way of providing for any known liability of which the amount cannot be determined with 'substantial accuracy'.

Revenue reserves (p. 182): A balance of profits retained available to pay cash dividends including an amount voluntarily transferred from the profit and loss appropriation account by debiting it, reducing the amount of profits left for cash dividend purposes, and crediting a named reserve account, such as a general reserve.

Capital reserve (p. 182): A reserve which is a balance of profit retained that can never be used for the payment of cash dividends. These are normally created specifically under the provisions of the Companies Acts. Examples include a capital redemption reserve and a share premium account.

Main points to remember

1   Provisions involve uncertainty over the precise amount involved, it being impossible to determine the amount with 'substantial' accuracy.

2   Liabilities can be determined with 'substantial' accuracy.

3   There are two main categories of reserves:
    (*a*) revenue reserves (can be freely distributed); and
    (*b*) capital reserves (subject to restrictions on their distribution).

Review question

12.1 An extract from the draft accounts of Either Ltd at 30 November 19X5 shows the following figures before allowing for any dividend which might be proposed:

	£000
Ordinary shares of £1 each	400
6% preference shares of £1 each	150
Capital redemption reserve	300
Revaluation reserve	125
General reserve	80
Profit and loss account	13
	1,068
Operating profit before taxation for the year	302
Taxation	145
	£157

Additional information includes:
(*a*) The revaluation reserve consists of an increase in the value of freehold property following a valuation in 19X3. The property concerned was one of three freehold properties owned by the company and was subsequently sold at the revalued amount.
(*b*) It has been found that a number of stock items have been included at cost price, but were being sold after the balance sheet date at prices well below cost. To allow for this, stock at 30 November 19X5 would need to be reduced by £35,000.
(*c*) Provision for directors' remuneration should be made in the sum of £43,000.

(d) Included on the balance sheet is £250,000 of research and development expenditure carried forward.

(e) No dividends have yet been paid on either ordinary or preference shares for the year to 30 November 19X5, but the directors wish to pay the maximum permissible dividends for the year.

(f) Since the draft accounts were produced it has been reported that a major customer of Either Ltd has gone into liquidation and is unlikely to be able to pay more than 50p in the £ to its creditors. At 30 November 19X5 this customer owed £60,000 and this has since risen to £180,000.

(g) It has been decided that the depreciation rates for plant and machinery are too low but the effect of the new rates has not been taken into account in constructing the draft accounts. The following information is available:

	£
Plant and machinery	
Purchases at the commencement of the business on	
1 December 19X1 cost	100,000
Later purchases were: 1 June 19X3	25,000
29 February 19X4	28,000
31 May 19X4	45,000
1 December 19X4	50,000

In the draft financial statements depreciation has been charged at the rate of 25 per cent using the reducing balance method and charging a full year's depreciation in the year of purchase. It has been decided to change to the straight line method using the same percentage but charging only an appropriate portion of the depreciation in the year of purchase. There have been no sales of plant and machinery during the period.

Required:

(a) Calculate the maximum amount which the directors of Either Ltd may propose as a dividend to be paid to the ordinary shareholders whilst observing the requirements of the Companies Acts. Show all workings and state any assumptions made.

(b) Outline and discuss any differences which might have been made to your answer to (a) if the company were a public limited company.

For the purposes of this question you may take it that corporation tax is levied at the rate of 50 per cent.

(*Chartered Association of Certified Accountants*)

13

The increase and reduction of the share capital of limited companies

Objectives

After you have studied this chapter, you should:

- *be aware of the various ways in which a limited company may alter its share capital*

- *know the difference between a 'bonus' issue and a 'rights' issue of shares*

- *understand why a company may introduce a scheme for the reduction of its capital*

- *be aware of the effect upon the balance sheet of bonus issues, rights issues and schemes for the reduction of capital*

13.1 Alteration of capital

A limited company may, if so authorised by its articles, and if the correct legal formalities are observed, alter its share capital in any of the following ways.

1 Increase its share capital by new shares, e.g. increase authorised share capital from £5,000 to £15,000.
2 Consolidate and divide all or any of its share capital into shares of a larger amount than its existing shares, for instance to make 5,000 ordinary shares of £1 each into 1,000 ordinary shares of £5 each.
3 Convert all or any of its paid-up shares into stock, and reconvert that stock into shares of any denomination, e.g. 10,000 ordinary shares of £1 each made into 10,000 ordinary stock.
4 Subdivide all, or any, of its shares into shares of smaller denominations, e.g. 1,000 ordinary shares of £6 each made into 2,000 ordinary shares of £3 each, or 3,000 ordinary shares of £2 each, etc.
5 Cancel shares which have not been taken up. This is 'diminution' of capital, not to be confused with reduction of capital described later in the chapter. Thus a firm with an authorised capital of £10,000 and an issued capital of £8,000 can alter its capital to be authorised capital £8,000 and issued capital £8,000.

13.2 Bonus shares

These are shares issued to existing shareholders free of charge. An alternative name is **scrip issue**.

If the articles give the power, and the requisite legal formalities are observed, the following may be applied in the issuing of bonus shares:

1 the balance of the profit and loss appropriation account;
2 any other revenue reserve;
3 any capital reserve, e.g. share premium.

This thus comprises all of the reserves.

The reason why this should ever be needed can be illustrated by taking the somewhat exaggerated example shown in Exhibit 13.1.

Exhibit 13.1

A company, Better Price Ltd, started business 50 years ago with 1,000 ordinary shares of £1 each and £1,000 in the bank. The company has constantly had to retain a proportion of its profits to finance its operations, thus diverting them from being used for cash dividend purposes. Such a policy has conserved working capital.

The firm's balance sheet as at 31 December 19X7 is shown as:

Better Price Ltd

Balance Sheet as at 31 December 19X7
(before bonus shares are issued)

	£
Fixed assets	5,000
Current assets *less* current liabilities	5,000
	10,000
Share capital	1,000
Reserves (including profit and loss appropriation balance)	9,000
	10,000

If in fact an annual profit of £1,500 was now being made, this being 15 per cent on capital employed, and £1,000 could be paid annually as cash dividends, then the dividend declared each year would be 100 per cent, i.e. a dividend of £1,000 on shares of £1,000 nominal value. It is obvious that the dividends and the share capital have got out of step with one another. Employees and trade unions may well become quite belligerent, as owing to the lack of accounting knowledge, or even misuse of it, it might be believed that the firm was making unduly excessive profits. Customers, especially if they are members of the general public, may also be deluded into thinking that they are being charged excessive prices, or, even though this could be demonstrated not to be true because of the prices charged by competitors, they may well still have the feeling that they are somehow being duped.

In point of fact, an efficient firm in this particular industry or trade may well be only reasonably rewarded for the risks it has taken by making a profit of 15 per cent on capital employed. The figure of 100 per cent for the dividend is due to the very misleading convention in accounting in the UK of calculating dividends in relationship to the nominal amount of the share capital.

If it is considered, in fact, that £7,000 of the reserves could not be used for dividend purposes, due to the fact that the net assets should remain at £8,000, made up of fixed assets £5,000 and working capital £3,000, then besides the £1,000 share capital which cannot be returned to the shareholders there are also £7,000 reserves which cannot be rationally returned to them. Instead of this £7,000 being called reserves, it might as well be called capital, as it is needed by the business on a permanent basis.

To remedy this position, as well as some other needs less obvious, bonus shares were envisaged. The reserves are made non-returnable to the shareholders by being converted into share capital. Each holder of one ordinary share of £1 each will receive seven bonus shares (in the shape of seven ordinary shares) of £1 each. The balance sheet, if the bonus shares had been issued immediately, would then appear:

Better Price Ltd

Balance sheet as at 31 December 19X7
(after bonus shares are issued)

	£
Fixed assets	5,000
Current assets *less* current liabilities	5,000
	10,000
Share capital (£1,000 + £7,000)	8,000
Reserves (£9,000 – £7,000)	2,000
	10,000

When the dividends of £1,000 per annum are declared in the future, they will amount to:

$$\frac{£1,000}{£8,000} \times \frac{100}{1} = 12.5 \text{ per cent}$$

This will cause less disturbance in the minds of employees, trade unions and customers.

Of course the issue of bonus shares may be seen by any of the interested parties to be some form of diabolical liberty. To give seven shares of £1 each free for one previously owned may be seen as a travesty of social justice. In point of fact the shareholders have not gained at all. Before the bonus issue there were 1,000 shareholders who owned between them £10,000 of net assets. Therefore, assuming just for this purpose that the book 'value' is the same as any other 'value', each share was worth £10. After the bonus issue each previous holder now has eight shares for every one share he held before. If he had owned one share only, he now owns eight shares. He is therefore the owner of $^8/_{8,000}$ part of the firm, i.e. a one thousandth part. The 'value' of the net assets are £10,000, so that he owns £10 of them, so his shares are worth £10. This is exactly the same 'value' as that applying before the bonus issue was made.

It would be useful, in addition, to refer to other matters for comparison. Anyone who had owned a £1 share 50 years ago, then worth £1, would now have (if he was still living after such a long time) eight shares worth £8. A new house of a certain type 50 years ago might have cost £x; it may now cost £8x. The cost of a bottle of beer may now be y times greater than it was 50 years ago, a packet of cigarettes may be z times more and so on. Of course, the firm has brought a lot of trouble on itself by waiting so many years to capitalise reserves. It should have been done by several stages over the years.

This is all a very simplified, and in many ways an exaggerated version. There is, however, no doubt that misunderstanding of accounting and financial matters has caused a great deal of unnecessary friction in the past and will probably still do so in the future. Yet another very common misunderstanding is that the assumption the reader was asked to accept, namely that the balance sheet values equalled 'real values', is often one taken by the reader of a balance sheet. Thus a profit of £10,000 when the net assets' book values are £20,000 may appear to be excessive, yet in fact a more realistic value of the assets may be saleable value – in this case the value may be £100,000.

The accounting entries necessary are to debit the reserve accounts utilised, and to credit a bonus account. The shares are then issued and the entry required to record this is to credit the share capital account and to debit the bonus account. The journal entries would be:

The Journal

	Dr	Cr
	£	£
Reserve account(s) (show each account separately)	7,000	
Bonus account		7,000
Transfer of an amount equal to the bonus payable in fully paid shares		
Bonus account	7,000	
Share capital account		7,000
Allotment and issue of 7,000 shares of £1 each, in satisfaction of the bonus declared		

13.3 Rights issue

A company can also increase its share capital by making a **rights issue**. This is the issue of shares to existing shareholders at a price lower than the ruling market price of the shares.

The price at which the shares of a very profitable company are quoted on the Stock Exchange is usually higher than the nominal value of the shares. For instance, the market price of the shares of a company might be quoted at £2.50 while the nominal value per share is only £1.00. If the company has 8,000 shares of £1 each and declares a rights issue of one for every eight held at a price of £1.50 per share, it is obvious that it will be cheaper for the existing shareholders to buy the rights issue at this price instead of buying the same shares in the open market for £2.50 per share. Assume that all the rights issue were taken up, then the number of shares taken up will be 1,000 (i.e. 8,000 ÷ 8), and the amount paid for them will be £1,500. The journal entries will be:

The Journal

	Dr	Cr
	£	£
Cash	1,500	
Share capital		1,000
Share premium		500
Being the rights issue of 1 for every 8 shares		
held at a price of £1.50 nominal value being £1.00.		

It is to be noted that because the nominal value of each share is £1.00 while £1.50 was paid, the extra 50p constitutes a share premium to the company.

Notice also that the market value of the shares will be reduced or 'diluted' by the rights issue, as was the case for bonus shares. Before the rights issue there were 8,000 shares at a price of £2.50, giving a market capitalisation of £20,000. After the issue there are 9,000 shares and the assets have increased by £1,500. The market value may therefore reduce to £2.39 [(20,000 + 1,500)/9,000)], although the precise market price at the end of the issue will have been influenced by the information given surrounding the sale about the future prospects of the company and may not be exactly the amount calculated.

13.4 Reduction of capital

Where capital is not represented by assets

Any scheme for the reduction of capital needs to go through the legal formalities via the shareholders and other interested parties, and must receive the consent of the court. It is assumed that all of this has been carried out correctly.

Capital reduction means in fact that the share capital – all of it if there is only one class such as ordinary shares, or all or part of it if there is more than one class of shares – has been subjected to a lessening of its nominal value, or of the called-up part of the nominal value. Thus:

(a) a £4 share might be made into a £3 share;
(b) a £5 share might be made into a £1 share;
(c) a £3 share, £2 called up, might be made into a £1 share fully paid up;
(d) a £5 share, £3 called up, might be made into a £3 share £1 called up;

plus any other variations.

Why should such a step be necessary? The reasons are rather like the issue of bonus shares in reverse. In this case the share capital has got out of step with the assets, in that the share capital is not fully represented by assets. Thus Robert Ltd may have a balance sheet as follows:

Robert Ltd

Balance Sheet as at 31 December 19X7

	£
Net assets	30,000
Ordinary share capital	
10,000 ordinary shares of £5 each fully paid	50,000
Less Debit balance – profit and loss account	20,000
	30,000

The net assets are shown at £30,000, it being felt in this particular firm that the book value represented a true and fair view of their 'actual value'. The company will almost certainly be precluded from paying dividends until the debit balance on the profit and loss appropriation account has been eradicated and a credit balance brought into existence. Some firms, in certain circumstances, may still pay a dividend even though there is a debit balance, but it is to be assumed that Robert Ltd is not one of them. If profits remaining after taxation are now running at the rate of £3,000 per annum, it will be more than seven years before a dividend can be paid. As the normal basic reason for buying shares is to provide income, although there may well enter another reason such as capital appreciation, the denial of income to the shareholders for this period of time is serious indeed.

A solution would be to cancel, i.e. reduce, the capital which was no longer represented by assets. In this case there is £20,000 of the share capital which can lay no claim to any assets. The share capital should therefore be reduced by £20,000. This is done by making the shares into £3 shares fully paid instead of £5 shares. The balance sheet would become:

Robert Ltd
Balance Sheet as at 31 December 19X7

	£
Net assets	30,000
	30,000
Ordinary share capital	30,000
	30,000

Now that there is no debit balance on the profit and loss appropriation account the £3,000 available profit next year can be distributed as dividends.

Of course, the firm of Robert Ltd is very much a simplified version. Very often both preference and ordinary shareholders are involved and sometimes debenture holders as well. Even creditors occasionally sacrifice part of the amount owing to them, the idea being that the increase in working capital so generated will help the firm to achieve prosperity, in which case the creditors hope to enjoy the profitable contact that they used to have with the firm. The whole of these capital reduction schemes are matters of negotiation between the various interested parties. For instance, preference shareholders may be quite content for the nominal value of their shares to be reduced if the rate of interest they receive is increased. As with any negotiation the various parties will put forward their points of view and discussions will take place, until eventually a compromise solution is arrived at. When the court's sanction has been obtained, the accounting entries are:

(a) For amounts written off assets:
     Debit Capital reduction account.
     Credit Various asset accounts.
(b) For reduction in liabilities (e.g. creditors):
     Debit Liability accounts.
     Credit Capital reduction account.
(c) The reduction in the share capital:
     Debit Share capital accounts (each type).
     Credit Capital reduction account.
(d) If a credit balance now exists on the capital reduction account:
     Debit Capital reduction account (to close).
     Credit Capital reserve.

It is very unlikely that there would ever be a debit balance on the capital reduction account, as the court would very rarely agree to any such scheme which would bring about that result.

Capital reduction schemes for private companies will be used less frequently with the advent of powers to companies to purchase their own shares. The new powers given will normally be more suitable for private companies.

Where some of the assets are no longer needed

Where some of the firm's assets are no longer needed, probably due to a contraction in the firm's activities, a company may find itself with a surplus of liquid assets. Subject to the legal formalities being observed, in this case the reduction of capital is effected by returning cash to the shareholders, i.e.:

(*a*) *Debit*   Share capital account (with amount returnable).
    Credit Sundry shareholders.
(*b*) *Debit*   Sundry shareholders.
    Credit Bank (amount actually paid).

Such a scheme could be objected to by the creditors if it affected their interests.

New terms

Bonus shares (p. 189): Shares issued to existing shareholders free of charge. (Also known as 'scrip' issues.)

Rights issue (p. 191): Shares issued to existing shareholders at a price below their current market price.

Main points to remember

1 A limited company may alter its share capital if it is authorised to do so by its Articles of Association.

2 Alterations to share capital can be made by a limited company:
   (*a*) issuing new shares;
   (*b*) consolidating all or any of its share capital into shares of a higher nominal value;
   (*c*) converting paid-up shares into debentures and then reconverting the debentures back into shares of another denomination;
   (*d*) subdividing all or any of its share capital into shares of a lower nominal value;
   (*e*) cancelling shares that have not been 'taken up' – the difference between the 'authorised share capital' and the 'issued share capital'.

3 Where share capital is overvalued in relation to assets, a capital reduction scheme may be adopted in order to bring the share capital into line with the underlying asset value of the business as reported in the balance sheet.

Review questions

13.1 The Merton Manufacturing Co Ltd has been in business for many years making fitted furniture and chairs. During 19X4 and 19X5 substantial losses have been sustained on the manufacture of chairs and the directors have decided to concentrate on the fitted furniture side of the business which is expected to produce a profit of a least £22,500 per annum before interest charges and taxation. A capital reduction scheme has been proposed under which:
(*i*)   a new ordinary share of 50p nominal value will be created;
(*ii*) the £1 ordinary shares will be written off and the shareholders will be offered one new ordinary share for every six old shares held;
(*iii*) the £1 6 per cent redeemable preference shares will be cancelled and the holders will be offered for every three existing preference shares, one new ordinary share and £1 of a new 8 per cent debenture;
(*iv*) the existing 11½ per cent debenture will be exchanged for a new debenture yielding 8 per cent and in addition existing debenture holders will be offered one new ordinary share for every £4 of the old debenture held;
(*v*)   existing reserves will be written off;
(*vi*) goodwill is to be written off;

(*vii*) any remaining balance of write off which is necessary is to be achieved by writing down plant and equipment; and

(*viii*) existing ordinary shareholders will be invited to subscribe for two fully paid new ordinary shares at par for every three old shares held.

The balance sheet of the Merton Manufacturing Co Ltd immediately prior to the capital reduction is as follows:

	£	£
Fixed intangible assets		
Goodwill at cost less amounts written off		50,000
Fixed tangible assets		
Freehold land and buildings at cost		95,000
Plant and equipment at cost	275,000	
Less Depreciation to date	89,500	
		185,500
		330,500
Current assets		
Stocks	25,000	
Debtors	50,000	
	75,000	
Current liabilities	£	
Creditors	63,500	
Bank overdraft	15,850	
		79,350
Excess of current liabilities		(4,350)
		326,150
Long-term loan		
11½ per cent debenture, secured on the freehold land and buildings		100,000
		226,150
		£
Share capital and reserves		
£1 ordinary shares fully paid		90,000
6 per cent £1 redeemable preference shares fully paid		150,000
Share premium account		25,000
Profit and loss account		(38,850)
		226,150

On a liquidation, freehold land and buildings are expected to produce £120,000, plant and equipment £40,000, stocks £15,000 and debtors £45,000. Goodwill has no value.

There are no termination costs associated with ceasing the manufacture of chairs.

Required:

(*a*) Assuming that the necessary approval is obtained and that the new share issue is successful, produce a balance sheet of the company showing the position immediately after the scheme has been put into effect.

(*b*) Show the effect of the scheme on the expected earnings of the old shareholders.

(*c*) Indicate the points which a preference shareholder should take into account before voting on the scheme.

Corporation tax may be taken at 33⅓ per cent. The tax credit on dividends may be taken at 25 per cent.

(*Chartered Association of Certified Accountants*)

13.2 Deflation Ltd, which had experienced trading difficulties, decided to reorganise its finances.

On 31 December 19X5 a final trial balance extracted from the books showed the following position:

	£	£
Share capital, authorised and issued:		
150,000 6 per cent cumulative preference shares of £1 each		150,000
200,000 ordinary shares of £1 each		200,000
Share premium account		40,000
Profit and loss account	114,375	
Preliminary expenses	7,250	
Goodwill (at cost)	55,000	
Trade creditors		43,500
Debtors	31,200	
Bank overdraft		51,000
Leasehold property (at cost)	80,000	
,, (provision for depreciation)		30,000
Plant and machinery (at cost)	210,000	
,, (provision for depreciation)		62,500
Stock in hand	79,175	
	577,000	577,000

Approval of the Court was obtained for the following scheme for reduction of capital:

1   The preference shares to be reduced to £0.75 per share.
2   The ordinary shares to be reduced to £0.125 per share.
3   One £0.125 ordinary share to be issued for each £1 of gross preference dividend arrears; the preference dividend had not been paid for three years.
4   The balance on share premium account to be utilised.
5   Plant and machinery to be written down to £75,000.
6   The profit and loss account balance, and all intangible assets, to be written off.

At the same time as the resolution to reduce capital was passed, another resolution was approved restoring the total authorised capital to £350,000, consisting of 150,000 6 per cent cumulative preference shares of £0.75 each and the balance in ordinary shares of £0.125 each. As soon as the above resolutions had been passed 500,000 ordinary shares were issued at par, for cash, payable in full upon application.

You are required:
(a) to show the journal entries necessary to record the above transactions in the company's books; and
(b) to prepare a balance sheet of the company, after completion of the scheme.

(*Institute of Chartered Accountants*)

13.3   On 31 March 19X6 the following was the balance sheet of Finer Textiles.

Balance Sheet

	£	£
Fixed assets		
Goodwill and trade marks as valued	225,000	
Plant and machinery (at cost *less* depreciation)	214,800	
Furniture and fittings (at cost *less* depreciation)	12,600	
		452,400
Current assets:		
Stock-in-trade	170,850	
Sundry debtors	65,100	
Cash in hand	150	
		236,100
		688,500
Authorised capital:		
150,000 7 per cent preference shares of £1 each	150,000	
2,100,000 ordinary shares of £0.5 each	1,050,000	
		1,200,000
Issued and fully paid capital		
150,000 7 per cent preference shares of £1 each	150,000	
1,200,000 ordinary shares of £0.5 each	600,000	
		750,000
Capital reserve		48,000
		798,000
Deduct profit and loss account (debit balance)		183,900
		614,100
Current liabilities		
Sundry creditors		31,800
Bank overdraft		42,600
		688,500

The following scheme of capital reduction was sanctioned by the Court and agreed by the shareholders:

(*i*)   Preference shares were to be reduced to £0.75 each.

(*ii*)   Ordinary shares were to be reduced to £0.2 each.

(*iii*) The capital reserve was to be eliminated.

(*iv*) The reduced shares of both classes were to be consolidated into new ordinary shares of £1 each.

(*v*)   An issue of £150,000 8 per cent debentures at par was to be made to provide fresh working capital.

(*vi*) The sum written off the issued capital of the company and the capital reserve to be used to write off the debit balance of the profit and loss account and to reduce fixed assets by the following amounts:

Goodwill and trade marks	£210,000
Plant and machinery	£45,000
Furniture and fittings	£6,600

(*vii*) The bank overdraft was to be paid off out of the proceeds of the debentures which were duly issued and paid in full.

A further resolution was passed to restore the authorised capital of the company to 1,200,000 ordinary shares of £1 each.

Prepare journal entries (cash transactions to be journalised) to give effect to the above scheme and draw up the balance sheet of the company after completion of the scheme.

13.4A The balance sheet of Planners Ltd on 31 March 19X6 was as follows:

Balance Sheet

	£	£
Goodwill		20,000
Fixed assets		100,000
		120,000
Current assets:		
Stock	22,000	
Work in progress	5,500	
Debtors	34,000	
Bank	17,500	
		79,000
Capital expenses:		
Formation expenses		1,000
		200,000
Issued share capital:		
120,000 ordinary shares of £1 each		120,000
50,000 6 per cent cumulative preference shares of £1 each		50,000
		170,000
Less Profit and loss account debit balance		40,000
		130,000
6 per cent debentures		50,000
Current liabilities:		
Creditors		20,000
		200,000

The dividend on the preference shares is £9,000 in arrears. A scheme of reconstruction was accepted by all parties and was completed on 1 April 19X6.

A new company was formed, Budgets Ltd, with an authorised share capital of £200,000, consisting of 200,000 ordinary shares of £1 each. This company took over all the assets of Planners Ltd. The purchase consideration was satisfied partly in cash and partly by the issue, at par, of shares and debentures by the new company in accordance with the following arrangements:

1   The creditors of the old company received, in settlement of each £10 due to them, £7 in cash and three fully paid ordinary shares in the new company.
2   The holders of preference shares in the old company received seven fully paid ordinary shares in the new company to every eight preference shares in the old company and three fully paid ordinary shares in the new company for every £5 of arrears of dividend.
3   The ordinary shareholders in the old company received one fully paid share in the new company for every five ordinary shares in the old company.
4   The holders of 6 per cent debentures in the old company received £40 cash and £60 6 per cent debentures issued at par for every £100 debenture held in the old company.
5   The balance of the authorised capital of the new company was issued at par for cash and was fully paid on 1 April 19X6.
6   Goodwill was eliminated, the stock was valued at £20,000 and the other current assets were brought into the new company's books at the amounts at which they appeared in the old company's balance sheet. The balance of the purchase consideration represented the agreed value of the fixed assets.

You are required to show:
(*a*)   The closing entries in the realisation account and the sundry shareholders account in the books of Planners Ltd.
(*b*)   Your calculation of:
    (*i*)   the purchase consideration for the assets; and
    (*ii*)   the agreed value of the fixed assets.
(*c*)   The summarised balance sheet of Budgets Ltd as on 1 April 19X6.

13.5A The summarised balance sheet of Owens Ltd at 31 December 19X9 was as follows:

	£
Freehold premises	60,000
Plant	210,000
Stock	64,000
Debtors	70,000
Development expenditure	75,000
Cash at bank	6,000
Profit and loss account	85,000
	570,000
Issued capital:	
150,000 6 per cent preference shares of £1 each	150,000
300,000 ordinary shares of £1 each	300,000
Creditors	120,000
	570,000

A capital reduction scheme has been sanctioned under which the 150,000 preference shares are to be reduced to £0.75 each, fully paid, and the 300,000 ordinary shares are to be reduced to £0.10 each, fully paid.

Development expenditure and the debit balance on profit and loss account are to be written off, the balance remaining being used to reduce the book value of the plant.

Prepare the journal entries recording the reduction scheme and the balance sheet as it would appear immediately after the reduction. Narrations are not required in connection with journal entries.

14

Accounting Standards and related documents

Objectives

After you have studied this chapter, you should:

- *know of the measures being taken by the Accounting Standards Board to develop a framework for the preparation and presentation of financial statements*

- *be aware of the full range of accounting standards currently in issue, and of their aims and objectives*

14.1 Introduction

The external users of accounts need to be sure that reliance can be placed on the methods used by a business in calculating its profits and balance sheet values. In the late 1960s there was a general outcry that the methods used by different businesses were showing vastly different profits on similar data. In the UK, a controversy had arisen following the takeover of AEI Ltd by GEC Ltd. In fighting the takeover bid made by GEC, the AEI directors had produced a forecast, in the tenth month of their financial year, that the profit before tax for the year would be £10 million. After the takeover, the accounts of AEI for that same year showed a loss of £4.5 million. The difference was attributed to being £5 million as 'matters substantially of fact' and £9.5 million to 'adjustments which remain matters substantially of judgement'.

There was a general outcry in the financial pages of the national press against the failure of the accounting profession to lay down consistent principles for businesses to follow.

In December 1969, the Institute of Chartered Accountants in England and Wales issued a *Statement of Intent on Accounting Standards in the 1970s*. The Institute set up the Accounting Standards Steering Committee in 1970. Over the following six years, they were joined by the five other UK and Irish accountancy bodies and, in 1976, the committee became the Accounting Standards Committee (ASC). The six accountancy bodies formed the Consultative Committee of Accountancy Bodies (CCAB).

Prior to the issue of any accounting standard issued by the ASC, a great deal of preparatory work was done culminating in the publication of an exposure draft (ED). Copies of the exposure draft were then sent to those with a special interest in the topic. The journals of the CCAB also give full details of the exposure drafts. After full and proper consultation, when it was seen to be desirable, an accounting standard on the topic was issued. The Standards issued by the ASC were called Statements of Standard Accounting Practice (SSAPs).

Because the ASC had to obtain approval from its six professional accountancy body members, it did not appear to be as decisive and independent as was desired and, in 1990, a new body, the Accounting Standards Board (ASB), took over the functions of the ASC. The ASB is more independent of the accounting bodies and can issue its recommendations, known as Financial Reporting Standards (FRSs), without approval from any other body. The ASB has accepted the SSAPs in force and these will remain effective until replaced by an FRS. As with the ASC, the ASB issues exposure drafts – FREDs! – developed in a similar fashion to before.

While there is no general law compelling observation of the standards, accounting standards have had statutory recognition since the Companies Act 1989 was issued. As a result, apart from entities exempted from certain standards or sections within standards – SSAPs 13 (Research and development) and 25 (Segmental reporting), and FRS 1 (Cash flow statements), for example, all contain exemption clauses based on company size – accounting standards must be complied with when preparing financial statements intended to present a true and fair view. The Companies Acts state that failure to comply with the requirements of an accounting standard must be explained in the financial statements.

The main method of ensuring compliance with the standards has been through the professional bodies' own disciplinary procedures on their members. The ASB has, however, set up a Review Panel that has power to prosecute companies under civil law where their financial statements contain a major breach of the standards.

This book deals with the main outlines of all SSAPs and FRSs issued to October 1995. It does not deal with all the many detailed points contained in the standards and exposure drafts. It would be a far larger book if this was attempted. Students at the later stages of their professional examinations will need to get full copies of all standards and study them thoroughly (*see also* J Blake, *Accounting Standards* and A Sangster, *Workbook of Accounting Standards* (Pitman Publishing)).

This chapter deals with all the current SSAPs, FRSs and related documents which are not covered in detail elsewhere.

14.2 International Accounting Standards

The International Accounting Standards Committee (IASC) was established in 1973. Representatives from each of the founder members, which include the UK, sit on the committee, as well as co-opted members from other countries.

The need for an IASC has been said to be mainly due to the following:

(a) The considerable growth in international investment means it is desirable to have similar methods the world over so that investment decisions are more compatible.

(b) The growth in multinational firms which have to produce accounts covering a large number of countries. Standardisation between countries makes the accounting work easier, and reduces costs.

(c) As quite a few countries now have their own standard setting bodies, it is desirable that their efforts should be harmonised.

(d) For poor countries which cannot afford to have standard setting bodies, the IASC can help by letting them use the international standards instead of setting their own standards.

In the United Kingdom the FRSs have precedence over International Accounting Standards. In fact, most of the provisions of International Accounting Standards are incorporated into existing SSAPs or FRSs. Each FRS indicates the level of compliance with the relevant IAS.

14.3 Statement of Principles

In 1991, the Accounting Standards Board proposed a statement of the principles that underlie accounting and financial reporting. In its initial parts this closely followed the IASC text *Framework for the Preparation and Presentation of Financial Statements*. The objective of the ASB draft *Statement of Principles* is to assist the ASB, and all other users of financial statements, by clarifying the concepts that underlie the preparation and presentation of such statements. The *Statement of Principles* is not, however, an accounting standard and does not override any standard.

Scope

The ASB has indicated the following topics that will be covered in relation to financial statements (balance sheets, profit and loss accounts, cash flow statements and, following the issue of FRS 3: *Reporting financial performance*, the statement of total recognised gains and losses):

1 objectives;
2 attributes necessary to fulfil purpose;
3 elements making them up;
4 when items should be recognised;
5 how net resources and performance are measured and changes in these;
6 how items can best be presented;
7 the principles underlying consolidations and related matters.

The users identified by the ASB are the same as those shown in Chapter 34, and they are not reproduced here.

Objectives

'The objective of Financial Statements is to provide information about the financial position, performance and financial adaptability of an enterprise, that is useful to a wide range of users in making economic decisions.'

It is recognised, however, that financial statements alone will not be sufficient for economic decision making since they portray past events and may not include important non-financial information.

The assessment of management stewardship is also recognised, i.e. accountability of management for resources entrusted to it.

In covering the areas of financial position, performance and cash flow the *Statement of Principles* deals with those areas included in the analysis of accounts through ratios, e.g. liquidity and profitability, and indicates that the accounts should assist such analysis.

Qualitative characteristics of financial information

Exhibit 14.1 shows in diagrammatic form the structure adopted. The numbers in each box refer to explanations given below.

Note 1

Materiality means that if omission or mis-statement of some information would influence a decision, then it is material. Information which is not material is therefore not useful and beyond the threshold for inclusion.

Exhibit 14.1

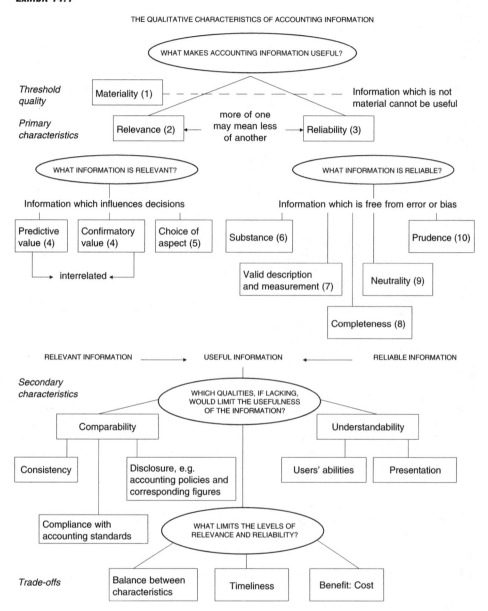

THE QUALITATIVE CHARACTERISTICS OF ACCOUNTING INFORMATION

Reproduced with the permission of the Accounting Standards Board

Note 2

To be useful, information must be relevant to the decision-taking needs of users. Relevance relates to the influence of the information on the user's evaluation of events – past, present or future. This evaluation can be influenced by the way items in accounts are presented.

Note 3

Reliability means information free from material error and bias and which can be relied on by users to conform with descriptions given.

It is clear that information may be very relevant but unreliable – e.g. a betting tip at a horse race. Reliability may not ensure relevance, e.g. reliable analysis of last year's performance may exclude very important indicators of future potential, such as new management in position. *Relevance* and *reliability* are primary characteristics of accounting information. They are broken down into further characteristics as follows:

Relevance
Note 4

Predictive value means using an analysis of current or past performance to predict a future outcome. The same information can be used to confirm whether predictions in past periods have come true.

Confirmatory value is this second part, i.e. checking past predictions.

Note 5

The term 'Choice of aspect' implies that there may be significant choice for the preparer of accounts as to which aspects of transactions to represent. For example, a business might acquire a new building in a good position for trading and on which it owns the freehold. Another relevant piece of information is that the property is in an area proposed for a new motorway and could well be the subject of a compulsory purchase order. To be relevant to a user who wishes to value the business for future prospects, both aspects of the information are relevant. Note that a simple statement that the property was owned and showing its purchase price would be a valid description and measurement and therefore reliable – so far as it went.

Reliability
Note 6

Substance indicates that information should represent the events it purports to represent. Sometimes complex legal arrangements may be entered into to obscure the ownership of assets. To be reliable the true operation and ownership of the assets re the substance must be reflected in the accounts. Artificial legal transactions should not obscure the substance.

Note 7

Although the title indicates the intention, it is important to relate this aspect of reliability to Note 5 'Choice of aspect'. 'Valid description and measurement' needs to be applied to the appropriate aspects of events.

Note 8

This indicates that incomplete information may make it false or misleading and thus not relevant.

Note 9

Neutrality implies freedom from bias. This indicates that accounts should not be prepared with the intention of influencing decisions in any particular way.

Note 10

Prudence is the concept already described in the earlier chapters and in relation to SSAP 2. It implies a degree of caution (anticipating losses) in the valuation of assets. In many cases this is subjective as it relates to the future, e.g. in predicting doubtful debts. This aspect should not be used to overestimate potential losses and thus misrepresent the affairs of an organisation.

In the second part of the chart, secondary characteristics which, if lacking, would limit the usefulness of the information are shown. The titles of these are self-explanatory and are not discussed further in this text.

14.4 SSAP 1: Accounting for associated companies

This standard is dealt with as a separate topic in Chapter 31 of this book.

14.5 SSAP 2: Disclosure of accounting policies

This standard, issued in 1971, does not set out to give a basic theoretical framework of accounting. It accepts the view that there may well be more than one accounting method which could be adopted in many cases, as the circumstances of different organisations will vary. Such varying practices may well be suitable in particular cases, but the users of accounting statements should be made aware of which practice has been used in each case.

SSAP 2 requires disclosure when the generally accepted accounting concepts are not complied with. The ones specifically mentioned as being generally applied are *accruals*, *consistency*, *going concern* and *prudence*. SSAP 2 does not mention other concepts and conventions generally recognised in the academic world, described in Volume 1, although it accepts that there are other concepts than the four mentioned. This has been confirmed since SSAP 2 was first issued, a number of other concepts having been formally introduced by the Companies Acts and other accounting standards: the Companies Act 1985 introduced the concept of 'separate determination' – each item included in the financial statements must be evaluated separately before being included in the total for its class. FRS 2: *Accounting for subsidiary undertakings* introduced the 'control' concept, and FRS 5: *Reporting the substance of transactions* introduced the 'substance over form' concept.

Accounting bases are the methods which could be used in applying the concepts. It should be recognised that these are subject to limitations imposed by adherence to legislation and accounting standards. At the same time, management must exercise its own judgement in choosing the bases to apply in their particular circumstances.

Accounting policies are the accounting bases judged by management to be the most appropriate. There should be a note attached to the accounts explaining the policies chosen. Five examples are given to illustrate where judgements may easily vary:

1 methods of depreciating fixed assets;
2 the valuation of stocks and of work-in-progress;
3 capitalisation of development expenditure;
4 the recognition of profit on long-term contracts;
5 hire purchase or instalment transactions.

14.6 SSAP 3: Earnings per share

This SSAP was revised both in 1974 and also by part of FRS 3: *Reporting financial performance*, issued in 1992. FRS 3 revised the definition of earnings per share. This is the new definition:

The profit in pence attributable to each equity share, based on the profit (or in the case of a group the consolidated profit) of the period after tax, minority interests and extraordinary items and after deducting preference dividends and other appropriations in respect of preference shares, divided by the number of equity shares in issue and ranking for dividend in respect of the period.

Students taking examinations which cover SSAP 3 in detail should read the actual standard. It gives detailed instruction as to how the following items shall be taken into account in the calculations: taxation charges; changes in capital structure; future dilutions of share capital.

Earnings per share (EPS) is a widely used stock market measure. The SSAP tries to bring about a more consistent method to aid comparability and reduce mis-understandings.

Basically, EPS is the profit per share calculated as follows:

	£	£
Profit on ordinary activities after taxation		XXXX
Extraordinary activities (less tax)		XXXX
		XXXX
Less Minority interest (see chapters on group accounts)	XXXX	
Preference dividends	XXXX	
		XXXX
Profit available to equity shareholders		XXXX

$$\text{EPS} = \frac{\text{Profit available to equity shareholders}}{\text{Number of equity shares}} = \text{EPS in pence}$$

As you will see later, minority interest only exists where the company controls another undertaking, and outsiders own part of that undertaking. Before the FRS 3 amendment, profits or losses from extraordinary activities were excluded, whereas they are now included.

14.7 SSAP 4: Accounting for government grants

Many different types of grant are or have been obtainable from government departments. Where these relate to revenue expenditure, e.g. subsidies on wages, they should be credited to revenue in the period when the revenue is incurred. The principle is that the grants should be recognised in the profit and loss account so as to match with the expenditure to which they are intended to contribute.

Where there are grants relating to capital expenditure, then SSAP 4 states that they should be credited to revenue *over the expected useful economic life of the asset*. This may be achieved by treating the amount of the grant as a deferred income, a portion of which is credited to the profit and loss account annually, over the life of the asset, on a basis consistent with depreciation. The amount of the deferred credit should, if material, be shown separately. It should not be shown as part of shareholders' funds.

The same effect as treating the grant as deferred income would be achieved by crediting the grant to the fixed asset account and depreciating only the net balance of the cost of the asset over its lifetime (depreciation is thus reduced by the grant). However, although this method is acceptable in principle, it is considered to be illegal under the Companies Act 1985, para. 17 of Schedule 4, which requires the balance sheet value of a fixed asset to be its purchase price or production cost.

14.8 SSAP 5: Accounting for value added tax

All that needs to be noted here is that Volume 1 of this book fully complies with SSAP 5. There is no need here to go into further detail.

14.9 SSAP 6: Extraordinary items and prior year adjustments

This standard has now been replaced by FRS 3 (*see* p. 235).

14.10 SSAP 7: Accounting for changes in the purchasing power of money

This was the original standard on inflation accounting, later replaced by SSAP 16.

14.11 SSAP 8: Treatment of tax under the imputation system

This can be understood by reference to Chapter 11 of this book which adheres throughout to this SSAP.

14.12 SSAP 9: Stocks and long-term contracts

Due to the many varying kinds of businesses and conditions in companies, there simply cannot be one system of valuation for stocks and work in progress. All that the standard can do is to narrow down the different methods that could be used.

Stocks should be stated at the total of the lower of cost and net realisable value of the separate items of stock or of groups of similar items. Profit should not, except in the case of long-term contracts, be recognised in advance, but immediate account should be made for anticipated losses.

In the balance sheet (or in the notes), stocks should be sub-classified so as to indicate the amounts held in each of the main categories in the standard balance sheet formats (as adapted where appropriate) of the Companies Act 1985. (These categories are *raw materials and consumables, work in progress, finished goods and goods for resale*, and *payments on account*.)

Net realisable value consists of the expected selling price less any expenses necessary to sell the product. This may be below cost because of obsolescence, deterioration and similar factors. SSAP 9 also defines 'cost' and certainly in the case of a manufacturing business it will also include overhead expenses, so that prime cost could not be used. **Cost** is defined in SSAP 9 in relation to the different categories of stocks and work in progress as being:

> *that expenditure which has been incurred in the normal course of business in bringing the product or service to its present location and condition. This expenditure should include, in addition to cost of purchase* [as defined later] *such costs of conversion* [as defined later] *as are appropriate to that location and condition.*

Cost of purchase comprises purchase price including import duties, transport and handling costs and any other directly attributable costs, less trade discounts, rebates and subsidies.

Cost of conversion comprises:

(a) costs which are specifically attributable to units of production, i.e. direct labour, direct expenses and subcontracted work;
(b) production overheads (as defined later);
(c) other overheads, if any, attributable in the particular circumstances of the business to bringing the product or service to its present location and condition.

Production overheads based on the normal level of activity, taking one year with another, should all be included including fixed production overheads. Obviously, neither selling nor general administration costs should be included in cost.

Notice that abnormal costs should not be included, as they should not have the effect of increasing stock valuation.

The LIFO and base stock methods should not be used, as they do not provide an up-to-date valuation. Although LIFO is not accepted by the SSAP, the Companies Act 1985 accepts its use.

The Standard does accept that replacement cost may, in certain circumstances, be acceptable and therefore the lower of replacement or net realisation value may be used since, again, this is in accord with the Companies Act 1985.

Long-term contract work

Chapter 19 of this book deals with long-term contracts.

14.13 SSAP 10: Statement of source and application of funds

This has been replaced by FRS 1: *Cash flow statements*, covered in Chapter 18 of this book.

14.14 SSAP 11: Deferred tax

The original standard on deferred tax, replaced in 1978 by SSAP 15 (*see* Chapter 11).

14.15 SSAP 12: Accounting for depreciation

This standard applies to all fixed assets, except for:

1 investment properties, dealt with in SSAP 19;
2 goodwill, dealt with in SSAP 22;
3 development costs, dealt with in SSAP 13;
4 investments.

First of all some terms are defined:

● **Depreciation:** is the measure of wearing out, consumption or other reduction in the useful economic life of a fixed asset whether arising from use, effluxion of time or obsolescence through technological or market changes.

- **Useful economic life:** of an asset is the period over which the present owner will derive economic benefits from its use.
- **Residual value:** is the realisable value of the asset at the end of its economic life, based on prices prevailing at the date of acquisition or revaluation, where this has taken place. Realisation costs should be deducted in arriving at residual values.
- **Recoverable amount:** is the greater of the net realisable value of an asset (at the date of the balance sheet) and where appropriate, the amount recoverable from its further use.

Depreciation should be provided in respect of all fixed assets which have a finite useful economic life. It should be provided by allocating the cost less net realisable value over the periods expected to benefit from the use of the asset being depreciated. No depreciation method is prescribed, but the method selected should be that which produces the most appropriate allocation of depreciation to each period in relation to the benefit being received in that period through use of the asset. The depreciation should be calculated on the value as shown on the balance sheet and not on any other figure. It *must* be charged against the profit and loss account, and *not* against reserves.

Useful economic lives should be reviewed on a regular basis, normally at least every five years. Where the amended asset life would materially distort future results if treated normally, it should be treated as an exceptional item as defined by FRS 3: *Reporting financial performance* and included under the same statutory format heading as the ongoing depreciation charge.

The depreciation method may only be changed when to do so will result in an improvement in the true and fair view. A change in method does not constitute a change in accounting policy. When the method is changed, the net book value should be depreciated over the remaining useful economic life of the asset, commencing with the period when the change occurred. Where a change of method occurs, the effect, if material, should be shown as a note attached to the financial statements.

Urgent Issues Task Force (UITF) Abstract 5, issued in July 1992, introduced rules relating to situations where current assets are included in the balance sheet at the lower of cost and net realisable value. Specifically, it addressed the question of an appropriate transfer value when a current asset becomes a fixed asset through its being retained for use on a continuing basis. (This could arise, for example, when a motor dealer removes a second-hand car from sale and provides it as a company car to the company secretary.) To avoid entities being able to effect transfers from current assets to fixed assets at above net realisable value and subsequently write down the value through a debit to a revaluation reserve, UITF 5 requires that all such transfers are done at the lower of cost and net realisable value, with any diminution in value at that point being charged in the profit and loss account.

Asset revaluation

Asset revaluation is recommended and if a policy of revaluation is adopted, the valuations should be kept up to date. Any permanent reduction should be written off immediately, the remainder being written off over the asset's remaining useful economic life. Such adjustments are via the profit and loss account.

Depreciation should be charged irrespective of when the asset was revalued. According to paragraph 21 of FRS 3: *Reporting financial performance*, the profit or loss on the disposal of an asset should be accounted for in the profit and loss account of the period in which the disposal occurs as the difference between the net sale proceeds and the net carrying amount, whether carried at historical cost (less any provisions made) or at a valuation.

An increased value arising from a revaluation does not mean that depreciation should not be charged. The new value is the one on which future depreciation should be based. Depreciation charged before revaluation should not be credited back to profit and loss.

Land and buildings

Freehold land

As this normally lasts forever there is no need to depreciate, unless subject to depletion or loss of value for reasons which may be applicable in certain circumstances, such as desirability of location, land erosion, extraction of minerals, dumping of toxic waste, etc.

It is rare to encounter circumstances under which freehold land should be subject to depreciation. The problem that most often occurs is the distinction between the cost/value of freehold land and the cost/value of the buildings upon it. SSAP 12 implies that the distinction should be made as only the buildings should be depreciated. Failure to separate the two elements of the cost/value will result in non-compliance with the standard.

Buildings

These should be depreciated, except that if the amount is not material and their life is expected to be very long then there will be no need to charge depreciation. If estimated residual value equals or is more than net value depreciation can be ignored.

Notes to accounts

The following should be disclosed:

1 method of depreciation used;
2 economic life or depreciation rate in use;
3 total depreciation for period;
4 depreciable assets – gross amount and accumulated depreciation.

14.16 SSAP 13: Accounting for research and development

SSAP 13 divides research and development expenditure under three headings, except for the location or exploitation of oil, gas or mineral deposits, or where all expenditure will be reimbursed by a third party. The three headings are:

(a) **pure (or basic) research:** experimental or theoretical work undertaken primarily to acquire new scientific or technical knowledge for its own sake rather than directed towards any specific aim or application;
(b) **applied research:** original or critical investigation undertaken in order to gain new scientific or technical knowledge and directed towards a specific practical aim or objective;
(c) **development:** use of scientific or technical knowledge in order to produce new or substantially improved materials, devices, products or services, to install new processes or systems prior to the commencement of commercial production or commercial applications, or to improve substantially those already produced or installed.

Expenditure incurred on pure and applied research can be regarded as part of a continuing operation required to maintain a company's business and its competitive position. In general, one particular period rather than another will not be expected to benefit and therefore it is appropriate that these costs should be written off as they are incurred.

The development of new and improved products is, however, distinguishable from pure and applied research. Expenditure on such development is normally undertaken with a reasonable expectation of specific commercial success and of future benefits arising from the work, either from increased revenue and related profits or from reduced costs. However, development expenditure should be written-off in the year of expenditure, except in the following circumstances when it may be deferred to future periods:

1 there is a clearly defined project; and
2 the related expenditure is separately identifiable; and
3 the outcome of such a project has been assessed with reasonable certainty as to:
   (a) its technical feasibility; and
   (b) its ultimate commercial viability considered in the light of factors such as:
        (i)   likely market conditions (including competing products);
        (ii)   public opinion;
        (iii) consumer and environmental legislation;
4 furthermore, a project will be of value only if:
   (a) the aggregate of the deferred development cost and any further development costs to be incurred on the same project together with related production, selling and administration costs is reasonably expected to be exceeded by related future revenues; and
   (b) adequate resources exist, or are reasonably expected to be available, to enable the project to be completed and to provide any consequential increases in working capital.

The elements of uncertainty inherent in the considerations set out in points 1 to 4 are considerable. There will be a need for different persons having differing levels of judgement to be involved in assessing the technical, commercial and financial viability of the project. Combinations of the possible different assessments which they might validly make can produce widely differing assessments of the existence and amounts of future benefits.

If these uncertainties are viewed in the context of the concept of prudence, the future benefits of most development projects would be too uncertain to justify carrying the expenditure forward. Nevertheless, in certain industries it is considered that there are numbers of major development projects that satisfy the stringent criteria set out above.

The Standard says that if the criteria are satisfied then expenditure may be deferred to the extent that its recovery can reasonably be regarded as assured. It is also required that where this policy is adopted, all projects meeting the criteria should be included.

If development costs are deferred, they should be amortised over the period of sale or use of the product.

At each accounting date the unamortised balance of development expenditure should be examined project by project to ensure that it still fulfils the criteria. Where any doubt exists as to the continuation of those circumstances the balance should be written-off.

Fixed assets may be acquired or constructed in order to provide facilities for research and/or development activities. The use of such fixed assets will usually extend over a number of accounting periods and accordingly they should be capitalised and written off over their usual life.

The Standard requires that accounting policy on research and development expenditure should be stated and explained. The total amount of research and development expenditure charged in the profit and loss account should be disclosed, analysed between the current year's expenditure and amounts amortised from deferred expenditure.

Movement on deferred expenditure and the amount carried forward at the beginning and end of the period should be disclosed. Deferred development expenditure should be disclosed under intangible fixed assets in the balance sheet.

14.17 SSAP 14: Group accounts

This Standard was replaced in 1992 by FRS 2: *Accounting for subsidiary undertakings* (*see* Chapter 31).

14.18 SSAP 15: Accounting for deferred taxation

The description of the methods of accounting for deferred taxation is given in Chapter 11. It follows SSAP 15 exactly and there is no need to repeat it here.

14.19 SSAP 16: Current cost accounting

The outlines of this outdated and suspended SSAP are given in Chapter 36 of this book.

14.20 SSAP 17: Accounting for post-balance sheet events

Quite often there will be events occurring after a balance sheet date which will provide evidence of the value of assets, or of the amounts of liabilities, as at the balance sheet date. Obviously any event up to the balance sheet date will have affected the balance sheet. Once the board of directors have formally approved the financial statements it becomes impossible to alter them. However, there is the period between these dates during which events may throw some light upon the valuation of assets or amounts of liabilities. SSAP 17 directs its attention to such events during this period.

SSAP 17 brings in two new terms – 'adjusting events' and 'non-adjusting events'.

Adjusting events

These are events which provide additional evidence relating to conditions existing at the balance sheet date. They require changes in amounts to be included in financial statements. Examples of adjusting events are now given:

(a) **Fixed assets.** The subsequent determination of the purchase price or of the proceeds of sale of assets purchased or sold before the year end.
(b) **Property.** A valuation which provides evidence of a permanent diminution in value.
(c) **Investments.** The receipt of a copy of the financial statements or other information in respect of an unlisted company which provides evidence of a permanent diminution in the value of a long-term investment.

(*d*) **Stocks and work in progress:**
    (*i*)   the receipt of proceeds of sales after the balance sheet date or other evidence concerning the net realisable value of stocks;
    (*ii*) the receipt of evidence that the previous estimate of accrued profit on a long-term contract was materially inaccurate.

(*e*) **Debtors.** The renegotiation of amounts owing by debtors, or the insolvency of a debtor.

(*f*) **Dividends receivable.** The declaration of dividends by subsidiaries and associated companies relating to periods prior to the balance sheet date of the holding company.

(*g*) **Taxation.** The receipt of information regarding rates of taxation.

(*h*) **Claims.** Amounts received or receivable in respect of insurance claims which were in the course of renegotiation at the balance sheet date.

(*i*) **Discoveries.** The discovery of errors or frauds which show that the financial statements were incorrect.

Non-adjusting events

These are events which arise after the balance sheet date and concern conditions which did not exist at that time. Consequently they do not result in changes in amounts in financial statements. They may, however, be of such materiality that their disclosure is required by way of notes to ensure that financial statements are not misleading. Examples of non-adjusting events which may require disclosure are now given:

(*a*) **Mergers and acquisitions.**

(*b*) **Reconstructions** and proposed reconstructions.

(*c*) **Issues** of shares and debentures.

(*d*) **Purchases and sales of fixed assets** and investments.

(*e*) **Loss of fixed assets** or stocks as a result of a catastrophe such as fire or flood.

(*f*) **Opening new trading activities** or extending existing trading activities.

(*g*) **Closing a significant part** of the trading activities if this was not anticipated at the year end.

(*h*) **Decline in the value** of property and investments held as fixed assets, if it can be demonstrated that the decline occurred after the year end.

(*i*) **Changes in rates of foreign exchange.**

(*j*) **Government action,** such as nationalisation.

(*k*) **Strikes** and other labour disputes.

(*l*) **Augmentation of pension benefits.**

14.21 SSAP 18: Accounting for contingencies

The definition given in SSAP 18 is that a contingency is:

> *a condition which exists at the balance sheet date, where the outcome will be confirmed only on the occurrence or non-occurrence of one or more uncertain future events. A contingent gain or loss is a gain or loss dependent on a contingency.*

The overriding concern is the concept of prudence. Quite simply, if one is in doubt then contingent losses must be taken into account but contingent gains are left out. If there is a material contingent loss then it should be accrued if it can be estimated with reasonable accuracy. Otherwise it should be disclosed by way of notes to the financial statements.

14.22 SSAP 19: Accounting for investment properties

Under the accounting requirements of SSAP 12: *Accounting for depreciation*, fixed assets are generally subject to annual depreciation charges to reflect on a systematic basis the wearing out, consumption or other loss of value whether arising from use, effluxion of time or obsolescence through technology and market changes. Under those requirements it is also accepted that an increase in the value of such a fixed asset does not generally remove the necessity to charge depreciation to reflect on a systematic basis the consumption of the asset.

A different treatment is, however, required where a significant proportion of the fixed assets of an enterprise is held not for consumption in the business operations but as investments, the disposal of which would not materially affect any manufacturing or trading operations of the enterprise. In such a case the current value of these investments, and changes in that current value, are of prime importance rather than a calculation of systematic annual depreciation. Consequently, for the proper appreciation of the financial position, a different accounting treatment is considered appropriate for fixed assets held as investments (called in this standard 'investment properties').

Investment properties may be held by a company which holds investments as part of its business such as an investment trust or a property investment company.

Investment properties may also be held by a company whose main business is not the holding of investments.

Where an investment property is held on a lease with a relatively short unexpired term, it is necessary to recognise the annual depreciation in the financial statements to avoid the situation whereby a short lease is amortised against the investment revaluation reserve whilst the rentals are taken to the profit and loss account.

This statement requires investment properties to be included in the balance sheet at open market value. The statement does not require the valuation to be made by qualified or independent valuers, but calls for disclosure of the names or qualifications of the valuers, the bases used by them and whether the person making the valuation is an employee or officer of the company. However, where investment properties represent a substantial proportion of the total assets of a major enterprise (e.g. a listed company) the valuation thereof would normally be carried out:

(*a*) annually by persons holding a recognised professional qualification and having recent post-qualification experience in the location and category of the properties concerned; and

(*b*) at least every five years by an external valuer.

14.23 SSAP 20: Foreign currency translation

The rules of SSAP 20 are already shown in Chapter 4 of this book. There is only need here for a few extra comments.

Hyper-inflation

If there is hyper-inflation the methods described in Chapter 4 may not give a fair view of the results. In these cases it may first of all be necessary to produce accounts adjusted for inflation. However, no guidance is provided in the standard as to how to define a 'high rate' of inflation or how to perform the adjustment to current price. UITF 9: *Accounting for operations in hyper-inflationary economies*, was issued in June 1993 in order to clarify this area.

UITF 9 confirmed that adjustments are required when the hyper-inflationary impact will affect the true and fair view. It also states that adjustments are required where the cumulative inflation rate over three years is approaching or exceeds 100 per cent – effectively a 'rule-of-thumb' definition of the term hyper-inflation.

It suggested two methods that could be adopted in order to eliminate the distortions caused by hyper-inflation. (If neither was deemed suitable, the reason(s) should be stated and another method should be adopted.) Either the local currency financial statements should be adjusted to reflect current price levels before being translated, or a relatively stable currency (e.g. the US dollar or sterling) should be used as the currency of measurement (the *functional* currency) for the relevant foreign operations. In the latter case, the functional currency would effectively be the *local* currency as defined in SSAP 20; and, if the transactions are not initially recorded in the functional currency, they must be measured in that currency by applying the temporal method based on the functional currency.

Hedging against exchange losses

Losses incurred may be set off against profits made in the computation of exchange dealings.

Disclosure

The method used to translate currencies should be disclosed. Net profits/net losses on translation must be disclosed, irrespective of whether they are shown in the profit and loss account or as a movement of reserves.

14.24 SSAP 21: Accounting for leases and hire purchase contracts

Details of SSAP 21 are given in Chapter 5.

14.25 SSAP 22: Accounting for goodwill

Although this is contained in Volume 1, it is repeated here for the benefit of those not having that volume in their possession. In addition, a note follows which is applicable for those who will be studying Chapters 21 to 31 on consolidated (group) financial statements.

A brief summary of SSAP 22 is as follows:

1   No amount should be attributed to non-purchased goodwill in the balance sheet of companies or groups.
2   Where goodwill is purchased, the account should be the difference between the fair value of the consideration given (the price paid) and the aggregate of the fair value of the net assets acquired.
3   The amount attributed to purchased goodwill should not include any value for intangible items. The amount paid for these should be included under the heading for intangible assets in the balance sheet.

4 Purchased goodwill should not remain on the balance sheet as a permanent item. It may either be:

(a) written-off immediately on acquisition against reserves; or

(b) amortised by charges against the profit and loss on ordinary activities over its useful economic life.

5 Where the fair value of the assets acquired exceeds the fair value of the consideration given (negative goodwill), the excess should be credited directly to reserves.

6 It should not be revalued but, if there is a permanent diminution in its value, it should be written-down immediately through the profit and loss account to its estimated recoverable amount.

Note: In the chapters dealing with consolidated financial statements, a figure for goodwill will often be calculated. It must be borne in mind that this is subject to the contents of SSAP 22 just as much as for a company simply buying the business of a sole trader or partnership.

14.26 SSAP 23: Accounting for acquisitions and mergers

This Standard was replaced by FRS 6: *Acquisitions and mergers* in 1994 (*see* Chapter 30).

14.27 SSAP 24: Accounting for pension costs

The details will have to be studied if you proceed to a higher level in accounting. Basically the objective is that the employer should recognise the expected cost of providing pensions on a 'systematic and rational basis' over the period during which he/she derives benefit from the employees' services.

14.28 SSAP 25: Segmental reporting

This Standard was introduced to help interpret the requirement of the Companies Act 1985 that the information in the accounts should be broken down (segmented) in two principal ways – by class of business and geographically. A **class of business** is a distinguishable component of an entity that provides a separate product or service. A **geographical segment** is an area comprising an individual country or group of countries in which an entity operates.

The main provisions of the Standard can be summarised in brief as follows. If an entity has two or more classes of business and operates in two or more geographical segments, then it should report for each class and segment:

(a) **turnover** – split between that to external activities and that to other segments;

(b) **result**, i.e. profit before taxation, minority interest and extraordinary items;

(c) **net assets**.

14.29 Statements of Recommended Practice and UITF Consensus Pronouncements

In 1986 the Accounting Standards Committee (ASC) issued the first Statement of Recommended Practice (SORP). It is important to note that they are different from accounting standards. Provisions in standards must be carried out, unless there is sufficient and adequate evidence to prove otherwise and, in addition, any non-compliance must be clearly stated. A SORP simply sets out what is considered to be the best practice on a particular topic, in respect of which it is not considered suitable to issue a standard at that time. Companies are simply encouraged to use the SORP. No action will be taken by the accounting bodies if a SORP is not followed.

A sub-category of SORPs was introduced, called 'franked SORPs'. Generally these refer to topics which are of limited application for a specific industry and they are not included in this text.

The Accounting Standards Board has announced that it will not issue its own SORPs. In the event that the ASB's own authority is required to standardise practice within a specialised industry, the ASB's preference is to issue an industry standard if the issue cannot be resolved under the existing accounting standards.

The ASB set up a committee in 1991 known as the Urgent Issues Task Force (UITF). This committee assists the ASB in areas where an accounting standard or Companies Act provision exists but where unsatisfactory or conflicting interpretations have developed or seem likely to do so. In these circumstances, the UITF issues a 'consensus pronouncement' (or 'abstract'). The ASB considers that compliance with consensus pronouncements will form an important element in detecting whether accounts give a true and fair view. Consequently, they have the same status as accounting standards and *must* be observed. As at October 1995, 13 UITF Abstracts had been issued, of which ten were still in force (the others having been withdrawn following the issue of FRSs 3 and 4). Wherever appropriate, UITFs are included in this book when the topic to which they relate is being discussed.

14.30 FRS 1: Cash flow statements

See Chapter 18.

14.31 FRS 2: Accounting for subsidiary undertakings

See Chapter 31.

14.32 FRS 3: Reporting financial performance

See Chapter 15, p. 235.

14.33 FRS 4: Capital instruments

FRS 4 is concerned with accounting for capital instruments by the entities that issue them. A capital instrument is anything issued to raise finance. This includes shares, debentures, loans and debt instruments, and options and warrants that give the holder the right to subscribe for or obtain capital instruments. The term includes those issued by subsidiaries, except when held by another member of the group. Leases, warrants issued under employee share schemes, and equity shares issued as part of a business combination that is accounted for as a merger are not covered by FRS 4. Nor are investments in capital instruments issued by other entities.

The objective of FRS 4 is to ensure that financial statements provide a clear, coherent and consistent treatment of capital instruments, in particular in relation to:

- the classification of capital instruments;
- treating the costs associated with capital instruments in a manner consistent with their classification (and allocated to accounting periods on a fair basis over the period the instrument is in issue, in the case of redeemable instruments);
- ensuring that financial statements provide relevant information concerning the nature and amount of the entity's sources of finance and the associated costs, commitments and potential commitments.

All capital instruments should be accounted for in the balance sheet within one of the following categories:

- shareholders' funds;
- liabilities; or, for consolidated financial statements,
- minority interests.

Shares and warrants should be reported as part of shareholders' funds. When issued, the net proceeds should be reported in the reconciliation of movements in shareholders' funds. When repurchased or redeemed, shareholders' funds should be reduced by the value of the consideration given. The balance sheet should show the total amount of shareholders' funds, analysed between the amount attributable to non-equity interests (i.e. the aggregate of amounts relating to all classes of non-equity shares and warrants for non-equity shares) and the amount attributable to equity interests (i.e. the difference between total shareholders' funds and the total amount attributable to non-equity interests). When the entitlement to dividends in respect of non-equity shares is calculated by reference to time, the dividends should be reported as appropriations of profit and accounted for on an accruals basis except when ultimate payment is remote (for example, when profits are insufficient to justify a dividend and the dividend rights are non-cumulative). Where the finance costs of non-equity shares are not equal to the dividends, the difference should be accounted for in the profit and loss account as an appropriation of profit. The finance costs for non-equity shares should be calculated on the same basis as the finance costs for debt.

All capital instruments other than shares should be classified as liabilities if they contain an obligation to transfer economic benefits. Otherwise, they should be reported within shareholders' funds. Convertible debt should be reported separately within liabilities from non-convertible debt. Debt should be analysed on the basis of its maturity distinguishing between debt with up to one year, one to five years, and five or more years to maturity, maturity being determined on the basis of the earliest date on which the lender can require payment. The finance cost of convertible debt should be calculated on the basis that the debt will never be converted. When converted, the amount recognised in shareholders' funds in respect of the shares issued should be the amount at which the liability for the debt is stated at the date of conversion, and therefore no gain or loss should be recognised. When issued, debt should be stated at the amount of the net proceeds and its finance cost should be allocated over the term of the debt at a constant rate on the carrying amount, charged in the profit and loss account (unless the entity is an investment company, in which case it may be included in the statement of total gains and losses to the extent that it relates to capital). The carrying amount of debt should be increased by the finance cost in respect of the reporting period and reduced by payments made in respect of the debt in that period. Accrued finance costs may be included in accruals (rather than in the carrying amount of debt) to the extent that the period costs have accrued in one period and will be paid in cash in the next. However, in the event that the debt is repurchased or settled early, any such accrual should be included in the carrying amount of the debt for the purposes of calculating finance costs and gains and losses on the transaction, and any such gains or losses should be recognised in the profit and loss account in the period during which the transaction occurs.

Where subsidiaries have issued shares outside the group, those shares should be reported as minority interests, unless the group as a whole has an obligation to transfer economic benefit in connection with the shares. In such cases, they should be accounted for as liabilities within the consolidated financial statements. The amount of minority interests in the balance sheet should be split between the amounts attributable to equity and non-equity interests, the calculation of the amounts attributed to non-equity minority interests (and their associated finance costs) being calculated in the same way as those for non-equity shares. The finance costs associated with such interests should be included in minority interests in the profit and loss account.

14.34 FRS 5: Reporting the substance of transactions

The purpose of FRS 5 is to ensure that the substance of an entity's transactions is reported in its financial statements. The commercial effect of the entity's transactions, and any resulting assets, liabilities, gains or losses, should be faithfully represented in its financial statements.

The standard does not apply to:

- forward contracts and futures;
- foreign exchange and interest rate swaps;
- contracts where a net amount will be paid or received based on a movement in a price or an index;
- expenditure commitments and orders placed, until the earlier of delivery or payment;
- employment contracts.

In determining the substance of a transaction, all its aspects and implications should be identified and greater weight given to those more likely to have a commercial effect in practice. Where a group or series of transactions achieve, or are intended to achieve, an overall commercial effect, they should be viewed as a whole, not as individual transactions.

The substance of a transaction depends upon whether it has given rise to new assets or liabilities for the reporting entity, and whether it has changed the entity's existing assets and liabilities. An entity has rights or other access to benefits (and therefore has an asset) if the entity is exposed to the risks inherent in the benefits, taking into account the likelihood of those risks having a commercial effect. Evidence that an obligation to transfer benefits (i.e. a liability) exists is shown if there is some circumstance in which the entity cannot avoid, legally or commercially, an outflow of benefits.

Where an asset or a liability results from a transaction, it should be recognised in the balance sheet if there is sufficient evidence of its existence (including, where relevant, any future inflow or outflow of benefit), and if it can be measured at a monetary amount with sufficient reliability.

Where transactions have no significant effect upon either the entity's rights or other access to benefits arising from a previously recognised asset, or to the entity's exposure to the risks inherent in those benefits, the entire asset should continue to be recognised.

When the transactions transfer *all* the significant rights or other access to benefits *and all* the significant exposure to risk, the entire asset should cease to be recognised. Where a stage between nil and full effect is found, and it is a significant change, the description or monetary amounts relating to an asset should be changed and a liability recognised for any obligations to transfer benefits that are assumed. However, the standard also states that this partial case arises in only three situations:

1 a transfer of only part of the item;
2 a transfer of all of the item for only part of its life;
3 a transfer of all of the item for all of its life but where the entity retains some significant right to benefits or exposure to risk.

Where a transaction is in substance a financing of a recognised asset (whether previously recognised or not) the finance should be shown deducted from the gross amount of the item it finances on the face of the balance sheet within a single asset caption of 'linked presentation'. The gross amounts of both the item and the finance should be shown on the face of the balance sheet. Profit on a linked presentation should be recognised on entering into the arrangement only to the extent that the non-returnable proceeds received exceed the previous carrying value of the item. Thereafter, any profit or loss arising should be recognised in the period in which it arises, both in the profit and loss account and in the notes.

Assets and liabilities should not be offset, except where they do not constitute separate assets and liabilities.

Where an entity has a quasi-subsidiary (i.e. a company, trust, partnership or other vehicle that is directly or indirectly controlled by the reporting entity, but that is not a subsidiary, and which gives rise to benefits for the reporting entity that are in substance no different from those that would arise were the vehicle a subsidiary) the substance of the transactions entered into by the quasi-subsidiary should be reported in the consolidated statements. The fact that a quasi-subsidiary has been included in the consolidated financial statements should be disclosed and a summary of the financial statements of the quasi-subsidiary should be provided in the notes.

Disclosure of a transaction in the financial statements should be sufficient to enable the user of those statements to understand its commercial effect. Where a transaction has resulted in the recognition of assets or liabilities whose nature differs from that of items usually included under the relevant balance sheet heading, the differences should be explained.

14.35 FRS 6: Acquisitions and mergers

See Chapter 30.

14.36 FRS 7: Fair values in acquisition accounting

See Chapter 27.

14.37 FRS 8: Related party disclosures

This FRS requires disclosure of all material related party transactions. The FRS extends the disclosure requirements contained in the Companies Acts, thus providing guidance in an area that had previously not been covered adequately by either statute or the Stock Exchange rules.

Main points to remember

1 Accounting standards have statutory recognition and must, therefore, be complied with when preparing financial statements intended to present a true and fair view.

2 As at October 1995, there were 25 Accounting Standards (18 SSAPs and 7 FRSs) and 10 UITF Abstracts in force.

Review questions

14.1 In preparing its accounts for the year to 31 May 19X7, Whiting plc had been faced with a number of accounting problems, the details of which were as follows:

(i) The company had closed down its entire American operations which represented a significant part of Whiting plc's business.

(ii) The corporation tax for the year to 31 May 19X6 had been over-provided by £5,000.

(iii) Land and buildings had been revalued at an amount well in excess of the historic cost (note: the current value is to be adjusted in the accounts).

(iv) A trade debtor had gone into liquidation owing Whiting plc an amount equivalent to 20 per cent of Whiting's turnover for the year. It is highly unlikely that any of this debt will ever be repaid.

(v) During the year, the company changed its method of valuing stock. If the same method had been adopted in the previous year, the profits for that year would have been considerably less than had previously been reported.

Required:

(a) being careful to give your reasons, explain how each of the above matters should be treated in the financial statements of Whiting plc for the year to 31 May 19X7 if the company follows the requirements of FRS 3; and

(b) outline the provisions of SSAP 22 (accounting for goodwill) for the treatment of both non-purchased and purchased goodwill in the balance sheets of companies and groups of companies.

(*Association of Accounting Technicians*)

14.2 The directors are preparing the published accounts of Dorman plc for the year to 31 October 19X5. The following information is provided for certain of the items which are to be included in the final accounts.

(i) *Stocks of raw material, monolite:*

	£
Cost	26,500
Replacement cost	48,100

(ii) *Stocks of finished goods:*

	Paramite £	Paraton £
Direct costs	72,600	10,200
Proportion of fixed factory overhead	15,300	4,600
Proportion of selling expenses	6,870	1,800
Net realisable value	123,500	9,520

(iii) *Plant and machinery.* An item of plant was shown in the 19X4 accounts at a net book value of £90,000 (£160,000 cost less accumulated depreciation £70,000). The plant was purchased on 1 November 19X2 and has been depreciated at 25 per cent reducing balance. The directors now consider the straight line basis to be more appropriate: they have estimated that at 1 November 19X4 the plant had a remaining useful life of six years and will possess zero residual value at the end of that period.

(iv) *Freehold property.* The company purchased a freehold property for £250,000 11 years ago, and it is estimated that the land element was worth £50,000 at that date.

The company has never charged depreciation on the property but the directors now feel that it should have done so; the building is expected to have a total useful life of forty years.

(v)   *Research expenditure:* incurred in an attempt to discover a substitute for raw materials currently purchased from a politically sensitive area of the world amounted to £17,500 during the year.

(vi) *Development expenditure:* on Tercil, which is nearly ready for production, amounted to £30,000. Demand for Tercil is expected significantly to exceed supply for at least the next four years.

(vii) *Accident.* On 1 December 19X5 there was a fire in the warehouse which damaged stocks, other than the items referred to in (i) and (ii) above. The book value of these stocks was £92,000. The company has discovered that it was under-insured and only expects to recover £71,000 from the insurers.

(viii) *Investments.* Dorman purchased 30,000 ordinary shares in Lilleshall Ltd on 1 November 19X4 for £96,000, and immediately succeeded in appointing two of its directors to Lilleshall's board. The issued share capital of Lilleshall consists of 100,000 ordinary shares of £1 each. The profits of Lilleshall for the year to 31 October 19X5 amounted to £40,000. (Ignore taxation.)

Required:
Explain how each of the above items should be dealt with in the published financial statements of Dorman plc.

(*Institute of Chartered Secretaries and Administrators*)

14.3A In preparing the published financial statements of a company, briefly state the significant accounting/disclosure requirements you would have in mind in ensuring that the financial statements comply with best accounting practice as embodied in accounting standards concerning:

(a) Value added tax.
(b) Earnings per share.
(c) The disclosure requirements of each major class of depreciable assets.
(d) Research expenditure.
(e) Capital-based grants relating to fixed assets.
(f) Goodwill on consolidation.
(g) The disclosure requirements relating to generally accepted fundamental accounting concepts.
(h) The accounts of a subsidiary undertaking having similar activities to that of the parent undertaking.

(*Association of Accounting Technicians*)

14.4A   Oldfield Enterprises Limited was formed on 1 January 19X5 to manufacture and sell a new type of lawn mower. The bookkeeping staff of the company have produced monthly figures for the first ten months to 31 October l9X5 and from these figures together with estimates for the remaining two months, Barry Lamb, the managing director, has drawn up a forecast profit and loss account for the year to 31 December 19X5 and a balance sheet as at that date.

These statements together with the notes are submitted to the board for comment. During the board meeting discussion centres on the treatment given to the various assets. The various opinions are summarised by Barry Lamb who brings them, with the draft accounts, to you as the company's financial adviser.

Oldfield Enterprises Ltd

Draft Profit and Loss Account for the year to 31 December 19X5

	£000s	£000s
Sales		3,000
Cost of sales		1,750
Gross profit		1,250
Administration overheads	350	
Selling and distribution overheads	530	
		880
Net profit before taxation		370

Draft Balance Sheet at 31 December 19X5

Fixed assets – tangible	Cost £000s	Depreciation and amortisation £000s	Net £000s
Leasehold land and buildings	375	125	250
Freehold land and buildings	350	–	350
Plant and machinery	1,312	197	1,115
	2,037	322	1,715
Fixed assets – intangible			
Research and development			375
Current assets			
Stock		375	
Debtors		780	
		1,155	
Current liabilities			
Creditors	250		
Bank overdraft	125	375	
			780
			2,870
Share capital			2,500
Net profit for year			370
			2,870

Notes

(a) Administration overheads include £50,000 written-off research and development.

(b) The lease is for 15 years and cost £75,000. Buildings have been put up on the leasehold land at a cost of £300,000. Plant and machinery has been depreciated at 15 per cent. Both depreciation and amortisation are included in cost of sales.

Opinions put forward

Leasehold land and buildings:

The works director thinks that although the lease provides for a rent review after three years the buildings have a 50-year life. The buildings should therefore be depreciated over 50 years and the cost of the lease should be amortised over the period of the lease.

The managing director thinks that because of the rent review clause the whole of the cost should be depreciated over three years.

The sales director thinks it is a good idea to charge as much as the profits will allow in order to reduce the tax bill.

Freehold land and buildings:
The works director thinks that as the value of the property is going up with inflation no depreciation is necessary.

The sales director's opinion is the same as for leasehold property.

The managing director states that he has heard that if a property is always kept in good repair no depreciation is necessary. This should apply in the case of his company.

Plant and machinery:
The managing director agrees with the 15 per cent for depreciation and proposes to use the reducing balance method.

The works director wants to charge 25 per cent straight line.

Research and development:
The total spent in the year will be £425,000. Of this £250,000 is for research into the cutting characteristics of different types of grass, £100,000 is for the development of an improved drive system for lawn mowers and £75,000 is for market research to determine the ideal lawn mower characteristics for the average garden.

The managing director thinks that a small amount should be charged as an expense each year.

The works director wants to write-off all the market research and 'all this nonsense of the cutting characteristics of grass'.

The sales director thinks that, as the company has only just started, all research and development expenditure relates to future sales so all this year's expenditure should be carried forward.

Stock:
Both the managing director and the works director are of the opinion that stock should be shown at prime cost.

The sales director's view is that stocks should be shown at sales price as the stock is virtually all sold within a very short period.

Required:
(a) You are asked to comment on each opinion stating what factors should be taken into account to determine suitable depreciation and write off amounts.
(b) Indicate what amounts should, in your opinion, be charged to profit and loss and show the adjusted profit produced by your recommendations, stating clearly any assumptions you may make.

(*Chartered Association of Certified Accountants*)

14.5 The accountant of Hook, Line and Sinker, a partnership of seven people, has asked your advice in dealing with the following items in the partnership accounts for the year to 31 May 19X7.
(a) (i) Included in invoices prepared and dated in June 19X7 were £60,000 of goods despatched during the second half of May 19X7.
  (ii) Stocks of components at 31 May 19X7 include parts no longer used in production. These components originally cost £50,000 but have been written-down for purposes of the accounts to £25,000. Scrap value of these items is estimated to be £1,000. Another user has expressed interest in buying these parts for £40,000.
(b) After May 19X7 a customer who accounts for 50 per cent of Hook, Line and Sinker sales suffered a serious fire which has disrupted his organisation. Payments for supplies are becoming slow and Hook, Line and Sinker sales for the current year are likely to be substantially lower than previously. This customer owed £80,000 to Hook, Line and Sinker at 31 May 19X7.
(c) During the year to 31 May Hook, Line and Sinker commenced a new advertising campaign using television and expensive magazine advertising for the first time. Sales

during the year were not much higher than previous years as the partners consider that the effects of advertising will be seen in future years.

Expenditure on advertising during the year is made up of:

	£
Television	50,000
Advertisements in magazines	60,000
Advertisements in local papers	25,000

All the expenditure has been treated as expense in the accounts but the partners wish to carry forward three-quarters of the television and magazine costs as it is expected that this cost will benefit future years' profits and because this year's profits will compare unfavourably with previous years if all the expenditure is charged in the accounts.

(d) Three projects for the construction of sinkers have the following cost and revenue characteristics:

	Project A	Project B	Project C
Degree of completion	75%	50%	15%
	£	£	£
Direct costs to date	30,000	25,000	6,000
Sales price of complete project	55,000	50,000	57,500
Overheads allocated to date	4,000	2,000	500
Costs to complete – Direct	10,000	25,000	40,000
– Overheads	2,000	2,000	3,000

No profits or losses have been included in the accounts.

(e) After considerable discussion with management, the sales of a newly developed special purpose hook have been given the following probabilities:

First year of production

Sales	Probability
£	
15,000	0.2
30,000	0.5
40,000	0.3

Second year of production

Increase over first year	Probability
£	
10,000	0.1
20,000	0.5
30,000	0.4

Second year sales may be assumed independent of first year levels.

Cost-volume-profit analysis shows that the breakeven point is £50,000.

Production of the special purpose hook started prior to the end of the accounting year and stocks of the finished product are included at cost amounting to £20,000. It has been decided that if there is less than 0.7 probability of breakeven being reached in the second year then stocks should be written down by 25 per cent.

(f) During the year it was discovered that some stock sheets had been omitted from the calculations at the previous year end. The effect is that opening stock for the current year, shown as £35,000, should be £42,000. No adjustment has yet been made.

Required:

Discuss the treatment of each item with reference to relevant accounting standards and accounting concepts and conventions. Recommend the appropriate treatment for each item showing the profit effect of each recommendation made.

(*Chartered Association of Certified Accountants*)

14.6 The chief accountant of Uncertain Ltd is not sure of the appropriate accounting treatment for a number of events occurring during the year 19X5/6.

(*i*) A significant number of employees have been made redundant, giving rise to redundancy payments of £100,000 which have been included in manufacturing cost of sales.

(*ii*) One of Uncertain Ltd's three factories has been closed down. Closure costs amounted to £575,000. This amount has been deducted from reserves in the balance sheet.

(*iii*) The directors have changed the basis of charging depreciation on delivery vehicles. The difference between the old and new methods amounts to £258,800. This has been charged as a prior period adjustment.

(*iv*) During October 19X6 a fire occurred in one of the remaining factories belonging to Uncertain Ltd and caused an estimated £350,000 of additional expenses. This amount has been included in manufacturing cost of sales.

(*v*) It was discovered on 31 October 19X6 that a customer was unable to pay his debt to the company of £125,000. The £125,000 was made up of sales in the period July to September 19X6. No adjustment has been made in the draft accounts for this item.

Uncertain Ltd

Draft Profit and Loss Account for the year ended 30 September 19X6

	£	£
Sales		5,450,490
Manufacturing cost of sales		3,284,500
Gross profit		2,165,990
Administration expenses	785,420	
Selling expenses	629,800	
		1,415,220
		750,770
Corporation tax (50%)		375,385
		375,385
Proposed dividend on ordinary shares		125,000
		250,385
Prior period adjustment	258,800	
Corporation tax	129,400	
		129,400
		120,985

Required:

(*a*) Write a report to the chief accountant of Uncertain Ltd with suggestions for appropriate treatment for each of the items (*i*) to (*iv*), with explanations for your proposals.

(*b*) Amend the draft profit and loss account to take account of your proposals.

(*Chartered Association of Certified Accountants*)

14.7 With reference to SSAP 17 (Accounting for post balance sheet events) and SSAP 18 (Accounting for contingencies):

(*a*) define the following terms:
  (*i*) post-balance sheet events;
  (*ii*) adjusting events;
  (*iii*) non-adjusting events; and
  (*iv*) contingent gain/loss;

(*b*) give FOUR examples of adjusting events, and FOUR examples of non-adjusting events; and

(*c*) state how
  (*i*) a material contingent loss, and
  (*ii*) material contingent gains should be accounted for in financial statements.

(*Association of Accounting Technicians*)

15

The final accounts of limited companies: profit and loss accounts, related statements and notes

Objectives

After you have studied this chapter, you should:

- be aware of the alternative presentation formats available under the Companies Acts that must be used when preparing profit and loss accounts for external reporting purposes

- know how to present information under the most commonly used of the Companies Act formats

- be aware of the differences between the statutory format and formats generally adopted for internal use

- be aware of the FRS 3 requirements that relate to the profit and loss account concerning:
  - continuing operations
  - acquisitions
  - discontinued operations
  - sale or termination of an operation
  - reorganisation and restructuring costs
  - profits and losses on disposal of fixed assets
  - exceptional and extraordinary items
  - prior period adjustments

- be aware of the impact of FRS 3 upon the Companies Act format

- be aware of the format of the Statement of Total Recognised Gains and Losses

- be aware of the format of the Note of Historical Cost Profits and Losses

15.1 Introduction

When a company draws up its own final accounts, purely for internal use by directors and the management, it can draft them in any way it wishes. Students should be aware that drawing up a trading and profit and loss account and balance sheet for the firm's own use is not necessarily the same as drawing up such accounts for examination purposes. If a firm wishes to charge something in the trading account which perhaps in theory ought to be shown in the profit and loss account, then there is nothing to prevent the firm from so doing. The examinee, on the other hand, must base his/her answers on accounting theory and not on the practice of his/her own firm.

When it comes to publication, i.e. when the final accounts are sent to the shareholder or to the Registrar of Companies, then the Companies Acts lay down the information which must be shown, and also how it should be shown. Prior to 1981, provided the necessary information was shown it was completely up to the company exactly how it did so. The provisions of the 1981 Act brought the United Kingdom into line with the Fourth Directive of the EC, and the freedom previously available to companies on how to show the information was removed. There are, however, some advantages to be gained from such standardisation.

15.2 Layout of accounts

The Companies Acts do, nevertheless, give companies the choice of two alternative formats (layouts) for balance sheets, and four alternative formats for profit and loss accounts. As the reader for this chapter will most probably be studying this for the first time, it would be inappropriate to give all the details of all the formats. Only the far more advanced student would need such details. In this book, therefore, the reader will be shown an internal profit and loss account which can easily be adapted to cover publication requirements under the Acts, along with a balance sheet.

All companies, even the very smallest, have to produce accounts for shareholders giving the full details required by the Acts. 'Small' and 'medium-sized' companies can, however, file summarised accounts with the Registrar of Companies, but they must still prepare full accounts for their shareholders. In addition, listed companies may send their shareholders summary financial statements in place of the full version, unless a shareholder specifically requests a full version. These points will be examined later.

(Currently, a 'small' company is one for which two of the following are true: turnover does not exceed £2.8 million; the balance sheet total does not exceed £1.4m; the average number of employees does not exceed 50. For 'medium-sized' companies, the equivalent limits are £11.2 million, £5.6 million, and 250 employees.)

Of the four formats which could be used, the format that will be used for the published profit and loss account in this book is Format 1. It is in a vertical style, which is much more modern and also more likely to gain extra marks from examiners and, in addition, it is much more like common UK practice before 1981. The other Formats, not shown in this book, are Format 2 (vertical style) and Formats 3 and 4 (horizontal style).

15.3 Format 1

The Companies Acts show Format 1 as in Exhibit 15.1.

Exhibit 15.1

Profit and loss account

Format 1

1 Turnover
2 Cost of sales
3 Gross profit or loss
4 Distribution costs
5 Administrative expenses
6 Other operating income
7 Income from shares in group undertakings
8 Income from participating interests
9 Income from fixed asset investments
10 Other interest receivable and similar income
11 Amounts written off investments
12 Interest payable and similar charges
13 Tax on profit or loss on ordinary activities
14 Profit or loss on ordinary activities after taxation
15 Extraordinary income
16 Extraordinary charges
17 Extraordinary profit or loss
18 Tax on extraordinary profit or loss
19 Other taxes not shown under the above items
20 Profit or loss for the financial year

This is simply a list and it does not show where sub-totals should be placed. The important point is that the items 1 to 20 have to be displayed in that order. If some items do not exist for the company in a given year, then those headings will be omitted from the published profit and loss account. Thus, if the company has no investments, items 7, 8, 9, 10, and 11 will not exist, and item 6 will be followed by item 12 in that company's published profit and loss account. The category reference numbers on the left-hand side of items do not have to be shown in the published accounts.

15.4 Accounts for internal use

Exhibit 15.2 shows a trading and profit and loss account drawn up for internal use by a company. There are no statutory rules concerning how financial statements are drawn up for internal use. However, if the internal accounts were drawn up in a completely different fashion to those needed for publication, then there would be quite a lot of work needed in order to reassemble the figures into a profit and loss account for publication. In Exhibit 15.2 the internal accounts have been drawn up in a style which makes it much easier to get the figures for the published profit and loss account. Examination questions on this topic often ask for both (*a*) internal and (*b*) published accounts and it therefore makes it simpler for students if the internal and published accounts follow a similar order of display.

Exhibit 15.2 (accounts for internal use)

Block plc

Trading and Profit and Loss Account for the year ended 31 December 19X6

	£000	£000	£000
Turnover			800
Less Cost of sales:			
Stock 1 January 19X6		100	
Add Purchases		525	
		625	
Less Stock 31 December 19X6		125	500
Gross profit			300
Distribution costs:			
Salaries and wages	30		
Motor vehicle costs: Distribution	20		
General distribution expenses	5		
Depreciation: Motors	3		
Machinery	2	60	
Administrative expenses			
Salaries and wages	25		
Motor vehicle costs: Administration	2		
General administration expenses	7		
Auditors' remuneration	2		
Depreciation: Motors	3		
Machinery	1	40	
			100
			200
Other operating income			30
			230
Income from shares in group undertakings		20	
Income from participating interests		10	
Income from shares from non-related companies		5	
Other interest receivable		15	
			50
Amounts written off investments			280
		4	
Interest payable:			
Loans repayable within five years	10		
Loans repayable in ten years' time	6		
		16	
			20
Profit on ordinary activities before taxation			260
Tax on profit on ordinary activities			95
Profit on ordinary activities after taxation			165
Retained profits brought forward from last year			60
			225
Transfer to general reserve		40	
Proposed ordinary dividend		100	
			140
Retained profits carried forward to next year			85

15.5 Accounts for publication

Note that there are no items in Exhibit 15.2 that would appear under items 15 to 19 in Companies Act Format 1. Exhibit 15.3 redrafts Exhibit 15.2 into a form suitable for publication according to Format 1. However, as before, the category reference numbers to the left-hand side of Exhibit 15.3 are for the benefit of the reader of this book – they do not have to be included.

Exhibit 15.3 (Accounts for publication presented according to Format 1)

Block plc

Profit and Loss Account for the year ending 31 December 19X6

		£000	£000
1	Turnover		800
2	Cost of sales		500
3	Gross profit		300
4	Distribution costs	60	
5	Administrative expenses	40	
			100
			200
6	Other operating income		30
			230
7	Income from shares in group undertakings	20	
8	Income from participating interests	10	
9	Income from fixed asset investments	5	
10	Other interest receivable and similar income	15	
			50
			280
11	Amounts written off investments	4	
12	Interest payable and similar charges	16	
			20
	Profit or loss on ordinary activities before taxation		260
13	Tax on profit or loss on ordinary activities		95
14	Profit or loss on ordinary activities after taxation		165
	Retained profits from last year		60
			225
	Transfer to reserves	40	
	Dividends paid and proposed	100	
			140
	Retained profits carried to next year		85

It would be legally possible for the internal accounts, as shown in Exhibit 15.2, to be published just as they are, because all the items are shown in the correct order. This would not have been possible if the internal accounts were drafted in a different order. However, the Companies Act does not force companies to publish fully detailed accounts (for example, as detailed as Exhibit 15.2), because their competitors may thereby be given information which would lead to them being placed in a better competitive position. The law therefore states the minimum information which must be disclosed. A company can show more than the minimum should it so wish.

15.6 Definition of items in Format 1

Format Item 1

Turnover is defined as the amounts derived from the provision of goods and services falling within the company's ordinary activities, net after deduction of VAT and trade discounts.

Format Items 2, 4 and 5

The figures for cost of sales, distribution costs and administrative expenses must include any depreciation charges connected with these functions. In the case of Block plc, because of the type of business, there are depreciation charges as part of distribution costs and administration expenses, but not cost of sales.

Format Item 6

This is operating income which does not fall under Item 1. Such items as rents receivable or royalties receivable might be found under this heading.

Format Item 7

In Chapter 21 of this book the reader will be introduced to parent and subsidiary undertakings. A parent is able to exert a dominant influence (i.e. control) over the activities of the subsidiary usually, but not necessarily, as a result of its owning a majority of the voting rights in the subsidiary. The parent and all its subsidiaries are a 'group'. Any dividends received by a company from its investments in shares in any member of the 'group' have to be shown separately.

Format Item 8

The term 'participating interest' means one where the parent company has a long-term holding of shares or their equivalent in an undertaking for the purpose of securing a contribution to the investor's own activities by the exercise of control or influence arising from or related to that interest. Where the equity stake exceeds 20 per cent, there is a presumption of such influence unless the contrary is shown.

Format Item 12

This includes bank interest on loans and overdrafts, debenture interest, etc.

The profit and loss account produced will not appear precisely as presented in Exhibit 15.1. As can be seen in Exhibit 15.3, the published profit and loss account for Block plc contains no items in categories 15, 16, 17, 18, 19 or 20. In addition, after item 14, there are several more lines, those of retained profits brought forward and carried forward, transfer to reserves, and proposed dividends. Although the format omits them, they are required according to the detailed rules accompanying the format. This also applies to line 20 'Profit or loss for the financial year' shown in Exhibit 15.1, when that line is included.

It would also have been possible to amalgamate items, for instance 4 and 5 could have been shown together as 'Net operating expenses £100,000'. In this case, included in the notes appended to the accounts would be an item showing the composition of the figure of £100,000.

In the notes attached to the profit and loss account, the Companies Acts require that the following be shown separately:

(*a*) interest on bank loans, overdrafts and other loans:
    (*i*) repayable within 5 years from the end of the accounting period;
    (*ii*) finally repayable after 5 years from the end of the accounting period;
(*b*) amounts set aside for redemption of share capital and for redemption of loans;
(c) rents from land, if material;
(d) costs of hire of plant and machinery;
(e) auditors' remuneration, including expenses.

Where a company carries on business of two or more classes differing substantially from each other, a note is required of the amount of turnover for each class of business, and the division of the profit and loss before taxation between each class. Information also has to be given of the turnover between geographical markets.

Notes are also required concerning numbers of employees, wages and salaries, social security costs, and pension costs.

Three further disclosure requirements of the Companies Act are expanded by FRS 3:

- the effect must be stated of any amount relating to any preceding financial year included in any item in the profit and loss account;
- particulars must be given of any extraordinary income or charges arising in the financial year; and
- the effect of any transaction of exceptional size or incidence that falls within the ordinary activities of the company must be stated.

15.7 Layout of the profit and loss account

Had Block plc had items relevant to the other Format 1 categories, the profit and loss account would have been presented as shown in Exhibit 15.4. Note that the lines added have been included simply to show what the statement would look like. Where a category has no value, it would normally be omitted from the statement, as was the case in Exhibit 15.3. In addition, Exhibit 15.4 shows the extra lines that must be included, but were not shown in Format 1 in the Companies Act. It is also worthwhile noting that the four lines in Format 1 that relate to *extraordinary items* are virtually eliminated as a result of the definition of the term that was introduced in FRS 3: *Reporting financial performance*. As a result of their issuing FRS 3, the Accounting Standards Board do not expect any company to identify an item as 'extraordinary' in their financial statements and so items 15–18 are unlikely to be seen in any future published profit and loss accounts. (This will be covered in greater detail in section 15.11.)

Exhibit 15.4

Block plc

Profit and Loss Account for the year ending 31 December 19X6

		£000	£000
1	Turnover		800
2	Cost of sales		500
3	Gross profit		300
4	Distribution costs	60	
5	Administrative expenses	40	
			100
			200
6	Other operating income		30
			230
7	Income from shares in group undertakings	20	
8	Income from participating interests	10	
9	Income from fixed asset investments	5	
10	Other interest receivable and similar income	15	
			50
			280
11	Amounts written off investments	4	
12	Interest payable and similar charges	16	
			20
	Profit or loss on ordinary activities before taxation		260
13	Tax on profit or loss on ordinary activities		95
14	Profit or loss on ordinary activities after taxation		165
15	Extraordinary income	0	
16	Extraordinary charges	0	
17	Extraordinary profit or loss	0	
18	Tax on extraordinary profit or loss	0	
			0
			165
19	Other taxes not shown under the above items		0
20	Profit or loss for the financial year		165
	Retained profits from last year		60
			225
	Transfer to reserves	40	
	Dividends paid and proposed	100	
			140
	Retained profits carried to next year		85

15.8 Allocation of expenses

It will be obvious under which heading most expenses will be shown, whether they are

(a) cost of sales; or
(b) distribution costs; or
(c) administrative expenses.

However, as the Companies Acts do not define these terms, some items are not so easy to allocate with certainty. Some companies may choose one heading for a particular item, while another company will choose another. These items can now be examined.

1   **Discounts received.** These are for prompt payment of amounts owing by us. Where they are for payments to suppliers of goods they could be regarded as either being a reduction in the cost of goods or, alternatively, as being a financial recompense – i.e. the reward for paying money on time. If regarded in the first way they would be deducted from cost of sales, whereas the alternative approach would be to deduct them from administrative expenses. However, these discounts are also deducted when paying bills in respect of distribution costs or administrative expenses, and it would also be necessary to deduct from these headings if the cost of sales deduction approach is used. As this raises complications in the original recording of discounts received, it would be more suitable in this book if all cash discounts received are deducted in arriving at the figure of administrative expenses.

2   **Discounts allowed.** To be consistent in dealing with discounts, this should be included in administrative expenses.

3   **Bad debts.** These could be regarded as an expense connected with sales: after all, they are sales which are not paid for. The other point of view is that for a debt to become bad, at least part of the blame must be because the proper administrative procedures in checking on customers' creditworthiness has not been thorough enough. In this book all bad debts will be taken as being part of administrative expenses.

15.9 FRS 3: Reporting financial performance

Accounting is not a static subject. Changes occur over the years as they are seen to be necessary, and also get general agreement as to their usefulness. Since the advent of SSAPs and FRSs the number of changes that practitioners and students have had to learn has increased at a very fast rate. A prime example of this is the introduction of FRS 3, which necessitates changes to the formats of profit and loss accounts when certain events have occurred.

This Standard superseded SSAP 6: *Extraordinary items and prior year adjustments*, amended SSAP 3: *Earnings per share*, and also made changes as a consequence to various other accounting standards.

Suppose that you are considering the affairs of a business over the years. The business has not changed significantly, there have been no acquisitions, no discontinued operations, no fundamental reorganisation or restructuring of the business, nor have there been any extraordinary items affecting the accounts. In these circumstances, when comparing the accounts over the years, you are comparing like with like, subject to the problem of the effect of inflation or deflation.

On the other hand, suppose that some of the things mentioned have occurred. When trying to see what the future might hold for the company, simply basing your opinions on what has happened in the past can be very confusing.

To help you to distinguish the past and the future, and to give you some idea as to what changes have occurred, FRS 3 requires that the following are highlighted in the profit and loss account if they are material in amount:

(*a*) *What the results of continuing operations are, including the results of acquisitions.* Obviously acquisitions affect future results, and are therefore included in continuing operations.

(*b*) *What the results have been of discontinued operations.* This should help distinguish the past from the future.

(*c*) *The profits or losses on the sale or termination of an operation, the costs of fundamental reorganisation or restructuring, and the profits and losses on the disposal of fixed assets.* The profits and losses concerning these matters are not going to happen again, and so this also helps us distinguish the past from the future.

We can see how FRS 3 requires (*a*), (*b*) and (*c*) to be shown on the face of the profit and loss account in Exhibit 15.5. Not only is the turnover split to show the figures relevant to continuing operations, acquisitions and discontinued operations, the operating profit is split in a similar fashion. In addition any profit or loss on the disposal of the discontinued operations would also be shown. Exhibit 15.5 is restricted to the first 6 categories of Format 1 as this is the part of the statement affected by these FRS 3 requirements. Once again, it uses Block plc for the example.

Exhibit 15.5

Block plc

Profit and Loss Account for the year ending 31 December 19X6 (extract)

		£000	£000
1	Turnover		
	Continuing operations	520	
	Acquisitions	110	
		630	
	Discontinued operations	170	
			800
2	Cost of sales		500
3	Gross profit		300
4	Distribution costs	60	
5	Administrative expenses	40	
			100
	Operating profit		
	Continuing operations	160	
	Acquisitions	60	
	(*a*)	220	
	Discontinued operations (loss) (*b*)	(20)	
			200
	Profit on disposal of discontinued operations (*c*)		10
			210
6	Other operating income		20
	Profit or loss on ordinary activities before interest		230

The items marked (*a*), (*b*) and (*c*) can be described as exceptional items. They are material in amount, they fall within the ordinary activities of the firm, and need to be shown so that the accounts will give a 'true and fair view'.

They are exceptional in that they are not the ordinary daily occurrence, but remember that they fall within the ordinary activities of the company. FRS 3 requires that three categories of exceptional items be shown separately on the face of the profit and loss account after operating profit and before interest, and included under the appropriate heading of continued or discontinued operations:

- profits or losses on the sale or termination of an operation;
- costs of a fundamental reorganisation or restructuring having a material effect on the nature and focus of the reporting entity's operations;
- profits or losses on the disposal of fixed assets.

Other exceptional items should be credited or charged in arriving at the profit or loss on ordinary activities by inclusion under the heading to which they relate. The amount of each exceptional item should be disclosed in a note, or on the face of the profit and loss account, if necessary in order to give a true and fair view.

15.10 Other statements and notes required by FRS 3

1 Statement of total recognised gains and losses

The *statement of total recognised gains and losses* is one of two new primary statements introduced by FRS 3. It shows the extent to which shareholders' funds have increased or decreased from all the various gains and losses recognised in the period, and enables users to consider all recognised gains and losses of a reporting entity in assessing its overall performance; an example of what would be included in the statement would be unrealised gains on fixed asset revaluations. Exhibit 15.6 presents an example of the statement using the data from Block plc. (*Note*: only the profit figure can be found in the profit and loss account. The others have been inserted to demonstrate what the statement looks like. Also, as with all these statements, including the profit and loss account, comparative figures would also be shown.)

Exhibit 15.6

Block plc

Statement of Total Recognised Gains and Losses

	19X6 £000
Profit for the financial year	165
Unrealised surplus on revaluation of properties	12
Unrealised (loss)/gain on trade investment	(8)
	169
Currency translation differences on foreign currency investments	(5)
Total recognised gains and losses relating to the year	164
Prior period adjustment	(19)
Total gains and losses recognised since last annual report	145

2 Note of historical cost profits and losses

Where assets have been revalued, which obviously affects depreciation, it may have a material effect upon the results shown in the accounts using the revalued figures. If this is the case, FRS 3 requires that there should also be shown as a note what the profit and loss account would have been if the account had been shown using historical (i.e. not revalued) figures. The note should also show how the reported profit on ordinary activities (using accounts with revalued assets) can be reconciled with that calculated using historical figures, and should also show the retained profit figure for the financial year reported on the historical cost basis. The note should be presented immediately following the profit and loss account or the statement of total recognised gains and losses. An example of the note is presented in Exhibit 15.7. (*Note*: as with the statement of total recognised gains and losses, only the profit figure can be identified in the profit and loss account. Also, comparative figures should be shown.)

Exhibit 15.7

Block plc

Note of Historical Cost Profits and Losses

	19X6
	£000
Reported profit on ordinary activities before taxation	260
Realisation of property revaluation gains of previous years	12
Difference between a historical cost depreciation charge and the actual depreciation charge of the year calculated on the revalued amount	1
Historical cost profit on ordinary activities before taxation	273
Historical cost profit for the year retained after taxation, minority interests, extraordinary items and dividends (273 – 95 – 100)	78

3 Reconciliation of movements in shareholders' funds

The profit and loss account and the statement of total recognised gains and losses reflect the performance of a reporting entity in a period, but there are other changes that can occur in shareholders' funds that these two statements do not disclose, and which can be important in understanding the change in the financial position of the entity – for example, a new share issue or goodwill written-off. For this reason, FRS 3 also gave the *reconciliation of movements in shareholders' funds* the status of a primary statement, its purpose being to highlight these other changes in the financial position. When shown as a primary statement (there is an option to show it as a note), the reconciliation should be shown separately from the statement of total recognised gains and losses. Exhibit 15.8 presents an example of the statement. (*Note:* the figures can be found in the other statements except for the new share capital, the goodwill written off and the opening shareholders' funds amounts. As before, comparative figures should also be presented.)

Exhibit 15.8

Block plc

Reconciliation of Movements in Shareholders' Funds

	19X6
	£000
Profit for the financial year	165
Dividends	(100)
	65
Other recognised gains and losses relating to the year (net)	(1)
New share capital subscribed	20
Goodwill written off	(25)
Net addition to shareholders' funds	59
Opening shareholders' funds (originally £321,000 before deducting prior period adjustment of £19,000)	302
Closing shareholders' funds	361

15.11 FRS 3 and extraordinary items

You have just seen that in FRS 3 some of the exceptional items have to be highlighted on the face of the profit and loss account, whilst others can be put under appropriate headings with notes giving details being attached to the accounts.

In Exhibit 15.3 all of these exceptional items will have been dealt with by the time that item 14, profit for the year on ordinary activities after taxation, has been reached. Extraordinary items, as per Format 1, would be shown after that as items 15, 16, 17 and 18.

Before FRS 3, the distinction between what was an exceptional item and what was an extraordinary item was not as well defined as it could have been. This led to directors of companies sometimes manipulating the figures for their own ends whilst keeping within the necessary legal boundaries.

They did this because the profit per item 14 was a very well-used figure for assessing how well, or otherwise, a company was being managed. It was a vital part of calculating the earnings per share (EPS) which is a main indicator to many people of the company's performance. If a favourable item could be called an 'exceptional item' it would increase the size of the profit per 14. On the other hand, should an item be unfavourable, and therefore lower the figure of profit per 14, then perhaps it could be (and it often was) called an 'extraordinary item' instead. In this way the profit per 14 could be shown at a higher figure than was really justified. Such actions could affect the stock exchange values of the company's shares.

FRS 3 is more strict about what is, or is not, an extraordinary item, and thus to be shown after item 14 in the profit and loss account. Extraordinary items should be:

(*a*) material items possessing a high degree of abnormality which arise from events or transactions that fall outside the ordinary activities of the business, and

(*b*) are not expected to recur, and

(*c*) do not include exceptional items, and

(*d*) do not include items relating to a prior period merely because they relate to a prior period.

Extraordinary items fall *outside* the 'ordinary' activities of a company, whereas exceptional items fall *within* them. 'Ordinary activities' are any activities undertaken by a reporting entity as part of its business and such related activities in which the reporting entity engages in furtherance of, incidental to or arising from these activities. Ordinary activities include the effects on the reporting entity of any event in the various environments in which it operates. It is little wonder that the ASB did not believe that anything could ever be described as an extraordinary item after the introduction of FRS 3.

15.12 FRS 3 and prior period adjustments

A prior period adjustment is a material adjustment applicable to prior periods arising from changes in accounting policies or from the correction of fundamental errors. They do not include normal recurring adjustments or corrections of accounting estimates made in prior periods.

They are accounted for by restating the comparative figures for the preceding period in the primary statements and notes and adjusting the opening balance of reserves for the cumulative effect. The cumulative effect of the adjustments should also be noted at the foot of the statement of total recognised gains and losses of the current period (*see* Exhibit 15.6). The effect of prior period adjustments on the results for the preceding period should be disclosed where practicable.

15.13 FRS 3 and comparative figures

Comparative figures should be shown for all items in the primary statements and the notes to the statements required by FRS 3. The comparative figures in respect of the profit and loss account should include in the continuing category only the results of those operations included in the current period's continuing operations.

Main points to remember

1   There are set formats for the preparation of published financial statements.

2   Accounts for internal use need not comply with these set formats.

3   FRS 3: *Reporting financial performance* has altered the set format for the profit and loss account by requiring further details to be disclosed concerning:
    (*a*) continuing and discontinued operations;
    (*b*) restructuring; and
    (*c*) disposal of fixed assets.

4   In addition, by defining extraordinary items out of existence, it has effectively made obsolete a number of the categories contained in the set format profit and loss accounts relating to extraordinary items.

5   FRS 3 introduced two additional primary financial statements:
    (*a*) the statement of total recognised gains and losses; and
    (*b*) the reconciliation of movements in shareholders' funds (may be shown as a note).

6   It also introduced a new note – the note of historical cost profits and losses.

Advice

It is important for you to know that the published profit and loss account of a company must show certain items in a given order.

The contents of FRS 3 are likely to attract quite a lot of questions in future. In particular the new definition of extraordinary items per FRS 3 will undoubtedly see quite a crop of questions. Some will come in the form of the directors of a company wanting to classify something as extraordinary, and therefore shown after item 14, 'Profit or loss on ordinary activities after taxation'.

Review questions

15.1 From the following selected balances of Rogers plc as at 31 December 19X2 draw up (*i*) a trading and profit and loss account for internal use, and (*ii*) a profit and loss account for publication.

	£
Profit and loss account as at 31 December 19X1	15,300
Stock 1 January 19X2	57,500
Purchases	164,000
Sales	288,000
Returns inwards	11,500
Returns outwards	2,000
Carriage inwards	1,300
Wages and salaries (*see* note (*b*))	8,400
Rent and rates (*see* note (*c*))	6,250
General distribution expenses	4,860
General administrative expenses	3,320
Discounts allowed	3,940
Bad debts	570
Debenture interest	2,400
Motor expenses (*see* note (*d*))	7,200
Interest received on bank deposit	770
Income from shares in related companies (gross)	660
Motor vehicles at cost: Administrative	14,000
Distribution	26,000
Equipment at cost: Administrative	5,500
Distribution	3,500
Royalties receivable	1,800

Notes:
(*a*) Stock at 31 December 19X2 £64,000.
(*b*) Wages and salaries are to be apportioned: Distribution costs ⅓, Administrative expenses ⅔.
(*c*) Rent and rates are to be apportioned: Distribution costs 60 per cent, Administrative expenses 40 per cent.
(*d*) Apportion Motor expenses equally between Distribution costs and Administrative expenses.
(*e*) Depreciate Motor vehicles 25 per cent and Equipment 20 per cent on cost.
(*f*) Accrue auditors' remuneration of £500.
(*g*) Accrue corporation tax for the year on ordinary activity profits £30,700.
(*h*) A sum of £8,000 is to be transferred to general reserve.
(*i*) An ordinary dividend of £30,000 is to be proposed.

15.2 You are given the following selected balances of Federal plc as at 31 December 19X4. From them draw up (*i*) a trading and profit and loss account for the year ended 31 December 19X4 for internal use and (*ii*) a profit and loss account for publication.

	£
Stock 1 January 19X4	64,500
Sales	849,000
Purchases	510,600
Carriage inwards	4,900
Returns inwards	5,800
Returns outwards	3,300
Discounts allowed	5,780
Discounts received	6,800
Wages (putting goods into saleable condition)	11,350
Salaries and wages: Sales and distribution staff	29,110
Salaries and wages: Administrative staff	20,920
Motor expenses (*see* note (*c*))	15,600
Rent and rates (*see* note (*d*))	25,000
Investments in related companies (market value £66,000)	80,000
Income from shares in related companies	3,500
General distribution expenses	8,220
General administrative expenses	2,190
Bad debts	840
Interest from government securities	1,600
Haulage costs: Distribution	2,070
Debenture interest payable	3,800
Profit and loss account: 31 December 19X3	37,470
Motor vehicles at cost: Distribution and sales	75,000
Administrative	35,000
Plant and machinery at cost: Distribution and sales	80,000
Administrative	50,000
Production	15,000
Directors' remuneration	5,000

Notes:
(*a*) The production department puts goods bought into a saleable condition.
(*b*) Stock at 31 December 19X4 £82,800.
(*c*) Apportion Motor expenses: Distribution ⅔, Administrative ⅓.
(*d*) Apportion Rent and rates: Distribution 80 per cent, Administrative 20 per cent.
(*e*) Write £14,000 off the value of investments in related companies.
(*f*) Depreciate Motor vehicles 20 per cent on cost, Plant and machinery 10 per cent on cost.
(*g*) Accrue auditors' remuneration £2,000.
(*h*) Accrue corporation tax on ordinary activity profits £74,000.
(*i*) A sum of £20,000 is to be transferred to debenture redemption reserve.
(*j*) An ordinary dividend of £50,000 is to be proposed.

15.3 The following information has been extracted from the books of account of Rufford plc for the year to 31 March 19X6:

	Dr £000	Cr £000
ACT (paid on 14 October 19X5)	3	
Administration expenses	97	
Deferred taxation		24
Depreciation on office machinery (for the year to 31 March 19X6)	8	
Depreciation on delivery vans (for the year to 31 March 19X6)	19	
Distribution costs	33	
Dividends received (from a UK listed company on 31 July 19X5)		14
Factory closure expenses (closed on 1 April 19X5)	12	
Interest payable on bank overdraft (repayable within five years)	6	
Interim dividend (paid on 30 September 19X5)	21	
Interest receivable		25
Purchases	401	
Retained profit at 31 March 19X5		160
Sales (net of VAT)		642
Stock at 1 April 19X5	60	

Additional information:
1 Administrative expenses include the following items:

	£000
Auditors' remuneration	20
Directors' emoluments	45
Travelling expenses	1
Research expenditure	11
Hire of plant and machinery	12

2 It is assumed that the following tax rates are applicable for the year to 31 March 19X6:

	%
Corporation tax	50
Income tax	30

3 There was an overprovision for corporation tax of £3,000 relating to the year to 31 March 19X5.
4 Corporation tax payable for the year to 31 March 19X6 (based on the profits for that year) is estimated to be £38,000. The company, in addition, intends to transfer a further £9,000 to its deferred taxation account.
5 A final dividend of £42,000 for the year to 31 March 19X6 is expected to be paid on 2 June 19X6.
6 Stock at 31 March 19X6 was valued at £71,000.
7 As a result of a change in accounting policy, a prior year charge of £15,000 (net of tax) is to be made.
8 The company's share capital consists of 420,000 ordinary shares of £1 each. There are no preference shares, and no change had been made to the company's issued share capital for some years.

Required:
(*a*) In so far as the information permits, prepare the company's published profit and loss account for the year to 31 March 19X6 in the vertical format in accordance with the Companies Act and with related statements of standard accounting practice.
(NB A statement of the company's accounting policies is not required.)

(b) Prepare balance sheet extracts in order to illustrate the balances still remaining in the following accounts at 31 March 19X6:

(i) corporation tax;
(ii) advance corporation tax;
(iii) proposed dividend; and
(iv) deferred taxation.

(NB: a detailed balance sheet is not required.)

(*Association of Accounting Technicians*)

15.4A The following balance has been extracted from the books of Falconer plc as on 31 August 19X4. From them draw up (i) a trading and profit and loss account, for internal use, for the year ended 31 August 19X4, also (ii) a profit and loss account for publication for the year.

	£
Purchases	540,500
Sales	815,920
Returns inwards	15,380
Returns outwards	24,620
Carriage inwards	5,100
Wages – productive	6,370
Discounts allowed	5,890
Discounts received	7,940
Stock 31 August 19X3	128,750
Wages and salaries: Sales and distribution	19,480
Wages and salaries: Administrative	24,800
Motor expenses: Sales and distribution	8,970
Motor expenses: Administrative	16,220
General distribution expenses	4,780
General administrative expenses	5,110
Rent and rates (*see* note (*c*))	9,600
Directors' remuneration	12,400
Profit and loss account: 31 August 19X3	18,270
Advertising costs	8,380
Bad debts	1,020
Hire of plant and machinery (*see* note (*b*))	8,920
Motor vehicles at cost: Sales and distribution	28,000
Administrative	36,000
Plant and machinery: Distribution	17,500
Debenture interest payable	4,800
Income from shares in group companies	12,800
Income from shares in related companies	10,500
Preference dividend paid	15,000
Profit on disposal of investments	6,600
Tax on profit on disposal of investments	1,920

Notes:

(a) Stock at 31 August 19X4 £144,510.
(b) The hire of plant and machinery is to be apportioned: Productive £5,200, Administrative £3,720.
(c) Rent and rates to be apportioned: Distribution ⅔, Administrative ⅓.
(d) Motors are to be depreciated at 25 per cent on cost, Plant and machinery to be depreciated at 20 per cent on cost.
(e) Auditors' remuneration of £1,700 to be accrued.
(f) Corporation tax on profit from ordinary activities for the year is estimated at £59,300, excluding tax on disposal of investments.
(g) Transfer £25,000 to general reserve.
(h) Ordinary dividend of £60,000 is proposed.

15.5A   From the following balance of Danielle plc you are to draw up (*i*) a trading and profit and loss account for the year ended 31 December 19X6, for internal use, and (*ii*) a profit and loss account for publication:

	£
Plant and machinery, at cost (*see* note (*c*))	275,000
Bank interest receivable	1,850
Discounts allowed	5,040
Discounts received	3,890
Hire of motor vehicles: Sales and distribution	9,470
Hire of motor vehicles: Administrative	5,710
Licence fees receivable	5,100
General distribution expenses	11,300
General administrative expenses	15,800
Wages and salaries: Sales and distribution	134,690
Administrative	89,720
Directors' remuneration	42,000
Motor expenses (*see* note (*e*))	18,600
Stock 31 December 19X5	220,500
Sales	880,000
Purchases	405,600
Returns outwards	15,800
Returns inwards	19,550
Profit and loss account as at 31 December 19X5	29,370

Notes:
(*a*) Stock at 31 December 19X6 £210,840.
(*b*) Accrue auditor's remuneration £3,000.
(*c*) Of the Plant and machinery, £150,000 is distributive in nature, whilst £125,000 is for administration.
(*d*) Depreciate plant and machinery 20 per cent on cost.
(*e*) Of the Motor expenses ⅔ is for Sales and distribution and ⅓ for Administration.
(*f*) Corporation tax on ordinary profits is estimated at £28,350.
(*g*) Proposed ordinary dividend is £50,000.
(*h*) A sum of £15,000 is to be transferred to general reserve.

15.6A Bunker plc is a trading company; it does not carry out *any* manufacturing operations. The following information has been extracted from the books of account for the year to 31 March 19X0:

	£000
Auditors' remuneration	30
Corporation tax: based on the accounting profit	
for the year to 31 March 19X0	7,200
overprovision for the year to 31 March 19X9	200
United Kingdom corporation tax relief on	
overseas operations: closure costs	30
Delivery expenses	1,200
Dividends: final (proposed – to be paid 1 August 19X0)	200
interim (paid on 1 October 19X9)	100
Fixed assets at cost:	
Delivery vans	200
Office cars	40
Stores plant and equipment	5,000
Franked investment income (amount received from listed companies)	1,200
Office expenses	800
Overseas operations: closure costs of entire operations on 1 April 19X9	350
Purchases (net of value added tax)	24,000
Sales (net of value added tax)	35,000
Stocks at cost:	
at 1 April 19X9	5,000
at 31 March 19X0	6,000
Storeroom costs	1,000
Wages and salaries:	
Delivery staff	700
Directors' emoluments	300
Office staff	100
Storeroom staff	400

Additional information:
1 Depreciation policy:
   Depreciation is provided at the following annual rates on a straight line basis: delivery vans 20 per cent; office cars 7.5 per cent; stores plant and equipment 10 per cent.
2 The following taxation rates may be assumed:
   corporation tax 35 per cent; income tax 25 per cent; value added tax 15 per cent.
3 The franked investment income arises from investments held in fixed asset investments.
4 It has been decided to transfer an amount of £150,000 to the deferred taxation account.
5 There were 1,000,000 ordinary shares of £1 each in issue during the year to 31 March 19X0. There were no preference shares in issue.

Required:
Insofar as the information permits, prepare Bunker plc's published profit and loss account for the year to 31 March 19X0 in accordance with the minimum requirements of the Companies Act 1985 and related accounting standards.

Note: A statement of accounting policies is NOT required, but where appropriate, other formal notes SHOULD be attached to your profit and loss account. Detailed workings should also be submitted with your answer.

(Association of Accounting Technicians)

15.7A Fresno Group plc have prepared their financial statements for the year ended 31 January 19X4. However, the financial accountant of Fresno Group plc had difficulty in preparing the statements required by FRS 3: *Reporting financial performance*, and approached you for help in preparing those statements. The financial accountant furnished you with the following information:

(*i*)   **Fresno Group plc**
                    Profit and Loss Account extract for year ended 31 January 19X4

	£ million
Operating profit – continuing operations	290
Profit on sale of property in continuing operations	10
Profit on ordinary activities before taxation	300
Tax on ordinary activities	(90)
Profit after taxation	210
Dividends	(15)
Retained profit for year	195

The financial accountant did not provide for the loss on any discontinued operations in the profit and loss account. (However, you may assume that the taxation provision incorporated the effects of any provision for discontinued operations.)

(*ii*) The shareholders' funds at the beginning of the financial year were as follows:

	£ million
Share capital – £1 ordinary shares	350
Merger reserve	55
Revaluation reserve	215
Profit and loss reserve	775
	1,395

(*iii*) Fresno Group plc regularly revalues its fixed assets and at 31 January 19X4, a revaluation surplus of £375 million had been credited to revaluation reserve. During the financial year, a property had been sold on which a revaluation surplus of £54 million had been credited to reserves. Further, if the company had charged depreciation on a historical cost basis rather than the revalued amounts, the depreciation charge in the profit and loss account for fixed assets would have been £7 million. The current year's charge for depreciation was £16 million.

(*iv*) The group has a policy of writing off goodwill on the acquisition of subsidiaries directly against a merger reserve. The goodwill for the period amounted to £250 million. In order to facilitate the purchase of subsidiaries, the company had issued £1 ordinary shares of nominal value £150 million and share premium of £450 million. The premium had been taken to the merger reserve. All subsidiaries are currently 100 per cent owned by the group.

(*v*)   During the financial year to 31 January 19X4, the company had made a decision to close a 100 per cent owned subsidiary, Reno plc. However, the closure did not take place until May 19X4. Fresno Group plc estimated that as at 31 January 19X4 the operating loss for the period 1 February 19X4 to 31 May 19X4 would be £30 million and that in addition redundancy costs, stock and plant write-downs would amount to £15 million. In the event, the operating loss for the period 1 February 19X4 to 31 May 19X4 was £65 million, but the redundancy costs, stock and plant write-downs only amounted to £12 million.

(*vi*) The following information relates to Reno plc for the period 1 February 19X4 to 31 May 19X4.

Reno plc

	£ *million*
Turnover	175
Cost of sales	(195)
Gross loss	(20)
Administrative expenses	(15)
Selling expenses	(30)
Operating loss before taxation	(65)

Required:

(*a*) Prepare the following statements in accordance with current statutory requirements and FRS 3: *Reporting financial performance* for Fresno Group plc for the year ending 31 January 19X4:
   (*i*)   statement of total recognised gains and losses;
   (*ii*) reconciliation of movements in shareholders' funds;
   (*iii*) analysis of movements on reserves;
   (*iv*) note of historical cost profits and losses.

(*b*) Explain to the financial accountant:
   (*i*) how the decision to close the subsidiary, Reno plc, affects the financial statements of Fresno Group plc for the year ended 31 January 19X4;
   (*ii*) how the subsidiary, Reno plc, should be dealt with in the financial statements of Fresno Group plc for the year ended 31 January 19X5.

(*Chartered Association of Certified Accountants*)

16

The final accounts of limited companies: balance sheets

Objectives

After you have studied this chapter, you should:

● *be aware of the alternative presentation formats available under the Companies Acts that must be used when preparing balance sheets for external reporting purposes*

● *know how to present information under the most commonly used of the Companies Acts formats*

● *be aware of the differences between the statutory format and formats generally adopted for internal use*

● *be aware of the exemptions available to 'small' and 'medium-sized' companies in respect of filing modified accounts*

● *be aware of the option available to plcs to send members a summary financial statement*

16.1 Balance sheet formats

The Companies Acts set out two formats for the balance sheet, one vertical and one horizontal. The method chosen for this book is that of Format 1 because this most resembles previous UK practice. As it is the vertical style format it will also be looked upon with favour by examiners.

Format 1 is shown as Exhibit 16.1. Monetary figures have been included to illustrate it more clearly.

Exhibit 16.1

Balance Sheet – Format 1

			£000s	
		£	£	£
A	CALLED-UP SHARE CAPITAL NOT PAID*			10
B	FIXED ASSETS			
I	Intangible assets			
	1 Development costs	20		
	2 Concessions, patents, licences, trade marks			
	and similar rights and assets	30		
	3 Goodwill	80		
	4 Payments on account	5	135	
II	Tangible assets			
	1 Land and buildings	300		
	2 Plant and machinery	500		
	3 Fixtures, fittings, tools and equipment	60		
	4 Payments on account and assets in course			
	of construction	20	880	
III	Investments			
	1 Shares in group companies	15		
	2 Loans to group companies	10		
	3 Shares in related companies	20		
	4 Loans to related companies	5		
	5 Other investments other than loans	30		
	6 Other loans	16		
	7 Own shares	4	100	1,115
C	CURRENT ASSETS			
I	Stock			
	1 Raw materials and consumables	60		
	2 Work in progress	15		
	3 Finished goods and goods for resale	120		
	4 Payments on account	5	200	
II	Debtors			
	1 Trade debtors	200		
	2 Amounts owed by group companies	20		
	3 Amounts owed by related companies	10		
	4 Other debtors	4		
	5 Called-up share capital not paid*	–		
	6 Prepayments and accrued income**	–	234	
III	Investments			
	1 Shares in group companies	40		
	2 Own shares	5		
	3 Other investments	30		
			75	
IV	Cash at bank and in hand		26	
			535	
D	PREPAYMENTS AND ACCRUED INCOME**		15	
			550	

E CREDITORS: AMOUNTS FALLING DUE WITHIN ONE YEAR

1	Debenture loans	5	
2	Bank loans and overdrafts	10	
3	Payments received on account	20	
4	Trade creditors	50	
5	Bills of exchange payable	2	
6	Amounts owed to group companies	15	
7	Amounts owed to related companies	6	
8	Other creditors including taxation and social security	54	
9	Accruals and deferred income***	–	162

F NET CURRENT ASSETS (LIABILITIES)   388
G TOTAL ASSETS LESS CURRENT LIABILITIES   1,513
H CREDITORS: AMOUNTS FALLING DUE AFTER MORE
    THAN ONE YEAR

1	Debenture loans	20	
2	Bank loans and overdrafts	15	
3	Payments received on account	5	
4	Trade creditors	25	
5	Bills of exchange payable	4	
6	Amounts owed to group companies	10	
7	Amounts owed to related companies	5	
8	Other creditors including taxation and social security	32	
9	Accruals and deferred income***	–	116

I PROVISIONS FOR LIABILITIES AND CHARGES

1	Pensions and similar obligations	20	
2	Taxation, including deferred taxation	40	
3	Other provisions	4	64

J ACCRUALS AND DEFERRED INCOME***   20   200
                                                                1,313

K CAPITAL AND RESERVES
I   Called-up share capital   1,000
II Share premium account   100
III Revaluation reserve   20
IV Other reserves:

1	Capital redemption reserve	40	
2	Reserve for own shares	10	
3	Reserves provided for by the articles of association	20	
4	Other reserves	13	83

V PROFIT AND LOSS ACCOUNT   110
                                                                1,313

(*) (**) (***) These items may be shown in any of the positions indicated.

It should be noted that various items can be shown in alternative places, i.e.:

- **called-up share capital not paid,** either in position A or position CII 5;
- **prepayments and accrued income,** either CII 6 or as D;
- **accruals and deferred income,** either E9 or H9, or in total as J.

Items preceded by letters or roman numerals must be disclosed on the face of the balance sheet, e.g. B Fixed assets, KII Share premium account, whereas those shown with arabic numerals (you may call them ordinary numbers, 1, 2, 3, 4, etc.) may be combined where they are not material or the combination facilitates assessment of the company's affairs. Where they are combined, the details of each item should be shown in the notes accompanying the financial statements. The actual letters, roman numerals or arabic numbers do *not* have to be shown on the face of the published balance sheets.

16.2 Further details for Format 1

The following also apply to the balance sheet in Format 1.

BI Intangible assets are assets not having a 'physical' existence compared with tangible assets which do have a physical existence. For instance, you can see and touch the tangible assets of land and buildings, plant and machinery, etc., whereas goodwill does not exist in a physical sense.

For each of the items under fixed assets, whether they are intangible assets, tangible assets or investments, the notes accompanying the accounts must give full details of (*a*) cost, at beginning and end of financial year, (*b*) effect on that item of acquisitions, disposals, revaluations, etc. during the year, and (*c*) full details of depreciation, i.e. accumulated depreciation at start of year, depreciation for year, effect of disposals on depreciation in the year and any other adjustments.

All fixed assets, including property and goodwill, must be depreciated over the period of the useful economic life of each asset. Prior to this many companies had not depreciated property because of rising money values of the asset. Costs of research must not be treated as an asset, and development costs may be capitalised only in special cases. Any hire purchase owing must not be deducted from the assets concerned. Only goodwill which has been purchased can be shown as an asset; internally generated goodwill must not be capitalised. (This does not refer to goodwill in consolidated accounts – *see* Chapter 22.)

Where an asset is revalued, normally this will be fixed assets being shown at market value instead of cost. Any difference on revaluation must be debited or credited to a revaluation reserve – *see* KIII in the Format.

Investments shown as CIII will be in respect of those not held for the long term.

Two items which could previously be shown as assets, (*a*) preliminary expenses (these are the legal expenses etc. in forming the company), and (*b*) expenses of and commission on any issue of shares or debentures, must not now be shown as assets. They can be written off against any share premium account balance; alternatively they should be written off to the profit and loss account.

Full details of each class of share capital, and of authorised capital, will be shown in notes accompanying the balance sheet.

16.3 Choice of formats

The Acts leave the choice of a particular format for the balance sheet and the profit and loss account to the directors. Once adopted, the choice must be adhered to in subsequent years except in the case that there are special reasons for the change. If a change is made, then full reasons for the change must be stated in the notes attached to the accounts.

16.4 Fundamental accounting principles

The Companies Acts set out the accounting principles (or 'valuation rules' as they are called in the Fourth Directive of the EC) to be followed when preparing company financial statements.

The following principles are stated in the Acts. The reader is referred to Chapter 10 of *Business Accounting 1* for a fuller discussion of some of them.

(*a*) A company is presumed to be a going concern.

(*b*) Accounting policies must be applied consistently from year to year.

(*c*) The prudence concept must be followed.

(*d*) The accruals concept must be observed.

(*e*) Each component item of assets and liabilities must be valued separately. As an instance of this, if a company has five different types of stock, each type must be valued separately at the lower of cost and net realisable value, rather than be valued on an aggregate basis.

(*f*) Amounts in respect of items representing assets or income may *not* be set off against items representing liabilities or expenditure. Thus an amount owing on a hire purchase contract cannot now be deducted from the value of the asset in the balance sheet, although this was often done before 1981.

16.5 True and fair view

If complying with the requirements of the Companies Acts would cause the financial statements not to be 'true and fair' then the directors must set aside such requirements. This should not be done lightly, and it would not be common to find such instances.

16.6 Reporting requirements for small and medium-sized companies

Small and medium-sized companies do not have to file a full set of final accounts with the Registrar of Companies. They could, if they wished, send a full set of final accounts, but what they *have* to file is a minimum of 'modified accounts'. They would still have to send a full set to their own shareholders – the 'modified accounts' refer only to those filed with the Registrar. However, there is no longer an audit requirement for small companies with a turnover under £90,000, unless 10 per cent or more of shareholders sign a formal notice requesting an audit and lodge this at the registered office.

The definition of 'small' and 'medium-sized' companies is if, for the financial year in question and the previous year, the company comes within the limits of at least two of the following three criteria:

	Small	*Medium-sized*
Aggregate turnover not more than	£2.8 million net/ £3.36 million gross	£11.2 million net/ £13.44 million gross
Aggregate gross assets not more than	£1.4 million net/ £1.68 million gross	£5.6 million net/ £6.72 million gross
Aggregate employees not more than	50	250

16.7 Modified accounts of small companies

(*a*) Neither a profit and loss account nor a directors' report has to be filed with the Registrar.

(*b*) A modified balance sheet showing only those items to which a letter or roman numeral are attached (*see* Format 1, Exhibit 16.1) has to be shown. For example, the total for CI Stock has to be shown but not the figures for each of the individual items comprising this total.

16.8 Modified accounts of medium-sized companies

(a) The profit and loss account per Format 1 does not have to show item 1 (Turnover), or item 2 (Cost of sales) or item 6 (Other operating income). It will therefore begin with the figure of gross profit or loss.

(b) The analyses of turnover and profit normally required as notes to the accounts need not be given.

(c) The balance sheet, however, must be given in full.

Notes to the accounts: review questions on published company accounts including notes required by law are shown at the end of Chapter 17.

16.9 Summary financial statements

A plc may send a summary financial statement to members in place of the full statements, but any member who requests the full statements must be sent them. The summary statement must:

(a) state that it is only a summary of information in the company's financial statements and the directors' report;

(b) contain a statement by the company's auditors of their opinion as to whether the summary financial statement is consistent with those financial statements and that report and complies with the requirements of the section in the Companies Act (CA 85, section 251) that permits the distribution of this summary financial statement and the regulations made under it;

(c) state whether the auditors' report on the financial statements was unqualified or qualified, and if it was qualified set out the report in full together with any further material needed to understand the qualification;

(d) state whether the auditors' report on the annual accounts contained a statement under either:

- CA 85, section 237(2) – accounting records or returns inadequate or financial statements not agreeing with records or returns; or
- CA 85, section 237(3) – failure to obtain necessary information and explanations;

and, if so, set out the statement in full.

Main points to remember

1 There are set formats for the preparation of published financial statements.

2 Accounts for internal use need not comply with these set formats.

3 Accounting standards have statutory recognition and must, therefore, be complied with when preparing financial statements intended to present a true and fair view.

4 'Small' and 'medium-sized' companies may file modified accounts with the Registrar if they wish.

5 Plcs may send a summary financial statement to members in place of the full statements, but any member who requests the full statements must be sent them.

Review questions

16.1 The following balances remained in the books of Owen Ltd on 31 December 19X1, *after* the profit and loss account and appropriation account had been drawn up. You are to draft the balance sheet as at 31 December 19X1 in accordance with the Companies Acts.

	Dr £	Cr £
Ordinary share capital: £1 shares		50,000
Preference share capital: 50p shares		25,000
Calls account (ordinary shares)	150	
Development costs	3,070	
Goodwill	21,000	
Land and buildings – at cost	48,000	
Plant and machinery – at cost	12,500	
Provision for depreciation: Buildings		16,000
Provision for depreciation: Plant and machinery		5,400
Shares in related companies	35,750	
Stock: Raw materials	3,470	
Stock: Finished goods	18,590	
Debtors: Trade	17,400	
Amounts owed by related companies	3,000	
Prepayments	1,250	
Debentures (*see* note 1)		10,000
Bank overdraft (repayable within 6 months)		4,370
Creditors: Trade (payable within 1 year)		12,410
Bills payable (*see* note 2)		3,600
Share premium		20,000
Capital redemption reserve		5,000
General reserve		4,000
Profit and loss account		8,400
	164,180	164,180

Notes:
1 Of the debentures £6,000 is repayable in 3 months' time, while the other £4,000 is repayable in 5 years' time.
2 Of the bills payable, £1,600 is in respect of a bill to be paid in 4 months' time and £2,000 for a bill payable in 18 months' time.
3 The depreciation charged for the year was: Building £4,000, Plant and machinery £1,800.

16.2 After the profit and loss appropriation account has been prepared for the year ended 30 September 19X4, the following balances remain in the books of Belle Works plc. You are to draw up a balance sheet in accordance with the Companies Acts.

	£	£
Ordinary share capital		70,000
Share premium		5,000
Revaluation reserve		10,500
General reserve		6,000
Foreign exchange reserve		3,500
Profit and loss		6,297
Patents, trade marks and licences	1,500	
Goodwill	17,500	
Land and buildings	90,000	
Provision for depreciation: Land and buildings		17,500
Plant and machinery	38,600	
Provision for depreciation: Plant and machinery		19,200
Stock of raw materials: 30 September 19X4	14,320	
Work in progress: 30 September 19X4	5,640	
Finished goods: 30 September 19X4	13,290	
Debtors: Trade	11,260	
Debtors: Other	1,050	
Prepayments and accrued income	505	
Debentures (redeemable in 6 months' time)		6,000
Debentures (redeemable in 4½ years' time)		12,000
Bank overdraft (repayable in 3 months)		3,893
Trade creditors (payable in next 12 months)		11,340
Trade creditors (payable after 12 months)		1,260
Bills of exchange (payable within 12 months)		4,000
Corporation tax (payable in 9 months' time)		14,370
National insurance (payable in next month)		305
Pensions contribution owing		1,860
Deferred taxation		640
	193,665	193,665

16.3 The following trial balance has been extracted from the books of Baganza plc as at 30 September 19X7:

	£000	£000
Advance corporation tax (paid on interim dividend)	87	
Administrative expenses	400	
Called up share capital		
(1,200,000 ordinary shares of £1 each)		1,200
Cash at bank and in hand	60	
Corporation tax		
(overpayment for the year to 30 September 19X6)		20
Deferred taxation (at 1 October 19X6)		460
Distribution costs	600	
Dividends received (on 31 March 19X7)		249
Extraordinary item (net of tax)		1,500
Freehold property:		
at cost	2,700	
accumulated depreciation (at 1 October 19X6)		260
Interim dividend (paid on June 19X7)	36	
Investments in United Kingdom companies	2,000	
Plant and machinery:		
at cost	5,200	
accumulated depreciation (at 1 October 19X6)		3,600
Profit and loss account (at 1 October 19X6)		2,109
Purchases	16,000	
Research expenditure	75	
Stock (at 1 October 19X6)	2,300	
Tax on extraordinary item		360
Trade creditors		2,900
Trade debtors	2,700	
Turnover		19,500
	£32,158	£32,158

Additional information:
1 The stock at 30 September 19X7 was valued at £3,600,000.
2 Depreciation for the year to 30 September 19X7 is to be charged on the historic cost of the fixed assets as follows:
     Freehold property: 5 per cent
     Plant and machinery: 15 per cent
3 The basic rate of income tax is assumed to be 27 per cent.
4 The directors propose a final dividend of 60p per share.
5 The company was incorporated in 1970.
6 Corporation tax based on the profits for the year at a rate of 35 per cent is estimated to be £850,000.
7 A transfer of £40,000 is to be made to the deferred taxation account.
8 The ACT rate is 20 per cent.

Required:
Insofar as the information permits, prepare Baganza plc's profit and loss account for the year to 30 September 19X7, and a balance sheet as at that date in accordance with the Companies Act 1985 and appropriate accounting standards.

However, formal notes to the accounts are not required, although detailed workings should be submitted with your answer, which should include your calculation of earnings per share.

(*Association of Accounting Technicians*)

16.4A The trial balance of Payne Peerbrook plc as on 31 December 19X6 is as follows:

	Dr £	Cr £
Preference share capital: £1 shares		50,000
Ordinary share capital: 50p shares		60,000
General reserve		45,000
Exchange reserve		13,600
Profit and loss account as on 31 December 19X5		19,343
Stock 31 December 19X5	107,143	
Sales		449,110
Returns inwards	11,380	
Purchases	218,940	
Carriage inwards	2,475	
Wages (putting goods into a saleable condition)	3,096	
Wages: Warehouse staff	39,722	
Wages and salaries: Sales staff	28,161	
Wages and salaries: Administrative staff	34,778	
Motor expenses (*see* note *ii*)	16,400	
General distribution expenses	8,061	
General administrative expenses	7,914	
Debenture interest	10,000	
Royalties receivable		4,179
Directors' remuneration	18,450	
Bad debts	3,050	
Discounts allowed	5,164	
Discounts received		4,092
Plant and machinery at cost (*see* note *iii*)	175,000	
Provision for depreciation: Plant and machinery		58,400
Motor vehicles at cost (*see* note *ii*)	32,000	
Provision for depreciation: Motors		14,500
Goodwill	29,500	
Development costs	16,320	
Trade debtors	78,105	
Trade creditors		37,106
Bank overdraft (repayable any time)		4,279
Bills of exchange payable (all due within 1 year)		6,050
Debentures (redeemable in 5 years' time)		80,000
	845,659	845,659

Notes:
(*i*) Stock of finished goods on 31 December 19X6 £144,081.
(*ii*) Motor expenses and depreciation on motors to be apportioned: Distribution ¾, Administrative ¼.
(*iii*) Plant and machinery depreciation to be apportioned: Cost of sales ⅕, Distribution ⅗, Administrative ⅕.
(*iv*) Depreciate the following fixed assets on cost: Motor vehicles 25 per cent, Plant and machinery 20 per cent.
(*v*) Accrue corporation tax on profits of the year £14,150. This is payable 1 October 19X7.
(*vi* A preference dividend of £5,000 is to be paid and an ordinary dividend of £10,000 is to be proposed.

You are to draw up:
(*a*) a trading and profit and loss account for the year ended 31 December 19X6 for internal use, and
(*b*) a profit and loss account for publication, also a balance sheet as at 31 December 19X6.

16.5A   You are presented with the following information relating to Plott plc for the year to 31 March 19X1:

	£000
Advance corporation tax (paid on 14 June 19X0)	70
Bank overdraft	500
Called-up share capital (issued and fully paid)	2,100
Corporation tax (based on the profit for the year to 31 March 19X1)	900
Creditors	300
Debtors	200
Deferred taxation (credit)	150
Fixed assets: at cost	3,800
accumulated depreciation (at 31 March 19X1)	1,400
Fixed asset investments: at cost	100
Profit and loss account (at 1 April 19X0: credit)	1,200
Proposed dividend	420
Retained profit (for the year to 31 March 19X1)	585
Share premium account	315
Stocks: at cost (at 31 March 19X1)	400
Trade creditors	2,000
Trade debtors	5,300

Additional information:
1   The above information has been obtained after the compilation of the company's profit and loss account for the year to 31 March 19X1.
2   Details of fixed assets for the year to 31 March 19X1 are as follows:

		£000
(*a*)	At cost	
	At 1 April 19X0	3,400
	Additions	600
	Disposals	200
(*b*)	Accumulated depreciation	
	At 1 April 19X0	1,200
	Additions	500
	Disposals	300

3   The market value of the fixed asset investments at 31 March 19X1 was £110,000. There were no purchases or sales of fixed asset investments during the year.
4   Stocks comprise finished goods. The replacement cost of these goods is similar to the value indicated in the balance sheet.
5   Assume that the basic rate of income tax is 25 per cent.
6   The authorised share capital of the company consists of 2,500,000 ordinary shares of £1 each.
7   The ACT rate is 20 per cent.

Required:
Insofar as the information permits, prepare Plott plc's balance sheet as at 31 March 19X1 in accordance with the *minimum* requirements of the Companies Act 1985 and related accounting standards.

Notes:
1   Where appropriate, formal notes must be attached to your balance sheet; and
2   detailed working should be submitted with your answer.

(*Association of Accounting Technicians*)

16.6A The following information has been extracted from the books of Quire plc as at 30 September 19X1.

	£000	£000
Advance corporation tax	20	
Bank overdraft		2,400
Called-up share capital (ordinary shares of £1 each)		4,000
Deferred taxation		200
Delivery expenses	2,800	
Fixed assets: at cost	3,500	
accumulated depreciation (at 1 October 19X0)		1,100
Fixed asset investments	100	
Franked investment income (amount received)		40
Interest payable	400	
Interim dividend paid	60	
Office expenses	3,000	
Other creditors		180
Other debtors	160	
Profit and loss account (at 1 October 19X0)		820
Purchases	12,000	
Sales		19,000
Stocks (at 1 October 19X0)	500	
Trade creditors		100
Trade debtors	5,300	
	£27,840	£27,840

The following additional information is to be taken into account:
1   Stocks at 30 September 19X1 were valued at £400,000.
2   All items in the above trial balance are shown net of value added tax.
3   At 30 September 19X1, £130,000 was outstanding for office expenses, and £50,000 had been paid in advance for delivery van licences.
4   Depreciation at a rate of 50 per cent is to be charged on the historic cost of the tangible fixed assets using the reducing balance method: it is to be apportioned as follows:

	%
Cost of sales	60
Distribution	30
Administration	10
	100

There were no purchases or sales of fixed assets during the year to 30 September 19X1.
5   The following rates of taxation are to be assumed:

	%
Corporation tax	35
Income tax	25
Value added tax	17.5
ACT	20

The corporation tax payable based on the profits for the year to 30 September 19X1 has been estimated at £80,000.
6   A transfer of £60,000 is to be made from the deferred taxation account.
7   The directors propose to pay a final ordinary dividend of 3p per share.

Required:
Insofar as the information permits, prepare Quire plc's profit and loss account for the year to 30 September 19X1, and a balance sheet as at that date in accordance with the MINIMUM requirements of the Companies Act 1985 and related accounting standards.

Note: Formal notes to the accounts are NOT required, but detailed workings should be submitted with your answer.

(Association of Accounting Technicians)

16.7A The following trial balance has been extracted from the books of Patt plc as at 31 March 19X0:

	Dr £000	Cr £000
Bank overdraft		25
Called-up share capital (ordinary shares of £1 each)		1,440
Creditors		55
Debtors	50	
Fixed assets: at cost	300	
accumulated depreciation (at 1 April 19X9)		120
Marketing expenses	100	
Office expenses	200	
Profit and loss account (at 1 April 19X9)		200
Production expenses	2,230	
Purchases (net of VAT)	3,700	
Sales (amounts invoiced, net of VAT)		7,000
Stocks (at 1 April 19X9)	130	
Trade creditors		160
Trade debtors	2,290	
	£9,000	£9,000

Additional information:
1 Following the preparation of the above trial balance, the following additional matters need to be taken into account:
   (*a*) stock at 31 March 19X0 was valued at £170,000;
   (*b*) at 31 March 19X0, £20,000 was owing for office expenses, and £15,000 had been paid in advance for marketing expenses;
   (*c*) a customer had gone into liquidation owing the company £290,000; the company does not expect to recover any of this debt;
   (*d*) the company decides to set up a provision for doubtful debts amounting to 5 per cent of the outstanding trade debtors as at the end of each financial year; and
   (*e*) depreciation is to be charged on the fixed assets at a rate of 20 per cent on cost; it is to be apportioned as follows:

	%
Marketing	20
Office	10
Production	70
	100%

Note: There were no acquisitions or disposals of fixed assets during the year to 31 March 19X0.

2 Corporation tax (based on the accounting profit for the year at a rate of 35 per cent) is estimated to be £160,000. The basic rate of income tax is assumed to be 25 per cent. The ACT rate is 20 per cent.
3 The directors are to recommend the payment of a dividend of 10p per ordinary share.

Required:
Insofar as the information permits, prepare Patt plc's profit and loss account for the year to 31 March 19X0, and a balance sheet as at that date in accordance with the Companies Act 1985 and related accounting standards.

Notes:
(*i*) Where appropriate, formal notes should be attached to your profit and loss account and balance sheet. However, a statement of accounting policies is NOT required.
(*ii*) Detailed workings should also be submitted with your solution. They should be clearly designated as such, and they must not form part of your formal notes.

(Association of Accounting Technicians)

17

Published accounts of limited companies: accompanying notes

Objectives

After you have studied this chapter, you should:

- *be aware of the additional notes to published financial statements that are required by the Companies Acts*

- *be aware of the requirement to include a directors' report with the published financial statements*

17.1 Notes to accompany the balance sheet

The Companies Acts require that the following additional notes are given to accompany the published balance sheet.

1 Particulars of turnover

An analysis of turnover into:

(a) each class of business; and by
(b) geographical markets;

and, in addition, the amount of profit or loss before taxation, in the opinion of the directors, attributable to each class of business.

Such disclosure does not have to made if it would be prejudicial to the business of the company. The fact of non-disclosure would have to be stated. An example of such a note might be as in Exhibit 17.1:

Exhibit 17.1

Analysis of Turnover

	Turnover £	Profit £
Motors	26,550,000	2,310,000
Aircraft	58,915,000	4,116,000
	85,465,000	6,426,000

The geographical division of turnover is:	£
United Kingdom	31,150,000
The Americas	43,025,000
Rest of the World	10,290,000
	85,465,000

It should be noted that these requirements were extended by SSAP 25: *Segmental reporting*, but only for:

- plcs or parent undertakings that have one or more plcs as a subsidiary
- banking and insurance companies or groups
- private companies and other entities that exceed the criteria, multiplied in each case by ten, for defining a medium-sized company under section 247 of the Companies Act 1985. (*See* Chapter 16, section 16.6 for a table of these criteria.)

It requires that for each segment, turnover (analysed between sales to external customers and sales between segments), results and net assets should be disclosed. Geographical segmental analysis should, in the first instance, be on the basis of source (i.e. the geographical location of the supplying segment). In addition, turnover to third parties should be segmentally reported on the basis of destination (i.e. the geographical location of the receiving segment).

Where associated undertakings account for at least 20 per cent of the total results or net assets of the reporting entity, additional disclosure should be made in aggregate for all associated undertakings. This comprises segmental disclosure of the reporting entity's share of the aggregate profits or losses before tax, minority interests and extraordinary items of the associated undertakings, and the reporting entity's share of the net assets of the associated undertakings (including goodwill to the extent that it has not been written off) after attributing, where possible, fair values to the net assets at the date of acquisition of the interest in each associated undertaking.

2 Particulars of staff

(*a*) Average number employed by the company (or by group in consolidated accounts), divided between categories of workers, e.g. between manufacturing and administration.

(*b*) (*i*) Wages and salaries paid to staff.
(*ii*) Social security costs of staff.
(*iii*) Other pension costs for employees.

(*c*) Number of employees (excluding those working wholly or mainly overseas) earning over £30,000, analysed under successive multiples of £5,000. Exclude pension contributions.

Exhibit 17.2 is an example of a note concerning higher-paid employees.

Exhibit 17.2

The number of employees earning over £30,000 was 28, analysed as follows:

Gross salaries	*Number of employees*
£30,001–35,000	16
£35,001–40,000	8
£40,001–45,000	4
	28

3 Directors' emoluments

(*a*) Aggregate amounts of:
   (*i*)   emoluments, including pension contributions and benefits in kind. Distinction to be made between those emoluments as fees and those for executive duties;
   (*ii*) pensions for past directors;
   (*iii*) compensation for loss of office.
(*b*) The chairman's emoluments and those of the highest paid director, if paid more than the chairman. In both cases pension contributions are to be excluded.
(*c*) Number of directors whose emoluments, excluding pension contributions, fall within each bracket of £5,000.
(*d*) Total amounts waived by directors and numbers concerned.

The disclosures under (*b*) and (*c*) above are not needed for a company being neither a parent nor subsidiary undertaking where its directors' emoluments under (*a*) do not exceed £60,000. The disclosures under (*b*) and (*c*) are also not necessary for directors working wholly or mainly overseas.

An illustration is now given in Exhibit 17.3:

Exhibit 17.3

Name	Fee (as directors)	Remuneration (as executives)	Pension contributions
A (Chairman)	£5,000	£85,000	£20,000
B	£2,500	£95,000	£30,000
C	£2,500	£55,000	£15,000
D	£1,500	£54,000	£12,500
E	£1,500	£30,000	£10,000

Note to accounts:
Directors' remuneration: the amounts paid to directors were as follows:

Fees as directors	£13,000
Other emoluments, including pension contributions	£406,500

Emoluments of the Chairman – excluding pension contributions – amounted to £90,000, and those of the highest paid director to £97,500. Other directors' emoluments were in the following ranges:

£30,001 to £35,000	1
£55,001 to £60,000	2

4 Various charges to be shown as notes

(*a*) Auditors' remuneration, including expenses.
(*b*) Hire of plant and machinery.
(*c*) Interest payable on (*i*) bank loans, overdrafts and other loans repayable by instalments or otherwise within five years; (*ii*) loans of any other kind.
(*d*) Depreciation:
   (*i*)   amounts of provisions for both tangible and intangible assets;
   (*ii*) effect on depreciation of change of depreciation method;
   (*iii*) effect on depreciation of revaluation of assets.

5 Income from listed investments

6 Rents receivable from land, after deducting outgoings

7 Taxation (see also SSAP 8: Treatment of tax under the computation system)

(a) Tax change split between:
    (i)   UK corporation tax, and basis of computation;
    (ii) UK income tax, and basis of computation;
    (iii) irrecoverable VAT;
    (iv) tax attributable to franked investment income.
(b) If relevant, split between tax on ordinary and tax on extraordinary activities.
(c) Show, as component part, charge for deferred tax.
(d) Any other special circumstances affecting tax liability.

8 Extraordinary and exceptional items and prior period adjustments

See FRS 3.

9 Redemption of shares and loans

Show amounts set aside for these purposes.

10 Earnings per share (listed companies only)

See SSAP 3.

11 Statement showing movements on reserves

17.2 The directors' report

As well as a balance sheet and profit and loss account, the shareholders must also receive a directors' report. The contents of the report are given in the Companies Acts, but no formal layout is given. Such a report is additional to the notes, which have to be attached to the accounts; the directors' report does not replace such notes.

(a) A fair review of the development of the business of the company (and its subsidiaries) during the financial year and of the position at the end of the year. The dividends proposed and transfers to reserves should be given.
(b) Principal activities of the company and any changes therein.
(c) Post-balance sheet events, i.e. details of important events affecting the company (and its subsidiaries) since the end of the year.
(d) Likely future developments in the business.
(e) An indication of research and development carried on.
(f) Significant changes in fixed assets. In the case of land, the difference between book and market values, if significant.
(g) Political and charitable contributions; if, taken together, these exceed £200 there must be shown:
    (i)   separate totals for each classification;
    (ii) where political contributions exceeding £200 have been made, the names of recipients and amounts.
(h) Details of own shares purchased.

(*i*) Employees:
  (*i*) statement concerning health, safety and welfare at work of company's employees;
  (*ii*) for companies with average workforce exceeding 250, details of employment of disabled people.
(*j*) Indication of activities in research and development.
(*k*) Directors:
  (*i*) names of all persons who had been directors during any part of the financial year;
  (*ii*) their interests in contracts;
  (*iii*) for each director, the name; also:
    ● the number of shares held at the start of the year;
    ● the number of shares held at the end of the year;
    ● for each director elected in the year there shall also be shown shares held when elected;
    ● all the above to show nil amounts where appropriate.

Note: Under the Companies Acts the directors' report is subject to external audit. If the external auditors' judgement is that the directors' report is inconsistent with the audited company accounts, then this must be stated in the auditors' report.

17.3 Illustrative company accounts: specimen question 1

F Clarke Ltd are specialist wholesalers. This is their trial balance at 31 December 19X4.

	Dr £	Cr £
Ordinary share capital: £1 shares		1,000,000
Share premium		120,000
General reserve		48,000
Profit and loss account as at 31.12.19X3		139,750
Stock: 31.12.19X3	336,720	
Sales		4,715,370
Purchases	2,475,910	
Returns outwards		121,220
Returns inwards	136,200	
Carriage inwards	6,340	
Carriage outwards	43,790	
Warehouse wages (average number of workers 59)	410,240	
Salesmen's salaries (average number of workers 21)	305,110	
Administrative wages and salaries	277,190	
Plant and machinery	610,000	
Motor vehicle hire	84,770	
Provisions for depreciation: plant and machinery		216,290
General distribution expenses	27,130	
General administrative expenses	47,990	
Directors' remuneration	195,140	
Rents receivable		37,150
Trade debtors	1,623,570	
Cash at bank and in hand	179,250	
Trade creditors (payable before 31.3.19X5)		304,570
Bills of exchange payable (payable 28.2.19X5)		57,000
	6,759,350	6,759,350

Notes:

(*a*) Stock at 31.12.19X4: £412,780, consists of goods for resale.

(*b*) Plant and machinery is apportioned: distributive 60 per cent; administrative 40 per cent.

(*c*) Accrue auditors' remuneration: £71,000.

(*d*) Depreciate plant and machinery: 20 per cent on cost.

(*e*) Of the motor hire, £55,000 is for distributive purposes.

(*f*) Corporation tax on profits, at a rate of 35 per cent, is estimated at £238,500, and is payable on 1.10.19X5.

(*g*) There is a proposed ordinary dividend of 37½ per cent for the year.

(*h*) All of the sales are of one type of goods. Net sales of £3,620,000 have been made in the UK with the remainder in Europe, and are shown net of VAT.

(*i*) Pension contributions for staff amounted to £42,550 and social security contributions to £80,120. These figures are included in wages and salaries in the trial balance. No employee earned over £30,000.

(*j*) Plant of £75,000 had been bought during the year.

(*k*) Directors' remuneration has been as follows:

	£
Chairman	46,640
Managing Director	51,500
Finance Director	46,000
Marketing Director	43,000
	187,140

In addition each of them drew £2,000 as directors' fees. Pensions are the personal responsibility of directors.

Required:

Subject to the limits of the information given you, draw up a profit and loss account for the year ended 31 December 19X4, and a balance sheet as at that date. They should be in published form and accompanied by the necessary notes prescribed by statute.

Specimen answer 1

F Clarke Ltd: Workings

	£		£	£
Turnover: Sales	4,715,370	Cost of sales:		
Less Returns in	136,200	Opening stock		336,720
	4,579,170	*Add* Purchases	2,475,910	
		Less Returns out	121,220	
			2,354,690	
		Add Carriage in	6,340	2,361,030
				2,697,750
		Less Closing stock		412,780
				2,284,970
Distribution costs:		Administrative expenses:		
Warehouse wages	410,240	Wages and salaries		277,190
Salesmen's salaries	305,110	Motor hire		29,770
Carriage out	43,790	General expenses		47,990
General expenses	27,130	Directors' remuneration		150,140
Motor hire	55,000	Auditors' remuneration		71,000
Depreciation: plant	73,200	Depreciation: plant		48,800
				624,890
Marketing Director's				
remuneration	45,000			
	959,470			

(a) F Clarke Ltd

Profit and Loss Account for the year ended 31 December 19X4

	£	£
Turnover		4,579,170
Cost of sales		2,284,970
Gross profit		2,294,200
Distribution costs	959,470	
Administrative expenses	624,890	1,584,360
		709,840
Other operating income		37,150
Profit on ordinary activities before taxation		746,990
Tax on profit on ordinary activities		238,500
Profit on ordinary activities after taxation		508,490
Retained profits from last year		139,750
		648,240
Proposed ordinary dividend		375,000
Retained profits carried forward to next year		273,240

(b) F Clarke Ltd

Balance Sheet as at 31 December 19X4

	£	£	£
Fixed assets			
Tangible assets			
Plant and machinery			271,710
Current assets			
Stock			
Finished goods and goods for resale		412,780	
Debtors			
Trade debtors		1,623,570	
Cash at bank and in hand		179,250	
		2,215,600	
Creditors: amounts falling due within one year			
Trade creditors	304,570		
Bills of exchange payable	57,000		
Other creditors including taxation and social security	684,500	1,046,070	
Net current assets			1,169,530
Total assets less current liabilities			1,441,240
Capital and reserves			
			£
Called-up share capital			1,000,000
Share premium account			120,000
Other reserves:			
General reserve			48,000
Profit and loss account			273,240
			1,441,240

Notes to the accounts

1 Turnover

This is the value, net of VAT, of goods of a single class of business. Turnover may be analysed as follows:

	£
United Kingdom	3,680,000
Europe	899,170
	4,579,170

2 Employees

Average number of workers was:

Warehousing	59
Sales	21
	80

Remuneration of employees was:

	£
Wages and salaries	869,870
Social security costs	80,120
Pension contributions	42,550
	992,540

3 Directors' remuneration

The amounts paid to directors were as follows:

	£
Fees as directors	8,000
Other emoluments	187,140

Emoluments of the Chairman amounted to £46,640, and those of the highest paid director £51,500. Other directors' emoluments were in the following ranges:

£40,001–45,000	1
£45,001–50,000	1

4 Operating profit is shown after charging

	£
Auditors' remuneration	71,000
Hire of motors	84,770

5 Fixed assets

Plant and machinery	£	£
Cost at 1.1.19X4	535,000	
Additions	75,000	610,000
Depreciation to 31.12.19X3	216,290	
Charge for the year	122,000	338,290
		271,710

6 Other creditors including taxation

	£	£
Proposed dividend	375,000	
Auditors' remuneration	71,000	
Corporation tax	238,500	684,500

17.4 Illustrative company accounts: specimen question 2

The trial balance of Quartz plc on 31 December 19X3 was as follows:

	Dr £000	Cr £000
Preference share capital: £1 shares		200
Ordinary share capital: £1 shares		1,000
Exchange reserve		75
General reserve		150
Profit and loss account 31.12.19X2		215
Sales		4,575
Purchases	2,196	
Carriage inwards	38	
Stock 31.12.19X2	902	
Wages (adding value to goods)	35	
Wages: warehousing	380	
Wages and salaries: administrative	120	
Wages and salaries: sales	197	
Motor expenses	164	
Bad debts	31	
Debenture interest	40	
Bank overdraft interest	19	
General distribution expenses	81	
General administrative expenses	73	
Directors' remuneration	210	
Investments: related companies	340	
Income from shares in related companies		36
Discounts allowed and received	55	39
Buildings: at cost	1,200	
Plant and machinery: at cost	330	
Motor vehicles: at cost	480	
Provisions for depreciation:		
Land and buildings		375
Plant and machinery		195
Motors		160
Goodwill	40	
Patents, licences and trade marks	38	
Trade debtors and creditors	864	392
Bank overdraft (repayable any time)		21
Debentures 10 per cent		400
	7,833	7,833

Notes:
(*a*) Stock at 31.12.19X3: £1,103,000 at cost.
(*b*) Motor expenses and depreciation on motors to be apportioned: Distribution 75 per cent; Administrative 25 per cent.
(*c*) Depreciation on buildings and plant and machinery to be apportioned: Distribution 50 per cent; Administrative 50 per cent.
(*d*) Depreciate on cost: Motor vehicles 25 per cent; Plant and machinery 20 per cent.
(*e*) Accrue corporation tax on profits of the year £266,000. This is payable 1 October 19X4.

(*f*) A preference dividend of 10 per cent is to be paid and an ordinary dividend of 50 per cent is to be proposed.

(*g*) During the year new vehicles were purchased at a cost of £60,000.

(*h*) During June 19X3 one of the buildings, which had originally cost £130,000, and which had a written-down value at the date of the sale of £80,000, was sold for £180,000. Depreciation on buildings to be charged against the year's profits £60,000. The buildings are revalued by B & Co., Chartered Surveyors, at £1,500,000 at 31.12.19X3 (and this figure is to be included in the accounts).

(*i*) Directors' remuneration was as follows:

	£
Marketing	42,000
Chairman	37,000
Managing	61,000
Finance	50,000
	190,000

In addition each director drew £5,000 fees.

(*j*) Of the goodwill, 50 per cent is to be written off during this year, and 50 per cent in the following year.

(*k*) The debentures are to be redeemed in five equal annual instalments, starting in the following year 19X4.

(*l*) The investments are in listed companies with a market value at 31 December 19X3 of £438,000.

(*m*) Auditors' remuneration, including expenses, was £7,000.

You are required to prepare a balance sheet as at 31 December 19X3. It should:

(*a*) conform to the requirements of the Companies Act 1985;
(*b*) conform to the relevant accounting standards;
(*c*) be shown in vertical form;
(*d*) give the notes necessary to the accounts.

Specimen answer 2

Quartz plc: workings

	£000		Dist. £000	Admin £000
Cost of sales:		Wages	577	120
Opening stock	902	Motor expenses	123	41
Add Purchases	2,196	General	81	73
Add Carriage in	38	Depreciation: plant	33	33
		motors	90	30
	3,136	buildings	30	30
Less Closing stock	1,103	Directors	47	163
		Discounts (net) 55–39		16
	2,033	Debenture interest		40
Wages (added value)	35	Bank interest		19
		Bad debts		31
	2,068		981	596

(a) Quartz plc

Profit and Loss Account for the year ended 31 December 19X4

	£000	£000
Turnover		4,575
Cost of sales		2,068
Gross profit		2,507
Distribution costs	981	
Administrative expenses	596	1,577
		930
Income from shares in related companies		36
Profit on ordinary activities before taxation		966
Tax on profit on ordinary activities		266
Profit for the year on ordinary activities after taxation		700
Retained profits from last year		215
		915
Goodwill written off	20	
Dividends paid and proposed	520	540
Retained profits carried to next year		375

(b) Quartz plc

Balance Sheet as at 31 December 19X3

	£000	£000	£000
Fixed assets			
Intangible assets			
Patents, licences and trade marks		38	
Goodwill		20	
		58	
Tangible assets			
Buildings	1,500		
Plant and machinery	69		
Vehicles	200	1,769	
Investments			
Shares in related companies		340	2,167
Current assets			
Stock	1,103		
Trade debtors	864	1,967	
Creditors: amounts falling due within one year			
Debenture loans	80		
Bank overdraft	21		
Trade creditors	392		
Other creditors	786		
	1,279		
Creditors: amounts falling due after more than one year			
Debenture loans	320	1,599	368
			2,535
Capital and reserves			
Called-up share capital			1,200
Revaluation reserve			735
Other reserves			225
Profit and loss account			375
			2,535

Notes to the accounts

1 Share capital called up

	£
200,000 10 per cent preference shares of £1 each	200,000
1,000,000 ordinary shares of £1 each	1,000,000
	1,200,000

2 Accounting policies

Goodwill has been written off £20,000 against this year. The directors intend to write off the remaining £20,000 against next year's profits.

3 Tangible assets

	Buildings £000	Plant £000	Vehicles £000
Cost at 1.1.19X4	1,330	330	480
Disposals (at cost)	(130)	–	–
Adjustment for revaluation	735		
	1,935	330	480
Depreciation at 1.1.19X4	425	195	160
Provided in year	60	66	120
Disposals	(50)		
	435	261	280
Net book values	1,500	69	200

4 Investments

The market value of investments at 31 December 19X3 was £438,000.

5 Ten per cent debenture loans

These are redeemable in five equal annual instalments, starting next year. Interest of £40,000 is charged in this year's accounts.

6 Other creditors including taxation

	£
Preference dividend proposed	20,000
Ordinary dividend proposed 50 per cent	500,000
Corporation tax based on year's profits	266,000
	786,000

7 Other reserves

	£
Exchange reserve	75,000
General reserve	150,000
	225,000

8 Directors' remuneration

The amounts paid to directors were as follows:

	£	£
Fees as directors	20,000	
Other emoluments	190,000	210,000

Emoluments of the chairman amounted to £42,000 and those of the highest paid director £66,000. Other directors' emoluments were in the following ranges:

£45,001 to £50,000	1
£50,001 to £55,000	1

9 Operating profit is shown after charging

	£
Auditors' remuneration	7,000
Bank overdraft interest	19,000

Main points to remember

1   The Companies Acts require that additional notes be prepared and included with the published financial statements.

2   In some cases, the contents of these notes have been extended through the issuing of an accounting standard. For example, SSAP 25: *Segmental reporting* extended the disclosure required of many entities concerning segmental performance.

3   Along with the notes to the financial statements, a directors' report must be presented that summarises the activities and performance of the entity, along with specific details on a number of matters, including directors' shareholdings and information concerning significant changes in fixed assets.

Review questions

17.1 The following trial balance of X Limited, a non-listed company, has been extracted from the books after the preparation of the profit and loss and appropriation accounts for the year ended 31 March 19X7.

	£000	£000
Ordinary share capital – authorised, allotted and		
called-up fully paid shares of £1 each		1,000
12% debentures (repayable in 9 years)		500
Deferred taxation		128
Provisions for depreciation:		
Plant and machinery at 31 March 19X7		650
Freehold properties at 31 March 19X7		52
Vehicles at 31 March 19X7		135
Investments (listed), at cost	200	
Trade debtors and prepayments	825	
Corporation tax		310
Advance corporation tax recoverable	70	
Proposed final dividend		280
Tangible fixed assets:		
Freehold properties at 31 March 19X7	1,092	
Plant and machinery at 31 March 19X7	1,500	
Vehicles at 31 March 19X7	420	
Profit and loss account – balance at 31 March 19X7		386
Share premium account		150
Trade creditors and accruals		878
Research and development costs	35	
Stocks:		
Raw materials	200	
Work-in-progress	50	
Finished goods	250	
Bank balance	439	
Revaluation reserve on freehold properties		612
	5,081	5,081

You are also provided with the following information:

1 Investments
The listed investments consist of shares in W plc quoted on the Stock Exchange at £180,000 on 31 March 19X7. This is not considered to be a permanent fall in the value of this asset.

2 Trade debtors and prepayments
The company received notice, during April 19X7, that one of its major customers, Z Limited, had gone into liquidation. The amount included in trade debtors and prepayments is £225,000 and it is estimated that a dividend of 24p in the £ will be paid to unsecured creditors.

3 Taxation
(*a*) *Corporation tax*
The figure in the trial balance is made up as follows:

	£000
Based on profits for the year	174
Tax on exceptional item (*see* note 4)	96
Advance corporation tax on proposed dividend (ACT rate = 20%)	70
	340
Less Advance corporation tax paid during the year	30
	310

(b) *Deferred taxation*

A transfer of £50,000 was made from the profit and loss account during the year ended 31 March 19X7.

4 Tangible fixed assets

(a) In arriving at the profit for the year, depreciation of £242,000 was charged, made up of freehold properties £12,000, plant and machinery £150,000 and vehicles £80,000.

(b) During the year to 31 March 19X7, new vehicles were purchased at a cost of £200,000.

(c) During March 19X7, the directors sold one of the freehold properties which had originally cost £320,000 and which had a written-down value at the date of the sale of £280,000. A profit of £320,000 on the sale, which was regarded as exceptional, has already been dealt with in arriving at the profit for the year. The estimated corporation tax liability in respect of the capital gain will be £96,000, as shown in note 3. After this sale, the directors decided to have the remaining freehold properties revalued, for the first time, by Messrs V & Co, Chartered Surveyors and to include the revalued figure of £1,040,000 in the 19X7 accounts.

5 Research and development costs

The company carries out research and development and accounts for it in accordance with the relevant accounting standard. The amount shown in the trial balance relates to development expenditure on a new product scheduled to be launched in April 19X7. Management is confident that this new product will earn substantial profits for the company in the coming years.

6 Stocks

The replacement cost of the finished goods, if valued at 31 March 19X7, would amount to £342,000.

You are required to prepare a balance sheet at 31 March 19X7 to conform to the requirements of the Companies Acts and relevant accounting standards in so far as the information given allows. The vertical format must be used.

The notes necessary to accompany this statement should also be prepared.

Workings should be shown, but comparative figures are not required.

(*Chartered Institute of Management Accountants*)

17.2 The following information has been extracted from the books of account of Billinge plc as at 30 June 19X6:

	Dr £000	Cr £000
Administration expenses	242	
Cash at bank and in hand	157	
Cash received on sale of fittings		3
Corporation tax (over-provision for the previous year)		10
Deferred taxation		60
Depreciation on fixtures, fittings, tools and equipment (1 July 19X5)		132
Distribution costs	55	
Factory closure costs	30	
Fixtures, fittings, tools and equipment at cost	340	
Profit and loss account (at 1 July 19X5)		40
Purchase of equipment	60	
Purchases of goods for resale	855	
Sales (net of VAT)		1,500
Share capital (500,000 authorised, issued and fully paid ordinary shares of £1 each)		500
Stock (at 1 July 19X5)	70	
Trade creditors		64
Trade debtors	500	
	£2,309	£2,309

Additional information:
1 The company was incorporated in 19X0.
2 The stock at 30 June 19X6 (valued at the lower of cost or net realisable value) was estimated to be worth £100,000.
3 Fixtures, fittings, tools and equipment all related to administrative expenses. Depreciation is charged on them at a rate of 20 per cent per annum on cost. A full year's depreciation is charged in the year of acquisition, but no depreciation is charged in the year of disposal.
4 During the year to 30 June 19X6, the company purchased £60,000 of equipment. It also sold some fittings (which had originally cost £20,000) for £3,000 and for which depreciation of £15,000 had been set aside.
5 The corporation tax based on the profits for the year at a rate of 35 per cent is estimated to be £100,000. A transfer of £40,000 is to be made to the deferred taxation account.
6 The company proposes to pay a dividend of 20p per ordinary share.
7 The standard rate of income tax is 30 per cent.
8 The ACT rate is 20 per cent.

Required
Insofar as the information permits, prepare Billinge plc's profit and loss account for the year to 30 June 19X6, and a balance sheet as at that date in accordance with the Companies Acts and appropriate accounting standards.

(*Association of Accounting Technicians*)

17.3A Cosnett Ltd is a company principally involved in the manufacture of aluminium accessories for camping enthusiasts.

The following trial balance was extracted from the books at 30 September 19X5.

	£	£
Issued ordinary share capital (£1 shares)		600,000
Retained profit at 1 October 19X4		625,700
Debentures redeemable 20X0		150,000
Bank loan		25,000
Plant and machinery at cost	1,475,800	
Accumulated depreciation to 30 September 19X5		291,500
Investments in UK companies at cost	20,000	
Turnover		3,065,800
Dividends from investments (amount received)		2,800
Loss arising on factory closure	86,100	
Cost of sales	2,083,500	
Political and charitable contributions	750	
Distribution costs	82,190	
Salaries of office staff	42,100	
Directors' emoluments	63,000	
Rent and rates of offices	82,180	
Hire of plant and machinery	6,700	
Travel and entertainment expenses	4,350	
General expenses	221,400	
Trade debtors	396,100	
Trade creditors and accruals		245,820
Stocks	421,440	
Bank	17,950	
Interim dividend paid	21,000	
Interest charged	19,360	
Provision for deferred taxation		45,100
Advance corporation tax	7,800	
	5,051,720	5,051,720

You are provided with the following additional information:
(a) The company's shares are owned, equally, by three brothers: John, Peter and Henry Phillips; they are also the directors.
(b) The bank loan is repayable by five equal annual instalments of £5,000 commencing 31 December 19X5.
(c) The investments were acquired with cash, surplus to existing operating requirements, which will be needed to pay for additional plant the directors plan to acquire early in 19X6.
(d) On 1 January 19X5 the company closed a factory which had previously contributed approximately 20 per cent of the company's total production requirements.
(e) Trade debtors include £80,000 due from a customer who went into liquidation on 1 September 19X5; the directors estimate that a dividend of 20p in the £ will eventually be received.
(f) Trade creditors and accruals include:
   (i) £50,000 due to a supplier of plant, of which £20,000 is payable on 1 January 19X6 and the remainder at the end of the year;
   (ii) accruals totalling £3,260.
(g) The mainstream corporation tax liability for the year is estimated at £120,000.
(h) The directors propose to pay a final dividend of 10.5p per share and to transfer £26,500 to the deferred tax account.

Note: An advance corporation tax rate of 20 per cent may be assumed.

Required:
The profit and loss account of Cosnett Ltd for the year to 30 September 19X5 and balance sheet at that date together with relevant notes attached thereto. The accounts should comply with the minimum requirements of the Companies Acts and accounting standards so far as the information permits.

(*Institute of Chartered Secretaries and Administrators*)

17.4A The following trial balance has been extracted from the books of Arran plc as at 31 March 19X7:

	£000	£000
Administrative expenses	95	
Advance corporation tax paid	6	
Called-up share capital (all ordinary shares of £1 each)		200
Cash at bank and in hand	25	
Debtors	230	
Deferred taxation (at 1 April 19X6)		60
Distribution costs	500	
Fixed asset investments	280	
Franked investment income		12
Interim dividend paid	21	
Overprovision of last year's corporation tax		5
Land and buildings at cost	200	
Land and buildings: accumulated depreciation at 1 April 19X6		30
Plant and machinery at cost	400	
Plant and machinery: accumulated depreciation at 1 April 19X6		170
Profit and loss account (at 1 April 19X6)		235
Profit on exceptional item		50
Purchases	1,210	
Sales		2,215
Stocks at 1 April 19X6	140	
Trade creditors		130
	£3,107	£3,107

Additional information
1   Stocks at 31 March 19X7 were valued at £150,000.
2   Depreciation for the year to 31 March 19X7 is to be charged against administrative expenses as follows:

	£000
Land and buildings	5
Plant and machinery	40

3   Assume that the basic rate of income tax is 30 per cent.
4   Corporation tax of £180,000 is to be charged against profits on ordinary activities for the year to 31 March 19X7.
5   £4,000 is to be transferred to the deferred taxation account.
6   The company proposes to pay a final ordinary dividend of 30p per share.
7   The ACT rate is 20 per cent.

Required:
Insofar as the information permits, prepare the company's profit and loss account for the year to 31 March 19X7 and a balance sheet as at that date in accordance with the Companies Acts and related accounting standards. (*Note*: Profit and loss account and balance sheet notes are not required, but you should show the basis and computation of earnings per share at the foot of the profit and loss account, and your workings should be submitted.)

(*Association of Accounting Technicians*)

17.5A   The following trial balance has been extracted from the books of account of Greet plc as at 31 March 19X8:

	Dr £000	Cr £000
Administrative expenses	210	
Called up share capital (ordinary shares of £1 fully paid)		600
Debtors	470	
Cash at bank and in hand	40	
Corporation tax (overprovision in 19X7)		25
Deferred taxation (at 1 April 19X7)		180
Distribution costs	420	
Exceptional item		60
Fixed asset investments	560	
Franked investment income (amount received)		72
Plant and machinery:		
At cost	750	
Accumulated depreciation (at 31 March 19X8)		220
Profit and loss (at 1 April 19X7)		182
Purchases	960	
Stock (at 1 April 19X7)	140	
Trade creditors		261
Turnover		1,950
	£3,550	£3,550

Additional information:
1 Stock at 31 March 19X8 was valued at £150,000.
2 The following items (*inter alia*) *are already included* in the balances listed in the above trial balance:

	Distribution costs £000	Administrative expenses £000
Depreciation (for the year to 31 March 19X8)	27	5
Hire of plant and machinery	20	15
Auditors' remuneration	–	30
Directors' emoluments	–	45

3 The following rates of taxation are to be assumed:

	%
Corporation tax	35
Income tax	27
ACT	20

4 The corporation tax charge based on the profits for the year is estimated to be £52,000.
5 A transfer of £16,000 is to be made to the credit of the deferred taxation account.
6 The exceptional item relates to the profit made on the disposal of a factory in Belgium following the closure of the company's entire operations in that country.
7 The company's authorised share capital consists of 1,000,000 ordinary shares of £1 each.
8 A final ordinary payment of 50p per share is proposed.
9 There were no purchases or disposals of fixed assets during the year.
10 The market value of the fixed assets investments as at 31 March 19X8 was £580,000. There were no purchases or sales of such investments during the year.

Required:

Insofar as the information permits, prepare the company's published profit and loss account for the year to 31 March 19X8 and a balance sheet as at that date in accordance with the Companies Acts and with related accounting standards.

Relevant notes to the profit and loss account and balance sheet and detailed workings should be submitted with your answer, but a statement of the company's accounting policies is not required.

(*Association of Accounting Technicians*)

17.6 The accountant of Scampion plc, a retailing company listed on the London Stock Exchange, has produced the following draft financial statements for the company for the year to 31 May 19X7.

Profit and Loss Account for year to 31 May 19X7

	£000	£000
Sales		3,489
Income from investments		15
		3,504
Purchases of goods and services	1,929	
Value added tax paid on sales	257	
Wages and salaries including pension scheme	330	
Depreciation	51	
Interest on loans	18	
General administration		
expenses – Shops	595	
– Head office	25	
		3,205
Net profit for year		299
Corporation tax at 40%		120
Profit after tax for year		179

Balance Sheet at 31 May 19X7

	£000	£000
Fixed assets		
Land and buildings		1,178
Fixtures, fittings, equipment and motor vehicles		194
Investments		167
		1,539
Current assets		
Stock	230	
Debtors	67	
Cash at bank and in hand	84	
	381	
Current liabilities		
Creditors	487	
		(106)
		1,433
Ordinary share capital (£1 shares)		660
Reserves		703
Loans		70
		1,433

You discover the following further information:

(*i*)   Fixed assets details are as follows:

	Cost £000	Depreciation £000	Net £000
Freehold land and buildings	1,212	34	1,178
Fixtures, fittings and equipment	181	56	125
Motor vehicles	137	68	69

Purchases of fixed assets during the year were freehold land and buildings £50,000, fixtures, fittings and equipment £40,000, motor vehicles £20,000. The only fixed asset disposal during the year is referred to in note (*x*). Depreciation charged during the year was £5,000 for freehold buildings, £18,000 for fixtures, fittings and equipment and £28,000 for motor vehicles. Straight-line depreciation method is used assuming the following lives: Freehold buildings 40 years, fixtures, fittings and equipment 10 years and motor vehicles 5 years.

(*ii*)   A dividend of 10 pence per share is proposed.

(*iii*) A valuation by Bloggs & Co Surveyors shows the freehold land and buildings to have a market value of £1,350,000.

(*iv*)   Loans are:
£20,000 bank loan with a variable rate of interest repayable by 30 September 19X7;
£50,000 12 per cent debenture repayable 20X1;
£100,000 11 per cent debenture repaid during the year.
There were no other loans during the year.

(*v*)   The income from investments is derived from fixed asset investments (shares in related companies) £5,000 and current asset investment (government securities) £10,000.

(*vi*)   At the balance sheet date the shares in related companies (cost £64,000) are valued by the directors at £60,000. The market value of the government securities is £115,000 (cost £103,000).

(*vii*) After the balance sheet date but before the financial statements are finalised there is a very substantial fall in share and security prices. The market value of the government securities had fallen to £50,000 by the time the directors signed the accounts. No adjustment has been made for this item in the accounts.

(*viii*) Within two weeks of the balance sheet date a notice of liquidation was received by Scampion plc concerning one of the company's debtors. £45,000 is included in the balance sheet for this debtor and enquiries reveal that nothing is likely to be paid to any unsecured creditor. No adjustment has been made for this item in the accounts.

(*ix*)   The corporation tax charge is based on the accounts for the year and there are no other amounts of tax owing by the company.

(*x*)   Reserves at 31 May 19X6 were:

	£
Revaluation reserve	150,000
Share premium account	225,000
Profit and loss account	149,000

The revaluation reserve represents the after-tax surplus on a property which was valued in last year's balance sheet at £400,000 and sold during the current year at book value.

Required:
A profit and loss account for the year to 31 May 19X7 and a balance sheet at that date for Scampion plc complying with the Companies Acts insofar as the information given will allow.
  Ignore advance corporation tax and related tax credit on investment income.

(*Chartered Association of Certified Accountants*)

17.7A The Companies Acts and accounting standards (SSAPs) require a great deal of information to be disclosed in a company's annual report and accounts.

Required:
List the disclosure requirements for the following items:
(*i*)   employees;
(*ii*)   directors' emoluments; and
(*iii*) fixed assets.

(*Association of Accounting Technicians*)

18
FRS 1: Cash flow statements

Objectives

After you have studied this chapter, you should be able to:

● *discuss the purpose of cash flow information*

● *understand the difference between cash flow and profit*

● *prepare a cash flow statement for a company following the format given in FRS 1*

18.1 Introduction

Volume 1 introduced cash flow statements. This chapter is concerned with the accounting standard relating to these statements – FRS 1: *Cash flow statements*. The standard requires that a cash flow statement be prepared according to prescribed formats for all companies other than those exempt from doing so, either because they are 'small', as defined by the Companies Act (see Chapter 16), or because they are subsidiary undertakings and the group they belong to is publishing group accounts in the European Union. The standard requires that the statement be included as a primary statement within the financial statements, i.e. it has the same status as the profit and loss account and the balance sheet.

18.2 Standard headings

The objective of FRS 1 is to require entities to report their cash generation and absorption for a period on a standard basis and, by so doing, facilitate comparison of the cash flow performance of different entities. For this reason, the statement must show the flows of cash and cash equivalents for the period under the headings:

● operating activities;
● returns on investments and servicing of finance;
● taxation;
● investing activities; and
● financing.

The headings should be in that order and the statement should include a total for each heading and a total of the net cash inflow or outflow before 'financing'.

18.3 Cash flow

The cash flow statement reports cash flow. Cash flow is defined in paragraph 4 of FRS 1 as 'an increase or decrease in an amount of cash or cash equivalent resulting from a transaction'. Anything that falls outside this definition is not a cash flow and should not appear in the statement (though it could appear in the notes).

These two components of cash flow are further defined:

- **Cash** – cash in hand and deposits repayable on demand with any bank or other financial institution, including cash in hand and deposits denominated in foreign currency.
- **Cash equivalents** – short-term, highly liquid investments that are readily convertible into known amounts of cash without notice and which were within three months of maturity when acquired, less advances from banks repayable within three months from the date of the advance. They include investments and advances denominated in foreign currencies provided that they fulfil the above criteria. To qualify as a cash equivalent there must be no significant risk of changes in value owing to changes in interest rates, i.e. if a change in interest rates could have a significant effect on the realisable value of an amount invested, it will not be possible to state that it represents a known amount of cash, and it should not, therefore, be included in cash equivalents.

18.4 Operating activities and cash flows

Operating activities are generally the cash effects of transactions and other events relating to operating and trading activities. The net cash flow from operating activities represents the net increase or decrease in cash and cash equivalents resulting from the operations shown in the profit and loss account in arriving at operating profit.

In the cash flow statement, **operating cash flows** may be shown on either a **net** or a **gross** basis. The *net* basis uses the **indirect** method and would be laid out in a manner similar to that shown in Exhibit 18.1.

Exhibit 18.1

	£
Operating profit	12,000
Depreciation charges	500
Loss on sale of tangible fixed assets	10
Increase in stocks	(200)
Increase in debtors	(100)
Increase in creditors	300
Net cash inflow from operating activities	12,510

However, FRS 1 requires that a reconciliation be shown between the net cash flow from operating activities and the operating profit as shown in the profit and loss account, which is precisely what is produced if the *indirect* method is adopted. Consequently, by adopting the *net* basis, as the detailed information is to be included in a reconciliation, the main part of the statement may only include a single line 'net cash flow from operating activities'. Instead of being included in the body of the cash flow statement, the details shown in Exhibit 18.1 would be included in the notes to the statement. When the net basis is adopted, no details of the equivalent gross basis analysis is required.

On the other hand, when the *gross* basis is adopted for preparation of the statement, the reconciliation (i.e. the *indirect* method analysis) must also be prepared and included as a note to the statement. The *gross* basis, using the **direct** method, would produce an analysis in the cash flow statement similar to that shown in Exhibit 18.2.

Exhibit 18.2

Operating activities	£
Cash received from customers	120,000
Cash payments to suppliers	(40,000)
Cash paid to and on behalf of employees	(60,000)
Other cash payments	(7,490)
Net cash inflow from operating activities	12,510

It is generally easier for an entity to adopt the net basis – the figures are readily available from the profit and loss account and balance sheet data. The *gross* basis, on the other hand, requires that the cash book is analysed. Despite there being much more work involved in preparing it, FRS 1 recommends the use of the *gross* basis – it does help provide a far clearer view of cash flow than the bookkeeping adjustments to profit that are undertaken under the *net* basis. In an examination, if sufficient information on cash flows is provided for you to adopt the *gross* basis and use the *direct* method, you should assume that is the approach to take – however, you would probably still require to adopt the *net* basis in completing the reconciliation.

18.5 Returns on investment and servicing of finance

Generally, the standard endeavours to relate all cash flows to the underlying transaction. As a result, the 'Returns on investment and servicing of finance' section excludes any item that may be classified under one of the other headings. For example, interest paid and received including any related tax is entered in this section, along with dividends paid and received, but any related ACT is excluded and shown within the taxation section. Tax on interest is seen as relating to the original investment, whereas ACT is a tax on profits.

18.6 Taxation

Tax cash flows on revenue and capital profits are included under this section in the statement. Other tax cash flows should be included under the same heading as the cash flow which gave rise to them – VAT, for example, is seen as relating to 'Operating activities'. Consequently, the net amount of VAT paid to or received from the tax authorities is included under that section. The exception to this arises when VAT is irrecoverable, in which case it is added to the originating transaction value and not distinguished from it within the cash flow statement.

18.7 Investing activities

Cash flows relating to the acquisition and disposal of any asset held as either a fixed asset or a current asset investment (e.g. short-term bank deposits) are included in this section. Purchases and sales of fixed assets, purchases and sales of investments in subsidiaries and other entities, and transactions relating to loans to and from other entities would all appear in this section of the statement.

18.8 Financing

Receipts and repayments of the principal amounts (i.e. the advance, not the interest) to external providers of finance are entered in this section. Examples include receipts from issuing and payments towards the redemption of shares and debentures, the capital element of finance lease rental payments, and issue and commission expenses on any shares, debentures, loans, notes, bonds, or other financing.

The standard requires that the items shown in this section should be reconciled to the related item in the opening and closing balance sheets for the period.

18.9 Material transactions not resulting in any cash flows

FRS 1 also requires that details of material transactions that do not result in any cash flows should be included in a note if it is necessary for an understanding of the underlying transactions. A possible example would be an operating lease. It would involve the acquisition of an asset, but the reporting entity is paying rent, not purchasing the asset.

18.10 Reconciliation with balance sheet figures

In addition to the requirement to reconcile the items shown in the 'Financing' section to the opening and closing balance sheets, the movement of cash and cash equivalents should also be reconciled to the related items in the opening and closing balance sheets.

18.11 Extraordinary and exceptional items

Cash flows relating to items classed as exceptional in the profit and loss account should be shown under the appropriate standard headings, according to their nature. They should be sufficiently disclosed in a note to the statement to allow a user to gain an understanding of the effect of the underlying item(s) on the entity's cash flows.

Extraordinary items should be similarly treated, except that they should be shown separately within the headings and, where the headings are inappropriate, the cash flow should be shown within a separate section of the statement.

While this does not appear particularly complex, it is the nature of the underlying cash flows which determines where these exceptional and extraordinary items appear in the statement, not the nature of the items which gave rise to them. For example, the cash flows arising when an exceptional loss arose on the disposal of a building would be shown under investing activities even when the sale occurred because the company had to repay a long-term loan when the lender went into liquidation – a financing item.

In keeping with the approach of FRS 1 to taxes on revenue and capital profits, the tax flows related to extraordinary items should appear in the taxation section, rather than in the section where the extraordinary cash flow appears.

18.12 Two examples

Exhibits 18.3 and 18.4 illustrate how a cash flow statement is prepared. Some key points to remember include:

- It is amounts paid rather than charged or accrued that are included. Thus for both tax and dividends, it is the actual payments and receipts that occurred during the period that are included in the statement, not the amounts provided for that will be paid or received in a future period.

- Profit on sale of fixed assets is already included in the sale amount and should not be included a second time.

- Care should be taken to identify and eliminate non-cash adjustments to the original profit before tax figure, for example depreciation and bad debt provisions.

- If the layout presented in Exhibits 18.3 and 18.4 is followed, the entries in the 'Financing' section will have the opposite signs to the others, i.e. income will be shown with negative values, rather than positive as is the case in the other sections of the statement.

Exhibit 18.3

From the following profit and loss and balance sheet information, prepare a cash flow statement as required by FRS 1 *using the indirect method.*

Profit and Loss Account for the year ending 31 December 19X4

	£000	£000
Sales		10,000
Cost of goods sold		6,000
		4,000
Expenses		
Depreciation	600	
Interest	150	
Other expenses	2,100	
		2,850
Profit for the year before tax		1,150
Tax		200
Profit for the year after tax		950
Proposed dividend		150
Retained profit		800

Balance Sheet as at 31 December

	19X4		19X3	
	£000	£000	£000	£000
Fixed assets at cost		6,000		6,000
Less accumulated depreciation		3,000		2,400
Net book value		3,000		3,600
Current assets				
Stock	650		700	
Trade debtors	200		250	
Cash	1,610		150	
		2,460		1,100
Less current liabilities				
Trade creditors	310		300	
Taxation	200		150	
Proposed dividends	150		250	
		660		700
		4,800		4,000
Financed by				
Ordinary share capital		2,000		2,000
Revenue reserves		2,800		2,000
		4,800		4,000

Outline solution

Cash Flow Statement (using the indirect method) for the year ended 31 December 19X4

	£000	£000
Net cash inflow from operating activities		2,010
Returns on investments and servicing of finance		
Interest paid	(150)	
Dividends paid	(250)	
Net cash outflow from returns on investments and servicing of finance		(400)
Tax paid		(150)
Investing activities		–
Net cash inflow before financing		1,460
Financing		–
Increase in cash and cash equivalents		1,460

Notes to the cash flow statement

1. Reconciliation of operating profit to net cash inflow from operating activities:

Operating profit	1,300
Depreciation charges	600
Decrease in stocks	50
Decrease in debtors	50
Increase in creditors	10
Net cash inflow from operating activities	2,010

Working:
Operating profit = Retained profit (800) + Interest (150) + Dividend (150) + Tax (200)
= 1,300

Exhibit 18.4

From the summarised cash account and the fixed asset schedule of Thistle Ltd for 19X2, prepare a cash flow statement as required by FRS 1 *using the direct method.*

Summarised Cash Account

	£000		£000
Opening balance	500	Wages	1,350
Cash from cash sales	3,500	Other expenses	600
Cash from credit sales	5,750	Cash paid to suppliers	4,320
Cash from issue of shares	1,200	Tax paid	100
Cash from sale of building	970	Cash paid on finance lease	700
		Final dividend for 19X1	100
		Interim dividend 19X2	50
		Closing balance	4,700
	11,920		11,920

Fixed Asset Schedule

	Plant £000	Buildings £000	Total £000
Cost at 1.1.19X2	10,000	15,000	25,000
Acquisitions	4,730	–	4,730
Disposals	–	(5,000)	(5,000)
Cost at 31.12.19X2	14,730	10,000	24,730
Accumulated depreciation at 1.1.19X2	3,500	6,000	9,500
Charge for year	650	1,500	2,150
Disposals	–	(4,500)	(4,500)
Accumulated depreciation at 31.12.19X2	4,150	3,000	7,150

Other information

(a) The tax charge for the year was £400,000. The opening balance on the tax liability was £100,000.
(b) The proposed final dividend for 19X2 was £120,000.
(c) Other expenses include insurance, which is paid a year in advance, on 30 June. In 19X1, insurance of £300,000 was paid. The amount paid in 19X2 was £400,000.
(d) Accrued wages were £75,000 at 1.1.19X2, and £95,000 at 31.12.19X2.
(e) Stocks were £1,500,000 at 1.1.19X2, and £1,700,000 at 31.12.19X2.
(f) All £700,000 paid on the finance lease in 19X2 represented capital. This was the first year of the lease and interest was not paid until the second payment, which was made in 19X3. Interest of £403,000 was included in the 19X3 payment and was accrued in the 19X2 financial statements.
(g) Opening and closing trade debtors and trade creditors were:

	1.1.19X2	31.12.19X2
Trade debtors	300,000	450,000
Trade creditors	500,000	475,000

(h) 600,000 £1 ordinary shares were issued at a premium on 1.3.19X2.
(i) Retained profits for the year to 31.12.19X2 were £732,000.

Outline Solution
Cash Flow Statement (using the direct method) for Thistle Ltd for the year ended 31 December 19X2

	£000	£000
Operating activities		
Cash received from customers	9,250	
Cash paid to suppliers	(4,320)	
Cash paid to employees	(1,350)	
Other cash payments	(600)	
Net cash inflow from operating activities		2,980
Returns on investment and servicing of finance		
Interest paid	–	
Dividends paid	(150)	
Net cash flows from returns on investment and servicing of finance		(150)
Tax paid		(100)
Investing activities		
Sale of buildings	970	
Net cash outflow from investing activities		970
Net cash inflow before financing		3,700
Financing		
Issue of share capital	(1,200)	
Capital element of finance lease rental payments	700	
Net cash inflow from financing		(500)
Increase in cash and cash equivalents		4,200
		3,700

Note to the cash flow statement:

1 Reconciliation of operating profit to net cash inflow from operating activities:	£000
Operating profit	1,705
Depreciation charges	2,150
Profit on sale of building	(470)
Increase in stocks	(200)
Increase in debtors	(150)
Increase in prepayments	(50)
Decrease in creditors	(25)
Increase in accruals	20
Net cash inflow from operating activities	2,980

Workings

1 Dividends paid in 19X2 are the proposed dividends from the previous year, plus the interim dividend paid during 19X2. The dividend charge in the profit and loss account will be the interim dividend and the proposed dividend for 19X2.

2 Assume tax paid during 19X2 is the amount outstanding at the opening balance sheet date. The tax charge for 19X2 in the profit and loss account is £400,000.

3	£
Retained profit	732,000
Add Dividends	170,000
Add Tax	400,000
Add Interest	403,000
Operating profit	1,705,000

Main points to remember

1   The objective of FRS 1 is to require entities to report their cash generation and absorption for a period on a standard basis.

2   This aids comparison between entities.

3   The statement must show the flows of cash and cash equivalents for the period under the headings:
    - operating activities;
    - returns on investments and servicing of finance;
    - taxation;
    - investing activities; and
    - financing.

4   The headings should be in that order and the statement should include a total for each heading and a total of the net cash inflow or outflow before 'financing'.

5   Cash flow is an increase or decrease in cash or cash equivalent resulting from a transaction.

6   Operating activities are generally the cash effects of transactions and other events relating to operating and trading activities.

7   Operating cash flows can be show on either a *net* (using the *indirect* method) or *gross* (using the *direct* method) basis.

8   A reconciliation is required in the notes to the statement between the net cash flow from operating activities and the operating profit as shown in the profit and loss account.

9   FRS 1 recommends that the *gross* basis be used.

Review questions

18.1   List the five headings in the cash flow statement, as required by FRS 1.

18.2A   Give an example of the information to be included under each of the headings in the cash flow statement and indicate why this information might be useful.

18.3   Prepare a cash flow statement for Lee Ltd for the year ended 31 December 19X4 as required under FRS 1 using the direct method, together with note 1 to the statement. The profit and loss account, balance sheet and cash account for Lee Ltd for the year 19X4 are given below.

Profit and Loss Account for the year ending 31 December 19X4

	£	£
Sales		6,500
Less Cost of goods sold		3,000
		3,500
Less expenses		
Wages	2,000	
Other costs	600	
Depreciation	500	
Interest	100	
		3,200
Profit for the year		300
Proposed dividend		40
Retained profit		260

Balance Sheet as at 31 December

	19X4		19X3	
	£	£	£	£
Fixed assets at cost		4,500		3,800
Less Accumulated depreciation		2,300		1,800
Net book value		2,200		2,000
Current assets				
Stock	400		500	
Trade debtors	150		200	
Cash	200		100	
		750		800
Less current liabilities				
Trade creditors	275		250	
Accrued wages	25		50	
Proposed dividends	40		50	
		(340)		(350)
		2,610		2,450
Financed by				
Debentures		900		1,000
Ordinary share capital		1,000		1,000
Retained profits		710		450
		2,610		2,450

Cash Account for 19X4

	£		£
Opening balance	100	Wages	2,025
Cash from customers	6,550	Other expenses	600
		Cash paid to suppliers	2,875
		Interest paid	100
		Cash purchase of fixed assets	700
		Cash paid to debenture holders	100
		Dividends paid	50
		Closing balance	200
	6,650		6,650

18.4A The balance sheets and additional information relating to Pennylane Ltd are given below. Prepare a cash flow statement for Pennylane Ltd for the year ended 31 December 19X3 as required under FRS 1 using the indirect method, together with note 1 to the statement.

Pennylane Ltd

Balance Sheets as at 31 December

	19X3 £000	19X2 £000
Fixed assets		
Tangible assets	400	325
Intangible assets	230	180
Investments	–	25
	630	530
Current assets		
Stocks	120	104
Debtors	400	295
Short-term investments	50	–
Cash in hand	10	4
	580	403
Creditors: amounts falling due within one year		
Trade creditors	122	108
Bank overdraft	88	105
Taxation	120	110
Dividends proposed	100	80
	430	403
Net current assets	150	–
Total assets less current liabilities	780	530
Creditors: amounts falling due after one year		
Long-term loan	(100)	–
Provisions for liabilities and charges:		
Deferred taxation	(80)	(60)
	600	470
Capital and reserves		
Share capital (£1 ordinary shares)	200	150
Share premium account	160	150
Revaluation reserve	100	90
Profit and loss account	140	80
	600	470

Additional information:
(a) During the year interest of £75,000 was paid, and interest of £25,000 was received.
(b) The following information relates to tangible fixed assets.

At 31 December	*19X3*	*19X2*
	£000	£000
Cost	740	615
Accumulated depreciation	340	290
Net book value	400	325

(c) The proceeds of the sale of fixed asset investments were £30,000.
(d) Plant, with an original cost of £90,000 and a net book value of £50,000, was sold for £37,000.
(e) Tax paid to the Inland Revenue during 19X3 amounted to £110,000.

18.5 State the purposes of a cash flow statement.

(*Chartered Association of Certified Accountants*)

18.6 The following information has been extracted from the books of Nimmo Limited for the year to 31 December 19X9:

Profit and Loss Accounts for year to 31 December

	19X8	*19X9*
	£000	£000
Profit before taxation	9,500	20,400
Taxation	(3,200)	(5,200)
Profit after taxation	6,300	15,200
Dividends:		
Preference (paid)	(100)	(100)
Ordinary: interim (paid)	(1,000)	(2,000)
final (proposed)	(3,000)	(6,000)
Retained profit for the year	£2,200	£7,100

Balance Sheets at 31 December

	19X8	*19X9*
	£000	£000
Fixed assets		
Plant, machinery and equipment, at cost	17,600	23,900
Less: Accumulated depreciation	9,500	10,750
	8,100	13,150
Current assets		
Stocks	5,000	15,000
Trade debtors	8,600	26,700
Prepayments	300	400
Cash at bank and in hand	600	–
	14,500	42,100

Current liabilities

Bank overdraft	–	(16,200)
Trade creditors	(6,000)	(10,000)
Accruals	(800)	(1,000)
Taxation	(3,200)	(5,200)
Dividends	(3,000)	(6,000)
	(13,000)	(38,400)
	£9,600	£16,850

Share capital

Ordinary shares of £1 each	5,000	5,000
10% preference shares of £1 each	1,000	1,000
Profit and loss account	3,000	10,100
	9,000	16,100

Loans

15% debenture stock	600	750
	£9,600	£16,850

Additional information:

1 The directors are extremely concerned about the large bank overdraft as at 31 December 19X9 and they attribute this mainly to the increase in trade debtors as a result of alleged poor credit control.

2 During the year to 31 December 19X9, fixed assets originally costing £5,500,000 were sold for £1,000,000. The accumulated depreciation on these assets as at 31 December 19X8 was £3,800,000.

3 Advance corporation tax may be ignored.

Required:
Prepare a cash flow statement for the year to 31 December 19X9.

Author's note: Use the indirect method.

(Association of Accounting Technicians)

18.7 The following summarised balance sheets relate to Track Limited:

Balance Sheets at 30 June

	19X0	19X1
	£000	£000
Fixed assets at cost	500	650
Less Accumulated depreciation	200	300
	300	350
Investments at cost	200	50
Current assets		
Stocks	400	700
Debtors	1,350	1,550
Cash and bank	100	–
	1,850	2,250
Current liabilities		
Bank overdraft	–	(60)
Creditors	(650)	(790)
Taxation	(230)	(190)
Proposed dividend	(150)	(130)
	(1,030)	(1,170)
	£1,320	£1,480
Capital and reserves		
Called-up share capital (£1 ordinary shares)	500	750
Share premium account	150	200
Profit and loss account	670	530
	£1,320	£1,480

Additional information:

1 During the year to 30 June 19X1, some fixed assets originally costing £25,000 had been sold for £20,000 in cash. The accumulated depreciation on these fixed assets at 30 June 19X0 amounted to £10,000. Similarly, some of the investments originally costing £150,000 had been sold for cash at their book value.

2 The taxation balances disclosed in the above balance sheets represent the actual amounts agreed with the Inland Revenue. All taxes were paid on their due dates. Advance corporation tax may be ignored.

3 No interim dividend was paid during the year to 30 June 19X1.

4 During the year to 30 June 19X1, the company made a 1-for-2 rights issue of 250 ordinary £1 shares at 120p per share.

Required:
Prepare Track Ltd's cash flow statement for the year to 30 June 19X1 in accordance with the requirements of FRS 1.

Author's note: Use the indirect method.

(*Association of Accounting Technicians*)

18.8A You are presented with the following summarised information relating to Clinic plc:

Profit and Loss Account for the Year to 30 June 19X8

	£000
Net profit for the year before taxation	900
Taxation (*see* Note 1)	(651)
Profit for the year after taxation	249
Extraordinary item (after tax relief of £35,000)	(90)
Profit for the year after taxation and extraordinary item	159
Dividends paid and proposed	(119)
Retained profit for the year	£40

Balance Sheet at 30 June 19X8

	19X7	19X8
	£000	£000
Fixed assets (*see* Note 2)	1,515	1,810
Investments	40	40
Current assets		
Stocks	175	200
Debtors	100	60
Cash at bank and in hand	20	–
	295	260
Creditors: amounts falling due within one year		
Bank loans and overdrafts	–	(30)
Trade creditors	(130)	(100)
Other creditors including taxation and social security (*see* Note 3)	(500)	(619)
	(630)	(749)
Creditors: amounts falling due after more than one year		
Debenture loans	(200)	(50)
Provisions for liabilities and charges		
Taxation, including deferred taxation (*see* Note 4)	(120)	(211)
	£900	£1,100
Capital and reserves		
Called-up share capital	750	910
Profit and loss account	150	190
	£900	£1,100

Notes:

1 The taxation charge in the profit and loss account includes the following items:

	£000
Corporation tax based on the profit for the year	542
Overprovision of last year's corporation tax	(15)
Tax credit on franked investment income	24
Transfer to deferred taxation account	100
	£651

2 During the year to 30 June 19X8, Clinic sold an asset originally costing £150,000 for £5,000 in cash. The depreciation charged on this asset was £135,000. The total depreciation charged in the profit and loss account for the year to 30 June 19X8 was £384,000.

3 Other creditors including taxation and social security includes the following items:

	19X7	19X8
	£000	£000
Corporation tax	400	489
Proposed dividend	70	91
Advance corporation tax on the proposed dividend	30	39
	£500	£619

4 The deferred taxation balances include the following items:

	19X7	19X8
	£000	£000
Opening balance	100	120
Transfer from the profit and loss account	50	100
ACT paid offset against corporation tax	–	30
Advance corporation tax on the proposed dividend	(30)	(39)
	£120	£211

5 The standard rate of income tax is assumed to be 30 per cent.

Required:
Insofar as the information permits, prepare Clinic plc's statement of cash flow for the year to 30 June 19X8 in accordance with FRS 1.

(*Association of Accounting Technicians*)

18.9A The accountant of a private company has been able to get the use of a computer to produce the spreadsheets shown below but as yet the computer lacks a program to print out final accounts. The accountant nevertheless expects to use the spreadsheet data to reconstruct a summary profit and loss account and a cash flow statement for the year to 30 April 19X6.

Movements of Assets during the year 19X5/X6 (£000)

	Balance sheet value last year	Depreci- ation or amortis- ation for year	Additions during year	Sales during year	Other changes	Balance sheet value this year
Goodwill	–	–	40	–	–	40
Property	760	(36)	–	–	–	724
Plant and vehicles	540	(84)	420	(60)	–	816
Stocks	230	–	–	–	24	254
Debtors	254	–	–	–	76	330
Bank and cash	50	–	–	–	14	64
	1,834	(120)	460	(60)	114	2,228

Movement of Liabilities during the year 19X5/X6 (£000)

	Balance sheet value last year	New capital issued	Payments during year	Tranfers to reserves and for provisions	Other changes	Balance sheet value this year
Ordinary shares (£1 each)	1,060	440	–	–	–	1,500
Deferred taxation	36	–	–	176	–	212
General reserve	152	–	–	32	–	184
Creditors	136	–	–	–	24	160
Provision for corporation tax	340	–	(340)	52	–	52
Provision for net dividend	110	–	(110)	120	–	120
	1,834	440	(450)	380	24	2,228

Notes:

(*i*) Proceeds of £40,000 were received from the sale of plant and vehicles.

(*ii*) During the year the company redeemed 10,000 of its £1 ordinary shares for £125,000 wholly out of distributable profits and this transaction has not been included in the spreadsheets.

Required:

(*a*) Reconstruct the profit and loss account for the year to 30 April 19X6.

(*b*) Prepare a cash flow statement for the year to 30 April 19X6.

(*Institute of Chartered Secretaries and Administrators*)

18.10 You are presented with the following forecasted information relating to Blackley Limited for the three months to 31 March 19X7.

Forecasted profit and loss accounts (abridged) for the three months to 31 March 19X7:

	Jan 19X7 £000	Feb 19X7 £000	March 19X7 £000
Sales	250	300	350
Cost of goods sold	(200)	(240)	(280)
Gross profit	50	60	70
Depreciation	(3)	(20)	(4)
Administration, selling and distribution expenses	(37)	(40)	(42)
Forecasted net profit	£10	–	£24

Forecasted balances at	31 Dec 19X6 £000	31 Jan 19X7 £000	28 Feb 19X7 £000	31 March 19X7 £000
Debit balances				
Tangible fixed assets at cost	360	240	480	480
Investments at cost	15	5	5	10
Stocks at cost	40	30	40	55
Trade debtors	50	65	75	80
Cash at bank and in hand	80	–	–	–
Credit balances				
Debentures (10%)	–	–	–	50
Trade creditors	80	120	140	150
Taxation	8	–	–	–
Proposed dividend	15	–	–	–

Additional information:
1 Sales of tangible fixed assets in January 19X7 were expected to realise £12,000 in cash.
2 Administration, selling and distribution expenses were expected to be settled in cash during the month in which they were incurred.

Required:
(*a*) Calculate Blackley Limited's forecasted net cash position at 31 January, 28 February and 31 March 19X7 respectively; and
(*b*) prepare a forecasted statement of cash flow for the three months to 31 March 19X7.

(*Association of Accounting Technicians*)

18.11A The following information has been extracted from the draft financial information of V Ltd:

Profit and Loss Account for the year ended 31 December 19X3

	£000	£000
Sales		490
Raw materials consumed	(49)	
Staff costs	(37)	
Depreciation	(74)	
Loss on disposal	(4)	
		(164)
Operating profit		326
Interest payable		(23)
Profit before tax		303
Taxation		(87)
		216
Dividend		(52)
Profit retained for year		164
Balance brought forward		389
		553

Balance Sheets

	31 December 19X3		31 December 19X2	
	£000	£000	£000	£000
Fixed assets (*see below*)		1,145		957
Current assets:				
Stock	19		16	
Trade debtors	38		29	
Recoverable ACT	7		5	
Bank	19		32	
	83		82	
Current liabilities:				
Trade creditors	(12)		(17)	
Taxation	(79)		(66)	
Proposed dividend	(21)		(15)	
	(112)		(98)	
Working capital		(29)		(16)
		1,116		941
Long-term liabilities:				
Long-term loans		(70)		(320)
		1,046		621
Share capital		182		152
Share premium		141		80
Revaluation reserve		170		
Profit and loss		553		389
		1,046		621

	Land & buildings	Machinery	Fixtures & fittings	Total
	£000	£000	£000	£000
Fixed assets:				
Cost or valuation:				
At 31 December 19X2	830	470	197	1,497
Additions	–	43	55	98
Disposals	–	(18)	–	(18)
Adjustment on revaluation	70	–	–	70
At 31 December 19X3	900	495	252	1,647
Depreciation:				
At 31 December 19X2	(90)	(270)	(180)	(540)
Charge for year	(10)	(56)	(8)	(74)
Disposals	–	12	–	12
Adjustment on revaluation	100	–	–	100
At 31 December 19X3	0	(314)	(188)	(502)
Net book value:				
At 31 December 19X3	900	181	64	1,145
At 31 December 19X2	740	200	17	957

(a) **You are required** to prepare a cash flow statement for V Ltd for the year ended 31 December 19X3 in accordance with the requirements of Financial Reporting Standard 1 (FRS 1).

(b) It has been suggested that the management of long-term profitability is more important than short-term cash flow. Explain why this might be so.

(*Chartered Institute of Management Accountants*)

19

Contract accounts

Objectives

After you have studied this chapter, you should:

- *be aware of the factors that are involved in accounting for contracts*

- *be aware of how accounting records of contracts are maintained*

- *be aware of the need to apply prudence when assessing profit or loss on a contract that is still in progress*

19.1 Accounts and the business cycle

The span of production differs between businesses, and some fit into the normal pattern of annual accounts more easily than others do. A farmer's accounts are usually admirably suited to the yearly pattern, as the goods they produce are in accordance with the seasons, and therefore repeat themselves annually. With a firm whose production span is a day or two the annual accounts are also quite suitable.

On the other hand, there are businesses whose work does not conform to a financial year's calculation of profits. Assume that a firm of contractors has only one contract being handled, and that is the total construction of a very large oil refinery complex. This might take five years to complete. Not until it is completed can the actual profit or loss on the contract be correctly calculated. However, if the company was formed especially with this contract in mind, the shareholders would not want to wait for five years before the profit could be calculated and dividends paid. Therefore an attempt is made to calculate profits yearly. Obviously, most firms will have more than one contract under way at a time, and also it would be rare for a contract to take such a long time to complete.

19.2 Opening contract accounts

For each contract an account is opened. It is, in fact, a form of trading account for each contract. Therefore if the firm has a contract to build a new technical college it may be numbered Contract 71. Thus a Contract 71 Account would be opened. All expenditure traceable to the contract will be charged to the contract account. This is far easier than ascertaining direct expenses in a factory, as any expenditure on the site will be treated as direct, e.g. wages for the manual workers on the site, telephone rental for telephones on the site, hire of machinery for the contract, wages for the timekeepers, clerks, etc., on the site.

19.3 Certification of work done

The contractor is paid by agreement on the strength of architects' certificates in the case of buildings, or engineers' certificates for an engineering contract. The architect, or engineer, will visit the site at regular intervals and will issue a certificate stating his estimate of the value of the work done, in terms of the total contract price (the sale price of the whole contract). Thus he may issue a certificate for £10,000. Normally the terms governing the contract will contain a clause concerning retention money. This is the amount, usually stated as a percentage, which will be retained, i.e. held back, in case the contract is not completed by a stated date, or against claims for faulty workmanship, etc. A 10 per cent retention in the case already mentioned would lead to £9,000 being payable by the person for whom the contract was being performed.

19.4 Allocation of overheads

The administration overhead expenses not traceable directly to the sites are sometimes split on an arbitrary basis and charged to each contract. Of course, if there were only one contract then all the overhead expenses would quite rightly be chargeable against it. On the other hand if there are twenty contracts being carried on, any apportionment must be arbitrary. No one can really apportion on a 'scientific' basis the administration overhead expenses of the managing director's salary, the cost of advertising to give the firm the right 'image', or the costs of running accounting machinery for the records of the whole firm, and these are only a few of such expenses. In a fashion similar to the departmental accounts principle in Chapter 37 of Volume 1, it sometimes gives misleading results, and it is therefore far better left for the administrative overhead expenses which are obviously not chargeable to a contract to be omitted from the contract accounts. The surplus left on each contract account is thus the 'contribution' of each contract to administrative overhead expenses and to profit.

19.5 Example

Exhibit 19.1

Contract 44 is for a school being built for the Blankshire County Council. By the end of the year the following items have been charged to the Contract Account:

Contract 44

	£
Wages – labour on site	5,000
Wages – foreman and clerks on the site	600
Materials	4,000
Subcontractors on the site	900
Other site expenses	300
Hire of special machinery	400
Plant bought for the contract	2,000

The entries concerning expenditure traceable direct to the contract are relatively simple. These are charged to the contract account. These can be seen in the contract account shown on the next page.

Architects' certificates have been received during the year amounting to £14,000, it being assumed for this example that the certificates related to all work done up to the year end. A retention of 10 per cent is to be made, and the Blankshire County Council has paid £12,600. The £14,000 has been credited to a holding account called an Architects' Certificates Account and debited to the Blankshire County Council Account. The total of the Architects' Certificates Account now needs transferring to the Contract 44 Account. It is, after all, the 'sale' price of the work done so far, and the contract account is a type of trading account. The £12,600 received has been debited to the cash book and credited to Blankshire County Council Account, which now shows a balance of £1,400, this being equal to the retention money.

The cost of the stock of the materials on the site unused is not included in the value of the architects' certificates and is therefore carried forward to the next year at cost price. The value of the plant at the end of the year is also carried forward. In this case the value of the cost of the plant not yet used is £1,400. This means that £2,000 has been debited for the plant and £1,400 credited, thus effectively charging £600 for depreciation. Assume that the stock of unused materials cost £800.

The Contract 44 Account will now appear as follows:

Contract 44

	£		£
Wages – labour on site	5,000	Architects'certificates	14,000
Wages – foreman and clerks on		Stock of unused materials c/d	800
the site	600	Value of plant c/d	1,400
Materials	4,000		
Subcontractors on the site	900		
Other site expenses	300		
Hire of special machinery	400		
Plant bought for the contract	2,000		

19.6 Profit estimation

The difference between the two sides (Credit side £16,200, Debit side £13,200) can be seen to be £3,000. It would be a brave person indeed who would assert that the profit made to date was £3,000. The contract is only part completed, and costly snags may crop up which would dissipate any potential profit earned, or snags may have developed already, such as subsidence which has remained unnoticed as yet. The concept of prudence now takes over and the profit is reduced according to an 'appropriate' modifier. In the past, the custom developed of multiplying the profit by a fraction of two-thirds and then multiplying the result by the proportion of work certified for which cash had been received, as in the following example.

$$\text{Apparent profit} \times \frac{2}{3} \times \frac{\text{Cash received}}{\text{Work certified}} = \text{Amount available for dividends, etc.}$$

e.g. $£3,000 \times \frac{2}{3} \times \frac{12,600}{14,000} = £1,800$

When a revised version of SSAP 9: *Stocks and long-term contracts* was issued in 1988, this custom-based *rule of thumb* was replaced with a far more complex calculation that focuses upon turnover and the work certified valued in relation to the overall contract amount. It is beyond the scope of *Business Accounting*, where this topic is being introduced rather than developed in detail, to extend coverage of it to the level of complexity that would be required in order to cover the SSAP 9 rules adequately. Students who require a sound understanding of the SSAP 9 rules concerning long-term contracts should refer to the standard, where the appendix covers the topic in detail, or to a specialised text on the subject.

From the perspective of the review questions that follow at the end of this chapter, apart from question 19.5A, *unless otherwise indicated in the question*, you should apply the ⅔ rule of thumb given above. Doing so will develop an awareness of the complexity of contract accounts without the added complexity of applying the SSAP 9 rules. By adopting this approach students will be well-placed to progress to an understanding of the SSAP 9 rules, knowing well the underlying factors involved in contract accounts. The answer to question 19.5A is based on the SSAP 9 rules, and is provided for the benefit of any student who chooses to study those rules independently of this book.

On the basis of the £1,800 profit calculated above, the Contract 44 Account can now be completed:

Profit and Loss Account

	£
Profits from contracts:	
Contract 43	
Contract 44	1,800
Contract 45	

Contract 44

	£		£
Wages – labour on site	£5,000	Architects' certificates	14,000
Wages – foreman and clerks on the site	600	Stock of unused materials c/d	800
Materials	4,000	Value of plant c/d	1,400
Subcontractors on the site	900		
Other site expenses	300		
Hire of special machinery	400		
Plant bought for the contract	2,000		
Profit to the profit and loss account	1,800		
Reserve (the part of the apparent profit not yet recognised as earned) c/d	1,200		
	16,200		16,200
Stock of unused materials b/d	800	Reserve b/d	1,200
Value of plant b/d	1,400		

19.7 Anticipated losses

In the case shown there has been an apparent profit of £3,000, but the action would have been different if instead of revealing such a profit, the contract account had in fact shown a loss of £3,000. In such a case it would not be two-thirds of the loss to be taken into account but the whole of it. Thus £3,000 loss would have been transferred to the profit and loss account. This is in accordance with the concept of prudence which states that profits may be underestimated but never losses.

It is in fact not always the case that an engineer or architect will certify the work done up to the financial year end. He may call several days earlier than the year end. The cost of work done, but not certified at the year end, will therefore need carrying down as a balance to the next period when certification will take place.

New term

Work certified (p. 305): The value of work in progress on a contract as certified by, for example, an architect or engineer.

Main points to remember

1   Separate accounts should be opened in respect of every contract.

2   Profits or losses on contracts require to be estimated at the end of each accounting period.

3   Losses should be written off immediately they are identified.

4   An appropriate amount of any profit should be included in the financial statements.

5   The profit/loss ascertainment approach adopted in this chapter is necessarily simplified in order to ensure the topic is well understood; SSAP 9 should be consulted for the definitive approach to adopt.

Review questions

19.1 The final accounts of Diggers Ltd are made up to 31 December in each year. Work on a certain contract was commenced on 1 April 19X5 and was completed on 31 October 19X6. The total contract price was £174,000, but a penalty of £700 was suffered for failure to complete by 30 September 19X6.

The following is a summary of receipts and payments relating to the contract:

	During 19X5	During 19X6
Payments:		
Materials	25,490	33,226
Wages	28,384	45,432
Direct expenses	2,126	2,902
Purchases of plant on 1 April 19X5	16,250	–
Receipts		
Contract price (*less* penalty)	52,200	121,100
Sale, on 31 October 19X6, of all plant purchased on 1 April 19X5	–	4,100

The amount received from the customer in 19X5 represented the contract price of all work certified in that year less 10 per cent retention money.

When the annual accounts for 19X5 were prepared it was estimated that the contract would be completed on 30 September 19X6, and that the market value of the plant would be £4,250 on that date. It was estimated that further expenditure on the contract during 19X6 would be £81,400.

For the purposes of the annual accounts, depreciation of plant is calculated, in the case of uncompleted contracts, by reference to the expected market value of the plant on the date when the contract is expected to be completed, and is allocated between accounting periods by the straight-line method.

Credit is taken, in the annual accounts, for such a part of the estimated total profit, on each uncompleted contract, as corresponds to the proportion between the contract price of the work certified and the total contract price.

Required:
Prepare a summary of the account for this contract, showing the amounts transferred to profit and loss account at 31 December 19X5 and 31 December 19X6.

19.2 Stannard and Sykes Ltd are contractors for the construction of a pier for the Seafront Development Corporation. The value of the contract is £300,000, and payment is by engineer's certificate subject to a retention of 10 per cent of the amount certified; this is to be held by the Seafront Development Corporation for six months after the completion of the contract.

The following information is extracted from the records of Stannard and Sykes Ltd.

	£
Wages on site	41,260
Materials delivered to site by supplier	58,966
Materials delivered to site from store	10,180
Hire of plant	21,030
Expenses charged to contract	3,065
Overheads charged to contract	8,330
Materials on site at 30 November 19X8	11,660
Work certified	150,000
Payment received	135,000
Work in progress at cost (not the subject of a certificate to date)	12,613
Wages accrued to 30 November 19X8	2,826

Required:
Prepare the Pier Contract Account to 30 November 19X8, and suggest a method by which profit could be prudently estimated.

(*Chartered Association of Certified Accountants*)

19.3A Cantilever Ltd was awarded a contract to build an office block in London and work commenced at the site on 1 May 19X5.

During the period to 28 February 19X6, the expenditure on the contract was as follows:

	£
Materials issued from stores	9,411
Materials purchased	28,070
Direct expenses	6,149
Wages	18,493
Charge made by the company for administration expenses	2,146
Plant and machinery purchased on 1 May 19X5, for use at site	12,180

On 28 February 19X6, the stock of materials at the site amounted to £2,164 and there were amounts outstanding for wages £366 and direct expenses £49.

Cantilever Ltd has received on account the sum of £64,170 which represents the amount of Certificate No. 1 issued by the architects in respect of work completed to 28 February 19X6, after deducting 10 per cent retention money.

The following relevant information is also available:

(a) the plant and machinery has an effective life of five years, with no residual value, and
(b) the company only takes credit for two-thirds of the profit on work certified.

Required:
(a) prepare a contract account for the period to 28 February 19X6, and
(b) show your calculation of the profit to be taken to the credit of the company's profit and loss account in respect of the work covered by Certificate No 1.

(Institute of Chartered Accountants)

19.4A You are required to prepare the contract account for the year ended 31 December 19X0, and show the calculation of the sum to be credited to the profit and loss account for that year.

On 1 April 19X0 MN Ltd commenced work on a contract which was to be completed by 30 June 19X1 at an agreed price of £520,000.

MN Ltd's financial year ended on 31 December 19X0, and on that day expenditure on the contract totalled £263,000 made up as under:

	£
Plant	30,000
Materials	124,000
Wages	95,000
Sundry expenses	5,000
Head office charges	9,000
	263,000

Cash totalling £195,000 had been received by 31 December 19X0 representing 75 per cent of the work certified as completed on that date, but in addition, work costing £30,000 had been completed but not certified.

A sum of £9,000 had been obtained on the sale of materials which had cost £8,000 but which had been found unsuitable. On 31 December 19X0 stocks of unused materials on site had cost £10,000 and the plant was valued at £20,000.

To complete the contract by 30 June 19X1 it was estimated that:

(a) the following additional expenditures would be incurred:

	£
Wages	64,000
Materials	74,400
Sundry expenses	9,000

(b) further plant costing £25,000 would be required;
(c) the residual value of all plant used on the contract at 30 June 19X1 would be £15,000;
(d) head office charges to the contract would be at the same annual rate plus 10 per cent.

It was estimated that the contract would be completed on time but that a contingency provision of £15,000 should be made. From this estimate and the expenditure already incurred, it was decided to estimate the total profit that would be made on the contract and to take to the credit of the profit and loss account for the year ended 31 December 19X0, that proportion of the total profit relating to the work actually certified to that date.

(Chartered Institute of Management Accountants)

19.5A   *General information on the Lytax group of companies*

Lytax Ltd is a company in the building construction industry.

It has three regional offices, North Borders, Midlands and South Downs which are constituted as separate units for accounting purposes.

On 25 May 19X0 Lytax Ltd acquired 90 per cent of the ordinary share capital of Ceprem Ltd, a company which manufactures building materials.

Lytax Ltd has for 3 years held 15 per cent of the ordinary share capital of Bleco plc. This company carries out specialist research and development activities into building and construction materials, technology and techniques. It then sells the results of these activities to other companies.

Details of long-term contract work undertaken by Lytax Ltd

At 31 October 19X0, Lytax Ltd was engaged in various contracts including five long-term contracts, details of which are given below:

	1	2	3	4	5
	£000	£000	£000	£000	£000
Contract price	1,100	950	1,400	1,300	1,200
At 31 October 19X0:					
Cumulative costs incurred	664	535	810	640	1,070
Estimated further costs to completion	106	75	680	800	165
Estimated cost of post-completion guarantee/rectification work	30	10	45	20	5
Cumulative costs incurred transferred to cost of sales	580	470	646	525	900
Progress payments					
Cumulative receipts	615	680	615	385	722
Invoiced:					
Awaiting receipt	60	40	25	200	34
Retained by contractee	75	80	60	65	84

It is not expected that any contractees will default on their payments.

Up to 31 October 19X9, the following amounts had been included in the turnover and cost of sales figures.

	1	2	3	4	5
	£000	£000	£000	£000	£000
Cumulative turnover	560	340	517	400	610
Cumulative costs incurred transferred to cost of sales	460	245	517	400	610
Foreseeable loss transferred to cost of sales	–	–	–	70	–

It is the accounting policy of Lytax Ltd to arrive at contract turnover by adjusting contract cost of sales (including foreseeable losses) by the amount of contract profit or loss to be regarded as recognised, separately for each contract.

Required:

(a) Calculate the amounts to be included within the turnover and cost of sales figures of the profit and loss account of Lytax Ltd for the year ended 31 October 19X0, in respect of the long-term contracts.

(b) Prepare extracts from the balance sheet of Lytax Ltd at 31 October 19X0 incorporating the financial effects of the long-term contracts.

Your answer should comply with the requirements of SSAP 9 (Stocks and Long-Term Contracts) and should include any supporting notes required by that standard.

Workings for individual contracts which build up to the total for each item must be shown.

All calculations should be made to the nearest £1,000.

(*Chartered Association of Certified Accountants*)

20

Value added statements

Objectives

After you have studied this chapter, you should:

- *be aware of the benefits of presenting statements of value added*

20.1 The need for additional information

A great deal of discussion has taken place in recent years about the desirability of not simply interpreting results in terms of profits only. One way of doing this is in terms of the value added by the business itself to the resources acquired by it in transforming them into the final product. The production of such 'value added statements' was recommended in the *Corporate Report 1975*.

Such value added can be taken to represent in monetary terms the net output of an enterprise. This is the difference between the total value of its output and the value of the inputs of materials and services obtained from other enterprises. The value added is seen to be due to the combined efforts of capital, management and employees, and the statement shows how the value added has been distributed to each of these factors.

20.2 Example

As an example, the profit and loss account of Growth Ltd shown below is then restated in value added terms:

Growth Ltd

Profit and Loss Account for the year ended 31 December 19X1

	£	£
Turnover		765,000
Cost of sales*		439,000
Gross profit		326,000
Distribution costs*	93,000	
Administrative expenses*	108,000	201,000
		125,000
Interest payable		2,000
Profit on ordinary activities before taxation		123,000
Tax on profit on ordinary activities		44,000
Profit for the year on ordinary activities after taxation		79,000
Undistributed profits from last year		55,000
		134,000
Transfer to general reserve	15,000	
Proposed ordinary dividend	60,000	75,000
Undistributed profits carried to next year		59,000
Note: Costs* include:		£
Wages, pensions and other employee benefits		220,000
Depreciation		74,000
All other costs were bought in from outside		346,000
(£439,000 + £93,000 + £108,000)		£640,000

Growth Ltd

Statement of Value Added for the year ended 31 December 19X1

	£	£
Turnover		765,000
Bought in materials and services		346,000
Value added		419,000
Applied the following way:		
To pay employee wages, pensions and other benefits		220,000
To pay providers of capital:		
Interest on loans	2,000	
Dividends to shareholders	60,000	62,000
To pay government:		
Corporation tax payable		44,000
To provide for maintenance and expansion of assets:		
Depreciation	74,000	
Retained profits	19,000	93,000
		419,000

The reader can see that the retained profits figure of £19,000 is made up of the increase in undistributed profits (£59,000 − £55,000) £4,000 + transfer to general reserve £15,000 = £19,000.

The value added statement can be seen to be a means of reporting the income for all the groups which contribute to an organisation's performance. It is therefore relevant to the information needed by all of these groups, something which is not well served by an ordinary profit and loss account.

New term

Value added (p. 313): The difference between the total value of outputs and the total value of inputs.

Main points to remember

1   Traditional financial statements tend to focus on profit.

2   A statement of valued added focuses instead on the income contributed by each group within an organisation that is included in the statement.

Review questions

20.1   Manvers Ltd includes with its financial statements each year a statement of value added. The draft value added statement for the year ended 31 May 19X6 is as follows:

	£	£
Revenue from sales		204,052
Bought in materials and services		146,928
Value added by the company		57,124
Applied to:		
The benefit of employees		
Salaries	16,468	
Deductions for income tax and national insurance	3,352	
	13,116	
Pension schemes	2,810	
Employees' profit sharing schemes	525	
Welfare and staff amenities	806	
		17,257
Central and local government		
Value added tax	30,608	
Corporation tax	985	
Local rates	325	
Tax etc. deducted from salaries and loan interest	3,832	
		35,750
The providers of capital		
Interest on loan capital	1,600	
Income tax deducted	480	
	1,120	
Interest on bank overdrafts	250	
Dividends to shareholders of the company	500	
		1,870
The replacement of assets and the expansion of the business		
Depreciation	1,835	
Retained profits	412	
		2,247
		57,124

Discussion among the board of directors on the draft figures has revealed a wide variation of opinion on the usefulness of the value added statement to the readers of the accounts.

Some board members say that the added value statement is confusing as it is only a redrafting of the results which are shown in the profit and loss account which gives all the information necessary. Another view is that the statement of changes in financial position is far more important and this should be given in place of the value added statement.

Required:
(a) A report to the directors showing the advantages of the value added statement comparing it with the profit and loss account and the cash flow statement. Your report should deal specifically with the points raised in discussion by the directors.
(b) Construct a profit and loss account from the information given.
(c) Calculate the operating profit for use in a statement of changes in financial position.

(*Chartered Association of Certified Accountants*)

20.2.A The following information relates to the Plus Factors Group plc for the years to 30 September 19X8 and 19X9.

	Notes	19X9	19X8
		£000	£000
Associated company share of profit		10.9	10.7
Auditors' remuneration		12.2	11.9
Creditors for materials			
at beginning of year		1,109.1	987.2
at end of year		1,244.2	1,109.1
Debtors			
at beginning of year		1,422.0	1,305.0
at end of year		1,601.0	1,422.0
11% debentures	1	500.0	600.0
Depreciation		113.7	98.4
Employee benefits paid		109.9	68.4
Hire of plant, machinery and vehicles	2	66.5	367.3
Materials paid for in year		3,622.9	2,971.4
Minority interest in profit of the year		167.2	144.1
Other overheads incurred		1,012.4	738.3
Pensions and pension contributions paid		319.8	222.2
Profit before taxation		1,437.4	1,156.4
Provision for corporation tax		464.7	527.9
Salaries and wages		1,763.8	1,863.0
Sales	3	9,905.6	8,694.1
Shares at nominal value:			
Ordinary at 25p each fully paid	4	2,500.0	2,000.0
7% Preference at £1 each fully paid	4	500.0	200.0
Stocks of materials:			
beginning of year		804.1	689.7
end of year		837.8	804.1

Other information:
Ordinary dividends were declared as follows:
   Interim 1.12 pence per share (19X8 1.67p)
   Final 3.57 pence per share (19X8 2.61p)
Average number of employees was 196 (19X8 201)

Notes
1   £300,000 of debentures were redeemed at par on 31 March 19X9 and £200,000 new debentures at the same rate of interest were issued at 9 per cent on the same date.
     The new debentures are due to be redeemed on 31 March 19X4.
2   This is the amount for inclusion in the profit and loss account in accordance with SSAP 21.
3   All the group's sales are subject to value added tax at 15 per cent and the figures given include such tax. All other figures are exclusive of value added tax.
4   All shares have been in issue throughout the year.

Required:
(a) Prepare a statement of value added for the year to 30 September 19X9 and give comparative figures for 19X8. Include a percentage breakdown of the distribution of value added for both years.
(b) Produce ratios related to employees' interests, based on the statement in part (a), and explain how they might be of use.
(c) Explain briefly what are the difficulties of measuring and reporting financial information in the form of a statement of value added.

(*Chartered Association of Certified Accountants*)

Part 3

GROUPS

Introduction

This part is concerned with group accounts – how they are prepared, how various transactions should be dealt with, and how their presentation is regulated by the Companies Acts and accounting standards.

21

Group accounts: an introduction

Objectives

After you have studied this chapter, you should:

● *understand the difference between a parent undertaking and a subsidiary undertaking*

● *be aware of why it is important to produce consolidated financial statements*

● *know some of the alternative methods whereby control can be acquired by one company over another*

● *be aware of the relevance of 'dominant influence' to the identification of a parent–subsidiary relationship*

● *be aware of the relevance of 'significant influence' to the identification of the existence of an 'associated undertaking'*

21.1 Shareholders and their rights

The owners of a company are its shareholders. When someone buys ordinary shares in a company then they are usually given three rights. These are:

● voting rights at shareholders' meetings;
● a right to an interest in the net assets of the company;
● a right to an interest in the profits earned by the company.

Preference shareholders do not normally have such voting rights, but sometimes they can have such power. This could be when their dividends are in arrear, or their special rights are being changed by the company. Debenture holders have no rights at all to vote at general meetings.

By using their voting rights at shareholders' meetings, the shareholders are able to show their approval, or disapproval, of the election of directors. It is the directors who manage the affairs of the company. Therefore any group of shareholders, who between them own more than 50 per cent of the voting shares of the company, can control the election of directors. As a consequence they can therefore control the policies of the company through the directors. This would also be true if any one shareholder owned more than 50 per cent of the voting shares.

One company may hold shares in another company. Therefore if one company wishes to obtain control of another company it can do so by obtaining more than 50 per cent of the voting shares in that company.

21.2 Parent undertakings and subsidiary undertakings

- S Ltd has an issued share capital of 1,000 ordinary shares of £1 each.
- On 1 January 19X6, P Ltd buys 501 of these shares from Jones, a shareholder, for £600.
- P Ltd will now have control of S Ltd because it has more than 50 per cent of the voting shares.
- P Ltd is now called the 'parent undertaking'.
- S Ltd is now called the 'subsidiary undertaking' of P Ltd.

Just because the identity of S Ltd's shareholders has changed it does not mean that the balance sheet of S Ltd will be drafted in a different fashion. Looking only at the balance sheet of S Ltd no one would be able to deduce that P Ltd owned more than 50 per cent of the shares, or even that P Ltd owned any shares at all in S Ltd. After obtaining control of S Ltd both P Ltd and S Ltd will continue to maintain their own sets of accounting records and to draft their own balance sheets. If the balance sheets of P Ltd and S Ltd are looked at, both before and after the purchase of the shares, any differences can be noted.

Exhibit 21.1

(*a*) Before P Ltd acquired control of S Ltd.

P Ltd Balance Sheet as at 31 December 19X5	£	£
Fixed assets		2,000
Current assets:		
Stock-in-trade	2,900	
Debtors	800	
Bank	1,300	
		5,000
		7,000
Share capital		5,000
Profit and loss account		2,000
		7,000

S Ltd Balance Sheet as at 31 December 19X5	£	£
Fixed assets		400
Current assets:		
Stock-in-trade	400	
Debtors	200	
Bank	100	
		700
		1,100
Share capital		1,000
Profit and loss account		100
		1,100

(b) After P Ltd acquired control of S Ltd the balance sheets would appear as follows before any further trading took place:

P Ltd Balance Sheet as at 1 January 19X6

	£	£
Fixed assets		2,000
Investment in subsidiary		
undertaking		600
Current assets:		
Stock-in-trade	2,900	
Debtors	800	
Bank	700	
		4,400
		7,000
Share capital		5,000
Profit and loss account		2,000
		7,000

S Ltd Balance Sheet as at 1 January 19X6

	£	£
Fixed assets		400
Current assets:		
Stock-in-trade	400	
Debtors	200	
Bank	100	
		700
		1,100
Share capital		1,000
Profit and loss account		100
		1,100

The only differences can be seen to be those in the balance sheets of P Ltd. The bank balance has been reduced by £600, this being the cost of shares in S Ltd, and the cost of the shares now appears as 'Investment in subsidiary undertaking £600'. The balance sheets of S Ltd are completely unchanged.

We shall see later that FRS2: *Accounting for subsidiary undertakings* gives a much wider meaning to 'subsidiary undertaking' than we have seen so far. This has been deliberately excluded up to this point to let you see the basic structure without complicating it.

21.3 Profit and loss account

From the profit and loss account point of view, the appropriation section of S Ltd would also be completely unchanged after P Ltd takes control. P Ltd would however see a change in its profit and loss account when a dividend is received from S Ltd: in this case the dividends received would be shown as investment income in the profit and loss account. Remember that dividends payable are charged to the appropriation section of the paying company's profit and loss account, while dividends received are in the main part of the receiving company's profit and loss account.

The terms 'parent undertaking' and 'subsidiary undertaking' have been in use for only a fairly short time. Previously, a 'parent undertaking' was called a 'holding company', and a 'subsidiary undertaking' was a 'subsidiary company'. In Chapter 31 we will see exactly why the terms were changed. One of the reasons is that consolidated accounts used to be concerned only with companies. Now, as you will see, 'subsidiary undertakings' can include unincorporated businesses as well.

In the chapters which follow, 22 to 30 inclusive, we will show the consolidations only of companies, to demonstrate the principles involved. In addition we will often simply call a 'parent undertaking' by the title of 'parent' and a 'subsidiary undertaking' may also be shortened to 'subsidiary'.

In Chapter 31 we will examine Financial Reporting Standard 2 which covers the accounting needed for parent and subsidiary undertakings. This book, in the chapters which follow, fully complies with all the requirements of FRS 2.

21.4 The need for consolidated financial statements

Imagine being a shareholder of P Ltd. Each year you would receive a set of P Ltd's final accounts. After P's acquistion of the shares in S Ltd then £600 would appear as an asset in the balance sheet of P Ltd. It would be normal for it to be shown at cost £600, using the cost concept.

When you looked at the profit and loss account of P Ltd you would see the dividends received from S Ltd. This plus the cost of the investment in the balance sheet would therefore be the only things you would know about the subsidiary.

However, you have invested in P Ltd, and because of its majority shareholding in S Ltd you have in effect also invested in S Ltd as well. Just as you want to know how the assets and liabilities in P Ltd change over the years, you will now also like to know exactly the same for S Ltd.

You are not, however, a shareholder of S Ltd, and therefore you would not be sent a copy of its final accounts. If the situation were to stay like that, you could not get a proper view of your investment.

This would be even worse if in fact P Ltd was a parent undertaking with twenty subsidiaries, and held a different percentage stake in each of them. It would also be almost certain that the companies would trade with each other, and owe money to one another or be owed money by them. This would also raise complications.

Fortunately there is a remedy for this sort of problem. The Companies Acts provide for parent undertakings distributing to their shareholders a set of consolidated financial statements. These bring together all of the financial statements for the parent undertaking and its subsidiaries in such a way that the shareholders can get an overall view of their investments.

21.5 Different methods of acquiring control of one company by another

So far the acquisition of control in S Ltd was by P Ltd buying more than 50 per cent of the shares in S Ltd from Jones, i.e. buying shares on the open market. This is by no means the only way of acquiring control, so by way of illustration some of the other methods are now described.

(a) S Ltd may issue new shares to P Ltd amounting to over 50 per cent of the voting shares. P Ltd pays for the shares in cash.
(b) P Ltd could purchase over 50 per cent of the voting shares of S Ltd on the open market by exchanging for them newly issued shares of P Ltd.

Or, acting through another company:

(c) P Ltd acquires more than 50 per cent of the voting shares in S1 Ltd for cash, and then S1 Ltd proceeds to acquire all of the voting shares of S2 Ltd. S2 Ltd would then be a sub-subsidiary of P Ltd.

These are only some of the more common ways by which one company becomes a subsidiary of another company.

21.6 Control by dominant influence

The issue of FRS 2 in 1992 introduced a further way of looking at whether or not one company had control of another. If one company has 'the right to exercise a dominant influence' over another undertaking, then the company with the dominating influence is deemed to have control of the other. A dominant influence means that the holder of it has a right to give directions with regard to the operating and financial policies of another undertaking, and that the directors of that latter undertaking are obliged to comply, whether or not they are for the benefit of the undertaking.

In other words, if one undertaking can tell another undertaking what to do, both from an operating and financial point of view, and the directors of that latter undertaking have to carry out such instructions, then such an undertaking will be a subsidiary undertaking. This is a much wider definition than merely looking at the amounts of the shareholdings.

21.7 The nature of a group

Wherever two or more companies are in the relationship of parent and subsidiary undertakings then a 'group' is said to exist. When such a group exists then, besides the final accounts of the parent undertaking itself, to comply with legal requirements, there must be a set of financial statements prepared in respect of the group as a whole. These group accounts are usually known as **consolidated financial statements**, because the accounts of all the companies have had to be consolidated together to form one set of financial statements.

Sometimes parent undertakings carry on trading as well as investing in their subsidiaries. There are, however, other parent undertakings that do not trade at all, the whole of their activities being concerned with investing in other companies.

21.8 Subsidiary undertakings which are not limited companies

Until FRS 2, issued in 1992, group accounts consolidated only those accounts which belonged to limited companies. A subsidiary undertaking now can be other than a limited company. Basically, share of ownership or the dominant influence approach will determine whether or not it can be called a 'subsidiary undertaking'. These financial statements are then consolidated in a similar fashion to those of limited companies.

21.9 FRS 2: Accounting for subsidiary undertakings

The main changes brought about by FRS 2 were as follows:
(a) The concept of 'dominant influence' widened the scope of which companies could be seen as subsidiary undertakings, rather than relying on share ownership.
(b) Unincorporated businesses (i.e. not companies) were brought into its scope and came to be classed as subsidiary undertakings which have to have their financial statements consolidated with the rest of the group.

21.10 SSAP 1: Accounting for associated companies

Although, at present, the title of the SSAP has not changed, the term 'associated undertakings' would be more appropriate, as this is what they are defined as in the Companies Acts. Investments in such companies are too significant to be treated simply as trade investments, but on the other hand they do not qualify to be treated as investments in subsidiaries.

Basically, SSAP 1 says that B Ltd will be considered as an associated company of A Ltd if A Ltd can *significantly* influence the financial and operating decisions of B Ltd. As a normal rule the amount of B Ltd's equity shares that A Ltd would have to hold would be 20 per cent. This, however, is only a guideline. What is important is the presence or absence of significant influence.

The idea behind the SSAP was to ensure that if one company has invested in another company, and can significantly influence the affairs of that company, then ordinary investment accounting is not suitable. Rather than simply show dividends received as a measure of income, it would be much more realistic for the investing company's *full* share of the profit of that company to be incorporated in the investing company's accounts. The method of doing this is known as 'equity accounting'.

21.11 Teaching method

The method used in this book for teaching consolidated accounts is that of showing the reader the adjustments needed on the face of the consolidated balance sheet, together with any workings necessary shown in a normal arithmetical fashion. The reasons why this method of illustrating consolidated accounts has been chosen are as follows:

(a) The author believes that it is his job to try to help the reader understand the subject, and not just to be able to perform the necessary manipulations. He believes that, given understanding of what is happening, then the accounting entries necessary follow easily enough. Showing the adjustments on the face of the balance sheet gives a 'bird's-eye view' so that it is easier to see what is happening, rather than trace one's way laboriously through a complex set of double-entry adjustments made in ledger accounts.

(b) The second main reason is that this would be a much lengthier and more costly book if all of the double-entry accounts were shown. It is better for a first look at consolidated accounts to be an introduction to the subject only, rather than be at one and the same time both an introduction and a very detailed survey of the subject. If the reader can understand the consolidated accounts shown in this book, then he/she will have a firm foundation which will enable him/her to tackle the more difficult and complicated aspects of the subject.

New terms

Consolidation accounting (p. 325): This term means bringing together into a single balance sheet and profit and loss account the separate financial statements of a group of companies. Hence they are known as group financial statements.

Parent undertaking (p. 323): Although FRS 2 should be studied for a full and proper definition, the one that will suffice for the time being is 'an undertaking which controls or has a dominating influence over the affairs of another undertaking'.

Subsidiary undertaking (p. 324): An undertaking which is either controlled by another undertaking or where that other undertaking exercises a dominating influence over it.

Holding company (p. 323): The outdated term for what is now known as 'parent undertaking'.

Subsidiary company (p. 323): The outdated term for what is now known as a 'subsidiary undertaking'.

Main points to remember

1   Ordinary shareholders generally have voting rights, a right in the net assets of the company, and a right to an interest in profits earned.

2   Ordinary shareholders receive copies of the financial statements for the company whose shares they hold, but not for any company whose shares are owned by the company they hold their shares in.

3   Consolidated financial statements provide shareholders in parent undertakings with financial statements incorporating the relevant data for all companies in the group – not just the parent company's own accounts data.

4   The status of 'subsidiary undertaking' is dependent upon the existence of control over that undertaking by another entity.

5   'Control' is determined by whether 'dominant influence' can be exerted, not simply by the level of investment in the company.

6   Associated undertakings are not subsidiaries, and their existence is determined by the existence of a 'significant influence'.

Review questions

21.1   What determines whether or not one company is a subsidiary undertaking of another company?

21.2   How are incorporated businesses affected by the provisions of FRS 2?

21.3   What benefits accrue to the investor in a parent undertaking by the use of consolidated financial statements?

21.4   In what ways did FRS 2 change the ways in which consolidated financial statements should be drawn up?

22

Consolidation of balance sheets: basic mechanics I

Objectives

After you have studied this chapter, you should:

- understand the principle of cancellation that is adopted when preparing consolidated financial statements

- be aware of why goodwill and capital reserves may arise on consolidation

- understand what is meant by the term 'minority interest'

- be aware of how the existence of reserves at the time of acquisition affects the preparation of consolidated financial statements

22.1 Introduction

This chapter is concerned with the basic mechanics of consolidating balance sheets. The figures used will be quite small ones, as there is no virtue in obscuring the principles involved by bringing in large amounts. For the sake of brevity some abbreviations will be used. As the consolidation of the accounts of either two or three companies, but no more, will be attempted, then the abbreviations will be 'P' for the parent undertaking, 'S1' the first subsidiary undertaking, and 'S2' the second subsidiary undertaking. Where there is only one subsidiary undertaking it will be shown as 'S'. Unless stated to the contrary, all the shares will be ordinary shares of £1 each.

It will make the problems of the reader far easier if relatively simple balance sheets can be used to demonstrate the principles of consolidated accounts. To this end the balance sheets which follow in the next few chapters will usually have only two sorts of assets, those of stock and cash at bank. This will save a great deal of time and effort. If every time a consolidated balance sheet were to be drawn up the reader had to deal with assets of land, buildings, patents, motor vehicles, plant and machinery, stock, debtors and bank balances, then this would be an unproductive use of time.

22.2 The principle of cancellation

The various final accounts of the parent undertaking and its subsidiary undertakings have to be brought together and consolidated into one set of accounts for the whole of the group. Some items in one of the original sets of accounts will also be found to refer to exactly the same transactions in one of the other sets of original final accounts.

Let us look at some of the more common examples:

- An item which is a debtor in one balance sheet may be shown as a creditor in another balance sheet. If P Ltd had sold goods to S Ltd, its subsidiary, but S Ltd had not yet paid for them, then the item would be shown as a debtor in the balance sheet of P Ltd and as a creditor in the balance sheet of S Ltd.
- Sales by one of the group to another company in the group will appear as sales in one company's accounts and purchases in another company's accounts.
- Shares bought in one of the subsidiary undertakings by the parent undertaking will be shown as an investment on the assets side of the parent undertaking's balance sheet. In the balance sheet of the subsidiary, exactly those same shares will be shown as issued share capital.
- Dividends paid by a subsidiary undertaking to its parent undertaking will be shown as paid dividends in the final accounts of the subsidiary, and as dividends received in the final accounts of the parent undertaking.

The group or consolidated financial statements are supposed to show how the group as a whole has dealt with the world outside. Transactions which are simply within the group do not represent dealings with the outside world. When all of the separate accounts of the companies within the group are put together such items need to be deleted, and will not appear in the consolidated financial statements of the group.

This therefore is the principle of cancellation. Like things in different final accounts within the group should be cancelled out from each to arrive at the group's final accounts. All of the items already listed will therefore not appear in the consolidated financial statements.

This can be shown in the form of the diagram in Exhibit 22.1.

Exhibit 22.1 Consolidation of accounts of a group

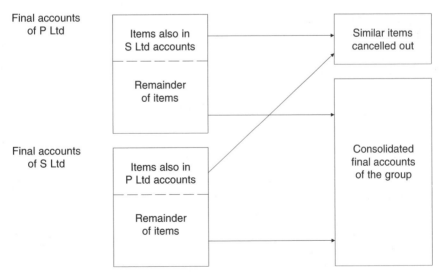

This means that a consolidated set of financial statements, where the subsidiaries are 100 per cent owned by the parent undertaking, will appear as follows:

Group Balance Sheet as at .....

	£	£
Fixed Assets (*less* Cancelled items)		xxxx
Current Assets (*less* Cancelled items)	xxxx	
Less Current liabilities (*less* Cancelled items)	xxxx	xxxx
		xxxx

Financed by

Share capital (of the parent undertaking only, as the purchase of shares in the subsidiaries have cancelled out)	xxxx
Reserves (*less* Cancelled items)	xxxx
	xxxx

22.3 Rule 1

The first rule is, therefore, that in consolidation like things cancel out each other. In fact **cancellation accounts** are what consolidation accounts are all about. It also helps the reader to see the issue more clearly if the consolidated balance sheet is constructed immediately after P has bought the shares in S. In fact this would not be done in practice, but it is useful to use the method from a teaching point of view.

Exhibit 22.2

100 per cent of the shares of S bought at balance sheet value.

P has just bought all the shares of S. Before consolidation the balance sheets of P and S appear as follows:

P Balance Sheet

	£
Investment in subsidiary S (A)	6
Bank	4
	10
Share capital	10
	10

S Balance Sheet

	£
Stock	5
Bank	1
	6
Share capital (B)	6
	6

Now the consolidated balance sheet can be drawn up. The rule about like things cancelling out each other can now be applied. As can be seen, item (A) in P's balance sheet and item (B) in S's balance sheet are concerned with exactly the same thing, namely the 6 ordinary shares of S, and for the same amount, for the shares are shown in both balance sheets at £6. These are cancelled when the consolidated balance sheet is drafted.

P & S Consolidated Balance Sheet

	£
Stock	5
Bank (£4 + £1)	5
	10
Share capital	10
	10

Exhibit 22.3

100 per cent of the shares of S bought for more than balance sheet value.

P Balance Sheet

		£
Investment in subsidiary S: 6 shares	(C)	9
Bank		1
		10
Share capital		10
		10

S Balance Sheet

		£
Stock		5
Bank		1
		6
Share capital	(D)	6
		6

Now (C) and (D) refer to like things, but the amounts are unequal. What has happened is that P has given £3 more than the book value for the shares of S. In accounting, where the purchase money for something exceeds the stated value then the difference is known as Goodwill. This is still adhered to in the consolidation of balance sheets. The consolidated balance sheet is therefore:

P and S Consolidated Balance Sheet

	£
Goodwill (C) £9 – (D) £6	3
Stock	5
Bank (£1 + £1)	2
	10
Share capital	10
	10

Exhibit 22.4

100 per cent of the shares of S bought for less than balance sheet value.

P Balance Sheet

		£
Investment in subsidiary S: 6 shares	(E)	4
Stock		5
Bank		1
		10
Share capital		10
		10

S Balance Sheet

		£
Stock		5
Bank		1
		6
Share capital	(F)	6
		6

P has bought all the shares of S, but has given only £4 for £6 worth of shares at balance sheet values. The £2 difference is the opposite of goodwill. Contrary to what many people would think, this is not 'badwill' as such a word is not an accounting term. The uninitiated might look upon the £2 as being 'profit' but your knowledge of company accounts should tell you that this difference could never be distributed as cash dividends. It is therefore a **capital reserve** and will be shown accordingly in the consolidated balance sheet. The consolidated balance sheet therefore appears as:

P and S Consolidated Balance Sheet

	£
Stock (£5 + £5)	10
Bank (£1 + £1)	2
	12
Share capital	10
Capital reserve (F) £6 – (E) £4	2
	12

22.4 Cost of control

In fact the expression **cost of control** could be used instead of goodwill. This expression probably captures the essence of the purchase of the shares rather than calling it goodwill. It is precisely for the sake of gaining control of the assets of the company that the shares are bought. However, the expression goodwill is more widely used and is correspondingly the one that will be used through the remainder of this book. Details of how to record entries in a 'cost of control' account can be seen in section 28.4, p. 402. (You can now attempt Review Questions 22.1, 22.2 and 22.3.)

Important note: Remember that SSAP 22: *Accounting for goodwill* applies to all the goodwill figures you will be calculating in the next few chapters. It will be up to the company exactly how it will apply SSAP 22.

22.5 Rule 2

This states that, although the whole of the shares of the subsidiary have not been bought, nonetheless the whole of the assets of the subsidiary (subject to certain inter-company transactions described later) will be shown in the consolidated balance sheet.

This rule comes about because of the choice made originally between two possible methods that could have been chosen. Suppose that P bought 75 per cent of the shares of S then the balance sheets could be displayed in one of two ways, e.g.

P and S Consolidated Balance Sheet

	£
Goodwill	xxxx
Assets of P: 100 per cent	xxxx
Assets of S: 75 per cent	xxxx
	xxxx
Share capital of P	xxxx
	xxxx

P and S Consolidated Balance Sheet

	£
Goodwill	xxxx
Assets of P: 100 per cent	xxxx
Assets of S: 100 per cent	xxxx
	xxxx
Share capital of P	xxxx
Claims of outsiders which equal 25 per cent of the assets of S	xxxx
	xxxx

It can be seen that both balance sheets show the amount of assets which P owns by virtue of its proportionate shareholding. On the other hand the second balance sheet gives a fuller picture, as it shows that P has control of all of the assets of S, although in fact it does not own all of them. The claims of outsiders come to 25 per cent of S and obviously they cannot control the assets of S, whereas P, with 75 per cent, can control the whole of the assets even though they are not fully owned by it. The second balance sheet method gives rather more meaningful information and is the method that is used for consolidated accounts in accordance with FRS 2.

Assume that S has 6 shares of £1 each and that it has one asset, namely stock £6. P buys 4 shares for £1 each, £4. If the whole of the assets of S £6 are to be shown on the assets side of the consolidated balance sheet, and the cancellation of only £4 is to take place on the other side, then the consolidated balance sheet would not balance. Exhibit 22.5 shows this in detail before any attempt is made to get the consolidated balance sheet to balance.

Exhibit 22.5

P Balance Sheet

	£
Investment in subsidiary: 4 shares (bought today)	4
Stock	5
Bank	1
	10
Share capital	10
	10

S Balance Sheet

	£
Stock	6
Share capital	6

Now as the two extra shares have not been bought by P then they cannot be brought into any calculation of goodwill or capital reserve. P has in fact bought four shares with a balance sheet value of £1 each, £4, for precisely £4. There is therefore no element of goodwill or capital reserve. But on the other hand the consolidated balance sheet per Rule 2 must show the whole of the assets of S. This gives a consolidated balance sheet as follows:

P and S Consolidated Balance Sheet

	£
Stock (£5 + £6)	11
Bank	1
Share capital	10

Quite obviously the balance sheet totals differ by £2. What is this £2? On reflection it can be seen to be the £2 shares not bought by P. These shares belong to outsiders, they are not owned by the group. These outsiders also hold less than 50 per cent of the voting shares of S. In fact, if they owned more, then S would probably not be a subsidiary company. The title given to the outside shareholders is the apt one therefore of **minority interest**. As the whole of the assets of S are shown in the consolidated balance sheet then part of these assets are owned by the minority interest. This claim against the assets is therefore shown on the capital side of the consolidated balance sheet. The consolidated balance sheet becomes:

P and S Consolidated Balance Sheet

	£
Stock (£5 + £6)	11
Bank	1
	12
Share capital	10
Minority interest	2
	12

This therefore is the convention of showing the whole of the assets of the subsidiary (less certain inter-company transactions) in the consolidated balance sheet, with the claim of the minority interest shown on the other side of the balance sheet.

Exhibit 22.6

Where less than 100 per cent of the subsidiary's shares are bought at more than book value.

P Balance Sheet

		£
Investment in subsidiary: 6 shares	(G)	8
Stock		11
Bank		1
		20
Share capital		20
		20

S Balance Sheet

		£
Stock		7
Bank		3
		10
Share capital	(I)	10
		10

P has bought 6 shares only, but has paid £8 for them. As the book value of the shares is £6, the £2 excess must therefore be goodwill. The cancellation is therefore £6 from (G) and £6 from (I), leaving £2 of (G) to be shown as goodwill in the consolidated balance sheet. The remaining £4 of (I) is in respect of shares held by the minority interest.

P and S Consolidated Balance Sheet

	£
Goodwill	2
Stock (£11 + £7)	18
Bank (£1 + £3)	4
	24
Share capital	20
Minority interest	4
	24

Exhibit 22.7

Where less than 100 per cent of the shares in the subsidiary are bought at less than book value.

P Balance Sheet

		£
Investment in subsidiary: 7 shares	(J)	5
Stock		13
Bank		2
		20
Share capital		20
		20

S Balance Sheet

		£
Stock		9
Bank		1
		10
Share capital	(K)	10
		10

Seven shares of S have now been bought for £5. This means that £5 of (J) and £5 of (K) cancel out with £2 shown as capital reserve. The remaining £3 of (K) is in respect of the shares held by the minority interest and will be shown as such in the consolidated balance sheet.

P and S Consolidated Balance Sheet

	£
Stock (£13 + £9)	22
Bank (£2 + £1)	3
	25
Shares	20
Capital reserve	2
Minority interest	3
	25

You can now attempt Review Questions 22.6 and 22.7.

22.6 Taking over subsidiaries with reserves

So far, for reasons of simplification, the examples given have been of subsidiaries having share capital but no reserves. When reserves exist, as they do in the vast majority of firms, it must be remembered that they belong to the ordinary shareholders. This means that if P buys all the 10 shares of S for £15, and S at that point of time has a credit balance of £3 on its profit and loss account and a general reserve of £2, then what P acquires for its £15 is the full entitlement/rights of the 10 shares measured by/shown as:

	£
10 Shares	10
Profit and loss	3
General reserve	2
	15

This means that the £15 paid and the £15 entitlements as shown will cancel out each other and will not be shown in the consolidated balance sheet. This is shown by the balance sheets shown in Exhibit 22.8.

Exhibit 22.8

Where 100 per cent of the shares are bought at book value when the subsidiary has reserves.

P Balance Sheet

		£
Investment in subsidiary: 10 shares	(L)	15
Stock		11
Bank		2
		28
Share capital		20
Profit and loss		5
General reserve		3
		28

S Balance Sheet

		£
Stock		9
Bank		6
		15
Share capital	(M1)	10
Profit and loss	(M2)	3
General reserve	(M3)	2
		15

P and S Consolidated Balance Sheet

	£
Stock (£11 + £9)	20
Bank (£2 + £6)	8
	28
Share capital	20
Profit and loss	5
General reserve	3
	28

The cost of the shares (L) £15 is cancelled out exactly against (M1) £10 + (M2) £3 + (M3) £2 = £15. These are therefore the only items cancelled out and the remainder of the two balance sheets of P and S are then combined to be the consolidated balance sheet.

Exhibit 22.9

Where 100 per cent of the shares are bought at more than book value when the subsidiary has reserves.

P Balance Sheet

		£
Investment in subsidiary: 10 shares	(N)	23
Stock		7
Bank		5
		35
Share capital		20
Profit and loss		9
General reserve		6
		35

S Balance Sheet

		£
Stock		15
Bank		2
		17
Share capital	(O1)	10
Profit and loss	(O2)	4
General reserve	(O3)	3
		17

P paid £23 (N) for the entitlements (O1) £10 + (O2) £4 + (O3) £3 = £17, so that a figure of £6 will be shown in the consolidated balance sheet for Goodwill.

P and S Consolidated Balance Sheet

	£
Goodwill	6
Stock (£7 + £15)	22
Bank (£5 + £2)	7
	35
Share capital	20
Profit and loss	9
General reserve	6
	35

Exhibit 22.10

Where 100 per cent of the shares in the subsidiary are bought at below book value when the subsidiary has reserves.

P Balance Sheet

		£
Investment in subsidiary: 10 shares	(Z)	17
Stock		10
Bank		8
		35
Share capital		20
Profit and loss		6
General reserve		9
		35

S Balance Sheet

		£
Stock		16
Bank		5
		21
Share capital	(Q1)	10
Profit and loss	(Q2)	8
General reserve	(Q3)	3
		21

P has paid £17 (Z) for the benefits of (Q1) £10 + (Q2) £8 + (Q3) £3 = £21. This means that there will be a Capital Reserve of £21 − £17 = £4 in the consolidated balance sheet, while (Z), (Q1), (Q2) and (Q3), having been cancelled out, will not appear.

P and S Consolidated Balance Sheet

	£
Stock (£10 + £16)	26
Bank (£8 + £5)	13
	39
Share capital	20
Profit and loss	6
General reserve	9
Capital reserve	4
	39

Exhibit 22.11

Where less than 100 per cent of the shares are bought in a subsidiary which has reserves, and the shares are bought at the balance sheet value.

P Balance Sheet

		£
Investment in subsidiary: 8 shares	(R)	24
Stock		15
Bank		6
		45
Share capital		20
Profit and loss		17
General reserve		8
		45

S Balance Sheet

		£
Stock		21
Bank		9
		30
Share capital	(T1)	10
Profit and loss	(T2)	5
General reserve	(T3)	15
		30

The items (R) and the parts of (T1), (T2) and (T3) which are like things need to be cancelled out. The cancellation takes place from the share capital and reserves of S as follows:

	Total at acquisition date	Bought by P 80 per cent	Held by minority interest
	£	£	£
Share capital	10	8	2
Profit and loss	5	4	1
General reserve	15	12	3
	30	24	6

The amount paid by P was £24, and as P acquired a total of £24 value of shares and reserves the cancellation takes place without there being any figure of goodwill or capital reserve. The consolidated balance sheet therefore appears:

P and S Consolidated Balance Sheet

	£
Stock (£15 + £21)	36
Bank (£6 + £9)	15
	51
Share capital	20
Profit and loss	17
General reserve	8
Minority interest	6
	51

22.7 Partial control at a price not equal to balance sheet value

In Exhibit 22.11 the amount paid for the 80 per cent of the shares of S was equal to the balance sheet value of the shares in that it amounted to £24. Very rarely will it be so, as the price is normally different from balance sheet value. If an amount paid is greater than the balance sheet value then the excess will be shown as goodwill in the consolidated balance sheet, while if a smaller amount than balance sheet value is paid then the difference is a capital reserve and will be shown as such in the consolidated balance sheet. Using the balance sheet figure of S in Exhibit 22.11 then if P had paid £30 for 80 per cent of the shares of S then the consolidated balance sheet would show a goodwill figure of £6, while if instead £21 only had been paid then the consolidated balance sheet would show £3 for capital reserve.

When the acquisition of two subsidiaries brings out in the calculations a figure of goodwill in respect of the acquisition of one subsidiary, and a figure for capital reserve in respect of the acquisition of the other subsidiary, then the net figure only will be shown in the consolidated balance sheet. For instance if P had acquired two subsidiaries S1 and S2 where the calculations showed a figure of £10 for goodwill on the acquisition of S1 and a figure of £4 for capital reserve on the acquisition of S2, then the consolidated balance sheet would show a figure for goodwill of £6. Given figures instead of £11 goodwill for S1 and £18 capital reserve for S2 then the consolidated balance sheet would show a capital reserve of £7.

The final exhibit in this chapter is a composite one, bringing in most of the points already shown.

Exhibit 22.12

Where two subsidiaries have been acquired, both with reserves, full control being acquired of one subsidiary and a partial control of the other subsidiary.

P Balance Sheet

		£
Investment in subsidiaries:		
S1 10 shares	(U)	37
S2 7 shares	(V)	39
Stock		22
Bank		2
		100
Share capital		40
Profit and loss		50
General reserve		10
		100

S1 Balance Sheet

		£
Stock		19
Bank		11
		30
Share capital	(W1)	10
Profit and loss	(W2)	12
General reserve	(W3)	8
		30

S2 Balance Sheet

		£
Stock		42
Bank		18
		60
Share capital	(X1)	10
Profit and loss	(X2)	30
General reserve	(X3)	20
		60

With the acquisition of S1 P has paid £37 for (W1) £10 + (W2) £12 + (W3) £8 = £30, giving a figure of £7 for goodwill. With the acquisition of S2 P has given £39 for 7/10 of the following: (X1) £10 + (X2) £30 + (X3) £20 = £60 × 7/10 = £42, giving a figure of £3 for capital reserve. As the net figure only is to be shown in the consolidated balance sheet then it will be Goodwill £7 − Capital reserve £3 = Goodwill (net) £4.

P and S1 and S2 Consolidated Balance Sheet

		£
Goodwill		4
Stock (£22 + £19 + £42)		83
Bank (£2 + £11 + £18)		31
		118
Share capital		40
Profit and loss		50
General reserve		10
Minority interest:		
3/10 of (X1)	3	
3/10 of (X2)	9	
3/10 of (X3)	6	
		18
		118

Now work through Review Questions 22.10 and 22.11.

New terms

Minority interests (p. 334): Shareholders in subsidiary undertakings other than the holding undertaking who are not therefore part of the group.

Cost of control (p. 332): An alternative expression to goodwill.

Capital reserve (p. 332): Where less than fair value has been paid for the shares of the subsidiary.

Main points to remember

1 Some items in the accounts of one of the group companies will refer to exactly the same transactions as in the accounts of one of the other group companies and they will need to be cancelled out when the consolidated financial statements are prepared (*Rule 1*).

2   Where the consideration exceeds the balance sheet value acquired, goodwill arises.

3   Where the consideration is less than the balance sheet value acquired, a capital reserve arises.

4   The treatment of goodwill is governed by SSAP 22: *Accounting for goodwill.*

5   Minority interests exist when less than 100 per cent of the share capital of a subsidiary is owned at the balance sheet date.

6   All the assets of a subsidiary are included in the consolidated financial statements, even where less than 100 per cent of the share capital has been acquired (*Rule 2*).

7   When a subsidiary has reserves at the date of acquisition, those reserves are treated as part of the capital acquired and the calculation of goodwill includes the relevant proportion of the reserves.

8   When goodwill arises in respect of consolidation of one subsidiary and a capital reserve arises on another, the two amounts should be offset in the consolidated financial statements, leaving a net balance to be shown.

Review questions

22.1   The following balance sheets were drawn up immediately P Ltd had acquired control of S Ltd. You are to draw up a consolidated balance sheet.

P Balance Sheet

	£
Investment in S: 100 shares	110
Stock	60
Bank	30
	200
Share capital	200
	200

S Balance Sheet

	£
Stock	80
Bank	20
	100
Share capital	100
	100

22.2 You are to draw up a consolidated balance sheet from the following balance sheets of P Ltd and S Ltd which were drawn up immediately P Ltd had acquired the shares in S Ltd.

P Balance Sheet

	£
Investment in S Ltd:	
3,000 shares	2,700
Fixed assets	2,000
Stock	800
Debtors	400
Bank	100
	6,000
Share capital	6,000
	6,000

S Balance Sheet

	£
Fixed assets	1,800
Stock	700
Debtors	300
Bank	200
	3,000
Share capital	3,000
	3,000

22.3 Draw up a consolidated balance sheet from the following balance sheets which were drawn up as soon as P Ltd had acquired control of S Ltd.

P Balance Sheet

	£
Investment in S Ltd: 60,000 shares	60,000
Fixed assets	28,000
Stock	6,000
Debtors	5,000
Bank	1,000
	100,000
Share capital	100,000
	100,000

S Balance Sheet

	£
Fixed assets	34,000
Stock	21,000
Debtors	3,000
Bank	2,000
	60,000
Share capital	60,000
	60,000

22.4A P Ltd acquires all the shares in S Ltd and then the following balance sheets are drawn up. You are to draw up a consolidated balance sheet.

P Balance Sheet

	£
Investment in S Ltd	29,000
Fixed assets	5,000
Stock	4,000
Debtors	3,000
Bank	1,000
	42,000
Share capital	42,000
	42,000

S Balance Sheet

	£
Fixed assets	12,000
Stock	6,000
Debtors	4,000
Bank	2,000
	24,000
Share capital	24,000
	24,000

22.5A Draw up a consolidated balance sheet from the balance sheets of P Ltd and S Ltd that were drafted immediately the shares in S Ltd were acquired by P Ltd.

P Balance Sheet

	£
Investment in S Ltd: 63,000 shares	50,000
Fixed assets	18,000
Stock	5,000
Debtors	4,000
Bank	3,000
	80,000
Share capital	80,000
	80,000

S Balance Sheet

	£
Fixed assets	48,000
Stock	6,000
Debtors	5,000
Bank	4,000
	63,000
Share capital	63,000
	63,000

22.6 P Ltd acquires 60 per cent of the shares in S Ltd. Balance sheets are then drafted immediately. You are to draw up the consolidated balance sheet.

P Balance Sheet

	£
Investment in S Ltd: 1,200 shares	1,500
Fixed assets	900
Stock	800
Debtors	600
Bank	200
	4,000
Share capital	4,000
	4,000

S Balance Sheet

	£
Fixed assets	1,100
Stock	500
Debtors	300
Bank	100
	2,000
Share capital	2,000
	2,000

22.7 P Ltd acquires 95 per cent of the shares of S Ltd. The following balance sheets are then drafted. You are to draw up the consolidated balance sheet.

P Balance Sheet

	£
Investment in S: 2,850 shares	2,475
Fixed assets	2,700
Stock	1,300
Debtors	1,400
Bank	125
	8,000
Share capital	8,000
	8,000

S Balance Sheet

	£
Fixed assets	625
Stock	1,700
Debtors	600
Bank	75
	3,000
Share capital	3,000
	3,000

22.8A P Ltd buys 66⅔ per cent of the shares in S Ltd. You are to draw up the consolidated balance sheet from the following balance sheets constructed immediately control had been achieved.

P Balance Sheet

	£
Investment in S: 600 shares	540
Fixed assets	1,160
Stock	300
Debtors	200
Bank	100
	2,300
Share capital	2,300
	2,300

S Balance Sheet

	£
Fixed assets	400
Stock	200
Debtors	240
Bank	60
	900
Share capital	900
	900

22.9A After P Ltd acquired 75 per cent of the shares of S Ltd the following balance sheets are drawn up. You are to draw up the consolidated balance sheet.

P Balance Sheet

	£
Investments in S Ltd: 1,200 shares	1,550
Fixed assets	2,450
Stock	1,000
Debtors	800
Bank	200
	6,000
Share capital	6,000
	6,000

S Balance Sheet

	£
Fixed assets	800
Stock	400
Debtors	250
Bank	150
	1,600
Share capital	1,600
	1,600

22.10 Immediately after P Ltd had acquired control of S1 Ltd and S2 Ltd the following balance sheets were drawn up. You are to draw up a consolidated balance sheet.

P Balance Sheet

	£
Investments in subsidiaries:	
S1 Ltd (3,000 shares)	3,800
S2 Ltd (3,200 shares)	4,700
Fixed assets	5,500
Current assets	2,500
	16,500
Share capital	10,000
Profit and loss account	6,500
	16,500

S1 Balance Sheet

	£
Fixed assets	2,200
Current assets	1,300
	3,500
Share capital	3,000
Profit and loss account	400
General reserve	100
	3,500

S2 Balance Sheet

	£
Fixed assets	4,900
Current assets	2,100
	7,000
Share capital	4,000
Profit and loss account	1,000
General reserve	2,000
	7,000

22.11 Immediately after P Ltd had acquired control of S1 Ltd and S2 Ltd the following balance sheets were drawn up. You are to draw up a consolidated balance sheet.

P Balance Sheet

	£
Investment in subsidiaries:	
S1 Ltd (1,800 shares)	4,200
S2 Ltd (2,000 shares)	2,950
Fixed assets	4,150
Current assets	2,100
	13,400
Share capital	10,000
Profit and loss account	2,000
General reserve	1,400
	13,400

S1 Balance Sheet

	£
Fixed assets	3,500
Current assets	2,500
	6,000
Share capital	3,000
Profit and loss account	1,200
General reserve	1,800
	6,000

S2 Balance Sheet

	£
Fixed assets	1,800
Current assets	1,400
	3,200
Share capital	2,000
Profit and loss account	500
General reserve	700
	3,200

22.12A Immediately after P Ltd had achieved control of S1 Ltd and S2 Ltd the following balance sheets are drawn up. You are to draw up the consolidated balance sheet.

P Balance Sheet

	£
Investments in subsidiaries:	
S1 Ltd 4,000 shares	6,150
S2 Ltd 6,000 shares	8,950
Fixed assets	3,150
Current assets	2,050
	20,300
Share capital	15,000
Profit and loss account	2,000
General reserve	3,300
	20,300

S1 Balance Sheet

	£
Fixed assets	5,300
Current assets	1,200
	6,500
Share capital	4,000
Profit and loss account	1,100
General reserve	1,400
	6,500

S2 Balance Sheet

	£
Fixed assets	6,000
Current assets	3,450
	9,450
Share capital	7,000
Profit and loss account	1,400
General reserve	1,050
	9,450

22.13A The following balance sheets of P Ltd, S1 Ltd and S2 Ltd were drawn up as soon as P Ltd had acquired the shares in both subsidiaries. You are to draw up a consolidated balance sheet.

P Balance Sheet

	£
Investments in subsidiaries:	
S1 Ltd 3,500 shares	6,070
S2 Ltd 2,000 shares	5,100
Fixed assets	2,030
Current assets	1,400
	14,600
Share capital	11,000
Profit and loss account	1,000
General reserve	2,600
	14,600

S1 Balance Sheet

	£
Fixed assets	4,800
Current assets	2,400
	7,200
Share capital	5,000
Profit and loss account	900
General reserve	1,300
	7,200

S2 Balance Sheet

	£
Fixed assets	2,800
Current assets	900
	3,700
Share capital	2,000
Profit and loss account	1,400
General reserve	300
	3,700

23

Consolidation of balance sheets: basic mechanics II

Objectives

After you have studied this chapter, you should:

● *understand the implications when the date of acquisition and the group balance sheet date do not coincide*

● *know that the calculation of goodwill is performed as at the date of acquisition*

● *be aware of the difference in treatment between pre- and post-acquisition reserves of subsidiary undertakings*

23.1 Introduction

In the last chapter the consolidation of balance sheets was looked at as if the consolidated balance sheets were drawn up immediately the shares in the subsidiary had been acquired. However, this is very rarely the case in practice, and therefore the consolidation of balance sheets must be looked at as at the time it actually takes place, i.e. at the end of the accounting period some time after acquisition has taken place. Correspondingly, the balance on the profit and loss account of the subsidiary, and possibly the balances on the other reserve accounts, will have altered when compared with the figures at the date of acquisition.

23.2 Goodwill in later years' accounts

In Chapter 22 the goodwill, or capital reserve, was calculated at the date of acquisition, and this calculation will stay unchanged as the years go by. It is important to understand this. Say, for instance, that the calculation was made of goodwill on 31 December 19X3 and that the figure was £5,000. Even if the calculation were made one year later, on 31 December 19X4, then the calculation must refer to the reserves etc. as on 31 December 19X3 as this is when they were acquired, and so the figure of goodwill will still be £5,000. This would be true even if five years went by before anyone performed the calculation. In practice, therefore, once the figure of goodwill has been calculated then there is absolutely no need to recalculate it every year. However, in examinations the goodwill figure will still have to be calculated by the student even though the consolidated balance sheet that he is drawing up is 5, 10 or 20 years after the company became a subsidiary. This has to be done because the previous working papers are not available to an examinee.

23.3 Capital reserves

It would be outside the law and good accounting practice for any company to return its capital to the shareholders, unless of course special permission were granted by the court.* Similarly, if a parent undertaking were to pay its money in acquiring a company as a subsidiary, and then distribute as dividends the assets that it had bought, then this would really be the same as returning its capital to its shareholders. This can best be illustrated by a simple example.

P pays £15 to acquire 100 per cent of the shares of S, and the share capital of S consists of £10 of shares and £5 profit and loss account. Thus to acquire a capital asset, i.e. ownership of S, the holding company has parted with £15. If the balance of the profit and loss account of S were merely added to the profit and loss balance of P in the consolidated balance sheet, then the £5 balance of S could be regarded as being distributable as cash dividends to the shareholders of P. As this £5 of reserves has been bought as a capital asset then such a dividend would be the return of capital to the shareholders of S. To prevent this, the balance of the profit and loss account of S on acquisition is capitalised, i.e. it is brought into the computation as to whether there is goodwill or capital reserve and not shown in the consolidated balance sheet as a profit and loss account balance. On the other hand the whole of any profit made by S since acquisition will clearly belong to P's shareholders as P owns 100 per cent of the shares of S.

Exhibit 23.1

Where the parent undertaking holds 100 per cent of the subsidiary undertaking's shares.

P acquires the shares on 31 December 19X4. The balance sheets one year later are as follows:

P Balance Sheet as at 31 December 19X5

		£
Investment in subsidiary: 10 shares bought 31.12.19X4	(A)	18
Stock		11
Bank		3
		32
Share capital		20
Profit and loss		12
		32

*Since the 1981 Companies Act powers have been given to companies to purchase their own shares.

S Balance Sheet as at 31 December 19X5

		£
Stock		14
Bank		2
		16
Share capital	(B)	10
Profit and loss:		£
As at 31.12.19X4	(C)	5
Profit for 19X5	(D)	1
		6
		16

The shares were acquired on 31 December 19X4, therefore the calculation of the goodwill or capital reserve is as the position of those firms were at that point in time. Thus for (A) £18 the firm of P obtained the following at 31 December 19X4: Shares (B) £10 and profit and loss (C) £5 = £15. Goodwill therefore amounted to £3. The profit of S made during 19X5 is since acquisition and does not therefore come into the goodwill calculation. The figure of (D) £1 is a reserve which belongs wholly to P, as P in fact owns all of the shares of S. This (D) £1 is added to the reserves shown in the consolidated balance sheet.

P Consolidated Balance Sheet as at 31 December 19X5

	£
Goodwill	3
Stock (£11 + £14)	25
Bank (£3 + £2)	5
	33
Share capital	20
Profit and loss (P £12 + S £1)	13
	33

Exhibit 23.2

Where the parent holds 100 per cent of the shares of the subsidiary and there is a post-acquisition loss.

P Balance Sheet as at 31 December 19X5

		£
Investment in subsidiary:		
10 shares bought 31.12.19X4	(E)	19
Stock		10
Bank		4
		33
Share capital		20
Profit and loss:		£
As at 31.12.19X4		7
Add Profit 19X5		6
		13
		33

S Balance Sheet as at 31 December 19X5

			£
Stock			9
Bank			2
			11
Share capital	(F)		10
Profit and loss		£	
As at 31.12.19X4	(G)	4	
Less Loss 19X5	(I)	3	
			1
			11

In calculating goodwill, against the amount paid (E) £19 are cancelled the items (F) £10 and (G) £4, thus the goodwill is £5. The loss (I) has been incurred since acquisition. A profit since acquisition, as in Exhibit 23.1, adds to the reserves in the consolidated balance sheet, therefore a loss must be deducted.

P Consolidated Balance Sheet as at 31 December 19X5

	£
Goodwill	5
Stock (£10 + £9)	19
Bank (£4 + £2)	6
	30
Share capital	20
Profit and loss (£13 – (I)£3)	10
	30

Exhibit 23.3

Where the parent acquires less than 100 per cent of the shares of the subsidiary and there is a post-acquisition profit.

P Balance Sheet as at 31 December 19X5

			£
Investment in subsidiary: 8 shares bought 31.12.19X4	(J)		28
Stock			7
Bank			3
			38
Share capital			20
Profit and loss		£	
As at 31.12.19X4		10	
Add Profit 19X5		8	
			18
			38

S Balance Sheet as at 31 December 19X5

			£
Stock			28
Bank			2
			30
Share capital	(K)		10
Profit and loss		£	
As at 31.12.19X4	(L)	15	
Add Profit 19X5	(M)	5	
			(N) 20
			30

P has given (J) £28 to take over 80 per cent of (K) + (L), i.e. 80 per cent of (£10 + £15) = £20. Therefore goodwill is £8. The profit for 19X5 (M) £5 is also owned 80 per cent by P = £4, and as this has been earned since the shares in S were bought the whole of this belongs to the shareholders of P and is also distributable to them, therefore it can be shown with other profit and loss account balances in the consolidated balance sheet.

The minority interest is 20 per cent of (K) £10 + (N) £20 = £6. It must be pointed out that, although the holding company splits up the profit and loss account balances into pre-acquisition and post-acquisition, there is no point in the minority interest doing likewise. It would, however, amount to exactly the same answer if they did, because 20 per cent of (K) £10 + (L) £15 + (M) £5 still comes to £6, i.e. exactly the same as 20 per cent of (N) £20 + (K) £10 = £6.

P Consolidated Balance Sheet as at 31 December 19X5

		£
Goodwill		8
Stock (£7 + £28)		35
Bank (£3 + £2)		5
		48
Share capital		20
Profit and loss (P £18 + £4)		22
Minority interest (shares £2 + profit and loss £4):		6
		48

If there had been a post-acquisition loss, then this would have been deducted from P's profit and loss account balance of £18 when the consolidated balance sheet was drawn up.

Main points to remember

1 Goodwill must be calculated on the basis of the balance sheet values at the date of acquisition.

2 Once calculated, there is no point in recalculating the goodwill on an acquisition at a future balance sheet date as the value determined will not alter.

3 Pre-acquisition reserves of a subsidiary are part of the capital acquired and are cancelled out on consolidation; they are not treated as reserves of the group.

4 The group's share of a subsidiary undertaking's post-acquisition profits and losses are included on consolidation with the reserves of the rest of the group.

Review questions

23.1 P Ltd buys 100 per cent of the shares of S Ltd on 31 December 19X5. The balance sheets of the two companies on 31 December 19X6 are as shown. You are to draw up a consolidated balance sheet as at 31 December 19X6.

P Balance Sheet as at 31 December 19X6

	£	£
Investment in subsidiary:		
4,000 shares bought 31.12.19X5		5,750
Fixed assets		5,850
Current assets		2,400
		14,000
Share capital		10,000
Profit and loss account:		
As at 31.12.19X5	1,500	
Add Profit for 19X6	2,500	
		4,000
		14,000

S Balance Sheet as at 31 December 19X6

	£	£
Fixed assets		5,100
Current assets		1,500
		6,600
Share capital		4,000
Profit and loss account:		
As at 31.12.19X5	800	
Add Profit for 19X6	1,800	
		2,600
		6,600

23.2 P Ltd buys 70 per cent of the shares of S Ltd on 31 December 19X8. The balance sheets of the two companies on 31 December 19X9 are as follows. You are to draw up a consolidated balance sheet as at 31 December 19X9.

P Balance Sheet as at 31 December 19X9

	£	£
Investment in S Ltd:		
7,000 shares bought 31.12.19X8		7,800
Fixed assets		39,000
Current assets		22,200
		69,000
Share capital		50,000
Profit and loss account:		
As at 31.12.19X8	4,800	
Add Profit for 19X9	9,200	
		14,000
General reserve		5,000
		69,000

S Balance Sheet as at 31 December 19X9

	£	£
Fixed assets		8,400
Current assets		4,900
		13,300
Share capital		10,000
Profit and loss account:		
As at 31.12.19X8	1,700	
Less Loss for 19X9	400	
		1,300
General reserve (unchanged since 19X5)		2,000
		13,300

23.3A P Ltd bought 55 per cent of the shares in S Ltd on 31 December 19X6. From the following balance sheets you are to draw up the consolidated balance sheet as at 31 December 19X7.

P Balance Sheet as at 31 December 19X7

	£	£
Investment in S Ltd: 2,750 shares		4,850
Fixed assets		13,150
Current assets		13,500
		31,500
Share capital		30,000
Profit and loss account:		
As at 31.12.19X6	900	
Add Profit for 19X7	600	
		1,500
		31,500

S Balance Sheet as at 31 December 19X7

	£	£
Fixed assets		4,600
Current assets		3,100
		7,700
Share capital		5,000
Profit and loss account:		
As at 31.12.19X6	700	
Add Profit for 19X7	500	
		1,200
General reserve (unchanged since 19X6)		1,500
		7,700

23.4 P buys shares in S1 and S2 on 31 December 19X4. You are to draft the consolidated balance sheet as at 31 December 19X5 from the following:

P Balance Sheet as at 31 December 19X5

	£	£
Investment:		
S1: 6,000 shares		8,150
S2: 8,000 shares		11,400
Fixed assets		21,000
Current assets		12,000
		52,550
Share capital		40,000
Profit and loss account:		
As at 31.12.19X4	2,350	
Add Profit for 19X5	5,200	
		7,550
General reserve		5,000
		52,550

S1 Balance Sheet as at 31 December 19X5

	£	£
Fixed assets		9,900
Current assets		4,900
		14,800
Share capital		10,000
Profit and loss account:		
As at 31.12.19X4	1,100	
Add Profit for 19X5	1,700	
		2,800
General reserve (same as 31.12.19X4)		2,000
		14,800

S2 Balance Sheet as at 31 December 19X5

	£	£
Fixed assets		6,000
Current assets		4,000
		10,000
Share capital		8,000
Profit and loss account:		
As at 31.12.19X4	500	
Less Loss for 19X5	300	
		200
General reserve (same as 31.12.19X4)		1,800
		10,000

23.5A P Ltd bought 40,000 shares in S1 Ltd and 27,000 shares in S2 Ltd on 31 December 19X2. The following balance sheets were drafted as at 31 December 19X3. You are to draw up a consolidated balance sheet as at 31 December 19X3.

P Balance Sheet as at 31 December 19X3

	£	£
Investments in subsidiaries		
S1 Ltd 40,000 shares		49,000
S2 Ltd 27,000 shares		30,500
Fixed assets		90,000
Current assets		80,500
		250,000
Share capital		200,000
Profit and loss account:		
As at 31.12.19X2	11,000	
Add Profit for 19X3	16,000	
		27,000
General reserve		23,000
		250,000

S1 Balance Sheet as at 31 December 19X3

	£	£
Fixed assets		38,200
Current assets		19,200
		57,400
Share capital		50,000
Profit and loss account:		
As at 31.12.19X2	3,000	
Less Loss for 19X3	1,600	
		1,400
General reserve (as at 31.12.19X2)		6,000
		57,400

S2 Balance Sheet as at 31 December 19X3

	£	£
Fixed assets		31,400
Current assets		14,600
		46,000
Share capital		36,000
Profit and loss account:		
As at 31.12.19X2	4,800	
Add Profit for 19X3	3,400	
		8,200
General reserve (as at 31.12.19X2)		1,800
		46,000

23.6A The following information relates to Heather Limited and its subsidiary, Thistle Limited.

1   *Heather Limited*
    Retained profits as at 31 March 19X8 £700,000.
    80,000 ordinary shares were purchased in Thistle Limited on 1 April 19X1 for £150,000.
2   *Thistle Limited*
    Retained profits as at 1 April 19X1 £50,000.
    Retained profits as at 31 March 19X8 £120,000.
    There were no other capital or revenue account balances at either of these dates.
    Issued share capital: 100,000 ordinary shares of £1 each.
3   Goodwill arising on consolidation is written off immediately on acquisition against reserves.

Required:
Make the following calculations:
(*a*) the goodwill arising on the acquisition of Thistle Limited;
(*b*) the retained profits to be shown in the Heather Group balance sheet as at 31 March 19X8;
(*c*) the minority interest in the Heather Group as at 31 March 19X8.

(*Association of Accounting Technicians*)

24

Inter-company dealings: indebtedness and unrealised profit in stocks

Objectives

After you have studied this chapter, you should:

- *know how to treat intra-group indebtedness upon consolidation*

- *know how to treat unrealised intra-group profits upon consolidation*

24.1 Inter-company debts

When a subsidiary owes money to the parent, then the amount owing will be shown as a debtor in the parent's balance sheet and as a creditor in the subsidiary's balance sheet. Such debts in fact have to be shown separately from other debts so as to comply with the Companies Acts. Such a debt between these two companies is, however, the same debt and, following the rule that like things cancel out, the consolidated balance sheet will show neither debtor nor creditor for this amount as cancellation will have taken place. The same treatment would apply to debts owed by the parent to the subsidiary, or to debts owed by one subsidiary to another subsidiary. The treatment is exactly the same whether the subsidiary is 100 per cent owned or not.

Exhibit 24.1

Where the subsidiary owes money to the parent.

P Balance Sheet

		£	£
Investment in subsidiary: 10 shares			10
Stock			13
Debtors:			
Owing from subsidiary	(A)	4	
Other debtors		7	
			11
Bank			1
			35
Share capital			20
Profit and loss			6
Creditors			9
			35

S Balance Sheet

		£	£
Stock			6
Debtors			13
Bank			3
			22
Share capital			10
Creditors:			
Owing to parent	(B)	4	
Other creditors		8	
			12
			22

P & S Consolidated Balance Sheet

	£
Stock (£13 + £6)	19
Debtors (£7 + £13)	20
Bank (£1 + £3)	4
	43
Share capital	20
Profit and loss	6
Creditors (£9 + £8)	17
	43

24.2 Unrealised profit in stock-in-trade

It is possible that companies in a group may not have traded with each other. In that case the stocks-in-trade at the balance sheet date will not include goods bought from another member of the group. Again it is also possible that the companies may have traded with each other, but at the balance sheet date all of the goods traded with each other may have been sold to firms outside the group, and the result is that none of the companies in the group will have any of such goods included in its stock-in-trade.

However, it is also possible that the companies have traded with each other, and that one or more of the companies has goods in its stock-in-trade at the balance sheet date which have been bought from another group member. If the goods have been traded between members of the group at cost price, then the consolidated balance sheet will not be altered just because of a change in the location of stocks-in-trade. This means that it will not offend accounting practice by adding together all of the stock figures and showing them in the consolidated balance sheet, as the total will be the total of the cost of the unsold goods within the group.

Conversely, goods are usually sold between members of the group at prices above the original cost price paid by the first member of the group to acquire them. If all such goods are sold by group members to firms outside by the balance sheet date then no adjustments are needed in the consolidated balance sheet, because the goods will not then be included in the stocks-in-trade. It would, however, be more usual to find that some of the goods had not been sold by one of the companies at the balance sheet date, so that company would include these goods in its stock-in-trade in its own balance sheet. Suppose that the parent owns all the shares in S, the subsidiary, and that P had sold goods which had cost it £12 to S for £20. Assume in addition that S had sold none of these goods by the balance sheet date. In the balance sheet of S the goods will be included in stock-in-trade at £20, while the profits made by P will include the £8 profit recorded in buying the goods for £12 and selling them for £20. Although this is true from each company's point of view, it most certainly is not true from the group viewpoint. The goods have not passed to anyone outside the group, and therefore the profit of £8 has not been realised by the group.

24.3 Realisation of profits

Going back to the basic accounting concepts, the realisation concept states that profit should not be recognised until the goods have been passed to the customer. As the consolidated accounts are concerned with an overall picture of the group, and the profits have not been realised by the group, then such profits should be eliminated. Accordingly the figure of £8 should be deducted from the profit and loss account of P on consolidation, and the same amount should be deducted from the stock-in-trade of S on consolidation. This cancels an unrealised intra-group profit.

If P had sold goods which had cost it £12 to S, a 100 per cent owned subsidiary, for £20, and S had sold ¾ of the goods for £22 by the balance sheet date then the picture would be different. P will have shown a profit in its profit and loss account for these sales of £8. In addition S will have shown a profit in its profit and loss account for the sales made of £7, i.e. £22 − ¾ of £20. The two profit and loss accounts show total profits of £8 + £7 = £15. So far, however, looking at the group as a whole, these goods have cost the group £12. Three-quarters of these have been sold to firms outside the group, so that the cost of goods sold outside the group is ¾ × £12 = £9, and as these were sold by S the profit realised by the group is £22 − £9 = £13. This is £2 less than that shown by adding up the separate figures for each company in the group. Thus the group figures would be overstated by £2 if the separate figures were merely added together without any adjustment. In addition the stock-in-trade would be overvalued by £2 if the two separate figures were added together because the remaining stock-in-trade of S includes one-quarter of the goods bought from P, i.e. ¼ × £20 = £5 but the original cost of the group was ¼ × £12 = £3. The adjustment needed is that in the consolidation process £2 will be deducted from the profit and loss balance of P and £2 will be deducted from the stock-in-trade of S, thus removing any unrealised intra-group profits.

This could be expressed in tabular form as:

		£
(a)	Cost of goods to P	12
(b)	Sold to S for	20
(c)	Sold by S, ¾ for	22
(d)	Stock of S at balance sheet date at cost to S ¼ of (b)	5
(e)	Stock of S at balance sheet date at cost to P ¼ of (a)	3
(f)	Excess of S balance sheet value of stock over cost to group (d) – (e)	2

(g) Profit shown in P profit and loss account (b) – (a) = £8
(h) Profit shown in S profit and loss account (c) £22 – ¾ of (b) = £7
(i) Profit shown in the profit and loss accounts of P and S = (g) + (h) = £15
(j) Actual profit made by the group dealing with outsiders (c) £22 less (¾ of (a) £12) £9 = £13
(k) Profit recorded by individual companies exceeds profit made by the group's dealing with outsiders (i) – (j) = £2

The action needed for the consolidated balance sheet is therefore to deduct (f) £2 from the combined stock figure, and to deduct (k) £2 from the combined profit and loss account figure.

Exhibit 24.2

Where the stock-in-trade of one company includes goods bought from another company in the group.

P Balance Sheet as at 31 December 19X3

		£	£
Investment in subsidiary:			
10 shares bought 31.12.19X2			16
Stock-in-trade			24
Bank			6
			46
Share capital			20
Profit and loss account:			
As at 31.12.19X2		8	
Profit for 19X3	(C)	18	
			26
			46

S Balance Sheet as at 31 December 19X3

		£	£
Stock-in-trade	(D)		22
Bank			3
			25
Share capital			10
Profit and loss account:			
As at 31.12.19X2		6	
Profit for 19X3		9	
			15
			25

During the year P sold goods which had cost it £16 to S for £28, i.e. recording a profit for P of £12. Of these goods two-thirds had been sold by S at the balance sheet date, leaving one-third in stock-in-trade. This means that the stock-in-trade of S (D) includes £4 unrealised profit ($\frac{1}{3} \times$ £12). The figure of P's profit for the year (C) £18 also includes £4 unrealised profit. When consolidating the two balance sheets £4 therefore needs to be deducted from each of those figures.

In Exhibit 24.2 the subsidiary has been wholly owned by the parent. The final figures would have been exactly the same if it had been the subsidiary which had sold the goods to the parent instead of vice versa.

P Consolidated Balance Sheet as at 31 December 19X3

	£
Stock-in-trade (S £22 – £4 + P £24)	42
Bank (P £6 + S £3)	9
	51
Share capital	20
Profit and loss accounts (S £9 + P £8 + £18 – £4)	31
	51

24.4 Partially owned subsidiaries and unrealised profits

In Exhibit 24.2 the unrealised profit in stock-in-trade was £4, and in that case the subsidiary was 100 per cent controlled. A few years ago there were three possible methods of dealing with the adjustments needed, two of the methods taking into account the actual percentage of shares owned. However, with FRS 2 the elimination of intra-group profits or losses is to be made in full.

This means that if in Exhibit 24.2 S had been owned 75 per cent by P it would still be the full inter-group profit of £4 that would be deducted from the stock-in-trade in the consolidated balance sheet, and the full £4 would also be deducted from the profit and loss account of P when it is consolidated, there being no adjustment for minority interest.

Main points to remember

1   Intra-group indebtedness must be eliminated upon consolidation, irrespective of the proportion of the holding in the subsidiary undertaking(s) involved.

2   Unrealised intra-group profits must be eliminated upon consolidation, irrespective of the proportion of the holding in the subsidiary undertaking(s) involved.

Review questions

24.1 You are to draw up a consolidated balance sheet from the following details as at 31 December 19X9.

P Balance Sheet as at 31 December 19X9

	£	£
Investment in subsidiary:		
1,000 shares bought 31.12.19X8		2,800
Fixed assets		1,100
Stock		1,200
Debtors		2,100
Bank		200
		7,400
Share capital		2,000
Profit and loss account:		
As at 31.12.19X8	1,500	
Profit for 19X9	2,200	
		3,700
General reserve		800
Creditors		900
		7,400

S Balance Sheet as at 31 December 19X9

	£	£
Fixed assets		1,200
Stock		900
Debtors		1,400
Bank		300
		3,800
Share capital		1,000
Profit and loss account:		
As at 31.12.19X8	950	
Profit for 19X9	1,150	
		2,100
Creditors		700
		3,800

During the year P had sold goods which had cost £150 to S for £240. None of these goods had been sold by the balance sheet date.
  At the balance sheet date P owes S £220.

24.2 Draw up a consolidated balance sheet as at 31 December 19X4 from the following:

P Balance Sheet as at 31 December 19X4

	£	£
Investment in subsidiary:		
6,000 shares bought 31.12.19X3		9,700
Fixed assets		9,000
Stock		3,100
Debtors		4,900
Bank		1,100
		27,800
Share capital		20,000
Profit and loss account:		
As at 31.12.19X4	6,500	
Loss for 19X5	2,500	
		4,000
Creditors		3,800
		27,800

S Balance Sheet as at 31 December 19X4

	£	£
Fixed assets		5,200
Stock		7,200
Debtors		3,800
Bank		1,400
		17,600
Share capital		10,000
Profit and loss account:		
As at 31.12.19X4	3,500	
Profit for 19X5	2,000	
		5,500
Creditors		2,100
		17,600

At the balance sheet date S owes P £600.

During the year P sold goods which had cost £300 to S for £500. Three-quarters of these goods had been sold by S by the balance sheet date.

24.3 Draw up a consolidated balance sheet from the following details as at 31 December 19X8.

P Balance Sheet as at 31 December 19X8

	£	£
Investment in subsidiaries:		
S1 30,000 shares bought 31.12.19X7		39,000
S2 25,000 shares bought 31.12.19X7		29,000
Fixed assets		22,000
Stock		26,000
Debtors		13,000
Bank		5,000
		134,000
Share capital		100,000
Profit and loss account		
As at 31.12.19X7	14,000	
Add Profit for 19X8	9,000	
		23,000
General reserve		2,000
Creditors		9,000
		134,000

S1 Balance Sheet as at 31 December 19X8

	£	£
Fixed assets		22,000
Stock		11,000
Debtors		8,000
Bank		3,000
		44,000
Share capital		30,000
Profit and loss account:		
As at 31.12.19X7	8,000	
Less Loss for 19X8	5,000	
		3,000
General reserve (as at 31.12.19X7)		4,000
Creditors		7,000
		44,000

S2 Balance Sheet as at 31 December 19X8

	£	£
Fixed assets		21,000
Stock		9,000
Debtors		7,000
Bank		1,000
		38,000
Share capital		30,000
Profit and loss account:		
As at 31.12.19X7	1,200	
Add Profit for 19X8	1,800	
		3,000
Creditors		5,000
		38,000

At the balance sheet date S2 owed S1 £500 and P owed S2 £900.

During the year P had sold goods costing £2,000 to S1 for £2,800. Of these goods one-half had been sold by the year end. P had also sold goods costing £500 to S2 for £740, of which none had been sold by the year end.

24.4A You are presented with the following information from the Seneley group of companies for the year to 30 September 19X6:

	Seneley plc £000	Lowe Ltd £000	Wright Ltd £000
Tangible fixed assets	225	300	220
Investments			
Shares in group companies:			
Lowe Ltd	450	–	–
Wright Ltd	130	–	–
	580	–	–
Current assets			
Stocks	225	150	45
Trade debtors	240	180	50
Cash at bank and in hand	50	10	5
	515	340	100
Creditors: amounts falling due within one year			
Trade creditors	(320)	(90)	(70)
Net current assets	195	250	30
	1,000	550	250
Capital and reserves			
Called-up share capital	800	400	200
Profit and loss account	200	150	50
	1,000	550	250

Additional information:
(a) The authorised, issued and fully paid share capital of all three companies consists of £1 ordinary shares.
(b) Seneley purchased 320,000 shares in Lowe Ltd on 1 October 19X3, when Lowe's profit and loss account balance stood at £90,000.
(c) Seneley purchased 140,000 shares in Wright Ltd on 1 October 19X5, when Wright's profit and loss account balance stood at £60,000.
(d) During the year to 30 September 19X6, Lowe had sold goods to Wright for £15,000. These goods had cost Lowe £7,000, and Wright still had half of these goods in stock as at 30 September 19X6. Minority interests are not charged with their share of any unrealised stock profits.
(e) Included in the respective trade creditor and trade debtor balances as at 30 September 19X6 were the following inter-company debts:
● Seneley owed Wright £5,000;
● Lowe owed Seneley £20,000; and
● Wright owed Lowe £25,000.
(f) Seneley writes off any goodwill arising on consolidation to reserves.

Required:
Prepare the Seneley group's consolidated balance sheet as at 30 September 19X6. Your workings should be submitted.

(Association of Accounting Technicians)

24.5A You are to draw up a consolidated balance sheet as at 31 December 19X3 from the following:

P Balance Sheet as at 31 December 19X3

	£	£
Investment in subsidiaries:		
S1 75,000 shares bought 31.12.19X2		116,000
S2 45,000 shares bought 31.12.19X2		69,000
Fixed assets		110,000
Stock		13,000
Debtors		31,000
Bank		6,000
		345,000
Share capital		300,000
Profit and loss account:		
As at 31.12.19X2	22,000	
Less Loss for 19X3	7,000	
		15,000
General reserve (as at 31.12.19X2)		7,000
Creditors		23,000
		345,000

S1 Balance Sheet as at 31 December 19X3

	£	£
Fixed assets		63,000
Stock		31,000
Debtors		17,000
Bank		3,000
		114,000
Share capital		75,000
Profit and loss account:		
As at 31.12.19X2	11,000	
Add Profit for 19X3	12,000	
		23,000
Creditors		16,000
		114,000

S2 Balance Sheet as at 31 December 19X3

	£	£
Fixed assets		66,800
Stock		22,000
Debtors		15,000
Bank		4,000
		107,800
Share capital		80,000
Profit and loss account:		
As at 31.12.19X2	12,800	
Less Loss for 19X3	2,400	
		10,400
General reserve (as at 31.12.19X2)		6,400
Creditors		11,000
		107,800

At the balance sheet date S1 owed P £2,000 and S2 £500, and P owed S2 £1,800.

P had sold goods which had cost £2,000 to S2 for £3,200, and of these goods one-half had been sold by S2 by the year end.

24.6 The following summarised information relates to the Pagg group of companies.

Balance Sheet at 31 March 19X0

	Pagg plc £000	Ragg Ltd £000	Tagg Ltd £000
Tangible fixed assets at net book value	2,000	900	600
Investments			
800,000 ordinary shares in Ragg Ltd	3,000	–	–
300,000 ordinary shares in Tagg Ltd	1,000	–	–
	4,000	–	–
Current assets			
Stocks	1,300	350	100
Debtors	3,000	200	300
Cash	200	20	50
	4,500	570	450
Current liabilities			
Creditors	(4,000)	(270)	(400)
	6,500	1,200	650
Capital and reserves			
Called-up share capital (all ordinary shares of £1 each)	5,500	1,000	500
Profit and loss account	1,000	200	150
	6,500	1,200	650

Additional information:

1 Pagg acquired its shareholding in Ragg Ltd on 1 April 19X5. Ragg's profit and loss account balance at that time was £600,000.

2 The shares in Tagg Ltd were acquired on 1 April 19X9 when Tagg's profit and loss account balance was £100,000.

3 All goodwill arising on consolidation is amortised in equal amounts over a period of 20 years commencing from the date of acquisition of each subsidiary company.

4 At 31 March 19X0, Ragg had in stock goods purchased from Tagg at a cost to Ragg of £60,000. These goods had been invoiced by Tagg at cost plus 20 per cent. Minority interests are not charged with any inter-company profit.

5 Inter-company debts at 31 March 19X0 were as follows:
Pagg owed Ragg £200,000 and Ragg owed Tagg £35,000.

Required:

Insofar as the information permits, prepare the Pagg group of companies' consolidated balance sheet as at 31 March 19X0 in accordance with the Companies Acts and standard accounting practice.

Note: Formal notes to the accounts are NOT required, although detailed working must be submitted with your answer.

(*Chartered Association of Certified Accountants*)

24.7A You are presented with the following summarised information relating to Block plc for the year to 30 September 19X8:

	Block plc	Chip Ltd	Knot Ltd
	£000	£000	£000
Fixed assets	8,900	3,240	2,280
Investments			
Shares in group companies:			
Chip Ltd	2,500	–	–
Knot Ltd	1,600	–	–
	4,100	–	–
Current assets			
Stocks	300	160	80
Trade debtors	1,600	130	50
Cash at bank and in hand	400	110	120
	2,300	400	250
Creditors: amounts falling due within one year			
Trade creditors	(200)	(90)	(110)
Proposed dividend	(100)	(50)	(20)
	(300)	(140)	(130)
	15,000	3,500	2,400
Capital and reserves			
Called-up share capital (ordinary shares of £1 each)	10,000	3,000	2,000
Profit and loss account	5,000	500	400
	15,000	3,500	2,400

Additional information:
1 Block purchased 80 per cent of the share capital of Chip on 1 October 19X3 when Chip's profit and loss account balance was £200,000 credit.
2 On 1 October 19X7 Block purchased 60 per cent of the share capital of Knot. Knot's profit and loss account balance at that date was £500,000 credit.
3 Goodwill is written off against reserves immediately on acquisition.
4 During the year to 30 September 19X8, Block sold goods costing £200,000 to Chip for £300,000. Half of these goods remained in stock at the year end.
5 Inter-company debts at the year end were as follows:

	£000
Chip owed Block	20
Knot owed Chip	30

Required:
Prepare the Block plc group of companies' consolidated balance sheet as at 30 September 19X8. Formal notes to the accounts are NOT required, although detailed working should be submitted with your answer.

(Chartered Association of Certified Accountants)

25

Consolidated financial statements: acquisition of shares in subsidiaries at different dates

Objectives

After you have studied this chapter, you should:

● *know how to calculate goodwill when an interest in a subsidiary undertaking was acquired in blocks over a period of time*

● *know how to calculate goodwill when a subsidiary undertaking was acquired part way through its accounting period*

25.1 Shares bought at different dates

Up to this point the shares in subsidiaries have all been bought at one point in time for each company. However, it is a simple fact that shares are often bought in blocks at different times, and that the first purchase may not give the buyer a controlling interest.

There used to be two possible methods of calculating pre-acquisition profits, and therefore goodwill or capital reserve. However, FRS 2 states that only one method should be used, and this is the method used in this book. FRS 2 requires that the consolidation be based on the fair values at the date the undertaking actually becomes a subsidiary, even though the acquisition has been made in stages.

For instance, a company, S, has an issued share capital of 100 ordinary shares of £1 each. The only reserve of S is the balance on the profit and loss account which was £50 on 31 December 19X4 and two years later on at 31 December 19X6 it was £80. P buys 20 shares on 31 December 19X4 for £36, and a further 40 shares on 31 December 19X6 for £79. The date that S became a subsidiary was therefore 31 December 19X6. The calculation of goodwill becomes:

	£	£
Shares bought (20 + 40)	60	
Profit and loss account of subsidiary, 60 per cent × £80 (date control achieved)	48	108
Paid 31.12.19X4	36	
Paid 31.12.19X6	79	115
Goodwill therefore £115 – £108 = £7		

25.2 Shares bought during an accounting period

In addition it has been conveniently assumed so far that all shares have been bought exactly on the last day of an accounting period. This will just not be so, most shares being bought part way through an accounting period. Unless specially audited accounts are drawn up as at the date of acquisition there is no up-to-date figure of profit and loss account as at the date of acquisition. As this is needed for the calculation of goodwill or capital reserve the figure has to be obtained somehow. Naturally enough, specially audited accounts would be the ideal for the purpose of the calculation, but if they are not available a second-best solution is necessary. In this instance the profit and loss balance according to the last balance sheet before the acquisition of the shares is taken, and an addition made (or deduction – if a loss) corresponding to the proportion of the year's profits that had been earned before acquisition took place. This is then taken as the figure of pre-acquisition profits for goodwill and capital reserve calculations.

Exhibit 25.1

Calculation of pre-acquisition profits, and goodwill, where the shares are bought part way through an accounting period.

P bought 20 of the 30 issued ordinary shares of S for £49 on 30 September 19X5. The accounts for S are drawn up annually to 31 December. The balance sheet of S as at 31 December 19X4 showed a balance on the profit and loss account of £24. The profit and loss account of S for the year ended 31 December 19X5 disclosed a profit of £12.

	£	£
Shares bought		20
Profit and loss account:		
Balance at 31.12.19X4	24	
Add Proportion of 19X5 profits before acquisition $\frac{9}{12} \times £12$	9	
	33	
Proportion of pre-acquisition profits		
20 shares owned out of 30, $\frac{2}{3} \times £33$		22
		42
Paid for shares £49		
Therefore goodwill is £49 – £42 = £7		

Main points to remember

1 When an interest in a subsidiary undertaking is acquired in blocks over a period of time, goodwill is calculated as if all the blocks had been purchased at the date when control was achieved.

2 When a subsidiary undertaking is acquired part way through its accounting period, in the absence of specially audited financial statements, the proportion of profit (or loss) applicable to that part of the financial period that preceded the acquisition date should be treated as being part of the pre-acquisition reserves for the calculation of goodwill upon consolidation.

Review questions

25.1 On 31 December 19X4 S Ltd had share capital of £40,000 ordinary £1 shares and reserves of £24,000. Two years later the share capital has not altered but the reserves have risen to £30,000. The following shares were bought by P Ltd: 10,000 on 31 December 19X4 for £23,500, and on 31 December 19X6 14,000 for £31,000. You are to calculate the figure of goodwill for the consolidated balance sheet as at 31 December 19X6.

25.2A On 31 December 19X6, S Ltd had share capital of £400,000 ordinary £1 shares and reserves of £260,000. Three years later the share capital is unchanged but the reserves have risen to £320,000. The following shares were bought by P Ltd: 100,000 on 31 December 19X6 for £210,000, and 200,000 on 31 December 19X9 for £550,000. Calculate the figure of goodwill for the consolidated balance sheet as at 31 December 19X9.

25.3 P Ltd bought 50,000 of the 80,000 issued ordinary £1 shares of S Ltd for £158,000 on 31 August 19X8. S Ltd accounts are drawn up annually to 31 December. The balance sheet of S Ltd on 31 December 19X7 showed a balance on the profit and loss account of £36,000. The profit and loss account of S Ltd for the year ended 31 December 19X8 showed a profit of £42,000. Calculate the figure for the goodwill to be shown in the consolidated balance sheet as at 31 December 19X8.

25.4A On 1 January 19X1 S Ltd had a share capital of £300,000, a profit and loss account balance of £28,000 and a general reserve of £20,000. During the year ended 31 December 19X1 S Ltd made a profit of £36,000, none of which was distributed. P Ltd bought 225,000 shares on 1 June 19X1 for £333,000. Calculate the figure of goodwill to be shown in the consolidated balance sheet as at 31 December 19X1.

26

Intra-group dividends

Objectives

After you have studied this chapter, you should:

● *know how to treat intra-group dividends*

● *know how to treat dividends from a newly acquired subsidiary undertaking that were proposed prior to the acquisition date*

● *know how to treat dividends proposed by subsidiary undertakings at the balance sheet date*

26.1 Not from pre-acquisition profits

Intra-group dividends are dividends paid by one member of a group to another, i.e. from one company in the group to another. They will, therefore, be shown in the receiving company's own profit and loss account as investment income, with a subsequent increase in the bank balance. From the point of view of the paying company's own accounts, it will show the dividend as a charge against its own profit and loss account, thus reducing the final balance on that account; when paid, there will be a reduction of the bank balance. If the dividend has been proposed, but not paid at the accounting year end, then it will be normal for the proposed dividend to be shown as a current liability in the subsidiary's balance sheet, and as a current asset on the parent undertaking's balance sheet as dividend owing from the subsidiary.

From the point of view of the consolidated balance sheet (making an assumption about pre-acquisition profit shown in detail later) no action is needed. It is a past event that is automatically cancelled when drafting the consolidated balance sheet, as they are like things.

26.2 If paid from pre-acquisition profits

In Chapter 23, the company law principle that dividends should not be paid out of capital was reiterated. To prevent this happening, the pre-acquisition profits were capitalised and brought into the goodwill or capital reserve calculation. A company cannot circumvent the principle by buying the shares of a company, part of the purchase price being for the reserves of the subsidiary, and then utilising those reserves by paying itself dividends, and consequently adding those dividends to its own profits and then declaring an increased dividend itself. The next two exhibits are drawn up to illustrate this.

Exhibit 26.1

Dividends paid from post-acquisition profits.

P buys 100 per cent of the shares of S on 31 December 19X4. In 19X5, S pays a dividend of 50 per cent = £5 which P receives. To simplify matters the dividend is declared for 19X5 and paid in 19X5.

P Balance Sheet as at 31 December 19X5

	£	£
Investment in subsidiary:		
10 shares bought 31.12.19X4		23
Stock		11
Bank		1
		35
Share capital		20
Profit and loss account:		
As at 31.12.19X4	7	
Add Profit for 19X5 (including dividend of £5 from S)	8	
		15
		35

S Balance Sheet as at 31 December 19X5

	£	£	£
Stock			19
Bank			7
			26
Share capital			10
Profit and loss account:			
As at 31.12.19X4		12	
Profit for 19X5	9		
Less Dividend paid to P	5	4	16
			26

The dividend is £5 out of profits made since the acquisition of £9. The dividend can be treated as being from post-acquisition profits, and can therefore be shown in the profit and loss account of P as investment income and so swell the profits of P available for dividend purposes.

P Consolidated Balance Sheet as at 31 December 19X5

	£
Goodwill (£23 − £10 − £12)	1
Stock (P £11 + S £19)	30
Bank (P £1 + S £7)	8
	39
Share capital	20
Profit and loss account:	
(P £7 + £8 + S £4)	19
	39

Exhibit 26.2

Dividends paid from pre-acquisition profits.

P Balance Sheet as at 31 December 19X4

	£
Investment in subsidiary:	
10 shares bought 31.12.19X4	23
Stock	7
Bank	1
	31
Share capital	20
Profit and loss account	11
	31

S Balance Sheet as at 31 December 19X4

	£
Stock	14
Bank	3
	17
Share capital	10
Profit and loss account	7
	17

P Consolidated Balance Sheet as at 31 December 19X4
(immediately after acquisition)

	£
Goodwill (P £23 – S £10 – S £7)	6
Stock	21
Bank (P £1 + S £3)	4
	31
Share capital	20
Profit and loss account	11
	31

The consolidated balance sheet already shown was drafted immediately after acquisition. The following balance sheets show the position one year later. It is helpful to remember that the calculation of goodwill does not alter.

P Balance Sheet as at 31 December 19X5

	£	£
Investment in subsidiary:		
(£23 originally calculated less dividend from pre-acquisition profits £7)		16
Stock		18
Bank		5
		39
Share capital		20
Profit and loss account:		
As at 31.12.19X4	11	
Add Profit for 19X5 (does not include the dividend from S)	8	
		19
		39

S Balance Sheet as at 31 December 19X5

	£	£
Stock		8
Bank		2
		10
Share capital		10
Profit and loss account:		
As at 31.12.19X4	7	
Add Profit for 19X5*	0	
Less Dividend paid	7	
		–
		10

*For simplicity the profit of S for 19X5 is taken as being exactly nil.

P Consolidated Balance Sheet as at 31 December 19X5

	£
Goodwill	6
Stock	26
Bank	7
	39
Share capital	20
Profit and loss	19
	39

It will be noticed that when a dividend is paid out of pre-acquisition profits it is in fact a return of capital to the parent company. Accordingly, the dividend is deducted from the original cost of the investment – it is a return of the purchase money – rather than treated as investment income of the holding company. A common practice of many examiners, or 'trick' if you prefer to call it that, would have been to treat the receipt as investment income instead of as a refund of capital. Thus the balance sheet of P as at 31 December 19X5 in this exhibit would have read 'Profit and loss account £26' instead of 'Profit and loss account £19', and the investment would be shown at £23 instead of £16. This means that the examiner really wants the examinee to adjust what is in fact an incorrect balance sheet, so that the only way is to adjust the parent's balance sheet before proceeding with the consolidation of the balance sheets of P and S.

26.3 Proposed dividend at date of acquisition of shares

Quite frequently there will be a proposed dividend as at the date of the acquisition of the shares, and the holding company will receive the dividend even though the dividend was proposed to be paid from profits earned before acquisition took place. The action taken is similar to that in Exhibit 26.2, in that it will be deducted from the price paid for the shares in order that the net effective price is calculated.

Exhibit 26.3

Shares acquired in a subsidiary at a date when a proposed dividend is outstanding.

P Balance Sheet as at 31 December 19X3

	£	£
Investment in subsidiary:		
10 shares bought 31.12.19X2	22	
Less Dividend from pre-acquisition profits	6	
		16
Stock		11
Bank		2
		29
Share capital		20
Profit and loss account:		
As at 31.12.19X2	4	
Profit for 19X3	5	
		9
		29

S Balance Sheet as at 31 December 19X3

	£	£
Stock		19
Bank		4
		23
Share capital		10
Profit and loss account:		
As at 31.12.19X2 (after deducting the proposed dividend £6)	5	
Add Profit for 19X3	8	
		13
		23

P Consolidated Balance Sheet as at 31 December 19X3

	£	£
Goodwill (see workings below)		1
Stock		30
Bank		6
		37
Share capital		20
Profit and loss account:		
(P £9 + S £8)		17
		37

Calculation of goodwill

	£	£
Paid		22
Less Shares taken over	10	
Less Profit and loss balance at 31.12.19X2	5	
Less Dividend paid from pre-acquisition profits	6	
		21
Goodwill		1

26.4 Proposed dividends

When a dividend is proposed by a company it will be shown as a current liability in its balance sheet. This is just as true for a subsidiary company as it would be for a company which is not controlled by another company. It is common practice for the parent to show a proposed dividend from a subsidiary for an accounting period as being receivable in the same accounting period. Thus the subsidiary will show the proposed dividend as a current liability and the parent will show it as a current asset. However, as this is merely another form of intra-group indebtedness, the amounts owing must be cancelled out when drawing up the consolidated balance sheet. Where the subsidiary is owned 100 per cent by the parent then the two items will cancel out fully.

When the subsidiary is only part-owned, there is the question of the minority interest. The cancellation of the part of the proposed dividend payable to the parent is effected, and the remainder of the proposed dividend of the subsidiary will be that part owing to the minority interest. This can be dealt with in two ways, both acceptable in accounting:

(a) The part of the proposed dividend due to the minority interest is added back to the minority interest figure in the consolidated balance sheet.
(b) The part of the proposed dividend due to the minority interest is shown as a current liability in the consolidated balance sheet.

It must be borne in mind that nothing that has been said refers in any way to the proposed dividends of the parent. These will simply be shown as a current liability in the consolidated balance sheet.

Method (b) would seem to be the better method. For instance, when considering the working capital or liquidity of the group it is essential that all current liabilities due to external parties should be brought into calculation. If the proposed dividend soon to be paid to persons outside the group was excluded, this could render the calculations completely invalid.

Exhibit 26.4

Where a subsidiary has proposed a dividend, and there is a minority interest share in the subsidiary.

This will be shown using method (*b*) just described.

P Balance Sheet as at 31 December 19X3

	£
Investment in subsidiary:	
6 shares bought 31.12.19X1	17
Stock	19
Proposed dividend receivable from S	3
Bank	1
	40
Share capital	20
Profit and loss account	11
Proposed dividend (of the holding company)	9
	40

S Balance Sheet as at 31 December 19X3

	£
Stock	23
Bank	7
	30
Share capital	10
Profit and loss account	15
Proposed dividend	5
	30

Note: At the date of acquisition of the shares on 31 December 19X1 the profit and loss account balance of S was £10, and there were no proposed dividends at that date.

P Consolidated Balance Sheet as at 31 December 19X3

	£	£
Goodwill (*see workings*)		5
Stock		42
Bank		8
		55
Share capital		20
Profit and loss account (*see workings*)		14
Minority interest:		
Shares	4	
Profit and loss ⅖	6	
Current liabilities:		10
Proposed dividends of parent	9	
Owing to minority interest	2	
		11
		55

	£	£	£
Workings:			
Profit and loss account:			
P's profit and loss balance			11
S's profit and loss balance		15	
Less Owned by minority interest: ⅖ × £15	6		
Less Pre-acquisition profits at 31.12.19X1 bought by parent: ⅗ × £10	6		
		12	
			3
			14
Goodwill:			
Paid			17
Less Shares bought		6	
Less Pre-acquisition profits ⅗ × £10		6	
			12
			5

If method (*a*) had been used then the consolidated balance sheet would be as shown except for Minority interest and Current liabilities. These would have appeared:

	£	£
Minority interest:		
Shares	4	
Profit and loss	8	12
Current liabilities:		
Proposed dividend		9

Main points to remember

1 Intra-group dividends paid out of post-acquisition reserves will not appear in the consolidated financial statements, the entries in the individual company financial statements cancelling out upon consolidation.

2 Dividends from a newly acquired subsidiary that were declared prior to the date of acquisition are treated as repayment of capital and the investment in the subsidiary in the parent company balance sheet is reduced by the amount received.

3 Where a subsidiary undertaking is 100 per cent owned, dividends proposed by the subsidiary undertaking that are unpaid at the balance sheet date will be cancelled out upon consolidation.

4 Where a subsidiary undertaking is not 100 per cent owned, dividends proposed by the subsidiary undertaking that are unpaid at the balance sheet date will be cancelled out upon consolidation to the extent that ownership is held; the remainder of the dividend (that relates to the minority interest in the subsidiary undertaking) is shown as either an addition to the minority interest figure in the consolidated balance sheet, or as a current liability in the consolidated balance sheet.

Review questions

26.1 The following balance sheets were drawn up as at 31 December 19X7. The person drafting the balance sheet of P Ltd was not too sure of an item and has shown it as a suspense amount.

P Balance Sheet as at 31 December 19X7

	£	£
Investment in subsidiary:		
20,000 shares bought 31.12.19X6		29,000
Fixed assets		40,000
Current assets		5,000
		74,000
Share capital		50,000
Profit and loss account:		
As at 31.12.19X6	8,000	
Add Profit for 19X7	11,000	
		19,000
Suspense*		5,000
		74,000

*The suspense item consists of the dividend received from S in January 19X7.

S Balance Sheet as at 31 December 19X7

	£	£
Fixed assets		17,000
Current assets		10,000
		27,000
Share capital		20,000
Profit and loss account:		
As at 31.12.19X6*	3,000	
Add Profit for 19X7	4,000	
		7,000
		27,000

*The balance of £3,000 is after deducting the proposed dividend for 19X6 of £5,000.

Draw up the consolidated balance sheet as at 31 December 19X7.

26.2A The following balance sheets of P Ltd and S Ltd were drawn up as at 31 December 19X4. Draw up the consolidated balance sheet as at that date.

P Balance Sheet as at 31 December 19X4

	£	£
Investment in subsidiary:		
100,000 shares bought 31.12.19X3		194,000
Fixed assets		250,000
Current assets		59,000
		503,000
Share capital		400,000
Profit and loss account:		
As at 31.12.19X3	39,000	
Add Profit for 19X4*	64,000	
		103,000
		503,000

*The profit figure for 19X4 includes the dividend of £20,000 received from S Ltd for the year 19X3.

S Balance Sheet as at 31 December 19X4

	£	£
Fixed assets		84,000
Current assets		49,000
		133,000
Share capital		100,000
Profit and loss account:		
As at 31.12.19X3*	11,000	
Add Profit for 19X4	22,000	
		33,000
		133,000

*The balance of £11,000 is after deducting the proposed dividend for 19X3 £20,000.

26.3 Draw up a consolidated balance sheet as at 31 December 19X9 from the following information.

P Balance Sheet as at 31 December 19X9

	£	£
Investment in subsidiary:		
30,000 shares bought 31.12.19X8		47,000
Fixed assets		44,000
Current assets		12,000
		103,000
Share capital		80,000
Profit and loss account:		
As at 31.12.19X8	14,000	
Add Profit for 19X9	9,000	
		23,000
		103,000

S Balance Sheet as at 31 December 19X9

	£	£
Fixed assets		36,000
Current assets		21,000
		57,000
Share capital		40,000
Profit and loss account:		
As at 31.12.19X8	4,000	
Add Profit for 19X9	7,000	
		11,000
Proposed dividend for 19X9		6,000
		57,000

The proposed dividend of S has not yet been brought into the accounts of P Ltd.

26.4A The balance sheets of P Ltd and S Ltd are as follows:

P Balance Sheet as at 31 December 19X4

	£	£
Investment in subsidiary:		
120,000 shares bought 31.12.19X3		230,000
Fixed assets		300,000
Current assets		75,000
		605,000
Share capital		500,000
Profit and loss account:		
As at 31.12.19X3	64,000	
Add Profit for 19X4	41,000	
		105,000
		605,000

S Balance Sheet as at 31 December 19X4

	£	£
Fixed assets		203,000
Current assets		101,000
		304,000
Share capital		200,000
Profit and loss account:		
As at 31.12.19X3	51,000	
Add Profit for 19X4	13,000	
		64,000
Proposed dividend for 19X4		40,000
		304,000

The proposed dividend of S has not yet been brought into the accounts of P Ltd. Draw up the consolidated balance sheet as at 31 December 19X4.

26.5   The following are the summarised balance sheets of P Ltd and S Ltd at 31 December 19X6.

	P Limited £	P Limited £	S Limited £	S Limited £
Tangible fixed assets (*see* note (*a*))		320,000		360,000
Loan to S Ltd		50,000		
Investment in S Ltd		250,000		
Current assets:				
Stocks	110,000		50,000	
Debtors	100,000		40,000	
Bank	30,000		10,000	
		240,000		100,000
Creditors: amounts falling due within one year:				
Trade creditors	190,000		22,000	
Proposed preference dividend	–		8,000	
		(190,000)		(30,000)
Total assets *less* current liabilities		£670,000		£430,000
Capital and reserves:				
Ordinary shares of £1 each, fully paid		500,000		200,000
8% preference shares of £1 each, fully paid		–		100,000
Reserves		170,000		80,000
Loan from P Ltd		–		50,000
		£670,000		£430,000

Notes:

(*a*) *Tangible fixed assets:*

P Limited

	Cost £	Cumulative Depreciation £	WDV £
Buildings	120,000	10,000	110,000
Plant and machinery	200,000	40,000	160,000
Motor vehicles	80,000	30,000	50,000
	400,000	80,000	320,000

Tangible fixed assets:
S Limited

	Cost £	Cumulative Depreciation £	WDV £
Buildings	300,000	100,000	200,000
Plant and machinery	120,000	30,000	90,000
Motor vehicles	130,000	60,000	70,000
	550,000	190,000	360,000

There were no additions or disposals of fixed assets by the group during the year.

(*b*)   P Limited acquired its holding on 1 January 19X6, when the balance on S Limited's reserves stood at £50,000. The investment consists of 150,000 ordinary shares of £1 each, fully paid, purchased for £250,000.

(*c*)   P Limited credited to its profit and loss account a dividend of £7,500 from S Limited in March 19X6, in respect of the shares acquired on 1 January 19X6. S Limited does not intend to pay an ordinary dividend for the year ended 31 December 19X6.

Required:
Prepare a consolidated balance sheet for P Limited and its subsidiary S Limited at 31 December 19X6.

Note: Ignore taxation.

(*Chartered Institute of Management Accountants*)

26.6 X plc acquired 80 per cent of the ordinary share capital of Y plc on 1 January 19X6 for £300,000.

The lists of balances of the two companies at 31 December 19X6 were as follows:

	X plc £000	Y plc £000
Called-up share capital:		
400,000 ordinary shares of £1 each, fully paid	400	
300,000 ordinary shares of £0.50 each, fully paid		150
Reserves as at 1 January 19X6	220	90
Retained profits for 19X6	20	18
Trade creditors	130	80
Taxation	30	14
Proposed final dividend	20	10
Depreciation provisions:		
Freehold property	12	6
Plant and machinery	40	12
Current account		14
	872	394
Tangible fixed assets:		
Freehold property, at cost	120	160
Plant and machinery, at cost	183	62
Investment in Y plc	300	
Stocks	80	70
Debtors	160	90
Bank	10	12
Current account	19	
	872	394

Notes:
(*a*) A remittance of £2,000 from Y plc to X plc in December 19X6 was not received by X plc until January 19X7.
(*b*) Goods, with an invoice value of £3,000, were despatched by X plc in December 19X6 but not received by Y plc until January 19X7. The profit element included in this amount was £400.
(*c*) Included in the stock of Y plc at 31 December 19X6 were goods purchased from X plc for £10,000. The profit element included in this amount was £2,000.
(*d*) It is group policy to exclude all profit on any intra-company transactions.
(*e*) No interim dividend was paid in 19X6 by either company.
(*f*) Ignore the ACT on the proposed final dividend.
(*g*) Goodwill is to be written off against reserves.

Required:
Prepare a consolidated balance sheet for X plc and its subsidiary Y plc as at 31 December 19X6.

(*Chartered Institute of Management Accountants*)

26.7A P plc acquired 80 per cent of the ordinary share capital of S plc for £150,000 and 50 per cent of the issued 10 per cent cumulative preference shares for £10,000, both purchases being effected on 1 May 19X7. There have been no changes in the issued share capital of S plc since that date. The following balances are taken from the books of the two companies at 30 April 19X8:

	P plc £000	S plc £000
Ordinary share capital (£1 shares)	300	100
10% cumulative preference shares (50p shares)	–	20
Share premium account	20	10
General reserve	68	15
Profit and loss account	50	35
Trade creditors	35	22
Taxation	50	30
Proposed dividends	15	10
Depreciation		
Freehold property	40	15
Plant and machinery	100	48
	678	305
Freehold property at cost	86	55
Plant and machinery at cost	272	168
Investment in S plc	160	–
Stocks	111	65
Debtors	30	15
Cash	19	2
	678	305

The following additional information is available:
(*a*) Stocks of P plc include goods purchased from S plc for £20,000. S plc charged out these stocks at cost plus 25 per cent.
(*b*) Proposed dividend of S plc includes a full year's preference dividend. No interim dividends were paid during the year by either company.
(*c*) Creditors of P plc include £6,000 payable to S plc in respect of stock purchases. Debtors of S plc include £10,000 due from P plc. The holding company sent a cheque for £4,000 to its subsidiary on 29 April 19X8 which was not received by S plc until May 19X8.
(*d*) At 1 May 19X7 the balances on the reserves of S plc were as follows:

	£000
Share premium	10
General reserve	20
Profit and loss account	30

(*e*) Goodwill is to be written off against reserves.

Required:
(*a*) Prepare a consolidated balance sheet for P plc and its subsidiary S plc at 30 April 19X8. Ignore the ACT on the proposed final dividend.

Notes to the accounts are not required. Workings must be shown.
(*b*) Explain what is meant by the term 'cost of control' and justify your treatment of this item in the above accounts.

(*Chartered Institute of Management Accountants*)

27

Consolidated balance sheets: sundry matters

Objectives

After you have studied this chapter, you should:

● *know how to calculate goodwill on the purchase of preference shares*

● *know how to treat unrealised profits and losses on intra-group asset sales*

● *be aware of the effect of 'fair value' on the calculation of goodwill and on the preparation of the consolidated financial statements*

27.1 Preference shares

It should be remembered that preference shares do not carry voting powers under normal conditions, nor do they possess a right to the reserves of the company. Contrast this with ordinary shares which, when bought, will give the parent company voting rights and also a proportionate part of the reserves of the company.

This means that the calculation of goodwill or capital reserve on the purchase of preference shares is very simple indeed. If 9 preference shares of £1 each are bought for £12 then goodwill will be £3, while if 20 preference shares of £1 each are bought for £16 then the capital reserve will be £4. The amount of goodwill or capital reserve on the purchase of preference shares is not shown separately from that calculated on the purchase of ordinary shares. Instead the figures will be amalgamated to throw up one figure only on the consolidated balance sheet.

Preference shares owned by the minority interest are simply shown as part of the minority interest figure in the consolidated balance sheet, each share being shown at nominal value.

27.2 Sale of fixed assets between members of the group

There is obviously nothing illegal in one company in the group selling items in the nature of fixed assets to another company in the group. If the sale is at the cost price originally paid for it by the first company, then no adjustment will be needed in the consolidated balance sheet. Rather more often, the sale will be at a price different from the original cost price. The intra-group unrealised profit must be eliminated in a similar fashion to that taken for the unrealised profit in trading stock as described in Chapter 24.

If the fixed asset is shown at its cost to the group in the consolidated balance sheet rather than at the cost to the particular company, then obviously the depreciation figure on that fixed asset should be adjusted to that based on the group cost rather than on the cost of the particular company.

Exhibit 27.1

P Balance Sheet as at 31 December 19X6

	£	£
Investment in S:		
50 shares bought 31.12.19X5		95
Fixed assets	78	
Less Depreciation	23	
		55
Current assets		20
		170
Share capital		100
Profit and loss account:		
As at 31.12.19X5	30	
For the year 19X6	40	
		70
		170

S Balance Sheet as at 31 December 19X6

	£	£
Fixed assets	80	
Less Depreciation	20	
		60
Current assets		35
		95
Share capital		50
Profit and loss account:		
As at 31.12.19X5	20	
For the year 19X6	25	
		45
		95

During the year P Ltd had sold a fixed asset which had cost it £20 to S Ltd for £28. Of the figure of £20 depreciation in the balance sheet of S, £7 refers to this asset and £13 to the other assets. The rate of depreciation is 25 per cent. The £8 profit is included in the figure of £40 profit for 19X6 in the balance sheet of P.

This means that the figure of £8 needs cancelling from the asset costs in the consolidated balance sheet and from the profit and loss account balance. In addition the figure of depreciation needs adjusting downward, from the £7 as shown on the balance sheet of S, to the figure of £5, i.e. 25 per cent depreciation based on the cost of the asset to the group. This in turn means that the figure of profit for S, £25, needs increasing by £2, as, instead of the expense of £7 depreciation, there will now be a reduced expense of £5. The consolidated balance sheet becomes:

P and S Consolidated Balance Sheet as at 31 December 19X6

	£	£
Goodwill		25
Fixed assets	150	
Less Depreciation	41	
		109
Current assets		55
		189
Share capital		100
Profit and loss account:		
(P £70 − £8 + S £25 + £2)		89
		189

27.3 Fair values in acquisition accounting

The consolidated balance sheet should give a picture that is not clouded by the method of drafting consolidated accounts. The consolidation process is looked at from the point of view that the parent undertaking acquires shares in a company, and thereby achieves control of that company. In addition, it is recognised that the reserves are also taken over. It has been said previously that the economic view is that of taking over the assets of another company – after all one does not buy such shares just to possess the share certificates. Rather, the exercise is for the assets which are taken over and used. The consolidated balance sheet should therefore give the same picture as that which would have been recorded if, instead of buying shares, the assets themselves had been bought directly.

Prior to the issue of FRS 6: *Acquisitions and mergers* and FRS 7: *Fair values in acquisition accounting* in September 1994, the way in which acquisitions were accounted for varied from case to case. One of the areas of greatest diversity was in the revaluation of assets and liabilities to 'fair values'. 'Fair value' is defined as the amount for which an asset or liability could be exchanged in an arm's length transaction (i.e. as in an exchange between strangers). Generally, acquiring companies set their own 'fair values' on the assets and liabilities acquired, and then followed the SSAP 22 (goodwill) rules that the amount to be attributed to purchased goodwill should be the difference between the 'fair value' of the consideration given and the aggregate of the 'fair values' of the separable net assets acquired. Where assets are revalued, this should apply to all the assets, i.e. including those attributable to minority interests.

These two standards, FRS 6 and FRS 7, reduced the flexibility available to companies. FRS 6 requires that, under acquisition accounting, the investment is shown at cost (= the 'fair value' given) in the parent company's own financial statements. On consolidation, if the fair value of the net assets (excluding goodwill) acquired is less than the fair value of the purchase consideration, the difference should be treated as goodwill and written off to reserves or capitalised and amortised; if the fair value of the net assets (excluding goodwill) acquired exceeds the fair value of the purchase consideration, the difference should be treated as a negative consolidation difference. This is similar to the treatment that has been adopted throughout the previous few chapters, the only difference being that 'fair values' should be used rather than the values as shown in the balance sheet of the acquired company.

FRS 7 seeks to ensure that upon acquisition, all assets and liabilities that existed in the acquired entity at that date are recorded at *fair values* reflecting their condition at that date. In addition it seeks to ensure that all changes to the acquired assets and liabilities, and the resulting gains and losses that arise after control of the acquired entity has passed to the acquirer, are reported as part of the post-acquisition financial performance of the reporting group.

There are a number of rules given in FRS 7 governing the determination of the appropriate fair value.

- The fair value of **tangible fixed assets** should be based upon either *market value* (if assets similar in type and condition are bought and sold on an open market) or *depreciated replacement cost* (reflecting the acquired business's normal buying process and the sources of supply and prices available to it). However, the fair value should not exceed the recoverable amount (i.e. the greater of the net realisable value and the value in use) of the asset.
- The fair value of **intangible assets** should be based on their *replacement cost*, which is normally their estimated market value.
- **Stocks**, including commodity stocks, that **the acquired entity trades on a market in which it participates as both a buyer and and seller** should be valued at *current market prices*.
- **Other stocks and work-in-progress** should be valued at the lower of *replacement cost* and *net realisable value*. As with the use of *depreciated replacement cost* for *tangible fixed assets*, *replacement cost* for stock should be the cost at which it would have been replaced by the acquired entity, reflecting the acquired business's normal buying process and the sources of supply and prices available to it. The standard suggests that this is synonymous with 'the current cost of bringing the stocks to their present location and condition'.
- **Quoted investments** should be valued at *market price*.
- **Monetary assets and liabilities**, including accruals and provisions, should take into account their timing and the amounts expected to be received and paid. The *fair value* should be determined by reference to *market prices*, or by discounting to present value.
- **Contingences** should be measured at *fair values* where these can be determined, using reasonable estimates of the expected outcome if necessary.

The cost of acquisition is defined in FRS 7 as the amount of cash paid and the fair value of other purchase consideration given by the acquirer, together with the expenses of the acquisition.

The effect of the use of 'fair values' can be seen from what would occur if 'fair values' were used by the acquiring company in arriving at the price it wished to pay, but then were never incorporated into the financial statements. For instance, if P buys all the 10 shares of S for £18 when the reserves are £5, then the goodwill calculation if 'fair values' are not used is:

	£	£
Cost		18
Less Shares	10	
Less Reserves	5	
		15
Goodwill		£3

However, P might have bought the shares of S because it thought that the 'fair value' of the net assets of S was £17.

In P's eyes, it is giving £18 for physical assets worth £17 and the goodwill figure is correspondingly £18 − £17 = £1. Assuming that the difference is in the recorded value of fixed assets, then the consolidated balance sheet will not be showing a true and fair view if it shows goodwill £3 and assets £15. The revaluation upwards of the fixed assets by £2, and the consequent reduction of the goodwill figure by £2 will correct the view. Where there are depreciation charges on the revalued assets, this will also require to be adjusted.

Exhibit 27.2

P Balance Sheet as at 31 December 19X6

	£	£
Investment in subsidiary:		
30 shares bought 31.12.19X5		56
Fixed assets	80	
Less Depreciation for the year	16	
		64
Current assets		26
		146
Share capital		100
Profit and loss account:		
As at 31.12.19X5	20	
Add Profit 19X6	26	
		46
		146

S Balance Sheet as at 31 December 19X6

	£	£
Fixed assets	50	
Less Depreciation for the year	10	
		40
Current assets		14
		54
Share capital		30
Profit and loss account:		
As at 31.12.19X5	3	
Add Profit 19X6	21	
		24
		54

At the time when P bought the shares in S, the assets in S were shown at a value of £33 in the balance sheet of S. In fact, however, P valued the fixed assets as being worth £20 higher than that shown. The consolidated balance sheet will therefore show them at this higher figure. In turn the depreciation, which is at the rate of 20 per cent, will be £4 higher. The consolidated balance sheet therefore appears:

P and S Consolidated Balance Sheet as at 31 December 19X6

	£	£
Goodwill		3
Fixed assets		
(£80 + £70)	150	
Less Depreciation (£16 + £14)	30	
		120
Current assets		40
		163
Share capital		100
Profit and loss account:		
(P £46 + S £21 – increased depreciation £4)		63
		163

Main points to remember

1 Goodwill on the purchase of preference shares is the difference between their nominal value and the amount paid.

2 Unrealised profit on the sale of fixed assets between companies in a group must be eliminated upon consolidation.

3 'Fair values' at the time of acquisition should be used in the calculation of goodwill, rather than the value shown in the balance sheet of the subsidiary, and the consolidation of the subsidiary undertaking should also be based on those 'fair values'.

4 'Fair value' is dependent upon the nature of the item being valued. However, the general rule is that it represents the amount for which an asset or liability could be exchanged in an arm's length transaction, i.e. as in an exchange between strangers.

Review questions

27.1 From the following balance sheets and further information you are to draw up a consolidated balance sheet as at 31 December 19X8.

P Balance Sheet as at 31 December 19X8

	£	£
Investment in S:		
200,000 shares bought 31.12.19X7		340,000
Fixed assets	300,000	
Less Depreciation	100,000	
		200,000
Current assets		103,000
		643,000
Share capital		500,000
Profit and loss account:		
As at 31.12.19X7	77,000	
Add Profit for 19X8	66,000	
		143,000
		643,000

S Balance Sheet as at 31 December 19X8

	£	£
Fixed assets	210,000	
Less Depreciation	40,000	
		170,000
Current assets		102,000
		272,000
Share capital		200,000
Profit and loss account:		
As at 31.12.19X7	40,000	
Add Profit for 19X8	32,000	
		72,000
		272,000

During the year P Ltd had sold a fixed asset, which had cost it £40,000 to S for £50,000. S has written off 20 per cent, i.e. £10,000 as depreciation for 19X8.

27.2A   From the following balance sheets and supplementary information you are to draw up a consolidated balance sheet as at 31 December 19X5.

P Consolidated Balance Sheet as at 31 December 19X5

	£	£
Investment in S:		
10,000 shares bought 31.12.19X4		23,000
Fixed assets	84,000	
Less Depreciation	14,000	
		70,000
Current assets		20,000
		113,000
Share capital		75,000
Profit and loss account:		
As at 31.12.19X4	15,000	
Add Profit for 19X5	23,000	
		38,000
		113,000

S Consolidated Balance Sheet as at 31 December 19X5

	£	£
Fixed assets	26,000	
Less Depreciation	10,000	
		16,000
Current assets		12,000
		28,000
Share capital		10,000
Profit and loss account:		
As at 31.12.19X4	6,000	
Add Profit for 19X5	7,000	
		13,000
General reserve		
(as at 31.12.19X4)		5,000
		28,000

During the year P sold a fixed asset to S. It had cost P £3,000 and it was sold to S for £5,000. S had written off £500 as depreciation during 19X5.

27.3

P Balance Sheet as at 31 December 19X7

	£	£
Investment in S:		
60,000 shares bought on 31.12.19X6		121,000
Fixed assets	90,000	
Less Depreciation for year	24,000	
		66,000
Current assets		40,000
		227,000
Share capital		150,000
Profit and loss account:		
As at 31.12.19X6	44,000	
Add Profit for 19X7	33,000	
		77,000
		227,000

S Balance Sheet as at 31 December 19X7

	£	£
Fixed assets	70,000	
Less Depreciation for year	7,000	
		63,000
Current assets		28,000
		91,000
Share capital		60,000
Profit and loss account:		
As at 31.12.19X6	17,000	
Add Profit for 19X7	14,000	
		31,000
		91,000

When P Ltd bought the shares of S Ltd it valued the fixed assets at £95,000 instead of the figure of £70,000 as shown in the balance sheet of S.

Draw up a consolidated balance sheet as at 31 December 19X7.

27.4A

P Balance Sheet as at 31 December 19X5

	£	£
Investment in S:		
30,000 shares bought 31.12.19X4		53,400
Fixed assets	60,000	
Less Depreciation for year	6,000	
		54,000
Current assets		10,600
		118,000
Share capital		80,000
Profit and loss account:		
As at 31.12.19X4	27,000	
Add Profit for 19X5	11,000	
		38,000
		118,000

S Balance Sheet as at 31 December 19X5

	£	£
Fixed assets	40,000	
Less Depreciation for year	4,000	
		36,000
Current assets		11,000
		47,000
Share capital		30,000
Profit and loss account:		
As at 31.12.19X4	8,000	
Add Profit for 19X5	9,000	
		17,000
		47,000

When P Ltd took control of S Ltd it valued the fixed assets at 31.12.19X4 at £50,000 instead of £40,000 as shown.

Draw up the consolidated balance sheet as at 31 December 19X5.

28

Consolidation of the accounts of a vertical group of companies

Objectives

After you have studied this chapter, you should:

- *understand how a company that is the subsidiary of another is also a subsidiary of its parent's own parent undertaking*

- *know how to consolidate groups that include subsidiaries of subsidiaries*

28.1 Subsidiaries that control other companies

So far we have considered the case of parent undertakings having a direct interest in their subsidiary undertakings. In each case the parent itself has bought the shares in its subsidiaries. In each case over 50 per cent of the voting shares have been bought. In a straightforward case, where the parent company, P1, has bought shares in subsidiaries S1 and S2, it could be represented by a diagram (Exhibit 28.1).

Exhibit 28.1

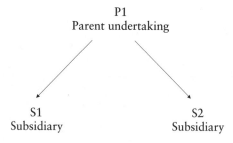

Suppose instead that P2 bought 100 per cent of the shares in S3, and that S3 then itself bought 100 per cent of the shares in S4. Because P2 controls S3 completely, and S3 controls S4 completely, therefore P2 controls both S3 and S4. This is shown as Exhibit 28.2.

If P3 owned S5 100 per cent, but S5 only owned 80 per cent of S6, then we can say that P3 owns 100 per cent of 80 per cent of S6 = 80 per cent (*see* Exhibit 28.3). Similarly if in another case P4 owned 75 per cent of S7, and S7 owns 80 per cent of S8, then P4 owns 75 per cent × 80 per cent = 60 per cent of S8 (*see* Exhibit 28.4).

Exhibit 28.2   *Exhibit 28.3*   *Exhibit 28.4*

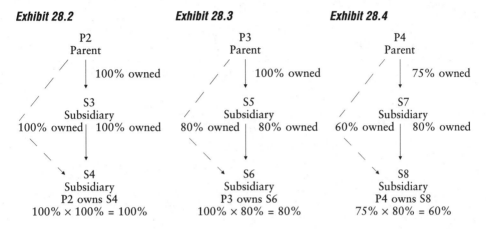

In Exhibits 28.2, 28.3 and 28.4 the eventual ownership by P of each subsidiary's subsidiary exceeds 50 per cent.

There will be cases where the ownership of the subsidiary of a subsidiary by the parent is less than 50 per cent. Exhibit 28.5 shows where P5 owns 80 per cent of S9, and S9 owns 60 per cent of S10. This means that P5 owns 80% × 60% = 48% of S10. Exhibit 28.6 similarly shows where P6 owns 60 per cent of S11 and S11 owns 55 per cent of S12. Therefore P6 owns 60% × 55% = 33% of S12.

Exhibit 28.5   *Exhibit 28.6*

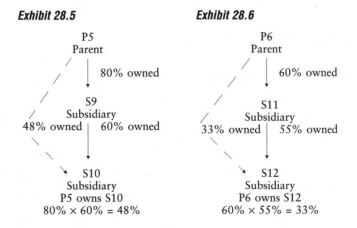

It might look as though S10 is not a subsidiary of P5, because P5 owns less than 50 per cent of S10. However, P5 controls S9 as its ownership is over 50 per cent, and in turn S9 controls S10 as it owns more than 50 per cent. Effectively, therefore, P5 controls S10, and as such S10 is its subsidiary.

28.2 Necessity for consolidated accounts and the Companies Act

Section 228 of the Companies Act 1985 exempts a wholly owned subsidiary from preparing consolidated accounts. For instance, in Exhibit 28.2 the subsidiary S3 would not have to prepare consolidated accounts; neither would S5 in Exhibit 28.3.

In each of cases S7, S9 and S11 in Exhibits 28.4, 28.5 and 28.6, there are minority shareholders. In practice, therefore, those subsidiary companies may have to prepare consolidated accounts, e.g. in Exhibit 28.4 consolidating S7 and S8 if sufficient of the minority interests demand it. See also Chapter 31 for FRS 2 re exemptions.

28.3 Methods of consolidating accounts

There are in fact two methods of consolidating the accounts.

(a) The 'indirect' or 'single-stage' method follows the reasoning already given in this chapter, i.e. computing the parent's interest in the subsidiaries and their subsidiaries and taking that percentage of the capital and reserves of these companies into the consolidation process. For instance, in Exhibit 28.5 the capital and reserves would give 100% of P5 + 80% of S9 + 48% of S10.

(b) The 'multi-stage' method first consolidates the balance sheets of the subsidiary and its subsidiary, and when that is done it is then consolidated with the balance sheet of the holding company. This recognises the fact that subsidiaries with minority interests have to produce consolidated accounts and is more generally used in practice than the indirect method.

For an examination method (a) is to be preferred. It is a quicker method, and usually you will be short of time in an examination. Also an examination question will almost certainly ask for consolidation for all the companies and therefore there will be no need to do the intermediate consolidation. This book will therefore use method (a) only.

28.4 Consolidation technique

We are concerned here with the **indirect** method. It follows mainly the same techniques as described in earlier chapters, but two points need stressing:

(a) **Cost of control account**, and the entry for the cost of investment:
  (i) For subsidiaries, debit total cost of investment to cost of control account.
  (ii) For subsidiaries of subsidiaries, debit cost of control account only with the proportion concerned with the parent's share in the subsidiary which controls the subsidiary. Debit minority interest account with the balance.

Given P investing £20,000 to buy 80 per cent of shares of S1, then S1 investing £10,000 to buy 60 per cent of shares of S2, the entries in the cost of control account (or its workings) would be:

Cost of Control

	£
Cost of shares in S1	20,000
Cost of shares in S2 (80%)	8,000

The remaining proportion of investment by S1 is then debited to a minority interest account (or its workings).

Minority Interest

	£
Cost of shares in S2 (20%)	2,000

(b) **Apportionment of share capital and reserves** to cost of control account and to minority interest account:
  (i) *Cost of control*: take only the group's ultimate share of subsidiary of subsidiary's share capital and reserves.
  (ii) *Minority interest*: include the balance of subsidiary of subsidiary's share capital and reserves.

In the illustration given in (a)(ii) where P bought 80 per cent of S1, and S1 bought 60 per cent of S2, the ultimate share of the group is 80% × 60% = 48%. Therefore, in the consolidated financial statements 48 per cent should come into group calculations and 52 per cent shown in minority interest workings. Double entry: Cr Cost of control account: Dr (appropriate) Reserve account.

28.5 A worked example (without proposed dividends)

Exhibit 28.7

P Ltd owns 80 per cent of the ordinary share capital of S1 Ltd. In turn S1 Ltd owns 75 per cent of the ordinary share capital of S2 Ltd. Both investments had been acquired on 31 December 19X4, one year previous to the following balance sheets:

Balance Sheets December 19X5

	P Ltd £000	P Ltd £000	S1 Ltd £000	S1 Ltd £000	S2 Ltd £000	S2 Ltd £000
Fixed assets		40		4		27
Investments:						
Shares in S1		41				
Shares in S2				25		
Net current assets		19		6		28
		100		35		55
Share capital		40		10		20
Profit and loss						
As at 31.12.19X4	24		5		15	
Add Profit 19X5	36	60	10	15	20	35
General reserve at 31.12.19X4				10		
		100		35		55

Ownership of P can be seen to be 80 per cent of S1 and 80% × 75% = 60 per cent of S2. Any goodwill on acquisition to be written off to profit and loss.

We now will prepare a consolidated balance sheet on 31 December 19X5, one year after both acquisitions. In previous chapters the illustrations have been given on the face of the balance sheets. In this more complicated example we will use double entry accounts for the main items.

P Ltd and its subsidiaries

Consolidated Balance Sheet as at 31 December 19X5

	£000
Fixed assets	71
Net current assets	53
	124
Share capital	40
Profit and loss (*see* account below)	60
	100
Minority interest (*see* account below)	24
	124

In the accounts which follow (*a*)(*i*), (*a*)(*ii*), (*b*)(*i*) and (*b*)(*ii*) refer to consolidation techniques already described.

Cost of Control

	£000		£000
Cost of shares in S1 (*a*)(*i*)	41	Share capital S1 80% × 10	8
Cost of shares in S2 80% (*a*)(*ii*)	20	Share capital S2 60% × 20 (*b*)(*i*)	12
		Pre-acquisition reserves:	
		Profit and loss S1 80% × 5	4
		Profit and loss S2 60% × 15	9
		General reserve S1 80% × 10	8
		Profit and loss: goodwill written off	20
	61		61

Minority Interest

	£000		£000
Cost of shares in S2 20% (*a*)(*ii*)	5	Share capital S1 20%	2
Balance to consolidated balance sheet	24	Share capital S2 40% (*b*)(*ii*)	8
		Profit and loss S1 20%	3
		Profit and loss S2 40% (*b*)(*ii*)	14
		General reserve S1 20% × 10	2
	29		29

Profit and Loss

	£000		£000
Minority interest S1	3	P	60
Minority interest S2	14	S1	15
Cost of control S1: pre-acquisition	4	S2	35
Cost of control S2: pre-acquisition	9		
Cost of control: goodwill written off	20		
Balance to consolidated balance sheet	60		
	110		110

General Reserve

	£000		£000
Cost of control 80% × 10	8	S1 balance b/f	10
Minority interest 20% × 10	2		
	10		10

28.6 A worked example (with proposed dividends)

Take the same companies as in Exhibit 28.7 but in this case the companies have proposed dividends at 31 December 19X5 of P Ltd £16,000, S1 Ltd £5,000, S2 Ltd £20,000. The balance sheets would have appeared:

Balance Sheets 31 December 19X5

	P Ltd £000	P Ltd £000	S1 Ltd £000	S1 Ltd £000	S2 Ltd £000	S2 Ltd £000
Fixed assets		40		4		27
Investments						
Shares in S1		41				
Shares in S2				25		
Net current assets (as before)		19		6		28
Dividends to be received	(80% of S1)	4	(75% of S2)	15		
		104		50		55
Share capital		40		10		20
Profit and loss as at 31.12.19X4	24		5		15	
Retained profits for 19X5						
(see below)	24	48	20	25	–	15
General reserve				10		
Proposed dividends		16		5		20
		104		50		55

Note:			
Retained profit	P	S1	S2
Net profits 19X5	36	10	20
Less Proposed dividends	16	5	20
	20	5	–
Add Dividends receivable			
P 80% of S1 × 5	4		
S1 75% of S2 × 20		15	
	24	20	

Now a consolidated balance sheet can be drawn up.

P Ltd and its subsidiaries

Consolidated Balance Sheet as at 31 December 19X5

	£000
Fixed assets	71
Net current assets	53
	124
Share capital	40
Profit and loss (*see* account below)	44
	84
Minority interest (*see* account below)	24
Proposed dividend	16
	˙124

The cost of control figures and goodwill in this exhibit are the same as for Exhibit 28.7 as circumstances at dates of acquisition had not changed.

Profit and Loss

	£000		£000
Minority interest:		Balances P	48
S1 20% × 25	5	S1	25
S2 40% × 15	6	S2	15
Cost of control (as before) S1	4		
Cost of control (as before) S2	9		
Cost of control: goodwill written off	20		
Balance to consolidated balance sheet	44		
	88		88

Minority Interest

	£000		£000
Cost of shares in S2 (20%)	5	Profit and loss S1	5
Balance to consolidated balance sheet	24	Profit and loss S2	6
		General reserve 20%	2
		Share capital S1 20%	2
		Share capital S2 40%	8
		Proposed dividends S1	1
		Proposed dividends S2 (*see* note (*a*))	5
	29		29

Proposed Dividends

	£000		£000
Minority interest S1	1	P	16
Minority interest S2 (25%)	5	S1	5
Consolidated balance sheet (P)	16	S2	20
Cancel against dividends receivable	19		
	41		41

Dividends Receivable

	£000		£000
P	4	Cancel against proposed dividends	
S1	15	(note (b))	19
	19		19

Notes:
(a) Credit is given to minority for 25 per cent of S2 dividend, not 40 per cent. This is because 25 per cent is the amount actually received by them, while 75 per cent is received by S1, and the minority interest in this dividend is automatically calculated when we calculate the S1 minority interest in profit and loss balance £25,000 at 20 per cent. As the £25,000 figure already includes the dividend from S2 it should not be double-counted.
(b) The balances on dividends proposed and receivable cancel out, so nothing appears in the consolidated balance sheet.
(c) It would have been possible to show the proposed dividends applicable to minority shareholders, S1 £1,000 and S2 £5,000, as a current liability in the consolidated balance sheet, rather than show it as part of minority interest. This would seem to be the better method. For instance, when considering the working capital or liquidity of the group it is essential that all current liabilities due to external parties should be brought into the calculation. If the proposed dividend soon to be paid to persons outside the group was excluded, this could render the calculations completely invalid.

Main points to remember

1   A company that is the subsidiary of another is also a subsidiary of its parent's own parent undertaking, even where the ultimate parent's shareholding is below 50 per cent.

2   There are two recognised methods of consolidating the financial statements of groups that contain subsidiaries of subsidiaries:
    (a) the multi-stage method is generally more common in practice, but
    (b) the indirect single-stage method is recommended for examinations.

3   The indirect method involves computing the parent undertaking's interest in the subsidiaries and their subsidiaries and taking that percentage of the capital and reserves of these companies into the consolidation process.

Review questions

28.1 From the following balance sheets you are to draft a consolidated balance sheet for the group of P, S1 and S2.

P Balance Sheet as at 31 December 19X7

	£	£
Investment in S1:		
9,000 shares bought 31.12.19X6		23,000
Fixed assets		99,000
Current assets		25,000
		147,000
Share capital		100,000
Profit and loss account:		
As at 31.12.19X6	15,000	
Add Profit for 19X7	22,000	
		37,000
General reserve		10,000
		147,000

S1 Balance Sheet as at 31 December 19X7

	£	£
Investment in S2:		
3,500 shares bought 31.12.19X6		6,000
Fixed assets		22,000
Current assets		5,000
		33,000
Share capital		10,000
Profit and loss account:		
As at 31.12.19X6	7,000	
Add Profit for 19X7	16,000	
		23,000
		33,000

S2 Balance Sheet as at 31 December 19X7

	£	£
Fixed assets		6,000
Current assets		3,000
		9,000
Share capital		5,000
Profit and loss account:		
As at 31.12.19X6	1,000	
Add Profit for 19X7	3,000	
		4,000
		9,000

28.2A From the following balance sheets prepare a consolidated balance sheet for the group of P, S1 and S2.

P Balance Sheet as at 31 December 19X9

	£	£
Investment in S1:		
16,000 shares bought 31.12.19X8		39,000
Fixed assets		200,000
Current assets		40,000
		279,000
Share capital		200,000
Profit and loss account:		
As at 31.12.19X8	43,000	
Add Profit for 19X9	36,000	
		79,000
		279,000

S1 Balance Sheet as at 31 December 19X9

	£	£
Investment in S2:		
7,000 shares bought 31.12.19X8		13,000
Fixed assets		16,000
Current assets		4,000
		33,000
Share capital		20,000
Profit and loss account:		
As at 31.12.19X8	6,000	
Add Profit for 19X9	4,000	
		10,000
General reserve (as at 31.12.19X8)		3,000
		33,000

S2 Balance Sheet as at 31 December 19X9

	£	£
Fixed assets		10,500
Current assets		5,500
		16,000
Share capital		10,000
Profit and loss account:		
As at 31.12.19X8	1,000	
Add Profit for 19X9	5,000	
		6,000
		16,000

28.3 On 1 April 19X1 Machinery Limited bought 80 per cent of the ordinary share capital of Components Limited and on 1 April 19X3 Machinery Limited was itself taken over by Sales Limited who purchased 75 per cent of the ordinary shares in Machinery Limited.

The balance sheets of the three companies at 31 October 19X5 prepared for internal use showed the following position:

	Sales Ltd £	Sales Ltd £	Machinery Ltd £	Machinery Ltd £	Components Ltd £	Components Ltd £
Fixed assets						
Freehold land at cost		89,000		30,000		65,000
Buildings at cost	100,000		120,000		40,000	
Less						
Accumulated depreciation	36,000		40,000		16,400	
		64,000		80,000		23,600
Plant and equipment at cost	102,900		170,000		92,000	
Less						
Accumulated depreciation	69,900		86,000		48,200	
		33,000		84,000		43,800
		186,000		194,000		132,400
Investments						
Shares in Machinery at cost		135,000				
Shares in Components at cost				96,000		
Current assets						
Stocks	108,500		75,500		68,400	
Debtors	196,700		124,800		83,500	
Cash at bank	25,200		–		25,400	
		330,400		200,300		177,300
		651,400		490,300		309,700
Current liabilities						
Creditors	160,000		152,700		59,200	
Bank overdraft	–		37,400		–	
Corporation tax	57,400		47,200		24,500	
Proposed dividends	80,000		48,000		12,000	
		297,400		285,300		95,700
		354,000		205,000		214,000
Ordinary shares		200,000		120,000		100,000
10% preference shares		–		–		40,000
Revenue reserves		154,000		85,000		74,000
		354,000		205,000		214,000

Additional information
(a) All ordinary shares are £1 each, fully paid.
(b) Preference shares in Components Ltd are 50p each fully paid.
(c) Proposed dividends in Components Ltd are:
on ordinary shares £10,000;
on preference shares £2,000.
(d) Proposed dividends receivable by Sales Ltd and Machinery Ltd are included in debtors.
(e) All creditors are payable within one year.
(f) Items purchased by Machinery Ltd from Components Ltd and remaining in stock at 31 October 19X5 amounted to £25,000. The profit element is 20 per cent of selling price for Components Ltd.

(g) Depreciation policy of the group is to provide for:
  (i) buildings – at the rate of 2 per cent on cost each year;
  (ii) plant and equipment – at the rate of 10 per cent on cost each year including full provision in the year of acquisition.
  These policies are applied by all members of the group.
  Included in the plant and equipment of Components Ltd is a machine purchased from the manufacturers, Machinery Ltd, on 1 January 19X4 for £10,000. Machinery Ltd recorded a profit of £2,000 on the sale of the machine.
(h) Intra-group balances are included in debtors and creditors respectively and are as follows:

			£
Sales Ltd	Creditors	– Machinery Ltd	45,600
		– Components Ltd	28,900
Machinery Ltd	Debtors	– Sales Ltd	56,900
Components Ltd	Debtors	– Sales Ltd	28,900

(i) A cheque drawn by Sales Ltd for £11,300 on 28 October 19X5 was received by Machinery Ltd on 3 November 19X5.
(j) At 1 April 19X1, reserves in Machinery Ltd were £28,000 and in Components Ltd £20,000. At 1 April 19X3 the figures were £40,000 and £60,000 respectively.

Required:
Prepare a group balance sheet at 31 October 19X5 for Sales Ltd and its subsidiaries complying, so far as the information will allow, with the accounting requirements of the Companies Acts.

(*Chartered Association of Certified Accountants*)

28.4A Bryon Ltd has held 1,500,000 shares in Carlyle Ltd for many years. At the date of acquisition, the reserves of Carlyle Ltd amounted to £800,000. On 31 March 19X6 Carlyle Ltd bought 400,000 shares in Doyle Ltd for £600,000 and a further 400,000 shares were purchased on 30 June 19X6 for £650,000.

At 30 September 19X6 the balance sheets of the three companies were:

	Bryon Ltd £	Bryon Ltd £	Carlyle Ltd £	Carlyle Ltd £	Doyle Ltd £	Doyle Ltd £
Freehold land and buildings						
– cost		950,000		1,375,000		300,000
Plant and equipment						
Cost	500,000		10,000,000		750,000	
Depreciation	280,000		7,500,000		500,000	
		220,000		2,500,000		250,000
		1,170,000		3,875,000		550,000
Investments						
1,500,000 shares in						
Carlyle Ltd		1,600,000				
800,000 shares in						
Doyle Ltd				1,250,000		
Stocks	50,000		2,050,000		850,500	
Debtors	325,000		2,675,000		1,700,000	
Cash at bank	25,500		–		16,500	
		400,500		4,725,000		2,567,000
		3,170,500		9,850,000		3,117,000
Creditors under 1 year	91,500		2,385,750		1,395,800	
Proposed dividend	200,000					
Bank overdraft	–		1,450,850		–	
		291,500		3,836,600		1,395,800
		2,879,000		6,013,400		1,721,200
10% debenture		–		2,000,000		–
		2,879,000		4,013,400		1,721,200
		£		£		£
Ordinary shares of						
£1 each		2,000,000				1,200,000
50p each				1,000,000		
8% redeemable preference						
shares of £1 each				2,000,000		
Reserves		879,000		1,013,400		521,200
		2,879,000		4,013,400		1,721,200

Proposed dividends have not yet been provided for on the shares in Carlyle Ltd and Doyle Ltd although Bryon Ltd has included dividends of 5p per share as receivable from Carlyle Ltd in debtors. Dividends on the preference shares were paid for one-half year on 1 April 19X6; the next payment date was 1 October 19X6. Dividends on the ordinary shares in Doyle Ltd are proposed at the rate of 10p per share and on Carlyle's shares as anticipated by Bryon.

Profits for the year in Doyle Ltd were £310,000, before making any adjustments for consolidation, accruing evenly through the year.

The directors of Bryon Ltd consider that the assets and liabilities of Carlyle Ltd are shown at fair values, but fair values for Doyle Ltd for the purposes of consolidation are:

	£	£
Freehold land and building		500,000
Plant and equipment – Valuation	968,400	
– Depreciation	639,600	
		328,800

Other assets and liabilities are considered to be at fair values in the balance sheet.

Additional depreciation due to the revaluation of the plant and equipment in Doyle Ltd amounts to £40,000 for the year to 30 September 19X6.

Included in stocks in Carlyle Ltd are items purchased from Doyle Ltd during the last three months of the year, on which Doyle Ltd recorded a profit of £80,000.

On 30 September 19X6 Carlyle Ltd drew a cheque for £100,000 and sent it to Doyle Ltd to clear the current account. As this cheque was not received by Doyle Ltd until 3 October, no account was taken of it in the Doyle Ltd balance sheet.

Required:
Prepare a balance sheet as at 30 September 19X6 for Bryon Ltd and its subsidiaries, conforming with the Companies Acts so far as the information given will permit.

Ignore taxation.

(Chartered Association of Certified Accountants)

29

Consolidated profit and loss accounts

Objectives

After you have studied this chapter, you should:

● *know how to prepare consolidated profit and loss accounts for groups with wholly owned subsidiaries*

● *know how to prepare consolidated profit and loss accounts for groups with partly owned subsidiaries*

29.1 Wholly owned subsidiaries

The consolidated profit and loss account is drawn up to show the overall profit (or loss) of the companies in the group, treating the group as a single entity. If all of the subsidiaries are owned 100 per cent, and there are no inter-company dividends or unrealised profits in stock, then it is simply a case of adding together all of the separate profit and loss accounts to form the consolidated profit and loss account. However, such a situation would very rarely be found.

Exhibit 29.1 shows the framework for a consolidated profit and loss account giving details of adjustments needed. Notes (*a*) to (*g*) follow the account.

Exhibit 29.1

Specimen Profit and Loss Account for the Year ended...

		£000	£000	
Turnover	(a)		200	Parent plus
Cost of sales	(b)		120	subsidiaries
Gross profit			80	less cancellation
Distribution costs		10		of
Administrative expenses		20	30	inter-company
Profit on ordinary activities before taxation			50	items
Tax on profit on ordinary activities	(c)		14	
Profit on ordinary activities after taxation			36	
Minority interest	(d)		4	
Profit for the financial year			32	
Retained profits from last year	(e)		7	
			39	
Proposed dividend	(f)	15		Parent only
Transfer to reserves	(g)	8	23	
Retained profits carried to next year			16	

Notes:

(a) Turnover. Sales within the group to be deducted.

(b) Cost of sales: (i) Deduct purchases within the group. This is the same figure as for (a), as the price at which sales are made by one group company is the same figure at which the other group company has bought them. (ii) Adjust for unrealised profit in stock, by reducing closing stock. As cost of sales = opening stock + purchases − closing stock, any reduction in closing stock will increase 'cost of sales'. The balance sheet stock figure will be reduced by unrealised profits.

(c) Tax on profit on ordinary activities. This is the sum of tax for all companies within the group.

(d) Minority interest:

   (i) If ordinary shares only issued by subsidiary: take requisite percentage of subsidiary's profits after taxation.

   (ii) If preference shares also issued by subsidiary found by:
   Minority interest percentage of preference share capital × total preference dividend for the year
   plus
   Minority interest percentage of ordinary share capital × balance of profits (i.e. after preference dividend) for the year
   e.g.
   Total preference shares £1,000: Minority interest £400.
   Total ordinary shares £2,000: Minority interest £500.
   Total preference dividend for year £150.
   Profit of subsidiary after tax but before dividend: £950.

   Minority interest is:

Share of preference dividend: 40% × £150	=	£60
Share of balance of profits: 25% × (£950 − £150)	=	£200
		£260

(e) This is parent's retained profits plus group's share of post-acquisition profit of subsidiaries.

(f) In respect of parent only.

(g) Those of the parent plus the group's share of the subsidiary's transfers to reserves.

We can now look at two examples:

(a) Exhibit 29.2: consolidation of accounts where subsidiary owned 100 per cent;

(b) Exhibit 29.3: consolidation where there is a minority interest in subsidiary company.

Exhibit 29.2

P Ltd owns 100 per cent of shares in S Ltd. Profit and loss accounts of these companies for the year to 31 December 19X4 are as follows:

Profit and loss accounts	P Ltd		S Ltd	
	£000	£000	£000	£000
Turnover		400		280
Cost of sales		270		190
Gross profit		130		90
Distribution costs	20		10	
Administrative expenses	30	50	15	25
Profit on ordinary activities before taxation		80		65
Tax on profit on ordinary activities		17		11
Profit on ordinary activities after taxation		63		54
Retained profits from last year		11		7
		74		61
Proposed dividend	40		30	
Transfer to reserves	5	45	2	32
Retained profits carried to next year		29		29

Notes:

(a) P Ltd had sold goods costing £10,000 to S Ltd for £15,000.

(b) At the balance sheet date 40 per cent of the goods in (a) had not been sold by S Ltd.

(c) Of the £7,000 retained profits from last year for S Ltd, £3,000 is in respect of post-acquisition profits.

The consolidated profit and loss of the group can now be drawn up.

P Ltd and subsidiary S Ltd

Consolidated Profit and Loss Account for the year ended 31 December 19X4

	£000	£000
Turnover (W1)		665
Cost of sales (W2)		447
Gross profit		218
Distribution costs	30	
Administrative expenses	45	75
Profit on ordinary activities before taxation		143
Tax on profit on ordinary activities		28
Profit on ordinary activities after taxation		115
Retained profits from last year (W3)		14
		129
Proposed dividend (W4)	40	
Transfer to reserves (W5)	7	47
Retained profits carried to next year		82

Workings:

Letters (*a*) to (*g*) refer to the descriptions given above and in Exhibit 29.1.

(W1)   P 400 + S 280 – 15 inter-company sales = 665 (*a*).

(W2)   P 270 + S 190 – 15 inter-company purchases + unrealised profit in stock (40% × 5)2 = 447 (*b*) (*i*) and (*ii*).

(W3)   P 11 + S 3 = 14. Only post-acquisition profits of S included. (*See* (*e*) in Exhibit 29.1.)

(W4)   Only dividend of P included as S dividend will be received by P and will cancel out. (*See* item (*f*) in Exhibit 29.1.)

(W5)   P 5 + S (100%)2 = 7. (*See* item (*g*) in Exhibit 29.1.)

29.2 Partly owned subsidiaries

Exhibit 29.3

P Ltd owns 80 per cent of shares in S Ltd. Profit and loss accounts of the companies for the year to 31 December 19X2 are as follows:

Profit and loss accounts	P Ltd		S Ltd	
	£000	£000	£000	£000
Turnover		640		330
Cost of sales		410		200
Gross profit		230		130
Distribution costs	35		20	
Administrative expenses	70	105	55	75
Profit on ordinary activities before taxation		125		55
Tax on profit on ordinary activities		26		10
Profit on ordinary activities after taxation		99		45
Retained profits from last year		29		35
		128		80
Proposed dividend	60		35	
Transfers to reserves	22	82	10	45
Retained profits carried to next year		46		35

Notes:
(a) S Ltd had sold goods costing £20,000 to P Ltd for £30,000.
(b) At the balance sheet date 30 per cent of the goods in (a) had not been sold by P Ltd.
(c) Of the £25,000 retained profits of S Ltd, £15,000 is in respect of post-acquisition profits.

P Ltd and subsidiary S Ltd

Consolidated Profit and Loss Account for the year ending 31 December 19X2

	£000	£000
Turnover (W1)		940
Cost of sales (W2)		583
Gross profit		357
Distribution costs	55	
Administrative expenses	125	180
Profit on ordinary activities before taxation		177
Tax on profit on ordinary activities		36
Profit on ordinary activities after taxation		141
Minority interest (W3)		9
Profit for the financial year		132
Retained profits from last year (W4)		41
		173
Proposed dividend (W5)	60	
Transfer to reserves (W6)	30	90
Retained profits carried to next year		£83

Workings:
Letters (a) to (g) refer to the descriptions given above and in Exhibit 29.1.
(W1) P 640 + S 330 – inter-company sales 30 = 940 (a).
(W2) P 410 + S 200 – inter-company purchases 30 + unrealised profit in stock (30% × 10)3
        = 583 (b) (i) and (ii).
(W3) 20 per cent × 45: profit after taxation of S Ltd = 9 (d) (i).
(W4) P 29 + S (80% × 15)12 = 41 (e).
(W5) Only the dividend of P shown. *See* (f).
(W6) P 22 + S (80% × 10)8 = 30 (g).

Main points to remember

1 When consolidating profit and loss accounts for groups with wholly-owned subsidiaries with no intra-group transactions or indebtedness, it is simply a case of adding together all the separate profit and loss accounts to form the consolidated profit and loss account.

2 When consolidating profit and loss accounts, adjustments for unrealised profits on intra-group transactions and for intra-group indebtedness must be made where they exist (as per Chapters 24, 26, and 27).

3 When consolidating profit and loss accounts for groups with partly owned subsidiaries, the approaches detailed in Chapters 22 and 28 should be followed.

Review questions

29.1 The following information relates to the Brodick group of companies for the year to 30 April 19X7:

	Brodick plc £000	Lamlash Ltd £000	Corrie Ltd £000
Turnover	1,100	500	130
Cost of sales	(630)	(300)	(70)
Gross profit	470	200	60
Administrative expenses	(105)	(150)	(20)
Dividend from Lamlash Ltd	24	–	–
Dividend from Corrie Ltd	6	–	–
Profit before tax	395	50	40
Taxation	(65)	(10)	(20)
Profit after tax	330	40	20
Interim dividend	(50)	(10)	–
Proposed dividend	(150)	(20)	(10)
Retained profit for the year	130	10	10
Retained profits brought forward	460	106	30
Retained profits carried forward	£590	£116	£40

Additional information:
(a) The issued share capital of the group was as follows:
   Brodick plc: 5,000,000 ordinary shares of £1 each;
   Lamlash Ltd: 1,000,000 ordinary shares of £1 each; and
   Corrie Ltd: 400,000 ordinary shares of £1 each.
(b) Brodick plc purchased 80 per cent of the issued share capital of Lamlash Ltd in 19X0. At that time, the retained profits of Lamlash amounted to £56,000.
(c) Brodick plc purchased 60 per cent of the issued share capital of Corrie Ltd in 19X4. At that time, the retained profits of Corrie amounted to £20,000.
(d) Brodick plc recognises dividends proposed by other group companies in its profit and loss account.

Required:
In so far as the information permits, prepare the Brodick group of companies' consolidated profit and loss account for the year to 30 April 19X7 in accordance with the Companies Acts and related accounting statements. (*Note:* Notes to the profit and loss account are not required, but you should append a statement showing the make-up of the 'retained profits carried forward', and your workings should be submitted.)

(*Association of Accounting Technicians*)

29.2 You are presented with the following summarised information for Norbreck plc and its subsidiary, Bispham Ltd:

Profit and Loss Accounts for the year to 30 September 19X7

	Norbreck plc	Bispham Ltd
	£000	£000
Turnover	1,700	450
Cost of sales	(920)	(75)
Gross profit	780	375
Administration expenses	(300)	(175)
Income from shares in group company	120	–
Profit on ordinary activities before taxation	600	200
Tax on profit on ordinary activities	(30)	(20)
Profit on ordinary activities after taxation	570	180
Dividends paid	(90)	(50)
proposed	(270)	(100)
Retained profit for the year	210	30
Retained profit brought forward	220	70
Retained profit carried forward	£430	£100

Balance Sheets at 30 September 19X7

	Norbreck plc	Bispham Ltd
	£000	£000
Fixed tangible assets	1,280	440
Investments: Shares in group company	400	–
Current assets:		
Stocks	300	250
Debtors (including, for Norbreck plc,	280	150
the dividend proposed by the subsidiary)		
Cash at bank and in hand	40	10
	620	410
Creditors (amounts falling due within one year):		
Trade creditors	(80)	(160)
Other creditors, taxation and social security	(160)	(70)
Proposed dividend	(270)	(100)
	(510)	(330)
Net current assets	110	80
Total assets *less* current liabilities	1,790	520
Provisions for liabilities and charges		
Taxation, including deferred taxation	(460)	(20)
	£1,330	£500

	Norbreck plc	Bispham Ltd
	£000	£000
Capital and reserves:		
Called-up share capital (ordinary shares of £1 each)	900	400
Profit and loss account	430	100
	£1,330	£500

Additional information:
(a) Norbreck plc acquired 80 per cent of the shares in Bispham Ltd on 1 October 19X4. Bispham's profit and loss account balance as at that date was £40,000.
(b) Goodwill arising on acquisition is to be written off against the group's retained profits.
(c) Norbreck takes credit within its own books of account for any dividends receivable from Bispham.
(d) Ignore advance corporation tax.

Required:
Prepare Bispham plc's consolidated profit and loss account for the year to 30 September 19X7 and a consolidated balance sheet as at that date.

Note: Formal notes to the account are not required, although detailed workings should be submitted with your answer. You should also append to the consolidated profit and loss account your calculation of earnings per share and a statement showing the make-up of 'retained profits carried forward'.

(*Association of Accounting Technicians*)

29.3A The following figures for the year to 30 April 19X6 have been extracted from the books and records of three companies which form a group:

	Old plc	Field Ltd	Lodge Ltd
	£	£	£
Revenue reserves at 1 May 19X5	30,000	40,000	50,000
Stocks at 1 May 19X5	90,000	150,000	80,000
Sales	1,250,000	875,000	650,000
Purchases	780,000	555,000	475,000
Distribution expenses	125,000	85,000	60,000
Administration expenses	28,000	40,000	72,000
Interim dividends:			
Paid 31 July 19X5, ordinary	45,000	35,000	15,000
Paid 31 October 19X5, preference		4,000	
Share capital – fully paid ordinary shares of £1 each	450,000	350,000	200,000
8% preference shares of £1 each		100,000	
Stocks at 30 April 19X6	110,000	135,000	85,000

Profits are deemed to accrue evenly throughout the year.

Other information:
(a) Corporation tax of the following amounts is to be provided on the profits of the year:

Old plc	£125,000
Field Ltd	£75,000
Lodge Ltd	£20,000

(b) Final dividends proposed are:

Old plc	15p per share
Field Ltd	12.5p per share on the ordinary shares and a half-year's dividend on the preference shares
Lodge Ltd	7.5p per share

(c) Field Ltd sells goods for resale to both Old plc and Lodge Ltd. At 30 April 19X6, stocks of goods purchased from Field Ltd are:

in Old plc	£40,000
in Lodge Ltd	£28,000

The net profit percentage for Field Ltd on sales of these goods is 25 per cent.
Old plc has £36,000 of these goods in stock at 1 May 19X5.
Total sales in the year by Field Ltd to Old plc were £150,000 and to Lodge Ltd £120,000.

(d) Old plc acquired the whole of the ordinary shares in Field Ltd many years ago. 50,000 of the preference shares were acquired on 1 August 19X5. Old plc acquired 120,000 shares in Lodge Ltd on 1 August 19X5.

Required:

A consolidated profit and loss account for Old plc and its subsidiaries for the year ended 30 April 19X6, together with any relevant notes.

(*Chartered Association of Certified Accountants*)

29.4A The following are the trial balances of ATH Ltd, GLE Ltd, and FRN Ltd as on 31 December 19X8.

	ATH Ltd £	GLE Ltd £	FRN Ltd £
Ordinary share capital (shares of £1 each, fully paid)	100,000	30,000	20,000
7 per cent cumulative preference share capital (shares of £1 each, fully paid)	–	–	5,000
Profit and loss account – balance at 31.12.19X7	15,600	6,000	1,900
Current liabilities	20,750	15,900	18,350
Sales	194,000	116,000	84,000
Dividend received from GLE Ltd	1,200		
	331,550	167,900	129,250
Fixed assets	45,000	29,000	25,000
Current assets	46,000	27,500	22,500
24,000 ordinary shares in GLE Ltd at cost	33,700	–	–
20,000 ordinary shares in FRN Ltd at cost	21,250	–	–
Cost of goods sold	153,000	87,000	63,000
General expenses	32,600	22,900	18,750
Dividend for 19X8, paid on 31.12.19X8	–	1,500	–
	331,550	167,900	129,250

ATH Ltd acquired the shares in FRN Ltd on 31 December 19X6, when the credit balance on the profit and loss account of FRN Ltd was £700, and acquired the shares in GLE Ltd on 31 December 19X7. No dividend was paid by either ATH Ltd or GLE Ltd for the year 19X7.

No dividend has been paid by FRN Ltd for the years 19X6, 19X7 and 19X8 and none is proposed. The directors of ATH Ltd propose to pay a dividend of £7,000 for 19X8.

The sales of GLE Ltd for 19X8 (£116,000) include £1,000 for goods sold to FRN Ltd and this amount has been debited to purchases account in the books of FRN Ltd.

All these goods were sold by FRN Ltd during 19X8.

Required:

A consolidated trading and profit and loss account for the year 19X8 and a consolidated balance sheet as on 31 December 19X8 (not necessarily in a form for publication).

Ignore depreciation of fixed assets and taxation.

(*Institute of Chartered Secretaries and Administrators*)

30

Consolidated financial statements – FRS 6: Acquisitions and mergers

Objectives

After you have studied this chapter, you should:

● *know when merger accounting should be used*

● *know the difference between the acquisition and the merger methods of preparing consolidated financial statements*

30.1 Methods of combination of companies

When two limited companies are going to combine together in some way, then it is obvious that the shares must come under common ownership. There are two main methods of achieving this, with different possible methods of accounting for the combination: **acquisition accounting**, which would normally be applied (and which has been assumed throughout Chapters 21–29); and **merger accounting**, which is restricted to specific circumstances. Acquisition accounting is dealt with in FRS 2: **Accounting for subsidiary undertakings**; FRS 6: **Acquisitions and mergers**; and FRS 7: **Fair values in acquisition accounting**. FRS 6 presents the merger accounting approach.

Examples of combinations where it would be appropriate to adopt acquisition accounting

A common approach to the formation of new business combinations is for one company, A, to purchase the shares of another company, B. Often, this is achieved by A making a cash payment to shareholders in B. In accepting the cash, the shareholders sever their links with the company. Company A shareholders now control both companies.

Another common approach is where company A issues debentures (loan stock) to company B's shareholders in exchange for their shareholdings in B: the new debenture holders would have no voting power in the new group, which would be controlled by the shareholders of A.

In both of these cases, **acquisition accounting** should be used.

Exhibit 30.1 Requirements to be met if merger accounting is to be used

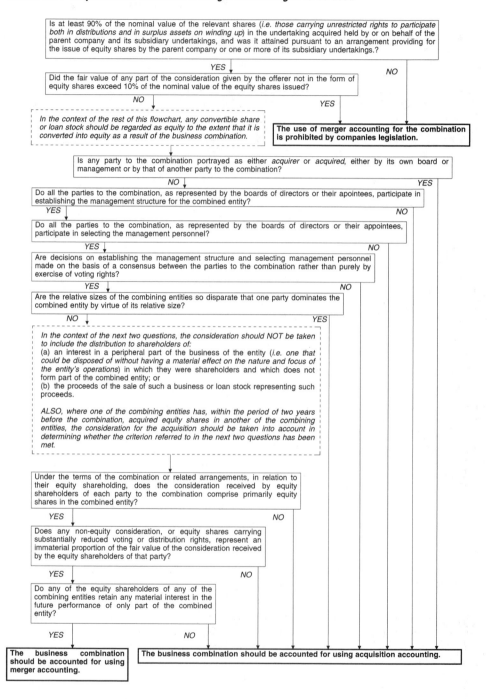

Examples of combinations where it would be appropriate to adopt merger accounting

When company A does not pay cash or issue debentures to the old shareholders of company B, but instead issues new equity (ordinary voting) shares to the old shareholders of B, this means that the shareholders of A and B have 'merged' into one, and between them have a joint interest in the new group. It is often called a pooling of interest.

A variation on this is the 'new entity' method of combination. Here a new company, C, is formed to take over A and B, giving the old shareholders of A and B new shares in C. Once again the shareholders have 'merged' into one.

In both these cases, **merger accounting** may be used, but only if a number of conditions contained in FRS 6 are met; otherwise, **acquisition accounting** must be used.

Exhibit 30.1 shows the conditions to be considered if merger accounting is to be used.

30.2 Acquisition accounting method

As mentioned above, this is the method that has been assumed in Chapters 21–29. In the books of the parent undertaking:

(*a*) shares purchased in a subsidiary should be shown at cost less dividends received out of pre-acquisition profits;
(*b*) dividends out of pre-acquisition profits cannot be regarded as available for distribution as dividends by the parent.

In the consolidated financial statements:

(*c*) assets and liabilities of the subsidiary at the date of acquisition should be shown in the balance sheet at their fair value at that date;
(*d*) the difference at the date of acquisition between the fair value of the purchase consideration and the fair value of the net assets is treated as goodwill, positive or negative;
(*e*) only post-acquisition profits of the subsidiary should be included in the consolidated reserves of the group.

The idea underlying these rules is to stop capital receipts, i.e. dividends from pre-acquisition profits, being paid out as dividends.

The consolidation of balance sheets using the **acquisition method** is now shown in Exhibit 30.2.

Exhibit 30.2

A Ltd has just made an offer of £270,000 for the whole of the share capital of B Ltd. and this has been accepted. Payment to be by cash. The 'fair value' placed on the tangible fixed assets of B Ltd for the purposes of the merger is £148,000. Following are the two companies' balance sheets, immediately before the merger on 31 December 19X3.

	A Ltd		B Ltd	
	£000	£000	£000	£000
Tangible fixed assets		400		120
Current assets	450		200	
Less Current liabilities	130	320	90	110
		720		230
Ordinary shares £1		500		150
Revenue reserves		220		80
		720		230

The balance sheets of A Ltd, and of the group, immediately following the merger, are as follows:

Balance Sheet at 31 December 19X3

		A Ltd			Group	
		£000	£000		£000	£000
Fixed assets						
Intangible (goodwill)		–		(W2)	12	
Tangible		400		(W3)	548	
Investments		270	670		–	560
Current assets	(W1)	180		(W4)	380	
Less Current liabilities		130	50		220	160
			720			720
Share capital			500			500
Reserves			220			220
			720			720

Workings (£000):
(W1) Original current assets 450 – cash paid 270 = 180
(W2) Paid for shares   270
 Less Net assets at takeover date   230
 Add Increase in value of fixed assets to a
  'fair value' 148 – 120 =   28   258
 Goodwill (intangible fixed asset)   12
(W3) Fixed assets A Ltd 400 + B Ltd 148 = 548
(W4) A Ltd (after payment) 180 + B Ltd 200 = 380

30.3 Merger accounting method

(*a*) Shares issued by the parent are merely the means of achieving the merger in a technical sense. Consequently, no share premium arises. They are shown in the parent's balance sheet (A Ltd) at nominal value, as addition to share capital.

(*b*) As share premium is not recognised in (a) the cost of the investment in the parent's balance sheet (A Ltd) is the nominal value of shares issued. If the nominal value of the shares is not the same as the Stock Exchange or similar market valuation then, obviously, the 'true' value of the subsidiary is not shown in the 'cost' of the investment.

(*c*) Any dividends received by the parent (A Ltd) from the subsidiary (B Ltd) can be distributed in full by the parent. This means that the whole of the subsidiary's reserves can be included in the consolidated balance sheet reserves.

(*d*) The assets of the subsidiary are not revalued at 'fair value' at the date of merger. It would not make sense to revalue B Ltd's assets while leaving A Ltd's assets valued at the old amounts. Sometimes, however, under the 'new entity' method of merger described on p. 425, both companies revalue their assets.

(*e*) Where the total nominal value of the shares issued by the parent, A Ltd, is more than the total nominal value of the shares of B Ltd, the difference is deducted from group reserves. If the total is less, then the shortfall becomes a non-distributable group reserve.

Exhibit 30.3

Taking the same firms, A Ltd and B Ltd, as in Exhibit 30.2, but instead of a cash offer of £270,000 the offer is 200,000 ordinary shares of £1 each at a stock exchange value of £270,000.

The balance sheets of A Ltd and the group immediately after the merger are now:

	A Ltd £000	A Ltd £000	Group £000	Group £000
Fixed assets				
Tangible	400			520
Investments	200	600		–
Current assets	450		650	
Less Current liabilities	130	320	220	430
		920		950

Workings:

(W1)	Reserve	A Ltd	220		
		B Ltd	80		300

Less Excess of nominal value shares issued by A Ltd over those
exchanged of B Ltd, i.e. 200 – 150

	50
	250

30.4 The advantages of merger accounting to a group

Merger accounting has a number of advantages from the perspective of the investing group:

(a) The subsidiary's results are included in the group for the whole accounting period, not just for the post-acquisition period. Consequently, the group can appear to the casual reviewer as more profitable than it was. However, as the amounts relating to pre- and post-merger must be disclosed, this is not as great an advantage as it may appear.

(b) The parent company can appear misleadingly successful if it is in receipt of pre-acquisition dividends which it treats as revenue income. (The investment is normally recorded at the nominal value of the holding company shares issued, plus any other consideration given, and is unlikely to need to be reduced to account for the pre-acquisition distribution.)

(c) Assets may be understated (compared to equivalent situations where **acquisition accounting** has been applied), providing an opportunity for instant earnings by selling assets, and resulting in higher returns on capital.

(d) Lower depreciation charges and an absence of goodwill will result in a correspondingly higher return on capital employed than would be the case were the **acquisition accounting** approach adopted.

(e) Most importantly, all the pre-acquisition distributable reserves of the companies involved are available for distribution to the group's shareholders (though this may be subject to a reduction resulting from the nominal value of the new shares exceeding the nominal value of the shares received).

However, despite these advantages, the merger method has only been used infrequently in the UK. Furthermore, with the release in September 1994 of FRS 6, which significantly tightened the restriction on its use, future adoption of merger accounting in the UK is likely to be very rare indeed.

30.5 Final points per FRS 6

Under **merger accounting**, per FRS 6, it is not necessary to adjust values of the subsidiaries' assets and liabilities to fair values. However, adjustments should be made to achieve uniformity of accounting policies within the group.

Remember that, in a merger, there is no such thing as **pre-acquisition profits**. The distribution of pre-acquisition profits is not restricted in the way it is under **acquisition accounting**.

Finally, while **acquisition accounting** will generally give rise to goodwill (positive or negative), **merger accounting** never does – not because a difference cannot arise between the consideration given and the value received, but because such differences arising under the merger accounting approach do not conform to the fair-value-based definition of goodwill given in SSAP 22: *Accounting for goodwill*.

Main points to remember

1 Merger accounting should be used only when certain conditions are met, and must be used when they are.

2 Otherwise, acquisition accounting should be used.

3 Under merger accounting, assets and liabilities do not require to be stated at their fair values on acquisition.

4 Goodwill can only arise under acquisition accounting.

5 No distinction is made between pre- and post-acquisition reserves under merger accounting.

Review questions

30.1 Large plc, a manufacturer and wholesaler, purchased 600,000 of the 800,000 issued ordinary shares of a smaller company, Small Ltd, on 1 January 19X5 when the retained earnings account of Small Ltd had a credit balance of £72,000.

The latest accounts of the two companies are:

Summary Profit and Loss Accounts for the year to 30 September 19X6 (£000s)

		Large plc		Small Ltd
Credit sales		10,830		2,000
Cost of sales and production services		3,570		1,100
Gross profit		7,260		900
Administrative and marketing expenses		2,592		180
(including depreciation, audit fee and directors' remuneration)				
Operating profit		4,668		720
Dividend received from Small Ltd		180		–
Net profit before tax		4,848		720
Taxation	2,304		200	
Net dividend	2,400		240	
		4,704		440
Profit retained		144		280
Brought forward from last year		1,200		192
Carried forward to next year		1,344		472

Summary Balance Sheets at 30 September 19X6 (£000s)

	Large plc	Small Ltd
Intangible assets:		
Research and development:		
– pure research	20	–
– applied research	30	–
– development	180	–
Goodwill – purchased (at cost less amounts written off)	48	–
– unpurchased	50	–
Fixed assets at cost less depreciation	3,920	728
Investment in Small Ltd	525	–
Current account with Large plc	–	75
Stock	594	231
Debtors	2,250	370
Bank	99	24
	7,716	1,428
Less Current account with Small Ltd	75	–
Creditors for goods and services	297	156
	7,344	1,272
Share capital	6,000	800
Retained earnings	1,344	472
	7,344	1,272

Notes:
The intangible asset section of the balance sheet of Large plc has not yet been amended prior to consolidation to take account of the provisions of the Companies Acts or the recommendations contained in accounting standards regarding intangible assets.

The stock of Large plc contained goods valued at £108,000 purchased from Small Ltd at production cost plus 50 per cent.

Required:
(a) Prepare the consolidated profit and loss account of Large plc and its subsidiary Small Ltd for the year to 30 September 19X6 using the acquisition (purchase) method of consolidation.
(b) Prepare the consolidated balance sheet of Large plc and its subsidiary Small Ltd at 30 September 19X6 using the acquisition method of consolidation.
(c) What would the reserves of the group be if the merger method of consolidation were used instead of the acquisition method? Briefly explain why there is a difference between the values of the reserves arising from the two methods of consolidation.

(Institute of Chartered Secretaries and Administrators)

30.2A Huge plc acquired a holding of 600,000 of the 800,000 ordinary £1 shares of Large plc on 1 October 19X5 when the revenue reserves of Large stood at £320,000.

On 1 October 19X6, the directors of Medium plc agreed to appoint the commercial manager of Huge as one of its directors to enable Huge to participate in its commercial, financial and dividend policy decisions. In exchange, Huge agreed to provide finance to Medium for working capital. On the same day, Huge acquired its holding of 100,000 of the 400,000 ordinary £1 shares of Medium when the revenue reserves of Medium were £150,000. Three months later, the directors of Small plc, who supplied materials to Large, heard of the arrangement between Huge and Medium and suggested that they would be pleased to enter into a similar relationship. The board of Huge were interested in the proposal and showed their good faith by acquiring a 10 per cent holding in Small which at that time had a debit balance of £2,000 on its profit and loss account.

Balance Sheets of the four companies on 30 September 19X7

	Huge £000	Large £000	Medium £000	Small £000
Property, plant and machinery	2,004	780	553	85
Investment in Large	650			
Investment in Medium	180			
Investment in Small	12			
Current a/c Medium	40			
Current a/c Small		10		
Stocks	489	303	72	28
Debtors	488	235	96	22
Bank/cash	45	62	19	5
	3,908	1,390	740	140
Less Liabilities due in one year:				
Creditors	318	170	90	10
	3,590	1,220	650	130
Ordinary share capital	2,400	800	400	80
Revenue reserves	1,190	420	210	40
Current a/c Huge			40	
Current a/c Large				10
	3,590	1,220	650	130

Required:

(a) Identify which of the four companies should be included in a group consolidation, explaining how and why the treatment of one company in the consolidation may be different from another. Mention any appropriate accounting standards or legislation applicable.

(b) Prepare the consolidated balance sheet of the group at 30 September 19X7 using the acquisition method of accounting.

(*Institute of Chartered Secretaries and Administrators*)

31

Standards covering subsidiary and associated undertakings

Objectives

After you have studied this chapter, you should:

● *understand the importance of the control concept*

● *know the circumstances under which a parent:subsidiary relationship is recognised*

● *know of the conditions whereby companies are exempt from preparing consolidated financial statements*

● *know of the conditions under which a subsidiary company should not be included in the consolidated financial statements*

● *know what to do when a company has investments in associated undertakings but does not prepare consolidated financial statements because it has no investments in subsidiary undertakings*

31.1 Introduction

The whole field of accounting relating to consolidated financial statements and groups in general has recently undergone considerable changes. FRS 2 has been introduced to clarify and extend business operations for which consolidated financial statements are needed, and to define those situations where exemptions from their preparation should apply. It also appears likely that SSAP 1: *Accounting for associated companies* will be revised in full in the reasonably near future.

31.2 FRS 2: Accounting for subsidiary undertakings

Financial Reporting Standard 2 superseded SSAP 14: *Group accounts*. Obviously it must comply with the law as laid down in the Companies Acts. It does, however, redefine the legal requirements by reducing the number of alternatives and by making the requirements and definitions more precise. This will obviously be of benefit in improving the standardisation of accounts.

As you will see, the main changes in recent times have concerned consolidated financial statements. Specifically:

(*a*) the definitions of parents and subsidiaries are now based upon control, rather than on ownership;

(*b*) instead of 'company' the term 'undertaking' is used. This means that unincorporated bodies are now covered;

(*c*) there are now more exemptions available from the need to prepare consolidated financial statements.

In the remainder of this chapter the more important provisions are discussed. As chapters 21 to 30 have already incorporated the actual mechanics of implementing FRS 2, those points will not be looked at again. While this chapter is concerned with the other most important aspects of FRS 2 and of SSAP 1, it does not cover every detail. This would be needed only in your studies at a later stage.

31.3 Parent and subsidiary relationship

In general terms, the main test as to the existence of a parent:subsidiary relationship is one of control. A group consists of all of the various enterprises, which may include unincorporated businesses as well as companies, under the control of the parent. If you can understand that, the detail contained in FRS 2 and the Companies Acts will become much clearer. In fact, control and ownership usually go together, but it is the exceptions to this that have brought about the need for the changes that have been made to the Companies Acts and that have led to the issue of replacement accounting standards.

FRS 2 states that an undertaking is a parent undertaking of another undertaking (this being the subsidiary undertaking) if any of the following can apply to it:

1 it holds a majority of the voting rights (i.e. shares carrying a right to vote) in the undertaking;

2 it is a member of the undertaking and has the right to appoint or remove directors holding a majority of the voting rights at meetings of the board on substantially all matters;

3 it has the right to exercise a 'dominant influence' over the undertaking. This could be by virtue of provisions in the undertaking's memorandum or articles, or by a control contract which must be in writing and be legally valid. By 'dominant influence' is meant influence that can be exercised to achieve the operating and financial policies desired by the holder of the influence, not withstanding the rights or influence of any other party – in other words, it has the right to give directions as to the functioning of the operating and financial policies of the undertaking, whether or not they are to the benefit of that undertaking;

4 it is a member of the undertaking and controls alone a majority of the voting rights by agreement with other members;

5 it has a 'participating interest' (i.e. an interest in the shares of the undertaking which is held for the long term for the purpose of securing a contribution to its activities by the exercise of control or influence arising from that interest – this would normally be a holding of more than 20 per cent of the shares of the undertaking) and either (a) it exercises a dominant influence over the undertaking, or (b) it and the undertaking are managed on a unified basis (i.e. where the whole of the operations of the

undertakings are integrated and they are managed as a single unit);
6   a parent undertaking is also treated as the parent undertaking of the subsidiary undertakings of its subsidiary undertakings.

Points 1 and 6 above are the more traditional and more usual ways of establishing the existence of a parent:subsidiary relationship in the UK.

31.4   Exemption from preparing consolidated financial statements

The Companies Act 1989 brought in new provisions which exempt some groups from having to prepare consolidated accounts. Exactly the same provisions are contained in FRS 2. The main points contained therein are:

1   Small and medium-sized groups can claim exemption on the grounds of size. They must comply with at least two of the following criteria:

	Small	*Medium-sized*
Aggregate turnover not more than	£2.8 million net/ £3.36 million gross	£11.2 million net/ £13.44 million gross
Aggregate gross assets not more than	£1.4 million net/ £1.68 million gross	£5.6 million net/ £6.72 million gross
Aggregate employees not more than	50	250

(This exemption does not apply to groups whose members include a plc, a bank, an insurance company, or an authorised person under the Financial Services Act (1986).)
   In the past small and medium-sized companies could file modified group accounts. This is no longer possible. Small and medium-sized companies now have to choose between filing *full* consolidated accounts or *individual* company accounts.
2   Except for companies who have any of their securities listed on any stock exchange in the European Union, any parent undertaking that is itself a wholly owned subsidiary whose immediate parent is established in the European Union does not have to prepare consolidated financial statements. Individual company accounts must still be prepared for the parent and they must include the name of its own parent undertaking; the country where its own parent is incorporated, if it is not the United Kingdom; and the fact that it is exempt from preparing group financial statements. As well as this, a copy of the audited consolidated financial statements of its own parent must be filed with its own individual company accounts. (This exemption can be overturned by minority shareholders who can require that consolidated accounts are prepared.)
3   If all of the subsidiary undertakings are permitted or required to be excluded from consolidation under the Companies Acts, consolidated financial statements are not required.

31.5   Exemption from the inclusion of a subsidiary in consolidated financial statements

There are three grounds for exclusion of a subsidiary given in FRS 2:

1 where severe long-term restrictions substantially hinder the rights of the parent undertaking over the assets or management of the subsidiary undertaking;
2 where the interest in the subsidiary undertaking is held exclusively for subsequent resale; and
3 where activities are so different from those of other undertakings to be included in the consolidation that their inclusion would be incompatible with the obligation to give a true and fair view.

A subsidiary that is excluded on the grounds of long-term restriction should be treated as a fixed asset investment. However, if the parent still exercises significant influence it should be treated as an associated undertaking.

Subsidiaries excluded on the grounds that they are being held exclusively for resale should be included as current assets at the lower of cost and net realisable value.

Where exclusion is due to the activities of the subsidiary being so different from those of other undertakings to be included in the consolidation that their inclusion would be incompatible with the obligation to give a true and fair view, they should be accounted for using the equity method.

31.6 SSAP 1: Accounting for associated companies

Although the title of the SSAP has not changed since the terminology changed, the term 'associated undertakings' would be more appropriate, as this is what they are defined as in the Companies Acts. Investments in such companies are too significant to be treated simply as trade investments but, on the other hand, they do not qualify to be treated as investments in subsidiaries.

SSAP 1 says that B Ltd will be considered to be an associated company of A Ltd if A Ltd can *significantly* influence the financial and operating decisions of B Ltd. As a normal rule the amount of B Ltd's equity shares that A Ltd would have to hold would be 20 per cent. This, however, is only a guideline. What is important is the presence or absence of *significant* influence.

The idea behind SSAP 1 was to ensure that if one company has invested in another company, and can significantly influence the affairs of that company, then ordinary investment accounting is not suitable. Rather than simply showing dividends received as a measure of income, it would be much more realistic that the investing company's *full* share of the post-acquisition retained earnings of that company should be incorporated in the investing company's accounts. The method of doing this is known as 'equity accounting'.

31.7 Equity accounting

Equity accounting is a modified form of consolidation that requires similar adjustments to be made as apply under FRS 2: *Accounting for subsidiary undertakings* for full, acquisition accounting-based consolidations. In the consolidated profit and loss account, the investing company should take into account the whole of its share of the earnings of the associate, whether or not the associate has distributed the earnings as dividends. In the consolidated balance sheet the investment is shown at cost, adjusted each year by the share of retained profits belonging to the investor, subject to an adjustment for any goodwill arising on acquisition written off.

We will shortly see how this is carried out. You will note that there are considerable differences between equity accounting and consolidation accounting of a subsidiary's results. With subsidiary accounting, the group would take credit for the whole of the turnover, cost of sales, etc. and then make a one-line adjustment to remove any minority share. With equity accounting, the associated company's turnover, cost of sales, etc. are not amalgamated with those of the group. Instead, only the items concerned with the group's share of the associated company's results are brought into account.

As it would be quite rare for the investing company not to have subsidiaries, we will use an example that brings the necessary equity accounting into a consolidated set of financial statements.

Effect upon consolidated profit and loss account

Take out:
(a) dividends received or receivable from the associate.

Include instead the group's share of the associate's:

(b) pre-tax profit;
(c) taxation charge;
(d) post-acquisition retained profits brought forward.

Effect upon consolidated balance sheet

Rather than   the cost of the investment
Show instead   the cost of the investment
          plus
     the group's share of associate's post-acquisition retained profit.

Exhibit 31.1 shows how the associated company's results are incorporated into a set of consolidated financial statements.

Exhibit 31.1

A Ltd is a holding company with subsidiaries. It also has 25 per cent of the equity share capital of B Ltd. This was bought for £100,000 three years ago when B Ltd had reserves (retained profits) of £20,000.

Profit and Loss Accounts for the year ending 31 December 19X3

	A Ltd & Subsidiaries (consolidated)		B Ltd Associate Comp.	
	£000	£000	£000	£000
Turnover		540		200
Cost of sales		370		130
Gross profit		170		70
Distribution costs	20		3	
Administrative expenses	40	60	7	10
		110		
Dividends receivable from B Ltd		(A) 10		
Profit on ordinary activities before taxation		120		(B) 60
Tax on profit on ordinary activities		28		(C) 16
Profit on ordinary activities after taxation		92		44
Retained profits from last year		43		40
		135		84
Proposed dividends		60		40
Retained profits carried to next year		75		44

Balance Sheet as at 31 December 19X3 (abbreviated)

	£000	£000
Fixed assets	145	130
Investment in B Ltd at cost	100	–
Net current assets	180	114
	425	244
Share capital (ordinary shares)	350	200
Reserves	75	44
	425	244

Now we can move to the consolidation of B Ltd with A Ltd. As you have already been told the items needing adjusting are:

Take out: (A) Dividends receivable
Include: (B) Group share of pre-tax profit
           (C) Group share of taxation
           (D) Group's share post-acquisition retained profit brought forward.

The answer is:

A Ltd Group

Consolidated Profit and Loss Account for the year ending 31 December 19X3

		£000	£000
Turnover			540
Cost of sales			370
			170
Distribution costs		20	
Administrative expenses		40	60
			110
Share of profit of associated company (*see* W1)	(B)		15
Profit on ordinary activities before taxation			125
Tax on profit on ordinary activities (*see* W2)	(C)		32
Profit on ordinary activities after taxation			93
Retained profits from last year (*see* W3)	(D)		48
			141
Proposed dividend			60
Retained profits carried to next year			81

Consolidated Balance Sheet as at 31 December 19X3

	£000
Fixed assets	145
Investment in B Ltd (*see* W4)	106
Net current assets	180
	431
Share capital	350
Reserves (*see* W5)	81
	431

Workings:
(W1) 25% of profit before taxation of B Ltd × £60 = £15
(W2) A £28 + 25% of B £16 = £32
(W3) A £33 + 25% of B's post-acquisition profits (£40 – £20) £20 = £48
(W4) Cost of 25% share in B =   100

Add Retained profits B c/fwd	44	
Less Pre-acquisition profits	20	
Post-acquisition profits	24	
25% share		6
		106

(W5) Reserves A	75	
Add 25% of post-acquisition		
profit of B (*see* W4)	6	81

31.8 Investing companies without subsidiaries

If no consolidated financial statements are produced by the investing company and it is not exempt from preparing consolidated statements, or would not be if it had subsidiaries, a separate profit and loss account (or a supplement to the investing company's own profit and loss account) should be prepared showing the information that would have been included in respect of the associated undertaking had consolidated financial statements been prepared. Similar requirements apply to the balance sheet. An example of a supplementary statement incorporating the results of associated companies is shown in Exhibit 31.2.

Exhibit 31.2

Example of a profit and loss account of a company without subsidiaries:

Profit and Loss Account of an Investing Company

	£000	£000
Turnover		2,000
Cost of sales		1,400
Gross profit		600
Distribution costs	175	
Administrative expenses	125	300
Profit on ordinary activities before taxation		300
Tax on profit on ordinary activities		85
Profit on ordinary activities after taxation		215
Dividends – proposed		80
Amount set aside to reserves		135

Supplementary statement incorporating results of associated companies:

	£000
Share of profits less losses of associated companies	50
Less Tax	15
Share of profits after tax of associated companies	35
Profit on ordinary share activites after taxation (as above)	215
Profit attributable to members of the investing company	250
Dividends – proposed	80
Net profit retained (£35,000 by associated companies)	170

Note: The earnings per share figure would be based on £250,000.

31.9 The control concept

The control concept underlies the presentation of consolidated financial statements for a group as a single economic entity. While the list given in section 31.3 can be used to identify a parent:subsidiary relationship, it may result in more than one undertaking being classified as the parent. However, FRS 2 states that control can only be held by one parent, and that the control that identifies undertakings as parent and subsidiary undertakings should be distinguished from shared control, for example as in a joint venture. If more than one undertaking is identified as the parent, their interests in the subsidiary are in effect interests in a joint venture, and no parent:subsidiary relationship exists.

On the other hand, one or more of these parents may exercise a non-controlling but significant influence over the company in which it has invested. In that case it would be appropriate to account for it as an associate undertaking.

New terms

Associated undertaking (p. 434): A company which is not a subsidiary of the investing group or company but in which the investing group or company has a long-term interest and over which it is in a position to exercise significant influence.

Equity accounting (p. 434): A method of accounting for associated undertakings that brings into the consolidated profit and loss account the investor's share of the investment undertaking's results and that records the investment in the consolidated balance sheet at the investor's share of the investment undertaking's net assets including any goodwill arising to the extent that it has not previously been written off.

Main points to remember

1 The existence of a parent:subsidiary relationship depends upon whether the 'parent' undertaking can exercise *dominant* influence over the 'subsidiary' undertaking.

2 The existence of a parent:associate relationship depends upon whether the 'parent' undertaking can exercise *significant* influence over the 'associate' undertaking.

3 There are some circumstances where groups are exempted from the preparation of consolidated financial statements.

4 Equity accounting is used when including associate undertakings in consolidated financial statements.

5 When a company has investments in associated undertakings but does not prepare consolidated financial statements because it has no investments in subsidiary undertakings, it should prepare a supplement to its financial statements detailing the information that would have been included in respect of the associated undertaking had consolidated financial statements been prepared.

6 Subsidiary undertakings can only have one parent; however, more than one parent may have a significant influence over an associated undertaking.

Review questions

31.1 Q plc has three subsidiaries: L Ltd, M Ltd, and N Ltd. All three were acquired on 1 January at the start of the financial year which has just ended. Q has a 55 per cent, 70 per cent, and 95 per cent holding respectively and holds a majority of the voting equity in L and M. It has changed the composition of both these companies' boards since they were acquired. However, despite its 95 per cent holding in N Ltd, it only has a 45 per cent holding of the voting equity and has so far failed in all its attempts to have a director appointed to the board. How should these three investee companies be treated in the Q group consolidated financial statements?

31.2 At the end of 19X5, a parent company, P plc, with one subsidiary had a holding representing 10 per cent of the equity of R Ltd, a clothing company. It had cost £80,000 when purchased at the start of 19X4. At the time of that investment, R Ltd had net assets of £560,000 which increased to £840,000 by the end of that year. At the start of the current year, the investment was increased by a further 11 per cent of the equity at a cost of £110,000.

(a) How would the investment be shown in the financial statements if it were treated as a *trade investment*?

(b) How would the investment be shown in the financial statements if it were treated as an *associated undertaking*?

31.3A Relevant balance sheets as at 31 March 19X4 are set out below:

	Jasmin (Holdings) plc £000	Kasbah plc £000	Fortran plc £000
Tangible fixed assets	289,400	91,800	7,600
Investments			
Shares in Kasbah (at cost)	97,600		
Shares in Fortran (at cost)	8,000		
	395,000		
Current assets			
Stock	285,600	151,400	2,600
Cash	319,000	500	6,800
	604,600	151,900	9,400
Creditors: amounts falling due within one year	289,600	238,500	2,200
Net current assets	315,000	(86,600)	7,200
Total assets less current liabilities	710,000	5,200	14,800
Capital and reserves			
Called up share capital			
Ordinary £1 shares	60,000	20,000	10,000
10% £1 Preference shares		4,000	
Revaluation reserve	40,000		1,200
Profit and loss reserve	610,000	(18,800)	3,600
	710,000	5,200	14,800

You have recently been appointed chief accountant of Jasmin (Holdings) plc and are about to prepare the group balance sheet at 31 March 19X4. The following points are relevant to the preparation of those accounts.

(a) Jasmin (Holdings) plc owns 90 per cent of the ordinary £1 shares and 20 per cent of the 10 per cent £1 preference shares of Kasbah plc. On 1 April 19X3 Jasmin (Holdings) plc paid £96 million for the ordinary £1 shares and £1.6 million for the 10 per cent £1 preference shares when Kasbah's reserves were a credit balance of £45 million.

(b) Jasmin (Holdings) plc sells part of its output to Kasbah plc. The stock of Kasbah plc on 31 March 19X4 includes £1.2 million of stock purchased from Jasmin (Holdings) plc at cost plus one-third.

(c) The policy of the group is to revalue its tangible fixed assets on a yearly basis. However, the directors of Kasbah plc have always resisted this policy, preferring to show tangible fixed assets at historical cost. The market value of the tangible fixed assets of Kasbah plc at 31 March 19X4 is £90 million. The directors of Jasmin (Holdings) plc wish to follow the requirements of FRS 2 'Accounting for Subsidiary Undertakings' in respect of the value of tangible fixed assets to be included in the group accounts.

(d) The ordinary £1 shares of Fortran plc are split into 6 million 'A' ordinary £1 shares and 4 million 'B' ordinary £1 shares. Holders of 'A' shares are assigned 1 vote and holders of 'B' ordinary shares are assigned 2 votes per share. On 1 April 19X3 Jasmin (Holdings) plc acquired 80 per cent of the 'A' ordinary shares and 10 per cent of the 'B' ordinary shares when the profit and loss reserve of Fortran plc was £1.6 million and the revaluation reserve was £2 million. The 'A' ordinary shares and 'B' ordinary shares carry equal rights to share in the company's profit and losses.

(e) The fair values of Kasbah plc and Fortran plc were not materially different from their book values at the time of acquisition of their shares by Jasmin (Holdings) plc.

(f) Goodwill arising on acquisition is amortised over five years.

(g) Kasbah plc has paid its preference dividend for the current year but no other dividends are proposed by the group companies. The preference dividend was paid shortly after the interim results of Kasbah plc were announced and was deemed to be a legal dividend by the auditors.

(h) Because of its substantial losses during the period, the directors of Jasmin (Holdings) plc wish to exclude the financial statements of Kasbah plc from the group accounts on the grounds that Kasbah plc's output is not similar to that of Jasmin (Holdings) plc and that the resultant accounts therefore would be misleading. Jasmin (Holdings) plc produces synthetic yarn and Kasbah plc produces garments.

Required:

(a) List the conditions for exclusion of subsidiaries from consolidation for the directors of Jasmin (Holdings) plc and state whether Kasbah plc may be excluded on these grounds.

(b) Prepare a consolidated balance sheet for Jasmin (Holdings) Group plc for the year ending 31 March 19X4. (All calculations should be made to the nearest thousand pounds.)

(c) Comment briefly on the possible implications of the size of Kasbah plc's losses for the year for the group accounts and the individual accounts of Jasmin (Holdings) plc.

(Chartered Association of Certified Accountants)

Part 4

PLANNING, CONTROL AND DECISION MAKING

Introduction

This part considers how accounting information is used for planning, control and decision making.

32

Budgeting and budgetary control

Objectives

After you have studied this chapter, you should:

● *have an awareness of the budgetary process*

● *be aware of the importance of budgets for planning and control*

● *be aware of the importance of effective co-ordination of budgets for the organisation*

● *be aware of the benefits of operating a system of flexible budgeting*

Part one: An introduction

It can be stated that management control is needed to try to ensure that the organisation achieves its objectives. Once the objectives have been agreed, plans should be drawn up so that the progress of the firm can be directed towards the ends specified in the objectives. Now it must not be thought that plans can be expressed only in accounting terms. For example, quality of the product might be best shown in engineering terms, or social objectives shown in a plan concerned with employee welfare. But some of the objectives, such as the attainment of a desired profit, or the attainment of a desired growth in assets, can be expressed in accounting terms. When a plan is expressed quantitatively it is known as a **budget** and the process of converting plans into budgets is known as **budgeting**. In this book we are concerned primarily with budgets shown in monetary terms, i.e. financial budgets.

The budgeting process may be quite formal in a large organisation with committees set up to perform the task. On the other hand in a very small firm the owner may jot down his budget on a piece of scrap paper or even on the back of a used envelope. Some even manage without writing anything down at all – they have done the budgets in their heads and can easily remember them. This book is concerned with budgeting in a formal manner.

32.1 Budgets and people

Probably in no other part of accounting is there a greater need for understanding other people than in the processes of budgeting. Budgets are prepared in order to try to guide the firm towards its objectives. There is no doubt that some budgets that are drawn up are even more harmful to a firm than if none were drawn up at all.

Budgets are drawn up for control purposes, that is, as an attempt to control the direction that the firm is taking. Many people, however, look upon them, not as a guide, but as a straitjacket. We can look at a few undesirable actions that can result from people regarding budgets as a straitjacket rather than as a guide.

(a) The sales manager refuses to let a salesman go to Sweden in response to an urgent and unexpected request from a Swedish firm. The reason – the overseas sales expenses budget has already been spent. The result – the most profitable order that the firm would have received for many years is taken up instead by another firm.

(b) The works manager turns down requests for overtime work, because the budgeted overtime has already been exceeded. The result – the job is not completed on time, and the firm has to pay a large sum under a penalty clause in the contract for the job which stated that if the job was not finished by a certain date then a penalty of £20,000 would become payable.

(c) Towards the end of the accounting year a manager realises that he has not spent all of his budget for a particular item. He then launches on a spending spree, completely unnecessary items being bought, on the basis that 'If I don't spend this amount this year they will cut down next year when I will really need the money.' The result: a lot of unusable and unnecessary equipment.

(d) The education budget has been spent, therefore the education manager will not let anyone go on courses for the rest of the year. The result: the firm starts to fall behind in an industry which is highly technical, the staff concerned become fed up, and the better ones start to look for jobs in other firms which are more responsive to the need to allow personnel to keep in touch with changing technology.

Studies have shown that the more that managers are brought into the budgeting process, then the more successful budgetary control is likely to be. A manager on whom a budget is imposed, rather than a manager who had an active part in the drafting of his budget, is more likely to pay less attention to the budget and use it unwisely in the control process.

Having sounded the warning that needs to be borne in mind constantly when budgeting, we can now look at the positive end of budgeting – to see the advantages of a good budgetary control system.

32.2 Budgets and profit planning

The methodology of budgetary control is probably accountancy's major contribution to management. Before we get down to the mechanics of constructing budgets we should first of all look at the main outlines of drafting budgets.

When the budgets are being drawn up the two main objectives must be uppermost in the mind of top management, that is that the budgets are for:

(a) **Planning.** This means a properly co-ordinated and comprehensive plan for the whole business. Each part must interlock with the other parts.

(b) **Control.** Just because a plan is set down on paper does not mean that the plan will carry itself out. Control is exercised via the budgets, thus the name budgetary control. To do this means that the responsibility of managers and budgets must be so linked that the responsible manager is given a guide to help him to produce certain desired results, and the actual achieved results can be compared against the expected, i.e. actual compared with budget.

32.3 Preparation of estimates

The first thing to establish is what the limiting factors are in a firm. It may well be the fact that sales cannot be pushed above a certain amount, or it might be the fact that the firm could sell as much as it can produce, but the productive capacity of the firm sets a limit. Whatever the limiting factor is, there is no doubt that this aspect of the firm will need more attention than probably any other. There would not, for instance, be much point in budgeting for the sale of 1,000 units a year if production could not manufacture more that 700, or to manufacture 2,000 a year if only 1,300 of them could be sold.

There is no doubt that usually the most difficult estimate to make is that of sales revenue. This can be done by using one of two methods:

(a) Make a statistical forecast on the basis of the economic conditions applying with reference to the goods sold by the company, and what is known about the actions of competitors.

(b) The opposite is to make an internal forecast. This is usually done by asking each salesman, or group of salesmen, to estimate the sales in their own areas, and then total the estimates. Sometimes the salesmen are not asked at all.

Now we should remember that much of the subject matter that you have read about, or are currently reading, in Economics is very relevant here. A knowledge of elasticity of demand, whether the product is a complementary product, e.g. the price of egg-cups is linked to the demand for eggs, or whether it is a substitute, e.g. that a rise in the price of butter may induce housewives to turn to other commodities instead, is very relevant in this area. Factors such as whether the firm has a monopoly, whether the firm has many small customers, a few large customers, or even one large customer, are of crucial importance. Estimating sales revenue is very much a matter of taking all the economic factors into account allied to other factors.

The sales budget is, however, more than just a sales forecast. Budgets should show the actions that management is taking to influence future events. If an increase in sales is desired the sales budget may show extra sales, which may well be an indication of the action that management is going to take by means of extra television advertising, making a better product, or giving retailers better profit margins and pushing up sales in that way.

32.4 The production budget

The production budget stems from the sales budget, but the first question that has to be settled is that of the level of the stock of finished goods which will be held by the firm.

If sales are even over the year, then production can also be in keeping with the sales figure, and the stock figure can remain constant. Suppose that the firm sells 50 units every month, then the firm can produce 50 units per month. In almost every firm, a stock level will have to be maintained, the amount of stock being dependent on factors such as amount of storage space, the estimated amount needed to cater for breakdowns in production or for delays in receiving raw materials, etc. Nonetheless, if the stock level was to be a minimum of 70 units it would still mean that production was at the rate of 50 units per month.

On the other hand sales may not be constant. Sales may average 50 units per month, but the figures may well be as follows:

January	20 units	February	30 units	March	60 units
April	80 units	May	70 units	June	40 units

This would mean that if production levels were kept at 50 units per month the stock levels would usually have to be more than 100 units, whilst if the stock levels were to be kept at 100 units minimum the production figures each month would equal the sales figures. We can now compare the two levels of production.

32.5 Even production flow

The problem here is to find the stock level that the firm would need on 1 January if (a) sales are as shown, (b) the stock must not fall below 100 units, (c) production is to be 50 units per month. It can be found by trial and error. For instance, if you decided to see what would happen if the firm started off with 100 units in stock at 1 January, you would find that, after adding production and deducting sales each month, the stock level would fall to 90 units in May. As 100 units of stock is the minimum needed you would need to start off on 1 January with 110 units. The method is that if you start off your calculation with an estimated figure of stock, which must at least be the minimum figure required, then if you find that the lowest figure of stock shown during the period is 10 units less than the minimum stock required, go back and add 10 units to the stock to be held on 1 January. If the lowest figure is 30 units less than required add 30 units to the 1 January stock, and so on. We can now look at the figures in Exhibit 32.1.

Exhibit 32.1

Units	January	February	March	April	May	June
Opening stock	110	140	160	150	120	100
Add Units produced	50	50	50	50	50	50
	160	190	210	200	170	150
Less Sales	20	30	60	80	70	40
Closing stock	140	160	150	120	100	110

Before we look at the implications of maintaining an even production flow we can look at another example. Try to work it out for yourself before looking at the answer in Exhibit 32.2. The sales are expected to be January 70, February 40, March 50, April 120, May 140 and June 70. The stock level must not fall below 120 units and an even production flow of 80 units is required. What stock level would there have to be on 1 January?

Exhibit 32.2

Units	January	February	March	April	May	June
Opening stock	140	150	190	220	180	120
Add Units produced	80	80	80	80	80	80
	220	230	270	300	260	200
Less Sales	70	40	50	120	140	70
Closing stock	150	190	220	180	120	130

It is more important in many firms to ensure a smooth production flow than to bother unduly about stock levels, assuming that the minimum stock level is always attained. If the work is skilled then that type of labour force may take several years to become trained, and skilled labour in many industries does not take kindly to being sacked and re-employed as the demand for the goods fluctuates. This is not always true with skilled labour. For instance, in the building industry such craftsmen as bricklayers may go to a builder until he has completed a contract such as building a college, a hospital or a housing estate, and then leave and go to another employer on the completion of the job.

On the other hand, a skilled engineer concerned with the manufacture of, say, diesel engines would not expect to be fired and re-employed continuously. The bricklayer has a skill that is easily transferable to many other building employers in an area, whereas the diesel engineer may have only one firm within fifty miles of his home where he can perform his skills properly. A man employed as a labourer might work on a building site in one part of the year and then transfer to an engineering factory as a labourer in another part of the year. Whether a firm could carry on production with widely uneven production levels depends so much on the type of firm and the type of labour involved. A firm would only sack skilled labour which it needed again shortly if it could persuade the men or women to come back when required. If the people who had been sacked were likely to find other employment, and not return to the firm when required, then this would mean that the firm would probably keep them on its payroll and production would continue and stocks of finished goods would begin to pile up. Many firms do in fact realise their social obligations by only laying off workers when no other alternative is at all reasonable. In many organisations there are probably more workers from time to time than the firm actually needs – this is known as 'organisational slack', so that there is a leeway between the increasing of production and having to take on extra workers.

32.6 Uneven production levels

Some firms by their very nature will have uneven production levels, and this will be accepted by their labour force. An ice-cream firm would find sales at the highest levels in summer, tailing off in winter. It is not really possible to build up stocks of ice-cream very much in the winter for summer sales! Even if it could be done technically, the costs of refrigerating large quantities of ice-cream for several months could hardly be economic. The large labour force used in the summer months will probably include quite a few students occupying their vacation periods profitably, and not able anyway to work at the job all the year round even if they wanted to. Such a kind of firm will normally have a far greater relationship between current stock levels and current sales than a firm which has even production levels. The calculation of the quantity to be produced is then:

Opening stock + Units produced – Sales = Closing stock

This means that if the opening stock will be 80 units, the sales are expected to be 100 units and the desired closing is 50 units the quantity to be produced becomes:

	Units
Opening stock	80
Add Production	?
Less Sales	100
Closing stock	50

Production will, therefore, be the missing figure, i.e. 70 units (80 + Production 70 = 150 for sale less actually sold 100 = closing stock 50).

Exhibit 32.3 shows the units to be produced if the following information is known – Stock required 1 January 40, at end of each month, January 60, February 110, March 170, April 100, May 60, June 20. Sales are expected to be January 100, February 150, March 110, April 190, May 70, June 50.

Exhibit 32.3

Units	January	February	March	April	May	June
Opening stock	40	60	110	170	100	60
Production required (?)	120	200	170	120	30	10
	160	260	280	290	130	70
Less Sales	100	150	110	190	70	50
Closing stock	60	110	170	100	60	20

Linked with the production budget will be a materials purchase budget. It may well be that an order will have to be placed in January, received in March and issued to production in April. The purchase of materials will have to be planned as scientifically as possible.

You are now in a position to be able to tackle review questions 32.1 to 32.6 inclusive.

Part two: Cash budgets

It is no use budgeting for production and for sales if during the budget period the firm runs out of cash funds. When talking about cash in budgets we are also usually including bank funds, and therefore in this book we will not be differentiating between cash and cheque payments or between cash and cheques received. Cash is, therefore, also budgeted for, so that any shortage of cash can be known in advance and action taken to obtain permission for a loan or a bank overdraft to be available then, rather than wait until the shortage or deficiency occurs. Bank managers, or anyone concerned with the lending of money, certainly resent most strongly one of their customers needing a bank overdraft without prior warning, when in fact the customer could have known if he had drawn up a cash budget in advance which revealed the need for cash funds on a particular date.

The finance needed may not just be by way of borrowing from a bank or finance house; it may well be a long-term need that can only be satisfied by an issue of shares or debentures. Such issues need planning well in advance, and a cash budget can reveal (*a*) that they will be needed, (*b*) how much is needed and (*c*) when it will be needed.

We can now look at a very simple case. Without being concerned in this first exhibit with exactly what the receipts and payments are for, just to keep matters simple at this stage, we can see the dangers that are inherent in not budgeting for cash.

Exhibit 32.4

Mr Muddlem had a meeting with his accountant on 1 July 19X3. He was feeling very pleased with himself. He had managed to get some very good orders from customers, mainly because he was now allowing them extra time in which to pay their accounts. Sprite, the accountant, said, 'Can you afford to do all that you are hoping to do?'

Muddlem laughed, 'Why, I'll be making so much money I won't know how to spend it.'

'But have you got the cash to finance everything?' asked Sprite.

'If I'm making a good profit then of course I'll have the cash,' said Muddlem. 'I know the bank manager says that any bank overdraft could not be more than £1,000, but I doubt if I need it.'

'Don't let's rely on guesses,' says Sprite. 'Let's work it out.'

After an hour's work the following facts emerge.

(*a*) Present cash balance (including bank balance) £800.

(*b*) Receipts from debtors will be: July £2,000, August £2,600, September £5,000, October £7,000, November £8,000, December £15,000.

(*c*) Payments will be July £2,500, August £2,700, September £6,900, October £7,800, November £9,900, December £10,300.

This is then summarised:	*Jul*	*Aug*	*Sep*	*Oct*	*Nov*	*Dec*
	£	£	£	£	£	£
Balance at start of the month:	+800	+300	+200			
Deficit at the start of the month:				−1,700	−2,500	−4,400
Receipts	2,000	2,600	5,000	7,000	8,000	15,000
	2,800	2,900	5,200	5,300	5,500	10,600
Payments	2,500	2,700	6,900	7,800	9,900	10,300
Balance at end of the month:	+300	+200				+300
Deficit at the end of the month:			−1,700	−2,500	−4,400	

'I'm in an awkward position now,' says Muddlem. 'I just cannot borrow £4,400 nor can I cut down on my sales, and anyway I don't really want to as these new sales are very profitable indeed. If only I'd known this, I could have borrowed the money from my brother only last week but he's invested it elsewhere now.'

'Come and see me tomorrow,' says Sprite. 'There may well be something we can do.'

Fortunately for Muddlem his luck was in. He arrived to see his accountant the following morning waving a cheque. 'My wife won £5,000 on a jackpot bingo last night,' he said.

'Thank goodness for that. At least in future you'll learn to budget ahead for cash requirements. You can't be lucky all the time,' says Sprite.

32.7 Timing of cash receipts and payments

In drawing up a cash budget it must be borne in mind that all the payments for units produced would very rarely be at the same time as production itself. For instance, the raw materials might be bought in March, incorporated in the goods being produced in April, and paid for in May. On the other hand the raw materials may have been in hand for some time, so that the goods are bought in January, paid for in February, and used in production the following August. Contrary to this, the direct labour part of the product is usually paid for almost at the same time as the unit being produced. Even here a unit may be produced in one week and the wages paid one week later, so that a unit might be produced on, say, 27 June and the wages for the direct labour involved paid for on 3 July.

Similarly the date of sales and the date of receipt of cash will not usually be the same, except in many retail stores. The goods might be sold in May and the money received in August, or even paid for in advance so that the goods might be paid for in February but the goods not shipped to the buyer until May. This is especially true, at least for part of the goods, when a cash deposit is left for specially made goods which will take some time to manufacture. A simple example of this would be a made-to-measure suit on which a deposit would be paid at the time of order, the final payment being made when the completed suit is collected by the buyer.

Exhibit 32.5

A cash budget for the six months ended 30 June 19X3 is to be drafted from the following information.

(*a*) Opening cash balance at 1 January 19X3 £3,200.

(*b*) Sales, at £12 per unit, cash received three months after sale: in units.

	19X2			19X3								
	Oct	Nov	Dec	Jan	Feb	Mar	Apr	May	Jun	Jul	Aug	Sep
	80	90	70	100	60	120	150	140	130	110	100	160

(*c*) Production: in units.

	19X2			19X3								
	Oct	Nov	Dec	Jan	Feb	Mar	Apr	May	Jun	Jul	Aug	Sep
	70	80	90	100	110	130	140	150	120	160	170	180

(*d*) Raw materials used in production cost £4 per unit of production. They are paid for two months before being used in production.

(*e*) Direct labour, £3 per unit paid for in the same month as the unit produced.

(*f*) Other variable expenses, £2 per unit, ¾ of the cost being paid for in the same month as production, the other ¼ paid in the month after production.

(*g*) Fixed expenses of £100 per month are paid monthly.

(*h*) A motor van is to be bought and paid for in April for £800. Schedules of payments and receipts are as follows:

Payments (the month shown in brackets is the month in which the units are produced):

January	£	*February*	£
Raw materials: 130 (March) × £4	520	140 (April) × £4	560
Direct labour: 100 (January) × £3	300	110 (February) × 3	330
Variable: 100 (January) × ¾ × £2	150	110 (February) × ¾ × £2	165
90 (December) × ¼ × £2	45	100 (January) × ¼ × £2	50
Fixed	100	Fixed	100
	£1,115		£1,205

March	£	*April*	£
Raw materials: 150 (May) × £4	600	120 (June) × £4	480
Direct labour: 130 (March) × £3	390	140 (April) × £3	420
Variable: 130 (March) × ¾ × £2	195	140 (April) × ¾ × £2	210
110 (February) × ¼ × £2	55	30 (March) × ¼ × £2	65
Fixed	100	Fixed	100
		Motor van	800
	£1,340		£2,075

May	£	*June*	£
Raw materials: 160 (July) × £4	640	170 (August) × £4	680
Direct labour: 150 (May) × £3	450	120 (June) × £3	360
Variable: 150 (May) × ¾ × £2	225	120 (June) × ¾ × £2	180
140 (April) × ¼ × £2	70	150 (May) × ¼ × £2	75
Fixed	100	Fixed	100
	£1,485		£1,395

Receipts: (the month shown in brackets is the month in which the sale was made):

				£
January	80	(October)	× £12	960
February	90	(November)	× £12	1,080
March	70	(December)	× £12	840
April	100	(January)	× £12	1,200
May	60	(February)	× £12	720
June	120	(March)	× £12	1,440

Cash budget

	Jan £	Feb £	Mar £	Apr £	May £	Jun £
Balance from previous month	3,200	3,045	2,920	2,420	1,545	780
Add Receipts (per schedule)	960	1,080	840	1,200	720	1,440
	4,160	4,125	3,760	3,620	2,265	2,220
Less Payments (per schedule)	1,115	1,205	1,340	2,075	1,485	1,395
Balance carried next month	3,045	2,920	2,420	1,545	780	825

You should now be able to tackle all of review questions 32.7 to 32.10 inclusive.

Part three: Co-ordination of budgets

The various budgets have to be linked together and a **master budget**, which is really a budgeted set of final accounts, drawn up. We have looked at the sales, production and cash budgets. There are, however, many more budgets for parts of the organisation; for instance, there may be:

1 a selling budget,
2 an administration expense budget,
3 a manufacturing overhead budget,
4 a direct labour budget,
5 a purchases budget,

and so on. In this book we do not wish to get entangled in too many details, but in a real firm with a proper set of budgeting techniques there will be a great deal of detailed backing for the figures that are incorporated in the more important budgets.

Now it may be that when all the budgets have been co-ordinated, or slotted together, the master budget shows a smaller profit than the directors are prepared to accept. This will mean recasting budgets to see whether a greater profit can be earned, and if at all possible the budgets will be altered. Eventually there will be a master budget that the directors can agree to. This then gives the target for the results that the firm hopes to achieve in financial terms. Remember that there are other targets such as employee welfare, product quality, etc. that cannot be so expressed.

The rest of this chapter is concerned with the drawing up of budgets for an imaginary firm, Walsh Ltd, culminating in the drawing up of the master budget.

To start with we can look at the last balance sheet of Walsh Ltd as at 31 December 19X4. This will give us our opening figures of stocks of raw materials, stock of finished goods, cash (including bank) balance, creditors, debtors etc.

Walsh Ltd

Balance Sheet as at 31 December 19X4

Fixed assets	Cost £	Depreciation to date £	Net £
Machinery	4,000	1,600	2,400
Motor vehicles	2,000	800	1,200
	6,000	2,400	3,600

Current assets			
Stocks: Finished goods (75 units)		900	
Raw materials		500	
Debtors (19X4 October £540 + November £360 + December £450)		1,350	
Cash and bank balances		650	
		3,400	
Less Current liabilities			
Creditors for raw materials (November £120 + December £180)	300		
Creditors for fixed expenses (December)	100	400	
Working capital			3,000
			6,600

Financed by		
Share capital: 4,000 shares £1 each		4,000
Profit and loss account		2,600
		6,600

The plans for the six months ended 30 June 19X5 are as follows:

(a) Production will be 60 units per month for the first four months, followed by 70 units per month for May and June.

(b) Production costs will be (per unit):

	£
Direct materials	5
Direct labour	4
Variable overhead	3
	£12

(c) Fixed overhead is £100 per month, payable always one month in arrears.

(d) Sales, at a price of £18 per unit, are expected to be:

	January	February	March	April	May	June
No. of units	40	50	60	90	90	70

(e) Purchases of direct materials (raw materials) will be:

	January £	February £	March £	April £	May £	June £
	150	200	250	300	400	320

(*f*) The creditors for raw materials bought are paid two months after purchase.

(*g*) Debtors are expected to pay their accounts three months after they have bought the goods.

(*h*) Direct labour and variable overheads are paid in the same month as the units are produced.

(*i*) A machine costing £2,000 will be bought and paid for in March.

(*j*) 3,000 shares of £1 each are to be issued at par in May.

(*k*) Depreciation for the six months: Machinery £450, Motor vehicles £200.

We must first of all draw up the various budgets and then incorporate them into the master budget. Some of the more detailed budgets which can be dispensed with in this illustration will be omitted.

Materials Budget

	January	*February*	*March*	*April*	*May*	*June*
Opening stock £	500	350	250	200	200	250
Add Purchases £	150	200	250	300	400	320
	650	550	500	500	600	570
Less Used in production:						
Jan–April 60 × £5	300	300	300	300		
May and June 70 × £5					350	350
Closing stock £	350	250	200	200	250	220

Production Budget (in units)

	January	*February*	*March*	*April*	*May*	*June*
Opening stock (units)	75	95	105	105	75	55
Add Produced	60	60	60	60	70	70
	135	155	165	165	145	125
Less Sales	40	50	60	90	90	70
Closing stock	95	105	105	75	55	55

Production Cost Budget (in £s)

	January	*February*	*March*	*April*	*May*	*June*	*Total*
Materials cost £	300	300	300	300	350	350	1,900
Labour cost £	240	240	240	240	280	280	1,520
Variable overhead £	180	180	180	180	210	210	1,140
	720	720	720	720	840	840	4,560

Creditors Budget

	January	*February*	*March*	*April*	*May*	*June*
Opening balance £	300	330	350	450	550	700
Add Purchases £	150	200	250	300	400	320
	450	530	600	750	950	1,020
Less Payments £	120	180	150	200	250	300
Closing balance £	330	350	450	550	700	720

Debtors Budget

	January	February	March	April	May	June
Opening balances £	1,350	1,530	2,070	2,700	3,600	4,320
Add Sales £	720	900	1,080	1,620	1,620	1,260
	2,070	2,430	3,150	4,320	5,220	5,580
Less Received £	540	360	450	720	900	1,080
Closing balances £	1,530	2,070	2,700	3,600	4,320	4,500

Cash Budget

	January	February	March	April	May	June
Opening balance £	+650	+550	+210			+1,050
Opening overdraft £				−2,010	−2,010	
Received (see schedule) £	540	360	450	720	3,900	1,080
	1,190	910	660	−1,290	1,890	2,130
Payments (see schedule) £	640	700	2,670	720	840	890
Closing balance £	+550	+210			+1,050	+1,240
Closing overdraft £			−2,010	−2,010		

Cash Payments Schedule

		January	February	March	April	May	June
Creditors for goods bought two months previously £		120	180	150	200	250	300
Fixed overhead £		100	100	100	100	100	100
Direct labour £		240	240	240	240	280	280
Variable overhead £		180	180	180	180	210	210
Machinery £				2,000			
	£	640	700	2,670	720	840	890

Cash Receipts Schedule

	January	February	March	April	May	June
Debtors for goods sold three months previously £	540	360	450	720	900	1,080
Shares issued £					3,000	
					3,900	

Master Budget
Forecast Operating Statement for the Six Months ended 30 June 19X5

			£
Sales			7,200
Less Cost of goods sold:			
Opening stock of finished goods		900	
Add Cost of goods completed		4,560	
		5,460	
Less Closing stock of finished goods		660	4,800
Gross profit			2,400
Less			
Fixed overhead		600	
Depreciation: Machinery	450		
Motors	200	650	1,250
Net profit			1,150

Forecast Balance Sheet as at 30 June 19X5

		Depreciation	
Fixed assets			
Tangible assets	*Cost*	*to date*	*Net*
	£	£	£
Machinery	6,000	2,050	3,950
Motor vehicles	2,000	1,000	1,000
	8,000	3,050	4,950

Current assets			
Stocks: Finished goods		660	
Raw materials		220	
Debtors		4,500	
Cash and bank balances		1,240	
		6,620	
Creditors: amounts falling due within 1 year			
Creditors for goods	720		
Creditors for overheads	100	820	
Net current assets			5,800
Total assets less current liabilities			10,750
Capital and reserves			
Called-up share capital			7,000
Profit and loss account (2,600+1,150)			3,750
			10,750

32.8 Capital budgeting

The plan for the acquisition of fixed assets such as machinery, buildings, etc. is usually known as a **capital budget**. Management will evaluate the various possibilities open to it, and will compare the alternatives. This is a very important part of budgeting. So far in this book it has been assumed that the capital budgeting has already been done.

Review questions 32.11 and 32.12 could now be attempted by you.

Part four: Further thoughts on budgets

The process of budgeting with the necessary participation throughout management, finally producing a profit plan, is now a regular feature in all but the smallest firms. Very often budgeting is the one time when the various parts of management can really get together and work as a team rather than just as separate parts of an organisation. When budgeting is conducted under favourable conditions, there is no doubt that a firm which budgets will tend to perform rather better than a similar firm that does not budget. Budgeting means that managers can no longer give general answers affecting the running of the firm; they have to put figures to their ideas, and they know that in the end their estimated figures are going to be compared with what the actual figures turn out to be.

It has often been said that the act of budgeting is possibly of more benefit than the budgets which are produced. However, the following benefits can be claimed for good budgeting:

1 The strategic planning carried out by the board of directors or owners can be more easily linked to the decisions by managers as to how the resources of the business will be used to try to achieve the objectives of the business. The strategic planning has to be converted into action, and budgeting provides the ideal place where such planning can be changed into financial terms.

2 Standards of performance can be agreed for the various parts of the business. If sales and production targets are set as part of a co-ordinated plan, then the sales department cannot really complain that production is insufficient if they had agreed previously to a production level and this is being achieved, nor can production complain if its production exceeds the amount budgeted for and it remains unsold.

3 The expression of plans in comparable financial terms. Some managers think mainly in terms of, say, units of production, or of tons of inputs or outputs, or of lorry mileage, etc. The effect that each of them has upon financial results must be brought home to them. For instance, a transport manager might be unconcerned about the number of miles that his haulage fleet of lorries covers until the cost of doing such a large mileage is brought home to him, often during budgeting, and it may be then and only then that he starts to search for possible economies. It is possible in many cases to use mathematics to find the best ways of loading vehicles, or to plan routes taken by vehicles so that fewer miles are covered and yet the same delivery service is maintained. This is just one instance of many when the expression of the plans of a section of a business in financial terms sparks off a search for economies, when otherwise such a search may never be started at all.

4 Managers can see how their work slots into the activities of the firm. It can help to get rid of the feeling of 'I'm only a number not a person', because managers can identify their positions within the firm and can see that their jobs really are essential to the proper functioning of the firm.

5 The budgets for a firm cannot be set in isolation. This means that the situation of the business, the nature of its products and its workforce, etc., must be seen against the economic background of the country. For instance it is no use budgeting for extra labour when labour is in extremely short supply, without realising the implications, possibly that of paying higher than normal wage rates. Increasing the sales target during a 'credit squeeze' needs a full investigation of the effect of the shortage of money upon the demand for the firm's goods and so on.

The charges made against budgeting are mainly that budgets bring about inflexibility, and that managers will not depart from budget even though the departure would bring about a more desirable result. Too many budgets are set at one level of sales or production when in fact flexible budgets (discussed below) ought to be used. It is very often the case that budgeting is forced upon managers against their will. Instead the firm should really set out first of all to do a 'selling job' to convince managers that budgets are not the monsters so often thought. A trial run for part of a business is far superior to starting off by having a fully detailed budget set up right away for the whole of the business. Learning to use budgets is rather like learning to swim. Let a child get used to the water first and remove its fear of the water, then it will learn to swim fairly easily. For most children (but not all), if the first visit to the baths meant being pushed into the deep end immediately, then reaction against swimming would probably set in. Let a manager become used to the idea of budgeting, without the fear of being dealt with severely during a trial period, and most managers will then become used to the idea and participate properly.

32.9 Flexible budgets

So far in this book budgets have been drawn up on the basis of one set of expectations, based on just one level of sales and production. Later, when the actual results are compared with the budgeted results expected in a fixed budget, they will have deviated for two reasons:

1   While the actual and budgeted volumes of production and sales may be the same there may be a difference on actual and budgeted costs.
2   The volumes of actual and budgeted units of sales and production may vary, so that the costs will be different because of different volumes.

The variations, or variances as they are more commonly known, are usually under the control of different managers in the organisation. Variances coming under (1) will probably be under the control of the individual department. On the other hand variances under (2) are caused because of variations in plans brought about by top management because of changing sales, or at least the expectation of changing sales.

Budgets are used for control purposes, therefore a manager does not take kindly to being held responsible for a variance in his spending if the variance is caused by a type (2) occurrence if he is working on a fixed budget. The answer to this is to construct budgets at several levels of volume, and to show what costs etc. they should incur at different levels. For instance, if a budget had been fixed at a volume of 500 units and the actual volume is 550, then the manager would undoubtedly feel aggrieved if his costs for producing 550 units were compared with the costs he should have incurred for 500 units. Budgets which do allow for changing levels are called **flexible budgets**.

To draft a full set of flexible budgets is outside the scope of this book, but an instance of one department's flexible budget for manufacturing overhead is shown in Exhibit 32.6.

Exhibit 32.6

Data Ltd
Budget for Manufacturing Overhead, Department S
(This would in fact be in greater detail)

Units	400	450	500	550	600
	£	£	£	£	£
Variable overhead	510	550	600	680	770
Fixed overhead	400	400	400	400	400
Total overhead (A)	£910	£950	£1,000	£1,080	£1,170
Direct labour hours (B)	200	225	250	275	300
Overhead rates (A) divided by (B)	£4.55	£4.22	£4.0	£3.92	£3.9

Notice that the variable costs in this case do not vary in direct proportion to production. In this case once 500 units production have been exceeded they start to climb rapidly. The flexible budget makes far greater sense than a fixed budget. For instance, if a fixed budget had been agreed at 400 units, with variable overhead £510, then if production rose to 600 units the manager would think the whole system unfair if he were expected to incur only £510 variable overhead (the figure for 400 units). On the contrary, if the comparison was on a flexible budget then costs at 600 units production would instead be compared with £770 (the figure at 600 units).

New terms

Budget (p. 443): A plan quantified in monetary terms in advance of a defined time period – usually showing planned income and expenditure and the capital employed to achieve a given objective.

Flexible budget (p. 457): A budget which, by recognising the difference in behaviour between fixed and variable costs in relation to fluctuations in output, turnover or other factors, is designed to change appropriately with such fluctuations.

Main points to remember

1 Budgets are prepared in order to guide the firm towards its objectives.

2 They should be drawn up within the context of *planning* and *control*.

3 While budgets are drawn up for control purposes, a budget should not be seen as a straitjacket.

4 There are a number of budgets that together comprise the 'master budget' and they must all reconcile to each other and to the master budget.

5 Budget preparation is often an iterative process as the master budget is focused more and more tightly to the objectives of the organisation.

6 Flexible budgeting permits managers to adjust their budgets in the light of variations in plan, often involving items over which they have no control.

Review questions

32.1 What would the production levels have to be for each month if the following data was available:

Units 19X5	Jan	Feb	Mar	Apr	May	Jun
(a) Stocks levels wanted at the end of each month	690	780	1,100	1,400	1,160	940
(b) Expected sales each month	800	920	1,090	1,320	1,480	1,020

(c) The stock level at 1 January, 19X5 will be 740 units.

32.2 For the year ended 31 December 19X9 the sales of units are expected to be:

January	110	July	70
February	180	August	30
March	170	September	170
April	150	October	110
May	120	November	150
June	100	December	190

The opening stock at 1 January 19X9 will be 140 units. The closing stock desired at 31 December 19X9 is 150 units.

Required:
(a) What will production be per month if an even production flow is required and stock levels during the year could be allowed to fall to zero?
(b) Given the same information plus the constraint that stock levels must never fall below 80 units, and that extra production will be undertaken in January 19X9 to ensure this, what will be the January production figure?

32.3A
(a) For each of the following, state three reasons why a firm may wish to keep:
  (i) a minimum stock level of finished goods, and
  (ii) an even level of production in the face of fluctuating demand.
(b) The sales forecast for Douglas & Co for July–December 19X7 is:

	J	A	S	O	N	D
Units	280	200	260	360	400	420

Produce a production budget showing monthly opening and closing stock figures if the firm wishes to maintain an even level of producing 300 units each month, and a minimum stock level of 150 units.
  What must the opening stock be at 1 July to achieve this?
(c) Under what circumstances, in budgetary control, may a firm's productive capacity prove to be its limiting or key factor?

(Associated Examining Board: GCE 'A' level)

32.4   Ukridge comes to see you in April 19X3. He is full of enthusiasm for a new product that he is about to launch on to the market. Unfortunately his financial recklessness in the past has led him into being bankrupted twice, and he has only just got discharged by the court from his second bankruptcy.

'Look here laddie,' he says, 'with my new idea I'll be a wealthy man before Christmas.'

'Calm down,' you say, 'and tell me all about it.'

Ukridge's plans as far as cash is concerned for the next six months are:

(*a*) Present cash balance (including bank) £5.

(*b*) Timely legacy under a will – being received on 1 May 19X3, £5,000. This will be paid into the business bank account by Ukridge.

(*c*) Receipts from debtors will be: May £400, June £4,000, July £8,000, August £12,000, September £9,000, October £5,000.

(*d*) Payments will be: May £100, June £5,000, July £11,000, August £20,000, September £12,000, October £7,000.

You are required:

(*a*) To draw up a cash budget, showing the balances each month, for the six months to 31 October 19X3.

(*b*) The only person Ukridge could borrow money from would charge interest at the rate of 100 per cent per annum. This is not excessive considering Ukridge's past record.
Advise Ukridge.

32.5   Draw up a cash budget for N Morris showing the balance at the end of each month, from the following information for the six months ended 31 December 19X2:

(*a*) Opening cash (including bank) balance £1,200

(*b*) Production in units:

19X2									19X3	
April	*May*	*June*	*July*	*Aug*	*Sept*	*Oct*	*Nov*	*Dec*	*Jan*	*Feb*
240	270	300	320	350	370	380	340	310	260	250

(*c*) Raw materials used in production cost £5 per unit. Of this 80 per cent is paid in the month of production and 20 per cent in the month after production.

(*d*) Direct labour costs of £8 per unit are payable in the month of production.

(*e*) Variable expenses are £2 per unit, payable one-half in the same month as production and one-half in the month following production.

(*f*) Sales at £20 per unit:

19X2									
Mar	*April*	*May*	*June*	*July*	*Aug*	*Sept*	*Oct*	*Nov*	*Dec*
260	200	320	290	400	300	350	400	390	400

Debtors to pay their accounts three months after that in which sales are made.

(*g*) Fixed expenses of £400 per month payable each month.

(*h*) Machinery costing £2,000 to be paid for in October 19X2.

(*i*) Will receive a legacy £2,500 in December 19X2.

(*j*) Drawings to be £300 per month.

32.6 Richard Toms has agreed to purchase the business of Norman Soul with effect from 1 August 19X7. Soul's budgeted working capital at 1 August 19X7 is as follows:

	£	£	£
Current assets			
Stock at cost	13,000		
Debtors	25,000		
		38,000	
Current liabilities			
Creditors	10,000		
Bank overdraft	20,000		
		30,000	
			8,000

In addition to paying Soul for the acquisition of the business, Toms intends to improve the liquidity position of the business by introducing £10,000 capital on 1 August 19X7. He has also negotiated a bank overdraft limit of £15,000. It is probable that 10 per cent of Soul's debtors will in fact be bad debts and that the remaining debtors will settle their accounts during August subject to a cash discount of 10 per cent. The opening creditors are to be paid during August. The sales for the first four months of Toms' ownership of the business are expected to be as follows: August £24,000, September £30,000, October £30,000 and November £36,000. All sales will be on credit and debtors will receive a two-month credit period. Gross profit will be at a standard rate of 25 per cent of selling price. In addition, in order to further improve the bank position and to reduce his opening stock, Toms intends to sell on 1 August 19X7 at cost price £8,000 of stock for cash. In order to operate within the overdraft limit Toms intends to control stock levels and to organise his purchases to achieve a monthly rate of stock turnover of 3. He will receive one month's credit from his suppliers.

General cash expenses are expected to be £700 per month.

Required:
(a) A stock budget for the four months ending 30 November 19X7 showing clearly the stock held at the end of each month.
(b) A cash budget for the four months ending 30 November 19X7 showing clearly the bank balance at the end of each month.

(*Associated Examining Board: GCE 'A' level*)

32.7A Ian Spiro, formerly a taxi-driver, decided to establish a car-hire business after inheriting £50,000.

His business year would be divided into budget periods each being four weeks.

He commenced business on a Monday the first day of period 1, by paying into a business bank account £34,000 as his initial capital.

All receipts and payments would be passed through his bank account.

The following additional forecast information is available on the first four budget periods of his proposed business venture.

1 At the beginning of period 1 he would purchase 6 saloon cars of a standard type; list price £6,000 each, on which he had negotiated a trade discount of 11 per cent.
2 He estimates that four of the cars will be on the road each Monday to Friday inclusive, and at weekends all six cars will be on the road. Hire charges as follows:

Weekday rate £10 per day per car
Weekend rate £18 per day per car

He estimates that this business trading pattern will commence on the Monday of the second week of period 1, and then continue thereafter.

All hire transactions are to be settled for cash.

Note: a weekend consists of Saturday and Sunday. All remaining days are weekdays.

3 An account was established with a local garage for fuel, and it was agreed to settle the account two periods in arrear. The forecast gallon usage is as follows:

Period 1	Period 2	Period 3	Period 4
200	200	400	500

The fuel costs £1.80 per gallon.

4 Servicing costs for the vehicles would amount to £300 per period, paid during the period following the service. Servicing would commence in period 1.

5 Each of his vehicles would be depreciated at 25 per cent per annum on a reducing balance basis.

6 Fixed costs of £200 per period would be paid each period.

7 He had agreed with a local firm to provide two cars on a regular basis, Monday to Friday inclusive, as chauffeur driven cars. The agreed rate was £60 a day (per car), payment being made in the following period.

This contract would not commence until the first day of period 2, a Monday.

8 Drawings: Periods 1 & 2   £400 a period.

                      Periods 3 &4   £800 a period.

9 Wages and salaries:

(a) Initially he would employ 3 staff, each on £320 a budget period. Employment would commence at the beginning of period 1.

(b) On commencement of the contract the two additional staff employed as chauffeurs would each receive £360 a budget period. Payments are to be made at the end of the relevant period.

10 In anticipation of more business being developed he planned to buy a further three cars for cash in period 4. The cars would cost £6,500 each and it was agreed he would be allowed a trade discount of 10 per cent.

Required:

(a) A detailed cash budget for the first four budget periods.

(b) An explanation as to why it is important that a business should prepare a cash budget.

(c) Identify how a sole proprietor may finance a forecast cash deficit distinguishing between internal and external financial sources.

(*Associated Examining Board: GCE 'A' level*)

32.8A A company's estimated pattern of costs and revenues for the first four months of 19X7 is as follows:

Cost and Revenues: January–April 19X7
(£000)

Month	Sales	Materials	Wages	Overheads
January	410.4	81.6	16.2	273.6
February	423.6	84.8	16.8	282.4
March	460.8	93.6	18.3	306.7
April	456.3	91.2	18.6	304.5

1 One-quarter of the materials are paid for in the month of production and the remainder two months later: deliveries received in November 19X6 were £78,400, and in December 19X6 £74,800.

2 Customers are expected to pay one-third of their debts a month after the sale and the remainder after two months: sales expected for November 19X6 are £398,400, and for December 19X6, £402,600.

3   Old factory equipment is to be sold in February 19X7 for £9,600. Receipt of the money is expected in April 19X7. New equipment will be installed at a cost of £38,000. One-half of the amount is payable in March 19X7 and the remainder in August 19X7.

4   Two-thirds of the wages are payable in the month they fall due, and one-third a month later: wages for December 19X6 are estimated at £15,900.

5   £50,000 of total monthly overheads are payable in the month they occur, and the remainder one month later: total overheads for December 19X6 are expected to be £265,200.

6   The opening bank balance at 1 January 19X7 is expected to be an overdraft of £10,600.

Required:

(*a*) Using the information above, prepare the firm's cash budget for the period January–April, 19X7.

(*b*) Provide a statement to show those items in part (*a*) which would appear in a budgeted balance sheet as at 30 April 19X7.

(*University of London: GCE 'A' level*)

32.9 D Smith is to open a retail shop on 1 January 19X4. He will put in £25,000 cash as capital. His plans are as follows:

(*i*)   On 1 January 19X4 to buy and pay for Premises £20,000, Shop fixtures £3,000, Motor van £1,000.

(*ii*)   To employ two assistants, each to get a salary of £130 per month, to be paid at the end of each month. (PAYE tax, National Insurance contributions, etc., are to be ignored.)

(*iii*) To buy the following goods (shown in units):

	Jan	Feb	Mar	Apr	May	Jun
Units	200	220	280	350	400	330

(*iv*)   To sell the following number of units:

	Jan	Feb	Mar	Apr	May	Jun
Units	120	180	240	300	390	420

(*v*)   Units will be sold for £10 each. One-third of the sales are for cash, the other two-thirds being on credit. These latter customers are expected to pay their accounts in the second month following that in which they received the goods.

(*vi*)   The units will cost £6 each for January to April inclusive, and £7 each thereafter. Creditors will be paid in the month following purchase. (Value stock-in-trade on FIFO basis.)

(*vii*) The other expenses of the shop will be £150 per month payable in the month following that in which they were incurred.

(*viii*) Part of the premises will be sub-let as an office at a rent of £600 per annum. This is paid in equal instalments in March, June, September and December.

(*ix*)   Smith's cash drawings will amount to £250 per month.

(*x*)   Depreciation is to be provided on Shop fixtures at 10 per cent per annum and on the Motor van at 20 per cent per annum.

You are required to:

(*a*) Draw up a cash budget for the six months ended 30 June 19X4, showing the balance of cash at the end of each month.

(*b*) Draw up a forecast trading and profit and loss account for the six months ended 30 June 19X4 and a balance sheet as at that date.

32.10A The summarised balance sheet of Newland Traders at 30 May 19X7 was as follows:

	£000	£000
Fixed assets at cost		610
Less depreciation		264
		346
Current assets		
Stocks	210	
Debtors	315	
Cash at bank and in hand	48	
	573	
Less Current liabilities		
Creditors	128	445
		791
Capital and reserves		
Issued capital		600
General reserve		150
Profit and loss account		41
		791

Selling and materials prices at 30 May 19X7 provide for a gross profit at the rate of 25 per cent of sales.

The creditors at 30 May 19X7 represent the purchases for May 19X7, and the debtors the sales for April of £150,000 and May of £165,000.

Estimates of sales and expenditure for the six months to 30 November 19X7 are as follows:

(i) Sales for the period at current prices will be £800,000. Sales for the months of September and October will each be twice those of the sales in each of the other months.

(ii) Stock at the end of each month will be the same as at 30 May 19X7 except that at 30 November 19X7 it will be increased to 20 per cent above that level.

(iii) Creditors will be paid one month after the goods are supplied and debtors will pay two months after the goods are supplied.

(iv) Wages and expenses will be £20,000 a month and will be paid in the month in which they are incurred.

(v) Depreciation will be at the rate of £5,000 a month.

(vi) There will be capital expenditure of £80,000 on 1 September 19X7. Depreciation, in addition to that given in (v) above, will be at the rate of 10 per cent per annum on cost.

(vii) There will be no changes in issued capital, general reserve or prices of sales or purchases.

Required:

(a) Sales and purchases budgets and budgeted trading and profit and loss accounts for the six months ended 30 November 19X7.

(b) A budgeted balance sheet as at 30 November 19X7.

(c) A cash flow budget for the six months ended 30 November 19X7 indicating whether or not it will be necessary to make arrangements for extra finance and, if so, your recommendation as to what form it should take.

Show all your calculations.

(*Welsh Joint Education Committee: GCE 'A' level*)

32.11 The balance sheet of Gregg Ltd at 30 June, 19X6 was expected to be as follows:

Balance Sheet 30 June 19X6

	Cost	Depreciation to date	Net
Fixed assets			
Land and buildings	40,000	–	40,000
Plant and machinery	10,000	6,000	4,000
Motor vehicles	6,000	2,800	3,200
Office fixtures	500	220	280
	56,500	9,020	47,480
Current assets			
Stock-in-trade: Finished goods		1,800	
Raw materials		300	
Debtors (19X6 May £990 + June £900)		1,890	
Cash and bank balances		7,100	11,090
			£58,570
Financed by			
Share capital			50,000
Profit and loss account			7,820
			57,820
Current Liabilities			
Creditors for raw materials			
(April £240 + May £140 + June £160)		540	
Creditors for variable overhead		210	750
			£58,570

The plans for the six months to 31 December 19X6 can be summarised as:

(*i*) Production costs per unit will be:

	£
Direct materials	2
Direct labour	5
Variable overhead	3
	£10

(*ii*) Sales will be at a price of £18 per unit for the three months to 30 September and at £18.5 subsequently. The number of units sold would be:

	Jul	Aug	Sep	Oct	Nov	Dec
Units	60	80	100	100	90	70

All sales will be on credit, and debtors will pay their accounts two months after they have bought the goods.

(*iii*) Production will be even at 90 units per month.

(*iv*) Purchases of direct materials – all on credit – will be:

	Jul	Aug	Sep	Oct	Nov	Dec
	£	£	£	£	£	£
	220	200	160	140	140	180

Creditors for direct materials will be paid three months after purchase.

(*v*) Direct labour is paid in the same month as production occurs.

(*vi*) Variable overhead is paid in the month following that in which the units are produced.

(*vii*)   Fixed overhead of £90 per month is paid each month and is never in arrears.
(*viii*) A machine costing £500 will be bought and paid for in July. A motor vehicle costing £2,000 will be bought and paid for in September.
(*ix*)   A debenture of £5,000 will be issued and the cash received in November. Interest will not start to run until 19X7.
(*x*)   Provide for depreciation for the six months: Motor vehicles £600, Office fixtures £30, Machinery £700.

You are required to draw up as a minimum:
(*a*)   Cash budget, showing figures each month.
(*b*)   Debtors' budget, showing figures each month.
(*c*)   Creditors' budget, showing figures each month.
(*d*)   Raw materials budget, showing figures each month.
(*e*)   Forecast operating statement for the six months.
(*f*) Forecast balance sheet as at 31 December 19X6.

In addition you may draw up any further budgets you may wish to show the workings behind the above budgets.

32.12A Len Auck and Brian Land trade as partners in Auckland Manufacturing Company making components for minicomputers. To cope with increasing demand the partners intend to extend their manufacturing capacity but are concerned about the effect of the expansion on their cash resources during the build-up period from January to April 19X6.

The following information is available.

(*a*)   The balance sheet of Auckland Manufacturing Company at 31 December 19X5 is expected to be:

	£	£
Fixed assets		
Plant and machinery at cost		65,000
Less depreciation		28,000
		37,000
Current assets		
Stocks – raw materials	10,500	
– finished goods	18,500	
Debtors	36,000	
Cash at bank	4,550	
	69,550	
Current liabilities		
Creditors	27,550	
		42,000
		£79,000
Partners' capital accounts		
Len Auck		40,000
Brian Land		39,000
		£79,000

(*b*)   Creditors at 31 December 19X5 are made up of:

Creditors for materials supplied in November and December at		
£13,000 per month	26,000	
Creditors for overheads	1,550	
	£27,550	

(c) New plant costing £25,000 will be delivered and paid for in January 19X6.

(d) Raw material stocks are to be increased to £12,000 by the end of January 19X6, thereafter raw material stocks will be maintained at that level. Payment for raw materials is made two months after the month of delivery. Finished goods stocks will be maintained at £18,500 throughout the period. There is no work in progress.

(e) Sales for the four months are expected to be:

	£
January	18,000
February	22,000
March	22,000
April	24,000

Sales for several months prior to 31 December had been running at the rate of £18,000 per month. It is anticipated that all sales will continue to be paid for two months following the month of delivery.

(f) The cost structure of the product is expected to be:

	%
Raw materials	50
Direct wages	20
Overheads, including depreciation	17½
Profit	12½
Selling price	100

(g) Indirect wages and salaries included in overheads amount to £900 for the month of January and £1,000 per month thereafter.

(h) Depreciation of plant and machinery (including the new plant) is to be provided at £700 per month and is included in the total overheads.

(i) Wages and salaries are to be paid in the month to which they relate; all other expenses are to be paid for in the month following the month to which they relate.

(j) The partners share profits equally and drawings are £400 per month each.

(k) During the period to April an overdraft facility is being requested.

Required:

(a) A forecast profit and loss account for the four months January to April 19X6 and a balance sheet as at 30 April 19X6.

(b) A month by month cash forecast for the four months showing the maximum amount of finance required during the period.

(c) A calculation of the month in which the overdraft facility would be repaid on the assumption that the level of activity in April is maintained.

For the purposes of this question taxation and bank interest may be ignored.

(*Chartered Association of Certified Accountants*)

33

Discounting techniques

Objectives

After you have studied this chapter, you should:

- *know why interest rates are important in financial decision making*

- *understand the difference between simple and compound interest*

- *know what is meant by and be able to calculate the annual percentage rate (APR)*

- *be able to calculate the present value of a series of cash flows*

- *be able to calculate and compare the net present value (NPV), internal rate of return (IRR), and payback of a series of cash flows*

- *be able to choose between alternative projects on the basis of NPV, IRR and payback*

- *understand and compute the effects of taxation upon capital project appraisal*

- *know what an annuity is and be able to calculate the value of ordinary annuities*

- *be able to calculate the annualised amount of a series of cash flows and select between alternative projects on that basis*

- *know the difference between operating and finance leases and be able to calculate the relevant figures for use in financial statements*

33.1 Different values

Would you rather be given £10 today or in 12 months' time? As time passes, money loses value due to the effects of inflation. When a transaction involves a delay in payment for the item purchased (e.g. a new car), the loss in value of the amount to be paid will be recovered by the seller charging the buyer interest. The delay also represents a period during which the seller could have invested the money and earned interest. This 'opportunity cost' of interest lost will also be charged to the buyer. The seller may have had to borrow money in order to provide the item purchased, and the interest cost incurred will be charged to the buyer. The seller will also add interest to the amount due in order to compensate for risk – the risk that the buyer will not pay the debt when due. Thus, the amount the buyer will be required to pay depends upon both the market rate of interest and the degree of risk in the debt, as perceived by the seller.

33.2 Interest rates

If a seller adds 10 per cent interest to a debt of £100, the required payment if made 1 year later is £100 + (10 per cent × £100 = £10) = £110. The interest in this case is known as 'simple interest' – 'simple' because the rate (10 per cent) is for one year, which matches the length of the debt. Interest rates generally indicate the percentage of the amount due that will be charged as interest if the debt is unpaid for a year.

If a 10 per cent interest rate is used, but the buyer is given two years to pay the debt, the second year's interest must be based on the amount due at the end of the first year – £110 (i.e. the original debt of £100 plus the £10 interest charged for the first year). The interest for the second year is therefore 10 per cent × £110 = £11, and the amount due at the end of the second year is the original debt (£100) + the first year's interest (£10) + the second year's interest (£11) = £121. This is known as 'compound interest' – 'compound' because the amount of interest due for years beyond the first year is calculated on the basis of how much is owed at the start of each year, i.e. the original amount plus all the interest to that date.

If the buyer offers to pay £121 in two years' time, instead of paying £100 today, providing the seller charges debtors 10 per cent interest, the value to the seller of the £121 in two years' time is £100 today. However, if the seller uses a 20 per cent interest rate, the £121 will only be worth £84.03. On the other hand, if the seller uses a 5 per cent interest rate, the £121 will be worth £109.75. These different values can be checked by applying the same approach as with the 10 per cent interest rate.

At 20 per cent, the interest for the first year on a debt of £84.03 will be £16.80, and the amount due at the end of one year will be £100.84. The second year's interest will be 20 per cent of £100.84, i.e. £20.17, and the total due at the end of the second year will be £121.

At 5 per cent, the interest for the first year on a debt of £109.75 will be £5.49, and the amount due at the end of one year will be £115.24. The second year's interest will be 5 per cent of £115.24, i.e. £5.76, and the total due at the end of the second year will be £121.

33.3 Simple interest

Simple interest on a debt of one year is, therefore, calculated using the formula:

$$\text{Amount of interest (Y)} = \text{Amount due (A)} \times \text{Interest rate (}r\text{)}$$

However, simple interest also applies to periods of less than a year. In order to calculate the interest on a shorter period, the period in question is expressed as a proportion of a year, and the formula is adjusted to:

$$\text{Amount of interest (Y)} = \text{Amount due (A)} \times \text{interest rate (}r\text{)} \times \text{fraction of a year (}t\text{)}$$

Example

Interest on a debt of £100 is to be charged at 10 per cent per annum. The debt will be repaid after 60 days. The interest due can be calculated using the formula:

$$Y = £100 \times 10\% \times (60/365) = £10 \times (60/365) = £1.64$$

33.4 Annual percentage rate (APR)

Sometimes, an interest rate that appears to be a 'simple interest' rate does not actually represent the 'real' rate charged. This can arise where, for example, a 10 per cent rate is charged on a debt for a year, but part of the debt must be repaid after six months, and the interest charge ignores the fact that there is early payment of part of the debt. This 'real' rate is known as the Annual Percentage Rate (APR). Hire purchase agreements are examples of debts where APR must be calculated in order to determine the 'real' cost incurred by the debtor.

Example

Interest on a debt of £100 is to be charged at 10 per cent per annum. However, £40 must be paid after six months, and the balance plus the interest at the end of the year.

					£
•	The interest to be paid is	10% of £100	$= y$	=	10
•	The amount due is	£100 for ½ year	=		50
		£ 60 for ½ year	=		30
•	The equivalent amount due for a year is		$= q$	=	80
•	The 'real' rate of interest		$= r$	=	Y/q
				=	10/80
				=	12.5% = the APR

Another typical example of APR arises when a business is owed money by its customers and it decides to sell the debt to a factor in order to obtain cash now. In these cases, the factor will pay the business an amount equal to the amount of the debt less a discount.

Example

A business is due £10,000 from a customer and the customer has agreed to make the payment in 90 days' time. The business approaches a debt factor who agrees to pay the amount due now, less a discount rate of 10 per cent. Applying the formula for debts of less than one year

Amount of interest (Y) = Amount due (A) × Interest rate (r) × Fraction of a year (t)

the discount charged is:

$$Y = £10,000 \times 10\% \times (90/365) = £1,000 \times (90/365) = £246.58$$

The debt factor will pay the business £10,000 less £246.58, i.e. £9,753.42. However, £246.58 does not represent a charge based on the amount of the advance (£9,753.42). Rather, it is based on the higher original amount of the customer's debt of £10,000. As a proportion of the £9,753.42 advanced by the debt factor, £246.58 represents an interest rate of 10.25 per cent. This can be seen by rewriting the formula for debts of less than one year to:

$$r = \frac{Y}{(A \times t)}$$

which, substituting the example values, gives:

$$r = \frac{246.58}{9,753.42 \times (90/365)}$$

$$= 10.25\%$$

A similar approach must be adopted with *bills of exchange* and *trade bill* interest rate calculations.

33.5 Compound interest

When more than a year is involved, the interest due is compounded, i.e. each year's interest charge is based on the amount outstanding, including all previous years' interest, at the beginning of the year. The graph shown in Exhibit 33.1 illustrates the difference between two investments of £1,000 at 10 per cent per annum for 20 years. In the first case, the interest is reinvested at the same 10 per cent rate and the final value of the investment is £6,727.50. In the other case, the interest is withdrawn as soon as it is paid, leaving only the original £1,000 invested, which is also the final value of the investment. However, 20 times £100, i.e. £2,000, has been received in interest over the 20 years, resulting in the overall value (ignoring inflation) being £3,000.

Exhibit 33.1

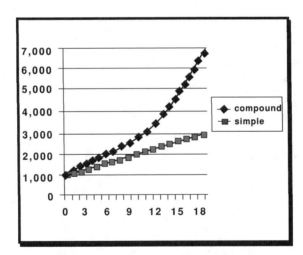

The final value of an investment that is subject to compound interest can be calculated laboriously by calculating the value at the end of the first year, calculating the interest on that amount for the next year, adding that interest to the amount at the start of the year to get the amount at the end of the year, and repeating the process for each year. However, there is a formula which enables the amount to be calculated swiftly:

Final value (V) = Amount invested (I) $\times (1 + r)^n$, where n = the number of years

Example

£10,000 invested today for five years at 10 per cent would have a final value (V) of:

$$
\begin{aligned}
V &= £1{,}000 \times (1+0.10)^5 \\
&= £1{,}000 \times (1.1)^5 \\
&= £1{,}000 \times 1.61051 \\
&= £1{,}610.51
\end{aligned}
$$

Calculations of this type are easily performed on most calculators, or by the use of tables. Where such calculations are performed regularly, it is quite common for a spreadsheet to be used to perform the calculation, often using the structure of a compound interest table within the spreadsheet to make it clear how the numbers used were derived. A compound interest table is included in Appendix II, but a shorter example is reproduced in Exhibit 33.2.

Exhibit 33.2 An example of a compound interest table

Compound Interest Table

Period
Length £1 *compounded at the end of each period at the interest rate shown*

n	1%	2%	3%	4%	5%	6%	7%	8%	9%	10%	n
1	1.010	1.020	1.030	1.040	1.050	1.060	1.070	1.080	1.090	1.100	1
2	1.202	1.040	1.061	1.082	1.103	1.124	1.145	1.166	1.188	1.210	2
3	1.030	1.061	1.093	1.125	1.158	1.191	1.225	1.260	1.295	1.331	3
4	1.041	1.082	1.126	1.170	1.216	1.262	1.311	1.360	1.412	1.464	4
5	1.051	1.104	1.159	1.217	1.276	1.338	1.403	1.469	1.539	1.611	5
6	1.062	1.126	1.194	1.265	1.340	1.419	1.501	1.587	1.677	1.772	6
7	1.072	1.149	1.230	1.316	1.407	1.504	1.606	1.714	1.828	1.949	7
8	1.083	1.172	1.267	1.369	1.477	1.594	1.718	1.851	1.993	2.144	8
9	1.094	1.195	1.305	1.423	1.551	1.689	1.838	1.999	2.172	2.358	9
10	1.105	1.219	1.344	1.480	1.629	1.791	1.967	2.159	2.367	2.594	10

n	11%	12%	13%	14%	15%	16%	17%	18%	19%	20%	n
1	1.110	1.120	1.130	1.140	1.150	1.160	1.170	1.180	1.190	1.200	1
2	1.232	1.254	1.277	1.300	1.323	1.346	1.369	1.392	1.416	1.440	2
3	1.368	1.405	1.443	1.482	1.521	1.561	1.602	1.643	1.685	1.728	3
4	1.518	1.574	1.630	1.689	1.749	1.811	1.874	1.939	2.005	2.074	4
5	1.685	1.762	1.842	1.925	2.011	2.100	2.192	2.288	2.386	2.488	5
6	1.870	1.974	2.082	2.195	2.313	2.436	2.565	2.700	2.840	2.986	6
7	2.076	2.211	2.353	2.502	2.660	2.826	3.001	3.185	3.379	3.583	7
8	2.305	2.476	2.658	2.853	3.059	3.278	3.511	3.759	4.021	4.300	8
9	2.558	2.773	3.004	3.252	3.518	3.803	4.108	4.435	4.785	5.160	9
10	2.839	3.106	3.395	3.707	4.046	4.411	4.807	5.234	5.695	6.192	10

Example

If you want to know how much will be held at the end of seven years if you invest £100 at 6 per cent compound interest per annum, the table in Exhibit 33.2 shows that it would be £100 times 1.504 = £1,504.

Sometimes, interest accumulates more frequently than once a year. It will often be paid every three months. If so, the rate of interest used in the formula must be changed to reflect this. To do this, the number of periods is multiplied by the number of payments being made each year, and the interest rate used is divided by the same amount. The formula can then be used with these adjusted values.

Example

If £100 is invested for two years at 12 per cent compound interest paid quarterly, the interest rate used in the calculation is 3 per cent (i.e. 12 per cent divided by four). The number of periods to use is eight (i.e. two multiplied by four). Looking up the table, the amount accumulated at the end of the two years will be £126.70. Compare that to the compounded amount if interest was paid annually, £125.40. The difference is very small. However, the investment was for a short period of time. Had it been for a longer period, the difference would have become progressively greater. When large amounts of money are being invested over a long period, an increased frequency of interest payments will have a significant effect upon the amount of interest received.

Over time, most investments change their value. Investments in the stock market or in houses, for example, are made without knowing what the rate of return (interest) will be. When the investment is ended and the final amount received is known, it is often useful to know what the rate of return over the period of the investment was. This can be done using the table. If an investment was made for five years, it is the five year row in the table that would be consulted. In that row, you would search for the number that represented the proportion that the final amount represented of the initial investment. The interest rate column in which that proportion lay would represent the average rate of return on the investment.

Example

If a house were bought for £100,000 on 1 January 19X1 and sold for £140,300 on 31 December 19X5, a five-year investment was made. The proportion that £140,300 represents of the £100,000 invested is 1.403:1. Looking up the table in the row where $n = 5$, a value of 1.403 can be seen in the 7 per cent interest rate column. The rate of return is equivalent to 7 per cent compound per annum. Where the proportion calculated is not shown in the table, the table can be used to identify an approximate rate which can then be adjusted in order to arrive at the accurate rate.

Example

If a house were bought for £100,000 on 1 January 19X1 and sold for £160,000 on 31 December 19X4, a four-year investment was made. The proportion that £160,000 represents of the £100,000 invested is 1.6:1. Looking up the table in the row where $n = 4$, a value of 1.574 can be seen in the 12 per cent column and 1.630 can be seen in the 13 per cent column. The difference between these two values is 0.056 (i.e. 1.630 − 1.574). The difference between 1.574 and the amount being searched for of 1.6 is 0.026, which represents 46 per cent of the total difference of 0.056 between the 12 per cent and 13 per cent amounts. Adding 0.46 to 12 produces a percentage return of 12.46 per cent.

Rather than using the tables to identify the rate of return, a formula can be used which is the final value formula (Final value (V) = Amount invested (I) $\times$ $(1 + r)^n$, where n = the number of years) rewritten to identify r:

$$r = \sqrt[n]{(V/I)} - 1$$

Substituting the values from the last example:

$$r = \sqrt[4]{(160{,}000/100{,}000)} - 1$$

$$= 12.46\%$$

33.6 Present value

Present value is the amount that a future cash flow is worth in terms of today's money. The £1,000 invested in the previous section for five years at 10 per cent compound resulted a final amount of £1,610.51, but what would be the value of that £1,610.51 at the date of the initial investment (i.e. today)? If it were known, it would be possible to tell whether the investment might be worthwhile.

To calculate present value, the formula to use has the same variables as that used to calculate compound interest, but it is rewritten to reflect that it is really the reciprocal of the compound interest formula:

$$\text{Amount invested (I)} = \frac{\text{Final value (V)}}{(1 + r)^n}$$

However, it would be more appropriate to describe the amount calculated as 'present value' rather than 'amount invested' and the formula becomes:

$$\text{Present value (PV)} = \frac{\text{Final value (V)}}{(1 + r)^n}$$

Example

A bank is offering a guaranteed return at the end of five years of £1,500 for every £1,000 invested. If you could usually expect to obtain a rate of interest of 8 per cent on your investments, what would be the present value of investing £1,000 in the bank?

$$\text{PV} = \frac{£1,500}{(1.08)^5} = £1,020.87$$

The 8 per cent interest rate used in this example is generally referred to as the 'discount rate', i.e. the rate at which the future flow of cash is discounted to arrive at its present value. As with compound interest, present value tables are generally used, and will often be created and used on spreadsheets. A present value table is included in Appendix II, but an extract is reproduced in Exhibit 33.3.

Exhibit 33.3 An example of a present value table

Present Value Table

Period
Length PV of £1 discounted over the period at the rate shown

n	1%	2%	3%	4%	5%	6%	7%	8%	9%	10%	n
1	0.990	0.980	0.971	0.961	0.952	0.943	0.935	0.926	0.917	0.909	1
2	0.980	0.961	0.943	0.925	0.907	0.890	0.873	0.857	0.842	0.826	2
3	0.971	0.942	0.915	0.889	0.864	0.840	0.816	0.794	0.772	0.751	3
4	0.961	0.924	0.889	0.855	0.823	0.792	0.763	0.735	0.708	0.683	4
5	0.951	0.906	0.863	0.822	0.784	0.747	0.713	0.681	0.650	0.621	5
6	0.942	0.888	0.838	0.790	0.746	0.705	0.666	0.630	0.596	0.564	6
7	0.933	0.871	0.813	0.760	0.711	0.665	0.623	0.583	0.547	0.513	7
8	0.923	0.853	0.789	0.731	0.677	0.627	0.582	0.540	0.502	0.467	8
9	0.914	0.837	0.766	0.703	0.645	0.592	0.544	0.500	0.460	0.424	9
10	0.905	0.820	0.744	0.676	0.614	0.558	0.508	0.463	0.422	0.386	10

n	11%	12%	13%	14%	15%	16%	17%	18%	19%	20%	n
1	0.901	0.893	0.885	0.877	0.870	0.862	0.855	0.847	0.840	0.833	1
2	0.812	0.797	0.783	0.769	0.756	0.743	0.731	0.718	0.706	0.694	2
3	0.731	0.712	0.693	0.675	0.658	0.641	0.624	0.609	0.593	0.579	3
4	0.659	0.636	0.613	0.592	0.572	0.552	0.534	0.516	0.499	0.482	4
5	0.593	0.567	0.543	0.519	0.497	0.476	0.456	0.437	0.419	0.402	5
6	0.535	0.507	0.480	0.456	0.432	0.410	0.390	0.370	0.352	0.335	6
7	0.482	0.452	0.425	0.400	0.376	0.354	0.333	0.314	0.296	0.279	7
8	0.434	0.404	0.376	0.351	0.327	0.305	0.285	0.266	0.249	0.233	8
9	0.391	0.361	0.333	0.308	0.284	0.263	0.243	0.226	0.209	0.194	9
10	0.352	0.322	0.295	0.270	0.247	0.227	0.208	0.191	0.176	0.162	10

Frequently, the cash flows arising from an investment arise throughout the period of the investment, not simply at the end. To calculate the overall present value of all the cash flows, each is calculated separately, and all the resulting present values are added together.

Example

An investment of £10,000 is made for five years. The net cash flows at the end of each of the five years are:

Period	Amount £
1	2,000
2	3,000
3	4,000
4	3,000
5	1,000

If the discount rate used is 10 per cent, the overall present value of the net cash flows is calculated as:

Period	Amount £	Discount factor 10%	Present value £
1	2,000	0.909	1,818
2	3,000	0.826	2,478
3	4,000	0.751	3,004
4	3,000	0.683	2,049
5	1,000	0.621	621
		Overall present value of cash flows	9,970

When compared to the initial investment of £10,000, it can be seen that this investment would lose £30 (i.e. £10,000 − £9,970). To make it easier to see this figure, these calculations usually incorporate the initial investment (which is not discounted as it is already at today's value) and produce a figure known as the **net present value**, or NPV. Incorporating the initial investment into this example produces the following table:

Period	Amount £	Discount factor 10%	Present value £
0	(10,000)	1.000	(10,000)
1	2,000	0.909	1,818
2	3,000	0.826	2,478
3	4,000	0.751	3,004
4	3,000	0.683	2,049
5	1,000	0.621	621
		Net present value	(30)

Many businesses have a rate of return that they require to achieve on investments. If a potential investment is not expected to achieve that rate of return, the investment will not be made. It is always possible to adopt the NPV approach in order to determine whether the return exceeds the required rate (which is shown by a positive NPV). However, it is often useful to know what the actual rate of return is – the proposed investment may, for example, require that some additional financing be obtained that would be at a higher rate than the business's normal rate of return.

The actual rate of return is known as the **internal rate of return,** or IRR. It is the discount rate that results in an NPV of zero. It can be calculated very easily using a spreadsheet – a table similar to the one above would be written in the spreadsheet, but the discount factor would be left blank. Then, by instigating an appropriate command, the spreadsheet would identify and insert the IRR into the table so as to arrive at an NPV of zero.

However, spreadsheets are not always available and IRR may need to be calculated manually. The method to adopt is similar to that adopted in the final example in section 33.5 – a guess is made as to an appropriate IRR and the NPV calculation is made using that rate. If the NPV is positive, a higher rate is selected (a lower rate is selected if the NPV is negative) and the NPV is again calculated. This continues until one positive NPV and one negative NPV are identified. The absolute difference between the two NPVs is calculated and the proportion of that difference that represents the difference between the NPV of the lower of the rates involved and zero is added to the lower rate to produce the IRR.

Example

You have been asked if you would be willing to lend £10,000 to a taxi company in order that it may expand its fleet of taxis. The money would be repaid at the rate of £3,000 per annum for four years. What is the IRR?

Step one is to select a rate that may be approximately correct. There is no simple way to select such a rate, and what would often be done is that the same rate would be used as the first step with most IRR calculations, and then the choice of the second rate to use would depend on how close to zero the first attempt came, and on whether the NPV it gave was positive or negative. If an 8 per cent rate is used, the following results:

Period	Amount £	Discount factor 8%	Present value £
0	(10,000)	1.000	(10,000)
1	3,000	0.926	2,778
2	3,000	0.857	2,571
3	3,000	0.794	2,382
4	3,000	0.735	2,205
		Net present value	(64)

Using the 8 per cent rate resulted in an NPV that was less than zero. The next rate chosen must, therefore, be less than 8 per cent. A 7 per cent rate produces the following:

Period	Amount £	Discount factor 7%	Present value £
0	(10,000)	1.000	(10,000)
1	3,000	0.935	2,805
2	3,000	0.873	2,619
3	3,000	0.816	2,448
4	3,000	0.763	2,289
		Net present value	161

Therefore, the IRR lies between 7 per cent and 8 per cent. The difference between the two NPVs is 225 (i.e. 64 + 161). A zero NPV will result if the rate is set to 7 per cent plus 161/225 (as 7 per cent is 161 away from zero). Expressed as a decimal, 161/225 = 0.72 and the IRR is, therefore, 7.72 per cent.

33.7 Annuities

Annuities are often thought of as a form of life assurance whereby, in return for the payment of a single lump sum, the 'annuitant' receives regular amounts of income over a predefined term (i.e. number of years). The frequency of the payments to the annuitant will depend upon the agreement reached, but would generally be either monthly, quarterly, six-monthly or annually. In some cases, the original investment will be repaid at the end of the agreed term, in others it is not. It is also possible for the agreement to include the annuitant making a number of payments, rather than paying everything in a single lump sum.

The timing of the payments to the annuitant vary from annuity to annuity – for example, some involve the regular payments to the annuitant being made at the start of each period, others have the payments at the end of each period.

There is a large range of possible arrangements that can be incorporated into an annuity, and it is not possible to describe how to deal with each of them. However, by concentrating upon one specific form of annuity – one in which equal payments are made to the annuitant at the end of each period – the basic principles to be applied can be identified. These principles can then be applied to more complex situations and, as a result, there should be very few circumstances when, with a little thought, it should not be possible to perform the appropriate calculation.

Many forms of business transaction are annuity-like, and a knowledge of the calculation of annuities can be useful, for example when considering rental agreements, hire purchase and leases.

33.8 Calculation of the value of ordinary annuities

When calculating the value of an annuity, it can be helpful to think of it as being similar to the calculation of compound interest, but one period in arrears. Thus, when considering compound interest, it would be assumed that an investment of £1,000 in year two was made at the start of the year. For an annuity, all the payments are assumed to arise at the end of a year, and interest on a payment made in year two would only start to accumulate during year three – there would be no interest in year two on that part of the annuity.

The following formula may be used to calculate the value of an annuity:

$$\text{Value} = \text{Annuity per period} \times \frac{(1+r)^n - 1}{r}$$

It can be applied to calculate the final value of a series of regular payments where a set rate of interest is being earned. For example, if £1,000 is being saved at the end of each year for five years and the interest rate is 10 per cent, the amount accumulated at the end of the fifth year will be:

$$
\begin{aligned}
\text{Value} &= £1,000 \times \frac{(1+0.10)^5 - 1}{5} \\
&= £1,000 \times 6.1051 \\
&= £6,105.10
\end{aligned}
$$

This can be confirmed by treating each of the five payments as individual compound interest calculations:

Year	Invested £	Formula	Value £
1	1,000	£1,000 × (1 + 0.10)^4	1,464.10
2	1,000	£1,000 × (1 + 0.10)^3	1,331.00
3	1,000	£1,000 × (1 + 0.10)^2	1,210.00
4	1,000	£1,000 × (1 + 0.10)^1	1,100.00
5	1,000	£1,000 × (1 + 0.10)	1,000.00
			6,105.10

Tables can also be used. The one provided in Appendix II also confirms that the value of an annuity of £1 for five years at 10 per cent would be £6.105, i.e. £1 times the multiplier of 6.105 given in the table.

Example

As an alternative to calculating the value of an annuity when the amounts paid are known, it can often be useful to know how much should be set aside regularly in order to accumulate a certain amount at the end of a given period. For example, if it was intended to purchase equipment estimated to cost £10,000 in five years' time, and a 10 per cent interest rate was being offered for regular investments over a five-year period, the annuity formula can be rewritten so as to provide the amount to set aside:

$$\text{Annuity per period} \quad = \quad \frac{\text{Value} \times (r)}{(1 + r)^n - 1}$$

$$= \quad \frac{£10,000 \times 0.10}{(1.10)^5 - 1}$$

$$= \quad £1,637.97$$

As mentioned previously, the multiplier given in the annuity table for a five-year annuity at 10 per cent is 6.105. If £1,637.97 is multiplied by 6.105, it confirms the annuity has a final value (to the nearest £1) of £10,000. It is also possible to confirm the annuity per period does result in the correct final value of £10,000 by creating a payment plus interest table:

Annuity paid	Payment £	Interest £	Increase in fund £	Balance of fund £
end of year 1	1,637.97	–	1,637.97	1,637.97
end of year 2	1,637.97	163.80	1,801.77	3,439.74
end of year 3	1,637.97	343.97	1,981.94	5,421.68
end of year 4	1,637.97	542.17	2,180.14	7,601.82
end of year 5	1,637.97	760.18	2,398.15	9,999.97

33.9 Calculation of the present value of ordinary annuities

If faced with a choice of paying for something now, or paying for it in instalments over the next year, it is useful to know which is the cheaper of the two alternatives. For example, a business may purchase a new computer costing £1,000 and have a choice of paying £1,000 now, or £200 per month for six months. It seems that the second option will be more expensive because £1,200 (i.e. six times £200) would be paid instead of £1,000.

In order to be able to compare the two alternatives, the payments must all be discounted to arrive at their cost expressed in terms of today's money, i.e. to arrive at their present values. Whether it really is more expensive to pay by instalments will depend on the discount rate used in the calculation.

As with the calculation of the value of an ordinary annuity, tables are available for the calculation of the present value of an ordinary annuity. A full table is provided in Appendix II and it shows the value now of £1 per period for n periods when an organisation uses a discount rate of r. When payments are made more frequently than once per annum, the discount rate used should be reduced accordingly – that is, if payments are half-yearly, the rate is halved; if they are made every month, the rate is divided by 12.

The formula for calculating the present value of an ordinary annuity is:

$$\text{Present value} \quad = \quad \text{payment} \times \left[\dfrac{1 - \dfrac{1}{(1+r)^n}}{r}\right]$$

If a 12 per cent rate were used with the above example, the rate of 12 per cent would be divided by 12 for the calculation and the present value would be:

$$\text{Present value} \quad = \quad £100 \times \left[\dfrac{1 - \dfrac{1}{(1+0.01)^6}}{0.01}\right]$$

$$= \quad £579.55$$

The multiplier in the table in Appendix II for 1 per cent over 6 periods is 5.795 which, when multiplied by the payment of £100, confirms a present value of £579.50.

It can be shown that this is the amount required if a table of interest and withdrawals is constructed (interest is at the same rate as above – 1 per cent per month):

Period	Balance b/f £	Interest £	Payment £	Balance c/f £
1	579.55	5.80	(100)	485.35
2	485.35	4.85	(100)	390.20
3	390.20	3.90	(100)	294.10
4	294.10	2.94	(100)	197.04
5	197.04	1.97	(100)	99.01
6	99.01	0.99	(100)	–

33.10 Capital project appraisal

If you had £5,000 to spend today and had the choice of investing it in a five-year bond with a bank, or lending it to a friend who had just opened a restaurant and who offered you 10 per cent of the profits for five years, plus the return of your £5,000 at the end of the five years, which alternative would you choose?

Organisations make vast numbers of short-term decisions. They make comparatively few long-term decisions. These long-term decisions involve investing resources in something and then receiving the benefits. Examples include:

- building a new production facility;
- buying a new delivery truck;
- sponsoring a local football team for three years;
- building a bridge;
- buying an airline;
- making a new product;
- starting a new business.

Generally, only the incremental cash payments and receipts arising from the decision to invest are relevant. The relevant costs include interest, but not items that normally appear in the calculation of profit but which do not involve cash – depreciation, for example. There are two aspects of the incremental cash flows that should be distinguished: the cash outflows resulting from the decision to invest, and the cash inflows arising as a result of investing. The difference between these two groups of incremental cash flows determines whether or not an investment is made.

The techniques used to aid the selection of the appropriate long-term decision are referred to collectively as **capital project appraisal**. There are three generally acceptable capital project appraisal techniques in common use. Two have already been introduced in section 33.6 – **net present value** and **internal rate of return**. Collectively, these two are known as **discounted cash flow (DCF) techniques**, as they involve the discounting of future net cash flows of a capital project to find their present value. Both techniques assume that all cash flows occur at the end of a period.

The third technique, **payback**, involves selecting the alternative that repays the initial investment in the shortest time, providing that it does not exceed the business's maximum acceptable payback period – its payback hurdle period. It is useful when cash resources are limited and swift repayment of the investment is vital for the maintenance of working capital. Also, because risks of problems arising increase with the length of an investment, payback reduces the risk by minimising the relevant length of investment. In contrast to the DCF techniques, payback assumes all cash flows occur evenly over a period.

A fourth technique, accounting rate of return (ARR), having once been very popular, is now falling into disuse as technology becomes more sophisticated, and those performing these calculations become more aware of the benefits of using the other three techniques in preference to ARR. The technique uses profits rather than cash flows and it involves dividing the average return by the average investment over the period, i.e. if £10,000 is invested and the return is £30,000 over a ten-year period, there would be a return of £3,000 per year (£30,000 ÷ 10). If the £10,000 is repaid at the end of the ten years, the average investment is £10,000 (i.e. [£10,000 + £10,000] ÷ 2). Therefore, the (annual) accounting rate of return is £3,000 divided by £10,000, i.e. 30 per cent. Although it is generally easy to calculate, ARR produces a percentage figure that is of little practical use. It cannot, for example, be compared to an organisation's cost of capital in order to assess whether a project would achieve a greater return than the cost of the capital that financed it. It also ignores the timing of cash flows – a project whose profits all arose at the start would be rejected in favour of one with a higher ARR whose profits all came at the end, even if inflation meant that those later period profits were worth significantly less in present value terms than the earlier profits of the rejected project.

Example

When considering a capital project proposal, the first step is to identify all the incremental cash flows that would arise were the decision taken to proceed with the investment. As most decisions of this type involve cash flows over a number of years, once identified, the cash flows are then mapped against the year in which they arise.

A new machine would cost £10,000 and installation would cost a further £1,000. It would replace an existing machine that would be sold for £2,000. The machine would generate cash income of £2,500 per annum for four years, at the end of which it would be sold for £3,000.

The cash flows are:

Period		Amount
		£
0	purchase + installation – sale proceeds	(9,000)
1	income	2,500
2	income	2,500
3	income	2,500
4	income (including sale proceeds)	5,500
		4,000

If the business's cost of capital is 10 per cent, that would be the discount rate used and the net present value (as previously illustrated in section 33.6) would be:

Period	Amount £	Discount factor 10%	Present value £
0	(9,000)	1.000	(9,000.00)
1	2,500	0.909	2,272.50
2	2,500	0.826	2,065.00
3	2,500	0.751	1,877.50
4	5,500	0.683	3,756.50
		Overall net present value of cash flows	971.50

As the NPV is positive, the internal rate of return is higher than 10 per cent. A 15 per cent discount factor produces a negative NPV of £144:

Period	Amount £	Discount factor 15%	Present value £
0	(9,000)	1.000	(9,000)
1	2,500	0.870	2,175
2	2,500	0.756	1,890
3	2,500	0.658	1,645
4	5,500	0.572	3,146
		Overall net present value of cash flows	(144)

Interpolating between these two values, as in section 33.6, the IRR is found to be 14.35 per cent. (The absolute difference is £1,115.50 (i.e. £971.50 + £144), of which approximately 87 per cent (£971.50) is represented by the proportion relating to the 10 per cent NPV. Multiplying the difference between the two discount rates (15% – 10% = 5%) by 87 per cent gives an answer to two decimal places of 4.35 per cent. This is then added to 10 per cent to produce the IRR of 14.35 per cent.) On the basis that the business's cost of capital is 10 per cent, this project will be financially beneficial. Substituting the discount rate of 14.35 per cent into the table produces a net present value of minus 10, the failure to reach a value of zero being due to rounding.

Period	Amount £	Discount factor 14.35%	Present value £
0	(9,000)	1.000	(9,000.00)
1	2,500	0.875	2,187.50
2	2,500	0.765	1,912.50
3	2,500	0.669	1,672.50
4	5,500	0.585	3,217.50
		Overall net present value of cash flows	(10.00)

These two DCF techniques generally arrive at selection of the same alternative when faced with a choice between two or more alternative projects. However, they can produce different choices and when they do, it is the NPV choice that should be selected.

As the following schedule shows, payback on the machine occurs after 3.27 years:

Period	Amount £	Balance £	
0	(9,000)	(9,000)	
1	2,500	(6,500)	
2	2,500	(4,000)	
3	2,500	(1,500)	
4	5,500	–	Payback at 3 plus 1,500/5,500 years = 3.27 years

This will then be compared to the business's hurdle period for payback. If it is later than the hurdle period, the project will be rejected. When cash flow is important, for example when the cost of capital is high, or when the risks in a project increase significantly the longer it runs, payback provides a measure of how quickly the investment in the project will be repaid, any subsequent cash flows being viewed as a bonus. However, it can result in a project being selected that is considerably less profitable than another that happens to take longer to repay the investment in it. It also ignores the time value of money. ('Real' payback will always be later than revealed by calculation as later receipts are not worth so much in today's money as early ones due to inflation.)

Closer inspection of the approach reveals that payback ignores everything after the (first) breakeven point. Applied blindly, it is not concerned about whether a project breaks even overall – only that the amount invested in a project is reduced to zero at some stage. If a project breaks even in three years, but then requires more investment in year five, only finally breaking even in year six, this can easily be overlooked when calculating payback.

These deficiencies in the payback approach can be addressed by discounting all cash flows to their present values, and by ensuring that the calculation includes a check for there being multiple payback points. While the first is generally sensible, the second is essential if payback is to be effectively applied.

33.11 Taxation

One factor often overlooked in consideration of capital projects is taxation. Items of equipment acquired will give rise to tax allowances that can be used to reduce tax payable, and any incremental profits arising from a capital project will give rise to payments of tax. Once calculated, the impact of taxation on the incremental cash flows is taken into account in the same way as any other item of incremental income or expenditure.

Example

A new machine costing £10,000 has an estimated useful economic life of four years, after which it will be scrapped. During those four years, it is expected to generate sales of £5,000 per annum. Production costs are anticipated to be 40 per cent of sales revenue. Working capital of £3,000 will be required for this activity, all of which will be recovered when the machine is scrapped. Depreciation is by the straight line method, i.e. £2,500 per annum starting in year one. Corporation tax of 40 per cent is paid nine months after the end of each accounting period. A writing-down allowance of 25 per cent (reducing balance) will be available if the machine is acquired.

The expected annual profit is:

	£	£
Sales		5,000
Production costs	2,000	
Depreciation	2,500	
		(4,500)
		500
Corporation tax		(200)
Net profit after tax		£300

The expected cash flows that would be used for the capital project appraisal are:

Investment (£)	Year: 1	2	3	4	5
Machine	(10,000)				
Working capital	(3,000)			3,000	
Tax allowance		1,000	750	562.50	1,687.50
	(13,000)	1,000	750	3,562.50	1,687.50
Cash flows (£)					
Sales	5,000	5,000	5,000	5,000	
Production costs	(2,000)	(2,000)	(2,000)	(2,000)	
Tax (40% × £3,000)		(1,200)	(1,200)	(1,200)	(1,200)
	3,000	1,800	1,800	1,800	(1,200)
Net cash flows (£)	(10,000)	2,800	2,550	5,362.50	487.50

(The overall tax allowances are £4,000, which is 40 per cent of the cost of the equipment, for which it has been assumed that there will be no scrap proceeds. Also, the cost of the machine and additional working capital would be treated as having arisen in year zero for the purposes of the capital project appraisal techniques. They are shown in year one in the above table so as to clarify the timing of the tax and tax allowance cash flows.)

33.12 Annualised figures

It can be difficult comparing projects that have different lengths. To overcome this complication, it is possible to use annualised amounts. Notionally, this approach assumes that the comparison would then be made over a period that represented the lowest common multiple of the projects – a twelve-year cycle would be used for two projects, one of three years' duration, the other four. However, as will be seen, once the annualised amounts are calculated, the decision can be taken without reference to any particular length of time.

The first step is to calculate the present value of the projects and then identify the amount of the annuity for the period of each project that has the same present value as that project's NPV. For example, if a discount rate of 10 per cent is used and the NPV of the three-year project is £500, the annuity multiplier (from the table in Appendix II) is 2.487 and the three-year annuity with a present value of £500 is therefore £201 (i.e. £500 ÷ 2.487). If the four-year project has an NPV of £800, the four-year annuity is £252 (i.e. £800 ÷ 3.170). On the basis of these annualised amounts, the four-year project would be selected.

33.13 Leasing

Under a lease, the lessee agrees to pay a rental to the lessor for use of something for a period of time. Lease rental payments are treated as allowable expenses for tax, whereas assets that are purchased are only eligible for a partial deduction against tax in the form of a capital allowance. The lessor claims the capital allowances on the assets leased. The lessee charges all the lease rental payments against income.

Leasing exists because both lessee and lessor can benefit from the arrangement as a result of their differing tax positions and capital raising abilities. A small company may find it very expensive, possibly impossible, to borrow £200,000 for some new equipment, whereas a large leasing company would be able to raise the funds at a very competitive rate.

An organisation acquiring an asset will often consider whether leasing may be preferable to outright purchase. As the cost, expected useful economic life, anticipated scrap value, and leasing charges can all be identified, it is possible to identify the APR of the lease. That can then be used to assess whether it would be preferable to lease rather than buy the asset.

Example

A printing machine costing £200,000 has an expected useful economic life of ten years. Scrap value of the machine is expected to be zero, as the rate of obsolescence on machinery of this type is very high. The machine could be leased for £32,547 per annum. The APR is the interest rate that is found when the cost of the machine is equal to the present value of the annual rental payments. That is, it is the interest rate for which the ten-year multiplier will convert £32,547 into £200,000. £200,000 divided by £32,547 is 6.145. In the 10 year row of the annuity table in Appendix II, 6.145 is the multiplier for an interest rate of 10 per cent which is, therefore, the APR of the lease. If the multiplier being sought lay part-way between two values in the annuity table, the APR would be identified by interpolation, as in the calculation of IRR.

Normally, tax would be taken into account in identifying the APR of a lease. Ignoring the time lags inherent in the tax system, as the expense is charged directly against income, if the tax rate is 40 per cent, in the above example the net of tax cost of the lease would be 60 per cent of £32,547 (i.e. £19,528) and the APR would be 60 per cent of 10 per cent, i.e. 6 per cent. This could then be compared to the organisation's cost of capital after tax in order to assess whether to lease or purchase the machine.

So far as the option to purchase is concerned, an annualised cost approach can be used. The cost of £200,000 would be assumed to occur at year zero. If 100 per cent capital allowances were available on the machine, at a tax rate of 40 per cent, there would be a tax saving equivalent to 40 per cent of £200,000 in year one. If the organisation's net of tax cost of capital is 8 per cent, the £80,000 tax saving would be discounted to £74,080 (i.e. £80,000 × 0.926), leaving a net present value of £125,920. The annualised cost is, therefore, £125,920 ÷ 6.710 (which is the annuity multiplier for 10 years at 8 per cent), i.e. £18,766. When compared to the net of tax cost of the lease of £19,528, this suggests that it might be preferable to purchase the machine.

As an alternative, the £125,920 net present value of buying the machine (as derived in the annualised cost calculation) can be compared to the NPV of the lease payments. The net of tax NPV of leasing is the net of tax rental (£19,528) multiplied by the present value multiplier of a ten-year annuity at 8 per cent (6.710), i.e. £131,033.

33.14 Financial implications of leasing

Despite the existence of a legal obligation to continue paying rental on a lease, neither the extent of the obligation to the lessor, nor the benefits obtainable under the lease normally appear on the face of the lessee's balance sheet. However, a lease often represents the equivalent of a loan. The equivalent loan is the NPV of the outstanding lease payments discounted at the pre-tax rate of interest. For example, the NPV of a ten-year lease with rental of £32,547 and a pre-tax rate of interest of 10 per cent would be £32,547 × 6.145 = £200,000.

33.15 Accounting for leases

Leases are either **finance** leases or **operating** leases. SSAP 21: *Accounting for leases and hire purchase contracts* defines the difference between them. The principal characteristic of a finance lease is that substantially all the risks and rewards of ownership are transferred to the lessee. Various steps are described in SSAP 21 that should be followed in order to determine whether a finance lease exists. These involve determining whether the present value of the minimum lease payments amount to substantially all (normally 90 per cent) of the fair value of the asset.

However, if the substance of the lease is to have the opposite effect, then it should be categorised accordingly. At the end of the day, it is the substance (i.e. what is actually happening to the risks and rewards of ownership) rather than the form of the transaction that decides whether there exists a finance or an operating lease.

Hire purchase contracts will usually be of a financing nature and treated in the same way as finance leases.

When a lease is classified as 'operating', it is deemed to still be an asset of the lessor. Both lessor and lessee take the rentals to the profit and loss account. The lessor should also record the fixed asset and depreciate it over its useful life.

An asset held under a finance lease is deemed to 'belong' to the lessee, who should capitalise it and make a corresponding entry in creditors. The initial value used should be the present value of the minimum lease payments. Depreciation should then be provided over the shorter of the lease term and the asset's useful life, except in the case of a hire purchase contract, under which circumstances the asset should be depreciated over its useful life. As each payment is made, the proportion which relates to the creditor balance should be applied to reduce that balance. The rest of the payment should be treated as a lease charge in the profit and loss account for the period.

Lessors should initially record the amount due under a finance lease as a debtor using the amount of the net investment in the lease. As each payment is received, the proportion which relates to payment of the debtor balance should be applied to reduce that balance. The rest of the receipt should be treated as lease income in the profit and loss account for the period.

Operating leases are accounted for in the same way as most revenue expenditure and income. Finance leases, however, are much more complex. The rental payments comprise a mixture of capital and revenue, and they must be separated and recorded differently. An approach called the actuarial method is generally used. Under this approach, it is first necessary to calculate the real rate of interest implied in the lease. This requires that information is available concerning the rental payments, the lease period and the cash value of the asset at the start of the lease.

Example

Quarterly rental on a leased computer is £400, the lease period is 12 quarters from 1 January 19X4, and the cash value of the computer at 1 January 19X4 is £4,000. The interest rate implied in the lease is that which produces a present value for the 12 payments of £400 equal to £4,000. Note, the first payment is at the start of the lease, yet ordinary annuity calculations relate to payments at the end of periods. In order to bring the example into line with this assumption, the first payment is offset against the cash value, reducing it to £3,600, and the annuity is calculated over 11 periods rather than 12.

The factor for 11 periods is $\dfrac{£3,600}{400} = 9$

From the tables   3%   =   9.253

                      4%   =   8.760

By interpolation, the gap between 3 per cent and the rate is 253/493 = 0.513, therefore, the interest rate implied in the lease is 3.513 per cent This can be verified by substituting the rate and other information into the formula given in section 33.9:

$$\text{Present value} \quad = \quad \text{Payment} \times \left[\frac{1 - \dfrac{1}{(1+r)^n}}{r} \right]$$

$$3{,}600 \quad = \quad \pounds 400 \times \left[\frac{1 - \dfrac{1}{(1+0.035153)^{11}}}{0.03513} \right]$$

$$3{,}600 \quad = \quad \pounds 400 \times \quad 9$$

Applying the rate of interest of 3.513 to the lease data produces the data in Exhibit 33.4.

Exhibit 33.4 Calculation of the periodic finance charge in the lease

Quarter	Capital sum at start of period £	Rental paid £	Capital sum during period £	Finance charge (3.513% per quarter) £	Capital sum at end of period £
19X4 – 1	4,000	400	3,600	126	3,726
2	3,726	400	3,326	117	3,443
3	3,443	400	3,043	107	3,150
4	3,150	400	2,750	96	2,846
19X5 – 1	2,846	400	2,446	86	2,532
2	2,532	400	2,132	75	2,207
3	2,207	400	1,807	63	1,870
4	1,870	400	1,470	51	1,521
19X6 – 1	1,521	400	1,121	39	1,160
2	1,160	400	760	27	787
3	787	400	387	13	400
4	400	400	–	–	–
		4,800		800	

The finance charges for each year of the lease are:

	£
19X4 (126 + 117 + 107 + 96)	= 446
19X5 (86 + 75 + 63 + 51)	= 275
19X6 (39 + 27 + 13)	= 79
	800

The overall picture in each of the three years is:

Year	Total rental £	less	Finance charge £	=	Capital repayment £
19X4	1,600		446		1,154
19X5	1,600		275		1,325
19X6	1,600		79		1,521

In the balance sheet of the lessee, the liability under the finance lease would be:

Year	Obligations under finance lease at start of year £	less	Capital repayment £	=	Obligations under finance lease at end of year £
19X4	4,000		1,154		2,846
19X5	2,846		1,325		1,521
19X6	1,521		1,521		–

33.16 The rule of 78

Before spreadsheets became commonplace, these actuarial method lease calculations were often considered too complex and, in their place, a simple rule-of-thumb approach was adopted: the rule of 78.

The '78' is the sum of the numbers 1 to 12, and is used because these calculations originally focused on twelve-month periods. Each month receives a proportion in reverse to its position. Thus, month 1 of 12 would be accorded $12/78$ of the total, and month 12 of 12, $1/78$.

Similarly to the actuarial method, under the rule of 78, earlier periods will carry the majority of the allocation. For the purpose of lease calculations, the proportion is applied to the difference between the total payments under the leasing agreement and the cash value of the asset at the start.

Using the example from Exhibit 33.4, the rule of 78 produces the following:

Quarter	Rental payment number	Rule of 78	Allocation × £800	Annual allocation £
19X4 – 1	1	11	11/66 × £800 =133	
2	2	10	121	
3	3	9	109	
4	4	8	97	460
19X5 – 1	5	7	85	
2	6	6	73	
3	7	5	61	
4	8	4	49	268
19X6 – 1	9	3	36	
2	10	2	24	
3	11	1	12	
4	–	–	–	72
		66	800	800

(There is no allocation to the final quarter as the payments are made at the start of each quarter.) Comparison of the two methods shows that the rule of 78 provides a general indication of the flows.

Year	Actuarial method £	Rule of 78 £
19X4	446	460
19X5	275	268
19X6	79	72
	800	800

33.17 Uncertainty

Many of the values used in the calculations and formulae described in this chapter are, at best, objectively based estimates of future cash flows and interest rates. It is, for example, virtually inconceivable that the figures forecast in a capital project appraisal will be confirmed to have been 100 per cent accurate when the project is completed.

Proposers of a course of action tend to be over-optimistic and, in order to avoid the risk of non-achievement of forecasted results, a number of measures have been adopted. The two most common are the adoption of a higher cost of capital rate than is actually required in practice, and reducing estimates of income by a fixed percentage and using the same percentage to increase all costs. However, such arbitrary adjustments can no more guarantee accuracy than the original estimates, and they will often cause the decision taken to be different from that which the original, possibly more meaningful, data would have produced.

A more rational adjustment that can be adopted is to change the amounts forecast according to their subjective probabilities. The probabilities would be provided by the proposers of a project.

Example

Estimated sales £	× Probability of occurrence	= Expected sales £
2,000	0.2	400
4,000	0.5	2,000
6,000	0.2	1,200
8,000	0.1	800
	1.0	4,400

In this case, the expected value of £4,400 will be used, rather than the most likely value of £4,000. While this approach appears more rational than the other possible methods of dealing with uncertainty, it is dependent upon the probabilities used being soundly based.

33.18 Sensitivity analysis

One of the greatest benefits of spreadsheets is the facility to perform unlimited numbers of sensitivity analysis computations on a given set of data. Cash flows can be adjusted marginally to see if the change turns a positive NPV negative; interest rates can be altered to see if the same decision would be made; the timing of cash flows can be altered to see what the impact of doing so is upon NPV. Sensitivity analysis enables information generated using the formulae and methods described in this chapter to be manipulated in order to maximise the understanding of the flexibility and limits of that information.

The importance of discounting has been recognised by the Institute of Chartered Accountants in England and Wales, who have issued Technical Release 773, *The Use of Discounting in Financial Statements*. It is an excellent source of discussion on this topic, and on its application in practice.

Main points to remember

1   As time passes, money loses value and this loss of value must be allowed for when considering long-term investments.

2   Interest rates may be simple or compound, and interest may be paid at any appropriate frequency. Compound interest will generate significantly greater values than the same rate of simple interest the longer the time period involved and the greater the frequency of interest payments.

3   The real rate of interest often differs from the apparent rate and an annual percentage rate (APR) must be calculated in order to compare alternatives.

4   Annuity calculations are useful when considering rental agreements, hire purchase and leases.

5   Net present value (NPV) and internal rate of return (IRR) usually lead to the same selection being made between mutually exclusive projects. When they differ, it is the NPV selection that should be followed.

6   Accounting rate of return (ARR) is still used, but the rate it produces cannot be compared to the cost of capital and the technique is not recommended.

7   Where alternative projects are of unequal length, annualised amounts can be calculated to enable comparison.

8   Operating leases are accounted for differently from finance leases.

Review questions

33.1 (a) If you were lent £12,000 for 56 days at 9 per cent, how much interest would you pay?

(b) If a debt factor offered to discount a £6,000 bill of exchange at 15 per cent, and if the bill had an outstanding period of 80 days, how much would the debt factor pay for the bill?

33.2A What is the real rate of interest of discounting the bill of exchange in question 33.1?

33.3 Interest of £1,000 is charged and included in a loan of £3,000. The loan has to be repaid at £750 per quarter over the next 12 months. What is the real rate of interest of the loan?

33.4 If £1,000 is invested for five years at 12 per cent compound per annum, how much interest is earned over the five years?

33.5A If the interest on the investment in question 33.4 had been compounded every six months, how much interest would have been earned over the five years?

33.6A Shares bought on 1 January 19X2 for £2,000 were sold on 31 December 19X5 for £3,158. What was the rate of annual compound interest on the investment?

33.7 Should you accept an offer of £15,000 for your rights over the next four years to the £4,000 annual rent from shop premises you own and have leased to a local company? You could invest the £15,000 at 10 per cent per annum.

33.8A In relation to the rental income, what rate of interest does the offer made in question 33.7 represent?

33.9 A condition of a ten-year loan of £20,000 is that the borrower will pay equal annual amounts into a sinking fund so that it accumulates at the end of the ten years to the amount of the loan. The sinking fund will earn interest at 8 per cent per annum. How much should be paid into the sinking fund each year?

33.10A If the interest on the sinking fund in question 33.9 were at 10 per cent, how much would the annual payments into it be?

33.11 The following project costs have been estimated relating to the upgrading of some equipment; all the costs are being incurred solely because of the project:

19X2

			£
January	1	One year's rent on premises paid	6,000
	31	Equipment purchased	40,000
March	31	Installation of equipment completed and paid	12,000
December	31	Costs incurred in commissioning equipment	18,000

19X3

January	1	One year's rent on premises paid	6,000
March	31	Additional commissioning costs paid	10,000
May	31	Training costs paid	4,000
June	30	Additional working capital provided	14,000
December	31	Cash proceeds from sale of old equipment	10,000

Ignoring tax, prepare a statement showing the outlays of cash on the project in 19X2 and 19X3. The new facility will be in full use from 1 July 19X3.

33.12 Assume the company in question 33.11 pays tax at 40 per cent, on 30 September each year, nine months after the end of its financial period. The company receives 25 per cent writing-down allowances on the cost of equipment and will receive the allowances for 19X2 expenditure to be offset against the tax payable on the profits for 19X2. 100 per cent capital allowances were received on the old equipment sold in 19X3 and the receipts from the sale of the old equipment must, therefore, be treated as taxable income of 19X3. Show the impact on the cash flows of these tax items.

33.13 Assuming an interest rate of 10 per cent, what is the net present value of the net of tax cash flows in question 33.12 for 19X2, 19X3, 19X4 and 19X5?

33.14A The annual profit from a project is forecasted as:

	£	£
Sales		110,000
Labour, materials, and overheads	30,000	
Depreciation	20,000	
		50,000
Net profit before tax		60,000
Tax at 40%		24,000
Net profit after tax		36,000

Equipment with a five-year useful economic life and no residual value will be purchased on 1 September for £30,000. £15,000 additional working capital, which will be recovered in full at the end of the five years, will be required from 1 September. A 25 per cent writing-down allowance will be available throughout the period of the project. Tax at 40 per cent will be payable on 1 June each year, nine months after the end of the company's financial period on 31 August. Prepare a cash flow budget for the project.

33.15A If the interest rate is 10 per cent, what is the net present value of the net cash flows arising from the project in question 33.14?

33.16A If retained, a machine would be depreciated at £2,500 for the next four years, at which point it would be fully written down and scrapped. The machine could be sold at any point in the next year for £15,000, the gain being subject to tax at 40 per cent, payable the following year. If it were sold, a new machine costing £80,000 would be bought. The new machine would receive 25 per cent writing-down allowances to be offset annually against profits. It is estimated that the new machine would save material costs of £25,000 per year. Profits are subject to tax at 40 per cent, payable nine months after the end of the company's financial period. The new machinery would have a four-year life, with a residual value of zero, and would be depreciated straight line over that period. Prepare a cash flow statement for the replacement option, and indicate how the profits reported in the financial statements would be altered were the existing machine to be replaced.

33.17 What is the payback period on the following project cash flows? (Brackets indicate expenditure.)

	Net cash flows £
Year 0	(10,000)
1	8,000
2	4,000
3	2,000
4	1,000

33.18 Using a discount rate of 12 per cent, what is the net present value of the project in question 33.17?

33.19 What is the internal rate of return on the project in question 33.17?

33.20 What is the annualised amount of the net benefits from the project in question 33.17?

33.21A What is the payback on a project requiring £60,000 initial investment that has a net cash inflow of £40,000 in year 1, £25,000 in year two, and £15,000 in year three?

33.22A Using a discount rate of 10 per cent, what is the net present value of the project in question 33.21?

33.23A What is the internal rate of return on the project in question 33.21?

33.24A What is the annualised amount of the net benefits from the project in question 33.21?

33.25A The annual profit from a project is forecasted as:

	£	£
Sales		80,000
Labour, materials, and overheads	20,000	
Depreciation	15,000	
		35,000
Net profit before tax		45,000

The project requires that a new machine be purchased for £65,000. It will be depreciated using the straight line method over four years to a residual value of £5,000. The project will cease when the machine is sold for £5,000 at the end of the fourth year. Ignoring taxation, what is the accounting rate of return? (No additional working capital is required for this project.)

33.26A Assuming that all sales are for cash, what is the internal rate of return on the project in question 33.25?

33.27 Which of the following two mutually exclusive alternatives should be selected if a 10 per cent interest rate is used for the calculation of net present value?

	Net cash flow Year 0	Net cash flow Year 3
	£	£
Machine A project	(12,000)	22,000
Machine B project	(38,000)	66,000

33.28 Using internal rate of return, which of the two projects in question 33.27 would be preferred?

33.29A Which of the following two mutually exclusive alternatives should be selected if a 12 per cent interest rate is used for the calculation of net present value?

	Net cash flow Year 0	Net cash flow Year 1	Net cash flow Year 3
	£	£	£
Project A	(34,000)	16,000	26,000
Project B	(29,000)	22,000	12,000

33.30A Using internal rate of return, which of the two projects in question 33.29 would be preferred?

33.31 Equipment with an estimated useful economic life of five years has an NPV of £3,100 using a 10 per cent discount rate. What is the annualised equivalent of the £3,100 NPV?

33.32A Two mutually exclusive alternatives are available. Project A will require initial investment of £3,000 and run for two years at a cost of £500 per annum. Project B will require initial investment of £7,000 and last for four years at a cost of £800 for the first three years and £1,000 in the fourth. Calculate the annualised cost of both projects over a four-year period, assuming that reinvestment in project A would cost £2,500 at the end of year two and assuming an interest rate of 8 per cent. Which alternative should be selected?

33.33 What is the implied interest rate if equipment can be leased for four years at £20,000 per annum and the cash price is £64,800?

33.34 A machine with a five-year useful life could be purchased for £60,000. It would have zero residual value at the end of the five years. Alternatively, the machine could be rented at £14,633 per annum for five years. Assuming a tax rate of 40 per cent and that tax relief is obtained in the same period as the payments, what is the implicit interest rate in the lease?

33.35 The annual rental payments on a six-year lease are £4,000. If the rate of interest payable on borrowing for this purpose is 16 per cent, what is the capital value of the lease?

33.36 Roadwheelers Ltd were considering buying an additional lorry but the company had not yet decided which particular lorry to purchase. The lorries had broadly similar technical specifications and each was expected to have a working life of five years.
   The following information was available on the lorries being considered:

1   Lorries

	BN *Roadhog*	FX *Sprinter*	VR *Rocket*
Purchase price	£40,000	£45,000	£50,000
Estimated scrap value after 5 years	£8,000	£9,000	£14,000
Fixed costs other than depreciation	£	£	£
Year 1	2,000	1,800	1,500
Year 2	2,000	1,800	1,500
Year 3	2,200	1,800	1,400
Year 4	2,400	2,000	1,400
Year 5	2,400	2,200	1,400
Variable costs per road mile	6p	8p	7p

2   The company charges 25p per mile for all journeys irrespective of the length of journey and the expected annual mileages over the five-year period are:

	Miles
Year 1	50,000
Year 2	60,000
Year 3	80,000
Year 4	80,000
Year 5	80,000

3   The company's cost of capital is 10 per cent per annum.

4   It should be assumed that all operating costs are paid and revenues received at the end of year.

5   Present value of £1 at interest rate of 10 per cent per annum:

Year 1	£0.909
Year 2	£0.826
Year 3	£0.751
Year 4	£0.683
Year 5	£0.621

Required:
(a) (i)   Appropriate computations using the net present value method for each of the lorries under consideration.
   (ii)   A report to the directors of Roadwheelers Ltd advising them as to which specific lorry should be purchased.
(b) A brief outline of the problems encountered in evaluating capital projects.

(Associated Examining Board: GCE 'A' level)

33.37A Hirwaun Pig Iron Co. operate a single blast furnace producing pig iron. The present blast furnace is obsolete and the company is considering its replacement.

The alternatives the company is considering are:

(*i*) Blast furnace type Exco. Cost £2 million.

This furnace is of a standard size capable of a monthly output of 10,000 tonnes. The company expects to sell 80 per cent of its output annually at £150 per tonne on a fixed price contract. The remaining output will be sold on the open market at the following expected prices:

	19X8	19X9	19X0	19X1
Price per tonne	£150	£140	£140	£160

(*ii*) Blast furnace type Ohio. Cost £3.5 million.

This large furnace is capable of a monthly output of 20,000 tonnes. A single buyer has agreed to buy all the monthly output at a fixed price which is applicable from 1 January each year. The prices fixed for the next four years are as follows:

Payments per tonne of output

	19X8	19X9	19X0	19X1
Price per tonne	£130	£130	£140	£170

Additional information:

1 Blast furnaces operate continuously and the operating labour is regarded as a fixed cost. During the next four years the operating labour costs will be as follows:

Exco £1.2 million per annum
Ohio £2.5 million per annum

2 Other forecast operating payments (excluding labour) per tonne:

	19X8	19X9	19X0	19X1
Exco	£130	£130	£135	£135
Ohio	£120	£120	£125	£125

3 It can be assumed that both blast furnaces will have a life of 10 years.
4 The company's cost of capital is 12 per cent per annum.
5 It should be assumed that all costs are paid and revenues received at the end of each year.
6 The following is an extract from the present value table for £1:

	11%	12%	13%	14%
Year 1	£0.901	£0.893	£0.885	£0.877
Year 2	£0.812	£0.797	£0.783	£0.770
Year 3	£0.731	£0.712	£0.693	£0.675
Year 4	£0.659	£0.636	£0.613	£0.592

Required:

(*a*) The forecast budgets for each of the years 19X8–19X1 and for each of the blast furnaces being considered. Show the expected yearly net cash flows.

(*b* Appropriate computations using the net present value method for each of the blast furnaces, Exco and Ohio, for the first four years.

(*c*) A report providing a recommendation to the management of Hirwaun Pig Iron Co as to which blast furnace should be purchased. Your report should include a critical evaluation of the method used to assess the capital project.

(*Associated Examining Board: GCE 'A' level*)

33.38 Moray Ferries Ltd own a single ship which provides a short sea ferry service for passengers, private vehicles and commercial traffic. The present ship is nearing the end of its useful life and the company is considering the purchase of a new ship.

The forecast operating budgets using the present ship are as follows:

	19X6	19X7	19X8	19X9	19X0
	£m	£m	£m	£m	£m
Estimated revenue receipts					
Private traffic	2	3	4.5	6	7
Commercial traffic	3	4	4.5	5	6
	5	7	9.0	11	13
Estimated operating payments	4	5	6.5	7.5	9
	1	2	2.5	3.5	4

The ships being considered as a replacement are as described below.

1 Ship A. Cost £10m
   This ship is of similar capacity to the one being replaced, but being a more modern ship it is expected that extra business would be attracted from competitors. It is anticipated therefore that estimated revenue receipts would be 10 per cent higher in each year of the present forecast. There would be no change in operating payments.

2 Ship B. Cost £14m
   This modern ship has a carrying capacity 30 per cent greater than the present ship. It is expected that private traffic receipts would increase by £½m a year in each year of the forecast. Commercial traffic receipts are expected to increase by 15 per cent in each of the first two years and by 30 per cent in each of the remaining years.
   Operating payments would increase by 20 per cent in each year of the forecast.

Additional information:
3 The company's cost of capital is 15 per cent per annum.
4 It is company policy to assume that ships have a life of 20 years.
5 It should be assumed that all costs are paid and revenues received at the end of each year.
6 The following is an extract from the present value table for £1:

	12%	14%	15%	16%
Year 1	£0.893	£0.877	£0.870	£0.862
Year 2	£0.797	£0.769	£0.756	£0.743
Year 3	£0.712	£0.675	£0.658	£0.641
Year 4	£0.636	£0.592	£0.572	£0.552
Year 5	£0.567	£0.519	£0.497	£0.476

7 All calculations should be made correct to three places of decimals.

Required:
(a) Revised operating budgets for 19X6–19X0 for each of the alternatives being considered.
(b) Appropriate computations using the net present value method for each of the ships, A and B.
(c) A report providing a recommendation to the management of Moray Ferries Ltd as to which course of action should be followed. Your report should include any reservations that you may have.

(*Associated Examining Board: GCE 'A' level*)

33.39A The Rovers Football Club are languishing in the middle of the Premier Division of the Football League. The Club have suffered a loss of £200,000 in their last financial year and whilst receipts from spectators have declined over the last five years, recently receipts have stabilised at approximately £1,000,000 per season. The Club is considering the purchase of the services of one of two new football players, Jimmy Jam or Johnny Star.

Jimmy Jam is 21 years old and considered to be a future international footballer. He is prepared to sign a five-year contract with Rovers for a salary of £50,000 per annum. His present club would require a transfer fee of £200,000 for the transfer of his existing contract. With J Jam in the team the Rovers Club would expect receipts to increase by 20 per cent.

Johnny Star is 32 years old and a leading international footballer who is prepared to sign for Rovers on a two-year contract before retiring completely from football. He would expect a salary of £200,000 per annum and his present club would require a transfer fee of £100,000 for the transfer of his existing contract. Rovers believe that as a result of signing Star receipts would increase by 40 per cent.

The rate of interest applicable to the transaction is 12 per cent and the following is an extract from the present value table for £1:

	12%
Year 1	0.893
Year 2	0.797
Year 3	0.712
Year 4	0.636
Year 5	0.567

It should be assumed that all costs are paid and revenues received at the end of each year.

Required:
A report, incorporating an evaluation of the financial result of engaging each player by the net present value method, providing the Rovers Football Club with information to assist it in deciding which alternative to adopt. Indicate any other factors that may be taken into consideration.

(*Associated Examining Board: GCE 'A' level*)

34

Accounting ratios: a further view

Objectives

After you have studied this chapter, you should:

- know of the existence of various groups of accounting ratios, where they would be used, why they would be of interest, and to whom

- know how to calculate a number of commonly used accounting ratios

- be aware of some of the difficulties that may arise in the calculation and interpretation of accounting ratios

- be aware of the dangers in overtrading and of how ratio analysis can be used to identify it

34.1 Introduction

Accounting ratios and the interpretation of final accounts were introduced in Volume 1. This chapter takes that material forward, re-examining the material for reinforcement, and developing greater depth of knowledge and understanding.

Information is data organised for a purpose. Information contained in financial statements is organised so as to enable users of the financial statements to draw conclusions concerning the financial well-being and performance of the reporting entity. In the case of the financial statements of companies, independent auditors review the manner in which the data has been presented and provide a filter mechanism attesting to the reliability of the information presented. For partnerships and sole traders, there is generally no such independent review. However, as the financial statements are generally subject to review by the tax authorities, there is some justification in assuming that they are a reasonable reflection of reality.

Yet, being 'reasonably assured' of their reliability is not generally sufficient for tax authorities and they will review the financial statements of partnerships and sole traders to determine whether there may be cause to doubt their reliability. One of the key instruments at their disposal is ratios, and they use ratio analysis to compare those found in the entity under review with those typically existing in that sector of the economy. Hence, through ratio analysis, factors can be identified that would not otherwise be apparent.

Ratio analysis can also be used to review trends and compare entities with each other. A number of commercial organisations specialise in this service, providing detailed ratio analysis of the financial statements of plcs to subscribers and enabling analysts to see, at a glance, how one entity is performing, or how its financial structure compares to others of a similar nature.

Without ratios, financial statements would be largely uninformative to all but the very skilled. With ratios, financial statements can be interpreted and usefully applied to satisfy the needs of the reader.

There are, however, a vast number of parties interested in analysing financial statements – shareholders, lenders, customers, suppliers, employees, government agencies and competitors are just some of the groups who may all be interested in the financial statements of an entity. Yet, in many respects they will be interested in different things, and so there is no definitive, all-encompassing list of points for analysis that would be useful to all the groups. Nevertheless, it is possible to construct a series of ratios that together will provide all these groups with something that they will find relevant, and from which they can choose to investigate further, if necessary. Ratio analysis is a first step in assessing an entity which removes some of the mystique surrounding the financial statements and makes it easier to pinpoint items which it would be interesting to investigate further.

Exhibit 34.1 shows some of categories of ratios and indicates some of the groups that would be interested in them.

Exhibit 34.1

Ratio category	Examples of interested groups
Solvency	Shareholders, suppliers, creditors, competitors
Profitability	Shareholders, management, employees, creditors, competitors, potential investors
Efficiency	Shareholders, potential purchasers, competitors
Capital structure	Shareholders, lenders, creditors, potential investors
Shareholder	Shareholders, potential investors

34.2 Solvency

It is essential that a business is aware if a customer or borrower is at risk of not repaying the amount due. New customers are usually vetted prior to being allowed to trade on credit rather than by cash. For private individuals there are credit rating agencies with extensive records of the credit histories of many individuals. For a small fee a company can receive a report indicating whether a new customer might be a credit risk. Similarly, information can be purchased concerning companies that indicates their solvency, i.e. whether they are liable to be bad credit risks. The difference between these two sources of information is that, while the information on private individuals is based on their previous credit record, that of the companies is generally based on a ratio analysis of their financial statements. The ratio analysis will focus upon the solvency (or liquidity) ratios. Of these the best known are the current ratio and the acid test ratio.

Current ratio

This compares total current assets to total current liabilities and is intended to indicate whether there are sufficient short-term assets to meet the short-term liabilities. Traditionally, in order to provide some general guide, a value is given that may generally be taken to be the 'norm'. This has become increasingly less meaningful and is really more misleading (as it instils undue confidence) than helpful – the ratio is so sector-dependent as to be incapable of being defined as 'generally best if around x'. Consequently, no such guidance will be given here. Rather, a set of factors will be suggested that ought to be considered:

- What is the norm in this industrial sector?
- Is this company significantly above or below that norm?
- If so, can this be justified after an analysis of the nature of these assets and liabilities, and of the reasons for the amounts of each held?

The ratio when calculated may be expressed as either a ratio to 1, with current liabilities being set to 1, or as a 'number of times', representing the relative size of the amount of total current assets compared with total current liabilities.

Example

If total current assets are £40,000 and total current liabilities are £20,000, the current ratio could be expressed as either:

£40,000:£20,000   = 2:1

or as:

$$\frac{£40,000}{£20,000} = 2 \text{ times}$$

Acid test ratio

As with the current ratio, there is little benefit in suggesting a norm for the value to expect. The only difference in the items involved between the two ratios is that the acid test (or 'quick') ratio does not include stock. Otherwise, it is identical to the current ratio, comparing current assets, excluding stock, to current liabilities. Stock is omitted as it is considered to be relatively illiquid, because it depends upon prevailing and future market forces and may be impossible to convert to cash in a relatively short time.

Many companies operate with acid test ratios below 1:1. That is, they have insufficient liquid assets to meet their short-term liabilities. The great majority of companies in this situation have no problem paying their creditors when due. Consideration of a simple example should explain how this is possible.

Example

If total current assets, including stock of £22,000, are worth £40,000 and total current liabilities stand at £20,000, the acid test ratio will be £18,000:£20,000 = 0.9:1 (or 0.9 times). This means that at the balance sheet date, had all current liabilities been due for payment, it would not have been possible to do so without converting some assets (e.g. stock, or fixed assets) into cash that were likely to only be convertible into cash at a discount on their true value – that is, the company would have had to pay a premium in order to meet its obligations, and would not be able to continue to do so indefinitely.

However, the reality is generally that the current liabilities are due for payment at varying times over the coming financial period and some, for example a bank overdraft, may not, in reality, ever be likely to be subject to a demand for repayment.

The current assets, on the other hand, are within the control of the company and can be adjusted in their timing to match the due dates for payment to creditors. They can be renewed many times before one or other of the current liabilities is due for payment. For example, debtors may be on a ten-day cycle while trade creditors are paid after 90 days' credit has expired. Clearly, in this case, receipts from nine times the balance sheet debtors' figure could be received and available to meet the trade creditor figure shown in the balance·sheet.

As with the current ratio, when calculated, the acid test ratio should be compared to the norms for the industrial sector, and then the underlying assets and liabilities should be considered to determine whether there is any cause for concern in the result obtained.

34.3 Profitability

These measures indicate whether the company is performing satisfactorily. They are used, among other things, to measure the performance of management, to identify whether a company may be a worthwhile investment opportunity, and to determine a company's performance relative to its competitors.

There are a large number of these ratios. Some of the most commonly used are described below.

Gross profit:Sales

If gross profit is £120,000 and sales are £480,000, the ratio would be 25 per cent. (This should not be confused with the gross margin:sales ratio which compares the gross profit to the cost of sales which, in this case, would have a value of 33.33 per cent.)

Net profit after tax:Sales

If net profit is £38,400 and sales are £480,000, the ratio would be 8 per cent. The ratio indicates how much safety there is in the price, i.e. current prices could be reduced by up to 8 per cent without causing the company to make a loss. Of course, it is much more complex than this. As any student of economics knows only too well, if a commodity's price falls, generally demand for it rises. This could result in costs increasing (if unexpected demand has to be met in a hurry) or falling (as bulk discounts become available that were not previously obtainable due to the lower level of demand). Nevertheless, as a general guide, it is a sensible indicator of safety, as well as an indicator of success.

While a high value for this ratio may suggest successful performance, it is not always the case. It is possible for selling prices to be so high that demand is reduced causing overall profitability to be significantly lower than it could be were a lower price being used. In this circumstance, the ratio would produce a high percentage, but performance would certainly not be as good as it ought to have been.

Return on capital employed

This is one of the more awkward ratios to deal with. Unlike the current ratio, for example, there is no widely agreed definition of return on capital employed (ROCE). Hence, care must be taken when comparing this ratio as calculated for one company and as reported for another. Use of financial analysis bureaux that use the same formula to calculate the ratios of all the companies they consider is one way around this difficulty. Another is to ensure that the formula used by the companies being compared against is known and, where necessary, the result is revised to bring it into line with the internally calculated ratio.

The ratio compares the profit earned (usually before interest and tax) to the funds used to generate that return (often the total of shareholders' funds at the beginning of the accounting period plus long-term creditors – most simply defined as total assets minus current liabilities). Were the profit before interest and tax £40,000 and the opening capital employed shown in the balance sheet £800,000, the return on capital employed would be 5 per cent. In theory, the higher the ratio, the more profitably the resources of the company have been used.

Return on share capital

As with ROCE, there are a number of different ways in which this may be calculated. One is the comparison of profit on ordinary activities before tax with share capital and reserves. For example, if profit on ordinary activities before tax were £40,000 and the share capital and reserves at the start of the accounting period £720,000, the return on share capital (ROSC) would be 5.56 per cent. In theory, the higher the ratio, the more profitably the shareholders' investment in the company has been used, and it is often used to compare performance between accounting periods, rather than to draw comparison with the ROSC of other companies.

Net profit after tax:Total assets

Net profit after tax is compared to the total of all assets other than current assets, plus working capital (i.e. current assets less current liabilities). If working capital is £20,000 and all non-current assets total £820,000, total assets are £840,000. If net profit after tax is £30,000, the ratio is £30,000/£840,000, i.e. 3.57 per cent.

There are problems with the integrity of this ratio – some items of expenditure that are relevant, e.g. interest on debentures, will have been charged against the profit in arriving at the figure for profit after tax. Strictly speaking, these other payments to investors and creditors ought to be reviewed and included in the profit figure used in the ratio, otherwise the profit may be significantly understated, giving a less healthy view than would be appropriate to present.

Intangible assets, e.g. goodwill, are included in the value of total assets used in the ratio. However, many would argue that this is inappropriate as there is not an agreed view on how such assets should be valued, thus inter-company comparisons may be difficult.

Net operating profit:Operating assets

This is an alternative to *Net profit after tax:Total assets*. It takes the net profit before interest, taxes and dividends, and before inclusion of any investment income. This is then compared with the assets other than intangibles and investments outside the company. Working capital would be included, but bank overdrafts would be excluded from the current liabilities on the basis that they are not generally short-term in nature. If net operating profit before interest, tax and dividends is £36,000, tangible fixed assets excluding investments made outside the company are £600,000, working capital is £20,000, and there is a bank overdraft of £5,000, the ratio is:

$$\frac{£36,000}{£625,000} = 5.76\%$$

34.4 Efficiency ratios

Profitability is affected by the way that the assets of a business are used. If plant and machinery are only used for a few hours a day, the business is failing to utilise these assets efficiently. This may be because there is limited demand for the product produced. It could be due to the business restricting supply in order to maximise profitability per unit produced. On the other hand, it could be that there is a shortage of skilled labour and that there is no one to operate the plant and machinery the rest of the time. Alternatively, it could be that the plant and machinery is unreliable, breaking down a lot, and that the limited level of use is a precautionary measure designed to ensure that production targets are met.

In common with all accounting ratios, it is important that the results of efficiency ratio computations are not treated as definitively good or bad. They must be investigated further through consideration both of the underlying variables in the ratios, and of the broader context of the business and its relation to the industrial sector in which it operates.

These ratios include the following.

Asset turnover

This is a measure of how effectively the assets are being used to generate sales. It is one of the ratios that would be considered when interpreting the results of profitability ratio analyses like ROCE, but is of sufficient importance to be calculated and analysed irrespective of that fact. The calculation involves dividing sales by total assets less current liabilities.

As a general guide, where a company's asset turnover is significantly lower than those of its competitors, it suggests there may be over-investment in assets which could, in turn, make it vulnerable to takeover from a company interested in selling off any surplus assets while otherwise retaining the business in its current form. However, considerable care must be taken when interpreting this ratio: the assets may be much newer than those of other companies; the company may use a lower rate of depreciation than its competitors; or the company may purchase its plant and machinery, whereas the industry norm is to lease them. On the other side of the ratio, the result may be high because selling prices are being suppressed in order to maximise volume.

Stock turnover

Included in virtually every case where accounting ratios are being calculated, this measures the number of times (approximately) that stock is replenished in an accounting period. If stock is £100,000 and sales are £800,000, the stock turnover ratio would be 8 times. The ratio can also be expressed as a number of days – the number of days stock held. In this example, 365 would be divided by 8 producing a result of 45.6 days.

There are two major difficulties in computing this ratio: sales are expressed at selling prices; stock is expressed at cost price. This may be overcome by using cost of sales rather than sales in the computation.

In addition, there are at least three possible stock values that could be used – opening, closing and the average of these figures. The average figure would be the more commonly used, but use of any of the three can be justified.

Whichever approach is taken, the result will, at best, be a crude estimate. Due to seasonality of the business, stock, as shown in the balance sheet for example, may not be representative of the 'normal' level of stock. However, it is still useful for comparing trends over time and should be used mainly for that purpose. The result it produces needs careful consideration. A rising stock turnover may indicate greater efficiency, or it may be an indicator that stocks are being run down and that there may be problems in meeting demand in future. A falling stock turnover may indicate lower efficiency, perhaps with a build-up of obsolete stocks, or it could indicate higher stock volumes are being held because stock purchasing has become more efficient and the higher stock levels are financially beneficial for the company. In addition, it is important not to overlook that any change in the ratio may have nothing to do with the stock, but be due to changes in factors relating to the sales for the period.

Debtor days

This indicates how efficient the company is at controlling its debtors. If debtors are £50,000 and sales £800,000, debtors are taking, on average, 22.8 days credit, i.e.

$$\frac{£50,000}{£800,000} \times 365 = 22.8$$

Strictly speaking, the two figures are not comparable. Debtors include the VAT on sales; the figure for sales excludes VAT. However, the adjustment is not difficult to make if required for clarity.

As with stock, the amount shown in the balance sheet for debtors may not be representative of the 'normal' level. Nevertheless, this is generally a very useful ratio to calculate and comparison with those of other companies in the same industrial sector may be very interesting. However, as with stock turnover, its strength lies in trend analysis between periods.

Creditor days

This ratio indicates how the company uses short-term financing to fund its activities and further investigation will reveal whether or not the result is due to efficiency. It is calculated by dividing creditors by purchases, and multiplying the result by 365. The purchases figure is not usually available in published financial statements, and the cost of sales amount would be used in its place. As with stock turnover and debtor days, its strength lies in trend analysis between periods.

34.5 Capital structure ratios

There are a number of ratios that can be used to assess the way in which a company finances its activities. One, creditor days, was referred to in the last section. The ratios discussed in this section differ in that they are longer-term in nature, being more concerned with the strategic rather than the operational level of corporate decision making. Some of the more commonly analysed ratios of this type are described below.

Net worth:Total assets

This ratio indicates the proportion of fixed and current assets that are financed by net worth (the total of shareholders' funds, i.e. share capital plus reserves). If fixed assets are shown at a value of £500,000, current assets £100,000 and net worth is £300,000, 50 per cent of total assets are financed by shareholders' funds. As with many accounting ratios, it is the trend in this ratio between periods that is important.

Fixed assets:Net worth

This ratio focuses on the longer-term aspects of the net worth:total assets ratio. By matching long-term investment with long-term finance it is possible to determine whether borrowing has been used to finance some long-term investment in assets. Where this has occurred, there may be a problem when the borrowing is to be repaid (as the fixed assets it was used to acquire cannot be readily converted into cash). Again, this ratio is of most use when the trend over time is analysed.

Fixed assets:Net worth + Long-term liabilities

This ratio focuses on whether sufficient long-term finance has been obtained to meet the investment in fixed assets.

Debt ratio

This ratio compares the total debts to total assets and is concerned with whether the company has sufficient assets to meet all its liabilities when due. For example, if total liabilities are £150,000 and total assets are £600,000, the debts represent 25 per cent of total assets. Whether this is good or bad will, as with all accounting ratios, depend upon the norm for the industrial sector in which the company operates and on the underlying items within the figures included in the ratio.

Capital gearing ratio

This ratio provides the proportion of a company's total capital that has a prior claim to profits over those of ordinary shareholders. Prior claim (or prior charge) capital includes debentures and preference share capital and is any capital carrying a right to a fixed return. Total capital includes ordinary share capital and reserves, prior charge capital, and long-term liabilities.

Debt:Equity ratio

This is the ratio of prior charge capital to ordinary share capital and reserves.

Borrowing:Net worth

This ratio indicates the proportion that borrowing represents of a company's net worth. If long-term liabilities are £100,000 and current liabilities are £50,000, total borrowing is £150,000. If net worth is £300,000, the ratio is 1:2, or 50 per cent.

This and the *debt:equity ratio* indicate the degree of risk to investors in ordinary shares in a company. The higher these ratios are, the greater the possibility of risk to ordinary shareholders – both in respect of expectations of future dividends (especially in times of depressed performance where much of the profits may be paid to the holders of prior charge capital), and from the threat of liquidation should there be a slump in performance that leads to a failure to meet payments to holders of prior charge capital. Whether these risks may be relevant can be investigated by reference to the next ratio.

Interest cover

This ratio shows whether enough profits are being earned to meet interest payments when due. It is calculated by dividing profit before interest and tax by the interest charges.

Thus, if profit before interest and tax is £400,000 and the total interest charges are £20,000 the interest cover is 20 times. In this case, there would be little cause for immediate concern that there was any risk of the company failing to meet its interest charges when due. However, just because a company is making profits does not guarantee that there will be sufficient cash available to make the interest charge payments when due.

34.6 Shareholder ratios

These ratios are those most commonly used by anyone interested in an investment in a company. They indicate how well a company is performing in relation to the price of its shares and other related items including dividends and number of shares in issue. The ratios usually calculated are described below.

Dividend yield

This measures the real rate of return by comparing the dividend paid to the market price of a share. It is calculated as:

$$\frac{\text{Gross dividend per share}}{\text{Market price per share}}$$

Earnings per share (EPS)

This is the most frequently used of all the accounting ratios and is generally felt to give the best view of performance. It indicates how much of a company's profit can be attributed to each ordinary share in the company. The calculation is prescribed by SSAP 3: *Earnings per share*, as amended by FRS 3: *Reporting financial performance*, and is:

$$\frac{\text{Earnings after tax, minority interests and extraordinary items available for equity shareholders}}{\text{Number of equity shares in issue and ranking for dividend in the period}}$$

This is often simplified to:

$$\frac{\text{Net profit after tax and preference dividends}}{\text{Number of ordinary shares in issue}}$$

Dividend cover

This compares the amount of profit earned per ordinary share with the amount of dividend paid, thereby showing the proportion of profits that could have been distributed and were. It differs from EPS only in having a different denominator. The formula is:

$$\frac{\text{Net profit after tax and preference dividends}}{\text{Net dividend on ordinary shares}}$$

Price earnings (P/E) ratio

This relates the earnings per share to the market price of the shares. It is calculated by:

$$\frac{\text{Market price}}{\text{Earnings per share}}$$

and is a useful indicator of how the stock market assesses the company. It is also very useful when a company proposes an issue of new shares, in that it enables potential investors to better assess whether the expected future earnings make the share a worthwhile investment.

34.7 Overtrading

A very high proportion of new businesses fail within the first two years of trading. This can occur because there was insufficient demand for the goods or service provided, because of poor management, or a number of other reasons of which possibly the most common to arise would be **overtrading**. However, unlike the other common causes of business failure, overtrading often arises when a business is performing profitably. Furthermore, despite the introduction to this paragraph referring to 'new' businesses, overtrading can just as easily affect established businesses.

Overtrading occurs when there is insufficient control over working capital resulting in there being insufficient liquid funds to meet the demands of creditors. As the cash dries up, so do the sources of supply of raw materials and other essential inputs – they will not continue to supply a business that fails to settle its bills when due. Overtrading is generally the result of sales growth being at too fast a rate in relation to the level of trade debtors, trade creditors and stock.

Take an example where, over a twelve-month period, profits increased by 20 per cent, sales doubled from £1 million to £2 million, trade debtors doubled from £80,000 to £160,000, trade creditors quadrupled from £60,000 to £240,000, stock quadrupled from £50,000 to £200,000, and the bank balance moved from positive £20,000 to an overdraft of £80,000. No changes occurred during the period in long-term financing of the business, though £100,000 was spent on some new equipment needed as a result of the expansion.

Working capital was 2.5:1; now it is 1.125:1 and the acid test ratio is now 0.5:1 from 1.67:1. Liquidity appears to have deteriorated significantly (but may have been high previously compared to other businesses in the same sector). Debtor days are unchanged (as the ratio of sales to debtors is unaltered). However, creditor days have probably doubled (subject to a slight reduction due to some cheaper purchasing costs as a result of the higher volumes involved). If the bank overdraft is currently at its limit, the business would be unable to meet any requests from creditors for immediate payment, never mind pay wages and other regular expenses.

This situation can be addressed by raising long-term finance, or by cutting-back on the expansion – clearly, the first option is likely to be the more attractive one to the business.

Signals suggesting overtrading include:

- significant increases in the volume of sales;
- lower profit margins;
- deteriorating debtor, creditor and stock turnover ratios;
- increasing reliance on short-term finance.

34.8 Summary of ratios

Ratio category	*Formula*
Solvency	
Current ratio	$\dfrac{\text{Current assets}}{\text{Current liabilities}}$
Acid test ratio	$\dfrac{\text{Current assets} - \text{Stock}}{\text{Current liabilities}}$
Profitability	
Gross profit:Sales	$\dfrac{\text{Gross profit}}{\text{Sales}}$
Net profit after tax:Sales	$\dfrac{\text{Net profit after tax}}{\text{Sales}}$
Return on capital employed	$\dfrac{\text{Profit before interest and tax}}{\text{Total assets} - \text{Current liabilities}}$
Return on share capital	$\dfrac{\text{Profit before tax}}{\text{Share capital} + \text{Reserves}}$
Net profit after tax:Total assets	$\dfrac{\text{Net profit after tax}}{\text{Total assets} + \text{Working capital} - \text{Current assets}}$
Net operating profit:Operating assets	$\dfrac{\text{Net profit before interest, tax, dividends and investment income}}{\underset{\text{assets}}{\text{Total}} - \underset{\text{assets}}{\text{Intangible}} + \underset{\text{capital}}{\text{Working}} - \underset{\text{assets}}{\text{Current}} + \underset{\text{overdraft}}{\text{Bank}}}$
Efficiency	
Asset turnover	$\dfrac{\text{Sales}}{\text{Total assets} - \text{Current liabilities}}$
Stock turnover	$\dfrac{\text{Cost of goods sold}}{\text{Average stock}}$
Debtor days	$\dfrac{\text{Debtors}}{\text{Sales}} \times 365$
Creditor days	$\dfrac{\text{Creditors}}{\text{Purchases}} \times 365$
Capital structure	
Net worth:Total assets	$\dfrac{\text{Shareholders' funds}}{\text{Total assets}}$
Fixed assets:Net worth	$\dfrac{\text{Fixed assets}}{\text{Shareholders' funds}}$
Fixed assets:Net worth + Long-term liabilities	$\dfrac{\text{Fixed assets}}{\text{Shareholders' funds} + \text{Long-term liabilities}}$
Debt ratio	$\dfrac{\text{Total liabilities}}{\text{Total assets}}$
Capital gearing ratio	$\dfrac{\text{Prior charge capital}}{\text{Total capital}}$
Debt:Equity ratio	$\dfrac{\text{Prior charge capital}}{\text{Ordinary share capital and reserves}}$

Borrowing:Net worth $\dfrac{\text{Total borrowing}}{\text{Shareholders' funds}}$

Interest cover $\dfrac{\text{Profit before interest and tax}}{\text{Interest charges}}$

Shareholder ratios

Dividend yield $\dfrac{\text{Gross dividend per share}}{\text{Market price per share}}$

Earnings per share $\dfrac{\text{Net profit after tax and preference dividends}}{\text{Number of ordinary shares in issue}}$

Dividend cover $\dfrac{\text{Net profit after tax and preference dividends}}{\text{Net dividend on ordinary shares}}$

Price earnings ratio $\dfrac{\text{Market price}}{\text{Earnings per share}}$

Main points to remember

1 There are many different categories of accounting ratios and many different ratios within each category.

2 Ratios that are of interest to one group of readers of financial statements may not be of interest to another.

3 Ratios may be used in order to review reliability of financial statements.

4 Ratios may be used to review trends between periods for the same company.

5 Ratios may be used to compare a company to others in the same industrial sector.

6 Some ratios are in wide use for which there is no agreed 'correct' formula to calculate them. This makes comparison between analysis reported elsewhere of limited value unless the formula used can be identified.

7 The ratios derived can be misleading if taken at face value. It is essential that they are placed in context and that interpretation goes beyond a superficial comparison to general norms.

8 Used casually, accounting ratios can mislead and result in poor quality decision making.

9 Used carefully, accounting ratios can provide pointers towards areas of interest in an entity, and provide a far more complete picture of an entity than that given by the financial statements.

10 Overtrading can be financially disastrous for a business and ratios can be used to help detect it.

Review questions

34.1 Five categories of accounting ratios are described in this chapter. What are they?

34.2A Why should different groups of people be interested in different categories of accounting ratios?

34.3 Describe two accounting ratios from each of the five groups of ratios, including how to calculate them.

34.4A What is the purpose in using each of the following ratios:

(*a*) current ratio;
(*b*) net profit after tax:sales;
(*c*) asset turnover;
(*d*) interest cover;
(*e*) dividend cover?

34.5 If you wished to assess the efficiency of a company, which of the following ratios would you use:

(*a*) stock turnover;
(*b*) interest cover;
(*c*) return on capital employed;
(*d*) acid test ratio;
(*e*) dividend yield?

34.6A   A company has capital of 1 million ordinary shares of £1 each. It pays a dividend of 6 per cent out of its profits after tax of £480,000 on sales of £4 million. The market price of the shares is £2.40. What is the:

(*a*) net profit after tax:sales;
(*b*) dividend yield;
(*c*) earnings per share;
(*d*) price earnings ratio?

34.7 In respect of each of the following events, select all the effects resulting from that event that are shown in the list of effects:

(*i*) a bad debt written-off;
(*ii*) an increase in the bank overdraft;
(*iii*) a purchase of six months' stock;
(*iv*) payment of all amounts due to trade creditors that had been outstanding for longer than 90 days;
(*v*) an offer of 5 per cent discount to all customers who settle their accounts within two weeks.

List of effects
(*a*) increased current ratio
(*b*) reduced current ratio
(*c*) increased acid test ratio
(*d*) reduced acid test ratio

34.8A Using the following balance sheet and profit and loss accounts, calculate and comment on ten accounting ratios (ignore taxation):

Balance Sheet as at 31 December 19X1 (All values are £000s)

Fixed Assets			
Equipment at cost			6,000
Less Depreciation to date			2,000
			4,000
Current assets			
Stock		600	
Debtors		60	
Bank		–	
		660	
Less Current liabilities			
Creditors	90		
Dividends payable	80		
Bank overdraft	450		
		620	
			40
			4,040
Long-term liabilities			
10% debentures			500
			3,540
Financed by			
Share capital – £1 ordinary shares			2,000
Reserves			
General reserve			800
Profit and loss account			740
			3,540

Profit and Loss Account for period ending 31 December 19X1

(All values are £000s)

Sales			8,000
Less Cost of sales			
Opening stock		500	
Add Purchases		1,300	
		1,800	
Less Closing stock		600	
			1,200
Gross profit			6,800
Less Depreciation		800	
Other expenses		5,500	
			6,300
Net operating profit			500
Less Debenture interest			50
Net profit			450
Add Balance b/f			490
			940
Less Appropriations			
General reserve		120	
Dividend		80	
			200
			740

34.9   You are to study the following financial statements for two similar types of retail store and then answer the questions which follow.

Summary of Financial Statements

Trading and Profit and Loss Account	A £	£	B £	£
Sales		80,000		120,000
Less Cost of goods sold				
Opening stock	25,000		22,500	
Add Purchases	50,000		91,000	
	75,000		113,500	
Less Closing stock	15,000	60,000	17,500	96,000
Gross profit		20,000		24,000
Less Depreciation	1,000		3,000	
Other expenses	9,000	10,000	6,000	9,000
Net profit		10,000		15,000

Balance sheets		A		B
Fixed assets				
Equipment at cost	10,000		20,000	
Less Depreciation to date	8,000	2,000	6,000	14,000
Current assets				
Stock	15,000		17,500	
Debtors	25,000		20,000	
Bank	5,000		2,500	
	45,000		40,000	
Less Current liabilities				
Creditors	5,000	40,000	10,000	30,000
		42,000		44,000
Financed by				
Capitals				
Balance at start of year		38,000		36,000
Add Net profit		10,000		15,000
		48,000		51,000
Less Drawings		6,000		7,000
		42,000		44,000

Required:

(*a*) Calculate the following ratios:

    (*i*) gross profit as percentage of sales;
    (*ii*) net profit as percentage of sales;
    (*iii*) expenses as percentage of sales;
    (*iv*) stockturn;
    (*v*) rate of return of net profit on capital employed (use the average of the capital account for this purpose);

    (*vi*) current ratio;
    (*vii*) acid test ratio;
    (*viii*) debtor:sales ratio;
    (*ix*) creditor:purchases ratio.

(*b*) Drawing upon all your knowledge of accounting, comment upon the differences and similarities of the accounting ratios for A and B. Which business seems to be the most efficient? Give possible reasons.

34.10A Study the following accounts of two companies and then answer the questions which follow. Both companies are stores selling textile goods.

Trading and Profit and Loss Accounts

		R Ltd		T Ltd
	£	£	£	£
Sales		250,000		160,000
Less Cost of goods sold				
Opening stock	90,000		30,000	
Add Purchases	210,000		120,000	
	300,000		150,000	
Less Closing stock	110,000	190,000	50,000	100,000
Gross profit		60,000		60,000
Less Expenses				
Wages and salaries	14,000		10,000	
Directors' remuneration	10,000		10,000	
Other expenses	11,000	35,000	8,000	28,000
Net profit		25,000		32,000
Add Balance from last year		15,000		8,000
		40,000		40,000
Less Appropriations				
General reserve	2,000		2,000	
Dividend	25,000	27,000	20,000	22,000
Balance carried to next year		13,000		18,000

Balance Sheets

		R Ltd		T Ltd
Fixed assets				
Equipment at cost	20,000		5,000	
Less Depreciation to date	8,000	12,000	2,000	3,000
Motor lorries	30,000		20,000	
Less Depreciation to date	12,000	18,000	7,000	13,000
		30,000		16,000
Current assets				
Stock	110,000		50,000	
Debtors	62,500		20,000	
Bank	7,500		10,000	
	180,000		80,000	
Less Current liabilities				
Creditors	90,000		16,000	
		90,000		64,000
		120,000		80,000
Financed by				
Issued share capital		100,000		50,000
Reserves				
General reserve	7,000		12,000	
Profit and loss	13,000	20,000	18,000	30,000
		120,000		80,000

Required:

(a) Calculate the following ratios for each of R Ltd and T Ltd:

    (i)   gross profit as percentage of sales;   (vi)   current ratio;

    (ii) net profit as percentage of sales;   (vii) acid test ratio;

    (iii) expenses as percentage of sales;   (viii) debtor:sales ratio;

    (iv) stockturn;   (ix)   creditor:purchases ratio.

    (v) rate of return of net profit on capital employed (for the purpose of this question only, take capital as being total of share capitals + reserves at the balance sheet date);

(b) Comment briefly on the comparison of each ratio as between the two companies. State which company appears to be the most efficient, giving what you consider to be possible reasons.

34.11 The directors of L Ltd appointed a new sales manager towards the end of 19X2. This manager devised a plan to increase sales and profit by means of a reduction in selling price and extended credit terms to customers. This involved considerable investment in new machinery early in 19X3 in order to meet the demand which the change in sales policy had created.

The financial statements for the years ended 31 December 19X2 and 19X3 are shown below. The sales manager has argued that the new policy has been a resounding success because sales and, more importantly, profits have increased dramatically.

Profit and loss accounts	*19X2*	*19X3*
	£000	£000
Sales	900	2,800
Cost of sales	(360)	(1,680)
Gross profit	540	1,120
Selling expenses	(150)	(270)
Bad debts	(18)	(140)
Depreciation	(58)	(208)
Interest	(12)	(192)
Net profit	302	310
Balance b/fwd	327	629
	629	939

Balance sheets

	19X2		19X3	
	£000	£000	£000	£000
Fixed assets:				
Factory		450		441
Machinery		490		1,791
		940		2,232
Current assets:				
Stock	30		238	
Debtors	83		583	
Bank	12			
	125		821	
Current liabilities:				
Creditors	(36)		(175)	
Bank			(11)	
	(36)		(186)	
Current assets *less* Current liabilities		89		635
		1,029		2,867
Borrowings		(100)		(1,600)
		929		1,267
Share capital		300		328
Profit and loss		629		939
		929		1,267

(a) **You are required** to explain whether you believe that the performance for the year ended 31 December 19X3 and the financial position at that date have improved as a result of the new policies adopted by the company. You should support your answer with appropriate ratios.

(b) All of L Ltd's sales are on credit. The finance director has asked you to calculate the immediate financial impact of reducing the credit period offered to customers. Calculate the amount of cash which would be released if the company could impose a collection period of 45 days.

(*Chartered Institute of Management Accountants*)

35

Interpretation of financial statements

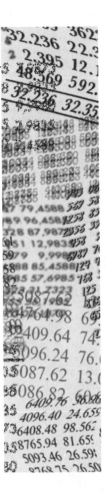

Objectives

After you have studied this chapter, you should:

- be aware of the importance of trend analysis when analysing financial statements

- appreciate that there is no such thing as a generally 'good' or 'bad' value for any ratio

- be aware of the need to compare 'like with like' if attempting to assess the quality of the result found from ratio analysis

- appreciate the existence of a pyramid of ratios that can be used in order to enhance the view obtained from ratio analysis

- be aware that different groups of users of financial statements have access to different sources of information that may help in developing an understanding of and explanation for the results of ratio analysis

35.1 Introduction

When shareholders receive the annual financial statements of a business, many simply look to see whether it has made a profit, and then put the document away. They are aware of only one thing – that the company made a profit of £x. They do not know if it was a 'good' profit. Nor do they know whether it was any different from the profit earned in previous years. (Even if they had noticed the previous period's profit figure in the comparative column, they would be unaware of the equivalent figures for the periods that preceded it.) In addition, they would have no perception of how the performance compared to those of other companies operating in the same sector.

In order that performance within a period can be assessed, ratio analysis may be undertaken, as explained in Chapter 34. However, such analysis is relatively useless unless a similar task is undertaken on the financial figures for previous periods. Trend analysis is very important in the interpretation of financial statements, for it is only then that the relative position can be identified, i.e. whether things are improving, etc.

Of similar importance if financial statements are to be usefully interpreted is comparison of the position shown with that of other companies operating in the same sector.

35.2 Sector relevance

The importance of ensuring that any comparison of analysis between companies is between companies in the same sector can best be illustrated through an extreme example – that of the contrast between service companies and manufacturing companies.

Stating the obvious, a firm of consultants that advise their clients on marketing strategies will have far fewer tangible assets than a company with the same turnover which manufactures forklift trucks. The service industry will need premises, but these could easily be rented, and in addition would need very little in the way of machinery. Some computer equipment and office equipment as well as motor cars would be all that would be needed.

Compared with the service industry firm, a manufacturing company, such as that making forklift trucks, would need a great deal of machinery as well as motor lorries and various types of buildings and so on. The manufacturing firm would also have stocks of materials and unsold trucks. The service firm would have very little in the way of stocks of tangible assets.

Especially with the service industries it is also likely that the number of people working for the firm, but who do most, sometimes all, of their work in their homes will grow apace. The need for people to turn up at offices at given times every day is falling dramatically with the wider use of computers and various communication and link-up devices.

All of this has an effect on the ratios of performance calculated from the accounts of manufacturers and service industry firms. The figure of return on capital employed for a service firm, simply because of the few tangible assets needed, may appear to be quite high. For a manufacturing firm the opposite may well be the case.

If this distinction between these completely different types of organisation is understood, then the interpreter of the accounts will judge them accordingly. Failure to understand the distinction will bring forth some very strange conclusions.

35.3 Trend analysis

What is important for a business is not just what the accounting ratios are for one year, but what the trend has been. In *Business Accounting 1*, the example was introduced of two companies G and H. The example is now reintroduced and further developed: Exhibit 35.1 presents four ratios derived from the financial statements of G over the past five periods.

Exhibit 35.1

	Period: X1	X2	X3	X4	X5 (now)
Gross profit as % of sales	40	38	36	35	34
Net profit as % of sales	15	13	12	12	11
Net profit as % of capital employed	13	12	11	11	10
Current ratio	3.0	2.8	2.6	2.3	2.0

If the trends in these four ratios are considered, it is clear that they are all deteriorating, but there is no indication whether there should be cause for concern as a result. For example, the industry may be becoming more competitive, causing margins to shrink, and the falling current ratio may be due to an increase in efficiency over the control of working capital.

A company with this trend of figures could state that these were the reasons for the decline in margins and for the reduction in liquidity. A reader of the financial statements could then accept the explanation and put the calculations away. However, there is no guarantee that an explanation of this kind actually indicates a beneficial situation, whether or not it is accurate. In order to gain a fuller view of the company, comparison with other comparable companies in the same sector is needed. Exhibit 35.2 presents the information from Exhibit 35.1 for company G plus information on another company of similar size operating in the same sector, company H.

Exhibit 35.2

	Period: X1	X2	X3	X4	X5 (now)
Gross profit as % of sales	G 40	38	36	35	34
	H 30	32	33	33	34
Net profit as % of sales	G 15	13	12	12	11
	H 10	10	10	11	11
Net profit as % of capital employed	G 13	12	11	11	10
	H 8	8	9	9	10
Current ratio	G 3.0	2.8	2.6	2.3	2.0
	H 1.5	1.7	1.9	1.9	2.0

Another way in which these results may be compared is through graphs, as shown by the example in Exhibit 35.3 which compares the trend in gross profit as a percentage of sales of the two companies. (Note that the vertical axis does not show the percentage below 30 as there is no percentage below that amount. Omitting the lower figures on the graph allows for a more informative display of the information.)

Exhibit 35.3

The trend of gross profit as a percentage of sales

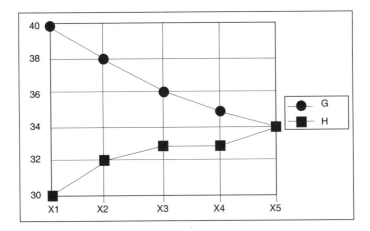

The companies have identical ratios for the current period – does that make them equally desirable as investments? Given one year's accounts it appears so, but the five-year trend analysis reveals a different picture.

From these figures, G appears to be the worse investment for the future, as the trend for it appears to be downwards, while that of H is upwards. It suggests that the explanation made earlier for the falling margins may not be valid. If the trend for G is continued it could be in a very dangerous financial situation in a year or two. H, on the other hand, is strengthening its position all the time.

While it would be ridiculous to assert that H will continue on an upward trend, or that G will continue downwards, a consistent trend of this type does suggest that the situation may well continue into the foreseeable future. It is certainly cause for further investigation.

35.4 Comparisons over time

As shown in the previous section, one of the best ways of using ratios is to compare them with the ratios for the same organisation in respect of previous years. Take another example, the net profit percentage of a company for the past six years, including the current year 19X8:

	19X3	*19X4*	*19X5*	*19X6*	*19X7*	*19X8 (now)*
Net profit %	5.4	5.2	4.7	4.8	4.8	4.5

This could be graphed as in Exhibit 35.4.

Exhibit 35.4

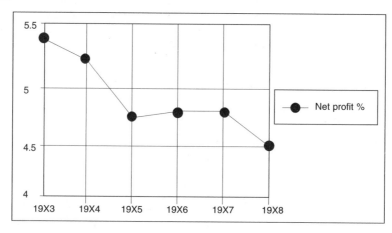

It is obvious that there is a long-term decline in net profit percentage. This prompts us to examine why this should be so. Without measuring against past years our understanding of the direction in which the business seems to be heading would be much diminished.

We would not look only at the long-term changes in net profit percentages, but would also compare similar long-term figures in relation to other aspects of the business.

In considering trends, problems may arise from the use of the historical cost accounting concept during a period of significant price increases because of inflation.

35.5 Comparisons with other businesses

No one can say in isolation that a firm is 'very profitable'. It could be the case that it has made £6 million a year, which to most people may seem profitable. On the other hand, if firms of a similar size in the same type of industry are making £20 million a year, then the firm making £6 million cannot be said to be 'very profitable'.

Ideally we would like to be able to compare the results of one firm with those of other similar firms in the same sort of industry. Then, and only then, would we really be able to judge how well, or how badly, it was doing.

The size of firm can have an important effect upon ratios. Just as we would not try to compare a chemist's shop with a building firm, it would also be wrong to judge a small supermarket against Sainsbury's, which owns hundreds of supermarkets.

Interfirm comparisons are also sometimes misleading because of the different accounting treatment of various items, and the location and ages of assets. Some industries have, however, set up interfirm comparisons with guidelines to the companies to ensure that the figures have been constructed using the same bases so that the information is properly comparable. The information does not disclose data which can be traced to any one firm, ensuring that full confidentiality is observed.

The information available may take the form shown in Exhibit 35.5.

Exhibit 35.5

Published ratios for the widget industry (extract)

	Solvency		*Efficiency*			
	Current	*Acid test*	*Asset T/O*	*Stock T/O*	*Debtor days*	*Creditor days*
19X6	2.4	0.7	5.4	8.2	56.4	80.4
19X7	2.2	0.8	5.7	9.3	52.6	66.8

The equivalent figures for the company being assessed can then be tabulated alongside the industry figures to enable comparisons to be made, as in Exhibit 35.6.

Exhibit 35.6

	Company ratios		*Industry ratios*	
	19X6	*19X7*	*19X6*	*19X7*
Current ratio	2.9	2.8	2.4	2.2
Acid test ratio	0.5	0.6	0.7	0.8
Asset turnover	5.2	5.3	5.4	5.7
Stock turnover	4.4	4.7	8.2	9.3
Debtor days	65.9	65.2	56.4	52.6
Creditor days	58.3	56.8	80.4	66.8

The financial status of the company is now much clearer. What appeared to be a situation of improving liquidity and efficiency is now clearly shown to be an increasingly poorer liquidity and efficiency position compared to the industry as a whole.

However, it should be borne in mind that the industry figures probably include many companies that are either much larger or much smaller than the company being assessed. To obtain a more complete picture, information is needed concerning companies of a similar size, such as in the comparison between G and H earlier in this chapter (section 35.3). This information may be available from the source of the interfirm comparison. If not, other sources would need to be used, for example the published financial statements of appropriate companies.

The other information missing from the above comparison is data from previous periods. While not so relevant to the current position, it can be useful in explaining why a situation has developed, and in determining whether the current position is likely to persist into the future.

35.6 Pyramid of ratios

Once ratios have been analysed and compared, explanations must be sought for the results obtained. Sometimes, it will be obvious why a certain result was obtained – for example, if a company has moved from traditional stock-keeping to a 'just-in-time' system during the period, its stock turnover will bear no resemblance to that which it had in the previous period.

For those inside the company – its directors and management – the management accounting records are available to assist in finding explanations, as are the company's staff. Outsiders – shareholders, analysts, lenders, suppliers, customers, etc. – do not have access to all this internal information (though some of these user groups will have access to more internal information than others – banks, for example, can usually obtain copies of a company's management accounts upon request). They must fall back upon other sources of information – newspaper reports and industry publications, for example. One source of additional information available to everyone is the **pyramid of ratios**. Most ratios can be further subdivided into secondary ratios, which themselves can also be subdivided. By following through the pyramid of a given ratio, the source of the original ratio can often be isolated, enabling a far more focused investigation than would otherwise be possible.

For example, one of the most important ratios is the return on the capital employed (ROCE). This ratio has not happened by itself. If the ratio of net profit to sales had not been a particular figure and the ratio of sales to capital employed had not been a particular figure, then the ROCE would not have turned out to be the figure that it is.

Thus, the ROCE comes about as a result of all the other ratios which have underpinned it. It is the final summation of all that has happened in the various aspects of the business. The ROCE pyramid of ratios is shown in Exhibit 35.7.

By itself the pyramid of ratios may not tell you much. It comes into full effect when compared with similar figures of the ratios for previous years, or with pyramids in respect of other firms. If the ROCE has been falling over the past year then a study of the pyramids for the two years may enable you to pinpoint exactly where the changes have been made to bring about the worsening position. Investigation of these matters may then give you some answers for action to be taken.

35.7 Return on capital employed: company policy

The pyramid of ratios in Exhibit 35.7 illustrates the interdependence of each ratio. This can be examined in greater detail by investigating the policies of two companies to achieve their desired return on capital employed.

The first part of the pyramid tells us that the ROCE is dependent on both net profit as a percentage of sales and also sales as a percentage of capital employed. This means that:

$$\text{ROCE} = \frac{\text{Net profit}}{\text{Capital employed}}$$

which by splitting the equation between profitability ratios and resource utilisation ratios means also that:

Exhibit 35.7

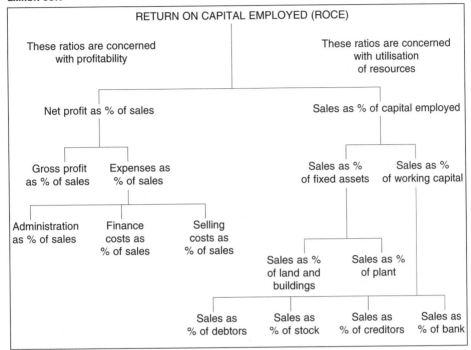

$$\text{ROCE} = \frac{\text{Net profit}}{\text{Sales}} \times \frac{\text{Sales}}{\text{Capital employed}}$$

This interrelationship of the subsidiary ratios can be illustrated through an example. At the same time, it can be seen that the result of computing a primary ratio is dependent upon the items comprising it; and that there is no guarantee that a value of x will be 'good', and y 'bad'. Whether the result obtained is 'good' or 'bad' depends on the underlying factors that give rise to the result obtained (what, for example, is the company's policy on depreciation and replacement of assets? This can significantly affect the ROCE), the sector in which the business operates and its relative size. Without knowledge of these items, comparison of the ratio analysis of two companies is likely to be misleading at best.

Two companies, both in the grocery business, may decide to aim for the same ROCE of 10 per cent. This can be achieved in completely different ways by the two companies.

A Ltd is a large company operating a supermarket. It seeks to attract customers by offering low prices and only makes a net profit of 1.25 per cent on sales. Its sales for the year are £8,000,000 on which its net profit is £100,000. Its capital employed is £1,000,000. The ROCE is, therefore, 10 per cent (i.e. £100,000 net profit on capital employed of £1,000,000). This can also be expressed as:

$$\text{ROCE} = \frac{\text{Net profit}}{\text{Sales}} \times \frac{\text{Sales}}{\text{Capital employed}}$$

$$= \frac{£100,000}{£8,000,000} \times \frac{£8,000,000}{£1,000,000} = 10\%$$

B Ltd by comparison, is a small local retailer. It seeks a higher margin per £100 sales, but because of higher prices it will achieve a lower volume of business. It makes a net profit of 5 per cent on sales. Its sales for the year amount to £200,000 on which it makes a net profit of £10,000. The capital employed is £100,000. The ROCE is therefore 10 per cent (i.e. £10,000 on capital employed of £100,000). This can also be expressed as:

$$\text{ROCE} = \frac{\text{Net profit}}{\text{Sales}} \times \frac{\text{Sales}}{\text{Capital employed}}$$

$$= \frac{\text{£}10,000}{\text{£}200,000} \times \frac{\text{£}200,000}{\text{£}100,000} = 10\%$$

It can be seen that two firms, despite different sizes of business and operating different pricing policies, can have the same ROCE.

Main points to remember

1 Ratios on their own are frequently misleading – they should not be considered in isolation from similar computations:
   (a) in previous periods; and/or
   (b) on similar sized firms in the same sector.

2 The items in the financial statements are affected by company policy – for example, the rate of depreciation to use, and the policy of asset replacement – and the policies adopted, therefore, directly affect the ratio analysis.

3 Companies of very different size and in very different sectors can have the same ratio results despite their being different in every respect.

4 The importance and impact of size, sector and company policies upon ratios mean that there is no such thing as a 'good' or 'bad' value that can be treated as a yardstick for any ratio.

5 All ratios are part of one or more pyramids of ratios.

6 When the results of ratio analysis are being investigated further, the relevant pyramid of ratios can be analysed in order to pinpoint the element giving rise to the situation being investigated.

Advice

This is a topic that causes more marks to be thrown away in exams than probably every other topic combined. No other topic is as concerned with understanding rather than knowledge, and examiners tend to expect students to be able to demonstrate their understanding rather than simply their ability to prepare the accounts or calculate the ratios.

There is no one set pattern to the questions, which depend upon the examiner's ingenuity and background experience. The usual shortcomings in the answers handed in by examinees, particularly on questions relating to this topic but also on questions in other areas, can be listed as follows:

1 Not following the instructions as laid down. If the question says 'list the' then the examiner expects a list as an answer, 'Discuss the' means exactly that, 'Write a report' needs a report as the answer, and so on. You will lose a lot of marks for not giving the examiner exactly what has been asked for.

2 Very often all the ratios etc. are calculated, but then the candidate does not offer any comments even though they have been asked for. *Make certain you cover this part of the question in an appropriate amount of detail.*

3 Even where students have written something about the ratios, they often repeat what the calculations are and offer nothing else, e.g. 'you can see that the gross profit ratio has increased from 18 to 20 per cent' and the answer has finished there. The examiner can already see from your calculations that the gross profit percentage has increased, and wants you to write about why it might have increased, what conclusions, if any, can be arrived at, or what further information may be needed to discover why it has changed.

4 Remember that when the examiner asks you 'what other information you would like to have' about a firm when trying to interpret the accounts so as to give advice to someone then, ideally, you would like to know more about the plans for the future of the business, how it compares with others in the same industry, whether or not there are going to be changes in the management and so on. We should not limit ourselves to information about the past, we really need to know as much about the future as we possibly can.

5 Do not restrict your examination answers to what you have read in a textbook. Keep your eyes and ears open as you go shopping, visit factories, work, buy petrol at the filling station, go to the theatre, and so on. Reading a 'quality' newspaper helps, as there are quite a lot of items about business. Bring all of this sort of knowledge and experience into your answers. You will impress the examiners. They are bored to death reading regurgitations of textbook learning with nothing else added.

6 Quite a few questions will concern the type of business of which you will have first-hand experience and can introduce your own personal knowledge into your answer. A typical instance would be comparing two grocery businesses. One would be a large supermarket and the other would be a small corner shop. The policies of the two firms would be quite different. The supermarket would have decided on a policy of attracting new customers by lowering sales margins and yet boosting ROCE. The corner shop might have a policy of high margins, but remain open on Sundays and late at nights, and thus be a 'convenience shop', i.e. customers might well go there when other shops are closed or are too far away to be worth the extra cost in petrol, etc. when compared with the extra cost of shopping at the corner shop.

7 Last, but not least, *show your workings.* If you make a mistake in your calculations and do not show your workings you cannot be awarded any credit for a partially incorrect calculation. Consider how much longer it takes to show the detail contained in section 35.7 above, rather than simply the result of the calculation – maybe 30 seconds. *Now consider whether you would rather spend five minutes in an exam showing the workings of ten ratio calculations, or six months studying to retake the exam you failed because you made a mistake in two of your calculations and lost five marks because the examiner could not tell why you got the answer wrong.*

Review questions

35.1 Adrian Frampton was considering the purchase of one of two businesses. However, Frampton had only been provided with limited information about the businesses, as follows:

Summarised financial information for the year ended 31 December 19X9

Information	Business X	Business Y
Cost of goods sold	£400,000	£600,000
Administrative expenses	£50,000	£60,000
Average stock at cost	£40,000	£50,000
Working capital as at 31 December 19X9	£90,000	£250,000
Selling and distribution expenses	£15,000	£35,000
Proprietor's capital at 1 January 19X9	£200,000	£350,000
Gross profit percentage mark-up on cost	20	25

Additional information
1. Average stock had been calculated by using the year's opening and closing stocks. Subsequently it was discovered that Business Y had overvalued its stock on 31 December 19X9 by £10,000.
2. Business X's administrative expenses included a payment for rent of £15,000 which covered a three-year period to 31 December 19X1.
3. A sum of £2,500 was included in the administrative expenses of Business Y in respect of a holiday taken by the owner and his family.
4. Cash drawings for the year ended 31 December 19X9 were:

	£
Business X	20,000
Business Y	25,000

5. The owners of the businesses had stipulated the following prices for their businesses:

	£
Business X	190,000
Business Y	400,000

Required:
(a) Based on the information available prepare comparative trading and profit and loss accounts for the year ended 31 December 19X9.
(b) Using the information provided and the accounting statements prepared in (a), calculate relevant accounting ratios in order to give Frampton a basis for assessing the performances of the two businesses. Comment on the results.
(c) What additional information is needed in order to assess more accurately
  (i) the liquidity of the businesses;
  (ii) the future prospects of the businesses?

(Associated Examining Board: GCE 'A' level)

35.2 Three companies have the capital structures shown below.

Company	A	B	C
	£000	£000	£000
Ordinary shares	600	400	50
12% debentures	–	200	550
	600	600	600

The return on capital employed was 20 per cent for each firm in 19X4, and in 19X5 was 10 per cent. Corporation tax in both years was assumed to be 55 per cent, and debenture interest is an allowable expense against corporation tax.

(a) Calculate the percentage return on the shareholders' capital for each company for 19X4 and 19X5. Assume that all profits are distributed.
(b) Use your answer to explain the merits and the dangers of high gearing.

(*University of London GCE 'A' level*)

35.3A Martha is the accountant of a trading business. During the past year she produced interim accounts for the six months ended 30 November 19X5, and draft final accounts for the year ended 31 May 19X6, as follows:

	Interim accounts £	Draft final accounts £
Sales (all on credit terms)	140,000	336,000
Cost of sales (note 1)	42,000	112,000
Gross profit	98,000	224,000
Less Expenses	56,000	168,000
Net profit	42,000	56,000
Fixed assets	70,000	63,000
Current assets (note 2)	42,000	71,000
Current liabilities (note 3)	(22,000)	(30,000)
	90,000	104,000
Share capital	30,000	30,000
Retained earnings	60,000	74,000
	90,000	104,000

Notes:
1 Average stock was £14,000 during the first six months.
2 Current assets were:

	30 Nov 19X5 £	31 May 19X6 £
Stock	16,000	25,000
Debtors	24,000	28,000
Bank	2,000	18,000
	42,000	71,000

3 Current liabilities consisted entirely of trade creditors.

Martha informs you that the business leased additional premises from 1 December 19X5, and that sales arising therefrom totalled £70,000 for the six months to 31 May 19X6, with an average mark-up on cost prices of 150 per cent being made on those goods.

Expenses relating to these additional premises totalled £21,000 for the period. Two-fifths of the closing stock of the business was located at these premises.

Prepare a report, using appropriate accounting ratios, to explain the changes in the financial situation of the business during the year ended 31 May 19X6.

(*University of London GCE 'A' level*)

35.4 John Jones is considering purchasing shares in one of two companies and has extracted the following information from the balance sheet of each company.

	Company A Plc £000	Company B Plc £000
Authorised share capital		
£1 ordinary shares	600	1,000
8% £1 preference shares	400	
Issued share capital		
£1 ordinary shares	300	800
8% £1 preference shares	200	
Reserves		
Share premium	300	400
Retained earnings	400	200
Loan capital		
10% debentures (19X0)		200
12% debentures (19X6)	400	

Required:
(a) Define the term 'gearing' stating clearly what is meant by a low gearing ratio.
(b) Calculate the gearing factor for each company.
(c) Explain to John Jones the significance of gearing to an ordinary shareholder in each of the companies above.
(d) Assuming for each company a trading profit of £200,000 before interest and an ordinary dividend of 15 per cent complete the profit and loss appropriation account for a year for each company. You should ignore taxation.

(*Associated Examining Board GCE 'A' level*)

35.5A The following are extracts from the balance sheets as at 31 March 19X4 and 31 March 19X5 of Glebe Ltd:

	31 March 19X4 £	£	31 March 19X5 £	£
Current assets				
Stocks	20,000		25,000	
Trade debtors	10,000		17,000	
Cash	5,000		3,000	
		35,000		45,000
Less				
Current liabilities				
Trade creditors	12,000		16,000	
Proposed dividends	6,000		5,000	
Bank overdraft	7,000		29,000	
		25,000		50,000
		10,000		(5,000)

Required:
(a) Calculate for each of the two years two ratios that indicate the liquidity position of the company.

(b) (i) From the information given, give reasons for the changes which have occurred in the working capital.

(ii) What other information regarding the current assets and current liabilities would you consider necessary to assess the ability of the business to continue in operation?

(c) Discuss any other information available from a balance sheet that may affect an assessment of the liquidity of a business.

(*Associated Examining Board GCE 'A' level*)

35.6 Colin Black is considering investing a substantial sum in the ordinary shares of Jacks Ltd. Having some accounting knowledge he has extracted the following information from the accounts for the last two financial years.

	As at 31 March 19X4 £	As at 31March 19X5 £
Issued share capital		
£1 ordinary shares, fully paid	100,000	150,000
Reserves		
Share premium	10,000	60,000
Retained earnings	140,000	160,000
Loan capital		
10% debentures 19X7–X9	40,000	40,000

	For year ended 31 March 19X4 £	For year ended 31 March 19X5 £
Net profit after tax	60,000	70,000

Because he was disappointed with the result he obtained when he calculated the return on the equity capital employed, Colin Black has asked for your advice.

Required:

(a) Calculate the figures which prompted Colin Black's reaction.

(b) Prepare a memorandum to Colin Black pointing out other information to be considered when comparing the return on equity capital employed over two years as a basis for his investment decision.

(c) Explain why a company builds up and maintains reserves.

(*Associated Examining Board*)

35.7A The following information has been extracted from the accounts of Witton Way Ltd:

Profit and Loss Account for the year to 30 April

	19X5 £000	19X6 £000
Turnover (all credit sales)	7,650	11,500
Less Cost of sales	(5,800)	(9,430)
Gross profit	1,850	2,070
Other expenses	(150)	(170)
Loan interest	(50)	(350)
Profit before taxation	1,650	1,550
Taxation	(600)	(550)
Profit after taxation	1,050	1,000
Dividends (all ordinary shares)	(300)	(300)
Retained profits	£750	£700

Balance Sheet at 30 April

	19X5 £000	19X6 £000
Fixed assets		
Tangible assets	10,050	11,350
Current assets		
Stocks	1,500	2,450
Trade debtors	1,200	3,800
Cash	900	50
	3,600	6,300
Creditors: Amounts falling due within one year	2,400	2,700
Net current assets	1,200	3,600
Total assets less current liabilities	11,250	14,950
Creditors:		
Amounts falling due after more than one year		
Loans and other borrowings	350	3,350
	£10,900	£11,600
Capital and reserves		
Called-up share capital	5,900	5,900
Profit and loss account	5,000	5,700
	£10,900	£11,600

Additional information:
During the year to 30 April 19X6, the company tried to stimulate sales by reducing the selling price of its products and by offering more generous credit terms to its customers.

Required:

(a) Calculate six accounting ratios specifying the basis of your calculations for each of the two years to 30 April 19X5 and 19X6 respectively which will enable you to examine the company's progress during 19X6.

(b) From the information available to you, including the ratios calculated in part (a) of the question, comment upon the company's results for the year to 30 April 19X6 under the heads of 'profitability', 'liquidity', 'efficiency' and 'shareholders' interests'.

(c) State what additional information you would require in order to assess the company's attempts to stimulate sales during the year to 30 April 19X6.

(*Association of Accounting Technicians*)

35.8 You are presented with the following information for three quite separate and independent companies:

Summarised Balance Sheets at 31 March 19X7

	Chan plc £000	Ling plc £000	Wong plc £000
Total assets *less* current liabilities	600	600	700
Creditors: amounts falling due after more than one year			
10% debenture stock	–	–	(100)
	£600	£600	£600
Capital and reserves:			
Called-up share capital			
Ordinary shares of £1 each	500	300	200
10% cumulative preference shares of £1 each	–	200	300
Profit and loss account	100	100	100
	£600	£600	£600

Additional information:
1 The operating profit before interest and tax for the year to 31 March 19X8 earned by each of the three companies was £300,000.
2 The effective rate of corporation tax for all three companies for the year to 31 March 19X8 is 30 per cent. This rate is to be used in calculating each company's tax payable on ordinary profit.
3 An ordinary dividend of 20p for the year to 31 March 19X8 is proposed by all three companies, and any preference dividends are to be provided for.
4 The market prices per ordinary share at 31 March 19X8 were as follows:

	£
Chan plc	8.40
Ling plc	9.50
Wong plc	10.38

5 There were no changes in the share capital structure or in long-term loans of any of the companies during the year to 31 March 19X8.

Required:
(a) Insofar as the information permits, prepare the profit and loss account for each of the three companies (in columnar format) for the year to 31 March 19X8 (formal notes to the accounts are not required);
(b) calculate the following accounting ratios for each company:
   (i) earnings per share;
   (ii) price earnings;
   (iii) gearing (taken as total borrowings (preference share capital and long-term loans) to ordinary shareholders' funds); and
(c) using the gearing ratios calculated in answering part (b) of the question, briefly examine the importance of gearing if you were thinking of investing in some ordinary shares in one of the three companies assuming that the profits of the three companies were fluctuating.

(Association of Accounting Technicians)

35.9A The chairman of a family business has been examining the following summary of the accounts of the company since it began three years ago.

Balance Sheet (at 30 June) £000s

	19X4 Actual		19X5 Actual		19X6 Actual	
Freehold land and buildings		150		150		150
Plant	150		150		450	
Less Depreciation	15	135	30	120	75	375
		285		270		525
Stock and work in progress	20		45		85	
Debtors	33		101		124	
Bank and cash	10		15		–	
	63		161		209	
Less Creditors	20		80		35	
Taxation	4		17		6	
Overdraft	–	39	–	64	25	143
		324		334		468
Less Loan		–		–		200
		324		334		468
Ordinary share capital (£1 shares)		300		300		400
General reserve		17		25		45
Deferred tax account		7		9		23
		324		334		468

Profit and Loss Account (for year to 30 June) £000s

	19X4 Actual		19X5 Actual		19X6 Actual	
Sales		260		265		510
Trading profit		53		50		137
Depreciation	15		15		45	
Loan interest	–	15	–	15	43	88
Net profit		38		35		49
Taxation (including transfer to or from deferred tax account)		11		15		15
Net profit after tax		27		20		34
Dividend (proposed*)		10		12		14*
Retained		17		8		20

The company's products are popular in the locality and in the first two years sales could have been higher if there had been extra machine capacity available.

On 1 January 19X6, additional share and loan capital was obtained which enabled extra machinery to be purchased. This gave an immediate increase in sales and profits.

Although 19X5/X6 showed the best yet results, the chairman is not very happy; the accountant has suggested that a dividend should not be paid this year because of the overdraft. The accountant has, however, shown a proposed dividend of £14,000 (£2,000 up on last year) for purposes of comparison pending a decision by the directors.

Naturally, the chairman is displeased and wants some explanations from the accountant regarding the figures in the accounts.

He specifically asks:
(i) Why, if profits are the best ever and considering the company has obtained extra capital during the year, has the company gone into overdraft? Can there really be a profit if there is no cash left in the bank to pay a dividend?
(ii) Why is the freehold still valued at the same price as in 19X4? The real value seems to be about £225,000. Why is this real value not in the balance sheet?

Required:
Write a report to the chairman:
(a) commenting on the state and progress of the business as disclosed by the accounts and the above information, supporting your analysis by appropriate key accounting ratios, and
(b) giving reasoned answers, in the context of recognised accounting law, rules and practices, to each of the questions raised by the chairman.

(*Institute of Chartered Secretaries and Administrators*)

35.10 The following information is provided for Bessemer Ltd which operates in an industry subject to marked variations in consumer demand.

(i) Shareholders' equity at 30 September 19X5:

	£000
Issued ordinary shares of £1 each fully paid	5,000
Retained profits	1,650
	6,650

There were no loans outstanding at the balance sheet date.

(ii) Profit and loss account extracts: year to 30 September 19X5:

	£000
Net profit before tax	900
Less Corporation tax	270
	630
Less Dividends	600
Retained profit for the year	30
Retained profit at 1 October 19X4	1,620
Retained profit at 30 September 19X5	1,650

(iii) The directors are planning to expand output. This will require an additional investment of £2,000,000 which may be financed either by issuing 1,000,000 ordinary shares each with a nominal value of £1, or by raising a 12 per cent debenture.

(iv) Forecast profits before interest charges, if any, for the year to 30 September:

	£000
19X6	1,800
19X7	500
19X8	2,200

A corporation tax rate of 30 per cent on reported profit before tax may be assumed; the directors plan to pay out the entire post-tax profit as dividends.

Required:
(a) The forecast profit and loss appropriation accounts for each of the next three years and year-end balance sheet extracts, so far as the information permits, assuming that the expansion is financed by:
   (i)   issuing additional shares, or
   (ii) raising a debenture.
(b) Calculate the forecast return on shareholders' equity, for each of the next three years, under the alternative methods for financing the planned expansion.
(c) An assessment of the merits and demerits of the alternative methods of finance based on the calculations made under (a) and (b) and any other relevant methods of comparison.

(*Institute of Chartered Secretaries and Administrators*)

35.11A An investor is considering the purchase of shares in either AA plc or BB plc whose latest accounts are summarised below. Both companies carry on similar manufacturing activities with similar selling prices and costs of materials, labour and services.

Balance Sheets at 30 September 19X7

	AA plc £000	AA plc £000	BB plc £000	BB plc £000
Freehold property at revaluation 19X5		2,400		–
Plant, machinery and equipment:				
at cost	1,800		1,800	
depreciation	1,200		400	
		600		1,400
Goodwill		–		800
Stocks: finished goods		400		200
work in progress		300		100
Debtors		800		500
Bank deposit		–		400
		4,500		3,400
Less Liabilities due within one year				
Creditors	600		900	
Overdraft	200		–	
	800		900	
Liabilities due after one year	1,400		1,000	
		2,200		1,900
		2,300		1,500
Ordinary £1 shares		1,000		500
Reserves		1,300		1,000
		2,300		1,500

Profit and Loss Accounts – Year to 30 September 19X7

	AA plc £000	AA plc £000	BB plc £000	BB plc £000
Sales		2,500		2,500
Operating profit		400		600
Depreciation – plant, machinery and equipment	180		180	
Loan interest	150		160	
		330		340
		70		260
Bank interest		–		100
		70		360
Taxation		20		90
Available to ordinary shareholders		50		270
Dividend		40		130
Retained		£10		£140
Price/earnings ratio	30		5	
Market value of share	£1.50		£2.70	

Required:
(a) Write a report to the investor, giving an appraisal of the results and state of each business, and
(b) advise the investor whether, in your opinion, the price earnings ratios and market price of the shares can be justified in the light of the figures in the accounts, giving your reasons.

(*Institute of Chartered Secretaries and Administrators*)

35.12 The following are the summarised accounts for B Limited, a company with an accounting year ending on 30 September.

Summarised Balance Sheets for	19X5/6		19X6/7	
	£000	£000	£000	£000
Tangible fixed assets – at cost				
Less Depreciation		4,995		12,700
Current assets:				
Stocks	40,145		50,455	
Debtors	40,210		43,370	
Cash at bank	12,092		5,790	
	92,447		99,615	
Creditors: amounts falling due within one year:				
Trade creditors	32,604		37,230	
Taxation	2,473		3,260	
Proposed dividend	1,785		1,985	
	36,862		42,475	
Net current assets		55,585		57,140
Total assets *less* current liabilities		60,580		69,840
Creditors: amounts falling due after more than one year:				
10% debentures 20X6/20X9		19,840		19,840
		40,740		50,000
Capital and reserves:				
Called-up share capital of £0.25 per share		9,920		9,920
Profit and loss account		30,820		40,080
Shareholders' funds		40,740		50,000

Summarised Profit and Loss Accounts for	19X5/6	19X6/7
	£000	£000
Turnover	486,300	583,900
Operating profit	17,238	20,670
Interest payable	1,984	1,984
Profit on ordinary activities before taxation	15,254	18,686
Tax on profit on ordinary activities	5,734	7,026
Profit for the financial year	9,520	11,660
Dividends	2,240	2,400
	7,280	9,260
Retained profit brought forward	23,540	30,820
Retained profit carried forward	30,820	40,080

You are required to:

(a) calculate, for each year, two ratios for each of the following user groups, which are of particular significance to them:
 (i) shareholders;
 (ii) trade creditors;
 (iii) internal management;

(b) make brief comments upon the changes, between the two years, in the ratios calculated in (a) above.

(*Chartered Institute of Management Accountants*)

35.13A The following are the financial statements of D Limited, a wholesaling company, for the year ended 31 December:

Profit and Loss Accounts	19X4	19X4	19X5	19X5
	£000	£000	£000	£000
Turnover – credit sales	2,200		2,640	
cash sales	200		160	
		2,400		2,800
Cost of sales		(1,872)		(2,212)
Gross profit		528		588
Distribution costs		(278)		(300)
Administration expenses		(112)		(114)
Operating profit		138		174
Interest payable		–		(32)
Profit on ordinary activities before tax		138		142

Balance Sheets as at 31 December	19X4	19X4	19X5	19X5
	£000	£000	£000	£000
Tangible fixed assets		220		286
Current assets: Stocks	544		660	
Debtors	384		644	
Cash at bank	8		110	
	936		1,414	
Creditors: amounts falling due within one year:				
Trade creditors	(256)		(338)	
Net current assets		680		1,076
Total assets *less* current liabilities		900		1,362
Creditors: amounts falling due after more than one year:				
Debenture loans				(320)
Shareholders' funds		900		1,042

The following information should be taken into consideration.

1 You may assume that:
 (i) The range of products sold by D Limited remained unchanged over the two years;
 (ii) the company managed to acquire its products in 19X5 at the same prices as it acquired them for in 19X4;
 (iii) the effects of any inflationary aspects have been taken into account in the figures.
2 Ignore taxation.
3 All calculations must be shown to one decimal place.

You are required, using the information above, to assess and comment briefly on the company, from the point of view of:

(*a*) profitability;

(*b*) liquidity.

(*Chartered Institute of Management Accountants*)

35.14 G plc is a holding company with subsidiaries that have diversified interests. G plc's board of directors is interested in the group acquiring a subsidiary in the machine tool manufacturing sector. Two companies have been identified as potential acquisitions, A Ltd and B Ltd. Summaries of both these companies' accounts are shown below:

Profit and Loss Accounts for the year ended 30 April 19X8

	A Ltd £000	B Ltd £000
Turnover	985	560
Cost of goods sold		
Opening stock	150	145
Materials	255	136
Labour	160	125
Factory overheads	205	111
Depreciation	35	20
Closing stock	(155)	(140)
	650	397
Gross profit	335	163
Selling and administration expenses	(124)	(75)
Interest	(35)	(10)
Profit before taxation	176	78
Taxation	65	25
Profit after taxation	111	53

Balance Sheets at 30 April 19X8

	A Ltd £000	A Ltd £000	B Ltd £000	B Ltd £000
Fixed assets		765		410
Current assets				
Stock	155		140	
Debtors	170		395	
Bank	50		45	
	375		580	
Current liabilities				
Trade creditors	235		300	
Other	130		125	
	365		425	
Net current assets		10		155
Debentures		(220)		(70)
		555		495
Share capital		450		440
Profit and loss account		105		55
		555		495

You are required to prepare a report for the board of G plc assessing the financial performance and position of A Ltd and B Ltd. Your report should be prepared in the context of G plc's interests in these two companies and should be illustrated with financial ratios where appropriate. You should state any assumptions you make as well as any limitations of your analysis.

(*Chartered Institute of Management Accountants*)

35.15A J plc supplies and fits car tyres, exhaust pipes and other components. The company has branches throughout the country. Roughly 60 per cent of sales are for cash (retail sales). The remainder are credit sales made to car hire companies and large organisations with fleets of company cars (business sales). Business sales tend to be more profitable than retail and the company is keen to expand in this area. There is, however, considerable competition. Branch managers are responsible for obtaining business customers and have some discretion over terms of trade and discounts.

The company's computerised accounting system has recently produced the following report for the manager of the Eastown branch for the six months ended 30 September 19X4:

	Eastown branch	Average for all branches
Return on capital employed	22%	16%
Gross profit	38%	45%
Selling and promotion costs/sales	9%	6%
Wages/sales	19%	14%
Debtors turnover (based on credit sales only)	63 days	52 days
Stock turnover	37 days	49 days

The Eastown branch manager has only recently been appointed and is unsure whether his branch appears well managed. He has asked for your advice.

You are required to compare the performance of the Eastown branch with the average for all branches. Suggest reasons for the differences you identify.

(*Chartered Institute of Management Accountants*)

35.16A Company managers are aware that the readers of financial statements often use accounting ratios to evaluate their performance. Explain how this could lead to decisions which are against the company's best interests.

(*Chartered Institute of Management Accountants*)

Part 5

ISSUES IN FINANCIAL REPORTING

36 Alternatives to historic cost accounting

37 Social accounting

38 Accounting as an information system

Introduction

This part looks at issues affecting accounting and financial reporting, and at the place of accounting information in the context of the environment in which business entities operate.

36

Alternatives to historic cost accounting

Objectives

After you have studied this chapter, you should:

- *know why historic cost accounts are deficient in times of rising prices*

- *understand different valuation methods*

- *know the purposes of specific price indices for assets and liabilities*

- *have an understanding of the adjustments necessary in order to convert historic costs to current costs*

- *be able to prepare a current cost balance sheet and current cost profit and loss account*

36.1 Introduction

Accounts have traditionally been prepared for two main purposes, stewardship and decision making. The Accounting Standards Board's Exposure Draft: Statement of Principles, published in 1991, outlined several user groups with varying needs, all of whom are interested in financial information. Shareholders are interested in different information than trade creditors. This information has traditionally been provided by financial statements prepared under the historic cost convention. However, there are circumstances when financial statements prepared under this traditional approach can present financial information in a misleading way.

Consider the following example. On 1 January 19X4, a company invests in 500 widgets for £1,000, that is £2 per unit. Shortly before the year end, when the replacement cost of a widget is £2.20 per unit, the stock is sold for £1,200. On a historic cost basis, the profit is recorded as follows:

	£
Sales	1,200
Cost of Sales	1,000
Profit	200

However, in order to maintain the same operating capacity, the company will need to invest in more widgets at a cost of £1,100 (500 × £2.20). If the company distributes the £200 as a dividend, it will only be left with £1,000 and cannot make this investment. From this simple example, one of the major criticisms of historic cost accounting is evident – its inability to reflect the effects of changing prices. Obviously, this criticism is dependent upon the level of inflation at the time.

An acceptable alternative to historic cost accounting has been sought by the accountancy profession in the United Kingdom for several years. The attempts of the Accounting Standards Committee (ASC) to introduce a system of inflation accounting, which are outlined in Chapter 45 of the first volume, failed. The culmination of great effort and numerous exposure drafts and standards was the ASC Handbook, *Accounting for the Effects of Changing Prices*, published in 1986. The remainder of this chapter considers several of the issues dealt with in the Handbook in the context of the preparation of a set of current cost accounts. It is worth noting that the ASB recognises that the present system of historic cost accounting, modified by voluntary revaluations of certain assets, is unsatisfactory. The ASB aims to tackle the issue, and current values are once again on the agenda. It is unlikely, however, that a system of current cost accounting will be introduced without difficulty.

36.2 Valuation

Under historic cost accounting, assets and liabilities are recorded at their actual cost at the date of transaction. For example, when a new machine is purchased, the price per the invoice can be recorded in the books of the business. Whilst this is a familiar and reasonably cheap method of recording the assets and liabilities of an entity, its main advantage is its objectivity. The historic cost of an item is an objective verifiable fact that can easily be ascertained from the records of the business. It is worth noting that there is some degree of subjectivity in the preparation of historic cost accounts. Consider, for example, the choice of suitable depreciation method for a fixed asset which is left to the discretion of the directors of the company. The size of the bad debts provision is also dependent upon the exercise of judgement. Notwithstanding this, it is fair to say that historic values have a high degree of reliability. The main disadvantage, particularly in times of changing prices, is their relevance, as demonstrated in the widget example in the previous section.

Current value accounting considers the following valuation methods which are covered in Chapter 45 of the first volume: **economic value, value to the business, replacement cost, net realisable value** and **recoverable amount**.

The **economic value** of an asset is the sum of the future expected net cash flows associated with the asset, discounted to its present value. **Value to the business**, or **deprival value**, can be considered an appropriate valuation basis for accounting purposes. If a business were deprived of an asset, it could either replace it, or choose not to. If the asset were replaced, then its current value to the business is its net current **replacement cost**. This is normally the current cost of a fixed asset, except where it has suffered a permanent diminution in value, in which case it will be written down to its **recoverable amount**. This may happen, for example, because there is no longer a market for the product. Alternatively, if the business would choose not to replace the asset, then it would sell it and its current cost is its **net realisable value**, i.e. the price at which it can be sold in the market.

How are these values determined by a business? The replacement cost of an asset can be approximated using a relevant index. Indices, published for example by the UK Government Statistical Service, are usually specific to a class of asset. A company may prepare its own index based on experience or, where it is not appropriate to use an index, a valuer may be relied upon. This is usual in the case of revaluing property. The index will indicate the change in value of the asset or class of asset.

Consider the following example. A machine was purchased on 1 January 19X2 for £75,000 when the relevant specific price index was 90. Its current value at 31 December 19X4, when the relevant specific price index is 120, is:

$$\frac{\text{Index at accounting date}}{\text{Index at date of purchases}} \times £75,000 = \frac{120}{90} \times £75,000 = £100,000$$

Replacement does not necessarily mean replacement of the asset with a similar asset. Rather, it focuses on replacement of the service potential of the asset and its contribution to the business.

Net realisable value is the price at which the asset could be sold in an arm's length transaction. A problem may arise where no market exists for the asset. The main problem with current values is the level of subjectivity involved in ascertaining valuations. A business may need to spend considerable time and effort ascertaining current values for its assets and liabilities.

36.3 Current cost accounts

The directors of Hillcrest Ltd are interested in preparing current cost accounts to reflect changing prices. They have prepared a historic cost balance sheet and profit and loss account (Exhibit 36.1). The relevant price indices for plant and machinery, stock, debtors and creditors, are given in Exhibit 36.2.

Exhibit 36.1

Hillcrest Ltd

Balance Sheet as at 30 June

		19X5 £000		19X4 £000
Fixed assets				
Plant and machinery				
Cost		800		800
Depreciation		320		240
Net book value		480		560
Current assets				
Stock	250		200	
Trade debtors	180		110	
Cash	105		75	
	535		385	
Current liabilities				
Trade creditors	(90)		(100)	
Net current assets		445		285
10% loan stock		(310)		(310)
		615		535
Financed by				
Ordinary shares		200		200
Reserves		415		335
Current cost reserve		615		535

Hillcrest Ltd

Profit and Loss Account for year ending 30 June 19X5

	£000	£000
Sales		1,700
Cost of sales		
Opening stock	200	
Purchases	1,375	
	1,575	
Less Closing stock	250	
		1,325
Gross profit		375
Interest	31	
Depreciation	80	
Other expenses	184	
		295
Net profit		80

Exhibit 36.2

Price index for stock at the end of each month:

March	19X4	109
April	19X4	112
June	19X4	114
December	19X4	116
March	19X5	122
April	19X5	126
June	19X5	130

Average for the year ending 30 June 19X5   126

Plant and machinery index			*Debtors and creditors index*		
June	19X1	80	June	19X4	110
June	19X2	90	June	19X5	200
June	19X3	100			
June	19X4	105			
June	19X5	110	Average for 19X5		255

In order to prepare current cost accounts, the first step is to calculate current values for the assets. Hillcrest Ltd's plant and machinery was purchased for £800,000 on 1 July 19X1. The current value of the plant and machinery at 30 June 19X5 is:

$$\text{Plant and machinery at cost} \times \frac{\text{Index at balance sheet date}}{\text{Index at date of purchase}} = £800,000 \times \frac{110}{80} = £1,100,000$$

The accumulated depreciation of £320,000 charged in the historic cost accounts, representing 40 per cent of the asset which has been consumed, is also restated. The current value of the depreciation is:

$$£320,000 \times \frac{110}{80} = £440,000$$

On average, Hillcrest Ltd's stock was acquired three months before the year end. Hence, its current value, rounded to the nearest £000, at 30 June 19X5 is:

$$£250,000 \times \frac{126}{122} = £258,000$$

Monetary assets, for example trade debtors and cash, and monetary liabilities, including trade creditors, are not restated. These items have a fixed monetary value which does not change. For example, if you borrow £1,000 today under an agreement to repay in 12 months, the monetary value of the amount borrowed will not change, that is you will repay £1,000. However, in times of rising prices, the market value of the amount will decrease. This gain will be dealt with later in the chapter.

36.4 Current cost reserve

Having revalued both plant and machinery and stock to their current values, the following revaluation gains are recorded:

	Plant and machinery £	Stock £
Current book value	660,000[1]	258,000
Historic book value	480,000	250,000
Surplus on revaluation	180,000	8,000

[1] Plant at current cost less accumulated depreciation,
   i.e. £1,100,000 − £440,000

The total gain of £188,000 (£180,000 + £8,000) is not a gain which has been realised through a transaction, for example sale of goods at a profit. In addition, Hillcrest Ltd cannot distribute this revaluation gain as a dividend if it wishes to maintain its operating capacity. In this example the gain of £188,000 will be credited to a non-distributable reserve called the Current Cost Reserve. The balance sheet incorporating these revaluations is shown in Exhibit 36.3.

Exhibit 36.3, however, does not incorporate the effect of changing prices on the profit for the year. The reserves figure of £415,000 includes historic cost profit of £80,000 for the year ended 30 June 19X5. We will now consider adjustments necessary in order to calculate the current cost profit for Hillcrest Ltd for the year.

Exhibit 36.3

Hillcrest Ltd

Balance Sheet as at 30 June

		19X5 £000
Plant and machinery		
Current value		1,100
Depreciation		440
Net book value		660
Current assets		
Stock	258	
Debtors	180	
Cash	105	
	543	
Current liabilities		
Trade creditors	(90)	
Net current assets		453
10% loan stock		(310)
		803
Financed by		
Ordinary shares		200
Reserves		415
Current cost reserve		188
		803

36.5 Cost of sales adjustment

In calculating the profit for an accounting period, the cost of the goods sold (or cost of sales) is charged against sales. In Exhibit 36.1, sales of £1,700,000 are recorded at their invoiced prices during the year to 30 June 19X5. Likewise, purchases of £1,375,000 are recorded at their actual cost prices during the year. If we assume that activity occurs evenly throughout the year, a reasonable assumption unless trade is seasonal, then these figures will reflect the average prices for the period. The opening and closing stock valuations, in times of rising prices, will not reflect average prices under the historic cost convention. It is therefore necessary to adjust these figures in order to calculate the current cost of sales. This is carried out using an averaging method.

Using the price index for stock, the current cost of sales for Hillcrest Ltd, to the nearest £000, is as follows:

		£
Opening stock at average prices: $£200,000 \times \dfrac{126}{109}$	=	231,000
Purchases (assume occur evenly through year)	=	1,375,000
Closing stock at average prices: $£250,000 \times \dfrac{126}{122}$	=	258,000
Current cost of sales	=	1,348,000

The cost of sales adjustment is the difference between the current cost of sales of £1,348,000 and the historic cost of sales of £1,325,000, i.e. £23,000. This is charged to the historic cost profit and loss account as an adjustment in order to arrive at the current cost profit. A corresponding amount will be credited to the current cost reserve.

36.6 Depreciation adjustment

Depreciation charged in the profit and loss account should be based on the value of the asset as stated in the balance sheet. Hence, an adjustment is necessary where depreciation has been based on the historic cost of a fixed asset. Consider the following example in which the depreciation charge is based on the value of the asset at the year end. A fixed asset is purchased on 1 January 19X3 for £10,000 when the relevant price index is 100. It is planned to depreciate this asset on a straight line basis at 20 per cent per annum. At the end of 19X3, when the index has moved to 110, the current value of the asset is:

$$£10,000 \times \frac{110}{100} = £11,000$$

and depreciation based on current cost of the asset is:

$$£10,000 \times \frac{110}{100} \times 20\% = £2,200$$

The net book value of the asset as stated in the current cost balance sheet is:

	£
Asset at current value	11,000
Accumulated depreciation	2,200
	8,800

At the end of 19X4 the relevant index is 120, and the current value of the asset is:

$$£10,000 \times \frac{120}{100} = £12,000$$

and the depreciation charge based on current cost is:

$$£10,000 \times \frac{120}{100} \times 20\% = £2,400$$

Hence, at the end of 19X4, the net book value of the asset in the current cost balance sheet is:

	£
Asset at current value	12,000
Accumulated depreciation	4,600
	7,400

Whilst 40 per cent of the value of the asset has been consumed at 31 December 19X4, it is noted that £4,600 is not 40 per cent of £12,000. This is due to an undercharge of £200 depreciation in 19X3 in current value terms. Hence, as the original cost of the asset is altered to reflect current values, so too must the aggregate depreciation. The term given to depreciation relating to earlier years is **backlog depreciation**. Backlog depreciation is not charged against this period's profit. As we saw in the Hillcrest example, only an adjustment for this year's depreciation is charged against profit. Backlog depreciation is charged to the current cost reserve.

For Hillcrest Ltd, depreciation charged at 10 per cent on the current value of the plant and machinery of £1,100,000 is £110,000. Comparing this with the historic cost depreciation charge in the historic cost profit and loss account of £80,000 gives an additional depreciation adjustment of £30,000. This is a charge in arriving at current cost profit for the year, the corresponding credit going to the current cost reserve.

36.7 Monetary working capital adjustment

The effect of changing prices on stock values has already been considered. In addition, during inflationary periods, the market value of monetary assets, e.g. trade debtors, trade creditors and cash, will change. In order for a business to maintain its operating capacity, this change needs to be reflected in the accounts. The **monetary working capital adjustment** represents the increase (or decrease) in finance necessary to provide an appropriate level of monetary working capital due to price changes, rather than a change in the volume of working capital. Cash is usually excluded from the calculation as the amount of cash held by a business may not relate to its operating activities. For example, cash may be held in order to make a capital investment. However, in the case of a bank, cash balances which are required to support daily operations are included in the **monetary working capital adjustment**.

Calculation of the monetary working capital adjustment is similar to the calculation of the cost of sales adjustment. The index for debtors should reflect changes in the cost of goods or services sold which are included in debtors. Likewise, the index for creditors should reflect changes in the cost of goods or services purchased which are included in creditors. A single index may be appropriate, and in some businesses, a fair approximation may be the index used for stock. Consider the following example:

	31 December 19X4	31 December 19X5
	£	£
Trade debtors	9,000	12,000
Trade creditors	7,500	11,000
Monetary working capital	1,500	1,000

Relevant indices applicable to the business are:

31 December 19X4	100
31 December 19X5	200
Average for the year	150

The monetary working capital at 31 December 19X4 in the historic cost accounts is £1,500 (£9,000 – £7,500). Stating this at average values for the year gives:

$$£1,500 \times \frac{150}{100} = £2,250$$

The monetary working capital at 31 December 19X5 in the historic cost accounts is £1,000 (£12,000 – £11,000). Stating this at average values for the year gives:

$$£1,000 \times \frac{150}{200} = £750$$

The historic cost accounts show a decrease in monetary working capital over the year of £500. However, at average values for the year the monetary working capital is reduced by £1,500 (£2,250 – £750). The difference between the change under the historic cost convention and under the current cost convention of £1,000 (£1,500 – £500) – the monetary working capital adjustment – represents the change in working capital due to price changes during the year.

For Hillcrest Ltd the monetary working capital adjustment is calculated as follows:

	19X5 £	19X4 £
Trade debtors	180,000	110,000
Trade creditors	90,000	100,000
Net monetary working capital	90,000	10,000

Hence, the increase in monetary working capital in historic cost terms is £80,000 (£90,000 – £10,000).

Restating opening monetary working capital at average prices gives (to the nearest £000):

$$£10,000 \times \frac{155}{110} = £14,000$$

The value of closing monetary working capital at average prices is (to the nearest £000):

$$£90,000 \times \frac{155}{200} = £70,000$$

The increase in monetary working capital which is due to change in volume is £56,000 (£70,000 – £14,000). The increase due to price changes – the monetary working capital adjustment – is £24,000 (£80,000 – £56,000).

36.8 Current cost operating profit

Hillcrest Ltd's current cost operating profit, having applied the above adjustments, is given in Exhibit 36.4.

Exhibit 36.4

Hillcrest Ltd

Current Cost Operating Profit for year ending 30 June 19X5

		£000
Sales		1,700
Trading profit (add back interest)		111
Adjustments		
Cost of sales adjustment	23	
Monetary working capital adjustment	24	
Additional depreciation adjustment	30	
		77
Current cost operating profit		34

From the point of view of a business and maintenance of its operating capacity, the current cost operating profit is relevant. However, maintenance of financial capital is also relevant where a business is not financed solely by equity. In this case, account should be taken of the capital structure of the business.

36.9 Gearing adjustment

If a company is financed by debt, and prices increase, whilst the monetary value of the loan has not changed, the market value has reduced. This gain for shareholders is recorded by making a gearing adjustment. The gearing adjustment is calculated in the following way.

Firstly, a gearing proportion is calculated. This is:

Average net borrowings for the year (L) : Shareholders' interest (S) + L

For Hillcrest Ltd, its net borrowings for the two years to 30 June 19X5 are:

	19X5	19X4
	£	£
Loan stock	310,000	310,000
Cash	105,000	75,000
Net borrowing	205,000	235,000

Hence, average net borrowings for the year to 30 June 19X5 are:

$$\frac{£205,000 + £235,000}{2} = £220,000$$

Shareholders' interest for both years are:

	19X5	19X4
	£	£
Ordinary shares	200,000	200,000
Reserves	415,000	335,000
	615,000	535,000

Average shareholders' interest (S) for the year to 30 June 19X5 is:

$$\frac{£615,000 + £535,000}{2} = £575,000$$

The gearing proportion is:

$$\frac{L}{L+S} = \frac{£220,000}{£220,000 + £575,000} = 27.67\%$$

To calculate the gearing adjustment, this proportion is applied to the sum of the current cost adjustments for the year, that is:

	£
Cost of sales adjustment	23,000
Depreciation adjustment	30,000
Monetary working capital adjustment	24,000
	77,000

The gearing adjustment for Hillcrest Ltd (to the nearest £000) is:

27.67% × £77,000 = £21,000

Exhibit 36.5 shows the current cost reserve having made the above adjustments.

Exhibit 36.5

Current cost reserve	£000
Surplus on revaluation of plant and machinery	180
Additional depreciation adjustment	30
Surplus on revaluation of stock	8
Cost of sales adjustment	23
Monetary working capital adjustment	24
Gearing adjustment	(21)
Balance at 30 June 19X5	244

The current cost profit for the year to 30 June 19X5 is given in Exhibit 36.6.

Exhibit 36.6

Hillcrest Ltd

Current Cost Profit and Loss Account for year ending 30 June 19X5

			£000
Sales			1,700
Trading profit (add back interest)			111
Adjustments			
Cost of sales adjustment	23		
Monetary working capital adjustment	24		
Additional depreciation adjustment	30		
			77
Current cost operating profit			34
Gearing adjustment		21	
Less Interest payable		31	
			(10)
Current cost profit			24

The balance sheet for Hillcrest Ltd for 30 June 19X5, based on current costs, is given in Exhibit 36.7.

Exhibit 36.7

Hillcrest Ltd

Current Cost Balance Sheet as at 30 June 19X5

		£000
Plant and machinery		
Cost		1,100
Depreciation		440
Net book value		660
Current assets		
Stock	258	
Debtors	180	
Cash	105	
	543	
Current liabilities		
Trade creditors	(90)	
Net current assets		453
10% loan stock		(310)
		803
Financed by		
Ordinary shares		200
Reserves		359
Current cost reserve		244
		803

Main points to remember

1   During inflationary periods, one of the main criticisms of historic cost accounting is its inability to reflect changing prices.

2   Deprival value is a suitable valuation basis for accounting purposes.

3   One of the major difficulties with current cost accounting is the level of subjectivity which can be involved in converting historic costs to current costs.

4   Relevant price indices, specific to an asset or class of assets, can approximate replacement cost.

5   The purpose of the cost of sales adjustment is to restate historic cost of sales in current cost terms by including opening and closing stock at average prices.

6   The depreciation adjustment ensures that the depreciation charge in the current cost profit and loss account is based on the current value of the asset as stated in the current cost balance sheet.

7   The monetary working capital adjustment reflects the change in the market value of monetary assets and liabilities, usually trade debtors and trade creditors, in the current cost accounts.

8   Gains or losses for shareholders, which arise due to debt financing in times of changing prices, are accounted for in the gearing adjustment.

9   Surpluses and deficits on revaluations are credited or charged to the current cost reserve, which is a non-distributable reserve.

Review questions

36.1 State whether you consider the following statements to be true or false:

(a) During inflationary periods, historic cost accounts do not reflect a true and fair view.
(b) The preparation of historic cost accounts does not involve subjectivity.
(c) Current cost accounting involves estimating future events.
(d) An index number must relate to a specific asset in order to be useful in converting historic cost accounts to current cost accounts.
(e) Where no market exists for an asset, conversion from historic cost to current cost can be difficult.

36.2A State whether you consider the following statements to be true or false:

(a) The current cost of plant and machinery is likely to be its net realisable value.
(b) A company should distribute dividends from the current cost reserve.
(c) The market value of a monetary asset, for example trade debtors, will decrease during inflationary periods.
(d) A gearing adjustment is necessary where a company is financed solely by equity capital.
(e) Backlog depreciation is charged to the current cost reserve.

36.3A What are the practical difficulties a company may encounter in ascertaining the current values of its assets?

36.4 Plant and machinery was purchased on 1 January 19X3 for £30,000, when the relevant specific price index was 90. What is the current cost value of the asset at 31 December 19X4 if the index at that date is 120?

36.5A The plant and machinery, details of which are given in question 36.4, is depreciated on a straight line basis at 10 per cent per annum. The depreciation charge is based on year-end values. What is the current cost depreciation charge for the year ended 31 December 19X5, if the index at that date is 160?

36.6 Calculate backlog depreciation at 31 December 19X5 for the plant and machinery whose details are given in question 36.5A.

36.7A A firm purchased machinery on 1 January 19X4 for £40,000, at which date the relevant price index for machinery was 100. Depreciation is charged on a straight line basis at 25 per cent per annum. The index at 31 December 19X4 had moved to 150, and at 31 December 19X5 it was 200. Show the current cost balance sheet entries for machinery at 31 December 19X4 and 31 December 19X5. Calculate the adjustments to the current cost reserve in respect of machinery.

36.8 The historic cost of sales figure for Apple Ltd for the year ended 31 December 19X3 is calculated as follows:

	£
Opening stock	50,000
Purchases	450,000
	500,000
Closing stock	70,000
Cost of sales	430,000

Price indices for stock are as follows:

Index at date of purchase of opening stock	80
Index at date of purchase of closing stock	120
Average index for 19X3	100
Index at 31 December 19X3	130

Assuming that purchases occur evenly throughout the year, calculate the cost of sales adjustment for Apple Ltd for 19X3.

36.9A The balance sheet of Seafield Ltd at 31 December 19X4 shows the following balances:

	31 December 19X4	31 December 19X3
	£	£
Trade debtors	35,000	30,000
Trade creditors	25,000	23,000

The relevant price indices for trade debtors and trade creditors are:

31 December 19X3	120
31 December 19X4	180
Average for the year ending 31 December 19X4	150

Using the above information, calculate the monetary working capital adjustment at 31 December 19X4 for Seafield Ltd.

36.10 If the relevant price indices for trade debtors and trade creditors are as follows, calculate the monetary working capital adjustment for Seafield Ltd, using the details given in question 36.9A.

31 December 19X3	200
31 December 19X4	280
Average for the year ending 31 December 19X4	240

36.11A The information given below has been extracted from the accounting records of Cedarwood Ltd for the year ended 30 June 19X4. Prepare a statement showing the current cost operating profit to 30 June 19X4.

	£
Sales	2,500,000
Historic cost operating profit	1,400,000
Current cost adjustments	
Additional depreciation adjustment	500,000
Cost of sales adjustment	750,000
Monetary working capital adjustment	25,000

36.12 The balance sheet for Cremore Ltd at 31 December 19X3 is given below:

	19X3 £000	19X3 £000	19X2 £000	19X2 £000
Plant and machinery				
Cost		800		800
Depreciation		320		160
		480		640
Current assets				
Stock	210		130	
Debtors	100		60	
Cash	145		50	
	455		240	
Current liabilities				
Trade creditors	(80)		(60)	
Net current assets		375		180
10% loan stock		(200)		(200)
		655		620
Financed by				
Ordinary shares		250		250
Reserves		370		340
Current cost reserve		35		30
		655		620

Using the above information, calculate the gearing adjustment percentage:

$$\frac{L}{L + S}$$

36.13A The following information has been extracted from the accounting records of Sycamore Ltd for the year ended 30 June 19X3.

	£
Sales	9,000,000
Historic cost trading profit	4,000,000
Interest payable	500,000
Corporation tax charge for the year	1,500,000
Ordinary dividend	600,000
Additional depreciation adjustment	200,000
Cost of sales adjustment	800,000
Monetary working capital adjustment	370,000
Gearing adjustment: $\dfrac{L}{L + S}$	20%

Prepare a current cost profit and loss account for Sycamore Ltd for the year ended 30 June 19X3.

36.14 During a period of inflation, many accountants believe that financial reports prepared under the historical cost convention are subject to the following major limitations:

1 stocks are undervalued;
2 depreciation is understated;
3 gains and losses on net monetary assets are undisclosed;
4 balance sheet values are unrealistic; and
5 meaningful periodic comparisons are difficult to make.

Required:
Explain briefly the limitations of historical cost accounting in periods of inflation with reference to each of the items listed above.

(*Association of Accounting Technicians*)

36.15A You are presented with the following information relating to Messiter plc:

Year to 31 December	19X4 £m	19X5 £m
Profit and loss accounts:		
Turnover, all on credit terms	1,300	1,400
Cost of sales	650	770
Gross profit	650	630
Profit before taxation	115	130
Balance sheets at 31 December:		
Fixed assets at cost	850	850
Less Accumulated depreciation	510	595
Net book value	340	255
Stock at cost	105	135
Trade debtors	142	190

Required:
(*a*) Using the historic cost accounts and stating the formulae you use, calculate the following accounting ratios for both 19X4 and 19X5:
  (*i*) Gross profit percentage;
  (*ii*) Net profit percentage;
  (*iii*) Stock turnover, stated in days;
  (*iv*) Trade debtor collection period, stated in days; and
  (*v*) Fixed asset turnover.

(*b*) Using the following additional information:
  (*i*) Restate the turnover for 19X4 and 19X5 incorporating the following average retail price indices:

Year to 31.12.19X4	85
Year to 31.12.19X5	111

  (*ii*) Calculate the additional depreciation charge required to finance the replacement of fixed assets at their replacement cost. The company's depreciation policy is to provide 10 per cent per annum on original cost, assuming no residual value.
  The replacement cost of fixed assets at 31 December was as follows:

	£ millions
19X4	1,140
19X5	1,200

(*iii*) Based upon these two inflation adjustments, why may it be misleading to compare a company's results for one year with that of another without adjusting for changes in general (RPI) or specific inflation?

(*Association of Accounting Technicians*)

37

Social accounting

Objectives

After you have studied this chapter, you should:

● *have an understanding of the term 'social accounting'*

● *be aware of the implications of 'social accounting' for the accounting function*

● *appreciate some of the difficulties in the measurement of qualitative factors*

● *be aware of the conflict between shareholders' interests and social considerations*

37.1 Introduction

Over time, the objective of financial statements has changed. In addition to reporting to shareholders of the company, directors are aware of a wide range of other user groups who are interested in accounting information. These user groups include employees of the company and, more controversially, the public at large. The controversy arises when considering whether or not organisations are responsible for 'social actions', that is actions which do not have purely financial implications.

37.2 Costs and measurement

One of the problems associated with actions of this type is the difficulty of identifying costs and measuring the effects of (often intangible) factors that contribute to the 'value' of an organisation. It is obvious that employee loyalty and commitment to quality performance increase this value, but how are such intangibles to be measured using objective and verifiable techniques?

Some of the input costs of 'social' activities can be evaluated reasonably accurately. Providing 'social' information required under the 1985 Companies Act is not particularly difficult – it requires information regarding employees to be presented in the accounts, including numbers of employees, wages and salaries data, and details regarding the company's policy on disabled persons. Also, even where 'social' actions are required by legislation, they can often be costed reasonably accurately. For example, there are a large number of European Union directives which have been implemented in the UK relating to social and environmental policies, including the monitoring and control of air and water pollution. The costs of complying with these disclosure requirements and operational control measures can be high and, as the numbers of regulations increase, these costs will become a basic and essential part of financial statements. It will become increasingly important that not only the costs are reported, but also the benefits, and this is where the difficulties arise – how can the benefits of controlling pollution from a factory be evaluated? Indeed, should an attempt be made to evaluate them at all? Would they be better reported in qualitative or non-financial quantitative terms?

As soon as a company seeks to incorporate social criteria alongside other more traditional performance measures, problems of objectivity, comparability and usefulness arise. For example, social criteria for a paper manufacturer may include environmental issues concerning reforestation. An oil extraction company would include the environmentally safe disposal of oil rigs at the end of their useful economic lives among its social criteria.

However, issues of this type become problematic when viewed using conventional capital appraisal techniques. Not only may the measurable financial payback be so long as to be immaterial – as in the case of an environmental project such as reforestation – it may be virtually non-existent, as in the case of the disposal of obsolete oil rigs. Assessment of issues of this type require different techniques from those traditionally used, and organisations' accounting information systems will need to take this into account, not just in terms of using more qualitative value criteria, but also in selecting the information which is sought in order to assist in the decision making process.

37.3 The pressure for social actions and social accounting

Despite the existence of many environmental laws, much of the pressure for social actions comes from pressure groups like Greenpeace. These groups can have an enormous impact upon an organisation's profitability, in ways that governments have singularly failed to do. For example, an air pollution law may concentrate on monitoring the quality of air around a factory, rather than on measuring emissions from the factory, making it far more difficult to enforce action against the factory as it can always argue that another factory is the cause of any pollution found. Also, powerful cartels can influence legislation to create enormous delays in introducing socially responsible legislative controls. A pressure group, on the other hand, can stop demand for a company's products, make it difficult for it to send its products to its customers, and may give it so much negative publicity that it can find its public image materially and irreversibly altered in a very short time.

While pressure groups are not a new phenomenon, their power is now far greater than it has ever been. Organisations need to be aware of the social, particularly environmental issues inherent in and/or related to their activities, and must be in a position to assess how best to approach these issues. They can only do so if they identify all the variables, both quantitative and qualitative, and both the inputs (costs) and the outputs (effects) of these variables, and determine methods with which to determine what actions to take. Social accounting is concerned with how to report upon the application of the social policies adopted by an organisation, and upon how they have impacted upon the organisation and its environment. An organisation that does so effectively will not only be providing user groups with rich information from which to form a view concerning its social ethos, it will also be enhancing its ability to take decisions appropriate for its own longer-term survival and prosperity.

37.4 Corporate social reporting

The reporting of the social effects of a company's activities became an issue in the UK in the 1970s. The reporting of non-financial information usually takes the form of narrative disclosure, sometimes supported by a statistical summary. As much social reporting is non-mandatory, comparison with other companies is difficult, if not virtually pointless and misleading. This is partially due to a positive bias in what is reported – most companies tend to report only 'good news' in their social reports. It is also due to the lack of standards governing what to include and how to present social reports.

Environmental issues have been firmly on the political agenda since the early 1980s and large corporations have responded to public demands for more information about 'green issues'. Oil companies, in particular, produce a notable amount of additional information in their annual reports. This environmental information usually includes details about the company's waste disposal practices, attitudes towards pollution and natural resource depletion, as well as the overall corporate environmental policy. However, many continue to avoid any non-mandatory social reporting, and many instances have been reported of organisations claiming to be socially responsible, when they were, in fact, anything but.

37.5 Types of social accounting

Social accounting can be divided into five general areas:

- national social income accounting;
- social auditing;
- financial social accounting in profit-oriented organisations;
- managerial social accounting in profit-oriented organisations;
- financial and/or managerial social accounting for non-profit organisations.

37.6 National social income accounting

Such accounts have now been in existence for many years. The measure of the nation's productivity recorded in the accounts – basically in sales terms – gives an income called the Gross National Product, usually referred to as GNP.

To an outsider an increase in GNP would seem to indicate a betterment or progress in the state of affairs existing in the country. This is not necessarily true. The following example illustrates this point.

A new chemical factory is built in a town. Fumes are emitted during production which cause houses in the surrounding areas to suffer destruction of paintwork and rotting woodwork, and it also causes extensive corrosion of bodywork on motor vehicles in the neighbourhood. In addition it also affects the health of the people living nearby. An increase in GNP results because the profit elements in the above add to GNP. These profit elements include:

- to construction companies and suppliers of building materials: profit made on construction of plant;
- to house paint dealers and paint manufacturers, painters and decorators, joiners and carpenters: profit made on all work effected in extra painting, woodwork, etc.;
- to garages and car paint manufacturers: profit made on all extra work needed on motor vehicles;
- to chemists and medical requirement manufacturers: profit made on dealing with effects on residents' health, because of extra medical purchases, etc.

However, in real terms one can hardly say that there has been 'progress'. Obviously the quality of life has been seriously undermined for many people.

As national income accounts do not record the 'social' well-being of a country, other national measures have been proposed. The one most often mentioned is a system of 'social indicators'. These measure social progress in such ways as:

- national life expectancies;
- living conditions;
- levels of disease;
- nutritional levels;
- amount of crime;
- road deaths.

Thus if national life expectancies rose, or road deaths per 100,000 people decreased, etc. there could be said to be social progress, while the converse would apply were the opposite signals found to be occurring.

The main difficulty with this approach is that (given present knowledge and techniques) it cannot be measured in monetary terms. Because of this, the national social income accounts cannot be adjusted to take account of social indicators. On the level of an individual organisation, however, social indicators similar to the above are used in planning, programming, budgeting systems (PPBS). This will be discussed later.

37.7 Social auditing

Whilst national social accounting would measure national social progress, many individual people or organisations are interested in their own social progress. This form of social progress is usually called 'social responsibility'.

To discover which of their activities have to be measured a 'social audit' is required. This is an investigation into:

(a) which of their activities contribute to, or detract from, being socially responsible;
(b) measurement of those activities;
(c) a report on the results disclosed by the investigation.

An example of this might be to discover how the organisation had performed in respect of such matters as:

- employment of women;
- employment of disabled people;
- occupational safety;
- occupational health;
- benefits at pensionable age;
- air pollution;
- water pollution;
- charitable activities;
- help to third world countries.

Social audits may be carried out by an organisation's own staff or by external auditors. The reports may be for internal use only or for general publication.

37.8 Financial social accounting in profit-oriented organisations

This is an extension to normal financial accounting. The objective may either be to show how the social actions have affected financial performance, or otherwise to put a social value on the financial statements of the organisations. The two main types of financial social accounting envisaged to date are those of human resource accounting and how the organisation has responded to governmental or professional bodies' regulations concerning environmental matters.

Human resource accounting

One of the main limitations of normal financial accounting is the lack of any inclusion of the 'value' of the workforce to an organisation. The value may be determined by either:

● capitalising recruitment and training costs of employees and apportioning value over employees' period of employment; or
● calculating the 'replacement cost' of the workforce and taking this as the value of human resources; or
● extending either of the above to include the organisation's suppliers and customers.

It is contended that such measurements have the benefits that (a) financial statements are more complete, and (b) managerial decisions can be made with a fuller understanding of their implications.

For instance, suppose that a short-term drop in demand for a firm's goods led to a manufacturer laying off part of the workforce. This might mean higher profits in the short term because of wages and salaries saved. In the long term it could do irreparable damage, because recruitment could then be made difficult in future, or because of the effect on the morale of the rest of the workforce, or changes in attitudes of suppliers and customers.

Compliance costs of statutory/professional requirements

As the effects of organisations upon societies are more widely recognised there will be more and more regulations with which to comply. The costs of compliance will obviously then become a basic and essential part of financial statements.

37.9 Managerial social accounting in profit-oriented organisations

All that has been described has an effect upon the accounting information systems of an organisation. They will have to be established on an ongoing basis, rather than be based purely on adjustments to the financial accounts at the year end.

The information will be used to affect the day-to-day decisions needed to run the organisation.

37.10 Financial and/or managerial social accounting for non-profit organisations

As profit is not a measure in these organisations it can be difficult to measure how well they are performing. Two approaches to measurement have been used, **planning, programming, budgeting systems (PPBS)**, and **social programme measurement**.

Both of these approaches can be said to be part of what politicians in recent years have called 'value for money'. The general attitude is that whilst there may be a need for all sorts of social programmes, including health, there is a great need for ensuring that money is not wasted in doing this. The demand is that we should ensure that we get 'value for money' in that the outputs from such schemes should be worth the amount of money expended in carrying them out.

Planning, programming, budgeting systems (PPBS)

It has been said that in the past there was a great deal of confusion between planning and budgeting. Annual budgeting takes a short-term financial view. Planning on the other hand should be long-term and also be concerned with strategic thinking.

PPBS enables management of non-profit organisations to make decisions on a better-informed basis about the allocation of resources to achieve their overall objectives. PPBS works in four stages:

1 Review organisational objectives.
2 Identify programmes to achieve objectives.
3 Identify and evaluate alternative ways of achieving each specific programme.
4 On the basis of cost-benefit principles, select appropriate programme.

PPBS necessitates the drawing up of a long-term corporate plan. This shows the objectives which the organisation is aiming to achieve. Such objectives may not be in accord with the existing organisational structure.

For instance, suppose that the objective of a local government authority, such as a city, is the care of the elderly. This could include providing:

- services to help them keep fit;
- medical services when they are ill;
- old people's housing;
- 'sheltered' accommodation;
- recreational facilities;
- educational facilities.

These services will usually be provided by separate departments, e.g. housing, welfare, education. PPBS relates the total costs to the care of the elderly, rather than to individual departmental budgets.

Management is therefore forced by PPBS to identify exactly which services or activities should be provided, otherwise the worthiness of the programme could not be evaluated. PPBS also provides information which enables management to assess the effectiveness of their plans, such as giving them a base to decide whether for every thousand pounds they are giving as good a service as possible.

As the structure of the programme will not match up with the structure of the organisation, e.g. the services provided will cut across departmental borders, one particular individual must be made responsible for controlling and supervising the programme.

Social programme measurement

The idea that governmental social programmes should be measured effectively is, as yet, in its infancy.

A government auditor would determine whether the agency had complied with the relevant laws, and had exercised adequate cost controls. The auditor would determine whether or not the results expected were being achieved and whether there were alternatives to the programmes at a lower cost.

There should be cost-benefit analyses to show that the benefits are worth the costs they incur. However, the benefit side of the analysis is often very difficult to measure. How, for instance, do you measure the benefits of not dumping a particular substance or an obsolete oil rig into the sea?

As a consequence, so far most social programmes do not yet measure results (benefits). Instead they measure 'outputs', e.g. how many prosecutions for dumping waste. Therefore, a high number of prosecutions is 'good', a low number 'bad'. This is hardly a rational way of assessing results, and quite a lot of research is going into better methods of audit.

37.11 Conflict between shareholders' interests and social considerations

Obviously, an organisation has to come to a compromise about how far it should look after the interests of its shareholders and how far it should bother about social considerations. For instance, a company could treat its employees so well in terms of pay, pensions and welfare that the extra costs would mean very low profits or even losses.

On the other hand there must be instances that, no matter what the effects on profits, the expenses just have to be incurred. If the company has a chemical plant which could easily explode, causing widespread destruction and danger to people, then there cannot be any justification for not spending the money either to keep the plant safe or to demolish it. The full severity of the law must bear down on transgressors of the law in such cases of wilful neglect.

All the facts of the particular case must be brought into account. Let us look at a typical case where the answer may seem obvious, but perhaps there may be other factors which may make the answer not so obvious. Workers in underdeveloped countries are usually paid far lower wages than those in the developed countries. What happens if a large multinational company pays its workers in a given country three or four times as much as home-based companies? Immediately everyone wants to work for the multinational company, which can afford high wages, and leave the home-based companies which cannot. Is that sensible? What chance is there for the development of the country's own home-based industries if the outside companies constantly take all the best brains and more able people?

In such a case it would probably make more sense for the multinational company to pay wages more in keeping with the particular economy, and to help that country in other ways such as by improving the health care generally for all, better education for all, and so on. Obviously a topic such as this will engender discussions and arguments for some considerable time.

37.12 Reports from companies

Companies, mainly those in the USA at first, have begun to declare their philosophy towards such matters as the environment. These are usually included in the annual reports which accompany the accounts.

One company, for instance, has stated that it has ten principles of environmental policy. These, briefly, were as follows:

1 To comply with both governmental and community standards of environmental excellence.
2 To use only materials and packaging selected to be good for the health of consumers, and for the safety and quality of the environment.
3 To keep energy use per unit of output down to a low level.
4 To minimise waste.
5 To get to as low a level as possible the discharge of pollutants.
6 To use other firms in business which have shown commitment to environmental excellence.
7 To research fully the ecological effect of the company's products and packaging.
8 To carry on business operations in an open, honest and co-operative manner.
9 To make certain that on the board of directors there would be scientifically knowledgeable directors, and ensure that they were provided with environmental reports regularly.
10 To ensure that all the above principles are fully observed and that challenges posed by the environment are vigorously and effectively pursued.

Main points to remember

1 To whom organisations are responsible is a controversial area, and there is no exact definition of 'social accounting'.

2 Social indicators measure social progress, but as yet, given their inability to measure progress in monetary terms, they cannot be incorporated into social income accounts.

3 A social audit will test the social responsibility of an organisation, including compliance with regulations, for example legislation relating to employees.

4 If an organisation wishes to take account of social and environmental factors, these items need to be incorporated into its accounting information system.

5 There is a conflict between shareholders' interests, for example profit maximisation, and social considerations.

6 Corporate social reporting is the reporting of a company's activities and how they are related to social, including environmental, issues.

7 There are five areas into which social accounting can be divided:
   (a) national social income accounting;
   (b) social auditing;
   (c) financial social accounting in profit-oriented organisations;
   (d) managerial social accounting in profit-oriented organisations;
   (e) financial and/or managerial social accounting for non-profit organisations.

8 Social accounting is as yet in its infancy. There is obviously a great difficulty in trying to put money values on the various aspects of being 'better off' or 'worse off'. There are also problems connected with exactly what 'better off' and 'worse off' mean. One person's 'worsening' in some way may be someone else's 'betterment'.

Review questions

37.1 Describe how an increase in Gross National Product may not have a positive effect on the well-being of the country.

37.2 What types of measures could be used to measure social well-being? What difficulties would be discovered in trying to use accounting in measuring these?

37.3 What aspects of an organisation's activities could be measured in a 'social audit'?

37.4 Describe how there could be conflicts between short-term and long-term benefits.

37.5 Describe how PPBS may conflict with departmental budgets.

37.6A Review a set of company accounts for social disclosures. Consider the usefulness of such disclosures to different user groups.

37.7 Why has the traditional model of income measurement failed to account for the impact of business activities on the environment?

(*Chartered Association of Certified Accountants*)

38

Accounting as an information system

Objectives

After you have studied this chapter, you should:

● *be aware of some of the deficiencies of financial accounting if it were used for management control purposes*

● *be aware of the need to avoid potential conflicts between alternative or competing objectives that may be adopted within an organisation*

● *know that decision making should involve more than just the financial figures involved*

● *be aware that the information needs of organisations are, in part at least, a function of their size*

● *understand the difference between the three areas in which management operates, and their different information needs*

● *be aware that accounting information is only one part of the overall system in which organisations operate*

● *understand that the accounting system is affected by the surrounding environment both inside and outside the organisation in which it operates*

38.1 The part played by financial accounting

So far your studies have been concerned primarily with the recording function of accounting, often called bookkeeping, and the drafting of the final accounts of different types of organisations, such as partnerships or limited companies. The term generally used for your studies up to this point is that of **financial accounting**. Much of it is concerned with legal requirements, such as complying with the provisions of the Companies Acts when drafting final accounts, or keeping an accounting record of a customer's legal indebtedness, i.e. a debtor's account.

With companies the final accounts represent the account given to the shareholders by the directors of their running of the company during a particular year, in other words it is a statement of the directors' 'stewardship'. These accounts are also given to other interested parties such as the bankers to the firm, creditors, Inspectors of Taxes, etc.

Whilst financial accounting is necessary from a legal point of view, it cannot be said to be ideal from the point of view of controlling the activities of a firm. Your studies would therefore be incomplete if you had seen only the 'stewardship' function of accounting. The use of accounting for controlling the activities of a firm is probably more important. In this chapter, we shall briefly consider accounting for 'management control' purposes.

The word 'management' does not necessarily mean that the firm is a limited company, although most of the large organisations in the private sector of industry would in fact be limited companies. It means instead the people who are managing the affairs of the firm, whether they are directors, partners, sole traders or 'managers' classified as those employees who are in charge of other employees.

38.2 Deficiencies of financial accounting

Before starting to examine accounting for management control let us look first at the deficiencies of financial accounting when we want to control the activities of an organisation.

Its first deficiency is that it deals with operations that have already occurred: it deals with the past, not the future. It is possible to control something whilst it is happening, and control can be arranged for something that is going to happen, but when it has already happened without being controlled then the activity has ended and we are too late to do anything about control. In this way if a company incurs a loss and we do not realise it until long after the event then the loss cannot be prevented.

What we really want to do is to control affairs so that a loss is not incurred if at all possible, and we should be able to call on accounting techniques to help in the control of activities. However, it certainly does not mean that we are not interested in the past. We can learn lessons from the past which can be very useful in understanding what is going on now, and what is likely to be happening in the future.

The second deficiency of financial accounting is that it is concerned with the whole of the firm. Thus the trading account of a firm may show a gross profit of £60,000, and whilst it is better to know that than to have no idea at all of what the gross profit is, it does not tell management much about past transactions. Suppose that in fact the firm manufactures three products – watches, pens and cigarette lighters. Some possibilities of how much profit (or loss) was attributable to each of the products might be as in Exhibit 38.1.

Exhibit 38.1

	Various possibilities of profits and loss for each product			
	1	2	3	4
Watches	20,000	5,000	30,000	(30,000)*
Pens	20,000	70,000	28,000	65,000
Lighters	20,000	(15,000)*	2,000	25,000
Total gross profit	£60,000	£60,000	£60,000	£60,000

*Losses are shown in brackets

These are only some of the possible figures of profit and loss for each product which could result in an overall gross profit of £60,000. Just the figure of total gross profit would give you very few clues as to what lessons can be learned from studying the past to help you control the firm in the future. If possibility number 2 was in fact the correct solution then it would stimulate further discussion and investigation as to why these results had occurred.

It could result in the closing down of the section of the firm which makes cigarette lighters if, after investigation, it was found to be in the interests of the firm to cease manufacturing them. Many more lessons can therefore be learned from events if the firms' activities can be examined for each part of its activities instead of just the whole of its activities.

This means that financial accounting is of little use by itself for management control purposes. It does not mean that it is of no use at all for control purposes, as for instance the financial accounting system may reveal that the debtors at a point in time are £50,000. Management need to know this if they are to control their finances properly, but although this is true of some accounting figures in financial accounting, many of the other accounting figures may not be much use in controlling the business. For example, if a building was bought in 1930 for £20,000 it may well be worth £200,000 today, whilst if we rented a similar building now it might cost us £30,000 a year. We would surely not use the original cost of £20,000 as the deciding factor as to what we will do now with the building. The original cost is now completely irrelevant for the control of the business now or in the future.

38.3 Objectives of the firm

If we want to discuss management control we must first of all ask ourselves what is its purpose. We can only have control if it is for a particular purpose, otherwise how can we possibly draw up any plans?

It might seem obvious to you that the objectives of an organisation should be spelled out clearly and unambiguously. In fact the writing down of objectives is not done by quite a few organisations. This means that all the employees of the firm could well be pulling in different directions, as they all have different ideas as to the firm's objectives.

Let us look at some of the possible objectives:

- To ensure that the maximum profit is made. This still is not clear; do we mean profits in the long term or the short term?
- To obtain a given percentage share of the market for our sort of goods or services.
- To achieve a high quality in the goods being manufactured or services offered.
- To ensure that our customers are fully satisfied with our goods and services.
- To ensure full employment for our employees.
- To ensure that our employees' welfare is maintained at a high level, in terms of back-up facilities and other things such as adequate pension schemes.
- To ensure that our employees receive the best training and are kept fully up to date with the latest technology for our sort of business.
- To cause as little damage as possible ecologically.

38.4 Conflicts between objectives

Each objective of the firm is not 'mutually exclusive'. By that we mean that one objective may affect another objective, and that it cannot be considered completely on its own.

Let us take the case of the objective of maximum profit with that of causing as little damage as possible ecologically. We could have to spend a lot of money ensuring that dangerous chemical substances are not released into the atmosphere. This could mean less profits. There would be a conflict here if the improvements were being made voluntarily by the firm instead of being forced on it by the authorities.

Similarly, to maintain a very high quality of goods could mean lower profits if a large number of items manufactured are scrapped because they are not up to this standard. Lowering the quality could possibly increase profits.

This could again be interpreted in more than one way. Lowering the quality could possibly increase the profits in the short term, but it could mean less profits in the long term if our customers deserted us because our goods were second-rate. This could apply similarly to services.

It is thus essential to ensure that the objectives are very clearly spelled out. Otherwise people will easily misunderstand them and because of this the firm may not proceed in the direction that is desired.

38.5 People and management control

It is also important to point out that the most important resource of any firm is the people who work in it. A danger exists that a great deal of care and attention may be given to designing a management control system and operating it, but this is absolutely of no use to management if it does not result in action by the human beings in the firm. Systems and figures do not themselves do anything; instead it is the people in the firm who take (or do not take) the necessary action.

You must bear in mind that figures thrown up by systems are only part of the evidence available when a decision has to be made as to the necessary action. A particular department may be incurring losses now, but the sales manager may give as his considered opinion that sales will increase soon and that the department will become profitable. If people accepted accounting figures as the only criteria on which action should be based then there would be some very bad actions by management. Many of the now very successful products have started off by incurring losses in the early stages, and have been eventually successful because the firm has persevered with the product because it had the faith that it would eventually make the grade.

If it was possible to have exactly the same system of management control in three different firms, it might be found in firm A that the control system was useless because no one acted on the data produced. In firm B the control system might result in damage being done to the firm because management used the data as though it were the only criterion in gauging the actions it should take. In firm C it might be an extremely good system because the management saw the data as a useful guide in the planning and control of the firm, and had also made certain that the rest of the organisation took the same view.

How human beings react to a management control system is therefore right at the heart of the problem of ensuring that an effective management control system is in use.

38.6 Different sizes of organisations

Part of this book is about information which is intended to be used by the management of an organisation. For a small and simple organisation the information needs of management may be limited and can be obtained by direct observation – using eyes to look and the voice to ask questions. For example, a person managing a greengrocery stall on a market can often operate effectively without formal records to help him. What he buys is determined by the goods available in the local wholesale market and his personal knowledge of what his customers are prepared to buy at a given price. His records will probably centre around the recording of cash – the details of his sales and expenditures in order to prepare financial accounts. However, apart from the essential requirement of maintaining proper cash levels these records do not help him in the day-to-day management of his business operations.

If in contrast we look at the manager responsible for buying greengrocery for a large supermarket chain certain differences emerge. The basic decision about what to buy at a given price remains the same. However, in the large organisation there is a much wider choice of where and how to buy than in the small organisation. The large buyer may, for example, be able to enter into contracts directly with growers and to enter forward contracts for the supply of produce (for example, a farmer agrees to sell all his potatoes at the end of the summer to the firm at a fixed price).

In the large organisation the buyer will not be in direct contact with the many different sales outlets and therefore needs written information to keep him in touch with demand. He does not have to listen to complaining customers! Similarly because the sources of supply are likely to be much wider for the big firm, he needs more formal information to keep him in touch with market prices.

One of the other features about the large organisation which distinguishes it from the small is that responsibility for running the business is shared between many different people. In order to ensure that the operations of the firm are carried out efficiently and effectively there needs to be some criterion to measure the performance of the managers. In a small firm the inadequate proprietor will either make a very poor living or become a bankrupt. Thus his success or failure is clearly his own responsibility. In a large firm the same things can happen overall, but the situation may be obscured by a swings and roundabouts effect of some good sections making up for some bad. A management information system should help identify these problems in an organisation.

38.7 The management process

The way that management operates in an organisation may be conveniently described by a division into three areas:

- forecasting and planning;
- controlling operations;
- evaluating performance.

Forecasting and planning

Forecasting and planning is the process by which senior management decide on major overall issues concerning what the business is going to do, and how it is going to do it. It involves an assessment of information about the future which is called forecasting. When the forecast has been prepared, then the company can plan how to achieve the objectives set by management based on the forecast. Planning is the process of co-ordinating the resources available to attain an objective.

Controlling operations

Controlling operations involves management in a number of processes and requires several different kinds of information. It involves converting top management plans into an operating pattern which matches the parts into which a company is divided. This changes the overall plan into detailed operating plans which relate to the management structure of the company. This process is called budgeting.

When actual events occur, then the information recording the events needs to be measured in such a way that it can be compared with the plan. This important process of management gives a feedback on the success of the plan to those who set it up in the first instance.

Controlling operations effectively also requires information designed to help managers take the decisions which their jobs require. For example, information about the profit produced by one product as compared to another will enable a decision about how many of each product to make.

Evaluating performance

Evaluating performance involves the analysis and assessment of actual results. This is partly a process of comparison with plans but not exclusively. The information on which plans were based may have been wrong. Thus the analysis of performance, whilst involving comparison of actual with planned results, needs considerable judgement as to what the plans should have been had all the facts been known in advance.

The three elements we have described are by no means completely independent. One way of looking at them is as a cycle in which information is circulating continually from one area to another as in Exhibit 38.2.

In this diagram information is shown to flow around from one part into the other. Thus, for example, forecasts in one period may be improved by taking account of the analysis of what happened last period.

The diagram we have just considered only looks at internal information. In practice, information is being fed into the process from outside. Top management will have to take into account all the information it can about the outside environment such as competition, economic cutbacks, etc. The control of operations also receives information about actual events.

Exhibit 38.2

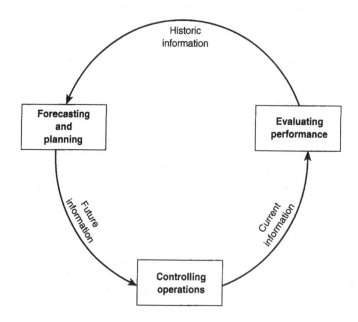

It is also useful to add to the diagram a time dimension as in Exhibit 38.3. Forecasting and planning must relate to the future. Controlling operations relates to concurrent events – the here and now. Evaluating performance can only be concerned with the past.

Exhibit 38.3

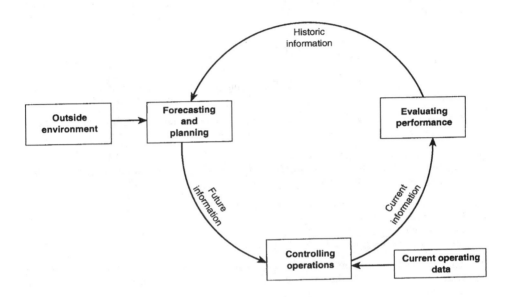

38.8 Types of management information

So far in this chapter no attempt has been made to describe the nature of the information which management requires. Information may come in many shapes and forms. In this book we are only concerned with information which is capable of being expressed in numerical terms, which in other words may be 'quantified'. Information of a more general nature about people's 'feelings' or 'views' may be very useful to management but cannot be quantified, and therefore is usually part of the informal rather than the formal information systems.

Within the body of quantified information it is normal to identify that part which can be measured in money terms. This is the part of the information system which is called accounting information. Accounting information is a very important element in the whole system since the organisation is basically an economic unit which must survive in conditions of economic scarcity and competition. In other words an organisation which does not meet its economic objectives will eventually fail or be taken over, hence the central importance of accounting information.

However, other quantified information may be very important for management. For example, if you are a farmer you will measure the yield of milk from your cows in the first instance as litres. A production manager will be very concerned to monitor the tonnages produced on his machines.

38.9 Quantitative methods in the information system

A modern management information system collects all the data together (into what is called a data bank) and issues that part which is important to each manager. Thus the distinction between accounting and other types of management information has tended to become less meaningful in modern data processing systems. The techniques of quantitative analysis (or statistics) apply to all the data in this system whether it be accounting data or not.

Main points to remember

1 Financial accounting fulfils a stewardship function by reporting past performance and financial position.

2 Financial accounting information is only of limited use for management control purposes, for which other forms of data and information are required.

3 It is important that organisational objectives are clearly defined and that the financial accounting information system is designed to meet and support those objectives in the most efficient and effective way.

4 Management is concerned with three areas of activity:
   (a) forecasting and planning;
   (b) control;
   (c) evaluating performance.

5 The financial accounting information system does not exist in a vacuum, it interacts with and is affected by the environment in which it is operating and must be designed accordingly.

Review questions

38.1 'Financial accounting looks behind, whilst management accounting looks ahead.' To what extent does this quotation accurately reflect the role of the two branches of accountancy?
(*University of London: GCE 'A' Level*)

38.2 'Financial accounting is non-dynamic, backward looking, conservative, as objective as possible, and subject to statutory and other regulation. Management accounting is future oriented, is dynamic, produces forward looking figures, should not be too concerned with objectivity, and is not generally subject to external regulation.' (Prof. Michael Bromwich)
   Justify this statement, giving examples to illustrate your answer.
(*University of London: GCE 'A' Level*)

38.3 What are some of the deficiencies of financial accounting?

38.4 Why is it important that the employees of an organisation should clearly understand what the objectives of the organisation are?

38.5 How can there be a conflict between the various objectives of an organisation?

38.6 Describe how the management process is carried out.

Appendix I

Examination techniques

If you were completely devoid of examination technique you would probably not have advanced to this stage of the examinations. All of the advice given to you in *Business Accounting 1* is still applicable. If you have not already read that advice you should try to borrow a copy of the book from a friend, or read it in a library.

A lot of what follows was written in *Business Accounting 1*. Don't avoid reading it just because you used it. In your first examination you were competing with people who had probably never sat an accounting examination before. A lot of them will not get past Stage 1. In Stage 2 you are competing against people who have already proved they have a certain degree of competence in the subject. You might have got away with a certain amount of poor examination technique at Stage 1, but that will not be as easy at Stage 2.

Here I want to concentrate on the main deficiencies noted by examiners. These have never changed for the past 40 years. Students really should read examiners' reports – they will learn a lot from them.

Students do not read the questions properly

A large number of students do not answer the questions as set by the examiner, because they have not read the question properly. They answer what they think the examiner wants, not what he is asking for.

Let me take a simple example. Suppose the examiner sets the following question: 'Describe the use of accounting ratios in assessing the performance of businesses.'

A lot of students will immediately start to describe how to calculate various accounting ratios. Marks which will be obtained – nil. The question asked for the *use* of accounting ratios, not *how to calculate* them.

Many other students will have concentrated on the word *use*. They will then write their answer based on comparing this year's accounting ratios in a business with those of last year. They may well even mention trend ratios which will earn them some extra marks. If they keep their discussion to comparing ratios in a business in the year with other years, however, they cannot get top marks, no matter how well they have written their answers.

Why not? Well, they picked up the word *use*, but from then on they stopped reading properly. The question does not in any way limit itself to the ratios of one business only. First of all you can compare the performance of a business with its own performance in the past. Secondly, you may be able to compare one business with another business of a similar kind. In addition, if you miss out mentioning interfirm comparisons you will lose marks.

Therefore, (a) *read* the question carefully, (b) *underline* the *key* words to get to the meaning of the question, (c) *think carefully* about how widespread your answer should be.

On the other hand there is no point in widening the question more than is needed. It is for the *use* of *accounting* ratios, *not* the use of *all types* of ratios. Besides accounting ratios there are marketing ratios – e.g. size of share of market, how long it takes to supply orders, ratios of defective goods etc. The question does not ask for all of these. If you give them, you will not get any extra marks.

Poor time management

Using time well to gain the highest possible marks is essential. Examiners constantly report that examinees are very poor in this aspect of tackling an examination. How then can you avoid the usual pitfalls?

First of all read the *rubric* carefully. These are the instructions at the top of the paper, e.g. 'Attempt four questions only: the three questions in Section A and one from Section B. Begin each answer on a separate page.'

You would be surprised to know that a lot of students would try to answer more than one question from Section B. If you tackle two questions from Section B you will get marks for only one of your answers. No examiner will mark both and then give you the marks for your highest marked answer. They will mark the first of the optional questions answered and ignore the next unnecessary answer.

Secondly, don't annoy the examiner by not starting your answer on a separate page. It is your job to make the examiner's work as easy as possible. Examiners are only human, and it would not be surprising if their annoyance did not result in it influencing the marking of your paper.

You really must attempt each and every question to fulfil the examination requirements. If you have to answer five questions then you must not tackle only four questions.

Students often feel that they would be better off by handing in the complete answers to only four questions, instead of five incomplete answers. In accounting examinations this is not true. Why is this so?

1   Examiners use positive marking in accounting examinations. If you have done 80 per cent of an answer worth 20 marks in total, and you have got it absolutely correct, then you get $80\% \times 20 = 16$ marks.
2   The first marks in a question are the easiest to obtain. Thus it is easier to get the first 10 marks out of 20 than it is to get the second lot of marks to get full marks. By ensuring that you get the easiest marks on every question it therefore makes your task easier.

To ensure that you tackle (not necessarily finish) each question you should mark the number of minutes to be allowed by *yourself* for each question. Thus a 20-mark question, in a 100-mark examination, should be given 20 per cent of the time, i.e. 3 hours × 20% = 36 minutes. When 36 minutes have gone by, *stop answering the question* unless it is the last question to be attempted, and go on to the next question.

If you don't know the answer, or part of an answer, you should guess. You don't lose marks for guessing, and if you guess correctly you get the marks. Intuition will often give the correct answer. Very often if you don't guess on part of a computational question you will be unable to go on to the remainder of the question which you can answer.

Workings

You may wonder why I have put this under a separate heading. I cannot emphasise enough how important it is that you should:

(*a*) submit all your workings; and
(*b*) ensure that the workings are set out so that the examiner can follow them.

A very high percentage of candidates in an examination are near the pass mark, within either a few percentage points above it or below it. You should know that from your study of natural curves in statistics. If you are one of these candidates, and, as we have said, there are a lot of them, handing in workings which can be understood by the examiner will often ensure you a pass mark. Conversely, no workings, or completely unintelligible workings may well ensure your failing the examination.

Tackle the easiest questions first

Never start off your examination by tackling a difficult question. You have got to be able to settle down properly, and not let your nerves get out of control. Starting off on the easiest question is the best way to enable you to get off to a good start. Much more about this was written in *Business Accounting 1*.

State your assumptions

It does happen that sometimes a question can contain ambiguities. Examination bodies try to prevent it happening, but it does occur occasionally. The questions do (unfortunately) sometimes contain errors.

In both of these cases you must point out the ambiguity/error. You should then make an assumption, based on what you thought the examiner meant, and carry on with your answer. You must, however, state what your assumption is. Try to make your assumption as sensible as possible. The examiner will then mark your answer accordingly. If you make a ridiculous assumption, it is unlikely that he will give you any marks for that part of your answer. Don't be sarcastic in your comments or complain about inefficiency – there are other times and places for that.

Answering written questions

The problem

Unlike computational-type answers you will not know whether your written answers are up to the mark until you receive your examination result. Likewise written questions lack the certainty and precision of accounting problems and it is often difficult to fathom out exactly what the examiners require of you. For this reason sound examination technique is absolutely essential together with precise knowledge of relevant law and regulations.

There are several major aspects to success in written papers. These are to *plan* your answer, to answer the question *as set*, to pay attention to good *layout* and to explain in clear and simple terms what you are doing. Remember you can only be marked on what you write down. You have no opportunity to explain some ambiguity or other and if what you write is unclear you will *not* get the benefit of the doubt.

Plan

First read the question and jot down the key *verb*, i.e. your instructions; this may be to discuss, explain, advise, set out, list, draft an audit programme, write a letter, etc.

If the question requires a discussion or an explanation it should be written in proper paragraph form. Each paragraph should be self-contained and explain the point it makes.

Sentences should be short and to the point. The ideal length for a paragraph is three sentences with four as a maximum. Over four and you are probably making more than one point and should have gone into two paragraphs.

Plan how many points you are going to make and what the answer is. This is essential as otherwise your answer will 'drift' as you struggle to come to some conclusion. The plan should consist of arrows connecting points to each other so that the answer will flow and be logical. The plan need not be too extensive; it is silly to waste time on a 'mini-answer'. It should consist of the *headings* you are going to use.

Layout

Whenever examiners meet to discuss results, or write down their commentary on students' performance, they all agree on the importance of good layout; yet students generally tend to take no notice. The range of marks between good papers and poor papers tends to be quite small. Anything you can do to put the examiner on your side will pay off in those few extra marks.

The main areas for good layout are:

1   *Tabulate* in numbered points, unless you are writing an essay-type question (as explained above).
2   Leave at least a clear line between each point or paragraph.
3   Use headings whenever possible to indicate what major point or series of points you are about to make. Make it easy for the examiner to read your work and follow what you are doing. A solid mass of material is difficult to read, provides no respite for the eye and shows a lack of discipline. Remember that you are taking a *professional* examination and there is no room for academic licence.
4   Take care with your *language*. Be objective and avoid the use of the words 'I' or 'we' at too frequent intervals. Be direct and concise, say what you mean, do not use pompous terminology and use technical words with their correct meaning.

 Short sentences are far more effective and punchy than long ones. An accounting programme or evaluation of an internal control system could well start with a series of *verbs*. Good ones are: test, examine, inspect, calculate, reconcile, compare, summarise, inquire, investigate. These key words will help you to make answers to these types of questions much more direct and to the point. If you start with them you are bound to avoid falling into the trap of being long-winded, or of padding out your answer. You only have a limited time and everything you write down must earn you marks.
5   *Think* while you are writing out your answer to make sure you are answering the question *as set*. Keep on reading the instructions and make sure you are following them. Use the question to help you to get the answer and, while this should be tackled at the planning stage, it is always possible that inspiration will strike while you are writing out your answer. In which case jot the point down on your plan, otherwise you might forget it and that can cause frustration. What you say should be relevant but if you are in doubt about the relevance but sure about the accuracy – give it to him! You cannot lose and it may be one of the key points he was looking for.

Key points

Do try to find a couple of key points to each question. These are points which you feel are vital to answer the question. You may well be right, and anyway jotting them down after you have read the question carefully can help to give your answer much needed direction.

Practice

You will need to practise the above routine. Written answers in fact need more practice than computational ones. Have a go at the question. Write out the answer as you would in the examination. Compare with the suggested answers.

Write out at the foot of your answer *what you left out* and *what you got wrong*.

Learn from the answers and from the work you do, so that when you see a similar question you will produce a better answer.

Time pressure

You will experience a lot of time pressure as you progress with written questions. Do not worry; this is a good sign.

In the examination spread your time sensibly. Start with the questions you like the look of most and if you have to go slightly over time do so. End with the question you think you cannot answer, but do give yourself time to have a reasonable go at it.

If a written question is included in a computational paper do not go over the time on it but do spend the allocated time. Examiners pay great attention to the written parts of computational papers, so do not skimp this part.

All this sounds formidable and, of course, it is. It requires skill and application and above all confidence. Practice makes perfect and once the skill is acquired then, like riding a bicycle, it will not be forgotten. Take pride in your work and be critical of your own efforts, but do not imagine your answers will have to be perfect to pass the examination. Suggested answers tend to be too long because tutors are afraid to reveal any signs of weakness or ignorance.

Go for the main points and make them well. That is the secret of success.

Appendix II

Interest tables

Table 1 Compound sum of £1

Year	1%	2%	3%	4%	5%	6%	7%	8%	9%	10%
1	1.010	1.020	1.030	1.040	1.050	1.060	1.070	1.080	1.090	1.100
2	1.020	1.040	1.061	1.082	1.103	1.124	1.145	1.166	1.188	1.210
3	1.030	1.061	1.093	1.125	1.158	1.191	1.225	1.260	1.295	1.331
4	1.041	1.082	1.126	1.170	1.216	1.262	1.311	1.360	1.412	1.464
5	1.051	1.104	1.159	1.217	1.276	1.338	1.403	1.469	1.539	1.611
6	1.062	1.126	1.194	1.265	1.340	1.419	1.501	1.587	1.677	1.772
7	1.072	1.149	1.230	1.316	1.407	1.504	1.606	1.714	1.828	1.949
8	1.083	1.172	1.267	1.369	1.477	1.594	1.718	1.851	1.993	2.144
9	1.094	1.195	1.305	1.423	1.551	1.689	1.838	1.999	2.172	2.358
10	1.105	1.219	1.344	1.480	1.629	1.791	1.967	2.159	2.367	2.594
11	1.116	1.243	1.384	1.539	1.710	1.898	2.105	2.332	2.580	2.853
12	1.127	1.268	1.426	1.601	1.796	2.012	2.252	2.518	2.813	3.138
13	1.138	1.294	1.469	1.665	1.886	2.133	2.410	2.720	3.066	3.452
14	1.149	1.319	1.513	1.732	1.980	2.261	2.579	2.937	3.342	3.797
15	1.161	1.346	1.558	1.801	2.079	2.397	2.759	3.172	3.642	4.177

Year	12%	14%	15%	16%	18%	20%	24%	28%	32%
1	1.120	1.140	1.150	1.160	1.180	1.200	1.240	1.280	1.320
2	1.254	1.300	1.323	1.346	1.392	1.440	1.538	1.638	1.742
3	1.405	1.482	1.521	1.561	1.643	1.728	1.907	2.097	2.300
4	1.574	1.689	1.749	1.811	1.939	2.074	2.364	2.684	3.036
5	1.762	1.925	2.011	2.100	2.288	2.488	2.932	3.436	4.007
6	1.974	2.195	2.313	2.436	2.700	2.986	3.635	4.398	5.290
7	2.211	2.502	2.660	2.826	3.185	3.583	4.508	5.629	6.983
8	2.476	2.853	3.059	3.278	3.759	4.300	5.590	7.206	9.217
9	2.773	3.252	3.518	3.803	4.435	5.160	6.931	9.223	12.166
10	3.106	3.707	4.046	4.411	5.234	6.192	8.594	11.806	16.060
11	3.479	4.226	4.652	5.117	6.176	7.430	10.657	15.112	21.199
12	3.896	4.818	5.350	5.936	7.288	8.916	13.215	19.343	27.983
13	4.363	5.492	6.153	6.886	8.599	10.699	16.386	24.759	36.937
14	4.887	6.261	7.076	7.988	10.147	12.839	20.319	31.691	48.757
15	5.474	7.138	8.137	9.266	11.974	15.407	25.196	40.565	64.359

Year	36%	40%	50%	60%	70%	80%	90%
1	1.360	1.400	1.500	1.600	1.700	1.800	1.900
2	1.850	1.960	2.250	2.560	2.890	3.240	3.610
3	2.515	2.744	3.375	4.096	4.913	5.832	6.859
4	3.421	3.842	5.062	6.544	8.352	10.498	13.032
5	4.653	5.378	7.594	10.486	14.199	18.896	24.761
6	6.328	7.530	11.391	16.777	24.138	34.012	47.046
7	8.605	10.541	17.086	26.844	41.034	61.222	89.387
8	11.703	14.758	25.629	42.950	69.758	110.200	169.836
9	15.917	20.661	38.443	68.720	118.588	198.359	322.688
10	21.647	28.925	57.665	109.951	201.599	357.047	613.107
11	29.439	40.496	86.498	175.922	342.719	642.684	1164.902
12	40.037	56.694	129.746	281.475	582.622	1156.831	2213.314
13	54.451	79.372	194.619	450.360	990.457	2082.295	4205.297
14	74.053	111.120	291.929	720.576	1683.777	3748.131	7990.065
15	100.712	155.568	437.894	1152.921	2862.421	6746.636	15181.122

Table 2 Present value of £1

Year	1%	2%	3%	4%	5%	6%	7%	8%	9%	10%	12%	14%	15%
1	0.990	0.980	0.971	0.961	0.952	0.943	0.935	0.926	0.917	0.909	0.893	0.877	0.870
2	0.980	0.961	0.943	0.925	0.907	0.890	0.873	0.857	0.842	0.826	0.797	0.769	0.756
3	0.971	0.942	0.915	0.889	0.864	0.840	0.816	0.794	0.772	0.751	0.712	0.675	0.658
4	0.961	0.924	0.889	0.855	0.823	0.792	0.763	0.735	0.708	0.683	0.636	0.592	0.572
5	0.951	0.906	0.863	0.822	0.784	0.747	0.713	0.681	0.650	0.621	0.567	0.519	0.497
6	0.942	0.888	0.838	0.790	0.746	0.705	0.666	0.630	0.596	0.564	0.507	0.456	0.432
7	0.933	0.871	0.813	0.760	0.711	0.665	0.623	0.583	0.547	0.513	0.452	0.400	0.376
8	0.923	0.853	0.789	0.731	0.677	0.627	0.582	0.540	0.502	0.467	0.404	0.351	0.327
9	0.914	0.837	0.766	0.703	0.645	0.592	0.544	0.500	0.460	0.424	0.361	0.308	0.284
10	0.905	0.820	0.744	0.676	0.614	0.558	0.508	0.463	0.422	0.386	0.322	0.270	0.247
11	0.896	0.804	0.722	0.650	0.585	0.527	0.475	0.429	0.388	0.350	0.287	0.237	0.215
12	0.887	0.788	0.701	0.625	0.557	0.497	0.444	0.397	0.356	0.319	0.257	0.208	0.187
13	0.879	0.773	0.681	0.601	0.530	0.469	0.415	0.368	0.326	0.290	0.229	0.182	0.163
14	0.870	0.758	0.661	0.577	0.505	0.442	0.388	0.340	0.299	0.263	0.205	0.160	0.141
15	0.861	0.743	0.642	0.555	0.481	0.417	0.362	0.315	0.275	0.239	0.183	0.140	0.123
16	0.853	0.728	0.623	0.534	0.458	0.394	0.339	0.292	0.252	0.218	0.163	0.123	0.107
17	0.844	0.714	0.605	0.513	0.436	0.371	0.317	0.270	0.231	0.198	0.146	0.108	0.093
18	0.836	0.700	0.587	0.494	0.416	0.350	0.296	0.250	0.212	0.180	0.130	0.095	0.081
19	0.828	0.686	0.570	0.475	0.396	0.331	0.276	0.232	0.194	0.164	0.116	0.083	0.070
20	0.820	0.673	0.554	0.456	0.377	0.319	0.258	0.215	0.178	0.149	0.104	0.073	0.061
25	0.780	0.610	0.478	0.375	0.295	0.233	0.184	0.146	0.116	0.092	0.059	0.038	0.030
30	0.742	0.552	0.412	0.308	0.231	0.174	0.131	0.099	0.075	0.057	0.033	0.020	0.015

Year	16%	18%	20%	24%	28%	32%	36%	40%	50%	60%	70%	80%	90%
1	0.862	0.847	0.833	0.806	0.781	0.758	0.735	0.714	0.667	0.625	0.588	0.556	0.526
2	0.743	0.718	0.694	0.650	0.610	0.574	0.541	0.510	0.444	0.391	0.346	0.309	0.277
3	0.641	0.609	0.579	0.524	0.477	0.435	0.398	0.364	0.296	0.244	0.204	0.171	0.146
4	0.552	0.516	0.482	0.423	0.373	0.329	0.292	0.260	0.198	0.153	0.120	0.095	0.077
5	0.476	0.437	0.402	0.341	0.291	0.250	0.215	0.186	0.132	0.095	0.070	0.053	0.040
6	0.410	0.370	0.335	0.275	0.227	0.189	0.158	0.133	0.088	0.060	0.041	0.029	0.021
7	0.354	0.314	0.279	0.222	0.178	0.143	0.116	0.095	0.059	0.037	0.024	0.016	0.011
8	0.305	0.266	0.233	0.179	0.139	0.108	0.085	0.068	0.039	0.023	0.014	0.009	0.006
9	0.263	0.226	0.194	0.144	0.108	0.082	0.063	0.048	0.026	0.015	0.008	0.005	0.003
10	0.227	0.191	0.162	0.116	0.085	0.062	0.046	0.035	0.017	0.009	0.005	0.003	0.002
11	0.195	0.162	0.135	0.094	0.066	0.047	0.034	0.025	0.012	0.006	0.003	0.002	0.001
12	0.168	0.137	0.112	0.076	0.052	0.036	0.025	0.018	0.008	0.004	0.002	0.001	0.001
13	0.145	0.116	0.093	0.061	0.040	0.027	0.018	0.013	0.005	0.002	0.001	0.001	0.000
14	0.125	0.099	0.078	0.049	0.032	0.021	0.014	0.009	0.003	0.001	0.001	0.000	0.000
15	0.108	0.084	0.065	0.040	0.025	0.016	0.010	0.006	0.002	0.001	0.000	0.000	0.000
16	0.093	0.071	0.054	0.032	0.019	0.012	0.007	0.005	0.002	0.001	0.000	0.000	
17	0.080	0.060	0.045	0.026	0.015	0.009	0.005	0.003	0.001	0.001	0.000	0.000	
18	0.069	0.051	0.038	0.021	0.012	0.007	0.004	0.002	0.001	0.000	0.000		
19	0.060	0.043	0.031	0.017	0.009	0.005	0.003	0.002	0.000	0.000			
20	0.051	0.037	0.026	0.014	0.007	0.004	0.002	0.001	0.000	0.000			
25	0.024	0.016	0.010	0.005	0.002	0.001	0.000	0.000					
30	0.012	0.007	0.004	0.002	0.001	0.000	0.000						

Table 3 Sum of an annuity of £1 for *n* years

Year	1%	2%	3%	4%	5%	6%	7%	8%
1	1.000	1.000	1.000	1.000	1.000	1.000	1.000	1.000
2	2.010	2.020	2.030	2.040	2.050	2.060	2.070	2.080
3	3.030	3.060	3.091	3.122	3.152	3.184	3.215	3.246
4	4.060	4.122	4.184	4.246	4.310	4.375	4.440	4.506
5	5.101	5.204	5.309	5.416	5.526	5.637	5.751	5.867
6	6.152	6.308	6.468	6.633	6.802	6.975	7.153	7.336
7	7.214	7.434	7.662	7.898	8.142	8.394	8.654	8.923
8	8.286	8.583	8.892	9.214	9.549	9.897	10.260	10.637
9	9.369	9.755	10.159	10.583	11.027	11.491	11.978	12.488
10	10.462	10.950	11.464	12.006	12.578	13.181	13.816	41.487
11	11.567	12.169	12.808	13.486	14.207	14.972	15.784	16.645
12	12.683	13.412	14.192	15.026	15.917	16.870	17.888	18.977
13	13.809	14.680	15.618	16.627	17.713	18.882	20.141	21.495
14	14.947	15.974	17.086	18.292	19.599	21.051	22.550	24.215
15	16.097	17.293	18.599	20.024	21.579	23.276	25.129	27.152
16	17.258	18.639	20.157	21.825	23.657	25.673	27.888	30.324
17	18.430	20.012	21.762	23.698	25.840	28.213	30.840	33.750
18	19.615	21.412	23.414	25.645	28.132	30.906	33.999	37.450
19	20.811	22.841	25.117	27.671	30.539	33.760	37.379	41.446
20	22.019	24.297	26.870	29.778	33.066	36.786	40.995	45.762
25	28.243	32.030	36.459	41.646	47.727	54.865	63.249	73.106
30	34.785	40.568	47.575	56.085	66.439	79.058	94.461	113.283

Year	9%	10%	12%	14%	16%	18%	20%	24%
1	1.000	1.000	1.000	1.000	1.000	1.000	1.000	1.000
2	2.090	2.100	2.120	2.140	2.160	2.180	2.200	2.240
3	3.278	3.310	3.374	3.440	3.506	3.572	3.640	3.778
4	4.573	4.641	4.779	4.921	5.066	5.215	5.368	5.684
5	5.985	6.105	6.353	6.610	6.877	7.154	7.442	8.048
6	7.523	7.716	8.115	8.536	8.977	9.442	9.930	10.980
7	9.200	9.487	10.089	10.730	11.414	12.142	12.916	14.615
8	11.028	11.436	12.300	13.233	14.240	15.327	16.499	19.123
9	13.021	13.579	14.776	16.085	17.518	19.086	20.799	24.712
10	15.193	15.937	17.549	19.337	21.321	23.521	25.959	31.643
11	17.560	18.531	20.655	23.044	25.738	28.755	32.150	40.238
12	20.141	21.384	24.133	27.271	30.350	34.931	39.580	50.895
13	22.953	24.523	28.029	32.089	36.766	42.219	48.497	64.110
14	26.019	27.975	32.393	37.581	43.672	50.818	59.196	80.496
15	29.361	31.722	37.280	43.842	51.659	60.965	72.035	100.815

Year	28%	32%	36%	40%	50%	60%	70%	80%
1	1.000	1.000	1.000	1.000	1.000	1.000	1.000	1.000
2	2.280	2.320	2.360	2.400	2.500	2.600	2.700	2.800
3	3.918	4.062	4.210	4.360	4.750	5.160	5.590	6.040
4	6.016	6.326	6.725	7.104	8.125	9.256	10.503	11.872
5	8.700	9.398	10.146	10.846	13.188	15.810	18.855	22.370
6	12.136	13.406	14.799	16.324	20.781	26.295	33.054	41.265
7	16.534	18.696	21.126	23.853	32.172	43.073	57.191	75.278
8	22.163	25.678	29.732	34.395	49.258	69.916	98.225	136.500
9	29.369	34.895	41.435	49.153	74.887	112.866	167.983	246.699
10	38.592	47.062	57.352	69.814	113.330	181.585	286.570	445.058
11	50.399	63.122	78.998	98.739	170.995	291.536	488.170	802.105
12	65.510	84.320	108.437	139.235	257.493	467.458	830.888	1444.788
13	84.853	112.303	148.475	195.929	387.239	748.933	1413.510	2601.619
14	109.612	149.240	202.926	275.300	581.859	1199.293	2403.968	4683.914
15	141.303	197.997	276.979	386.420	873.788	1919.869	4087.745	8432.045

Table 4 Present value of annuity of £1 per period

Year	1%	2%	3%	4%	5%	6%	7%	8%	9%	10%
1	0.990	0.980	0.971	0.962	0.952	0.943	0.935	0.926	0.917	0.909
2	1.970	1.942	1.913	1.886	1.859	1.833	1.808	1.783	1.759	1.736
3	2.941	2.884	2.829	2.775	2.723	2.673	2.624	2.577	2.531	2.487
4	3.902	3.808	3.717	3.630	3.546	3.465	3.387	3.312	3.240	3.170
5	4.853	4.713	4.580	4.452	4.329	4.212	4.100	3.993	3.890	3.791
6	5.795	5.601	5.417	5.424	5.076	4.917	4.766	4.623	4.486	4.355
7	6.728	6.472	6.230	6.002	5.786	5.582	5.389	5.206	5.033	4.868
8	7.652	7.325	7.020	6.733	6.463	6.210	6.971	5.747	5.535	5.335
9	8.566	8.162	7.786	7.435	7.108	6.802	6.515	6.247	5.985	5.759
10	9.471	8.983	8.530	8.111	7.722	7.360	7.024	6.710	6.418	6.145
11	10.368	9.787	9.253	8.760	8.306	7.887	7.499	7.139	6.805	6.495
12	11.255	10.575	9.954	9.385	8.863	8.384	7.943	7.536	7.161	6.814
13	12.134	11.348	10.635	9.986	9.394	8.853	8.358	7.904	7.487	7.103
14	13.004	12.106	11.296	10.563	8.899	9.295	8.745	8.244	7.786	7.367
15	13.865	12.849	11.938	11.118	10.380	9.712	9.108	8.559	8.060	7.606
16	14.718	13.578	12.561	11.652	10.838	10.106	9.447	8.851	8.312	7.824
17	15.562	14.292	13.166	12.166	11.274	10.477	9.763	9.122	8.544	8.022
18	16.398	14.992	13.754	12.659	11.690	10.828	10.059	9.372	8.756	8.201
19	17.226	15.678	14.324	13.134	12.085	11.158	10.336	9.604	8.950	8.365
20	18.046	16.351	14.877	13.590	12.462	11.470	10.594	9.818	9.128	8.514
25	22.023	19.523	17.413	15.622	14.094	12.783	11.654	10.675	9.823	9.077
30	25.808	22.397	19.600	17.292	15.373	13.765	12.409	11.258	10.274	9.427

Year	12%	14%	16%	18%	20%	24%	28%	32%	36%
1	0.893	0.877	0.862	0.847	0.833	0.806	0.781	0.758	0.735
2	1.690	1.647	1.605	1.566	1.528	1.457	1.392	1.332	1.276
3	2.402	2.322	2.246	2.174	2.106	1.981	1.868	1.766	1.674
4	3.037	2.914	2.798	2.690	2.589	2.404	2.241	2.096	1.966
5	3.605	3.433	3.274	3.127	2.991	2.745	2.532	2.345	2.181
6	4.111	3.889	3.685	3.498	3.326	3.020	2.759	2.534	2.339
7	4.564	4.288	4.089	3.812	3.605	3.242	2.937	2.678	2.455
8	4.968	4.639	4.344	4.078	3.837	3.421	3.076	2.786	2.540
9	5.328	4.946	4.607	4.303	4.031	3.566	3.184	2.868	2.603
10	5.650	5.216	4.833	4.494	4.193	3.682	3.269	2.930	2.650
11	5.988	5.453	5.029	4.656	4.327	3.776	3.335	2.978	2.683
12	6.194	5.660	5.197	4.793	4.439	3.851	3.387	3.013	2.708
13	6.424	5.842	5.342	4.910	4.533	3.912	3.427	3.040	2.727
14	6.628	6.002	5.468	5.008	4.611	3.962	3.459	3.061	2.740
15	6.811	6.142	5.575	5.092	4.675	4.001	3.483	3.076	2.750
16	6.974	6.265	5.669	5.162	4.730	4.033	3.503	3.088	2.758
17	7.120	5.373	5.749	4.222	4.775	4.059	3.518	3.097	2.763
18	7.250	6.467	5.818	5.273	4.812	4.080	3.529	3.104	2.767
19	7.366	6.550	5.877	5.316	4.844	4.097	3.539	3.109	2.770
20	7.469	6.623	5.929	5.353	4.870	4.110	3.546	3.113	2.772
25	7.843	6.873	6.907	5.467	4.948	4.147	3.564	3.122	2.776
30	8.055	7.003	6.177	5.517	4.979	4.160	3.569	3.124	2.778

Appendix III   Answers to review questions

Note: All the answers are the work of the author. None has been supplied by an examining body. The University of London Examinations and Assessment Council accepts no responsibility whatsoever for the accuracy or method of working in the answers given. In order to save space £ signs have been omitted from columns of figures except where the figures refer to £000, or where the denomination needs to be specified.

1.1

Ollier's Books (dates ignored)

Joint Venture with Avon

Cars	900	Sales	1,600
Repairs and respraying	60		
Profit on venture	237		
Balance c/d	403		
	1,600		1,600
Cash to Avon	403	Balance b/d	403

Avon's Books

Joint Venture with Ollier

Garage rental	20	Balance c/d	403
Advertising	10		
Licence and insurance	36		
Car	100		
Profit on venture	237		
	403		403
Balance b/d	403	Cash from Ollier	403

Memorandum Joint Venture Account

Cars	1,000	Sales	1,000
Repairs and respraying	60		
Garage rental	20		
Advertising	10		
Licence and insurance	36		
Profit on venture			
Ollier ½	237		
Avon ½	237	474	
	1,600		1,600

1.3

Plant's Books

Joint Venture with Hoe and Reap

Rent	156		
Labour: Planting	105		
Labour: Fertilising	36		
Sundries	10		
Labour	18		
Fertiliser	29		
Share of profit	266	Balance c/d	620
	620		620
Balance c/d	620	Cash from Reap	620

Hoe's Books

Joint Venture with Plant and Reap

Seeds	48		
Motor expenses	17		
Share of profit	114	Balance c/d	179
	179		179
Balance b/d	179	Cash from Reap	179

Reap's Books

Joint Venture with Plant and Hoe

Lifting	73	Sales	987
Sale expenses	39		
Share of profit	76		
Balances c/d	799		
	987		987
Cash to Plant	620	Balance b/d	799
Cash to Hoe	179		
	799		799

Plant, Hoe and Reap, Memorandum Joint Venture Account

Rent		Sales	156
Labour: Planting	105		
Labour: Fertilising	36		
Sundry expenses	18		
Lifting	73		
Fertiliser	29		
Motor expenses	17		
Seeds	48		
Sale expenses	39		
Sundries	10		
Profit shared: Plant	266		
Hoe	114		
Reap	76		
	456		
	987		987

2.1

(a) Gudgeon's books (years omitted)

R Johnson Ltd

Jul 1 Sales	2,460	Jul 1 Bills receivable	2,460

B Scarlet & Co Ltd

Jul 1 Sales	1,500	Jul 1 Bills receivable	1,500
Sep 4 Bills receivable (dishonour)	1,500		
" 4 Bank: Noting charge	6		

Bills Receivable

Jul 1 R Johnson Ltd	2,460	Jul 4 Bank	2,460
" 1 B Scarlet & Co Ltd	1,500	" 4 Bank	1,500

Bank

Jul 4 Bills receivable	2,460	Jul 4 Discounting charges	80
" 4 Bills receivable	1,500	" 4 Discounting charges	65
		Sep 4 B Scarlet (discounted bill)	1,500
		" 4 Noting charge (Scarlet)	6

Discounting Charges

Jul 4 Bank	80
" 4 Bank	65

(b) Johnson's books

N Gudgeon

Jul 1 Bills payable	2,460	Jul 1 Purchases	2,460

Bills Payable

	2,460	Jul 1 N Gudgeon	2,460

Bank

		Sep 1 Bills payable	2,460

(c) Scarlet's books

N Gudgeon

Jul 1 Bills payable	1,500	Jul 1 Purchases	1,500
		Sep 1 Bills payable	1,500
		" 4 Noting charge	6

Noting Charges

Sep 4 N Gudgeon	6

Bills Payable

Sep 1 N Gudgeon (discounted bill)	1,500	Jul 1 N Gudgeon	1,500

2.3

KC

Balance b/d	960	Bills receivable	960
Bank (dishonoured bill)	960	Bank	360
		Bad debts	600
	960		960

Bills Receivable

KC	960	Bank	960
	960		960

Bank

Bills receivable	960	Discounting charges	12
		KC (dishonoured bill)	960

Bad Debts

KC	600

Discounting Charges

Bank	12

2.4

Sales Ledger Control (years omitted)

Aug 1 Balances b/d	12,370	Aug 1 Balances b/d	105
" 31 Sales	16,904	" 31 Returns in	407
" 31 Bills receivable dishonoured	177	" 31 Bank	15,970
" 31 Balances c/d	88	" 31 Bills receivable	1,230
		" 31 Cash	306
		" 31 Bad debts	129
		" 31 Discounts allowed	604
		" 31 Balances c/d*	10,788
	29,539		29,539

*difference

2.5

Purchases Ledger Control

		£			£
Feb 1	Balances b/f	8,570	Feb 1	Balances b/f	11,375
,, 28	Returns outwards	33	,, 28	Purchases	
,, 28	Bills payable	568	,, 28	Bills payable dishonoured	800
,, 28	Bank	1,860	,, 28	Noting charges	20
,, 28	Cash	9,464	,, 28	Balances c/d	47
,, 28	Balances	177			
	(difference c/d)	8,710			
		20,812			20,812

3.1

Consignment to MB

	£		£
Goods	3,000	Sales	3,500
Carriage	147	Stock c/d	611
Insurance	93	20/120 × 3,666	
Freight	240		
Port charges	186		
	3,666		
Commission	175		
Profit	270		
	4,111		4,111

MB

	£		£
Sales	3,500	Freight	240
		Port charges	186
		Commission	175
		Bank	2,899
	3,500		3,500

3.3

Account Sales for Hughes of London
From Galvez of Madrid

	£	£
Bicycle sales 250 × £20 =	5,000	
50 × £18 =	900	
		5,900
Less Port and duty charges	720	
Storage and carriage	410	
Commission 6% of £5,900	354	
		1,484
		4,416

Consignment Inwards

	£		£
Port and duty charges	720	Sales 250 × £20	5,000
Storage and carriage charges	410	50 × £18	900
Commission	354		
Cash	4,416		
	5,900		5,900

3.4

Consignment to Rock

	£	£		£
Goods sent		12,000	Rock: Sales	10,600
Expenses			Value of stock c/d	3,921
Freight and insurance	720			
Rock: Expenses	350		Cost	12,000
		1,070	Add expenses	1,070
Selling expenses – Rock		245		13,070
Commission 5% of 10,600		530	30% × 13,070	3,921
Bank charges provision c/d		12		
Profit to profit and loss		664		
		14,521		14,521

	£		£
Value of stock b/d	3,921	Bank charges Provision b/d	12
Bank charges	12	Rock: Sales	4,800
Selling expenses	200		
Bad debts	120		
Commission 5% of £4,800	240		
Bank charges	9		
Profit and loss account	310		
	4,812		4,812

Rock

	£		£
Consignment	10,600	Commission	530
		Expenses	350
		Selling expenses	245
		Cash – draft	7,475
		Balance c/d	2,000
	10,600		10,600

	£		£
Balance b/d	2,000	Commission	240
Consignment	4,800	Selling expenses	200
		Bad debts	120
		Cash – draft	6,240
	6,800		6,800

4.1

Branch Stock (dates omitted)

	Memo			Memo	
Balance b/f	4,400	3,300	Branch debtors	21,000	21,000
Goods from head office	24,800	18,600	Cash sales	2,400	2,400
Gross profit		5,850	Returns to HO	1,000	750
			Goods stolen	600	450
			Profit and loss:		
			Normal wastage	100	75
			Profit and loss:		
			Excess wastage	152	114
			Balance c/f	3,948	2,961
	29,200	27,750		29,200	27,750

Branch Debtors

Balances b/fwd	3,946	Bad debts	148
Branch stock: Sales	21,000	Discounts allowed	428
		Bank	22,400
		Balance c/fwd	1,970
	24,946		24,946

4.2

(a) (dates omitted) Branch Current Account

Balance b/fwd	20,160	Cash	30,000
Goods sent	23,160	Goods returned	400
Expenses paid	6,000		
Net profit	3,500	Balance c/d	22,420
	52,820		52,820

(b) Proof:

Branch assets	xxx
Less Branch liabilities	xxx
= Balance of branch current account	
Indicates: Amount of money invested in branch	xxx

4.3

(a) (i) Branch Stock (Selling Prices)

Goods from head office		Cash sales	89,940
(82,400 + 10% 8,240 =		Sales: Branch debtors	1,870
90,640 + 25%)	113,300	Goods to other branches	3,300
		Branch stock adjustment:	
		Reductions	2,250
		Balance c/d	15,940
	113,300		113,300

(ii) *Branch Stock Adjustment* *(profit margin)

Goods to other branches	660	Branch stock	22,660
Branch stock: Reductions	2,250	(113,300 – 90,640)	
Profit and loss	16,562		
Balance c/d	3,188		
	22,660		22,660

*As cost to branch (original cost + 10%) is subject to further mark-up of 25%, therefore margin is 20%, and this is profit margin used in this account.

(b)

Book stock per branch stock account	15,940
Physical stock	14,850
	1,090

Four possible reasons for deficiency:
(i) thefts by customers;
(ii) thefts by staff;
(iii) wastages due to breakages, miscounting, etc.;
(iv) cash misappropriated.

(c) Figure to be taken for RST balance sheet:

Actual stock at selling price	14,850
Less 20% margin	2,970
Cost to branch	11,880
Less head office loading	
(+ 10% = 1/11th of adjusted figure) 1/11th	1,080
Actual cost to company	10,800

Therefore (ii) 10,800 is correct answer.

4.5

Packer & Stringer

Trading & Profit & Loss Account for the year ended 31 December 19X4

	HO		Branch	
Sales		39,000		26,000
Less Cost of goods sold				
Opening stock	13,000		4,400	
Add Purchases	37,000			
	50,000			
Goods to branch	17,200		17,200	
	32,800		21,600	
Less Closing stock	15,240		6,570	
		17,560		15,030
		21,440		10,970
Bad debt provision not required				20
				10,990
Salaries	4,500		3,200	
Administrative expenses	1,440		960	
Carriage	2,200		960	
General expenses	3,200		1,800	
Provision for bad debts	50			
Depreciation	150		110	
Manager's commission			360	
		11,540		7,390
Net profit		9,900		3,600

		13,500
Packer: Commission		900
Interest on capital: Packer	840	
Stringer	240	1,080
		1,980
Balance of profits: Packer ¾	8,640	
Stringer ¼	2,880	11,520
		13,500

Balance Sheet as at 31 December 19X4

Fixed assets		
Furniture		2,600
Less Depreciation		1,110
		1,490
Current assets		
Stock		21,810
Debtors	10,000	
Less Provision for bad debts	830	
		9,170
Cash and bank		3,000
		33,980
Less Current liabilities		
Creditors	6,200	
Bank overdraft	1,350	
Manager's commission	120	
		7,670
Working capital		26,310
		27,800

4.7

Nion

Trading and Profit and Loss Account for the year ended 31 October 19X1

	Head office		Branch	
	£000		£000	
Sales		914		437
Transfers to branch		8		
		922		
Less Cost of goods sold:				
Opening stock	850		20	
Add Purchases	380		375	
Add Goods from HO			395	
	1,230			
Less Closing stock	320		15	
		910		380
Gross profit		12		57
Less Expenses:				
Administrative	200		16.5	
Distribution	80.5		5	
Depreciation	35		10	
Changes in provision for bad debts	0.5		0.5	
		309.5		32
Net profit		(6)		25
		10.5		0.5

EG Company Ltd
Trading and Profit and Loss Accounts for the year ended 30 June 19X8

	Head office		Branch	
Sales		104,000		48,000
Less Cost of sales	58,400		38,600	
Depreciation	600		1,800	
	59,000			40,400
	35,000			
Goods to branch	24,000			
Gross profit		80,000		7,600
Administration costs	15,200		2,000	
Selling and distribution	23,300		3,200	
Provison for unrealised profit on branch stock	300			
Manager's commission	—		114	
		38,800		5,314
Net profit		41,200		2,286

Add Balance from last year	43,486
Balance carried forward to next year	2,000
	45,486

Balance Sheet as at 30 June 19X8

Fixed assets			
Freehold buildings at cost			23,000
Machinery at cost		24,000	
Less Depreciation		9,600	14,400
			37,400
Current assets			
Stock		30,040	
Debtors		13,360	
Bank		14,500	
Cash in transit		1,990	
		59,890	
Less Current liabilities			
Creditors*		9,809	
Working capital			50,081
			87,481
Financed by:			
Share capital: Authorised and issued			40,000
Reserves			
Difference on exchange		1,995	
Profit and loss		45,486	47,481
			87,481

*Creditors HO 9,500 + Branch 195 + Manager 114 = 9,809.

Balance Sheet as at 31 October 19X1

	£000	£000	£000
Fixed assets at cost			450
Less Depreciation to date			215
			235
Current assets			
Stocks (12 + 12 + 4*)		28	
Debtors	120		
Less Provision	6	114	
Cash and bank (15.5 + 13 + 50)		78.5	
		220.5	
Less Current liabilities			
Creditors		50	170.5
			405.5
Capital			
Balance at 1.11.19X0			410
Add Net profit			35.5
			445.5
Less Drawings			40
			405.5

*5 × 4/5

4.9

Conversion of Branch Trial Balance to Pounds Sterling

	Fl	Fl	Rate	£	£
Freehold buildings	63,000		7	9,000	
Debtors and creditors	36,000	1,560	8	4,460	195
Sales		432,000	9		48,000
Head office		504,260	Actual		60,100
Branch cost of sales	360,000		*below	40,400	
Depreciation: Machinery	56,700		7	8,100	
Administration costs	18,000		9	2,000	
Stock 30.6.19X8	11,520		8	1,440	
Machinery at cost	126,000		7	18,000	
Remittances	272,000		Actual	29,990	
Balances at bank	79,200		8	9,000	
Selling and distribution	28,800		9	3,200	
Profit on exchange			—		1,995
	994,520	994,520		118,390	118,390

*Cost of sales: Branch Fl 360,000

	Fl 12,600	+ 7 = £1,800
Less Depreciation	Fl 347,400	+ 9 = £38,600
		£40,400

4.9 (cont)

(HO Books) Branch Account

	£	Fl		£	Fl
Balance b/d	25,136	189,260	Cash from debtors	36	320
Components	35,000	315,000	Remittances	28,000	256,000
Net profit	2,286	*24,000	Cash in transit	1,990	16,000
Difference on exchange			Balance c/d	34,391	255,940
	1,995	—			
	64,417	528,260		64,417	528,260

*This represents the profit per branch profit and loss account if it had been drawn up using florins.

4.10

(a) Trial Balance as at 31 December 19X9

	Crowns	Rate	Crowns	£	£
Bank	66,000	4		16,500	
Creditors	92,400	4			23,100
Debtors	158,400	4		39,600	
Fixed assets	145,200	5		29,040	
Head office		Actual			65,280
Profit and Loss					18,000
Stocks	118,800	4.4		79,200	
Difference on exchange		4			8,460
	488,400		488,400	114,840	114,840

(b) (Books of head office) Highland Branch

Balance b/d	65,280	Balance c/d	91,740
Difference on exchange	8,460		
Net profit	18,000		
	91,740		91,740

(c) Balance Sheet as at 31 December 19X0

Fixed assets		68,640
Current assets:		
Stocks	56,100	
Debtors	58,080	
Bank	27,060	
	141,240	
Less Current liabilities		
Creditors	44,220	
Working capital		97,020
		165,660
Financed by:		
Issued share capital		86,400
Reserves		
Profit and loss	70,800	
Difference on exchange	8,460	79,260
		165,660

5.1

Machinery

19X3		
Jan 1	Vendor	6,000

Vendor's Account

19X3			19X3		
Jan 1	Bank	846	Jan 1	Machinery	6,000
Dec 31	Bank	2,000	Dec 31	HP interest	412
,, 31	Balance c/d	3,566			
		6,412			6,412
19X4			19X4		
Dec 31	Bank	2,000	Jan 1	Balance b/d	3,566
,, 31	Balance c/d	1,851	Dec 31	HP interest	285
		3,851			3,851
19X5			19X5		
Dec 31	Bank	2,000	Jan 1	Balance b/d	1,851
			Dec 31	HP interest	149
		2,000			2,000

Provision for Depreciation: Machinery

19X3				Profit and loss		600
Dec 31	Balance	c/d				
19X4						
Dec 31	Balance	c/d	1,140	Profit and loss		540
			1,140			1,140
19X5				Balance	b/d	1,140
Jan 1						
Dec 31	Balance	c/d	1,626	Profit and loss		486
			1,626			1,626

Balance Sheet as at 31 December 19X5

Machinery at cost 6,000
Less Depreciation 600
(Included in Liabilities) Owing on HP

5,400
3,566

5.3

(a)

Bulwell's books

Motor Lorries

19X1	Granby Garages	54,000

Hire Purchase Interest

19X1	Granby	11,250	19X1	Profit and loss	11,250
19X2	Granby	8,063	19X2	Profit and loss	8,063
19X3	Granby	4,078	19X3	Profit and loss	4,078

Bank

19X1	Granby (Jan 1)	9,000
19X1	Granby (Dec 31)	24,000
19X2	Granby	24,000
19X3	Granby	20,391

Granby Garages

19X1	Bank	9,000	19X1	Motor lorries	54,000
	Bank	24,000		HP interest	11,250
	Balance c/d	32,250			
		65,250			65,250
19X2	Bank	24,000	19X2	Balance b/d	32,250
	Balance c/d	16,313		HP interest	8,063
		40,313			40,313
19X3	Bank	20,391	19X3	Balance b/d	16,313
				Interest	4,078
		20,391			20,391

Depreciation

19X1	Balance c/d	12,500	19X1	Profit and loss		12,500
19X2	Balance c/d	25,000	19X2	Balance b/d		12,500
				Profit and loss		12,500
		25,000				25,000
19X3	Balance c/d	37,500	19X3	Balance b/d		25,000
				Profit and loss		12,500
		37,500				37,500
19X4	Balance c/d	50,000	19X4	Balance b/d		37,500
				Profit and loss		12,500
		50,000				50,000

Balance Sheet as at 31 December

	19X1	19X2	19X3	19X4
Motor lorries cost	54,000	54,000	54,000	54,000
Less Depreciation to date	12,500	25,000	37,500	50,000
	41,500	29,000	16,500	4,000
Liabilities:				
HP debt outstanding	32,250	16,313		
Charge against profit:				
HP interest	11,250	8,063	4,078	
Depreciation	12,500	12,500	12,500	12,500

NB: Calculation of interest
19X1 25% × £45,000 = £11,250
19X2 25% × £32,250 = £8,063
19X3 25% × £16,313 = £4,078

(b)

Granby's books

Bulwell Aggregates

19X1	HP sales	54,000	19X1	Bank – deposit		9,000
	HP interest	11,250		– instalment		24,000
				Balance c/f		32,250
		65,250				65,250
19X2	Balance b/d	32,250	19X2	Bank – instalment		24,000
	HP interest	8,063		Balance c/f		16,313
		40,313				40,313
19X3	Balance b/d	16,313	19X3	Bank – instalment		20,391
	HP interest	4,078				
		20,391				20,391

5.3 (cont)

Bank

19X1	Bulwell	9,000
19X2	Bulwell	24,000
19X3	Bulwell	24,000
	Bulwell	20,391

HP Interest

19X1	Bulwell	11,250	19X1	HP trading	11,250
19X2	Bulwell	8,063	19X2	HP trading	8,063
19X3	Bulwell	4,078	19X3	HP trading	4,078

Hire Purchase Trading

(19X1)

Cost of lorries	43,200	HP sales	54,000
Provision for unrealised profit c/f	6,450	HP interest	11,250
	49,650		
Gross profit	15,600		
	65,250		65,250

(19X2)

		HP interest	8,063
		Provision for unrealised profit b/f	6,450
		Less Provision for unrealised profit c/f	3,263
			3,187
		Gross profit	11,250

(19X3)

		HP interest	4,078
		Provision for unrealised profit b/f	3,263
		Gross profit	7,341

Working: Unrealised profit

$$\text{Profit margin} = \frac{10,800}{54,000} \times \frac{100}{1} = 20\%$$

20% × £32,250 = £6,450
20% × £16,313 = £3,263

Vehicles & Finance Co Ltd

19X7			19X7		
Dec 31	Cash	1,000	Dec 31	Motor lorry	3,081
Dec 31	Balance c/d	2,081			
		3,081			3,081
19X8			19X8		
Dec 31	Cash	1,199	Jan 1	Balance b/d	2,081
Dec 31	Balance c/d	1,090	Dec 31	HP interest 10% of 2,081	208
		2,289			2,289
19X9			19X9		
Dec 31	Cash	1,199	Jan 1	Balance b/d	1,090
		1,199	Dec 31	HP interest 10% of 1,090	109
					1,199

Motor lorry

19X7		
Dec 31	Vehicles and finance	3,081

Provision for Depreciation: Motor Lorry

19X7		
Dec 31	Profit and loss	770
19X8		
Dec 31	Profit and loss	578
19X9		
Dec 31	Profit and loss	433

Hire Purchase Interest

19X8					
Dec 31	Vehicles and finance	208	Dec 31	Profit and loss	208
19X9			19X9		
Dec 31	Vehicles and finance	109	Dec 31	Profit and loss	109

Balance Sheet as at 31 December 19X8

Motor lorry at cost		3,081
Less Depreciation to date		1,348
		1,733

(Included in Liabilities) Owing on hire purchase 1,090

5.6

S Craven

Hire Purchase Trading Account for the year ended 30 September 19X6

Sales at hire purchase price (1,900 × 100)			190,000
Purchases		120,000	
Less Stock (100 × 60)		6,000	
		114,000	
Provision for unrealised profit and interest*		42,560	
			156,560
Gross profit			33,440
Less Rent		4,500	
Wages		8,600	
General expenses		10,270	
			23,370
Net profit			10,070

*Cash yet to be collected 190,000 – 83,600 = 106,400

Therefore provision $\dfrac{106,400}{190,000} \times 76,000$ = 42,560

Balance Sheet as at 30 September 19X6

Fixed assets			10,000
Current assets			
Stock		6,000	
HP debtors	106,400		
Less Provision: unrealised profit and interest	42,560	63,840	
Bank		10,630	
		80,470	
Less Current liabilities			
Creditors		8,400	
Working capital			72,070
			82,070
Financed by:			
Capital			
Balance at 1.10.19X5			76,000
Add Net profit			10,070
			86,070
Less Drawings			4,000
			82,070

5.7

RJ

Hire Purchase Trading and Profit and Loss Account for the year ended 31 December 19X8

Sales at hire purchase price (850 × 300)		255,000
Purchases	180,000	
Less Stock (50 × 200)	10,000	
	170,000	
Cost of goods sold		
Provision of unrealised profit	59,500	
		229,500
Gross profit		25,500
Less Wages and salaries	12,800	
General expenses	5,500	
Bank interest	400	
		18,700
Net profit		6,800

Balance Sheet as at 31 December 19X8

Fixed assets			10,000
Current assets			
Stock in warehouse		10,000	
Hire purchase debtors	178,500		
Less Provision for unrealised profit	59,500	119,000	
		129,000	
Less Current liabilities			
Creditors		16,600	
Bank overdraft		19,600	
		36,200	92,800
			102,800
Financed by:			
Capital			100,000
Cash introduced			
Add Net profit			6,800
			106,800
Less Drawings			4,000
			102,800

5.11

(a)(i)

Machine Hire Purchase

1. 1.X8	Bank	2,000	1. 1.X8	Machine	10,000
30. 6.X8	Bank	3,056	1. 1.X8	HP interest	7,280
31.12.X8	Bank	3,056			
31.12.X8	Balance c/d	9,168			
		17,280			17,280
30. 6.X9	Bank	3,056	1. 1.X9	Balance b/d	9,168
31.12.X9	Bank	3,056			
31.12.X9	Balance c/d	3,056			
		9,168			9,168
30. 6.X0	Bank	3,056	1. 1.X0	Balance b/d	3,056

(ii)

Machine Hire Purchase (see workings)

1. 1.X8	Machine HP	7,280	31.12.X8	Profit and loss	4,368
			31.12.X8	Balance c/d	2,912
		7,280			7,280
1. 1.X9	Balance b/d	2,912	31.12.X9	Profit and loss	2,427
			31.12.X9	Balance c/d	485
		2,912			2,912
1. 1.X0	Balance b/d	485	31.12.X0	Profit and loss	485

(b)

(Extracts) Balance Sheets as at 31 December

	19X8	19X9	19X0
Fixed assets			
Machinery at cost	10,000	10,000	10,000
Less Depreciation to date	1,800	3,600	5,400
	8,200	6,400	4,600
Creditors:			
Falling due within 1 year			
Hire purchase*		3,685	2,571
Falling due after 1 year			
Hire purchase*		2,571	

Workings: Interest (sum of digits is 15)
To 31.12.19X8 (5/15 × 7,280) 2,427 + (4/15 × 7,280) = 4,368
To 31.12.19X9 (3/15 × 7,280) 1,456 + (2/15 × 7,280) 971 = 2,427
To 31.12.19X0 1/15 × 7,280 = 485
(19X8 3,056 + 3,056 − 2,427)
(19X9 3,056 − 485)
Depreciation (10,000 − 1,000) ÷ 5 = 1,800 p.a.

6.1

Appropriation Account S, W and M
for the year ended 31 December 19X6

Salaries: W	3,000		Net profit b/d		25,200
M	1,000	4,000			
Interest on capital					
S	600				
W	400				
M	200	1,200			
Balance of profits					
S 2/5	8,000				
W 2/5	8,000				
M 1/5	4,000	20,000			
		25,200			25,200

6.3

Realisation

Buildings	800	Cash: Debtors		2,700
Tools and fixtures	850	Buildings		400
Debtors	2,800	Tools etc.		950
Cash: Expenses	100	Discounts		200
		Loss on realisation:		
		Moore		150
		Stephens		150
	4,550			4,550

Capital Accounts

	Moore	Stephens		Moore	Stephens
Loss on realisation	150	150	Balance b/fwd	2,000	1,500
Cash	1,850	1,350			
	2,000	1,500		2,000	1,500

Cash

Balance b/fwd	1,800	Expenses realisation	100
Debtors	2,700	Creditors	2,550
Buildings	400	Capitals: Moore	1,850
Tools	950	Stephens	1,350
	5,850		5,850

6.4

(a)

Realisation

Fixed assets	14,000	Bank: Fixed assets	8,000
Stock	5,000	X: Fixed assets	7,000
Debtors	21,000	Bank: Stock	4,000
Bank: Dissolution costs	800	Bank: Debtors	3,000
		Discounts on creditors	500
		Loss: X 3/6 9,150	
		Y 2/6 6,100	
		Z 1/6 3,050	18,300
	40,800		40,800

(b)

Capitals

	X	Y	Z		X	Y	Z
Fixed assets taken over	7,000			Balances b/f	4,000	4,000	2,000
Loss shared	9,150	6,100	3,050	Deficiency shared:			
Deficiency	525	525		X			525
				Y			525
				Bank to settle	12,675	2,625	
	16,675	6,625	3,050		16,675	6,625	3,050

Bank (as proof only)

Balance b/f	8,000	Realisation: Fixed assets	13,000
Creditors	4,000	Stock	16,500
Realisation: Costs	3,000	Debtors	800
Capital: X	12,675		
Y	2,625		
	30,300		30,300

6.7

(a) (i)

Amis, Lodge & Pym
Trading and Profit and Loss Account for the year ended 31 March 19X8

Sales			404,500
Less Cost of goods sold:			
Opening stock		30,000	
Add Purchases		225,000	
Add Carriage inwards		4,000	
		259,000	
Less Closing stock		35,000	224,000
Gross profit			180,500
Add Bank interest		750	
Discounts received		4,530	5,280
			185,780
Less Office expenses (30,400 + 405)		30,805	
Rent, rates, light and heat (8,800 – 1,500)		7,300	
Carriage outwards		12,000	
Discounts allowed		10,000	
Provision for bad debts		295	
Depreciation: Motor		15,000	
Plant		20,000	95,400
Net profit			90,380
Add Interest on current accounts and drawings:			
Amis		1,000	
Lodge		900	
Pym		720	2,620
			93,000
Less Salary – Pym		13,000	
Interest on capitals: Amis	8,000		
Lodge	1,500		
Pym	500	23,000	
			70,000
Balance on profit shared:			
Amis 50%		35,000	
Lodge 30%		21,000	
Pym 20%		14,000	70,000

(a) (ii)

Current Accounts

	Amis	Lodge	Pym		Amis	Lodge	Pym
Balances b/f	1,000	500	400	Salary			13,000
Drawings	25,000	22,000	15,000	Interest on capital	8,000	1,500	500
Interest on drawings	1,000	900	720	Balance on profits	35,000	21,000	14,000
Transfer to capital	16,000	–	11,380	Transfer to capital		900	
	43,000	23,400	27,500		43,000	23,400	27,500

6.7 (cont)

(b)(i)

Realisation

Motors (80,000 – 35,000)	45,000	Discount on creditors	500
Plant (100,000 – 56,600)	43,400	Amis: Motor	5,000
Debtors (14,300 – 715)	13,585	Bank: Debtors	12,985
Stock	35,000	Fowles Ltd (75,000 + 63,500)	138,500
Profit on realisation			
Amis 50%	10,000		
Lodge 30%	6,000		
Pym 20%	4,000		
	20,000		
	156,985		156,985

(ii)

Bank

Balance b/f	4,900	Office expenses	405
Realisation: Debtors	12,985	Creditors	16,000
Rent rebate	1,500	Capital: Amis	76,000
Fowles Ltd	63,500		
Capitals: Lodge	4,900		
Pym	4,620		
	92,405		92,405

(iii)

Capitals

	Amis	Lodge	Pym		Amis	Lodge	Pym
Current a/c		900		Balances b/f	80,000	15,000	5,000
Fowles Ltd Shares	25,000	25,000	25,000	Current a/c	16,000		11,380
Realisation: Motor	5,000			Profit on real.	10,000	6,000	4,000
Bank	76,000			Bank		4,900	4,620
	106,000	25,900	25,000		106,000	25,900	25,000

6.9

(a)

Lock, Stock and Barrel

Profit and Loss Account for the six months ended 1 February 19X7

Sales of completed houses		280,000
Less Costs of completing houses		
Houses in course of construction at start	115,000	
Materials used	35,750	
Land used (75,000 × ⅓)	25,000	
Wages and subcontractors	78,000	253,750
Gross profit		26,250
Less Administration salaries	17,250	
General expenses	12,500	
Depreciation: Freehold land	300	
Plant and equipment (⁶⁄₁₂ × 10%)	7,500	
Vehicles (2.5% × ⁶⁄₁₂)	4,500	42,050
Net loss		15,800
Shared: Lock 40%	6,320	
Stock 30%	4,740	
Barrel 30%	4,740	15,800

Capitals

	Lock	Stock	Barrel		Lock	Stock	Barrel
Drawings	6,000	5,000	4,000	Balances b/f	52,000	26,000	3,500
Loss shared	6,320	4,740	4,740	Balance c/d			5,240
Balances c/d	39,680	16,260					
	52,000	26,000	8,740		52,000	26,000	8,740

Lock, Stock and Barrel

Balance Sheet as at 1 February 19X7

Fixed tangible assets	Cost	Depreciation	
Freehold land and buildings	20,000	3,300	16,700
Plant and equipment	150,000	89,500	60,500
Motor vehicles	36,000	27,500	8,500
	206,000	120,300	85,700

Current assets		
Stock of land for building	50,000	
Stocks of materials	7,500	
Debtors for completed houses	35,000	
	92,500	
Less Current liabilities		
Trade creditors	52,250	
Bank overdraft	75,250	127,500
Working capital		(35,000)
Net assets		50,700

Financed by:
Capitals: Lock   39,680
         Stock   16,260
         Barrel   (5,240)
                  50,700

(b) Amounts distributable to partners:
On 28 February there was only (6,200 + 7,000 + 72,500 – 75,250) 10,450 hence there was nowhere near enough to pay off the creditors, and so payment to partners could not be made.
On 30 April we treat it as though no more cash will be received.

(c) First distribution

	Lock	Stock	Barrel
Capital balances before dissolution	39,680	16,260	(5,240)
Loss if no further assets realised (85,700 + 92,500 – 6,000 – 6,200 – 7,000 – 72,500 – 35,000 – 50,000) = 1,500			
Loss shared in profit/loss ratios	(600)	(450)	(450)
Cars taken over	(2,000)	(2,000)	(2,000)
	37,080	13,810	(7,690)
Barrel's deficiency shared profit/loss ratio	4,394	3,296	7,690
Paid to partners	32,686	10,514	–

Second and final distribution

	Lock	Stock	Barrel
Capital balances before dissolution	39,680	16,260	(5,240)
Profit finally ascertained 100,000 – 1,500 = 98,500			
Shared	39,400	29,550	29,550
	79,080	45,810	24,310
Less Distribution and cars	34,686	12,514	2,000
Final distribution (100,000)	44,394	33,296	22,310

8.1

Bank

Application	20,000		
Allotment (30,000 less excess applications 5,000)	25,000		
First call (119,200 × 0.25)	29,800		
Second call (119,200 × 0.375)	44,700		
D Regan (800 × 0.9)	720	Balance c/d	120,220
	120,220		120,220

D Regan

Ordinary share capital	800	Bank	720
		Forfeited shares	80
	800		800

Application and Allotment

Ordinary share capital	45,000	Bank	20,000
		Bank	25,000
	45,000		45,000

Ordinary Share Capital

Forfeited shares	800	Application and allotment	45,000
Balance c/d	120,000	First call	30,000
		Second call	45,000
		D Regan	800
	120,800		120,800

First Call

Ordinary share capital	30,000	Bank	29,800
		Forfeited shares	200
	30,000		30,000

Second Call

Ordinary share capital	45,000	Bank	44,700
		Forfeited shares	300
	45,000		45,000

Forfeited Shares

First call	200	Ordinary share capital	800
Second call	300		
D Regan	80		
Transfer to share premium	220		
	800		800

Balance Sheet

Bank	120,220	Ordinary share capital	120,000
		Share premium	220
	120,220		120,220

8.2

Bank

Dr	£	Cr	£
Application (32,600 × 0.50)	16,300	Application and allotment:	1,300
Allotment (20,000 × 1.50 less excess application monies 5,000)	25,000	Refund of application monies	100,160
First call (19,900 × 2)	39,800	Balance c/d	480
Second call (19,880 × 1)	19,880		
B Mills (120 × 4)	480		
	101,460		101,460

Application and Allotment

Dr	£	Cr	£
Bank: Refunds	1,300	Bank	16,300
Ordinary share capital	40,000	Bank	25,000
	41,300		41,300

First Call Account

Dr	£	Cr	£
Ordinary share capital	40,000	Bank	39,800
		Forfeited shares	200
	40,000		40,000

Second Call Account

Dr	£	Cr	£
Ordinary share capital	20,000	Bank	19,880
		Forfeited shares	120
	20,000		20,000

Ordinary Share Capital

Dr	£	Cr	£
Forfeited shares	600	Application and allotment	40,000
Balance c/d	100,000	First call	40,000
		Second call	20,000
		B Mills	600
	100,600		100,600

Forfeited Shares

Dr	£	Cr	£
First call	200	Ordinary share capital	600
Second call	120		
B Mills	120		
Transfer to share premium	160		
	600		600

B Mills

Dr	£	Cr	£
Ordinary share capital	600	Bank	480
		Forfeited shares	120
	600		600

8.3

Cosy Fires Ltd

Application and allotment

Dr	£	Cr	£
Cash: Return of unsuccessful applications 5,000 × 0.60	3,000	Cash application for 65,000 × 0.60	39,000
Share capital: Due on application and allotment: 40,000 × 0.70	28,000	Cash: Balance due on allotment (see workings)*	1,975
Share premium: 40,000 × 0.25	10,000	Balance c/d: Due from allottee in respect of 500 shares:	
		500 × 0.35 = 175	
		Less o/paid on application	
		250 × 0.60 = 150	
		=	25
	41,000		41,000
Balance b/d	25	Forfeited shares	25

Share Capital

Dr	£	Cr	£
Forfeited shares: Amount called on shares forfeited: 500 × 0.70	350	Balance b/f	75,000
Balance c/fwd	115,000	Application and allotment	28,000
		Call	11,850
		Forfeited shares	500
	115,350		115,350

Share Premium

Dr	£	Cr	£
Balance c/fwd	10,375	Application and allotment	10,000
		Forfeited shares	375
	10,375		10,375

Forfeited Shares

Dr	£	Cr	£
Application and allotment	25	Share capital	350
Share capital	500	Cash: 500 × 1.10 per share	550
Share premium	375		
	900		900

Call

Dr	£	Cr	£
Share capital 39,500 × 0.30	11,850	Cash	11,850

Balance Sheet as at 31 May 19X7

Share capital		
Authorised: 160,000 ordinary shares of 1 each		160,000
Issued and fully paid: 115,000 ordinary shares of 1 each		115,000
Capital reserve:		
Share premium		10,375

Workings:

Due on application 0.60 × 40,000	24,000	
Due on allotment 0.35 × 40,000	14,000	
	39,000	
Received on application: 0.60 × 65,000	38,000	
Less Refunded 5,000 × 0.60	3,000	
	36,000	
Balance due on allotment		2,000
Less Amount due on		
application and allotment 500 × 0.95	475	
Received on application 750 × 0.60	450	25
		1,975

8.5

M Ltd

Ledger Accounts (dates omitted)

Cash

Application and allotment		Application and allotment	
(750,000 × 85p)	637,500	(Refund 125,000 × 85p)	106,250
Application and allotment	18,750		
(500,000 × 25p – overpaid			
125,000 × 85p)			
First and final call			
(495,000 × 50p)	247,500		
Forfeited shares	4,500		
(5,000 × 90p)			

Application and Allotment

Share capital	250,000	Cash	637,500
Share premium	300,000	Cash	18,750
Cash	106,250		
	656,250		656,250

Share Premium

		Application and allotment	300,000
Balance c/d	302,000	Forfeited shares	2,000
	302,000		302,000

Share Capital

Forfeited shares	5,000	Balance b/d	500,000
Balance c/d	1,000,000	Application and allotment	250,000
		First and final call	250,000
		Forfeited shares	5,000
	1,005,000		1,005,000

First and Final Call

Share capital	250,000	Cash	247,500
		Forfeited shares	2,500
	250,000		250,000

Forfeited Shares

First and final call	2,500	Share capital	5,000
Share capital	5,000	Cash	4,500
Share premium	2,000		
	9,500		9,500

Given format 1 of the Companies Act 1985, there are two places where uncalled capital can be shown. These are either place A or C II (5).

If C II(5) is chosen it becomes:

Current assets

II Debtors

(5) Called up share capital not paid	2,500
Issued share capital	
1,000,000 ordinary shares of £1 each	1,000,000
Reserves	
Share premium	302,000

The authorised share capital should be shown also as a note only. The increase in share premium would also be shown as a note in the statement showing changes in reserves.

9.1

(a)

		Dr	Cr
(A1)	Bank	5,000	
	(A2) Ordinary share applicants		5,000
Cash received from applicants.			
(B1)	Ordinary share applicants	5,000	
	(B2) Ordinary share capital		5,000
Ordinary shares allotted.			
(C1)	Preference share capital	5,000	
	(C2) Preference share redemption		5,000
Shares to be redeemed.			
(D1)	Preference share redemption	5,000	
	(D2) Bank		5,000
Payment made to redeem shares.			

	Balances before	Effect Dr	Effect Cr	Balances after
Net assets (except bank)	20,000			20,000
Bank	13,000	(A1) 5,000	(D2) 5,000	13,000
	33,000			33,000
Preference share capital	5,000	(C1) 5,000		–
Preference share redemption	–	(D1) 5,000	(C2) 5,000	–
Ordinary share capital	15,000		(B2) 5,000	20,000
Ordinary share applicants	–	(B1) 5,000	(A2) 5,000	–
Share premium	2,000			2,000
	22,000			22,000
Profit and loss	11,000			11,000
	33,000			33,000

(b)

		Dr	Cr
(A1)	Preference share capital	5,000	
	(A2) Preference share redemption		5,000
Shares to be redeemed.			
(B1)	Preference share redemption	5,000	
	(B2) Bank		5,000
Cash paid on redemption.			
(C1)	Profit and loss appropriation	5,000	
	(C2) Capital redemption reserve		5,000
Transfer per Companies Act.			

	Balances before	Effect Dr	Effect Cr	Balances after
Net assets (except bank)	20,000			20,000
Bank	13,000		(B2) 5,000	8,000
	33,000			28,000
Preference share capital	5,000	(A1) 5,000		15,000
Preference share redemption	–	(B1) 5,000	(A2) 5,000	–
Ordinary share capital	15,000			15,000
Capital redemption reserve	–		(C2) 5,000	5,000
Share premium	2,000			2,000
	22,000			22,000
Profit and loss	11,000	(C1) 5,000		6,000
	33,000			28,000

(c)

		Dr	Cr
(A1)	Bank	1,500	
(A2)	Ordinary share applicants		1,500
	Cash received from applicants.		
(B1)	Ordinary share applicants	1,500	
(B2)	Ordinary share capital		1,500
	Ordinary shares allotted.		
(C1)	Profit and loss appropriation	3,500	
(C2)	Capital redemption reserve		3,500
	Part of redemption not covered by new issue, to comply with Companies Act.		
(D1)	Preference share capital	5,000	
(D2)	Preference share redemption		5,000
	Shares to be redeemed.		
(E1)	Preference share redemption	5,000	
(E2)	Bank		5,000
	Payment made for redemption.		

	Balances before	Dr		Cr		Balances after
Net assets (except bank)	20,000					20,000
Bank	13,000	(A1) 1,500		(E2) 5,000		9,500
	33,000					29,500
Preference share capital	5,000	(D1) 5,000				–
Preference share redemption	–	(E1) 5,000		(D2) 5,000		–
Ordinary share capital	15,000			(B2) 1,500		16,500
Ordinary share applicants	–	(B1) 1,500		(A2) 1,500		–
Capital redemption reserve	–			(C2) 3,500		3,500
Share premium	2,000					2,000
	22,000					22,000
Profit and loss	11,000	(C1) 3,500				7,500
	33,000					29,500

(d)

		Dr	Cr
(A1)	Preference share capital	5,000	
(A2)	Preference share redemption		5,000
	Shares to be redeemed.		
(B1)	Profit and loss appropriation	1,250	
(B2)	Preference share redemption		1,250
	Premium on redemption of shares *not* previously issued at premium.		
(C1)	Profit and loss appropriation	5,000	
(C2)	Capital redemption reserve		5,000
	Transfer because shares redeemed out of distributable profits.		
(D1)	Preference share redemption	6,250	
(D2)	Bank		6,250
	Payment on redemption.		

	Balances before	Dr		Cr		Balances after
Net assets (except bank)	20,000					20,000
Bank	13,000			(D2) 6,250		6,750
	33,000					26,750
Preference share capital	5,000	(A1) 5,000				–
Preference share redemption	–	(D1) 6,250		(A2) 5,000		–
				(B2) 1,250		
Ordinary share capital	15,000			(C2) 5,000		15,000
Capital redemption reserve	–					5,000
Share premium	2,000					2,000
	22,000					22,000
Profit and loss	11,000	(C1) 5,000				4,750
	33,000	(B1) 1,250				26,750

9.1 (cont)

(e)

	Dr	Cr
(A1) Bank	7,000	
(A2) Ordinary share applicants		7,000
Cash received from applicants.		
(B1) Ordinary share applicants	7,000	
(B2) Ordinary share capital		7,000
Ordinary shares allotted.		
(C1) Preference share capital	5,000	
(C2) Preference share redemption		5,000
Shares being redeemed.		
(D1) Share premium account	1,500	
(D2) Preference share redemption		1,500
Amount of share premium account used for redemption.		
(E1) Profit and loss appropriation	500	
(E2) Preference share redemption		500
Excess of premium payable over amount of share premium account usable for the purpose.		
(F1) Preference share redemption	7,000	
(F2) Bank		7,000
Amount payable on redemption.		

	Balances before	Effect Dr	Effect Cr	Balances after
Net assets (except bank)	20,000			20,000
Bank	13,000	(A1) 7,000	(F2) 7,000	13,000
	33,000			33,000
Preference share capital	5,000	(C1) 5,000		–
Preference share redemption	–	(F1) 7,000	(C2) 5,000 (D2) 1,500 (E2) 500	–
Ordinary share capital	15,000		(B2) 7,000	22,000
Ordinary share applicants	–	(B1) 7,000	(A2) 7,000	–
Share premium account	2,000	(D1) 1,500	(E1) 500	500
	22,000			22,500
Profit and loss	11,000			10,500
	33,000			33,000

9.3

(a)

	Dr	Cr
(A1) Ordinary share capital	6,000	
(A2) Ordinary share purchase		6,000
Shares to be purchased.		
(B1) Ordinary share purchase	6,000	
(B2) Bank		6,000
Payment for shares purchased.		
(C1) Profit and loss	4,500	
(C2) Capital redemption reserve		4,500
Transfer of deficiency of permissible capital payment to comply with Companies Act.		

	Balances before	Effect Dr	Effect Cr	Balances after
Net assets (except bank)	12,500			12,500
Bank	13,000		(B2) 6,000	7,000
	25,500			19,500
Preference share capital	5,000			5,000
Ordinary share capital	10,000	(A1) 6,000		4,000
Ordinary share purchase	–	(B1) 6,000	(A2) 6,000	–
Non-distributable reserves	6,000			6,000
Capital redemption reserve	–		(C2) 4,500	4,500
	21,000			19,500
Profit and loss	4,500	(C1) 4,500		–
	25,500			19,500

(b)

	Dr	Cr
(A1) Ordinary share capital	6,000	
(A2) Ordinary share purchase		6,000
Shares to be purchased.		
(B1a) Profit and loss	4,500	
(B1b) Non-distributable reserves	1,500	
(B2) Ordinary share capital		6,000
Transfers of profit and loss and non-distributable reserves per Companies Act.		
(C1) Ordinary share purchase	12,000	
(C2) Bank		12,000
Payment to shareholders.		

9.5

	Balances before	Dr	Effect Cr	Balances after
Net assets (except bank)	12,500			12,500
Bank	13,000		(C2) 12,000	1,000
	25,500			13,500
Preference share capital	5,000			5,000
Ordinary share capital	10,000	(A1) 6,000	(A2) 6,000	4,000
Ordinary share purchase	–	(C1) 12,000	(B2) 6,000	–
Non-distributable reserves	6,000	(B1b) 1,500		4,500
	21,000			13,500
Profit and loss	4,500	(B1a) 4,500		
	25,500			13,500

Workings: Opening balance 10% debentures (a/c below)
Originally issued 375,000
Less Redeemed previously 150,000 225,000

10% Debentures

30/9 Debenture redemption	225,000	1/7 Balance b/f	225,000

Workings: Sinking fund investments (A/c below)

Appropriations to date 334,485
Interest invested (39,480 – 2,475) 37,005
371,490
Less Sold – at cost 144,915
226,575

Sinking Fund Investments

1/7 Balance b/f	226,575	2/8 Bank No 2 Sale	73,215
2/8 Sinking fund: Profit (73,215 – 69,322)	3,893	25/9 Bank No 2 Sale	160,238
25/9 Sinking fund: Profit (Cost 226,575 – 69,322 = 157,253. Sold for 160,238)	2,985		
	233,453		233,453

Workings: Sinking fund (a/c below)
Previous contributions 334,485
Interest on investments 39,480
Profit: Previous sales of investments (147,234 – 144,915) 2,328
Profit: Previous purchase debentures (150,000 – 147,243) 2,757
379,050
150,000
Less Transfer to general reserve sum equal to debentures redeemed 229,050

Sinking Fund A/c

30/9 Debentures redemption (Premium 1%)	2,250	1/7	Balance b/f	229,050
30/9 General reserve	236,889	7/7	No 2 Bank: Interest	1,756
		2/8	SF Investments: Profit	3,893
		13/9	No 2 Bank: Interest	1,455
		25/9	SF Investments: Profit	2,985
	239,139			239,139

No 2 Bank A/c

1/7	Balance b/f	2,475	30/9 W Bank plc (deposit)	15,150
7/7	Sinking fund: Interest	1,756	30/9 Debentures redemption	212,100
2/8	SF investments: Sale	73,215	30/9 No 1 Bank transfer of balance	11,889
13/9	Sinking fund: Interest	1,455		
25/9	SF investments: Sale	160,238		
		239,139		239,139

Debenture Redemption A/c

30/9 No 2 Bank (225,000 Debentures – 15,000 B Ltd = 210,000 at 1% premium)	212,100	30/9 10% Debentures	225,000
30/9 Balance c/d (15,000 outstanding at premium 1%)	15,150	30/9 Sinking fund (premium)	2,250
	227,250		227,250
		30/9 No 2 Bank	15,150

W Bank plc

30/9 No 2 Bank	15,150

9.7 (Dates omitted – all figures shown in £000)

Application and Allotment

Ordinary shares	80	Bank	60
Share premium	20	Bank	40
	100		100

Call Account

Ordinary shares	20	Bank	18
		Investments	2
	20		20

Investments (own shares)

Call	2	Bank	11
Share premium	9		
	11		11

9.9 (*Note:* some abbreviations are used)

10% Debentures

31.12.X8	Debenture redemption	12,000	1.4.X8	Balance b/d	100,000
31.3.X9	Balance c/d	88,000			
		100,000			100,000

Debenture Redemption Fund

31.12.X8	Reserve (equal to debentures redeemed)	12,000	1.4.X8	Balance b/d	20,000
			31.12.X8	DRFI (profit on redemption)	1,400
			31.12.X8	DR (profit on purchase)	900
			31.12.X8	Bank	1,600
			31.3.X9	Profit and loss (annual appropriation)	2,000
31.3.X9	Balance c/d	13,900			
		25,900			25,900

Debenture Redemption Fund Investment

1.4.X8	Balance b/d	20,000	31.12.X8	Bank (sale)	11,400
31.12.X8	DR Fund (profit on sale)	1,400			
31.3.X9	Bank (2,000 + 300 + 1,600)	3,900	31.3.X9	Balance c/d	13,900
		25,300			25,300

Debenture Redemption

31.12.X8	Bank (purchase)	11,400	31.12.X8	10% Debentures	12,000
31.12.X8	DR Fund (profit on redemption)	900	31.12.X8	Debenture interest accrued	300
		12,300			12,300

Debenture Interest

30.9.X8	Bank (10,000 × 10% ÷ 2)	5,000			
31.12.X8	Debenture redemption (interest included in price 12,000 × 10% × ¼)	300			
31.3.X9	Bank (10,000 × 88,000 × 2)	4,400	31.3.X9	Profit and loss	9,700
		9,700			9,700

10.1 (a)

Checkers Ltd

Profit and Loss Account for the year ended 31 December 19X5

	Total	Basis of allocation	Pre-incorporation	Post-incorporation
Gross profit	28,000	Turnover	8,000	20,000
Less				
Salaries of vendors	1,695	Actual	1,695	
Wages	8,640	Time	2,160	6,480
Rent	860	Time	215	645
Distribution	1,680	Turnover	480	1,200
Commission	700	Turnover	200	500
Bad debts	314	Actual	104	210
Interest	1,650	Time	990	660
Directors' remuneration	4,000	Actual		4,000
Directors' expenses	515	Actual		515
Depreciation*				
Motors	1,900	Actual	400	1,500
Machinery	575	Actual	125	450
Bank interest	168	Actual		168
	22,697		6,369	16,328
Net profit	5,303		1,631	3,672
	28,000		8,000	20,000

*Depreciation:
Motors to 31 March 19X5 20% × 3 months × 7,000 + 20% × 1 month × 3,000 = 400
After 20% × 9 months × 7,000 + 20% × 9 months × 3,000 = 1,500
(b) Transfer to capital reserve
(c) Charge to a goodwill account

10.2

Adjusted Profits

Profit per accounts		16,400		23,920		19,650
Add Motor expenses saved	620		660		700	
" Depreciation overcharged	1,500		700		60	
" Wrapping expenses saved	420		480		510	
" Bank interest	180		590		740	
" Preliminary expenses			690			
		2,720		3,120		2,010
		19,120		27,040		21,660
Less Extra management remuneration	1,500		1,500		1,500	
" Investment income	290		340		480	
" Rents received	940		420			
" Opening stock			1,900			
" Profit on property			4,800			
		2,730		8,960		1,980
Profits as adjusted		16,390		18,080		19,680

Average profit
$$16,390 + 18,080 + 19,680 = 54,150 \div 3 = 18,050$$

If 18,050 is a return of 25% on investment, then
$$\frac{18,050}{25} \times 100 = 72,200 \text{ purchase price.}$$

10.3

(a)

CK

Realisation

Freehold premises	8,000	CK Ltd: Value at which assets taken over	27,200
Plant	4,000	Discount on creditors	150
Stock	2,000		
Debtors	5,000		
Profit on realisation	8,350		
	27,350		27,350

Capital

CK Ltd: Shares	16,000	Balance b/d	24,150
Cash	8,350	Profit on realisation	200
	24,350		24,350

CK Ltd (not asked for in question)

Realisation

Realisation	27,200	Creditors	3,050
		Shares	24,150
	27,200		27,200

RP Ltd – Realisation

Freehold premises	4,500	CK Ltd: Value at which assets taken over	13,000
Plant	2,000		
Stock	1,600		
Debtors	3,400		
Profit on realisation	1,500		
	13,000		13,000

Sundry Shareholders

CK Ltd	5,000	Share capital	4,000
Cash	3,000	Profit on realisation	1,500
Shares	8,000	Revenue surplus	2,500
			8,000

CK Ltd (not asked for in question)

Realisation

Realisation	13,000	Bank overdraft	3,500
		Creditors	1,500
		Sundry shareholders: Cash	5,000
		Shares	3,000
	13,000		13,000

10.3 (cont)

Journal of CJK Ltd

(b) (Have omitted narratives)

Cash	5,000	
Share premium		3,000
Ordinary shares		2,000
Cash	7,840	
Discount on issue	160	
7 per cent debentures		8,000
Goodwill	7,000	
Freehold premises	10,000	
Plant	3,500	
Stock	2,000	
Debtors	5,000	
Provision for discounts receivable	150	
Creditors		3,200
Provision for bad debts		300
Ordinary shares		24,150
Goodwill	500	
Freehold premises	5,500	
Plant	2,000	
Stock	1,600	
Debtors	3,400	
Creditors		1,500
Bank overdraft		3,500
Cash		5,000
Ordinary share capital		3,000
Formation expenses	1,200	
Cash		1,200

(c)

CJK Ltd

Balance Sheet as at 1st January 19X0

Fixed assets: at cost			
Freehold premises			15,500
Plant			5,500
Goodwill			7,500
			28,500
Current assets			
Stock			3,600
Debtors		8,400	
Less Provision for bad debts		300	8,100
Cash at bank			3,140
			14,840
Less Current liabilities			
Creditors		4,700	
Less Provision		150	4,550
Working capital			10,290
			38,790

11.1

Debenture Interest

		£			£
19X3			19X3		
Dec 31	Bank	9,600	Dec 31	Profit and loss	12,800
„ 31	Income tax	3,200			
		12,800			12,800

Income Tax

		£			£
19X3			19X3		
Dec 31	Balance c/d	3,200	Dec 31	Debenture interest	3,200

Ordinary Dividends

		£			£
19X3			19X3		
Jul 1	Bank	20,000	Dec 31	Profit and loss	50,000
Dec 31	Accrued c/d	30,000			
		50,000			50,000

Deferred Taxation

		£			£
19X3			19X3		
Dec 31	Balance c/d	14,000	Dec 31	Profit and loss*	14,000

*35% of (£90,000 – £50,000) = £14,000

Corporation Tax

		£			£
19X3			19X3		
Dec 31	Balance c/d	90,000	Dec 31	Profit and loss	90,000

Advance Corporation Tax

19X3		£	19X3		£
Sept 30	Bank (25% × £20,000)	5,000	Dec 31	Balance c/d	5,000
		5,000			5,000

Profit and Loss Account (extracts) year to 31 December 19X3

	£	£
Net trading profit		220,000
Less Debenture interest		12,800
Profit on ordinary activities before taxation		207,200
Corporation tax	90,000	
Deferred tax	14,000	104,000
Profit on ordinary activities after taxation		103,200
Less Ordinary dividends: Interim	20,000	
Final proposed	30,000	50,000

Balance Sheet (extracts) as at 31 December 19X3

Creditors: Amounts falling due within one year	£
Proposed ordinary dividend	30,000
Corporation tax	90,000
Deferred tax (14,000 – ACT recoverable 5,000)	9,000
Income tax	3,200

11.3

Workings:

(W1) Tax deducted from franked investment income is

$$\frac{20}{100-20} \times £900 = \frac{1}{4} \times £900 = £225$$

Tax deducted from fixed interest income is $\frac{1}{3} \times £24,000 = £8,000$

(W2) Changes in deferred taxation account.

Timing difference:

	£
Capital allowances allowable for tax (E)	90,000
Depreciation actually charged (E)	50,000
	40,000

Transferred to deferred tax account £40,000 × 35% = £14,000

Deferred Tax

19X2		£	19X2		£
Dec 31	Balance c/d	81,000	Jan 1	Balance b/f (J)	67,000
			Dec 31	Tax on profit on ordinary activities (W2)	14,000
		81,000			81,000

Income Tax

19X2			£	19X2			£
Oct 31	Interest receivable	(C1)	8,000	Nov 30	Debenture interest	(B)	20,000
Dec 15	Bank		12,000				
			20,000				20,000

Interest Receivable

19X2		£	19X2			£
Dec 31	Profit and loss	32,000	Oct 31	Bank	(C1)	24,000
			" 31	Income tax	(C1)	8,000
		32,000				32,000

Debenture Interest

19X2			£	19X2		£
Nov 30	Bank	(B)	60,000	Dec 31	Profit and loss	80,000
" 30	Income tax	(B)	20,000			
			80,000			80,000

Franked Investment Income

19X2		£	19X2			£
Dec 31	Profit and loss	1,125	Sept 1	Bank	(C2)	900
			Sept 1	Tax on profit on ordinary activities*(W1)		225
		1,125				1,125

*See note following balance sheet.

Advance Corporation Tax

19X2		£	19X2			£
Jan 1	Balance b/f (N)	49,000	Sept 30	Corporation tax set-off of	(N)	49,000
May 31	Bank (ACT on (I))[1]	22,500				
Aug 31	Bank (ACT on (F))	4,500				
Sept 15	Bank (ACT on (G))[2]	18,525	Dec 31	Balance c/d[3]		45,525
		94,525				94,525

Notes:

1. The ACT on the final dividend for 19X1 cannot be set off against the corporation tax for 19X1. This is because it was paid in 19X2 and should therefore be set off against the 19X2 corporation tax payment.

Barnet Ltd

Profit and Loss (extracts) for the year ended 31 December 19X2

		£
Net trading profit	(A)	560,000
Add Fixed rate interest (C1) (gross)	32,000	
Franked investment income (C2) (gross)	1,125	33,125
		593,125
Less Debenture interest (B) (gross)		80,000
Profit on ordinary activities before taxation		513,125
Tax on profit on ordinary activities[1]		165,225
Profit on ordinary activities after taxation		347,900
Less Dividends:		
Preference dividend	18,000	
Ordinary: Interim	75,000	
Final	120,000	213,000

Note:

1. Notes attached to accounts giving make-up of this figure.

Balance Sheet (extracts) as at 31 December 19X2

	£
Creditors amounts falling due within one year	
Proposed ordinary dividend	120,000
Corporation tax	154,000
Deferred tax (81,000 – ACT recoverable 45,525)	35,475

A final point concerns the difference in treatment of tax on franked investment income as compared with tax on other income, such as interest. It is only the tax on franked investment income which is treated as part of the final tax costs, while the tax on interest is simply deducted from charges paid by the company. You would have to study taxation in detail to understand why this happens.

11.3 (cont)

2. The ACT on (G) is calculated $1/4 \times £75,000$ less tax credit on investment income (C2) £225 = £18,525.
3. Deductible against 19X2 tax payable in 19X3.

Corporation Tax

19X2			£	19X2			£
Sept 30	ACT set-off (N)		49,000	Jan 1	Balance b/f	(K)	115,000
" 30	Bank[1]		63,000	Dec 31	Tax on profit on ordinary activities	(L)	154,000
" 30	Tax on profit on ordinary activities[2]	(K)	3,000				
Dec 31	Balance c/d	(L)	154,000				
			269,000				269,000

Notes:

1. £115,000 owing – £3,000 reduction (K) – ACT set-offs deducted in 19X1, £49,000 = £63,000.
2. Adjustment for amendment in tax bill.

Tax on Profit on Ordinary Activities

19X2		£	19X2		£
Sept 1	Investment income (W1)	225	Sept 30	Corporation tax (K)	3,000
Dec 31	Corporation tax	154,000	Dec 31	Profit and loss	165,225
" 31	Deferred tax (W2)	14,000			
		168,225			168,225

Preference Dividends

19X2			£	19X2		£
Jun 30	Bank	(F)	18,000	Dec 31	Profit and loss	18,000

Ordinary Dividends

19X2			£	19X2			£
Mar 31	Bank	(I)	90,000	Jan 1	Accrued b/d	(I)	90,000
Jul 15	Bank	(G)	75,000	Dec 31	Profit and loss		195,000
Dec 31	Accrued c/d		120,000				
			285,000				285,000

11.5

BG Ltd

Profit and Loss Account for the year ended 31 December 19X7

	£000	£000
Trading profit		50,000
Income from shares in related companies	3,000	
Other interest receivable and similar income	1,100	
		4,100
		54,100
Interest payable and similar charges		3,600
Profit on ordinary activities before taxation		50,500
Tax on profit on ordinary activities		24,000
Profit on ordinary activities after taxation		26,500
Undistributed profits from last year		9,870
		36,370
Transfers to reserves	5,000	
Dividends proposed	21,000	
		26,000
Undistributed profits carried to next year		10,370

11.6

(All in £million)

Ordinary Dividends

			£				£
31.8.X9	Bank (X8 final)		28	1.4.X9	Balance b/d		28
31.12.X9	Bank (X9 interim)		12	31.3.X0	Profit and loss		48
31.3.X0	Balance c/d		36				
			76				76

Advance Corporation Tax

			£				£
14.10.X9	Bank (on 19X8 final)		7	1.4.X9	Balance b/d		7
14.1.X0	Bank (on 19X9 interim)		3	31.3.X0	Corporation tax		3
31.3.X0	Balance c/d		9	31.3.X0	Deferred tax (on 19X0 final)		9
			19				19

Deferred Taxation

			£				£
31.3.X0	Advance CT		9	1.4.X9	Balance b/d		3
31.3.X0	Balance c/d		6	31.3.X0	Corporation tax (on 19X9 proposed)		7
				31.3.X0	Profit and loss		5
			15				15

12.1

Either Ltd

		£000
Profit per draft accounts		157

		+	−
(i)	Stock: reduce to net realisable value		35
(ii)	Directors' remuneration		43
(iii)	Bad debt		30
(iv)	Corporation tax saved on (i) + (ii) + (iii) × 50%	54	
(v)	Depreciation adjustment (W1)		30
(vi)	Revaluation reserve (realised on sale)	125	
(vii)	General reserve	80	
(viii)	Loss brought forward (W2)		144
		259	282

net −23

134

Maximum possible dividend

Preference dividend 6%		£9,000
Ordinary dividend		£125,000

Research and development expenditure: assumed to have been carried forward in accordance with SSAP 13 and can be justified. Failing this it would have to be a realised loss.

For a plc no changes required, except that the payment should not reduce net assets below called-up share capital and undistributable reserves = 400 + 150 + 100 = 650. A further bad debt might change this position.

(W1) *Reducing balance*

	£	£
Cost 1.12.19X1		100,000
Depreciation 19X2	25,000	
		75,000
Cost 1.6.19X3	25,000	
		100,000
Depreciation 19X3	25,000	
		75,000
Cost 29.2.X4	28,000	
31.5.X4	45,000	
		148,000
Depreciation 19X4	37,000	
		111,000
Cost 1.12.19X4	50,000	
		161,000
Depreciation 19X5	40,250	
		120,750
		127,250

Total 25,000 + 25,000 + 37,000 + 40,250 =

12.1 (cont)

Straight line

	Cost	19X2	19X3	19X4	19X5
Cost 1.12.19X2	100,000	25,000	25,000	25,000	25,000
1.6.19X3	25,000		3,125	6,250	6,250
29.2.19X4	28,000			5,250	7,000
31.5.19X4	45,000			5,625	11,250
1.12.19X4	50,000				12,500
		25,000	28,125	42,125	62,000

Total 157,250

(W2) Extra depreciation 157,250 – 127,250 = 30,000

As profits after tax were £157,000 but were shown in the balance sheet as £13,000, this means that a deficit of £144,000 had been brought forward from last year.

13.1

(a)

Merton Manufacturing Co Ltd
Balance Sheet as at ...

Fixed tangible assets		
Freehold land and buildings at cost	(W1)	95,000
Plant and equipment at written-down value		104,350
		199,350
Current assets		
Stocks	25,000	
Debtors	50,000	
Bank	(W2) 14,150	
	89,150	
Creditors: Amounts falling due within one year		
Creditors	63,500	
Net current assets		25,650
Total assets *less* current liabilities		225,000
Long-term loans: 8 per cent debentures	(W3)	150,000
		75,000
Capital and reserves		
Called-up share capital		
150,000 50p ordinary shares	(W4)	75,000

Capital Reduction

Ordinary shares 50p (new)	7,500	Ordinary shares £1 (old)	90,000
(1 for 6 = 15,000 × 50p)		6% preference shares (old)	150,000
Ordinary shares 50p (new)	25,000	11½% debentures (old)	100,000
(1 for 3 – preference – 50,000 × 50p)		Share premium written off	25,000
8% debentures	50,000		
(1 for 3 preference)			
8% debentures	100,000		
(exchange for 11½%)			
Ordinary shares 50p	12,500		
(1 for every £4 old debenture)			
Goodwill written off	50,000		
Profit and loss written off	38,850		
Plant and equipment*	81,150		
	365,000		365,000

Workings:
(W1)
Shares issued 60,000 shares × 50p = 30,000
Cash 30,000 – overdraft 15,850 = balance 14,150
See capital reduction – debit side (W1) new debentures 50,000 + 100,000 = 150,000
See (W1) 7,500 + 25,000 + 12,500 + new shares issued for cash 30,000 = 75,000

*per (vii) of question – amount needed to balance.

(W2) Shares issued 60,000 shares × 50p = 30,000
Cash 30,000 – overdraft 15,850 = balance 14,150
(W3) See capital reduction – debit side (W1) new debentures 50,000 + 100,000 = 150,000
(W4) See (W1) 7,500 + 25,000 + 12,500 + new shares issued for cash 30,000 = 75,000

(b) (Main points)

	Old shareholdings	New shareholdings
Expected profit	22,500	22,500
Less Interest 11½%	11,500	
" 8%		12,000
Taxable profits	11,000	10,500
Less Corporation tax 33⅓%	3,667	3,500
Profits before dividends	7,333	7,000
Preference dividends – if profits sufficient	9,000	–

Before reconstruction

(Old) Preference shareholders

Before reconstruction it would have taken over 5 years at this rate before preference dividends payable, as probably deficit of 38,850 on the profit and loss account would have to be cleared off first.

(Old) Ordinary shares

Even forgetting the profit and loss account deficit, the preference dividends were bigger than available profits. This would leave nothing for the ordinary shareholder.

After reconstruction

The EPS (earnings per share) is £7,000 ÷ 150,000 = 4.67p
If all profits are distributed the following benefits will be gained:

By old preference shareholders		
50,000 shares × 4.67p	2,335	
£50,000 8% debentures	4,000	
	6,335	

Plus any benefits from tax credits.

By old ordinary shareholders	
15,000 shares × 4.67p	700

Plus any benefits from tax credits.

(c) Preference shareholders – points to be considered:

(i) What were prospects for income?
Based on projected earnings would have been no income for over 5 years, then earnings of 7,333 per annum if all profits distributed.

(ii) What are new prospects for income?
Total income of 6,333 per annum immediately.

(iii) Is it worth exchanging (i) for (ii)?
Obviously depends on whether forecasts are accurate or not. If the above are accurate would seem worthwhile.

(iv) What have preference shareholders given up?
Some of exchange consists of ordinary shares which are more risky than preference shares, both in terms of dividends and of payments on liquidation.

(v) What have they gained?
Debenture interest payable whether profits made or not.

13.2

(a)

(Narratives omitted)	Dr	Cr
Preference share capital	37,500	
Ordinary share capital	175,000	
Capital reduction		212,500

*Preference shares reduced 25p each (0.25 × 15,000) &
Ordinary shares reduced by 0.875 (200,000 × 0.875).*

	Dr	Cr
Capital reduction	3,375	
Ordinary share capital		3,375

Ordinary shares issued re preference dividend arrears, 27,000 × 0.125.

	Dr	Cr
Share premium	40,000	
Capital reduction		40,000

Share premium balance utilised.

	Dr	Cr
Provision for depreciation	62,500	
Capital redemption	72,500	
Plant and machinery		135,000

Plant and machinery written down to 75,000.

	Dr	Cr
Capital reduction	176,625	
Profit and loss		114,375
Preliminary expenses		7,250
Goodwill		55,000

Profit and loss account and intangible assets written off.

	Dr	Cr
Cash	62,500	
Ordinary share applicants		62,500

Applications for shares 500,000 × 0.125.

	Dr	Cr
Ordinary share applicants	62,500	
Ordinary share capital		62,500

500,000 ordinary shares issued.

13.2 (cont)

(b)

Balance Sheet as at 31 December 19X5

Fixed assets		
Leasehold property at cost	80,000	
Less Provision for depreciation	30,000	50,000
Plant and machinery at valuation		75,000
		125,000
Current assets		
Stock	79,175	
Debtors	31,200	
	110,375	
Less Current liabilities		
Bank overdraft	51,000	
Creditors	43,500	94,500
Working capital		15,875
		140,875
Financed by:		
Share capital:		
Preference shares		
150,000 shares £0.75		112,500
Ordinary shares		
227,000 ordinary shares £0.125		28,375
		140,875

13.3

The Journal (narratives omitted)

	Dr	Cr
(i) Preference share capital	37,500	
Capital reduction		37,500
(ii) Ordinary share capital	360,000	
Capital reduction		360,000
(iii) Capital reserve	48,000	
Capital reduction		48,000
(iv) Preference share capital	112,500	
Ordinary share capital	240,000	
New ordinary share capital		352,500
(v) (a) Debenture holders	150,000	
Debentures		150,000
(b) Cash	150,000	
Debenture holders		150,000
(vi) Capital reduction	445,500	
Goodwill etc.		210,000
Plant		45,000
Furniture		6,600
Profit and loss		183,900

Finer Textiles Ltd

Balance Sheet as at 31 March 19X6

Fixed assets			
Intangible: Goodwill			15,000
Tangible: Plant			169,800
Furniture			6,000
			190,800
Current assets			
Stock	170,850		
Debtors	65,100		
Bank	107,400		
Cash	150		
	343,500		
Creditors: Amounts falling due within 1 year			
Creditors	31,800		
Net current assets			311,700
Total assets less current liabilities			502,500
Creditors: Amounts falling due after more than 1 year			
Debentures			150,000
			352,500
Capital and reserves			
Called-up share capital			352,500

(v) Write off £17,500 to profit and loss (SSAP 13).

(vi) As this development expenditure is almost definitely going to be recovered over next 4 years it can be written off over that period (SSAP 13).

(vii) As this is unlikely to happen often it is an exceptional item. Charge to profit and loss on ordinary activities under the appropriate statutory heading (FRS 3).

(viii) As this is over 20 per cent, it is material and appears to be long-term. This means that Litreshall Ltd is an associated company and accounts should be prepared accordingly. The post-acquisition profits to be brought in are 30% × £40,000 = £12,000.

14.5 The fact that this is a partnership does not mean that accounting standards are not applicable; they are just as applicable to a partnership as they are to a limited company.

(a) (i) These should be included as Sales £60,000 in the accounts for the year to 31 May 19X7. This is because the matching concept requires that revenue, and the costs used in achieving it, should be matched up. Profits: increase of £60,000.

(ii) Stock values are normally based on the lower of cost or net realisable value. In this case it depends how certain it is that the stock can be sold for £40,000. If a firm order can definitely be anticipated, then the figure of £40,000 can be used as this then represents the lower figure of net realisable value. Profit: an increase of £15,000. However, should the sale not be expected, then the concept of prudence dictates that the scrap value of £1,000 be used. Profit: a reduction of £24,000.

(b) It is important to establish the probability of the payment of the debt of £80,000. If it is as certain as it possibly can be that payment will be made, even though it may be delayed then no provision is needed. Profit change: nil.

However, the effect on future profits can be substantial. A note to the accounts detailing the possibilities of such changes should be given.

(c) The concepts which are applicable here are (i) going concern, (ii) consistency, (iii) accruals, (iv) prudence.

Following on the revelations in (b) and the effect on sales so far of the advertising campaign, is the partnership still able to see itself as a going concern? This would obviously affect the treatment of valuations of all assets.

Given that it can be treated as a going concern, the next point to be considered is that of consistency. The treatment of the expense item should be treated consistently.

14.1 (a) Following is a brief answer:

(i) Such closure costs should be treated as an exceptional item, because:
- it is (probably) a material item;
- these are costs not likely to recur regularly or frequently.

(ii) This should be adjusted in tax charge for 19X7. Because it is not material (probably) it does not need to be disclosed separately.

(iii) The excess should be credited to a reserve account, and a note attached to the balance sheet. Depreciation to be based on revalued amount and on new estimate of remaining life of the asset, to be disclosed in a note to the accounts.

(iv) Treat as bad debt and write off to profit and loss. Because it is a material item it should be disclosed as an exceptional item in the profit and loss account.

(v) This is a prior period adjustment. The retained profit brought forward should be amended to allow for the change in accounting policy in the current year. The reasons: (a) it is material, (b) relates to a previous year, (c) as a result of change in accounting policy. The adjustment should be disclosed in a note to the financial statements.

(b) See pp. 215–16.

14.2 (i) The replacement cost is irrelevant. The stock should be shown at the cost of £26,500. This assumes historic cost accounts.

(ii) *Paramite:* Stock to be valued at direct costs £72,600 plus fixed factory overhead £15,300 = £87,900. Under no circumstances should selling expenses be included.
Paraton: As net realisable value is lower than the costs involved, this figure of £9,520 should be used (SSAP 9).

(iii) In this case there is a change of accounting policy. Accordingly a prior period adjustment will be made. On a straight line basis net book value would have been:

Cost 160,000 less 12½% × 2 years = 120,000
Value shown 90,000
Therefore prior period adjustment of 30,000
to be added to retained profit at 1 November 19X4.

For 19X5 and each of the following 5 years depreciation will be charged at the rate of £20,000 per annum (FRS 3).

(iv) The cost subject to depreciation is £250,000 less land £50,000 = £200,000. With a life of 40 years this is £5,000 per annum.
This also will result in a prior period adjustment, in this case 10 × £5,000 = £50,000. This will be debited to retained profits at 1 November 19X4. For 19X5 and each of the following 29 years the yearly charge of depreciation will be £5,000 (FRS 3).

14.5 (cont)

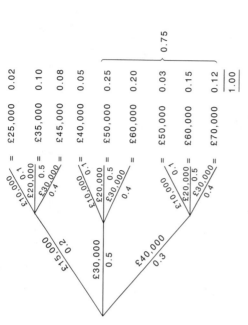

The accruals concept is concerned with matching up revenues and costs, and will affect the decision as to how much of the costs should be carried forward. Some revenue in future periods needs to be expected with a high degree of certainty before any of this expenditure should be carried forward. It does not seem highly likely that large revenues can be expected in future in this case. In any case 75 per cent is a very large proportion of such expenditure to be carried forward. There is no easy test of the validity of the partners' estimates. Granted that under SSAP 13 for development expenditure some of it, under very stringent conditions, can be carried forward. If the partners' estimates can be accepted under this, then profits would be increased by 75% × (50,000 + 60,000 + 25,000) = £82,500.

(d) The expected profit/loss is as follows:

	Project A	Project B	Project C
Direct costs to date	30,000	25,000	6,000
Overheads to date	4,000	2,000	500
Future expected direct costs	10,000	25,000	40,000
" overheads	2,000	2,000	3,000
Total of expected costs	46,000	54,000	49,500
Sale price of project	55,000	50,000	57,500
Expected total profit/loss	9,000	(4,000)	8,000
% complete	75%	50%	15%

When a project is sufficiently near completion then a proportion of the profits can be taken as being realised.

Project A is 75 per cent complete and this indicates profit being taken. Whether or not 75 per cent can be taken, i.e. £6,750, will depend on the facts of the case. If completion at the above figures can be taken for granted then it might be reasonable to do so. Prudence dictates that a lesser figure be taken.

With project B there is an expected loss. Following the prudence concept losses should always be accounted for in full as soon as they become known.

In project C it is too early in the project, 15 per cent completed, to be certain about the outcome. No profit should therefore be brought into account.

Profit, dependent on comments about project A, will therefore be increased by £6,750 – £4,000 = £2,750.

(e) This is a case where the examiner has dipped into topics from other subjects. What is needed here is a tree diagram to show the probabilities.

There is a probability of 0.75 of achieving £50,000 sales. As this is greater than the specified figure of 0.70 then the stocks should not be written down. Effect on profits: nil.

(f) The opening stock should be shown as the revised figure. If error had not been found this year's profit would have been £7,000 greater. The adjustment should be shown as a prior period adjustment in the current accounts.

14.6

(a)

Address
Date

The Chief Accountant
Uncertain Ltd

Dear Sir/Mr...,

Report on Draft Profit and Loss Account for the year ended 30 September 19X6.

Further to your letter/our meeting of . . . I would like to offer my suggestions for the appropriate accounting treatment of items (*i*) to (*v*).

(i) Redundancy payments: £100,000.
The reorganisation satisfies the requirements of FRS3, that it had a material effect on the nature and focus of the reporting entity's operations. As a result, the costs should be shown separately on the face of the profit and loss account after operating profit and before interest, and included under the heading of continuing operations. Relevant information regarding its effect on the taxation charge should be shown in a note to the profit and loss account. If there are other exceptional items in the financial period, and the tax effect differs between them, further information should be given, where practicable, to assist users in assessing the impact of the different items on the net profit or loss attributable to shareholders.

(ii) Closure costs of a factory
FRS 3 requires that material profits or losses on the termination of an operation should be treated as exceptional and shown separately on the face of the profit and loss account after operating profit and before interest, and included under the appropriate heading of continuing or discontinued operations. In calculating the profit or loss in respect of the termination, consideration should only be given to revenue and costs directly related to it. Clearly, the costs have been identified and are known and there is a loss on the termination. It should not have been deducted from reserves, it must go through the profit and loss account.

(iii) Change of basis of depreciation: £258,000
There should only be a change in the basis of depreciation if it brings about a change in the accounting results and financial position of the company – *see* SSAP 12. This SSAP also requires that the depreciation should be shown as normal expenses, rather than as a prior period adjustment.
Because the item is a material one, and makes comparison difficult, a note as to the details should be appended to the accounts.

(iv) Additional expenses covered by fire: £350,000
These expenses are covered by SSAP 17 as post-balance sheet non-adjusting events. The fire happened after the balance sheet date, and therefore did not affect conditions as at that date. The figures in this year's accounts should not therefore be altered.

If the event was such as to call into question the continuation of the business, then there should be a note to the accounts on the going-concern basis. In this particular instance this does not seem to be the case, but good practice, although not necessary, would be to give details of the event in notes to the accounts.

(v) Bad debt: £125,000
The accounts have not yet been approved by the directors, and it does affect the valuation of assets at the year end. SSAP 17 would be to treat it as a post-balance sheet adjusting event. It should therefore be written off as a bad debt.
Where it is considered to be a material and unusual event, there should also be a note attached to the accounts.

Should you like to have further discussions concerning any of the points raised, will you please contact me. I hope that you will find my comments to be of use.

Yours faithfully,

CACA

(b)

Uncertain Ltd

Draft profit and loss account for the year ended 30 September 19X6

Sales		5,450,490
Manufacturing cost of sales (W1)		2,834,500
		2,615,990
Administration expenses	785,420	
Selling expenses (W2)	1,013,600	
		1,799,020
Operating profit		816,970
Continuing operations – redundancy payments	100,000	
Discontinued operations – factory closure costs	575,000	
		675,000
Profit before tax		141,970
Corporation tax (50%) (W3)		70,985
		70,985
Proposed dividend on ordinary shares		125,000
Reduction in retained profits		(54,015)

(W1) £3,284,500 – £100,000 (*i*) – £350,000 (*iv*) = £2,834,500
(W2) £629,800 + £258,800 (*iii*) + £125,000 (*v*) = £1,013,600
(W3) 50% of profits before tax

14.7

(a) (i) Post-balance sheet events consists of those events, whether favourable or unfavourable, which take place between the date of the balance sheet and the date on which the financial accounts and notes are approved by the directors.

(ii) Adjusting events are post-balance sheet events which give extra evidence of what was happening at the balance sheet date. The events included may be included because they are either of a statutory nature or taken into account by convention.

(iii) Non-adjusting events are balance sheet events concerned with matters which did not exist at the balance sheet date.

(iv) Contingent gain/loss is concerned with something which seems to be apparent at the balance sheet date but can only be verified by future events which are uncertain.

(b) Adjusting entries: (i) debtor's inability to pay; (ii) subsequent discovery of frauds rendering accounts incorrect; (iii) when net realisable value is used for stock valuation later shown to be wrong when stock sold; (iv) subsequent discovery of errors rendering accounts incorrect.

Non-adjusting entries: (i) change in foreign exchange rates; (ii) strikes; (iii) nationalisation; (iv) share issues.

(c) (i) A material contingent loss should be accrued for where some future event will give evidence of the loss, subject to the fact that it should be able to be determined with reasonable accuracy when the accounts are agreed by the directors.

(ii) They should be disclosed in the financial statements if it is very probable that they will be realised.

15.1 (i) (for internal use)

Rogers plc

Trading and Profit and Loss Account for the year ended 31 December 19X2

Sales			288,000
Less Returns inwards			11,500
			276,500
Less Cost of sales:			
Stock 1 January 19X2		57,500	
Add Purchases	164,000		
Less Returns outwards	2,000	162,000	
Carriage inwards		1,300	
		220,800	
Less Stock 31 December 19X2		64,000	156,800
Gross profit			119,700
Distribution costs:			
Salaries and wages	2,800		
Rent and rates	3,750		
General distribution expenses	4,860		
Motor expenses	3,600		
Depreciation: Motors	6,500		
Equipment	700	22,210	
Administrative expenses:			
Salaries and wages	5,600		
Rent and rates	2,500		
General administrative expenses	3,320		
Motor expenses	3,600		
Auditors' remuneration	500		
Discounts allowed	3,940		
Bad debts	570		
Depreciation: Motors	3,500		
Equipment	1,100	24,630	46,840
			72,860
Other operating income: Royalties receivable			1,800
			74,660
Income from shares in related companies		660	
Interest on bank deposit		770	1,430
			76,090
Interest payable: Debenture interest			2,400
Profit on ordinary activities before taxation			73,690
Tax on profit on ordinary activities			30,700
Profit on ordinary activities after taxation			42,990
Retained profits from last year			15,300
			58,290
Transfer to general reserve		8,000	
Proposed ordinary dividend		30,000	38,000
Retained profits carried forward to next year			20,290

15.2 (i)

(for internal use)

Federal plc

Trading and Profit and Loss Account for the year ended 31 December 19X4

Sales			849,000
Less Returns inwards			5,800
			843,200
Less Cost of sales:			
Stock 1 January 19X4		64,500	
Add Purchases	510,600		
Less Returns outwards	3,300	507,300	
Carriage inwards		4,900	
		576,700	
Less Stock 31 December 19X4		82,800	
Cost of goods sold		493,900	
Wages		11,350	
Depreciation of plant and machinery		1,500	
			506,750
Gross profit			336,450
Distribution costs			
Salaries and wages	29,110		
Rent and rates	20,000		
Motor expenses	10,400		
General distribution expenses	8,220		
Haulage costs	2,070		
Depreciation: Motors	15,000		
Plant and machinery	8,000	92,800	
Administrative expenses			
Salaries and wages	20,920		
Rent and rates	5,000		
Motor expenses	5,200		
General administrative expenses	2,190		
Bad debts	840		
Discounts allowed	5,780		
Auditors' remuneration	2,000		
Directors' remuneration	5,000		
Depreciation: Motors	7,000		
Plant and machinery	5,000		
	58,930		
Less Discounts received	6,800	52,130	144,930
			191,520
Income from shares in related companies		3,500	
Interest from government securities		1,600	5,100
			196,620

(ii) (published accounts)

Rogers plc

Profit and Loss Account for the year ended 31 December 19X2

Turnover			276,500
Cost of sales			156,800
Gross profit			119,700
Distribution costs		22,210	
Administrative expenses		24,630	46,840
			72,860
Other operating income			1,800
			74,660
Income from shares in related companies		660	
Other interest receivable		770	1,430
			76,090
Interest payable			2,400
Profit on ordinary activities before taxation			73,690
Tax on profit on ordinary activities			30,700
Profit for the year on ordinary activities after taxation			42,990
Retained profits from last year			15,300
			58,290
Transfer to general reserve		8,000	
Proposed ordinary dividend		30,000	38,000
Retained profits carried forward to next year			20,290

Notes to accounts on debenture interest.

15.2 (cont)

Amount written off investment in related companies	14,000		
Debenture interest	3,800	17,800	
Profit on ordinary activities before taxation		178,820	
Tax on profit on ordinary activities		74,000	
Profit on ordinary activities after taxation		104,820	
Retained profits from last year		37,470	
		142,290	
Transfer to debenture redemption reserve	20,000		
Proposed ordinary dividend	50,000	70,000	
Retained profits carried forward to next year		72,290	

(ii) (published accounts)   Federal plc
Profit and Loss Account for the year ended 31 December 19X4

Turnover		843,200
Cost of sales		506,750
Gross profit		336,450
Distribution costs	92,800	
Administrative expenses	52,130	144,930
		191,520
Income from shares in related companies	3,500	
Other interest receivable	1,600	5,100
		196,620
Amounts written off investments	14,000	
Interest payable	3,800	17,800
Profit on ordinary activities before taxation		178,820
Tax on profit on ordinary activities		74,000
Profit on ordinary activities after taxation		104,820
Retained profits from last year		37,470
		142,290
Transfer to reserves	20,000	
Proposed ordinary dividend	50,000	70,000
Retained profits carried forward to next year		72,290

15.3 (a)   Rufford plc
Profit and Loss Account for the year ended 31 March 19X6

	Notes	£000	£000
Turnover	(1)		642
Cost of sales (60 + 401 − 71)			390
Gross profit			252
Distribution costs (33 + 19)		52	
Administrative expenses (97 + 8)		105	157

	Notes			
Operating profit – continuing operations	(2)			95
Loss on disposal of discontinued operations	(3)			12
				83
Income from other fixed asset investments	(4)			45
(14 × 100/70)		20		
Other interest receivable		25		
				128
Interest payable	(5)			6
Profit on ordinary activities before taxation				122
Tax on profit on ordinary activities	(6)			50
Profit for the year on ordinary activities after taxation				72
Retained profits brought forward from last year			160	
Prior period adjustment			15	
				145
				217
Dividends (21 + 42)	(7)			63
Retained profits carried forward to next year				154

Notes to the accounts:

1 Turnover is net of VAT.

2 Operating profit is shown after charging the following:

	£000	£000
Depreciation: distribution costs	19	
administrative expenses	8	27
Auditor's remuneration		20
Directors' emoluments		45
Hire of plant		12

3 Factory closure expenses.

4 Income from fixed asset investment is in respect of a listed company.

5 Interest payable is on a bank overdraft, repayable within 5 years.

6 Tax on profit on ordinary activities:

	£000
Corporation tax at 50% on profits	38
Tax credits on dividends received	6
Transferred to deferred taxation	9
Overprovision in 19X5	(3)
	50

7 Dividends:

	£000
Interim 5p per share	21
Final: proposed 10p per share	42
	63

8 Earnings per share:
EPS of 17.1p per share based on earnings of £72,000 and on average 420,000 shares on issue throughout the year (*see* FRS 3 amendment).

(b) *Balance Sheet extracts as at 31 March 19X6*

Creditors: amounts falling due within one year

	£	£
Debentures	6,000	
Bank overdrafts	4,370	
Trade creditors	12,410	
Bills of exchange payable	1,600	24,380
Net current assets		19,330
Total assets less current liabilities		118,400

Creditors: amounts falling due after one year

	£	£
Debentures	4,000	
Bills of exchange payable	2,000	6,000
		112,400

Capital and reserves

	£	£
Called-up share capital		75,000
Share premium account		20,000
Other reserves:		
Capital redemption reserve	5,000	
General reserve	4,000	9,000
Profit and loss account		8,400
		112,400

Notes:

(i) Called-up share capital consists of:

	£
50,000 £1 ordinary shares	50,000
50,000 preference shares of 50p each	25,000
	75,000

(ii) Land and buildings:

	£	£
Cost		48,000
Depreciation to 31 December 19X0	12,000	
Depreciation for year to 31 December 19X1	4,000	16,000
		32,000

(iii) Plant and machinery:

	£	£
Cost		12,500
Depreciation to 31 December 19X0	3,600	
Depreciation for year to 31 December 19X1	1,800	5,400
		7,100

(b) *Balance Sheet extracts as at 31 March 19X6*

	£000	£000
Creditors: Amounts falling due within one year		
Other creditors including taxation and social security (W1)		95
Provisions for liabilities and charges		
Taxation, including deferred taxation (W2)		15

Workings:

(W1) Corporation tax for year to 31 March 19X6

	£000
Corporation tax for year to 31 March 19X6	35
ACT paid on 14.10.19X5	3
	38
Proposed dividend	42
ACT on proposed dividend	18
	95

(W2) Deferred tax as given

	£000
Deferred tax as given	24
From profit and loss	9
	33
Less ACT on proposed dividend	18
	15

16.1

Owen Ltd
Balance Sheet as at 31 December 19X1

		£
Called-up share capital net paid		150
Fixed assets		
Intangible assets		
Development costs	3,070	
Goodwill	21,000	24,070
Tangible assets		
Land and buildings	32,000	
Plant and machinery	7,100	39,100
Investments		
Shares in related companies	35,750	98,920
Current assets		
Stock		
Raw materials and consumables	3,470	
Finished goods and goods for resale	18,590	22,060
Debtors		
Trade debtors	17,400	
Amounts owed by related companies	3,000	
Prepayments	1,250	21,650
		43,710

16.2

Belle Works plc

Balance Sheet as at 30 September 19X4

Fixed assets			
Intangible assets			
Concessions, patents, licences, trade marks and similar rights and assets	1,500		
Goodwill	17,500	19,000	
Tangible assets			
Land and buildings	72,500		
Plant and machinery	19,400	91,900	110,900
Current assets			
Stock			
Raw materials and consumables	14,320		
Work-in-progress	5,640		
Finished goods and goods for resale	13,290	33,250	
Debtors			
Trade debtors	11,260		
Other debtors	1,050		
Prepayments and accrued income	505	12,815	
		46,065	
Creditors: amounts falling due within one year			
Debenture loans	6,000		
Bank loans and overdrafts	3,893		
Trade creditors	11,340		
Bills of exchange payable	4,000		
Other creditors including taxation and social security	14,675	39,908	
Net current assets			6,157
Total assets less current liabilities			117,057
Creditors: amounts falling due after more than one year			
Debenture loans	12,000		
Trade creditors	1,260	13,260	
Provisions for liabilities and charges			
Pensions and similar obligations	1,860		
Taxation, including deferred taxation	640	2,500	15,760
			101,297
Capital and reserves			
Called-up share capital			70,000
Share premium account			5,000
Revaluation reserve			10,500
Other reserves			
General reserve	6,000		
Foreign exchange reserve	3,500	9,500	
Profit and loss account		6,297	
			101,297

Notes appended to the accounts on the details of Tangible assets and Depreciation, also exact details of items lumped under group descriptions.

16.3

Baganza plc

Profit and Loss Account for the year ended 30 September 19X7

	£000	£000
Turnover		19,500
Cost of sales (W1)		14,700
Gross profit		4,800
Distribution costs	600	
Administrative expenses (W2)	1,390	1,990
		2,810
Other operating income (W3)		341
Profit on ordinary activities before taxation		3,151
Tax on profit on ordinary activities (W4)		962
Profit on ordinary activities after taxation		2,189
Extraordinary item		1,500
Profit for the financial year		3,689
Retained profits from last year		2,109
		5,798
Dividends (W5)		756
Retained profits carried to next year		5,042
Earnings per share (W6)		182.4p

Workings (in £000s):
(W1) Opening stock 2,300 + Purchases 16,000 – Closing stock 3,600 = 14,700
(W2) Per trial balance 400 + Research 75 + Depreciation: Property (5% × 2,700) 135 + Plant (15% × 5,200) 780 = 1,390
(W3) Dividends received 249 + 27/73 of 249 = 341
(W4) Corporation tax 850 + Tax credit 92 + Deferred tax 40 – Overpayment last year 20 = 962
(W5) Dividends: Interim 36 + Final 720 = 756
(W6) EPS = Profit 3,689,000 ÷ Shares 1,200,000 = 307.4p
(FRS 3 now includes extraordinary items in calculation)

17.1

X Limited
Balance Sheet at 31 March 19X7

	£000	£000	£000
Fixed assets			
Intangible assets			
Development costs	35		
Tangible assets			
Freehold properties	1,040		
Plant and machinery	850		
Vehicles	285		
	2,175		2,410
Investments			
Investments in listed shares	200		
Current assets			
Stocks	500		
Debtors and prepayments (see workings)	654		
Cash at bank	439	1,593	
Creditors: amounts falling due within 1 year			
Trade creditors and accrual	878		
Other creditors (see workings)	590	1,468	
Net current assets			125
Total assets less current liabilities			2,535
Creditors: amounts falling due after more than 1 year			
12% debentures 19X6		500	
Provisions for liabilities and charges			
Deferred taxation		58	558
			1,977
Capital and reserves			
Called-up share capital			1,000
Share premium			150
Revaluation reserve			612
Profit and loss account (see workings)			215
			1,977

Workings:

	£000
Profit and loss	386
Less Bad debt (225,000 × 76%)	171
	215
Debtors	825
Less Bad debt (225,000 × 76%)	171
	654
Other creditors: Proposed dividend	280
Corporation tax	310
	590

Baganza plc
Balance Sheet as at 30 September 19X7

	£000	£000	£000
Fixed assets			
Tangible assets			
Land and buildings	2,305		
Plant and machinery	820	3,125	
Investments		2,000	
			5,125
Current assets			
Stocks		3,600	
Debtors		2,700	
Cash at bank		60	
		6,360	
Creditors: amounts falling due within one year			
Trade creditors	2,900		
Corporation tax (850 + 360 – 87)	1,123		
Other taxation and social security	180		
Proposed dividend (ACT ¼ × 720)	720	4,923	
Net current assets			1,437
Total assets less current liabilities			6,562
Taxation, including deferred taxation (460 + 40 – 180)			320
			6,242
Capital and reserves			
Called-up share capital			1,200
Profit and loss account			5,042
			6,242

17.1 (cont)

Notes to the balance sheet

1 Research and development

Research costs are written off immediately. Development costs are carried forward when there is a reasonable certainty of profitable outcome of the project and amortised over the useful life of the project.

2 Tangible assets

	Freehold property £000	Plant and machinery £000	Vehicles £000
Cost on 1 April 19X6*	800	1,500	220
Disposal at cost		(320)	
Addition			200
Revaluation adjustment	612		
On 31 March 19X7	1,092	1,500	420
Depreciation at 1 April 19X6*	80	500	55
Depreciation on disposals	(40)		
Provision in year	12	150	80
	52	650	135
Net book values	1,040	850	285

*Exam note only. Found by working backwards, leaving these figures as difference.

Note: Freehold property was valued by Messrs V & Co, Chartered Surveyors at a market value of £1,040,000 as compared with net book value of £428,000. The valuation figure has been included in balance sheet, and £612,000 has been credited to a revaluation reserve. Depreciation for 19X7 has been based on the revalued figure.

3 Investments

These had a market value of £180,000 on 31 March 19X7, but as this is not considered by the directors to be a permanent fall in value, the cost figure has been retained.

4 Stock

	£000
Finished goods	250
Raw materials	200
Work-in-progress	50
	500

The current replacement cost of goods is £342,000.

5 Deferred taxation

Provision as at 1 April 19X6	78
Add Provision during year	50
	128
Less ACT recoverable	70
	58

6 Share capital

1,000,000 ordinary shares of £1 each is the authorised capital, which has been fully issued and called up.

7 Reserves

	Profit and loss account	Share premium	Revaluation reserve
Balance at 1 April 19X6	?	150	–
Change during the year			612
	215	150	612

17.2

Billinge plc
Profit and Loss Account for the year to 30 June 19X6

	Notes	£000	£000
Turnover – continuing operations			1,500
Cost of sales (W1)			825
Gross profit			675
Distribution costs	(2)	55	
Administrative expenses (W2)		320	375
			300
Loss on disposal of discontinued operations	(3)		30
			270
Tax on profit on ordinary activities	(4)		130
Profit for the financial year			140
Retained profits from last year			40
			180
Dividends paid and proposed	(5)		100
Retained profits carried to next year			80
Earnings per share	(6)		28.0p

Billinge plc

Balance Sheet as at 30 June 19X6

	Notes	£000	£000	£000
Fixed assets				
Tangible assets	(7)			187
Fixtures and fittings				
Current assets				
Stocks: Finished goods and goods for resale		100		
Debtors		500		
Cash at bank		157		
		757		
Creditors: Amounts falling due within one year				
Trade creditors		64		
Other creditors, taxation and social security (W4)		100		
Advance corporation tax		25		
Proposed dividend		100	289	
Net current assets				468
				655
Total assets less current liabilities				
Provisions for liabilities and charges	(8)			
Taxation including deferred taxation				75
				580
Capital and reserves				
Called-up share capital	(9)			500
Profit and loss account				80
				580

Workings:

(W1)
Opening stock	70	
Purchases	855	925
Less Closing stock	100	825

(W2)
Depreciation	340	
Less disposals	20	320
Additions		60
		380
20% × 380	100	
Loss on disposals	20	
Less Depreciation	(15)	
		76

(W3)
C/T for year	100	
Deferred taxation	40	140
Less Previous overprovision	10	130
Less Cash	(3)	2
		78

(W4) Other creditors, taxation and social security:
Corporation tax	100
Administrative expenses	242
	320

Notes to the accounts:

1 Accounting policies
(a) The financial statements have been drawn up using the historical cost convention.
(b) Turnover consists of sales to external customers less VAT.
(c) Stocks are valued at lower of cost or net realisable value.
(d) Depreciation of fixed assets is based on cost, using the straight-line method over 5 years, salvage values being ignored.
(e) Deferred taxation is at the anticipated rate, taking into account the differing periods and the probability that a liability will occur.

2 Administrative expenses include depreciation £78,000.

3 Exceptional charges have arisen of £30,000 on the closure of a factory.

4 Taxation
	£000
Corporation tax at 35% on profit for the period	100
Deferred taxation	40
	140
Less Adjustment re last year's corporation tax	10
	130

5 Proposed ordinary dividend of 20p per share.

6 EPS calculated by dividing profit after taxation by number of ordinary shares on issue during the period.

7 Tangible fixed assets:
	£000	£000	£000
Fixtures etc. at 1.7.19X5	340		400
Additions	60		20
Less Disposals			380
Depreciation at 1.7.19X5	208		
For the period	132		193
Less Disposals	76	15	187

8
	£000	£000
Deferred taxation at 1.7.19X5	60	
Profit and loss charge	40	
	100	
ACT (¼ × 100,000)	25	75

9 Authorised, issued × fully paid ordinary £1 shares ... 500

17.6

Scampion plc
Profit and Loss Account for the year ended 31 May 19X7

	£000	£000
Turnover (3,489 – VAT 259)		3,232
Cost of sales (1,929 + 330 + 51)		2,310
Gross profit		922
Administrative expenses (595 + 25 + 45)		665
Operating profit		257
Income from shares in related companies	5	
Other interest receivable (note 2)	10	15
		272
Interest payable (note 3)	18	
Written off investments (note 7)	4	22
Profit on ordinary activities before taxation		250
Tax on profit on ordinary activities (note 4)		100
Profit on ordinary activities after taxation		150
Proposed ordinary dividend		66
Retained profits carried forward to next year		84

Earnings per share (note 5)   22.73p

Scampion plc
Balance Sheet as at 31 May 19X7

	£000	£000
Fixed assets		
Tangible assets (note 6)		1,372
Investments (note 7)		60
		1,432
Current assets		
Stock	230	
Debtors (67 – 45)	22	
Investments (market value £115,000)	103	
Cash at bank and in hand	84	
	439	
Creditors: amounts falling due within one year (note 8)	553	
Net current liabilities		(114)
Total assets less current liabilities		1,318
Creditors: amounts falling due after more than one year (note 9)		50
		1,268
Capital and reserves		
Called-up share capital		660
Share premium account		225
Profit and loss account (note 10)		383
		1,268

Notes:

1 Accounting policies

The historical cost convention has been used.

Provisions for depreciation are to write off the cost or valuation over the expected useful lives of the assets, by equal instalments, as follows:

Freehold buildings	40 years
Fixtures, fittings or equipment	10 years
Motor vehicles	5 years

Depreciation provisions have not been made on freehold land. The basis of the valuation of stock is the lower of cost or net realisable value.

2 Other interest receivable

This is income from government securities £10,000.

3 Interest payable

Interest on loans repayable within 1 year	12,000
Interest on loans repayable in more than 5 years' time	6,000
	£18,000

4 Taxation

(It has been assumed that 'tax charge based on the accounts for the year' means that the profit shown of £250 is same as the taxable profits.)
Corporation tax at the rate of 40 per cent on profits has been provided for.

5 Earnings per share = $\frac{150}{660}$ = 22.73p

6 Tangible assets (£000)

	Valuation or cost at 31.5.X6	Additions at cost	Less disposals	Depreciation to 31.5.X6	31.5.X7	Net
Freehold land and buildings	1,562	50	400	29	5	1,178
Fittings, fixtures and equipment	141	40		38	18	125
Motor vehicles	117	20		40	28	69
	1,820	110	400	107	51	1,372

7 Investments

Valuation by directors of shares in related companies	64,000
Less Written off during the year	4,000
	60,000

8 Creditors

Trade creditors (487,000 – Tax 120,000)	367,000
Corporation tax	100,000
Proposed dividend	66,000
Bank loan	20,000
	553,000

9 Creditors – amounts falling due after more than one year £50,000 12% debentures repayable in X years' time.

10 Reserves

	Revaluation	Profit and loss
Balance 31.5.19X6	150	149
Transfer to profit and loss	(150)	150
Retained profits for year to 31.5.X7	—	84
	—	383

18.1 See text of Chapter 18, section 18.2.

18.3 Cash Flow Statement (using the direct method) for
Lee Ltd for the year ended 31 December 19X4

Operating activities		
Cash received from customers	6,550	
Cash paid to suppliers	(2,875)	
Cash paid to employees	(2,025)	
Other cash payments	(600)	
Net cash inflow from operating activities		1,050
Returns on investment and servicing of finance		
Interest paid	(100)	
Dividends paid	(50)	
Net cash flows from returns on investment and servicing of finance		(150)
Tax paid		—
Investing activities		
Payments to acquire tangible assets	(700)	
Net cash outflow from investing activities		(700)
Net cash inflow before financing		200
Financing		
Repurchase of debentures	100	
Net cash outflow from financing		100
Increase in cash and cash equivalents		200

Notes to the cash flow statement

1 Reconciliation of operating profit to net cash inflow from operating activities:

Operating profit	400
Depreciation charges	500
Decrease in stocks	100
Decrease in debtors	50
Net cash inflow from operating activities	1,050

Working:
Operating profit = profit for the year (300) + interest (100) = 400

18.5 See text of Chapter 18, section 18.2.

18.6   **Nimmo Limited**
Cash Flow Statement (using the indirect method) for the year ended
31 December 19X9

	£000	£000
Net cash inflow from operating activities		2,150
Returns on investments and servicing of finance		
Dividends paid	(5,100)	
Net cash outflow from returns on investments and servicing of finance		(5,100)
Tax paid		(3,200)
Investing activities		
Purchase of fixed assets	(11,800)	
Sale of fixed assets	1,000	
Net cash outflow from investing activities		(10,800)
Net cash inflow before financing		(16,950)
Financing		
Issue of debenture stock	(150)	
Net cash outflow from financing		(150)
Decrease in cash and cash equivalents		(16,800)
		(16,950)

18.6 (cont)

Notes to the cash flow statement

1 Reconciliation of operating profit to net cash inflow from operating activities:

	£000
Operating profit	20,400
Depreciation charges	5,050
Loss on sale of fixed assets	700
Increase in stocks	(10,000)
Increase in trade debtors	(18,100)
Increase in prepayments	(100)
Increase in trade creditors	4,000
Increase in accruals	200
Net cash inflow from operating activities	2,150

Working:

Loss on sale of fixed assets = 1,000 − (5,500 − 3,800) = (700)

18.7

Track Limited

Cash Flow Statement (using the indirect method) for the year ended 30 June 19X1

	£000	£000
Net cash inflow from operating activities		(75)
Returns on investments and servicing of finance		
Dividends paid	(150)	
Net cash outflow from returns on investments and servicing of finance		(150)
Tax paid		(230)
Investing activities		
Purchase of fixed assets	(175)	
Sale of investments	150	
Sale of fixed assets	20	
Net cash outflow from investing activities		(5)
Net cash inflow before financing		(460)
Financing		
Issue of share capital	(300)	
Net cash outflow from financing		(300)
Decreasing in cash and cash equivalents		(160) (460)

Notes to the cash flow statement

1 Reconciliation of operating profit to net cash inflow from operating activities:

	£000
Operating profit	180
Depreciation charges	110
Profit on sale of fixed assets	(5)
Increase in stocks	(300)
Increase in trade debtors	(200)
Increase in trade creditors	140
Net cash inflow from operating activities	(75)

Workings:

Profit before tax: 670 − 530 = retained loss of 140 + tax (190) + dividends (130) = 180

Profit on sale of fixed assets = 20 − (25 − 10) = (5)

18.10

Blackley Limited

(a)

Forecasted net cash position for the three months ended 31 March 19X7

		Month to	
	31 Jan 19X7 £000	28 Feb 19X7 £000	31 Mar 19X7 £000
Receipts			
Trade debtors (W1)	235	290	345
Tangible fixed assets	12	–	–
Investments	10	–	–
Debentures	–	–	50
	257	290	395
Payments			
Trade creditors (W2)	150	230	285
Administration, selling and distribution expenses	37	40	42
Tangible fixed assets	–	240	–
Investments	–	–	5
Taxation	8	–	–
Dividend	15	–	–
	210	510	332
Forecasted net cash flow	47	(220)	63
Add Opening cash	80	127	(93)
Forecasted closing cash	127	(93)	(30)

Workings:

1 Trade debtors: forecasted cash receivable:

	31 Jan 19X7 £000	28 Feb 19X7 £000	31 Mar 19X7 £000
Sales	250	300	350
Less Closing trade debtors	65	75	80
	185	225	270
Add Opening trade debtors	50	65	75
Forecasted cash receipts from trade debtors	235	290	345

2 Trade creditors: forecasted cash payable

	31 Jan 19X7 £000	28 Feb 19X7 £000	31 Mar 19X7 £000
Opening stock	40	30	40
Purchases (by deduction)	190	250	295
	230	280	335
Less Closing stock	30	40	55
Cost of sales	200	240	280
Purchases (as above)	190	250	295
Less Closing trade creditors	120	140	150
	70	110	145
Add Opening trade creditors	80	120	140
Forecasted cash payments to trade creditors	150	230	285

(b)

Blackley Limited

Forecasted cash flow statement (using the direct method)
for the three months ended 31 March 19X7

	£000	£000
Operating activities		
Cash received from customers (W1)	870	
Cash paid to creditors (W2)	(665)	
Other cash payments (admin, selling & distribution)	(119)	
Net cash outflow from operating activities		86
Returns on investments and servicing of finance		
Dividends paid	(15)	
Net cash outflow from returns on investments and servicing of finance		(15)
Tax paid		(8)
Investing activities		
Purchase of fixed assets	(240)	
Purchase of investments	(5)	
Sale of fixed assets	12	
Sale of investments	10	
Net cash outflow on investing activities		(223)
Net cash inflow before financing		(160)
Financing		
Issue of debentures	(50)	
Net cash outflow from financing		(50)
Decrease in cash and cash equivalents		(110)
		(160)

Notes to the cash flow statement

1 Reconciliation of operating profit to net cash inflow from operating activities:

	£000
Operating profit	34
Depreciation charges	27
Increase in stocks	(15)
Increase in trade debtors	(30)
Increase in trade creditors	70
Net cash outflow from operating activities	86

19.1

Contract

Year 1:			Year 1:	
Plant	16,250		Work certified	58,000
Materials	25,490		Plant c/d	10,250
Wages	28,384		Stock and work-in-progress c/d	12,200
Direct expenses	2,126			
Gross profit to profit and loss	8,200			
	80,450			80,450
Year 2:			Year 2:	
Plant b/d	10,250		Work certified	116,000
Stock and work-in-progress b/d	12,200		Sale of plant	4,100
Materials	33,226			
Wages	45,432			
Direct expenses	2,902			
Penalty	700			
Gross profit to profit and loss	15,390			
	120,100			120,100

Workings:

Computation profit of Year 1:

Contract price		174,000
Less Actual expenditure		
25,490 + 28,384 + 2,126	56,000	
Estimated cost of plant (16,250 – 4,250)	12,000	
Estimated expenses Year 2	81,400	149,400
Estimated total contract profit: estimate made at end of year 1		24,600

Using formula given by question:

$$\frac{\text{Work certified}}{\text{Total contract price}} \times \text{Total estimated profit} = \text{Profit for Year 1}$$

$$= \frac{52,200 + 5,800}{174,000} \times 24,600 = 8,200$$

19.2

Stannard and Sykes Ltd
Pier Contract Account

Contract for Seafront Development Corporation valued at £300,000

Materials – direct	58,966		Materials on site carried down		11,660
– from store	10,180	69,146	Work-in-progress carried down		151,167
Wages		41,260			
Hire of plant		21,030			
Direct expenditure		3,065			
Overheads		8,330			
Wages accrued carried down		2,826			
		145,657			
Profit and loss account (proportion of profit to date)		17,170			
		162,827			162,827
Materials on site brought down		11,660	Wages accrued brought down		2,826
Work-in-progress brought down		151,167			

A suggested method for prudently estimating the amount of profit to be taken to November 30 is:

$$\frac{2}{3} \times \frac{\text{Cash received}}{\text{Value of work certified}} \times \text{Estimated profit (Value of work certified less cost of work certified)}$$

Total expenditure to date		145,657
Less Materials on site at November 30 19X8	11,660	
Cost of work not yet certified	12,613	24,273
Cost of work certified (*a*)		121,384
Value of work certified (*b*)		150,000
Total profit to date (*b*) – (*a*)		28,616

20.1 (a) Board of Directors
Manvers Ltd
Report on advantages of value added statement
Such statements were recommended for use in the *Corporate Report* as published by the professional accountancy bodies in 1975.
The advantages can be listed as:

1 It avoids using profit as the important factor. This is useful, as 'profit' is something misunderstood by many people.

2 Clarity. As it is concerned with linking revenue to the inputs and services paid for, it gives a clear picture of the operation of the business.

3 It illustrates interdependence between the various factors in a business.

4 Value added can also be related to capital employed.

The profit and loss account is legally necessary. The value added statement may use the same information, but it is used to demonstrate different factors and sheds light on matters which might have escaped attention otherwise.

The source and application funds statement is quite different. It is concerned with all items of a capital nature, whereas value added deals with performance on a revenue basis.

(b)
Manvers Ltd
Profit and Loss Account for the year ended 31 May 19X6

Turnover (204,052 − 30,608)		173,444
Less Expenses		
Materials and services	146,928	
Depreciation	1,835	
Pension scheme	2,810	
Salaries	16,468	
Profit sharing schemes	525	
Welfare and staff amenities	806	
Rates	325	
Bank interest	250	
Loan interest	1,600	171,547
Profits before taxation		1,897
Corporation tax		985
Profits after taxation		912
Dividends		500
Retained profits		412

(c)
Profits before tax	1,897
Add back non-cash item – depreciation	1,835
Operating profits	3,732

21.1 *See* text section 21.6.

21.2 *See* text section 21.8.

21.3 *See* text section 21.4.

21.4 *See* text section 21.9.

22.1 *P & S Consolidated Balance Sheet*

Goodwill	10
Stock	140
Bank	50
	200
Share capital	200
	200

22.2 *P & S Consolidated Balance Sheet*

Fixed assets	3,800
Stock	1,500
Debtors	700
Bank	300
	6,300
Share capital	6,000
Capital reserve	300
	6,300

22.3 *P & S Consolidated Balance Sheet*

Fixed assets	62,000
Stock	27,000
Debtors	8,000
Bank	3,000
	100,000
Share capital	100,000
	100,000

22.6

P & S Consolidated Balance Sheet

Goodwill	300
Fixed assets	2,000
Stock	1,300
Debtors	900
Bank	300
	4,800
Share capital	4,000
Minority interest	800
	4,800

22.7

P & S Consolidated Balance Sheet

Fixed assets	3,325
Stock	3,000
Debtors	2,000
Bank	200
	8,525
Share capital	8,000
Capital reserve	375
Minority interest	150
	8,525

22.10

P, S1 & S2 Consolidated Balance Sheet

Fixed assets	12,600
Current assets	5,900
	18,500
Share capital	10,000
Profit and loss	6,500
Capital reserve*	600
Minority interest	1,400
	18,500

*Goodwill S1 300, Capital reserve 900 = Net capital reserve 600.

22.11

P, S1 & S2 Consolidated Balance Sheet

Goodwill*	350
Fixed assets	9,450
Current assets	6,000
	15,800
Share capital	10,000
Profit and loss	2,000
General reserve	1,400
Minority interest	2,400
	15,800

*Goodwill (S1) 600, Capital reserve (S2) 250 = Net goodwill 350.

23.1

P & S Consolidated Balance Sheet as at 31 December 19X6

Goodwill	950
Fixed assets	10,950
Current assets	3,900
	15,800
Share capital	10,000
Profit and loss (P 4,000 + S 1,800)	5,800
	15,800

23.2

P & S Consolidated Balance Sheet as at 31 December 19X9

Fixed assets	47,400
Current assets	27,100
	74,500
Share capital	50,000
Profit and loss (14,000 – (400 × 70%) 280)	13,720
General reserve	5,000
Capital reserve	1,790
Minority interest (3,000 + 600 + 390)	3,990
	74,500

23.4

P, S1 & S2 Consolidated Balance Sheet as at 31 December 19X5

Goodwill		1,390
Fixed assets		36,900
Current assets		20,900
		59,190
Share capital		40,000
Profit and loss		8,270
General reserve		5,000
Minority interest		5,920
		59,190

Minority interest 40% of (10,000 + 2,800 + 2,000) = 5,920.
Goodwill S1 cost 8,150 – 60% of 10,000 + 1,100 + 2,000 = 290, S2 cost
11,400 – (8,000 + 500 + 1,800) = 1,100.
Profit and loss P 7,550 + S1 1,020 – S2 300 = 8,270.

24.1

P & S Consolidated Balance Sheet as at 31 December 19X9

Goodwill		850
Fixed assets		2,300
Current assets		
Stock (1,200 + 900 – 90)	2,010	
Debtors (2,100 + 1,400 – 220)	3,280	
Bank	500	
	5,790	
Less Current liabilities		
Creditors (900 + 700 – 220)	1,380	
Net current assets		4,410
		7,560
Financed by		
Share capital		2,000
Profit and loss		4,760
(P 3,700 – 90 + S 1,150)		
General reserve		800
		7,560

24.2

P & S Consolidated Balance Sheet as at 31 December 19X4

Goodwill		1,600
Fixed assets		14,200
Current assets		
Stock (3,100 + 7,200 – 50)	10,250	
Debtors (4,900 – 600 + 3,800)	8,100	
Bank	2,500	
	20,850	
Less Current liabilities		
Creditors (3,800 + 2,100 – 600)	5,300	
Net current assets		15,550
		31,350
Financed by		
Share capital		20,000
Profit and loss (P 4,000 – 50 + S 60% of 2,000)		5,150
Minority interest (40% of 10,000 + 5,500)		6,200
		31,350

24.3

P, S1 & S2 Consolidated Balance Sheet as at 31 December 19X8

Goodwill		
Fixed assets		65,000
Current assets		
Stock (£46,000 – £640)	45,360	
Debtors (£28,000 – £1,400)	26,600	
Bank	9,000	
	80,960	
Less Current liabilities		
Creditors (21,000 – 1,400)	19,600	
Net current assets		61,360
		126,360
Financed by:		
Share capital		100,000
Profit and loss account:		
(£23,000 – £400 – £240 – S1 £5,000 + S2 ⅖ths of £1,800)		18,860
General reserve		2,000
Minority interest (⅙th of £30,000 + £3,000)		5,500
		126,360

S1 Capital reserve: Cost £39,000 – £30,000 – £8,000 – £4,000 = £3,000.
S2 Goodwill: Cost £29,000 – ⅚ths of £30,000 + £1,200 = £2,800.
Net goodwill = £3,000 – £3,000 = Nil.

24.6

Pagg Group of Companies
Consolidated Balance Sheet as at 31 March 19X0

		£000
Fixed assets		
Intangible assets (Note 1)		1,898
Tangible assets		3,500
		5,398
Current assets		
Stocks (1,300 + 350 + 100 – 10)	1,740	
Debtors (3,000 + 300 + 200 – 200 – 35)	3,265	
Cash at bank and in hand	270	
	5,275	
Creditors falling due within 1 year (270 + 400 + 4,000 – 200 – 35)	4,435	
Net current assets		840
Total assets less current liabilities		6,238
Minority interests (Note 2)		500
		5,738
Capital and reserves		
Called-up share capital		5,500
Profit and loss		238
		5,738

Notes:

1 Cost of control

	Ragg	Tagg
Consideration	3,000	1,000
Less Shares (80%) 800 (80% × 600) 480		
(60%) 300 (60% × 100) 60		
Profit and loss	1,280	360
	1,720	640
Goodwill		
Total amount written off to 31.3.19X0 (5 years)	430	(1 year) 32
Amount not yet written off	1,290	608

1,898

2 Minority interests

	Ragg	Tagg
Share capital called up	1,000	500
Profit and loss (20%)	200	(40%) 150
	1,200	650
	240	260

500

3 Profit and loss:

Pagg	1,000
Ragg 80% × (200 – 600)	(320)
Tagg 60% × (150 – 100)	30
Goodwill (Note 1) 430 + 32	(462)
Inter-company profit on stock (¼ × 60)	(10)
	238

25.1

60% Share capital and reserves 31.12.19X6			
Shares bought 31.12.19X4	10,000	23,500	
Shares bought 31.12.19X6	14,000	31,000	
	24,000		56,400
			54,500
Negative goodwill			1,900

25.3

Shares bought		50,000
Profit and loss balance 31.12.19X7	36,000	
Add proportion 19X8 profits before acquisition 8/12 × 42,000	28,000	
	64,000	

Proportion of pre-acquisition profit:

$$\frac{50,000}{80,000} \times 64,000 = 40,000$$

Paid for shares 158,000

Therefore goodwill is 158,000 – 90,000 = 68,000.

26.1

P & S Consolidated Balance Sheet as at 31 December 19X7

Goodwill	1,000
Fixed assets	57,000
Current assets	15,000
	73,000
Share capital	50,000
Profit and loss account (H 19,000 + S 4,000)	23,000
	73,000

Workings: Goodwill: Cost 29,000 – 20,000 – 3,000 – Dividend 5,000 = 1,000.

26.3

P & S Consolidated Balance Sheet as at 31 December 19X9

Goodwill		14,000
Fixed assets		80,000
Current assets	33,000	
Less Current liabilities	1,500	
Net current assets		31,500
		125,500
Share capital		80,000
Profit and loss account: (P 23,000 + S ¾ of 6,000 + ¾ of 7,000)		32,750
Minority interest (¼ of 40,000 + 11,000)		12,750
		125,500

Workings: Goodwill: Cost 47,000 – ¾ of (40,000 + 4,000) = 14,000.

26.5

Consolidated Balance Sheet of P Ltd & S Ltd as at 31 December 19X6

Fixed assets				
Intangible assets				55,000
Goodwill (*see* Workings)				680,000
Tangible assets (Note 1)				
Current assets				
Stocks		160,000		
Debtors		140,000		
Bank		40,000		
		340,000		
Creditors: amounts falling due within 1 year				
Trade creditors	212,000			
Preference dividend proposed	8,000	220,000		
Net current assets				120,000
Total assets *less* current liabilities				855,000
Capital and reserves				
Called-up share capital: ordinary shares				
£1 fully paid				500,000
Reserves				185,000
Minority interest				170,000
				855,000

Note 1 Tangible fixed assets

	Cost	Depreciation to date	Net
Buildings	420,000	110,000	310,000
Plant and machinery	320,000	70,000	250,000
Motor vehicles	210,000	90,000	120,000
	950,000	270,000	680,000

Workings:

(a)

Goodwill		
Cost of investment		250,000
Less Ordinary shares (75%)	150,000	
Reserves (75%)	37,500	187,500
		62,500
Less Dividend from pre-acquisition profits		7,500
		55,000

(b)

Minority interest		
Preference shares		100,000
Reserves 25% × 80,000		20,000
Ordinary shares 25%		50,000
		170,000

The proposed preference dividend could be shown as part of the minority interest.

(c)

Reserves		
P Ltd		170,000
S Ltd 75% of extra reserves since acquisition 80,000 – 50,000 = 30,000		22,500
		192,500
Less Dividends received by P Ltd which were from pre-acquisition profits		7,500
		185,000

26.6 *Reconciliation of current accounts*

X					
Bal b/d	19		Bal b/d	14
			In transit	2
			Bank (1)	3
Bal c/d	19		Stock (2)	19
	19			19

Reserves			Y	
X			Bal b/d	220
19X6 retained profits	108			20
Proposed dividend Y 80%	0.4			8
80% Y profits for 19X6 × 18	2			14.4
	110.4			262.4

– Cost of control (above) written off 152
– Profit in goods in transit
– Profit in Y's stock

26.6 (cont)

Consolidated Balance Sheet for X plc & subsidiary Y plc as at 31 December 19X6

	Cost £000	Depreciation to date £000	Net £000
Tangible fixed assets			
Freehold property	280	18	262
Plant and machinery	245	52	193
	525	70	455
Current assets			
Stock (*see* Workings)		150.6	
Debtors		250	
Bank		24	
		424.6	
Less Current liabilities			
Trade creditors (130 + 80 + 2)	212		
Taxation	44		
Proposed dividends	20	276	148.6
			603.6
Called-up share capital			400
400,000 ordinary shares £1			
Reserves (*see* Workings)			152
			552
Minority interest (*see* Workings)			51.6
			603.6

Workings:

Cost of control (remember to calculate it as on 1.1.X6) £000

Cost of investment 300

Less Nominal value shares bought 80% 120
Reserves 80% × 90 72 192
108

Minority interest

20% of reserves at 1.1.X6 × 90 18
20% of 19X6 retained profit × 18 3.6
20% of shares × 150 30
51.6

Stock
X 80
Y 70
153
In transit 3
2
Less Profit element in Y's stock 0.4 2.4
150.6

"   " goods in transit

Bank X 10 + Y 12 + in transit 2 24

27.1

P & S Consolidated Balance Sheet as at 31 December 19X8

Goodwill			100,000
Fixed assets		500,000	
Less Depreciation		138,000	362,000
Current assets			205,000
			667,000
Share capital			500,000
Profit and loss account:			
(P 143,000 – 10,000 + S 32,000 + 2,000)			167,000
			667,000

27.3

P & S Consolidated Balance Sheet as at 31 December 19X7

Goodwill			19,000
Fixed assets		185,000	
Less Depreciation		33,500	151,500
Current assets			68,000
			238,500
Share capital			150,000
Profit and loss (P 77,000 + S 14,000 – 2,500)			88,500
			238,500

28.1

P, S1 & S2 Consolidated Balance Sheet as at 31 December 19X7

Goodwill			9,320
Fixed assets			127,000
Current assets			33,000
			169,320
Share capital			100,000
Profit and loss account			
(P 37,000 + S1 90% of 16,000 + S2 63% of 3,000)			53,290
General reserve			10,000
Minority interest			6,030
			169,320

Minority interest:

Shares in S1		1,000	
Shares in S2 37% of 5,000		1,850	2,850
Profit and loss S1 10% of 23,000		2,300	
S2 37% of 4,000		1,480	3,780
			6,630
Less Cost of shares in S2 for minority interest			
of S1 10% of 6,000			600
			6,030

Goodwill: Cost of shares to group in S1

in S2 90% of 6,000		23,000
Less Shares: In S1		5,400
In S2 63% of 5,000		9,000
Profit and loss S1 90% of 7,000	3,150	
S2 63% of 1,000	6,300	
	630	
		28,400
	19,080	
	9,320	

28.3

Sales Ltd & subsidiaries
Balance sheet as at 31 October 19X5

	Cost	Depreciation	Net
Fixed assets			
Buildings	184,000	–	184,000
Plant (W1)	260,000	92,400	167,600
	362,900	203,700	159,200
	806,900	296,100	510,800
Current assets			
Stock (W2)		247,400	
Debtors (W3)		275,200	
Bank		50,600	
		573,200	
Less Current liabilities			
Creditors (W4)	297,400		
Bank overdraft (W5)	26,100		
Corporation tax	129,100		
Proposed dividends	80,000		
Proposed dividends relating to minority interests (W6)	16,000	548,600	
Net current assets			24,600
			535,400
Ordinary share capital		200,000	
Revenue reserves (W7)		189,390	
Capital reserve (W8)		9,000	
		398,390	
Minority interest (W9)		137,010	
			535,400

Workings:
Note: S Ltd owns 75% of M Ltd & 75% × 80% = 60% of C Ltd

Plant 102,900 + 170,000 + 92,000 =		364,900
(W1) *Less* (Note (g)) inter-company profit		2,000
		362,900

(W1) Depreciation 69,900 + 86,000 + 48,200 =

		204,100
Less 2 years on inter-company profit element 10% × 2,000 × 2		400
		203,700

(W2) Stock 108,500 + 75,500 + 68,400

		252,400
– Unrealised profit (Note (f)) 20% × 25,000		5,000
		247,400

(W3) Debtors 196,700 + 124,800 – 83,500

		405,000
– Inter-indebtedness (Note (h))	56,900	
(Note (h))	28,900	
– Dividends: 80% of 10,000 (Note (h))	8,000	
75% of 48,000	36,000	
		129,800
		275,200

(W4) Creditors 160,000 + 152,700 + 59,200

		371,900
– Inter-indebtedness (Note (h))	28,900	
	45,600	
		74,500
		297,400

(W5) Overdraft

		37,400
– cheque in transit (Note (i))		11,300
		26,100

(W6) Minority interests: Shares of proposed dividends

Components Ltd: Ordinary 20% × 10,000		2,000
Preference		2,000
Machinery Ltd: Ordinary 25% × 48,000		12,000
		16,000

(W7) Reserves

S Ltd		154,000
M Ltd		85,000
C Ltd		74,000
		313,000
Add Reduction in depreciation of components 2,000 × 10% × 2yrs = 400 × 60% ownership of components		240
		313,240

28.3 (cont)

Less Profit on machinery	2,000	
Unrealised profit on stock	5,000	
Cost of control of C Ltd on 1.4.X3		
60% × 60,000	36,000	
Minority interest in C Ltd		
40% × 74,000	29,600	
Cost of control of M Ltd on 1.4.X3		
75% × 40,000	30,000	
Minority interest in M Ltd		
25% × 85,000	21,250	123,850
		189,390

(W8) Cost of control

C Ltd at date of purchase. Capital:		
Ordinary shares	100,000	
Reserves	60,000	
	160,000	

M Ltd had owned 80% =		128,000	
Then had paid		96,000	
Bringing about a capital reserve		32,000	
Of this 25% is owned by minority interest of M Ltd		8,000	24,000
M Ltd at date of purchase: Capital		120,000	
Reserve		40,000	
		160,000	

S Ltd owns 75%	120,000	
S Ltd paid	135,000	
Cost of control		15,000
Net figure for capital reserve		9,000

(W9) Minority interest

Ordinary shares: 25% M Ltd	30,000	
40% C Ltd	40,000	
		40,000
Preference shares		
Increase in profit because of depreciation change 40% × 400		160
25% revenue reserves M Ltd × 85,000		21,250
40% " C " × 74,000		29,600
		161,010
Less 2.5% payment made by M Ltd for investment in C Ltd × 96,000	24,000	137,010

29.1

Brodick plc & subsidiaries

Consolidated Profit and Loss Account for the year ended 30 April 19X7

	£000	£000
Turnover (1,100 + 500 + 130)		1,730
Cost of sales (630 + 300 + 70)		1,000
Gross profit		730
Administrative expenses (105 + 150 + 20)		275
Profit on ordinary activities before taxation		455
Tax on profit on ordinary activities (65 + 10 + 20)		95
Profit on ordinary activities after taxation		360
Minority interests (20% × 40 + 40% × 20)		16
Profit for the financial year		344
Retained profits from last year (W1)		506
		850
Dividends paid and proposed		200
Retained profits carried to next year (Note 1)		650

Note 1

Retained profits carried to next year comprise:

Brodick plc (*see* W1)	590
Subsidiaries (*see* W1)	60
	650

Workings:

(W1) Retained profits b/f

Brodick			460
Lamlash		106	
Less Minority (20%)		(21.2)	
Less Pre-acquisition (80% × 56)		(44.8)	30
Corrie		40	
Less Minority (40%)	12		
Less Pre-acquisition (60% × 20)	12	24	
			40
Retained profits for year (344 – 200)			6
			506
			144
			650

29.2 Norbreck plc & its subsidiary Bispham Ltd
Consolidated Profit and Loss Account for the year ended 30 September 19X7

	£000	£000
Turnover		2,150
Cost of sales		995
Gross profit		1,155
Administrative expenses		475
Profit on ordinary activities before taxation		680
Tax on profit on ordinary activities		50
Profit on ordinary activities after taxation		630
Minority interest (20% × 180)		36
Profit for the financial year		594
Retained profits from last year		196
		790
Dividends		360
Retained profits carried to next year		430

Earnings per share (594/900)   66p

Norbreck plc & its subsidiary Bispham Ltd
Consolidated Balance Sheet as at 30 September 19X7

	£000	£000	£000
Fixed assets			
Tangible assets			1,720
Current assets			
Stocks	550		
Debtors (280 + 150 – 80 dividend)	350		
Cash and Bank	50	950	
Creditors: amounts falling due within one year			
Trade creditors	240		
Other creditors, taxation and social security	230		
Proposed dividends (270 + 20% × 100)	290	760	
Net current assets			190
Total assets less current liabilities			1,910
Provisions for liabilities and charges			
Taxation, including deferred taxation			480
			1,430
Capital and reserves			
Called-up share capital			900
Profit and loss account			430
			1,330
Minority interest (20% × £500)			100
			1,430

Workings:

	£000	£000
Goodwill		
Investment		400
Nominal value of shares (80% × 400)	320	
Profit and loss (80% × 40)	32	352
Goodwill on acquisition		48
		220
Retained profits b/fwd		
Norbreck	70*	
Bispham	40	
– Pre-acquisition	30	
– Minority interest (20%)	6	24
		244
– Goodwill on acquisition (see above)		48
Retained profits of Group b/fwd		196
For the year (per consolidated P/L 594 – 360)		234
C/fwd		430

30.1 (a) Large Ltd & its subsidiary Small Ltd
Consolidated Profit and Loss Account for the year ended 30 September 19X6

	£000	£000
Turnover (10,830 + 2,000 – 108)		12,722
Cost of sales and production (3,570 + 1,100 – (108 × ⅔))		4,598
		8,124
Administrative and marketing expenses	2,772	
Unpurchased goodwill written off (per Companies Act 1985)	50	
Research costs written off (*see* SSAP 13)	50	2,872
Profit on ordinary activities before taxation		5,252
Tax on profit on ordinary activities		2,504
Profit on ordinary activities after taxation		2,748
Minority interests		121
		2,627
Retained profits from last year		1,290
		3,917
Dividend		2,400
Retained profits carried to next year		1,517

30.1 (cont)

(b)

Large Ltd & its subsidiary Small Ltd
Consolidated Balance Sheet as at 30 September 19X6

	£000	£000	£000
Fixed assets			
Intangible assets			
Development costs	180		
Goodwill	48		
		228	
Tangible assets			
At cost less depreciation		4,648	
			4,876
Current assets			
Stock (594 + 231 − 27)	798		
Debtors	2,620		
Bank	123		
		3,541	
Creditors: amounts falling due within one year			
Trade creditors		453	
Net current assets			3,088
			7,964
Capital and reserves			
Called-up share capital			6,000
Capital reserve (W1)			129
Profit and loss account			1,517
Minority interest (W2)			318
			7,964

Workings:

(W1)

Investment in Small cost			525
Less Share capital		600	
75% Retained earnings × 72		54	
			654
Capital reserve on acquisition			129

(W2)

Share capital		200
25% Retained earnings × 472		118
		318

(c) In this case merger accounting is not permitted. It can only be used when 90 per cent of the consideration is given as equity share capital, and here Large obtained 75 per cent for cash.

If merger treatment had been used the profits made before the merger could be distributed as dividends.

31.1

If Q plc is unable to exercise significant influence over N Ltd, the group comprises the parent undertaking (Q) and two subsidiaries (L and M). N Ltd should be excluded from consolidation (the grounds would be 'severe long-term restrictions') and treated as a fixed asset investment at cost. However, if Q plc is able to exercise significant influence over N Ltd, it should treat it as an associated undertaking using the equity method.

31.2

(a) There are two acquisition points. Any dividends received from the pre-acquisition (of the first investment) profits should be applied to reduce the initial investment of £80,000. Similar treatment should be applied to the £110,000 investment. The investment should be shown in the P's company balance sheet at cost of £190,000 less any such dividends received (or it could be shown at valuation). Dividends received and receivable should be shown in the profit and loss account after adjustment for any pre-acquisition element.

(b) At the time the investment became 21 per cent, the net assets of the clothing company were £840,000. The company's share of this is £176,400. The premium paid on acquisition, subject to adjustment for pre-acquisition reserves distributed, is £13,600 (£80,000 + £110,000 – £176,400) and, after any such adjustment required, it should either be written off to the reserves, or capitalised and amortised. Disclosure in the company's own financial statements is as for trade investments. The group profit and loss should show the company's share of the publishing company's pre-tax profits/losses and its attributable share of the associated undertaking's tax charge on those profits/losses. The group balance sheet carrying value in respect of this investment will comprise the cost of the investment plus the company's share of post-acquisition retained profits, less any amounts written-off either of these.

32.1

	Jan	Feb	Mar	Apr	May	Jun
Opening stock	740	690	780	1,100	1,400	1,160
Add Production	750	1,010	1,410	1,620	1,240	800
	1,490	1,700	2,190	2,720	2,640	1,960
Less Sales	800	920	1,090	1,320	1,480	1,020
Closing stock	690	780	1,100	1,400	1,160	940

32.2

(a)

Opening stock		140
Add Production	(C)	?
Less Sales total – see question	(B)	1,550
Closing stock		150

Missing figure (B) must be 1,700
Missing figure (C) must then be 1,560
Equal production per month 1,560 ÷ 12 = 130 units.

(b) Given figures per (a)

	(J)	(F)	(M)	(A)	(M)	(J)	(J)	(A)	(S)	(O)	(N)	(D)
Opening stock	140	160	130	70	110	50	60	90	150	210	230	210
Add Production	130	130	240	200	180	190	220	280	380	340	360	340
	270	290	370	270	290	240	280	370	530	550	590	550
Less Sales	110	180	170	130	70	100	190	170	320	340	150	150
Closing stock	160	110	200	140	220	140	90	200	210	210	440	400

Lowest closing figure is April 50 units.
If stock is not to fall below 80 units an extra 80 − 50 = 30 units will have to be produced in January making production for that month of 160 units.

32.4

(a) B Ukridge: Cash Budget

	May	Jun	Jul	Aug	Sep	Oct
Balance b/fwd		5,305	4,305	1,305		
Overdraft b/fwd					6,695	9,695
Receipts from debtors	400	4,000	8,000	12,000	9,000	5,000
Capital	5,005					
	5,405	9,305	12,305	13,305	2,305	(4,695)
Payments	100	5,000	11,000	20,000	12,000	7,000
Balance c/fwd	5,305	4,305	1,305			
Overdraft c/fwd				6,695	9,695	11,695

(b) There are the possibilities of delaying payments to creditors, delaying purchases or somehow getting debtors to pay up more quickly. Apart from these it is possible that a credit factoring firm could help in 'buying' the amounts of debtors from Ukridge.

If none of these is possible only a really fantastic product could warrant interest at 100 per cent per annum. This would rarely be the case, although there are many people whose optimism about their products exceeds the true profitability.

32.5 N Morris: Cash Budget

	Jul	Aug	Sep	Oct	Nov	Dec
Balance b/fwd	1,200		250			420
Overdraft b/fwd		260		160	540	
Receipts	4,000	6,400	5,800	8,000	6,000	9,500*
	5,200	6,140	6,050	7,840	5,460	9,080
Payments (see schedule)	5,460	5,890	6,210	8,380	5,880	5,410
Balance c/fwd		250				3,670
Overdraft c/fwd	260		160	540	420	

*Includes £2,500 legacy

Payments schedule

Jul
Raw materials 320 (Jul) × £4		1,280
300 (Jun) × £1		300
Direct labour 320 × £8		2,560
Variable 300 × £1 + 320 × £1		620
Fixed expenses		400
Drawings		300
		5,460

Aug
Raw materials 350 (Aug) × £4		1,400
320 (July) × £1		320
Direct labour 350 × £8		2,800
Variable 350 × £1 + 320 × £1		670
Fixed expenses		400
Drawings		300
		5,890

Sep
Raw materials 370 (Sep) × £4		1,480
350 (Aug) × £1		350
Direct labour 370 × £8		2,960
Variable 370 × £1 + 350 × £1		720
Fixed expenses		400
Drawings		300
		6,210

Oct
Raw materials 380 (Oct) × £4		1,520
370 (Sep) × £1		370
Direct labour 380 × £8		3,040
Variable 380 × £1 + 370 × £1		750
Fixed expenses		400
Drawings		300
Machinery		2,000
		8,380

Nov
Raw materials 340 (Nov) × £4		1,360
380 (Oct) × £1		380
Direct labour 340 × £8		2,720
Variable 340 × £1 + 380 × £1		720
Fixed expenses		400
Drawings		300
		5,880

Dec
Raw materials 310 (Dec) × £4		1,240
340 (Nov) × £1		340
Direct labour 310 × £8		2,480
Variable 310 × £1 + 340 × £1		650
Fixed expenses		400
Drawings		300
		5,410

32.6 (a) *Stock Budget 19X7*

		Aug	Sep	Oct	Nov
Opening stock	(A)	5,000*	7,000	8,000	7,000
Add Purchases	(B)	20,000	23,500	21,500	31,000
	(C)	25,000	30,500	29,500	38,000
Less Cost of sales	(D)	18,000	22,500	22,500	27,000
Closing stock	(E)	7,000	8,000	7,000	11,000

* After special sale of £8,000 goods at cost.
To work out missing figures:
August (A) is known. (D) is 24,000 – 25%

$$\text{(D) } 18,000$$

As stockturn is 3 therefore $\dfrac{(\text{A) } 5,000 + (\text{E) ?}}{2} = 3$

Therefore bottom line is 6,000 so (E) must be 7,000.
Repeat following months.

(b) *Cash Budget 19X7*

	Aug	Sep	Oct	Nov
Receipts:				
Capital	10,000			
Soul's debtors	20,250			
Debtors	–	–	24,000	30,000
Special sale	8,000			
	38,250	–	24,000	30,000
Payments:				
Creditors	10,000	20,000	23,500	21,500
General expenses	700	700	700	700
	10,700	20,700	24,200	22,200
Bank: Opening	(20,000)	7,550	(13,150)	(13,350)
Closing	7,550	(13,150)	(13,350)	(5,550)

32.9 *Cash Budget*

	Jan	Feb	Mar	Apr	May	Jun
Opening balance	25,000	+890	–370	–600	–740	–600
Opening overdraft						
Received (*see schedule*)	400	600	1,750	2,200	2,900	3,550
	25,400	1,490	1,380	1,600	2,160	2,950
Payments (*see schedule*)	24,510	1,860	1,980	2,340	2,760	3,460
Closing balance	+890					
Closing overdraft		–370	–600	–740	–600	–510

Cash Receipts Schedule

	Jan	Feb	Mar	Apr	May	Jun
Cash sales	400	600	800	1,000	1,300	1,400
Credit sales			800	1,200	1,600	2,000
Rent received			150			150
	400	600	1,750	2,200	2,900	3,550

Cash Payments Schedule

	Jan	Feb	Mar	Apr	May	Jun
Drawings	250	250	250	250	250	250
Premises	20,000					
Shop fixtures	3,000					
Motor van	1,000					
Salaries of assistants	260	260	260	260	260	260
Payments to creditors		1,200	1,320	1,680	2,100	2,800
Other expenses		150	150	150	150	150
	24,510	1,860	1,980	2,340	2,760	3,460

D Smith
Forecast Trading and Profit and Loss Accounts for the six months ended
30 June 19X4

Sales			16,500
Less Cost of goods sold:			
Purchases		11,410	
Less Closing stock (130 × £7)		910	
			10,500
Gross profit			6,000
Add Rent received			300
			6,300
Less Expenses:			
Assistants' salaries		1,560	
Other expenses		900	
Depreciation: Shop fixtures		150	
Motor van		100	
			2,710
Net profit			3,590

Balance Sheet as at 30 June 19X4

	Cost	Depn	Net
Fixed assets			
Premises	20,000	–	20,000
Shop fixtures	3,000	150	2,850
Motor van	1,000	100	900
	24,000	250	23,750

Current assets		
Stock-in-trade		910
Debtors		5,400
		6,310
Less Current liabilities		
Creditors	2,310	
Other expenses owing	150	
Bank overdraft	510	
		2,970
Working capital		3,340
		27,090
Financed by:		
Capital		25,000
Cash introduced		
Add Net profit		3,590
		28,590
Less Drawings		1,500
		27,090

(c) Creditors Budget (in £s)

	Jul	Aug	Sep	Oct	Nov	Dec
Opening balance	540	520	580	580	500	440
Add Purchases	220	200	160	140	140	180
	760	720	740	720	640	620
Less Payments	240	200	160	220	200	160
Closing balance	520	580	580	500	440	460

(d) Raw Materials Budget (in £s)

	Jul	Aug	Sep	Oct	Nov	Dec
Opening stock	300	340	360	340	300	260
Add Purchases	220	200	160	140	140	180
	520	540	520	480	440	440
Less Used in production	180	180	180	180	180	180
Closing stock	340	360	340	300	260	260

(e)

Gregg Ltd:
Forecast Operating Statement for the six months ended
31 December 19X6

Sales			9,130
Less Cost of goods sold			
Operating stock finished goods		1,800	
Add Cost of goods completed (£10 × 540)		5,400	
		7,200	
Less Closing stock finished goods (220 × £10)		2,200	
			5,000
Gross profit			4,130
Less Expenses:			
Fixed overhead		540	
Depreciation: Machinery	700		
Motor vehicles	600		
Office fixtures	30	1,330	
			1,870
Net profit			2,260

(f) Forecast Balance Sheet as at 31 December 19X6

		Depreciation	
Fixed assets	Cost	to date	Net
Tangible assets			
Land and buildings	40,000	–	40,000
Plant and machinery	10,500	6,700	3,800
Motor vehicles	8,000	3,400	4,600
Office fixtures	500	250	250
	59,000	10,350	48,650

32.11

Cash Payments Schedule

	Jul	Aug	Sep	Oct	Nov	Dec
Direct materials	240	140	160	220	200	160
Direct labour	450	450	450	450	450	450
Variable overhead	210	270	270	270	270	270
Fixed overhead	90	90	90	90	90	90
Machine	500					
Motor vehicle			2,000			
	1,490	950	2,970	1,030	1,010	970

Cash Receipts Schedule

	Jul	Aug	Sep	Oct	Nov	Dec
Debenture					5,000	
Receipts from debtors	990	900	1,080	1,440	1,800	1,850
	990	900	1,080	1,440	6,800	1,850

(a) Cash Budget (in £s)

	Jul	Aug	Sep	Oct	Nov	Dec
Opening balance	7,100	6,600	6,550	4,660	5,070	10,860
Add Receipts	990	900	1,080	1,440	6,800	1,850
	8,090	7,500	7,630	6,100	11,870	12,710
Less Payments	1,490	950	2,970	1,030	1,010	970
	6,600	6,550	4,660	5,070	10,860	11,740

(b) Debtors Budget (in £s)

	Jul	Aug	Sep	Oct	Nov	Dec
Opening balance	1,890	1,980	2,520	3,240	3,650	3,515
Add Sales	1,080	1,440	1,800	1,850	1,665	1,295
	2,970	3,420	4,320	5,090	5,315	4,810
Less Receipts	990	900	1,080	1,440	1,800	1,850
Closing balance	1,980	2,520	3,240	3,650	3,515	2,960

32.11 (cont)

Current assets

Stocks: Finished goods		2,200
Raw materials		260
		2,960
Debtors		11,740
Cash and bank		17,160

Creditors: amounts falling due within 1 year

Creditors for raw materials	460	
Creditors for variable overhead	270	
		730
Net current assets		16,430
Total assets less current liabilities		65,080

Creditors: amounts falling due after more than 1 year

Debentures		5,000
		60,080

Capital and reserves

Called-up share capital		50,000
Profit and loss account (7,820 + 2,260)		10,080
		60,080

33.1

(a) $12,000 \times 0.09 \times \dfrac{56}{365} = 165.70$

(b) $6,000 \times 0.15 \times \dfrac{80}{365} = 197.26$ discount, therefore amount paid = £5,802.74

33.3 The amount borrowed is:

$3,000 \times \frac{1}{4} =$		750.00
$2,250 \times \frac{1}{4} =$		562.50
$1,500 \times \frac{1}{4} =$		375.00
$750 \times \frac{1}{4} =$		187.50
Equivalent loan for 1 year		1,875.00

$r = \dfrac{1,000}{1,875} = 0.533$ or 53.3%

33.4 £1,000 will accumulate to $£1,000 \times (1 + 0.12)^5 = £1,762$

Interest is $£1,762 - £1,000 = £762$

33.7 The present value of an annuity of £4,000 p.a. for four years at 10%

$= £4,000 \times 3.170 = £12,680$ or:

Present value $= £4,000 \times \left[\dfrac{1 - \dfrac{1}{(1+0.1)^4}}{0.1} \right] = £12,680$

As it exceeds the present value of the rent, you should accept the offer of £15,000.

33.9 Paid in per year $= \dfrac{\text{Value} \times (r)}{(1+r)^n - 1}$

$= \dfrac{£20,000 \times 0.08}{(1.08)^{10} - 1}$

$= £1,380$ per year

33.11

	19X2	19X3
Equipment purchased	40,000	
Sale of old equipment		(10,000)
Installation of equipment completed and paid	12,000	10,000
Costs incurred in commissioning equipment	18,000	
Rent on premises up to completion date	6,000	(6 months)
Training costs		3,000
Working capital		4,000
		14,000
Net cash outlay	76,000	21,000

33.12

Capital cost 19X2		76,000	
19X2	25% WDA	19,000	@ 40% tax £7,600 received 19X3
	balance c/d	57,000	
New expenditure		17,000	excluding scrap value and
		74,000	additional working capital
19X3	25% WDA	18,500	@ 40% tax £7,400 received 19X4
	balance c/d	55,500	
19X4	25% WDA	13,875	@ 40% tax £5,550 received 19X5
	balance c/d	41,625	
19X5	25% WDA	10,406	@ 40% tax £4,162 received 19X6
	balance c/d	31,219	

This will continue over the life of the equipment. In 19X4 the cash received from the sale of old equipment will be taxed at 40 per cent, resulting in a tax outflow of £4,000.

	19X2	19X3	19X4	19X5	
Capital cash flow	(76,000)	(7,000)			
Tax relief		7,600	7,400	5,550	etc
Tax on sale			(4,000)		
Net cash flow	(76,000)	600	3,400	5,500	etc

33.13

	Net cash flow	Discount factor	Present value
		(10%)	
19X2	(76,000)	0.909	(69,084)
19X3	600	0.826	496
19X4	3,400	0.751	2,553
19X5	5,550	0.683	3,791
		NPV at start	(62,244)

33.17

Period	Amount	Balance
0	(10,000)	(10,000)
1	8,000	(2,000)
2	4,000	–
3	2,000	–
4	1,000	–

payback at 1 plus 2,000/4,000 years = 1.5 years

33.18

Period	Amount	Discount factor	Present value
		12%	
0	(10,000)	1.000	(10,000)
1	8,000	0.893	7,144
2	4,000	0.797	3,188
3	2,000	0.712	1,424
4	1,000	0.636	636
			2,392

Overall net present value of cash flows

33.19

Period	Amount	Discount factor (28%)	Present value	Discount factor (32%)	Present value
0	(10,000)	1.000	(10,000)	1.000	(10,000)
1	8,000	0.781	6,248	0.758	6,064
2	4,000	0.610	2,440	0.574	2,296
3	2,000	0.477	954	0.435	870
4	1,000	0.373	373	0.329	329
			15		(441)

28% discount rate gives NPV of 15
32% discount rate gives negative NPV of 441
456

The IRR is $\frac{15}{456} \times 4\% = 0.13\% + 28\% = 28.13\%$

33.20 The present value of an annuity of £1 for four years at 12% is 3.0.37. The NPV according to 33.18 is £2,382, therefore the annualised amount = 2,392/3,037 = 787.62

33.27

	Net present value (10%)
Machine A project	4,522
Machine B project	11,566

The Machine B project should be selected.

33.28

	Internal rate of return
Machine A project	22.4%
Machine B project	20.2%

The Machine A project would be preferred. However, comparing the NPV and IRR results, and remembering the rule of thumb that NPV should be followed when the two methods disagree, the Machine B project should be selected.

33.31 The present value of an annuity of £1 for five years at 10% is 3.791. Therefore the annualised amount = 3,100/3.791 = 817.73

33.33 £20,000 × present value factor of an annuity = £64,800. Therefore the present value factor = 64,800/20,000 = 3.24, which is 9% according to the tables.

33.34

Cost of machine £60,000 × (1 – 0.4) = 36,000
Cost of leasing £14,633 × (1 – 0.4) = 8,780

Present value for five years = $\frac{36,000}{8,780} = 4.1$

which is 7% according to the tables.

33.35 Factor present value of an annuity of £1 for six years at 16% is 3.685
£4,000 × 3.685 = £14,740 capital value of the lease.

33.36 (a)

BN Roadhog

	0	1	2	3	4	5
Cash inflow		12,500	15,000	20,000	20,000	20,000
Cash outflow						
fixed		2,000	2,000	2,200	2,400	2,400
variable		3,000	3,600	4,800	4,800	4,800
Operating cash flow		7,500	9,400	13,000	12,800	12,800
Capital	40,000					8,000
	40,000	7,500	9,400	13,000	12,800	20,800
	1.00	0.909	0.826	0.751	0.683	0.621
	40,000	6,817	7,764	9,763	8,742	12,916

NPV = 6,002 positive

FX Sprinter

	0	1	2	3	4	5
Cash inflow		12,500	15,000	20,000	20,000	20,000
Cash outflow						
fixed		1,800	1,800	1,800	2,000	2,200
variable		4,000	4,800	6,400	6,400	6,400
Operating cash flow		6,700	8,400	11,800	11,600	11,400
Capital	45,000					9,000
	45,000	6,700	8,400	11,800	11,600	20,400
	1.00	0.909	0.826	0.751	0.683	0.621
	45,000	6,090	6,938	8,862	7,923	12,668

NPV = 2,519 negative

VR Rocket

	0	1	2	3	4	5
Cash inflow		12,500	15,000	20,000	20,000	20,000
Cash outflow						
fixed		1,500	1,500	1,400	1,400	1,400
variable		3,500	4,200	5,600	5,600	5,600
		7,500	9,300	13,000	13,000	13,000
Capital	50,000					14,000
	50,000	7,500	9,300	13,000	13,000	27,000
	1.00	0.909	0.826	0.751	0.683	0.621
	50,000	6,817	7,682	9,763	8,879	16,767

NPV = 92 negative

To the Directors of Road Wheelers Ltd
The NPV anticipated for the three vehicles is as follows:

BN Roadhog	£6,002	Positive
FX Sprinter	£2,519	Negative
VR Rocket	£ 92	Negative

On the basis of NPV assessment using a discount rate of 10 per cent the BN Roadhog appears to be the best option.

The payback position on the three vehicles is as follows:

BN Roadhog	3 years	9.3 months
FX Sprinter	4 years	3.8 months
VR Rocket	4 years	3.2 months

This indicates that the BX Roadhog recovers the cash outlay faster than the other two options which is in its favour.

Since the capital outlay on the BX Roadhog is also significantly lower than the other options this indicates a lower risk and will enhance the ROC on the balance sheet figures.

The BN Roadhog appears to be the best choice.

(b) The problems in evaluating capital projects are essentially related to the estimates involved in forecasting the revenues and costs associated with the project. In this evaluation the relative performance of the three alternatives may be more reliable than overall estimates of the environment. In some situations important factors in the decision may not be readily quantified especially in areas of new technology where many factors are unknown.

The techniques of evaluating the cash flow data are well understood but care must be taken that an appropriate 'cost of capital' is chosen and that risk is taken into account.

33.38 (a) *Revised Operating Budget*

Ship A

	19X6	19X7	19X8	19X9	19X0
Estimated revenue receipts	5	7	9	11	13
Extra revenue 10%	0.5	0.7	0.9	1.1	1.3
	5.5	7.7	9.9	12.1	14.3
Operating payments	4.0	5.0	6.5	7.5	9.0
Net cash flow Ship A	1.5	2.7	3.4	4.6	5.3

Ship B

	19X6	19X7	19X8	19X9	19X0
Estimated revenue receipts:					
Private	2.5	3.5	5.0	6.5	7.5
Commercial	3.45	4.6	5.85	6.5	7.8
	5.95	8.1	10.85	13.0	15.3
Operating payments	4.8	6.0	7.9	9.0	10.8
Net cash flow Ship B	1.15	2.1	2.95	4.0	4.5

(b) *Cash flows*

Ship A

		Factor 15%	
0	(10.0)	1.0	(10.0)
19X6	1.5	0.870	1.3
19X7	2.7	0.756	2.0
19X8	3.4	0.658	2.2
19X9	4.6	0.572	2.6
19X0	5.3	0.497	2.6
NPV			0.7
	7.5	0.497	3.7
			4.4

Ship B

		Factor 15%	
0	(14.0)	1.0	(14.0)
19X6	1.15	0.87	1.0
19X7	2.1	0.756	1.6
19X8	2.95	0.658	1.9
19X9	4.0	0.572	2.3
19X0	4.5	0.497	2.2
			5.0
	10.5	0.497	5.2
			0.2

Assumed value of ship on market $15/20 \times$ cost

Note: The calculation has been done with a zero assumption about cash value of ships at the end of year 5 and then with an assumed value equal to the unexplained cost value based on a 20-year life.

(c) The evaluation assumes an interest rate of 15 per cent and evaluates cash flows over the first five years' life of the ships. If the assumption is that at the end of five years the ships will have no value then Ship A has a positive NPV of £0.7m whilst B has a negative NPV of £5.0m. However, it is unlikely that the ships would be valueless at the end of year 5 and if an assumption is made to take 15/20 of the cost as the realisable value then both NPVs become positive at £4.4m and £0.2m respectively.

From this evaluation Ship A looks to give a better return. It is worth noting, however, that Ship B does have much higher capacity. If operating revenues were to expand more than forecast over the five years and thereafter, this ship might provide much higher returns. This operating forecast and the likely market values of the two vessels should therefore be closely examined.

34.1 Solvency, profitability, efficiency, capital structure and shareholder.

34.3

Solvency	– *see* text sections 34.2 and 34.7.
Profitability	– *see* text sections 34.3 and 34.7.
Efficiency	– *see* text sections 34.4 and 34.7.
Capital structure	– *see* text sections 34.5 and 34.7.
Shareholder	– *see* text sections 34.6 and 34.7.

34.5 (a) Stock turnover.

34.7
(i) (b) and (d).
(ii) (b) and (d).
(iii) (d).
(iv) If current liabilities greater than current assets, (b) and (d); if current assets greater than current liabilities, (a) and (c).
(v) (b) and (d) but only after a customer takes up the offer.

34.9 (a)

(i) Gross profit as % of sales: $\dfrac{20{,}000}{80{,}000} \times \dfrac{100}{1} = 25\%$ $\dfrac{24{,}000}{120{,}000} \times \dfrac{100}{1} = 20\%$

(ii) Net profit as % of sales: $\dfrac{10{,}000}{80{,}000} \times \dfrac{100}{1} = 12.5\%$ $\dfrac{15{,}000}{120{,}000} \times \dfrac{100}{1} = 12.5\%$

(iii) Expenses as % of sales: $\dfrac{10{,}000}{80{,}000} \times \dfrac{100}{1} = 12.5\%$ $\dfrac{9{,}000}{120{,}000} \times \dfrac{100}{1} = 7.5\%$

(iv) Stockturn: $\dfrac{60{,}000}{(25{,}000+15{,}000) \div 2} = 3$ times $\dfrac{96{,}000}{(22{,}500+17{,}500) \div 2} = 4.8$ times

(v) Rate of return: $\dfrac{10{,}000}{(38{,}000+42{,}000)\div 2} \times \dfrac{100}{1} = 25\%$ $\dfrac{15{,}000}{(36{,}000+44{,}000)\div 2} \times \dfrac{100}{1} = 37.5\%$

(vi) Current ratio: $\dfrac{45{,}000}{5{,}000} = 9$ $\dfrac{40{,}000}{10{,}000} = 4$

(vii) Acid test ratio: $\dfrac{30{,}000}{5{,}000} = 6$ $\dfrac{22{,}500}{10{,}000} = 2.25$

(viii) Debtor/sales ratio: $\dfrac{25{,}000}{80{,}000} \times 12 = 3.75$ months $\dfrac{20{,}000}{120{,}000} \times 12 = 2$ months

(ix) Creditor/purchases ratio: $\dfrac{5{,}000}{50{,}000} \times 12 = 1.2$ months $\dfrac{10{,}000}{91{,}000} \times 12 = 1.3$ months approx.

34.9 (cont)

(b) Business B is the most profitable: both in terms of actual net profits £15,000 compared to £10,000, but also in terms of capital employed, B has managed to achieve a return of £37.50 for every £100 invested, i.e. 37.5 per cent. A has managed a lower return of 25 per cent. Reasons – possibly only – as not until you know more about the business could you give a definite answer.

(i) Possibly managed to sell far more merchandise because of lower prices, i.e. took only 20 per cent margin as compared with A's 25 per cent margin.

(ii) Maybe more efficient use of mechanised means in the business. Note that B has more equipment, and perhaps as a consequence kept other expenses down to £6,000 as compared with A's £9,000.

(iii) Did not have as much stock lying idle. Turned over stock 4.8 times in the year as compared with 3 for A.

(iv) A's current ratio of 9 far greater than normally needed. B kept it down to 4. A therefore had too much money lying idle and not doing anything.

(v) Following on from (iv) the acid test ratio for A also higher than necessary.

(vi) Part of the reason for (iv) and (v) is that A waited (on average) 3.75 months to be paid by customers. B managed to collect in 2 months on average. Money represented by debts is money lying idle.

(vii) A also paid creditors more quickly than did B, but not by much.

Put all these factors together, and it is obvious that business B is run far more efficiently, and is more profitable as a consequence.

34.11 (a) The ratios reveal that L Ltd's relative profitability has fallen between the two years. The gross and net profit margins have both fallen, but this may be due to the new sales manager's price-cutting policy, rather than because of any change in costs.

The fall in return on capital employed is not what was hoped for from the new sales price policy. A drop from 31 per cent to 18 per cent is very significant and suggests that the change in sales price policy and the related increased investment in new machinery, although with the related increased borrowings, have led to short-term depressed returns. If the increased market resulting from the new sales policy can be retained, it would be worthwhile considering an increase in sales price to a point where a higher rate of return would be achieved.

The company appears solvent – there is no shortage of liquid assets. However, it has taken on considerably more long-term debt in order to fund the market expansion. This will have to be serviced and the level of profit should be monitored to ensure that margins do not fall further, raising the current level of risk to unacceptable levels. As 38.2 per cent (£192,000) of net profits before interest (£502,000) are already being used to meet debt interest payments, compared to only 3.8 per cent in 19X2, it would not take very large changes in costs or selling price to cause this to become a major problem. The current level of gearing will also inhibit the company's ability to raise additional loan funding in future.

Profitability	19X2	19X3
Gross profit:sales	$\dfrac{540}{900} \times 100 = 60\%$	$\dfrac{1,120}{2,800} \times 100 = 40\%$
Net profit:sales	$\dfrac{302}{900} \times 100 = 34\%$	$\dfrac{310}{2,800} \times 100 = 11\%$
ROCE	$\dfrac{302 + 12}{929 + 100} = 31\%$	$\dfrac{310 + 192}{1,267 + 1,600} = 18\%$
Solvency		
Current ratio	$\dfrac{125}{36} = 3.47{:}1$	$\dfrac{821}{186} = 4.41{:}1$
Acid test ratio	$\dfrac{125 - 30}{36} = 2.63{:}1$	$\dfrac{821 - 238}{186} = 3.13{:}1$
Capital structure		
Capital gearing	$\dfrac{100}{100 + 929} = 10\%$	$\dfrac{1,600}{1,600 + 1,267} = 56\%$

(b) Current debtor collection period (i.e. debtor days) = $\dfrac{583}{2,800} \times 365 = 76$ days.

If the collection period were 45 days, the new debtors amount would be:

$$\dfrac{45}{76} \times 583,000 = 345,200$$

The amount released if a 45-day debtors collection period could be imposed would be £237,800.

35.1 (a) Trading and Profit and Loss Accounts for the year ended
31 December 19X9

	X		Y	
Sales		480,000		762,500*
Less Cost of goods sold		400,000		610,000
Gross profit		80,000		152,500
Less Admin. expenses	(−10,000) 40,000		(+10,000) 57,500	
Selling expenses	15,000	55,000	(−2,500) 35,000	92,500
Net profit		25,000		60,000

* Assumed 25 per cent mark-up despite wrong stock valuation.

(b) Profitability:

	X	Y
Gross profit %	20%	2.5%

Net profit % $\frac{25}{480} \times \frac{100}{1} = 5.2\%$ $\frac{60}{762.5} \times \frac{100}{1} = 7.87\%$

Stockturn $\frac{400,000}{40,000} = 10$ times $\frac{610,000}{45,000*} = 13.6$ times

*Adjusted to take into account inaccurate valuation.

Return on Capital Employed (ROCE) (previous owners)

$$\frac{25,000}{200,000} \times \frac{100}{1} = 12.5\% \qquad \frac{60,000}{350,000} \times \frac{100}{1} = 17.14\%$$

Based on purchase price of business the ROCE for Adrian Frampton would be:

X	Y
$\frac{25,000}{190,000} \times \frac{100}{1} = 13.15\%$	$\frac{60,000}{400,000} \times \frac{100}{1} = 15\%$

All ratios are favourable for Y. If gross profit ratios remained the same in future together with other expenses then Y business is best value.

However:
(i) Can gross profit ratios of X be improved as compared to those of Y?
(ii) Can stockturn be improved?
If so, then X could be cheapest business to buy as it gives a better ROCE.

(c) (i) Need to know current assets and current liabilities in detail.

(ii) Are these similar businesses?
Type of business
Areas in which situated
Competition
Prefer several years' accounts to gauge trends
Quality of staff and whether they would continue.

35.2 (a) 19X4

		A £000		B £000		C £000
19X4						
Return on capital of 20% = Profit*		120.0		120.0		120.0
Interest less tax		–	24.0		66.0	
			13.2	10.8	36.3	29.7
Profit for ordinary shares		120.0		109.2		90.3
Ordinary share capital		600		400		50
Profit return (%)		20		27.3		180.6
19X5						
Return on capital of 10% = Profit		60.0		60.0		60.0
Interest less tax		–	24.0		66.0	
			13.2	10.8	36.3	29.7
Profit for ordinary shares		60.0		49.2		30.3
Ordinary share capital		600		400		50
Profit return (%)		10		12.3		60.6

*Profit is assumed to be after tax but before interest.

(b) High gearing accentuates the rate of return to the ordinary shareholder. In the zero-geared position of A the return to the shareholder supply reflects the change in profits earned on trading. In the high-geared position of Company C the return to the shareholder decreases from 180.6 per cent to 60.6 per cent, i.e. to a reduction of 66.5 per cent as profits reduce by only 50 per cent. Company B reflects an intermediate position with a relatively moderate level of gearing.

High gearing increases risk to shareholders for two reasons. First if the profits earned are not sufficiently high to meet interest charges then the company may find itself failing since the lenders may seek a winding up order. Second the risk is increased simply because of exaggerated fluctuations in the returns which are accentuated in the high-geared situation.

However, it can be seen that if profits earned are higher than the interest rate, this will produce a significantly higher return to the shareholder in a high-geared company. The fact that interest is allowed as a deduction for tax purposes indicates that gearing may give an overall advantage. The market's assessment of the risk position will counter this, and will be based on the nature of the business and management.

35.4

(a) Refer to the text.

(b) To Mr C. Black

The reduction in profits from 24 per cent to 18.9 per cent of total equity needs to be analysed into its causal factors. During the year the net profits have increased but not as fast as the equity capital which has gone up by £120,000 over the year. If the increase reflected an investment late in 19X5 it would reduce returns because a full year's profit could not be earned.

It is therefore essential to examine the nature of the investment and the future. Before shares are bought it is essential to examine future prospects. If these are good the historic analysis may not be important. However, if the new funds were used – clearly prospects may not be good and shares should not be bought.

(c) Reserves are profits retained within the business. The profits may be from revenue, i.e. from profits which could be distributed as dividends to shareholders or capital – for example where fixed amounts are revalued upwards to reflect current market value.

The creation of reserves reflects an increase in capital in the organisation which would normally be to reflect an increasing scale of operation. In this sense reserves reflect an alternative to issuing new shares. In the case of capital reserves from revaluation – these are simply 'paper adjustments' to value which do not in themselves indicate more resources in the organisation.

Revenue reserves may in fact be distributed as dividends whereas capital reserves would not normally be available for this purpose and are more akin to share capital.

(b)

	Company A			B	
	£000	%		£000	%
Ordinary shares	300			800	
Revenue: Share premium	300			400	
Retained profit	400			200	
	1,000	62.5		1,400	87.5
8% preference shares	200			–	
10% loan – debentures	–			200	
12% loan – debentures	400			–	
	600	37.5		200	12.5
Total share capital and loan	1,600	100.0		1,600	100.0

Company A Debt/Equity $= \dfrac{37.5}{62.5} = 60\%$

B   " $= \dfrac{12.5}{87.5} = 14.3\%$

(c) Company A is more highly geared than B since it is committed to paying a higher proportion of fixed dividend and interest payments for its profits. A higher level of gearing increases risk. (Note the answer in 35.2 (b) is appropriate.)

(d)

	A	B
Trading profit before interest	200,000	200,000
Less Interest charges	48,000	20,000
Net profit after interest charge	152,000	180,000
Preference dividend	16,000	–
Ordinary dividend	45,000	120,000
	61,000	120,000
Retained profit	91,000	60,000

35.6

(a)

	19X4	19X5
Equity shares	100,000	150,000
Reserves	150,000	220,000
Total equity capital	250,000	370,000
Loans	40,000	40,000
Total capital employed	290,000	410,000
Profits (net after tax)	60,000	70,000
Return on total equity	24%	18.9%

35.8

(a) *Profit and Loss Accounts for the year to 31 March 19X8*

	Chan plc	Ling plc	Wong plc
	£000	£000	£000
Operating profit	300	300	300
Interest payable	–	–	(10)
Profit on ordinary activities before tax	300	300	290
Taxation (30%)	(90)	(90)	(87)
Profit on ordinary activities after tax	210	210	203
Dividends: Preference	–	(20)	(30)
Ordinary	(100)	(60)	(40)
	(100)	(80)	(70)
Retained profit for the year	£110	£130	£133

has to be set aside for both its debenture holders and its preference shareholders before any ordinary dividend can be declared. As a result, if the profits of the company are low, no ordinary dividend may be payable.

If profits are rising a high geared company may not be a particularly risky company in which to purchase some ordinary shares, but the reverse may apply if profits are falling.

For the year to 31 March 19X8, Chan, Ling and Wong's operating profit is identical. Wong is committed to paying interest on its debenture stock (which is allowable against tax), and both Ling and Wong have to pay a preference dividend (which is *not* allowable against tax).

In deciding whether to invest in any of the three companies, there are a great many other factors to be considered, including future prospects of all three companies. However, when profits are fluctuating an ordinary shareholder is more likely to receive a higher return by investing in Chan rather than by investing in either Ling or Wong. Similarly, an ordinary shareholder can expect a higher return by investing in Wong.

Based on the limited amount of information given in the question, therefore, an investor considering purchasing ordinary shares in only one of these three companies would be recommended to buy shares in Chan plc.

It should be noted that if profits were *increasing*, an investor would be recommended to buy shares first in Wong, then in Ling and finally in Chan. The earnings per share in both Ling and Wong are far higher than in Chan, so there is a much greater chance of an increase in the ordinary dividend, but this is not necessarily the case if profits are falling or fluctuating.

	Chan plc	Ling plc	Wong plc
(b) (i) Earnings per share			
$\dfrac{\text{Net profit after tax and preference dividend}}{\text{Number of ordinary shares in issue}} =$	$\dfrac{210}{500}$	$\dfrac{210-20}{300}$	$\dfrac{203-30}{200}$
	$\underline{\underline{42p}}$	$\underline{\underline{63.3p}}$	$\underline{\underline{86.5p}}$
(ii) Price/earnings ratio			
$\dfrac{\text{Market price of ordinary shares}}{\text{Earnings per share}} =$	$\dfrac{840}{42}$	$\dfrac{950}{63.3}$	$\dfrac{1038}{86.5}$
	$\underline{\underline{20}}$	$\underline{\underline{15}}$	$\underline{\underline{12}}$

(iii) Gearing ratio

$$\frac{\text{Loan capital} + \text{preference shares} \times 100}{\text{Shareholders' funds}} =$$

Chan plc $\underline{\underline{\text{Nil}}}$

Ling plc $= \dfrac{200}{300+100+130} \times 100 = \underline{\underline{37.7\%}}$

Wong plc $= \dfrac{300+100}{200+100+133} \times 100 = \underline{\underline{92.4\%}}$

(c) A gearing ratio expresses the relationship that exists between total borrowings (that is, preference share capital and long-term loans), and the total amount of ordinary shareholders' funds. It should be noted that other definitions of gearing are possible and are sometimes used.

Any company with a gearing ratio of, say, 70 per cent would be considered to be high geared, whilst a company with a gearing ratio of, say, 20 per cent would be low geared.

Gearing is an important matter to consider when investing in ordinary shares in a particular company. A *high-geared* company means that a high proportion of the company's earnings are committed to paying either interest on any debenture stock and/or dividends on any preference share capital *before* an ordinary dividend can be declared. If a company is low geared, then a high proportion of the company's earnings can be paid out as ordinary dividends.

Chan plc has not issued any long-term loans or any preference share capital. Gearing does not, therefore apply to this company, and all of the earnings may be paid out to the ordinary shareholders.

Ling plc is a relatively low-geared company. It has no debenture stock, and only a small proportion of its earnings are committed to paying its preference shareholders. The balance may then all be declared as an ordinary dividend.

Wong plc is an extremely high-geared company. A high proportion of borrowings (in this case consisting of both debenture stock and preference share capital) means that a high proportion of its earnings

35.10 (a) (i)

Forecast Profit and Loss Appropriation Accounts

	19X6 £000	19X7 £000	19X8 £000
Forecast profits	1,800	500	2,200
Less Corporation tax (30%)	540	150	660
	1,260	350	1,540
Less Dividends proposed	1,260	350	1,540

Balance sheet extracts

	19X6 £000	19X7 £000	19X8 £000
Shareholders' equity			
Issued ordinary shares of £1 each fully paid	6,000	6,000	6,000
Share premium account	1,000	1,000	1,000
Retained profits	1,650	1,650	1,650
	8,650	8,650	8,650
Current liabilities			
Dividends proposed	1,260	350	1,540

(ii)

Forecast Profit and Loss Appropriation Accounts

	19X6 £000	19X7 £000	19X8 £000
Forecast profits	1,800	500	2,200
Less interest (12% × £2m)	240	240	240
	1,560	260	1,960
Less Corporation tax (30%)	468	78	588
	1,092	182	1,372
Less Dividends proposed	1,092	182	1,372

Balance sheet extracts

	19X6 £000	19X7 £000	19X8 £000
Shareholders' equity			
Issued ordinary shares of £1 each fully paid	5,000	5,000	5,000
Retained profits	1,650	1,650	1,650
	6,650	6,650	6,650
Deferred liabilities			
12% debentures	2,000	2,000	2,000
Current liabilities			
Dividend proposed	1,092	182	1,372

(b) If planned expansion is financed by share issue, the forecast return on shareholders' equity for the next three years will be:

19X6 $1,260/8,650 \times 100$ = 14.6%
19X7 $350/8,650 \times 100$ = 4.0%
19X8 $1,540/8,650 \times 100$ = 17.8%

(ii) If planned expansion is financed by debenture issue, the forecast return on shareholders' equity for the next three years will be:

19X6 $1,092/6,650 \times 100$ = 16.4%
19X7 $182/6,650 \times 100$ = 2.7%
19X8 $1,372/6,650 \times 100$ = 20.6%

Note: All the above figures are, of course, net of tax and should be grossed by a factor of 100/70 if comparison with gross interest rates is to be made (on the assumption of 30 per cent tax rate).

(c) The return on shareholders' equity for the year ended 30 September 19X5 was $600/6,620 \times 100$ = 9.1 per cent, and it could have been 9.5 per cent if full distribution of the year's profit had been made. To have the return fluctuate between 2.7 per cent and 20.6 per cent, as it will do if the planned expansion is financed by the debenture issue, will surely unnerve all but the most sturdy shareholders. Such a violent swing from year to year will confuse, confound and alarm anyone looking at the shares as an investment.

To finance the planned expansion by a share issue does not improve matters greatly, as it will be seen that the return will still fluctuate between 4.0 per cent and 17.8 per cent. But since we are told that the industry is 'subject to marked variations in consumer demand' it does seem more appropriate to use share capital (by definition risk-bearing) rather than a debenture. The poor profits forecast for 19X7 suggest that it would not take much of a variation from the expected results to show no profit at all, and were this to occur, is there not a possibility that the debenture holders could not be paid their due interest? Failure to pay debenture interest on time would bring in a receiver (assuming the debentures were secured); his function would then be to collect not only the unpaid interest but the capital as well, as failure to pay interest would be a breach of the conditions under which the debenture was issued.

If shareholders are to miss a year's dividends as a result of there being no profits for distribution, the directors can expect a stormy annual general meeting, but that is far less dangerous than the entry of a receiver.

In practice, of course, it is unusual for a company to pay out all profits as dividends, and since shareholders will pay more attention usually to the level of dividends paid than to profits earned, it would make better financial sense if the 19X6 dividend were maintained at or slightly above the 19X5 level, enabling an addition to be made to retained profits. This in turn would enable a fund to be built up to supplement current profits for dividends and/or to redeem the debentures.

The all-shares or all-debentures choice is also an unrealistic one. Although there is much to be said for a broad share base to support what is obviously a risky business, it could make better sense to raise part of the required £2,000,000 by shares and part by debentures. A restrained dividend policy coupled with the use of the (probably enlarged) depreciation charge arising after the expansion had taken place could enable a debenture redemption programme to be established over the course of the next few years.

35.12 (a) (i) *Shareholders*

	19X6	19X7
Earnings per share (EPS)	$\dfrac{9,520}{39,680} = 24\text{p}$	$\dfrac{11,660}{39,680} = 29.4\text{p}$
Dividend cover (EPS ÷ dividend per share)	$\dfrac{24\text{p}}{(2,240 \div 39,680)}$	$\dfrac{24\text{p}}{(2,400 \div 39,680)}$
	$= \dfrac{24\text{p}}{5.6\text{p}} = 4.3$ times	$= \dfrac{29.4\text{p}}{6\text{p}} = 4.9$ times

(ii) *Trade creditors*

	19X6	19X7
Current ratio	$\dfrac{92,447}{36,862} = 2.5$	$\dfrac{99,615}{42,475} = 2.3$
Acid test	$\dfrac{40,210+12,092}{39,862} = 1.4{:}1$	$\dfrac{43,370+5,790}{42,475} = 1.2$

(iii) *Internal management*

	19X6	19X7
Debtor ratio/Sales*	$\dfrac{40,210}{486,300} \times 52 = 4.3$ weeks	$\dfrac{43,370}{583,900} \times 52 = 3.9$

*assumed credit sales

	19X6	19X7
Return on capital employed (before tax)	$\dfrac{15,254}{40,740} = 37.4\%$	$\dfrac{18,686}{50,000} = 37.4\%$

(b) *Shareholders*

EPS. An increase of 5.4p per share has occurred. This was due to an increase in profit without any increase in share capital.

Dividend cover. Increased by 0.6 times because increase in profit not fully reflected in dividends.

Trade creditors

Current ratio. This has fallen but only marginally and it still appears to be quite sound.

Acid test. This has also fallen, but still seems to be quite reasonable.

Internal management

Debtor ratio. There appears to have been an increase in the efficiency of our credit control.

Return on capital employed. This has stayed the same for each of the two years. The increase in capital employed has seen a proportional increase in profits.

35.14 To the Board of G plc

From   AN Other, Accountant

Subject: *Potential acquisition of either of companies A Ltd and B Ltd as subsidiaries in the machine tool manufacturing sector. Financial performances assessed.*

As instructed by you I have investigated the financial performances of these two companies to assist in the evaluation of them as potential acquisitions.

It should be borne in mind that financial ratio analysis is only partial information. There are many other factors which will need to be borne in mind before a decision can be taken.

The calculations of the various ratios are given as an appendix.

Profitability

While the main interest to the board is what G plc could obtain in profitability from A Ltd and B Ltd, all I can comment on at present is the current profitability enjoyed by these two companies.

Here the most important ratio is that of ROCE (Return on Capital Employed). A's ROCE is 27.2 per cent as compared with B's 15.6 per cent.

The great difference in ROCE can be explained by reference to the secondary ratios of profit and asset utilisation. Both ratios are in A's favour. The profit ratios are A 34 per cent: B 20 per cent. The asset utilisation ratios are A 0.9 per cent: B 0.6, showing that A is utilising its assets 50 per cent better than B. It is the effect of these two ratios that give the ROCE for each company.

The very low working capital employed by A Ltd very much affects the asset utilisation ratio. How far such a low working capital is representative of that throughout the whole year is impossible to say.

Liquidity

It would not be sensible to draw a final conclusion as to the liquidity positions of the two companies based on the balance sheet figures. As a balance sheet is based at one point in time it can sometimes be misleading, as a reading of figures over a period would be more appropriate.

35.14 (cont)

A Ltd does appear to have a short-term liquidity problem, as the current assets only just cover current liabilities. The 'quick' or 'acid test ratio' on the face of it appears to be very inadequate at 0.6.

By contrast, B Ltd with a current ratio of 1.4 and a 'quick ratio' of 1.0 would appear to be reasonably liquid.

However, much more light is shed on the position of the companies when the debtor collection period is examined. A collects its debts with a credit period of 9 weeks. In the case of B Ltd this rises to an astonishing 36.7 weeks. Why is this so? It could be due simply to very poor credit control by B Ltd. Such a long credit period casts considerable doubt on the real worth of the debtors. There is a high probability that many of the debts may prove difficult to collect. It might be that B Ltd, in order to maintain sales, has lowered its requirements as to the creditworthiness of its customers. If the credit period were reduced to a normal one for the industry it might be found that many of the customers might go elsewhere.

The problem with debtors in the case of B Ltd is also carried on to stock. In the case of A Ltd the stock turnover is 4.3 falling to 2.8 in B Ltd. There could be a danger that B Ltd has stock increasing simply because it is finding it difficult to sell its products.

Capital gearing

A Ltd is far more highly geared than B Ltd: 93.6 per cent as compared with 14.1 per cent. A comparison with this particular industry by means of interfirm comparison should be undertaken.

Limitations of ratio analysis

You should bear in mind the following limitations of the analysis undertaken:

(i) One year's accounts are insufficient for proper analysis to be undertaken. The analysis of trends, taken from, say, five years' accounts would give a better insight.
(ii) Differences in accounting policies between A Ltd and B Ltd will affect comparisons.
(iii) The use of historical costs brings about many distortions.
(iv) The use of industry interfirm comparisons would make the ratios more capable of being interpreted.
(v) The plans of the companies for the future expressed in their budgets would be of more interest than past figures.

Conclusions

Depending on the price which would have to be paid for acquisition, I would suggest that A Ltd is the company most suitable for takeover.

A N Other
Accountant

Appendix

(i) Return on capital employed

	A Ltd		B Ltd	
Profits before interest and tax / Capital employed	$\frac{211}{775} \times 100$	= 27.2%	$\frac{88}{565} \times 100$	= 15.6%

(ii) Assets utilisation ratios

	A Ltd		B Ltd	
Total assets turnover: $\frac{\text{Turnover}}{\text{Total assets}}$	$\frac{985}{1,140}$	= 0.9	$\frac{560}{990}$	= 0.6
Fixed assets turnover: $\frac{\text{Turnover}}{\text{Fixed assets}}$	$\frac{985}{765}$	= 1.3	$\frac{560}{410}$	= 1.4
Working capital turnover: $\frac{\text{Turnover}}{\text{Working capital}}$	$\frac{985}{10}$	= 98.5	$\frac{560}{155}$	= 3.6

(iii) Profitability ratios

	A Ltd		B Ltd	
Gross profit %: $\frac{\text{Gross profit}}{\text{Turnover}}$	$\frac{335}{985} \times 100$	= 34%	$\frac{163}{560} \times 100$	= 29%
Profit before taxation and interest as % turnover	$\frac{211}{985} \times 100$	= 21%	$\frac{88}{560} \times 100$	= 16%

(iv) Liquidity ratios

	A Ltd		B Ltd	
Current ratio: $\frac{\text{Current assets}}{\text{Current liabilities}}$	$\frac{375}{365}$	= 1.0	$\frac{580}{425}$	= 1.4
Acit test or 'quick ratio': $\frac{\text{Current assets} - \text{stock}}{\text{Current liabilities}}$	$\frac{220}{365}$	= 0.6	$\frac{440}{425}$	= 1.0
Debtor ratio: $\frac{\text{Trade debtors} \times 52}{\text{Credit sales}}$	$\frac{170}{985} \times 52$	= 9.0 wks	$\frac{395}{560} \times 52$	= 36.7 wks

(v) Capital structure

	A Ltd		B Ltd	
Gearing ratio: $\frac{\text{Long-term borrowing}}{\text{Shareholders' funds}}$	$\frac{220}{555} \times 100$	= 93.6%	$\frac{70}{495} \times 100$	= 14
Proprietary ratio: $\frac{\text{Shareholders' funds}}{\text{Tangible assets}}$	$\frac{555}{1,140}$	= 0.5	$\frac{495}{990}$	= 0.5

36.1 (a) T (b) F (c) T (d) F (e) T

36.4 £40,000

36.6 At 31 December 19X5, accumulated depreciation is:

$$30\% \times 30,000 \times \frac{160}{90} = 16,000$$

At 31 December 19X4, accumulated depreciation is:

$$20\% \times 30,000 \times \frac{120}{90} = 8,000$$

Depreciation charge for the year ended 31 December 19X5 is:

$$10\% \times 30,000 \times \frac{160}{90} = 5,333$$

Hence, depreciation provision at 31 December 19X5 is:

8,000 + 5,333 = 13,333

Backlog depreciation is 16,000 − 13,333 = 2,667

36.8

Opening stock at average prices = $50,000 \times \frac{100}{80}$	=	62,500
Purchases	=	450,000
Closing stock at average prices = $70,000 \times \frac{100}{120}$	=	58,333
Current cost of sales	=	454,167
Historic cost of sales	=	430,000
Cost of sales adjustment	=	24,167

36.10

Opening working capital	=	7,000
Closing working capital	=	10,000
Change in the year	=	3,000

At average values:

Opening working capital	=	$7,000 \times \frac{240}{200}$ = 8,400
Closing working capital	=	$10,000 \times \frac{240}{280}$ = 8,571
Change in the year	=	171

The monetary working capital adjustment is £3,000 − £171 = £2,829

36.12

	19X3 £000	19X2 £000
Loan stock	200	200
Cash	145	50
Net borrowings	55	150

Average net borrowings = $\dfrac{55,000 + 150,000}{2}$ = 102,500

	19X3 £000	19X2 £000
Ordinary shares	250	250
Reserves	370	340
Current cost reserve	35	30
Shareholder interest	655	620

Average shareholder interest = $\dfrac{655,000 + 620,000}{2}$ = 637,500

Gearing adjustment percentage is: $\dfrac{102,500}{102,500 + 637,500}$ = 13.85%

36.14 Many accountants believe that during a period of inflation financial reports prepared under the historical cost convention are subject to a number of severe limitations. The question lists five such limitations, and a brief explanation of each one is as follows:

1 *Stocks are undervalued.*
Stock values are normally based on historical costs. This means that the historic closing stock will usually have cost less than its current economic value. Hence the cost of sales will tend to be higher than it would be if the closing stock was revalued at its current cost. As a result, the gross profit will be higher, and the entity may then pay out a higher level of net profit.

If the entity pays out a high level of profit and at the same time it has to pay more for its stocks (because prices are rising), it may be left with insufficient funds for it to be able to replace its stocks with the same *quantity* of goods that it had sold during the previous period. Hence it will not be able to operate at the same level of activity as it had previously experienced.

2 *Depreciation is understated.*
Depreciation is usually based on the historic cost of fixed assets. Such assets will normally increase in price during a period of inflation. The annual depreciation charge, therefore, may not reflect the amount needed to be able to replace the assets at their increased cost. Consequently, the accounting profit tends to be overstated, and this may mean that too much profit is withdrawn from the business. The cash resources may then prove insufficient

36.14 (cont)

to replace the assets at the end of their useful life. Like the stock valuation problem, therefore, the business may not be able to operate at the same level of activity that it has previously experienced.

3 Gains or losses on net monetary assets are undisclosed.
Net monetary assets include both long and short-term loans made to and by the entity, for example, debentures, and trade debtors and trade creditors. During a period of inflation, an entity gains because although the amount originally borrowed will eventually be repaid at its face value, its purchasing power will have been reduced; for example, £5,000 borrowed in 19X1 will not purchase the same quantity of goods in 19X5 as it did in 19X1. In 19X5 the borrower may have to pay (say) £8,000 to purchase the same quantity of goods as he might have done in 19X1. Hence the entity will have, in effect, gained £3,000 by borrowing during an inflationary period, because it is effectively having to pay back less in purchasing power (or in real terms, as it is known) than it borrowed.

By contrast, if the entity has *loaned* money during a similar period (perhaps by allowing its customers to buy goods on credit), it loses money because the purchasing power of the respective debts (which are fixed in monetary terms) will purchase fewer goods when they are eventually settled than they would have done when they were first incurred.

In financial reports prepared under the historical cost system, neither the gross nor the net effect of these types of transactions is disclosed.

4 Balance sheet values are unrealistic.
Fixed assets are normally recorded in the balance sheet at their original cost, that is, at their historic cost. During a period of inflation, the historic cost of the assets may be far less than their *current* cost, that is, at the value the entity places on them at the time that the financial reports are prepared. Hence the financial reports give a misleading impression of the entity's net worth as at the time that they are prepared.

5 Meaningful periodic comparisons are difficult to make.
A meaningful comparison of financial reports prepared under the historic cost convention over several accounting periods may be misleading since such accounts will normally have been prepared using, say, pounds sterling in one period and pounds sterling in all subsequent periods.

Financial reports prepared in such a way are not, however, strictly comparable. For example, £100 in 19X1 is not the same as £100 in 19X5, because £100 would not purchase the same amount of goods in 19X5 as it did in 19X1. In fact the comparison is just as meaningless as comparing financial reports prepared, say, in dollars with, say, reports prepared in marks. It is obvious to most users of such reports that 100 dollars are not the same as 100 marks, but it is less obvious that £19X1 are not the same as £19X5.

In order to be able to make a meaningful comparison between financial reports prepared in different time periods, therefore, it is desirable to translate them into the same currency, that is, to use the same price base. The argument behind this point is similar in principle to that used in translating dollars into marks or marks into dollars.

37.1 *See* text section 37.6.

37.2 *See* text section 37.6. Difficulties lie in trying to give these measures a value in money that would get universal acceptance. How can you place a money value on living conditions, for example?

37.3 *See* text section 37.7.

37.4 Basically, there are many things that could be done to improve the various parts of 'social well-being'. However, (*a*) benefits cost a lot of money in the short term, and (*b*) beneficial effects are felt only in the long term. Examples are better education, and better housing.

37.5 *See* text section 37.10, social programme measurement.

37.7 The accountant's model of income measurement, with its reliance upon data that can be expressed in financial terms, can be said to be too narrow and fails to consider wider social and environmental issues. The air we breathe does not have a 'price' in financial terms. Yet, what businesses do may cause costs to be incurred by others as a result of their abuse of the air in their environment. Similarly, the true cost of a natural resource may never be accounted for – the rainforests being a very well known example: they are being removed upon payment of a financially stated price, but the price only satisfies the seller, it does little to replace the environment being destroyed. Thus the price being added into the cost of manufacturing paper from the trees in the rainforests does not include the social and environmental cost of their destruction.

Thus, in the income model, it could be argued only in a narrow sense of the term that 'capital' is being maintained. In reality, the destruction of natural resources that are not or cannot be replaced means that the 'capital' is being consumed and future consumption impaired as a result.

It is for reasons of this type that it can be argued that accountants ought to be involved in disclosing the effects of a company's business activities upon its environment, for only by doing so will a true view of a company's activities be revealed.

38.1 *See* text sections 38.1 and 38.2.

38.2 *See* text sections 38.1 and 38.2.

38.3 *See* text section 38.2.

38.4 *See* text section 38.3.

38.5 *See* text section 38.4.

38.6 *See* text section 38.7.

Index